BLUE-COLLAR WORLD

PRENTICE-HALL
INDUSTRIAL RELATIONS AND PERSONNEL SERIES
Dale Yoder, Editor

BLUE-COLLAR WORLD

Studies of the American Worker

edited by

Arthur B. Shostak

Department of Sociology
Wharton School of Finance and Commerce
University of Pennsylvania

and

William Gomberg

Department of Industry
Wharton School of Finance and Commerce
University of Pennsylvania

PRENTICE-HALL, INC., ENGLEWOOD CLIFFS, NEW JERSEY

To our wives, Susan and Addy

PRENTICE-HALL INTERNATIONAL, INC., *London*
PRENTICE-HALL OF AUSTRALIA, PTY., LTD., *Sydney*
PRENTICE-HALL OF CANADA, LTD., *Toronto*
PRENTICE-HALL OF INDIA (PRIVATE) LTD., *New Delhi*
PRENTICE-HALL OF JAPAN, INC., *Tokyo*

Second printing.....September, 1965

Library of Congress Catalog Card No.: 64–23481
Printed in the United States of America
[07770-C]

Contents

v

LEISURE

UNEMPLOYMENT AND RETIREMENT

TRENDS AND PROSPECTS

APPENDIX

List of Contributors

AIKEN, MICHAEL T. Assistant Professor in the Department of Sociology at the University of Wisconsin.

ANDERSON, CHARLES H. Graduate Student in Sociology at the University of Massachusetts. Assistant to Professor M. M. Gordon of the Department of Sociology at the University of Massachusetts.

BEAN, LEE L. Assistant Professor of Sociology at Yale University. Field Director of the research study, "A Ten Year Follow-Up of Psychiatric Patients," which is being conducted at Yale University.

BERG, IVAR. Associate Professor of Business Administration at the Graduate School of Business, Columbia University.

BOGERT, LEO, Ph.D. Vice President of Marketing Planning and Research of the Bureau of Advertising, American Newspaper Publishers Association (N.Y.C.). Author of *The Age of Television* and other books and articles.

BOWMAN, CLAUDE C. Professor of Sociology at Temple University.

BLUM, ALAN. Post-Doctoral Research Fellow in the Department of Psychiatry of the Harvard Medical School at the Massachusetts Mental Health Center.

CAPLOVITZ, DAVID. Senior Study Director of the National Opinion Research Center and Assistant Professor of Sociology at the University of Chicago. Formerly Research Assistant and Associate of the Bureau of Applied Social Research of Columbia University. Author of *The Poor Pay More*.

CHAPLIN, DAVID. Assistant Professor in the Department of Sociology at the University of Wisconsin.

COUSENS, FRANCES R., Ph.D. Research Associate with the Great Cities Program for School Improvement. Part-time Lecturer with the Department of Sociology at Wayne State University.

DANSEREAU, H. KIRK. Associate Professor of Sociology at the Pennsylvania State University.

DAVIS, ETHELYN. Professor and Director, Department of Sociology, Texas Woman's University.

DYER, WILLIAM G. Associate Professor of Sociology at Brigham Young University.

ENDLEMAN, ROBERT. Associate Professor and Acting Chairman of the Department of Sociology and Anthropology at Adelphi University.

FERMAN, LOUIS A. Research Associate in the Institute of Labor and Industrial Relations, University of Michigan-Wayne State University.

FOWLER, IRVING A. Associate Professor of Research at the School of Social Welfare, University of Buffalo.

FREEDMAN, LAWRENCE Z., Professor, Foundations Fund Research Professor in the Department of Psychiatry at the University of Chicago.

FREEMAN, HOWARD E. Associate Professor of Social Research and Director of the Research Center of the Florence Heller Graduate School for Advanced Studies in Social Welfare, Brandeis University. Co-Author of *The Mental Patient Comes Home* and co-editor of *The Handbook of Medical Sociology*.

FRIEDENBERG, EDGAR Z. Associate Professor of Education at Brooklyn College. Author of *The Vanishing Adolescent* and numerous articles.

GEISEL, PAUL N. Research Associate in the Graduate School of Public Health and Assistant Professor of Sociology at the University of Pittsburgh.

GOLDSTEIN, SIDNEY. Professor of Sociology at Brown University. Co-author with Professor Kurt B. Mayer of *The First Two Years: Problems of Small Firm Growth and Survival*.

GOMBERG, ADELINE. Assistant Professor of Education and Director of Reading Clinic at Beaver College.

GORDON, MILTON M. Professor of Sociology at the University of Massachusetts. Author of *Social Class in America* and numerous articles.

GROSS, RONALD, Ph.D. Assistant to the Executive Director of the Education Division of the Ford Foundation.

HAMILTON, RICHARD F. Assistant Professor in the Department of Sociology at Princeton University.

HANDEL, GERALD, Ph.D. Assistant Director of Social Research, Inc., in Chicago.

HARRISON, IRA E. Graduate Student in Sociology at Syracuse University, Assistant to Professor S. M. Miller of the Department of Sociology at Syracuse University.

HAUSKNECHT, MURRAY. Instructor in the Department of Sociology and Anthropology at Hunter College. Author of *The Joiners* and numerous articles.

HENDERSON, GEORGE. Program Coordinator for the Mayor's Committee on Community Action for Detroit Youth. Part-time Instructor in Sociology at Wayne State University.

HOULT, THOMAS F. Associate Professor of Sociology. Former Assistant Director of the Institute for Regional and Urban Studies and former Research Associate of the Urban Research Laboratory and the Detroit Area Traffic Study at Wayne State University.

HURVITZ, NATHAN, Ph.D. Certified Psychologist in Los Angeles, California. Lecturer at the University of Southern California and the University of Judaism in Los Angeles.

KARACKI, LARRY. Former graduate student in Sociology at Rutgers University. Former Assistant to Professor J. Toby of the Department of Sociology at Rutgers University.

LAMBERT, JR., CAMILLE. Assistant Professor of Social Research in the Florence Heller Graduate School for Advanced Studies in Social Welfare at Brandeis University. Director of research projects in the field of medical care.

LANTZ, HERMAN. Professor of Sociology at Southern Illinois University. Author of *People of Coal Town* and numerous articles.

LEGGETT, JOHN C. Assistant Professor in the Department of Sociology at the University of California, Berkeley.

LEVINSON, HARRY. Director, Division of Industrial Mental Health, Menninger Foundation. Co-author of *Human Understanding in Industry,* and numerous articles.

LOETHER, HERMAN J. Associate Professor of Sociology at Los Angeles State College.

LONDON, JACK. Associate Professor of Adult Education and Associate Research Sociologist at the University of California, Berkeley. Joint author of *The Worker Views His Union* and author of other books and articles.

MAYER, ALBERT J. Professor of Sociology at Wayne State University. Former Director of the Institute for Regional and Urban Studies, the Urban Research Laboratory, and the Detroit Area Traffic Study at Wayne State University.

MAYER, KURT B. Professor of Sociology at Brown University. Co-author with Professor Sidney Goldstein of *The First Two Years: Problems of Small Firm Growth and Survival.*

MILLER, S. M. Professor of Sociology and Senior Research Associate at Syracuse University. Affiliated with the Youth Development Center at Syracuse University.

MORLAND, J. KENNETH. Professor and Chairman, Department of Sociology and Anthropology, Randolph-Macon Woman's College. Author of *Millways of Kent.*

MYERS, JEROME K. Professor of Sociology at Yale University. Co-author of *Family and Class Dynamics in Mental Illness* and numerous articles.

PATTERSON, JAMES M. Associate Professor of Marketing in the Graduate School of Business, Indiana University. Co-author of *Marketing: The Firm's Viewpoint.*

PEPPER, MAX P. Director, State of Connecticut Mental Health Planning Project and Assistant Professor of Psychiatry, Public Health, and Sociology at Yale University.

POWLES, WILLIAM E., M.D. Assistant Professor of Psychiatry and a Clinical Instructor, Industrial Medicine Division, College of Medicine, University of Cincinnati.

PRICE, CHARLTON R. Staff Sociologist in the Department of Social Psychiatry, Menninger Foundation. Visiting Lecturer in Sociology at the University of Kansas.

PURCELL, THEODORE V., S.J. Acting Director, Institute of Social Order, National Jesuit Social Science Center at Saint Louis University.

RAINWATER, LEE. Associate Professor of Sociology and Anthropology at Washington University. Associate Director of Social Research, Inc. in Chicago.

RIESSMAN, FRANK. Chairman of the Department of Psychology at Bard College. Author of *The Culturally Deprived Child* and numerous articles.

RODMAN, HYMAN. Sociologist with the Merrill Palmer Institute in Detroit, Michigan.

ROGERS, DAVID. Assistant Professor of Sociology at the Graduate School of Business Administration, New York University.

ROSENBLATT, DANIEL, Ph.D. Director, Social Science Activities Program, N.Y.C. Health Department.

ROSENGREN, WILLIAM R. Associate Professor in the Department of Sociology and Anthropology, Western Reserve University.

RUBIN, MORTON. Associate Professor of Sociology at Northeastern University. Author of *Plantation County.*

SCHWARTZ, MICHAEL. Assistant Professor of Sociology and Psychology at Wayne State University, Research Coordinator for the Mayor's Committee on Community Action for Detroit Youth.

SEXTON, PATRICIA CAYO. Assistant Professor of Educational Sociology at New York University. Author of *Education and Income* and numerous articles.

SHEFFIELD, SUSAN. Sociology Graduate Student at the University of Michigan. Assistant to Professors A. J. Mayer and T. F. Hoult at Wayne State University.

SMITH, LUKE M. Chairman of the Department of Sociology at Alfred University.

SPINRAD, WILLIAM. Associate Professor in the Department of Social Science at Paterson State College.

STAMLER, ROSE S., M.A. Associated with the Chicago Board of Health, Division of Adult Health and Aging. Coordinator of Community Chronic Disease Detection Programs.

STREET, DAVID. Assistant Professor in the Department of Sociology at the University of Chicago.

SUCHMAN, EDWARD A. Professor of Sociology, University of Pittsburgh. Author of *Sociology and the Field of Public Health* and other books and articles.

TOBY, JACKSON. Professor of Sociology and Department Chairman at Rutgers University. Co-author of *Social Problems in America* and numerous articles.

VERNON, GLENN M. Professor and Chairman, Department of Sociology and Anthropology, University of Maine. Author of *Sociology of Religion* and numerous articles.

WENKERT, ROBERT. Assistant Research Sociologist at the University of California, Berkeley. Co-author with Professor J. London of *Some Reflections on Defining Adult Education.*

ZOLA, IRVING K. Assistant Professor in the Department of Sociology at Brandeis University.

Introduction

THIS collection of essays grew out of the conviction of both editors that there was a need for a picture of the members of the working class as people. Is the working class different from other groups? What is its special style of life, if any? What values does it attach to parenthood? How does the young worker experience adolescence? How does he see himself as citizen and community member? What are his moral values and religious convictions, his attitude toward physical well-being, his fears of illness? Does he partake of the middle-class preoccupation with mental health? Does he share the intellectual community's ambivalence about leisure-time pursuits? What terrors does unemployment instill, if any? What does he expect from retirement? Above all, who is he?

The question "Who am I?" is the most profound question posed by man. Scientists, novelists, dramatists, poets, and social observers have all wrestled with this problem.

THE PURPOSES OF THE COLLECTION

We have had four major concerns in preparing this book. The first has been to redress a serious imbalance in academic attention to the situation of the American worker as a person rather than as an instrument of production. The second concern was to encourage a new, integrated approach to the situation of the worker. The third was to stress the worker's contemporary situation and to derive from this some provocative and, we trust, meaningful projections. Finally, our desire has been to encourage researchers to re-examine materials they originally collected for other purposes—materials rich in insight into the situation of the worker. Essentially, what we are asking ourselves is, "Do the techniques developed in the social sciences tell us anything useful about the worker that can be ascribed to him as a member of a group?" This is the primary question to which we address ourselves. Is the classification "working class" meaningful in any other sense besides the fundamental classification of men working for an employer and receiving an income from that employer?

There is no lack of systematic study of the worker in the factory and at the workbench![1] The engineers, under the influence of Frederick W. Taylor and his followers, pursued studies on motivation in the factory. Social observers like Elton Mayo and his school extended their observations beyond the factory and the workbench, but again the central focus remained the effect of these nonfactory influences upon the worker as producer.[2] Nosow and Form are the latest of a long line of behavioral scientists whose focus of attention, in their own words, is the Sociology of Occupation. Our emphasis is placed elsewhere. It may be stated as follows:

> Is there a style of life peculiar to the blue-collar men who work for a living, and what are its characteristics? How does this style of life fit in with the worker's work experience?

WORKING CLASSES OLD AND NEW

A generation separates the senior editor of this book from the junior editor. One of us came to his majority in the depression-ridden 1930's, the other in the affluent 1950's. In other words, one of us was a contemporary of the working class of the 1930's; the other was a contemporary of the children of this generation who have now grown to manhood. Is the life style of the present generation of workers the same as that of its parents?

The senior editor recalls that when he was studying under the late Professor Rautenstrauch at Columbia, his attention was drawn to a photograph on the walls of Rautenstrauch's study. The photograph was labeled "Faithful Frank." The top of the muscular foreshoulders supported a rugged head. Deep lines of honest toil were etched upon the face. His trusting eyes looked directly at you. Both picture and title suggested the proletarian hero—the noble workman, loyal and honest, though exploited by employer and labor leader alike. No worker was dishonest. He was only exploited. If dishonesty did at times show its ugly self, it was the responsibility of those who exploited him. The worker was modern society's version of Rousseau's unspoiled *Natural Man*. Radicals endowed the working class with endless virtues in contradistinction to their exploiters, who were the embodiment of evil. Jack London expressed the spirit of the day when he wrote:

> I remembered my intellectuals and idealists, my unfrocked preachers, broken professors, and clean-minded, class-conscious workingmen. . . . And I saw before me, ever blazing and burning, the Holy Grail.[3]

Some fifty years and two generations later, a disenchanted philosopher, Raymond Aron, writes:

> Idealist revolutionaries assigned to the working class the superhuman mission of putting an end to the all-too-tangible evils of industrial society. They have not the honesty to admit that the proletarian, as it becomes gradually and inevitably

---

[1] See, for example, works ranging from Elton Mayo's *Human Relations of an Industrial Civilization*, written in the late 1920's to the collection of essays edited by Nosow and Form, *Man, Work and Society*, collected in 1962.

[2] See Robert Lampman, *The Share of Top Wealth Holders in National Wealth, 1922-1956* (Princton, N. J.: Princeton University Press, 1962); and Gabriel Kolko, *Wealth and Power in America* (New York: Frederick A. Praeger, 1962).

[3] Jack London, in Upton Sinclair, *The Cry for Justice* (New York: Upton Sinclair, 1915), p. 738.

more bourgeois, loses the virtue which seems to make it worthy of this high calling. The manual worker remains at the foot of the social ladder, not through the fault of capitalism or socialism, but through the determination of science applied to industry. The workers of the West have merely swelled the ranks of the petty bourgeoisie instead of bringing a renewal of station. They have tended toward the diffusion of a sort of secondhand culture. On both sides of the Iron Curtain, the culture peculiar to the working classes is dying out as more and more proletarians adopt bourgeois habits and values and avidly absorb the revolting literature of the so-called popular press, or of socialist realism. Technological progress, which replaces the hand by the machine and physical effort by know-how, does not advance him.[4]

THE WORKER AND THE FICKLE INTELLECTUAL

Well-intentioned and socially motivated sociologists have joined Mr. Aron. They, too, are disenchanted with the working class of late. This attitude is expressed in titles like *The End of Ideology*[5] and "Working-Class Authoritarianism." [6] Many of those who denigrate the working class today are the very ones who in former years were just as vehement in attributing a monopoly of virtue to the depressed workers, into whose hands they placed the hope for a new world.

Seymour M. Lipset notes many studies which suggest that the lower-class way of life produces individuals with rigid and intolerant approaches to politics. He then goes on to observe that it is the workers who have sought to limit immigration or to impose racial quotas in countries with open immigration. He calls attention to the mobs who engaged in race riots in Britain. He notes that many of the rank and file of these mobs were workers. He goes on to suggest that the workers everywhere are more liberal on economic issues— for example, higher wages, graduated income taxes, support of trade unions, and so forth. But when liberalism is defined in noneconomic terms as support of civil liberties and internationalism, the correlation is reversed. The more well-to-do are more liberal; the poorer are more intolerant. Why should this be surprising? The upper classes can afford to be tolerant. When schools are wrecked in the name of integration because of a misplaced hysterical demand that racial homogeneity is more important than ability homogeneity, it is the people who are dependent on these schools who see their schools wrecked— first the working class, then the middle class. The middle class, which has been abstractly dedicated to fashionable concepts of liberalism, loses its liberalism no less rapidly than the worker when it calls for something other than an abstract allegiance to a slogan that does not interfere with its everyday life.

The liberal observer's disenchantment with the working class is perhaps traceable to Professor Wilbert Moore's assessment of the structural-functionalist school within sociology. Professor Moore has observed that the school of the

---

[4] Raymond Aron, *The Opium of the Intellectuals* (New York: W. W. Norton & Company, Inc., 1962).

[5] Daniel Bell, *The End of Ideology* (New York: The Free Press of Glencoe, Inc., 1960), Ch. 13, "The Failure of American Socialism," p. 265.

[6] Seymour M. Lipset, *Political Man* (Garden City, N. Y.: Doubleday & Company, Inc., 1963), Ch. 4, "Working-Class Authoritarianism." (Anchor Books.)

structural functionalist in the field of sociology is technically correct in maintaining that statics must precede dynamics, but that its members are equally
unrealistic about their static propositions unless these statics are immediately
followed by dynamics. Thus we are presented with a picture of an authoritarian working class—no doubt as accurate a picture as one can gather from
a still photograph, but about as important and as revealing as a single frame
in the continuous sequence of a moving picture reel of a dynamic evolutionary
pattern. The pessimistic analysis of the working class in 1963 makes about as
much sense as a static analysis of the middle classes in precapitalist Poland,
where an examination of the pettifogging nature of business would have
endowed the middle class with a necessarily rude and ugly genetic, or at least
cultural, dishonesty. The ability to see the hereafter would have disclosed that
this pettifogging group would soon be superseded, because the very requirement of large-scale production imposed a primitive honesty and commercial
fair-dealing on business intercourse. Similarly, may we not conclude that the
obligation to improve and to promote their own status will impose upon the
working class a change of character and point of view? Many more will come
to understand what the active minority leadership already understands—that
they can attain their ends only by identifying with the progressive moral conscience of the community. Our investigation of the worker's way of life, his
style of living, and the method which he uses to gain his current satisfactions
constitutes an attempt to take inventory at one momentary scene in the moving
reel of his developing life. Greater investigators than we and more perceptive
observers will perhaps be able to discern in this information an intrinsic set
of dynamics of this segment of the population and to understand what Moore
has referred to as the lead of deliberate change and the lag of adversely
affected interests.

Neither of the editors subscribes to the nihilism of a value-free sociology.
The morality implicit in a poverty-stricken existence is expressed by George
Gissing in the following comment:

> The difference between the man with money and the man without is simply this:
> the one thinks, how shall I use my life; and the other, how shall I keep myself
> alive?[7]

Affluence is not a sufficient condition for improved morality, but it is certainly
a necessary condition for all except the occasional saint, and he would get lost
in any statistic of group measurement.

THE EFFECTS OF AFFLUENCE AND AUTOMATION

Our study has been motivated by two noteworthy developments in the
period under consideration: the advent of an affluent society, and the rapid
inroads of technological displacement which followed.

John Galbraith observed that the people whose incomes were below the
average for the country experienced increases in purchasing power of about
40 per cent between 1941 and 1950, compared with an increase of 20 per cent

---

[7] George Gissing, *The New Grub Street*, as quoted in Sinclair, *The Cry for Justice*, p. 104.

for those with above-average incomes in the same period. However, both Robert Lampman,[8] of the National Bureau of Economic Research, and Gabriel Kolko[9] provide evidence that this tendency toward equalitarianism has been subsequently arrested, and the old disparities may be reappearing. Similarly, in *The Other America,* Michael Harrington portrays a grim picture of poverty today.[10] He estimates that he is talking about one-fourth of the population rather than the two-thirds of the population of the 1930's. Part of this segment is made up of migratory workers in agriculture as well as the industrial group which dominated the scene of the 1930's.

Moreover, the rapid increase in the rate of technological displacement, loosely called *automation,* poses a new threat to the industrial group. Estimates of this displacement vary from 40,000 jobs per week, by John Snyder, President of United States Industries, to 4,000 jobs per week, the official United States Department of Labor estimate.[11] The essayists herein place both developments in perspective, uncover new meaning, and offer new insights into these matters.

THE PROBLEM OF METHOD

In choosing material for this book, the editors were always aware of the present disputes over authentic methodology. Workers in the field cover the area of a spectrum which ranges from the creative novelist at one extreme to a value-free manipulation of data modeled on physics at the other. Between these extremes are impressionists, journalists, and clinicians.

Novelists have attempted to capture the essence of the worker's complete life experience, both occupational and nonoccupational, ranging from Upton Sinclair's *Jungle* to Harvey Swados' *On the Line.* The novelist uses his intuitive insight to probe the character of his actors and to portray an impressionistic picture of an implicit group. On his part, the systematic investigator attempts to set up rigorous categories and criteria for classification in the hope that he may thereby portray meaningful and predictive behavior.

The relationship between the two methods of approach was underlined by Sigmund Freud. When Ernest Jones, Freud's biographer, was introducing the founder of psychoanalysis at a banquet to commemorate Freud's birthday, among the accolades that he bestowed upon Freud was the designation "Discoverer of the Unconscious." Freud arose and disclaimed this honor, stating that the insights of the unconscious were discovered long before his time by the poets, novelists, and dramatists. He went on to say that he had merely codified these insights into an organized scientific system.

As late as 1958, Professor Paul Lazarsfeld asks, "What has social research all added up to in the last fifty years? Is there any sociological finding that has not been anticipated by philosopher or novelist?" He replies that it is unlikely that any "surprising" discoveries will be made for some time to come, and

---

[8] Lampman, *op. cit.*

[9] Kolko, *op. cit.*

[10] Michael Harrington, *The Other America, Poverty in the United States* (New York: The Macmillan Company, 1963).

[11] *New York Times,* Wednesday, October 2, 1963, p. 1.

that the work of the social scientist will largely be confined to verifying by empirical methods the validity of these proverbs and intuitive insights.[12]

The exact area of delineation of human behavior marked out for study by a discipline is a source of great confusion. The senior editor recalls his attendance at a session of the Society for Applied Anthropology some years ago. An interdisciplinary session made up of psychiatrists, social psychologists, clinical psychologists, cultural anthropologists, and sociologists were dividing up the field on the bases of subject of study and method of approach. Quite obviously, there were marked areas of extensive overlap. Soon the observers became so spirited in staking out their exclusive areas of jurisdiction that the meeting resembled a conference of the Jurisdiction Committee of the AFL-CIO at which carpenters and metal workers were disputing who was entitled to install metal window frames. It may very well be that the multiplicity of professional titles indicating different disciplines reflects the bureaucratic needs of the observers rather than the intellectual "needs" of the subject matter. New disciplines create new university departments, which require new department heads and new budgets. Many departments, as a rule, may be made to justify more appointments than one single department. If this should be true, it would merely indicate how observers of human behavior are subject to the very forces they are seeking to discover.

The word *scientific* serves the same purpose in the twentieth century that *magic* did in the sixteenth. Professor Morris Raphael Cohen writes:

> For that matter, most of popular science is just a new form of superstition. What evidence is there that, because a man has read something about the romance of the atom, he really understands the world better; that he has attained a more scientific turn of mind? What evidence is there that, because a man talks freely about psychology or psychoanalysis and complexes and libidos and things of that sort, he really has scientific detachment and a sense of scientific evidence and scientific method? I should say that changes of lingo and various exercises of technical vocabulary do not indicate any growth of science—though the body of knowledge available today is larger than it was. People who want to use the material of science certainly have a better chance. But that does not mean that the great body of people today are more scientific than they were before.[13]

Wars are carried on among the behavioral-studies people about what constitutes scientific observation. Some have referred to general conclusions that were derived intuitively from clinical data as "scientific." Others have dismissed these methods and demanded rigorous quantified survey data which can be subjected to the rules of mathematical statistical inference. Still others have insisted that they can structure experiments which will tell more about people and their behavior than will clinical observation of actual situations.

It is amusing at times to read the comments of the self-styled scientific school on the work of their journalistic peers. A reviewer commenting upon Vance Packard's *The Pyramid Climbers* observed that Vance Packard 'made every methodological mistake that would be apparent to a student of Soci-

---

12 Paul F. Lazarsfeld, "Methodology," in *Sociology Today*, ed. by R. Merton, L. Broom and L. Cottrell (New York: Basic Books, Inc., 1958).

13 Morris R. Cohen, *The Faith of a Liberal* (New York: Holt, Rinehart, & Winston, Inc., 1946), p. 451.

ology I. This observation may tell us more about the sterility and pretentiousness of the professor's Sociology I than it does about Vance Packard.

We have urged our authors to sin bravely, and, given the choice between scholarly sterility and imaginative daring speculation, we have indicated our preference for the latter.

THE DURATION OF ANY GROUP PICTURE

Finally, though we would like to have a book that is definitive and of long-lasting value, we have the suspicion that the very concept of "working class" is middle-class. Since all other functional groups that arise out of nineteenth-century social taxonomy are subject to such extensive change, the best that we can hope for is a series of flashes from a moving-picture reel; the roles and functions of these groups are changing so rapidly under the impact of an explosive technology upon classic job descriptions and the men who occupy obsolete jobs that we are unable to arrive at a permanent picture.

The reader will probably note that the essays carry their share of jargon. We have allowed the authors to express themselves in their own way, although we have encouraged them to abandon jargon except where they felt it seemed indispensable. We have felt that we have to respect our essay writer's choice of jargon where he deemed no other words would convey the meaning that he wished to put across. In the choice between clarity of expression and aesthetics of writing, we have sometimes been forced to sacrifice the latter in order to grant our authors the right of their own methods of expression.

The editors have had their say. Now, let us look.

William Gomberg

ACKNOWLEDGMENTS

Our typists, Mrs. Ruth Hoffman and Mrs. Dorothy Tuohey, along with our editorial assistant, Miss Alberta Potter, contributed significantly to the completion of this project, and have our warm gratitude.

Our contributors cooperated wholeheartedly in meeting tight deadlines, accepting editorial guidance, and reading proof. We appreciate their support and would here thank them all publicly for "a job well done."

We also wish to express our appreciation to the publishers of *Social Problems, The Nation, Sociological Inquiry,* and *Commentary* for granting permission to reprint several of the essays appearing in this book.

Part I

WORKING CLASS:
NEW AND OLD

EVER since Marx and Engels proclaimed that history is the chronicle of class struggle and that the working class is predestined to cap its triumph with the abolition of all classes, the term *working class* has been a symbol inscribed upon a banner. Our object is much more modest. We want, in this section, to find out what the working class is in contemporary America. Accordingly, the first two of the five essays develop a distinction between the "new" working class of the urban "colored" poor and the "old" working class which is mainly white and has been urban manual for at least a generation. Miller describes the rise of the "new" group and stresses the relationship of their plight to the basic economic situation in America. In the second essay, he distinguishes among four types in the "new" group and links up specific reform proposals with each type. Attention turns thereafter to the "old" or "stable" working-class group, and Miller and Riessman discuss several basic themes in working-class life (such as the striving for stability and security). Rainwater and Handel follow with a discussion of style-of-life elements that have remained constant (such as approaches to child rearing) and those that have undergone change (such as evaluation of education). Finally, Hamilton considers the provocative question: Does financial and social success change the blue-collarite? He examines the situation of well-paid, high-status, skilled manual workers, and finds the effects of early socialization crucial in determining adult values and behavior.

The "New" Working Class*

S. M. MILLER

A few short years ago little attention was devoted to poverty and the poor. It was widely assumed that poverty was rapidly declining in "the affluent society," and that comparatively few people were touched by it. Indeed, it appeared that to think about the poor was to reveal that one was caught in a repetition-compulsion, unable to overcome the trauma of the 1930's despite the advent of prosperity and well-being. The great improvement in levels of living was presumed to have all but eliminated the vestiges of poverty among a "hard core."

More recently a spate of books has upset this complacent picture of the United States. Michael Harrington has feelingly portrayed the strain of poverty; Lampman, Kolko, Morgan, and Keyserling have revealed its extent.[1] The "income curtain" which separated the American "haves" from the American "have-nots" has been drawn back, and we can no longer assume that poverty affects few, that it is dwindling, or that it is far less destructive than the poverty of old. Nor do current trends furnish much optimism. The income of the poor generally and of Negroes in particular is not increasing relative

---

*I have had the benefit of comments from a great number of people: Martin Rein, Warren Haggstrom, Louis Kriesberg, Philip Norris, Hy Kornbluh, Seymour Bellin, Helen Icken, Arthur Pearl, Bernard Goldstein, Walter Goldstein, Ben Seligman, Irving Horowitz, Melvin Weiss, Irving Howe, Herbert Gans, and Martin Fleisher. I am particularly indebted to Frank Riessman and Patricia Sexton. None of the foregoing is responsible for the present formulations.

This essay is part of a larger chapter entitled "Poverty, Race and Politics," in Irving L. Horowitz, ed., *The New Sociology: Essays on Social Values and Social Theory in Honor of C. Wright Mills* (New York: Oxford University Press, 1964). The support of the Louis M. Rabinowitz Foundation is gratefully acknowledged.

[1] Conference on Economic Progress, *Poverty and Deprivation in the United States*, Washington, 1961; the main author of this analysis is Leon Keyserling, and it is known as the "Keyserling Report."

Michael Harrington, *The Other America: Poverty in the United States* (New York: The Macmillan Company, 1962).

Gabriel Kolko, *Wealth and Power in the United States* (New York: Frederick A. Praeger, Inc., 1962).

Robert J. Lampman, "The Low Income Population and Economic Growth," *Study Paper No. 12*, Joint Economic Committee of Congress, December 16, 1959.

James N. Morgan, *et al.*, *Income and Welfare in the United States* (New York: McGraw-Hill Book Company, Inc., 1962).

to that of those who are better off. World War II stimulated a great economic change in the United States, advantaging low-income groups.[2] But, since 1944, the income gap between the poor and the better-off has not been closing.[3]

Income inequality seems to be increasing rather than decreasing. Vast technological change (subsumed under the loose term "automation") is further reducing employment opportunities for the displaced and for low-educated youth. Coupled with limited economic growth, the effects are to prevent new jobs from emerging and to increase or maintain unemployment, especially of the disadvantaged—the young and the minority-group member.[4]

Poverty *is* an American problem, but has not as yet reached its full stature as a *political* problem. Whether poverty fully becomes the issue that it should depends largely on what the poor do. They will need allies if they are to be effective. But they are the likely "movers and shakers." The purpose of this essay is to set out the possibilities of political awareness and action among the poor. Because the obstacles to action are well-known, the effort is to stress these possibilities.

THE EXTENT OF POVERTY

How many people are poor in the United States depends on how poverty is defined. It is difficult to define what is a "poverty line"; Lampman, for example, employs $2,500 for a family of four as his base, while Keyserling uses $4,000 family income without reference to size of family. Estimates of poverty vary as a result. The minimal estimate appears to be about 16 per cent of the total population while the maximal estimate is about 25 per cent. Interpretation of the more detailed breakdown of the data has often been confused because the *incidence* of poverty within a given population (for example, over 65, nonwhite) has not always been recognized as different from the *composition* of poverty, that is, what percentage of the poor have a given characteristic (for example, over 65, nonwhite).[5]

The emphasis in most reports on the frequency of poverty—that is, what percentage of a given group is poor—has obscured some vital facts about poverty. Despite the great incidence of poverty among Negroes—35 per cent of Negro adults in Detroit were reported as unemployed in 1960—most poor are white (this is also true in the South). Similarly, although a high percentage of farm people are poor, almost 50 per cent of the poor are in urban communities.

An additional difficulty is that the data lend themselves to two opposing interpretations with quite different implications. One interpretation stresses the "differentness" of the poor; they are "special cases" requiring special help. The other view emphasizes the similarity of the poor to other groups. Lamp-

---

[2] Lampman, *op. cit.*, p. 12.

[3] Herman Miller, "Is the Income Gap Closing? No," *New York Times Magazine Section,* November 11, 1962.

[4] S. M. Miller, "Youth and the Changing Society," *Journal of Social Issues,* forthcoming.

[5] Martin Rein has made the most thoroughgoing analyses of the poverty data in a series of as yet unpublished studies.

man, for example, points out that 70 per cent of the poor have one or more of these four characteristics: over 65, nonwhite, in female-headed households, or in households headed by individuals with eight years of education or less. In the entire United States, 50 per cent had one or more of these characteristics. His conclusion is that the poor are different, whereas I am struck by the great overlap between the poor and the general population! His position is strengthened when only the first three characteristics are considered; then 50 per cent of the poor have one or more of these characteristics, although only 20 per cent of the total population is identifiable by these characteristics. The 50 per cent of the poor, however, who do not have any of these three characteristics are similar to 80 per cent of the general population.

Obviously, one can stress the distinctiveness of the poor or their similarity to the general population. (The lower the poverty line that is employed, the more "different" the poor appear.) The first position suggests that the poor's economic needs are different from those of the rest of society; the second underlines the coincidence of interests. This essay will overstress the latter point of view in an effort to compensate for a lack of attention to this position.

THE BACKGROUND OF THE POOR

In American life, the poor are probably a more varied group than ever before. The farm poor live in areas where the economic sustenance has withered with the technological development of agriculture and its economic concentration. The rural nonfarm, small-town, and small-city poor suffer from the demise of local industry, whether it be the coal mines of West Virginia or the dead one-industry textile towns of the East. Industrial centers like Detroit and Pittsburgh suffer from high productivity and limited demand. The youthful poor possess limited or outmoded skills and inadequate educational credentials in a high-technology, certificate-demanding economy.

Farms and small-town America are large producers of the poor; the big cities are increasingly the receivers of the poor (as well as generating a poor themselves). Many from "old America" move to the slum areas of large cities, where they join the leftover third-generation immigrant population and the other poor of the metropolis.[6]

Although farm and rural areas are pushing people toward the cities, the metropolises are not prepared to accept them. There is no pull from most of the urban centers. In contrast, an urban labor force was needed in the beginning stages of Britain's industrial progress and, as E. H. Carr argues, it was governmental policy to permit market forces to starve people off the land. In the contemporary case, our cities do not need the labor of the migrants or of the older urban poor. (I do not want to paint a gilded picture of industrializing Britain, for the urban jobs there provided a level of living that has been characterized as "grinding poverty.")

---

[6] See the rich discussion in Richard A. Cloward and Lloyd E. Ohlin, *Delinquency and Opportunity: A Theory of Delinquent Gangs* (New York: The Free Press of Glencoe, Inc., 1960), pp. 193-211.

Poverty is sad (and, in our kind of society, unforgivable) wherever it takes place, but I want to concentrate on the urban poor, particularly those in large cities. This urban poor is composed of many strands: refugees from the land and older settlers of the urban slums, Southern mountaineer whites and Southern Negroes, Puerto Ricans, and Mexican-Americans.

THE "NEW" WORKING CLASS

Despite their diversity, the poor in the largest urban centers are rapidly evolving into a "colored" poor of Negroes and the Spanish-speaking (Puerto Ricans and Mexican-Americans).[7] It is these groups who are most likely to be politicalized. *The confluence of class and race issues gives the poor a much greater political potential than is usually true of low-income, depressed populations.* Obviously, the term "colored" describes perceptions of and attitudes toward these groups rather than biological phenomena.

I shall be referring to the poor as the "new" working class.[8] The "old" working class, who still make up the bulk of skilled and semiskilled union members as well as the majority of blue-collar workers, is made up of "old-settler" Protestant recruits largely from farm and rural areas and the second- and third-generation emigrants from Catholic Eastern and Southern Europe.

Let me try to clarify how I see the relationship between the "new" working class and the poor, for a way of classifying a population is a way of thinking about them.

The poor are frequently referred to, following the lead of sociologists, as "lower class." For a variety of reasons, I am avoiding this designation. First, it has a negative connotation which an analytic term, at least, should avoid. Second, it is not a term that people use to designate themselves. This was sharply shown in Richard Centers' study of social-class identification which made an important discovery by offering people four choices for their social class (upper, middle, working, and lower class) rather than three (upper, middle, and lower); in the *Fortune* study which employed three categories, most people, including the poor and manual workers, put themselves in the middle class; in Centers' investigation, a slight majority of the total American population called themselves "working class," and an overwhelming proportion of the manual workers, including the poor, chose this term.[9] Third, "lower class" has been used to refer to a wide gamut of people from relatively highly paid, fairly well-educated skilled workers to third-

[7] Seymour Martin Lipset and Reinhard Bendix, *Social Mobility in Industrial Society* (Berkeley: University of California Press, 1959), p. 106.

[8] In Great Britain the term *new* working class has been used to refer to the more affluent manual workers. David Lockwood and John Goldthorpe, of Cambridge University, have carefully analyzed this group. The differences in immigration history and working-class economic and social conditions in the two countries have led to the contrasting usages of the term.

[9] Richard Centers, *The Psychology of Social Classes* (Princeton: Princeton University Press, 1949).

generation welfare families where the head of household has only inter-mittently worked and then in low-paid, marginal jobs.[10]

I prefer to use the term *"new" working class* in talking of the poor; the *"old" working class* largely includes those whose families have been urban manual for at least a generation. This "old" working class is more likely to be white, engaged in semiskilled and skilled occupations and employed in high-wage construction and manufacturing industries in the main economy than is the "new" working class. The latter is more frequently "colored," unskilled, in low-wage service and nonunionized industries (for example, hospitals) in the marginal economy of present-day United States. These distinctions are overstated, for obviously there are Negroes in unionized, skilled manufacturing occupations. (The election in 1962 of the first Negro to the executive board of the U.A.W. is indicative of the importance of Negroes in the high-wage, predominantly semiskilled and skilled manufacturing occupations covered by the contracts of this union.)

This formulation runs into another difficulty, because (using Keyserling's standards) 35 per cent of the heads of low-income families are not in the labor force—that is, they are not classified by Census statisticians as currently employed or actively engaged in looking for work if they are unemployed. This is not the place to analyze labor-force concepts, but I would emphasize that many of the adult poor who are outside of the labor force have worked and would work if jobs were available. The aged poor—a large percentage of the nonworkers—are less characterized by the orientation to work. They continue nonetheless to have many economic and political interests in common with the new working class. The welfare poor (particularly in families headed by women) are again probably limitedly oriented to working (but the reluc-tance should not be as casually assumed as it seems to be by many com-mentators today). Here, again, the long-run economic and political interests are frequently in common with the new working class. Moreover, when the welfare poor work, they are in the occupations which characterize the new working class. Many of the poor will be shifting back and forth between low-level unskilled work and government support; in both activities, they will have common interests in banding together to improve their conditions.

The concept of the "new" working class is more a fishing net than a hard container. Nevertheless, I prefer it to terms like *lower class, the poor, the lumpenproletariat, skid rowers,* and the like, because it points to economic and political issues rather than to personality deficiencies. It indicates that the poor are not a narrow segment of psychologically damaged individuals. The stratification term emphasizes common economic issues which many low-income people face in affluent America; it raises the possibility that they might move politically to do something about it. A less invidious term like *"new" working class* implies that low-income people are trying to get a foothold into urban industrial life. We should not ignore them by acting as though their plight were little involved in the basic economic situation of America.

---

[10] For a more extended analysis of the omnibus character of the term *lower class,* see S. M. Miller and Frank Riessman, "The Working-Class Subculture: A New View," *Social Problems,* Vol. IX (1961), pp. 86-97. Reprinted in this volume.

Harrington has pictured the poor as passive, inert, and apathetic, lacking generally the capacity for action. I find this portrait misleading. The aged have been active in political movements—from the Townsend Plan to the fight for Medicare. Mexican-Americans have recently won political control in Crystal City, a small Texas town. In many cities, the young and adult poor have organized to protest their conditions, as recently in Chicago, where women on welfare strongly demonstrated against the cessation of allowances. I shall be concentrating on Negroes, because they are a sizable proportion of the under-65, large-city poor, and because they are especially likely to become politicized.

In this century a radical change has taken place in the geographic distribution of Negroes. In 1910, 89 per cent of Negroes lived in the South; in 1960, the percentage had decreased to 60 per cent. Between these years a social revolution took place, liberating Negroes from the land and introducing them to the possibilities as well as the woes of urban life. In 1960, for the first time, a major city was predominantly Negro: in Washington, D.C. the Negro population was now 55 per cent of the total population. In many Northern cities, the Negro proportion is rapidly increasing. In the Borough of Manhattan in the City of New York, Negroes and Puerto Rican children are 70 per cent of the total elementary-school population; by 1980, the estimate is that 85 per cent of the elementary-school children will be Negro or Puerto Rican.

World War I was the breakthrough for the Southern Negro. During and immediately after the war, great numbers of Negroes left for the North, and in cities like New York and Chicago, Harlem and Bronzeville became Negro ghettos. In following years there was a steady if not spectacular movement of Negroes out of the South. Again a war led to a rapid change: during and after World War II, there was, and continues to be, a rapid movement of Negroes into urban centers, both North and South. The Negro is no longer a rural resident as he primarily was for generations: soon, a majority of Negroes will be living in the North and in large cities there.

The numerical importance of Negroes in the large Northern cities was demonstrated in the Kennedy victory in 1960. The almost solid Democratic vote in many Negro districts was important in swinging the populous industrial states into Kennedy's column. The increase in the number of Southern Negro voters accentuates the national role of Negroes. Legislative reapportionment, which increases the importance of the urban vote, will make the Negro vote more effective in state elections. With the rapid concentration of Negroes in central cities, they will become increasingly a power grouping there; in New York City, it now seems to be Democratic Party practice that the Borough President of Manhattan should be Negro. A Negro mayor of a large city is a distinct possibility in the next years.

Negroes, then, are developing a political "clout" which will give them the ability to demand and get services and help at both the federal and

The "New"
Working Class

local levels. We are witnessing the extension of citizenship rights to a new group and their groping utilization of the potential effectiveness of these rights. Historically, the trend in this nation has been toward the spread of citizenship rights. Formally, these rights have almost always been available to all; in practice, they have been accessible only to whites and more slowly to working-class whites. The white ethnics—first the Irish, later the Jews, and still more recently the Italians (the first Italian did not arrive in the United States Senate until shortly after World War II)—strengthened their citizenship rights through organization and pressure. They were able consequently to obtain a more equitable distribution of political and economic rewards. The same process is beginning with Negroes, and, at a slower rate, with many other members of the new working class. *It promises to be the decisive political condition of the 1960's in this country.*

A large-scale politicalization of Negroes and others of the poor is a real possibility because of the interweaving of class (economic) factors with ethnic and racial issues. The intermeshing of these concerns will likely lead to political mobilization. The racial-ethnic factors cement solidarity within some of the groups of the poor. Usually, the long-term economically depressed are unlikely candidates for a dynamic political movement, but the race/ethnic dimension, as well as the economic factor, is propelling the poor, whether Negro, Mexican-American, or Puerto Rican.

Many of the leaders of the poor will probably come from middle-class families of the racial/ethnic group, providing qualities and abilities that may not early emerge among the poor. E. Franklin Frazier's notion of a "black bourgeoisie" who in rising had cut itself off from feeling, contact, and identity with the mass of Negroes was probably overstated when he expressed it a few years ago; it undoubtedly is today. Less and less does "going up" mean "going out" of the Negro community: even those who are able to and do move out of the Negro ghetto frequently maintain ties with it and are deeply and actively concerned about the Negro poor. A generational factor is involved: the older, successful Negroes are less likely to be identified with poor Negroes and are more likely to emphasize "progress" than are younger, middle-class Negroes. But even the older frequently are being pushed along by the dynamism and pressure of the young and of the Negro community generally.[11]

The cohesion which comes from the race/ethnic issues may also separate each of the poor ethnic groupings from one another, leading each to be concerned only with issues particular to it. This self-centering pressure and inter-ethnic hostility may be overcome by the large number of issues which are common to all of the poor.

The high rate of unemployment among the new working class, their

---

[11] Obviously, contrasting patterns exist among Negroes and other ethnic groups of the poor. The middle-class Negro who does not want his children to have contact with low-income, educationally deficient Negro children is a frequently cited example of change within an ethnic group. My impression is that the general sweep of ethnic movement is today more compelling than interclass antagonism.

low wages, their inadequate housing as they suffer the bulk of the ravages (and reap few of the benefits) of urban redevelopment, the poor schooling offered their children, the neglect of public services in their neighborhoods, the frequent callousness of the police and welfare departments, their bilking by merchants—in short, their second-class economic and political citizenship—provide the issues which may mold the new working class into a potent political force.

The American Lower Classes: A Typological Approach*

S. M. MILLER

IN recent years, increasing attention has been directed to "the lower class" —those existing at the economic and social margins of society. The current concern with the limited economic prospects of dropouts,[1] the discussions of "hard-core" and "multiproblem" families,[2] the casualties of the welfare state,[3] the analysis of the numbers living below the "poverty line" in

---

* I am indebted to the Louis M. Rabinowitz Foundation for financial assistance. I have benefited from the suggestions and comments of Frank Riessman, Bernard Kramer, Bernard Goldstein, Helen Icken Safa, and Jerome Cohen. A version of this paper was presented at the annual meetings of the American Sociological Association, Los Angeles, August, 1963. Reprinted from *Sociology and Social Research,* an International Journal, Vol. 48, No. 3, April, 1964.

[1] Cf. Patricia Cayo Sexton, *Education and Income: Inequalities in our Public Schools* (New York: The Viking Press, Inc., 1961), pp. 10ff. S. M. Miller, Carolyn Comings, and Betty Saleem, *The School Dropout Problem—Syracuse* (Albany: New York State Division for Youth and the Syracuse University Youth Development Center, 1963). Herman P. Miller points out that the disadvantage of not having a college diploma grew from 1939 to 1958. See his "Money Value of an Education," *Occupational Outlook Quarterly* (September, 1961), p. 4.

[2] Janet E. Weinandy, *Families Under Stress* (Syracuse: Syracuse University Youth Development Center, 1962).

[3] Audrey Harvey, *Casualties of the Welfare State,* Fabian Tract 321 (London: Fabian Society, 1959).

America,[4] and the conditions of the "submerged fifth" in Britain[5]—all reflect the growing awareness of the "underprivileged" in presumably affluent welfare societies of high industrialization.

Much confusion exists in these discussions. Those concerned with psychological and social dislocations (disorganization is the commonly used word) tend to understress the importance of economic pressures, and those interested in economic deprivation frequently discount the role of social and psychological problems in preventing people from coping with their difficulties. Who is or is not "lower class" is a moot point, as different axes of demarcation are utilized. As I have explained elsewhere in this volume, I prefer to use such terms as the *new working class* rather than the *lower class*. Because most of the literature is couched in terms of the *lower class*, I use this term here despite my objections to it.

A way of classifying a population is a way of thinking about them. A frequent practice is to classify as "lower class"[6] the large number of people who are members of households where the breadwinner is not involved in some kind of white-collar (that is, middle-class) occupation. This category is then considered to have high homogeneity and is treated as though it constituted a group with great centrality of attitudinal and behavioral patterns. This orientation has probably led to much of the confusion and conflict in discussions of the characteristics of those at the lower end of the social structure. For example, the inconsistent child-rearing results may be due to the variations from study to study in those who are sampled as members of "the lower class."

It is becoming more common, although not a consistent practice, to mark off distinctions within the manual category. Frank Riessman and I[7] have argued that a working class of skilled and semiskilled regular workers should be distinguished from unskilled, irregular workers who might be called "lower class." Preferably, the latter group might be called by less invidious terms like "the unskilled," "marginal workers," or "underprivileged workers," restricting the latter term of Allison Davis to a narrow scope.[8] But even

---

[4] Michael Harrington, *The Other America: Poverty in the United States* (New York: The Macmillan Company, 1962) ; Conference on Economic Progress, *Poverty and Deprivation in the United States* (Washington: Conference on Economic Progress, 1961) ; the main author of this analysis is Leon Keyserling and it is known as the "Keyserling Report"; Gabriel Kolko, *Wealth and Power in the United States* (New York: Frederick A. Praeger, Inc., 1962); Robert J. Lampman, "The Low Income Population and Economic Growth," Study Paper No. 12, Joint Economic Committee, Congress of the United States, December 16, 1959 (Washington: Government Printing Office, 1959); James N. Morgan, *et al., Income and Welfare in the United States* (New York: McGraw-Hill, Inc., 1962) . These books are reviewed in S. M. Miller, "Poverty and Inequality in America: Implications for the Social Services," *Child Welfare*, Vol. XLII (November, 1963), pp. 442-45 (republished in the Syracuse University Youth Development Center Reprint Series.)

[5] Brian Abel-Smith, "Whose Welfare State?", in Norman MacKenzie, ed., *Conviction* (London: MacGibbon and Kee, 1957).

[6] "The terms 'lower class' and 'middle class' are used here to refer to systems of behavior and concerns rather than groups defined in conventional economic terms." William C. Kvaraceus and Walter B. Miller, *Delinquent Behavior: Culture and the Individual* (Washington: National Education Association, 1959), p. 62.

[7] S. M. Miller and Frank Riessman, "The Working-Class Subculture: A New View," *Social Problems*, Vol. IX (Summer, 1961) , pp. 86-97. Reprinted in this volume.

[8] Allison Davis, "The Motivation of the Underprivileged Worker," in William Foote Whyte, ed., *Industry and Society* (New York: McGraw-Hill, Inc., 1946), pp. 84-106.

where a distinction is made between the "working class" and the "lower class," the criteria of classification are frequently obscure or conflicting.

Two approaches, not always clearly noted, are employed in defining the "lower class." One approach emphasizes the definition of groups in terms of "class" characteristics, especially economic role or income. The other employs "cultural" or "status" criteria, such as style of life. The Hollingshead index—occupation, education, place of residence—is in the tradition of the first approach.[9] Walter Miller's discussion[10] of "the lower class subculture" is along the lines of the second. Social workers' discussions of "the lower-class client" and the "multiproblem family" almost always employ style-of-life indicators.

The two approaches intertwine but seem to make independent contributions to elucidating the characteristics of the "lower class" or the poor. Consequently, I have brought them together in an effort to move away from a broadly and vaguely defined "lower class" into a specification of types of lower-class individuals. The effort is to utilize class and status variables in categorizing a population. The combination of the two produces problems, but these may be overweighed by the difficulties and obscurities produced by the current shifting between the two sets of dimensions in discussing groupings and issues: Walter Miller's "lower class"[11] is not Lee Rainwater's.[12]

Obviously, other dimensions, like education and region, should also be employed. Class and status dimensions should be more carefully marked off than in the following discussion. Unfortunately, the material to do an adequate job is lacking. The purpose here is to show one way of approaching the problem of differentiation within the poor. The intent is to direct more attention to the recognition of variations among the poor.

THE CLASS CRITERION

The advantage of using an economic indicator in defining the lower class is that such an indicator specifies a political-economic category to which legislation and other remedial programs could be devoted. Emphasis on style-of-life indicators can be confusing, because the meaning of an attitude or behavior or what it leads to can be quite different for the rich, for the middling well-off, for those "getting by," and for the poor. The same behavior may have different roots and consequences in varying milieus.

---

[9] August B. Hollingshead and Frederick C. Redlich, *Social Class and Mental Illness: A Community Study* (New York: John Wiley & Sons, Inc., 1958), pp. 387-97.

[10] Walter B. Miller, "Lower Class Culture as a Generating Milieu of Gang Delinquency," *Journal of Social Issues*, Vol. XIV, No. 3 (1958), p. 6, footnote 3. In his penetrating analysis, Miller notes the existence of "subtypes of lower class culture" but does not pursue this point. While his emphasis is on cultural characteristics such as "female-based" household and "serial monogamy" mating patterns, he elsewhere employs educational, occupational, and income variables to define the lower class. See his "Implications of Urban Lower-Class Culture for Social Work," *Social Service Review*, Vol. XXXIII (September, 1959), pp. 229ff. His major stress is on cultural or status characteristics as defining the lower-class culture.

[11] *Ibid.*

[12] Lee Rainwater assisted by Karol Kane Weinstein, *And the Poor Get Children* (Chicago: Quadrangle Books, 1960). See also the distinctions made within the lower-lower class by Martin Loeb, "Social Class and the American Social System," *Social Work*, Vol. 6 (April, 1961), p. 16.

On the other hand, the class or occupational criterion is not so clear-cut as it appears. Some unskilled workers have stable, fairly well-paid jobs and are, thus, not a pressing social or economic problem. (This is particularly true where the unskilled worker is employed in a unionized, mass-production factory.) Many semiskilled and fewer skilled workers suffer some degree of irregularity of employment, especially owing to seasonal factors. Another problem is that a considerable number of poor families (35 per cent to 50 per cent) have no member in the labor force.[13]

Consequently, I would suggest that an income criterion is more useful today than an occupational criterion in the definition of the lower class. The recent analyses of poverty in the United States can be employed for this purpose.[14] They show remarkable agreement, despite their different procedures, in estimating that from one-quarter to one-fifth of the United States population lives below the poverty line. The level of income defining poverty varies, depending upon family size, composition, age, region, and type of community. For our purposes, we can ignore these complexities and put the poverty line at $4,000 family income, following Keyserling. It is this population which, if we want to use the term, could be called "lower class" or "low income" or "the poor."

The advantage of utilizing the economic criterion, and particularly the income definition, is that it specifies a socioeconomic category toward which policy can be directed. For example, Morgan reports,[15] following Lampman's earlier lead, that 10 billion dollars would bring all spending units now below the poverty line to an income level above poverty. Questions of the distribution of income and of social services can be pinpointed, then, in terms of how they affect this particular population.

Obviously, income levels and sources of income vary considerably among the "low-income" population. Keyserling distinguishes between the very poor, the poor, and a higher income group who suffer what he terms "deprivation" but not outright poverty. What income level is used affects deeply the characteristics of the poor. Lampman uses lower income limits than does Keyserling or Morgan. Consequently, he describes a poor population with 50 per cent of the heads of households out of the labor market; while the others, using a higher income level to define poverty, report only 35 per cent of the heads of households as out of the labor market. We do not have data, but it is reasonable to deduce that a higher percentage of Lampman's poor are on welfare than is true of Morgan's or Keyserling's.

Clearly, different income cutoff points shape the characteristics of those of "low income." The lower the income level used, the more economically and socially different are the poor.

Definitions of poverty and the poor are not technical problems but social and ideological issues. The low-income are not basically a "welfare poor." Only one-fifth of Morgan's poor receive welfare assistance. The social scientists and social-service specialists who write of the "welfare poor" are

---

[13] Keyserling, *op. cit.;* Lampman, *op. cit.*
[14] See footnote 4.
[15] Morgan, *op. cit.,* p. 3.

discussing only a slice of the poor; those concerned with "hard-core" and "multiproblem families" are, in turn, analyzing only a very thin wedge of this small slice.

The income criterion has several components: the level of income, the stability or regularity of income, and the source of income (employment or welfare). A number of observers believe that it makes a difference, holding income constant, whether a family is supported by welfare or not. The knowledge to make a fine classification of these components is lacking. I have resorted, therefore, to combining them into one indicator of economic security (roughly combining income and stability), and then dichotomizing this indicator into the two simple dimensions of high (security) and low (insecurity). Lumping together these components and dichotomizing them are inadequate.[16] But we cannot at present describe each of the cells of what should be an 8-fold or 16-fold table. I think, however, that the cells of a 4-fold table can be usefully discussed. This capsulated table should rapidly be expanded as we acquire more knowledge and understanding.

THE STYLE-OF-LIFE CRITERION

The style-of-life variable also offers difficulties. It refers, at least, to attitudes and behavior in the areas of family relationships and consumption patterns. A major difficulty is that the content of the "lower-class style of life" is debatable. Further, evaluative judgments (as implied in the concepts of "family disorganization," "social disorganization," and "family instability") are invariably involved. As yet, it is not possible to formulate a clear-cut classification which avoids cultural biases and still enables us to render a judgment about the impact of life style on individuals. For example, does the absence of a permanent male figure mean that the family is inevitably "unstable" and that children are necessarily psychologically deformed by living in such a family? Assessments such as these are difficult to make because much of our knowledge and theorizing about fatherless families are based on middle-class situations.

I employ the notion of "familial stability/instability," a dichotomization of style of life, to summarize a variety of elements. Familial stability patterns are characterized by families coping with their problems—the children are being fed, although not necessarily on a schedule; the family meets its obligations, so that it is not forced to keep on the move; children are not getting into much more trouble than other children of the neighborhood. These are not satisfactory indicators; they are, at best, suggestive of the kind of behavior which is characteristic of stability among the "low-income." The aim is to be able to describe the degrees of effectiveness of different styles of life in handling the same environment. Our vocabulary is inadequate for this task.

---

[16] Not all families receiving welfare assistance should automatically be classified in the economically insecure category. For the aged, perhaps, welfare assistance does not constitute a lack of security. In general, however, the fact of welfare assistance would put a family in the economically insecure category.

The two approaches can be welded together by cross-tabulating the two dimensions of the two variables of economic security and familial stability in a 2 x 2 table:

TYPES OF ECONOMIC SECURITY AND FAMILIAL STABILITY

		Familial	
		Stability	Instability
		+	−
Economic	Security +	++(1)	+−(2)
	Insecurity −	−+(3)	−−(4)

Cell 1 is referred to as *the stable poor*; cell 2, *the strained*; cell 3, *the copers*, and cell 4, *the unstable*.

To some extent, life-cycle stages may be involved here, as some young people escape from cell 4 via cell 2 or cell 3 to cell 1, a more stable pattern, and beyond. Or families may drop with age from cell 1 to cell 3, where they have lowered economic security but maintain family stability.

Each of the cells contains many variants. Although I believe that the four types are an improvement over analysis in terms of "*the* lower class," it is important to recognize that each type has many variations. One difference, of course, is whether the family is stationary in its particular pattern or moving to greater or less security-stability. *My general orientation is to emphasize flux rather than assuming a permanent position in a pattern.*

THE STABLE POOR

Cell 1 *(the stable poor)* is characterized by stability economically and familially. This cell points to the regularly employed, low-skill, stable-poor families.

Farm, rural nonfarm, and small-town persons undoubtedly make up the bulk of the stable poor, since they are the majority of the American poor: a recalculation of Morgan's data suggests that only 30 per cent of the poor live in metropolitan areas. The majority of all the poor and of the stable poor are white rural Southern populations. In addition, the nonurban poor are probably represented in this cell to a greater extent than they are among all the poor. Aged persons are also overrepresented and constitute a large part of the downwardly mobile poor, since most of them were better off at earlier points in their lives. Left-over third-generation immigrant populations in large cities are probably underrepresented.[17]

A number of Negro families are of the stable poor. They have higher social status in the Negro community than their economic counterparts have in the white community because of the general scaling down of incomes and occupational levels of Negroes in the United States. For reasons discussed

---

[17] Richard Cloward and Lloyd Ohlin, *Delinquency and Opportunity* (New York: The Free Press of Glencoe, Inc., 1960).

below, Negroes and other discriminated groups are probably becoming more important politically, as well as in relative size, among the urban stable poor.

The children of cell 1 families are most likely of all the children of the poor to be educationally and occupationally mobile. Cell 1 might be the "takeoff" cell—the phase necessary before many can really make a big advance. But this is a dangerous metaphor, for obviously many youth from families in more difficult circumstances are able to make considerable gains.

The stable poor, then, are a varied group; one component, the aged, has a poor economic future, except to the extent that Social Security and old-age payments improve, and a declining future as an intact family unit.

THE STRAINED

Cell 2 *(the strained)* portrays a secure economic pattern but an unstable family one. This might be a life-cycle problem; that is, at certain points, the families of low-wage, unskilled workers are likely to exhibit unstable patterns. Examples might be "wild" younger workers or alchoholic older workers who disturb family functioning. Or, the pattern could manifest the beginning of a move into cell 4, as a low-income family finds increasing difficulty in maintaining its economic security because of family and personal problems or the economic situation. Obviously, the two possibilities may be closely connected.

Movement may be viewed intergenerationally as well as in terms of life-cycle patterns. Many of the offspring of strained families "may fail to match the economic security of their parents" and experience intergenerational skidding.[18]

Strained familial relations may not, however, result in skidding. In earlier periods, immigrant groups faced considerable internal strain arising from the conflict between the younger and older generations in the course of acculturation. Nonetheless, the second generation generally improved its economic circumstances. The instability of today's strained families is regarded as more "pathological" than that of the immigrant populations, although some social-work accounts of families at the turn of the century differ little from current reports of "poor family functioning." The current stress is on fighting and drinking among parents, illicit sexual relations of parents, and neglect or brutality toward the children. Whether the economically secure and familially unstable are characterized by these patterns is not clear. If they are not, then the offspring of the strained family may not be as much prey to skidding. Further, not all children of deeply conflicted or hostile families are inevitably unable to maintain or improve their economic position.

I have looked at cell 2 as a transitional condition. This view may be misleading: many families persist with a low but steady income and a great deal of internal strain.

---

[18] Dennis Wrong, in a personal communication, has influenced this and the following paragraph. "Skidding" is discussed in Harold Wilensky and Hugh Edwards, "The Skidder: Ideological Adjustments of Downward Mobile Workers," *American Sociological Review,* Vol. 24 (April, 1959), pp. 215-31.

The American
Lower Classes:
A Typological
Approach

The copers of cell 3 manifest economic insecurity and familial stability —families and individuals having a rough time economically but managing to keep themselves relatively intact. This group probably increases considerably during extensive layoffs. Probably a considerable number of Negroes are in this group, and their children are more likely to be mobile than are those living in cell 2-type situations.

This cell probably contains a disproportionate number of families which have been downwardly mobile. Both Morgan[19] and I[20] have shown the sizable number of sons of nonmanual workers who end up in manual (and sometimes low-income) positions. In Great Britain, 40 per cent of those born in nonmanual families move into manual occupations. Many of these downwardly mobile are probably more likely to retain a stable family style than others in the same economic predicament. As in many other situations, however, a minority of the downwardly mobile may manifest extreme familial instability, which would place them in cell 4. Limited data suggest that children of downwardly mobile families have a better chance of rising occupationally than children of families which have been at this low level for some generations.

THE UNSTABLE

In cell 4, *the unstable* have neither economic nor personal stability. It is this group which is probably most generally called "the lower class," and Jerome Cohen has suggested to me that the term *lower class* might be usefully restricted to this group. Because this recommendation is unlikely to be consistently utilized by social workers, economists, sociologists, political scientists, and others interested in low-income populations, I have not adopted it, preferring to focus attention on the varied segments of the low-income population. Within the unstable group, there are degrees of stability and strain—*not every family is a "hard-core case" or has a "multi-agency problem."* Nor do we have sufficient longitudinal data to assert that, once in cell 4, always in cell 4. It may be that families and individuals occasionally manifest both economic and personal instability, then overcome these problems for a while. Later they may again suffer from illness, unemployment, emotional upset, or familial instability.

In some ways, it is as important to note that cell 4 is a very varied grouping as it is to distinguish cell 4 from the other three cells that make up the "lower class." Cell 4 comprises partially urbanized Negroes new to the North and to cities, remaining slum residents of ethnic groups which have largely moved out of the slums, long-term (intergenerational) poor white families, and the *déclassé* of Marx. Also included are the physically handi-

---

[19] Morgan, *op. cit.*

[20] S. M. Miller, "Comparative Social Mobility," *Current Sociology*, Vol. IX, No. 1 (1960), pp. 1-89.

capped and the aged who have dropped through the class structure. *The low-income class generally—and the unstable in particular—is a category of unskilled, irregular workers, broken and large families, and a residual bin of the aged, physically handicapped, and mentally disturbed.*

In some cases, such social characteristics as discrimination and recent rurality (resulting in unfamiliarity with urban problems and the lack of skills needed for dealing with them) handicap the low-income groups. These groups—Negroes and former mountaineer whites—would have the worst problems. Perhaps they would also have the greatest potential because elimination of their social limitations would lead to substantial change. Their handicaps are less self-inflicted and less self-sustaining. This may not be as true for mountaineer whites as for Negroes. In addition to people who drop into the poverty class along the life- and physical-cycle, the whites in the lower class who have no sound, social reason for being there are most likely to be intractable to change.

Hylan Lewis[21] has suggested the categories of *clinical, preclinical,* and *subclinical* to delineate patterns among the poor. I would substitute the word *chronic* for *clinical.* The *chronics* refer to the long-term dependents, part of whom would be the "hard-core"; the *prechronics* would be a high-risk group which is moving toward a chronic situation but have not yet become chronically dependent. The *subchronics* are those who have many characteristics of dependence but who also have a greater ability to cope with their problems.[22]

A number of forces can lead individuals into chronic dependence. *"Lower-class" life is crisis-life constantly trying to make do with string where rope is needed.* Anything can break the string. Illness is one of the most important —"Got a job but I got sick and lost it"; "We managed until the baby got sick." The great incidence of physical afflictions among the poor—frequently unknown to the victim—are obvious to any casual observer. Particularly striking are the poor teeth of many. The tendency of lower-class people to somaticize their emotional difficulties may be influenced by the omnipresence of illness.

Familial and personal instability may be the sources as well as the consequences of difficulties. Although some frequent concomitants of low-income life, such as matrifocality, do not inevitably produce grave difficulties in family life, they frequently do. Alchoholism, an inability to handle aggression, or hostility or dependence—one's own or that of another toward one—can deeply disturb family functioning. A variety of direct personal aid may be necessary.

Sophistication along these lines of analysis has frequently tended to denigrate the importance of structural factors in producing "personal

---

[21] Hylan Lewis, "Child Rearing Among Low Income Families," Washington Center for Metropolitan Studies, June 8, 1961. This paper and others by Lewis are among the most stimulating on the problems of low-income patterns. Also see Hyman Rodman, "The Lower-Class Value Stretch, *Social Forces,* Vol. 42 (December, 1963). Reprinted in revised form in this volume.

[22] I have used the terms *dependent* and *dependence* here for want of a sharper term; I find the concept of dependence murky and frequently used to cover a variety of conditions which a writer does not like.

The American
Lower Classes:
A Typological
Approach

inadequacies," "social disabilities," "familial instability." The work of Raymond Smith[23] and Edith Clarke[24] strongly suggests that illegitimacy is related to economic conditions—the better the economic conditions among the "lower-class" Negroes of the Caribbean, the lower the rate of illegitimacy. Kunstadter[25] similarly argues that matrifocality as a "lower-class" trait is related to a particular set of economic characteristics.

Prolonged unemployment, irregular employment, and low income are important forces leading to a chronic pattern. Low-paid and irregularly employed individuals do not develop an image of the world as something predictable and as something with which they are able to cope. Control or directing of events appears (and frequently is) an unattainable achievement. When they suffer long-term unemployment they are less likely than other unemployed, who have had the experience of fairly regular employment, to maintain a personal stability. (Maslow[26] has argued that those who have had a stable past are more able to manage in disastrous circumstances than those who have had considerable prior deprivation.) A high-employment economy has relatively fewer "hard-core" cases than a low-employment economy. The American community studies suggest that the "lower class" is smaller in numbers in times of prosperity than in periods of depression. Peter Townsend in an informal lecture recently declared that during the 1930's in England it was believed that 500,000 to 1,000,000 of those not working were "unemployable." In 1940, with the pressures of the war, it was discovered that only 100,000 were really unemployables. Structural change would be of great importance in reducing dependence.

STRATEGIES

Three basic policies are possible: (1) direct economic change, such as providing better employment, or directly raising incomes through the provision of a national minimum level of income; (2) direct services, such as casework activities to strengthen the ego-functioning of the individual, or family assistance through homemaker help; (3) indirect change by affecting the climate—social, psychological, or political—of the neighborhoods in which the poor live.

What would lead one type of low-income population in a given direction would not work at all for another type. A panacea does not work because there is no one thing which will have a pervasive impact in all cases if changed. What is dynamic for one type may be insignificant for others.

I find the concept of elasticity useful here.[27] It points to the extent of

[23] Raymond T. Smith, *The Negro Family in British Guiana* (London: Routledge & Kegan Paul, Ltd., 1956).

[24] Edith Clarke, *My Mother Who Fathered Me* (New York: Humanities Press, 1957).

[25] Peter Kunstadter, "A Survey of the Consanguine and Matrifocal Family," *American Anthropologist*, Vol. 65 (February, 1963), pp. 56-66.

[26] A. H. Maslow, *Motivation and Personality* (New York: Harper & Row, Publishers, 1954), pp. 80-106.

[27] Carlsson has reintroduced the concept of elasticity into sociological thinking. Gosta Carlsson, "Okonomische Ungleichheit und Lebenschanchen," *Kolner Zeitschrift fur Soziologie*, Vol. 5, 1961, pp. 189-99.

change resulting from the input of additional services or income. Some types of the poor have high income elasticity—a little change in income produces a big change in behavior; other types may have low income elasticity but high education elasticity or high casework elasticity. Still other types will respond rapidly and deeply to new housing, to a steady job, to counseling, or to a package of such ingredients rather than to, say, casework. The concept of elasticity introduces frontally the issues of variable remedies for different types. The issues of costs, substitution, and choice of different services or resources are made vivid by the notion of elasticity and productivity (the return per unit of expenditure).

The stable—those in cell 1—would be immediately helped if their incomes were raised so that they would come closer to the American standard of life. Unionization of their industries (especially in service trades and occupations), shifts from low-productivity land and industries to highly productive industries, and occupational retraining would be important. In some situations, individuals have to be prepared for retraining (where, for example, the level of literacy is low) or aided in moving to new localities where opportunities are greater. They may need help in adjusting to new urban conditions, but this adjustment would probably not be very difficult where jobs and housing are adequate. The stable poor, in short, would have a high income elasticity, rapidly improving and adjusting to increases in their income.

The inadequacy of social services and payments in the United States forces many into cell 1. Improving and extending Social Security, which keeps many in penury and does not help a substantial number in noncovered occupations and industries, would move many from cells 2, 3, and 4 into cell 1 and lead many of the stable poor into the main society. Harrington[28] and Titmuss[29] have pointed out that social services in the United States and Britain do not seem to be benefiting the poor as much as the middle-income population. Obviously, changes in social policy are necessary here.

Some of the strained of cell 2 might require some casework help in improving family conditions and operations, but other approaches might be effective. If they live in a locality that manifests high rates of disturbances, they might be helped by being moved to new areas. For some, an improvement in economic conditions may be necessary in order to get deeper family changes. Undoubtedly, a number are not sensitive to income changes or to neighborhood climate change, and for these sustained casework help would be necessary.

Familial instability may be a carryover from an earlier period when the family suffered from economic insecurity; the family has not caught up with its economic improvements. But, as Seymour S. Bellin and Jerome Cohen have pointed out, in some families where economic conditions have improved after a long period of economic deprivation and family difficulties, withdrawing

---

[28] Harrington, *op. cit.*

[29] Richard Titmuss, *Essays on 'The Welfare State'* (London: George Allen & Unwin, 1958), Ch. 2, "The Social Division of Welfare," in *Income Distribution and Social Change* (Toronto: University of Toronto Press, 1962). Although Titmuss is a seminal thinker in analyzing changes in the social structure of the modern society, he has been almost completely ignored by American sociologists.

the stress of economic insecurity may be insufficient. The toll of the stress frequently must be overcome. Special help may be necessary to bring about familial changes of great importance. Of importance would be the adaptation of social agencies to enable them to meet the requirements of these families at the time of need and to provide aid in ways which fit the outlook of these families.

The copers of cell 3, who maintain family stability in the face of grave economic difficulties, obviously need economic aid. Many of them would be helped by improvement in welfare payments and practices; others, where there is a working head of household, would be advanced by regularization of work and/or by shifting to more remunerative fields. The needs of the stable and the copers would seem to be similar. Improvement in the economic dimension would push more of the copers into the mobility possibilities of the stable poor of cell 1 and beyond.

Cell 4, containing the unstable, is the most discussed grouping of the poor today. Many, if not most, are on welfare allotments; women head many of the family units. A general improvement in economic conditions would not have much economic impact on the unstable, because they are largely out of the labor force and out of the economy. It is widely believed that unstable families do not have a high income elasticity, but the evidence is not strong. Specific programs aimed at this group would be important. Present-day welfare services are insufficient, since they have largely been budgetary and policing activities. Concentration on improving the educational achievement of the youth of these families would be more important, perhaps, than a diffuse effort to achieve better family functioning.[30] A number of interesting and aggressive casework services have been offered; their degree of long-term success is unclear. A variety of direct services may be effective with some of these families—including continuous homemaking and babysitting services, provision of nurseries, all-day schools, and consumer-buying protection.

It may be that a less direct approach would be effective. It would involve trying to mobilize politically the communities in which the unstable live with the more stable poor so as to provide greater feelings of strength and control. The anticipated but side effect would be the improving of family conditions. A general change in a low-income community, precipitated perhaps by the mobile, the strained, and the copers, may spread to affect the unstable of the community. The social-actionists, of whom Saul Alinsky is the best-known, utilize this implicit strategy.

In all of the strategies, it is necessary to be clear about who exactly is the target population. This is frequently determined on the basis of the numbers involved, although there is always the delicate choice between helping a lot of people a little and helping a few people a lot. The second step is to discover what works with whom. There is probably nothing that will help all "lower-class" people in one move, although, as suggested above, a steady, meaningful, well-paid job as a general base of action should not be underestimated. A decent level of living for all as the minimal responsibility of an affluent society, no matter what people do around this level, may be an important point to

---

[30] Cf. S. M. Miller, "Poverty and Inequality in America," *op. cit.*

maintain in a period when government welfare payments are under criticism. But there are some things that will help certain types. We have to find the right things for the right groups at the right time.

POLITICAL ACTION

The poor are not rapidly declining; income and wealth inequality appear to be increasing in recent years; the incomes of Negroes are no longer advancing relative to those of whites; pension and assistance schemes are maintaining many in poverty rather than providing a "Welfare State" standard. The decline in the number of poor between 1947 and 1957 was due, Lampman contends, to general economic advance rather than to a redistribution of income and wealth in favor of the poor. Improvements in social services and a decrease in inequality would require a shift in the allocation of national product toward improving the relative position of the bottom 20 per cent.

These issues are political ones. They will be affected by the possibility that the present American poor may prove to be more politically active than is usually true of the poor. If this happens, it will be because a large slice of the urban poor is made up of Negroes, who have ethnic as well as economic forces moving them. Samuel Lubell[31] has argued that Negroes in large cities will furnish a new base for Democratic ward machines. They are becoming more and more politically active and demanding. This self-organization is not only important in getting changes from the government, but is also serving to change "lower-class" Negro communities from within. Local leaders are developing, and the orientation of many community agencies to provide leadership and direction to "lower-class" communities will become increasingly ineffective. The conservative orientation of gaining change and social advance through an harmonious arrangement with local power forces is being superseded by disadvantaged groups themselves actively pressuring for the kinds of changes—in housing, in schools, and the like—that they believe to be important.

In the course of these pressures, it is likely that the *desegregation issue will emerge as a social-class issue* affecting all "lower-class" persons, and not only as a racial issue affecting Negroes alone. Mexican-Americans and Puerto Ricans, who with Negroes increasingly make the poor of the large metropolis a "colored poor," are increasingly moving into the stable and coping patterns and beginning to develop political effectiveness. Poverty may not be treated as a racial issue affecting only Negroes. *Even where Negroes operate alone, the impact of their demands will affect all the poor as they achieve better schools, better housing, better jobs, and better social services.*

CAUSE AND CONSEQUENCE

A good deal of the tone of discussions of the "lower class," even by sociologists, has a negative quality. On the other hand, a few seem to have a romantic feeling about the "lower class," particularly their juvenile de-

---

[31] In his syndicated column which appeared in the *Syracuse Herald-Journal* (November 14, 1961).

linquents, and see them as rebels against the horrors of middle-class, conformist America. The former view suffers from the assumption that they have little potential for change; the latter, that there is nothing better in present-day America to which they can change.

Among other things, the glorification theme ignores, as Riessman has pointed out, the impact on the "lower class" of its limited education.[32] The negative view frequently confuses, as Keyserling has noted, cause and consequence. The personal instability of many "lower-class" persons may be a consequence of economic instability as well as a cause of it. The chain of cause and effect over time frequently becomes blurred. Where is there an effective way of cutting into the chain so that change will occur? This becomes the issue. My feeling is that structural forces have been under-played recently as a mode of change, as "the culture of poverty" has been overstressed.[33]

The negative view has the danger of not seeing positive elements in "lower-class" life. By ignoring these elements, social policies can frequently worsen them. For example, in an exciting study of a Puerto Rican slum, Helen Icken Safa has reported the community and familial solidarity of the residents of a slum barrio. When families were moved into public housing, community ties were weakened. The project social workers centered on the wife. The husband's role and responsibility in the family and community diminished.[34]

It is perhaps a "heuristic" fallacy, as Frank Riessman has said, to believe that "lower-class" people are willing and capable of positive change. This is not always true, but if professionals and social reformers lack confidence in the poor, little can be accomplished in the social services or in political action. One might fail with this optimism—as we frequently do—but without it, it is doubtful if anything can be moved. Frequently, disenchantment and cynicism capture accurately a slice of life. They are also immobilizing, for they ignore the constructive and energizing role of hope.[35]

CONCLUSION

A clearly defined "lower class" does not exist—it is a varied, changing group, as Peter Townsend has noted:

> A misconception is that in a relatively prosperous society most individuals have the capacity to meet any contingency in life. Only a poor and handicapped minority need special protection or help. This ignores the infinite diversities and changing conditions to be found in any population. Men gain or fall in status

[32] Frank Riessman, *The Culturally Deprived Child* (New York: Harper & Row, Publishers, 1962).

[33] Harrington seems frequently to write and speak as though all low-income persons are bound in an immutable chain of apathy and ineffectiveness, characteristics of "the culture of poverty." He has obviously extended this term beyond the intent of Oscar Lewis, who introduced it in his *Five Families* (New York: Basic Books, Inc., 1959), and in *The Children of Sanchez* (New York: Random House, 1961). Warren Haggstrom has countered this view in his "The Power of the Poor," Syracuse University Youth Development Center, 1963.

[34] Helen Icken Safa, *From Shanty Town to Public Housing*, Syracuse University Youth Development Center, 1962. The peculiar stresses of public housing life may be functional equivalents of the economic conditions of matrifocality discussed by Kunstadter.

[35] Cf. S. M. Miller and Frank Riessman, "Working Class Authoritarianism: A Critique of Lipset," *British Journal of Sociology* (September, 1961).

and living standards; at one stage of their life their dependencies are minimal, at others unduly numerous; sometimes they need exceptional help to achieve qualifications and skills held to be desirable by society; and at all times they are susceptible to the vicissitudes of prolonged ill health, disability, redundancy of unemployment, and bereavement, which they are usually powerless to control or even reasonably anticipate. Unanticipated adversity is not the peculiar experience of one fixed section of the working class.[36]

In England, Dahrendorf contends, [37] the unskilled category is a temporary position—individuals at various stages of the life cycle may drop into it, but for only a comparatively few is it a permanent position. In the United States, this is not as true, and if caste pressures grow, it will be even less true.

The changing economy of America is producing new property relations; at the same time, it is producing new working classes and lower classes.[38] The analysis of data and the development of our concepts have not kept up with the increasing differentiation within these populations. Many pressures and counter-pressures exist in any stratum. Despite a modal pattern, considerable variety in values and behavior occurs. Because cross-pressures affect the "lower class" to a considerable extent,[39] we should look for *types* of behavior patterns even among people apparently very similar in objective characteristics. Those at the social bottom see only a vague and ill-defined "them" up there, whereas those above believe that those below are rather similar. But the tops know how much differentiation within the top actually takes place; the bottoms are aware of much more differentiation than are the outsiders looking in. In particular, what has been taken as typical of the most unstable bottom group has been generalized to apply to all who are poor or who are manual workers.

The label "the lower class" increasingly distorts complicated reality. We must begin to demarcate more sharply types of poor people if we are to understand and interpret behavior and circumstance and to develop appropriate social policies. Evaluations of commentators are frequently masked as description. *Ways of coping with hard reality are interpreted as normatively prescribed whereas frequently they are actually weakly dissanctioned behavior.*

The resurgence of interest in the poor augurs well for a rethinking of the new kind of poverty in the "welfare state" which is unlike the mass unemployment of the 1930's or the grinding poverty of the employed workers of the nineteenth century. Our "received wisdom" should be superseded by new categories and concepts. New wine is being poured into old conceptual bottles, and the specialness of the new is being lost.

---

[36] Peter Townsend, "Freedom and Equality," *New Statesmen,* Vol. LXI, No. 1570 (April 14, 1961), p. 574.

[37] Ralf Dahrendorf, *Unskilled Labour in British Industry,* unpublished Ph.D. thesis in sociology, London School of Economics, 1956, pp. 429-30.

[38] S. M. Miller, "Poverty, Race and Politics," in Irving Louis Horowitz, ed., *The New Sociology: Essays on Social Values and Social Theory in Honor of C. Wright Mills* (New York: Oxford University Press, Inc., 1964). This essay appears in this volume in revised form.

[39] See Miller and Riessman, "The Working-Class Subculture," and Hylan Lewis, *op. cit.*

The American
Lower Classes
A Typological
Approach

The Working-Class Subculture: A New View*

S. M. MILLER

FRANK RIESSMAN

A decade and a half ago the working class was depicted by Allison Davis and Robert J. Havighurst[1] as permissive and indulgent toward their children and free of the emotional strain of impulse-inhibition which characterized the middle class in the United States. Indeed, it was felt by many that the middle class had much to envy and imitate in the working class.[2] This romantic view of the working class has faded. It is now asserted that the working class (usually termed the "lower class") is incapable of deferring gratification[3] and consequently unable to make major strides in improving their conditions. Frequently accompanying this view is the belief that this lower class is "immoral," "uncivilized," "promiscuous," "lazy," "obscene," "dirty," and "loud." [4] With the rising plane and standard of living of workers has come the argument that workers are middle class in their outlook and desires;[5] the difficulties

---

* Presented at Annual Meetings of the American Sociological Association, New York, August 30, 1960. Reprinted from *Social Problems*, Vol. IX, No. 1 (Summer, 1961), pp. 86-97.

[1] Allison Davis and Robert J. Havighurst, "Social Class and Color Differences in Child Rearing," *American Sociological Review*, Vol. 11 (December, 1946), pp. 698-710.

[2] Cf. David Riesman in his introduction to Ely Chinoy's *American Workers and Their Dreams* (New York: Doubleday & Company, Inc., 1955).

[3] Louis Schneider and Sverre Lysgaard, "The Deferred Gratification Pattern: A Preliminary Study," *American Sociological Review*, Vol. 18 (April, 1953), pp. 142-49.

[4] These adjectives are taken from Rodman who then goes on to declare: "Lantz, Centers, Warner, *et al.*, Hollingshead, Drake and Cayton, West, and Davis, Gardner and Gardner make it clear that this is the way the lower class is viewed within the United States; the Henriques and Braithwaite studies make it clear that this is the way the lower class is viewed within the West Indies." Hyman Rodman, "On Understanding Lower-Class Behavior," *Social and Economic Studies*, Vol. 8 (December, 1959). Other authors state: "One of the most venerable stereotypes has been that applied by middle-class people to lower-class people. The qualities have from time to time included lack of thrift, intellectual inferiority, habitual dirtiness, licentiousness, and many that have derogatory implications." Robert R. Sears, Eleanor E. Maccoby, and Harry Levin, *Patterns of Child Rearing* (New York: Harper & Row, Publishers, 1957), p. 442. We have isolated five types of stereotypes of workers—anomic, depraved, incapable of deferring gratification, class conscious and middle-class oriented; these are discussed in S. M. Miller and Frank Riessman, "Images of Workers," a paper presented to the Eastern Sociological Society, New York, 1957.

[5] Daniel Bell, *The End of Ideology* (New York: The Free Press of Glencoe, Inc., 1959), and in various issues of *Fortune* magazine. On the other hand, see his path-breaking article, "The Subversion of Collective Bargaining," *Commentary* (March, 1960).

in attaining full middle-class status lead to juvenile delinquency on the part of those youths who fall back into the working and lower classes[6] and to authoritarianism on the part of those who rise into the middle class.[7] Recently, a further vigorous blow has felled any notions of desirable characteristics of workers: their economic liberalism is not paralleled by political liberalism for workers are said to be more authoritarian in outlook than are members of the middle class.[8] The free, spontaneous worker is now seen as an aggressive, authoritarian, yet fettered person.

The cyclothymic views of workers are more fitting as a topic in the sociology of knowledge than they are in the analysis of what workers actually believe and practice. In other work, we have criticized in some detail a number of prevailing interpretations of workers—the middle-class image,[9] the nondeferred gratification pattern,[10] the authoritarian view.[11] By the nature of criticism, we have not been able to present our view of what workers are like, for they are not simply the negative or opposite of prevailing views.

For example, because it is demonstrated that workers' behavior is not consistently characterized by an inability to postpone gratifications, we cannot therefore conclude that a major characteristic of the working class is *having* a deferred gratification pattern. It may very well be that the whole issue of deferred gratification does not have special relevance to workers' lives. The concept might stem from a sociocentric point of view, where the middle-class observer, in a sense, says, "If I were in the workers' boots, I wouldn't postpone gratification; I would enjoy myself while I could in the present and not worry about a future which is pretty vague and hopeless anyway." This thinking does not arise out of the context in which workers' behavior takes place, but rather is imposed upon it. In other words, the entire concept of deferred gratification may be inappropriate to understanding the essence of workers' lives.

In this paper, we can only present a few elements of what we believe is a more realistic picture of workers. This analysis is severely compressed and truncated in this presentation and it might be helpful therefore to indicate at the outset an important element of our general orientation. Our stress is much more on cognitive and structural factors than on the more commonly cited affectual and motivational ones. The nature of the conditions of working-class lives (jobs, opportunities, family structure) affects behavior more than has been frequently realized; similarly, modes of understanding the environment can be more important than deep-seated personality factors in be-

---

[6] Albert Cohen, *Delinquent Boys: The Culture of the Gang* (New York: The Free Press of Glencoe, Inc., 1955).

[7] Joseph Greenblum and Leonard I. Pearlin, "Vertical Mobility and Prejudice: A Socio-Psychological Analysis," in Reinhard Bendix and Seymour Martin Lipset, eds., *Class, Status and Power* (New York: The Free Press of Glencoe, Inc., 1953).

[8] Seymour Martin Lipset, *Political Man: The Social Bases of Politics* (New York: Doubleday & Company, Inc., 1960), Ch. IV.

[9] S. M. Miller and Frank Riessman, "Are Workers Middle Class?," *Dissent* (Autumn, 1961).

[10] S. M. Miller and Frank Riessman, "The Non-Deferred Gratification Pattern: A Critique," unpublished.

[11] S. M. Miller and Frank Riessman, " Working-Class Authoritarianism : A Critique of Lipset," *British Journal of Sociology* (September, 1961).

havioral patterns. (For example, workers' low estimates of opportunities and high expectations of risk and loss play a more crucial part in their unwillingness to undertake certain long-term actions than do personality inadequacies involved in a presumed inability to defer gratification.) This is not to argue that motivational-psychological-affectual variables are unimportant but that they have been overstressed, whereas cognitive and structural variables have been underemphasized. The recognition of the importance of the internal life of man has sometimes overshadowed the significance of the more manifest aspects of his existence.

Our definition of working class is simple: regular members of the non-agricultural labor force in manual occupations. Thus, we exclude the "lower class," irregular working people, although our analysis has some relevance to "the lower class," as mentioned below. One of the greatest sources of difficulty in understanding nonupper and nonmiddle class behavior is the social scientist's frequent use of the omnibus category of "lower class" to encompass the stable, and frequently mobile, fairly high-income skilled workers, the semiskilled factory worker, the worker in varied service trades, the unskilled worker, and the irregular worker. This collection is probably more a congeries of fairly disparate groups than it is a category with similar life chances and circumstances. It is especially important to distinguish from the other groupings, which are larger and have more in common, that segment which has irregular employment (and "voluntary" withdrawals from the labor force) and unskilled jobs in service occupations (and is largely Negro and Puerto Rican now).

We call this latter group of regular workers the "working class" despite the reluctance of many social scientists to use this historic term; the opprobrious term "lower class" might be applied to the irregular segment, although it would probably be better to use a less invidious term (perhaps "the unskilled").

This reluctance to make the distinction between "working class" and "lower class," despite useful discussions by Kahl[12] and others, not only is a topic worthy of independent study, but leads to error. For example, the findings of Hollingshead and Redlich in their important study[13] have been interpreted as: the lower the class, the higher the rate of mental illness. Close examination of their data reveals, however, that the working class (Class IV) is closer to the upper and middle classes (Classes I, II, and III) than to the lower class (Class V). Classes I through IV are similar, whereas Class V is quite dissimilar from all other classes, including the working class.

Within the working class, we are primarily interested in the *stable* working-class subculture. We believe there is considerable variation within the working

---

[12] Joseph A. Kahl, *The American Class Structure* (New York: Holt, Rinehart & Winston, Inc., 1959), pp. 205ff.

[13] For the original report, see A. B. Hollingshead and Frederick C. Redlich, *Social Class and Mental Illness* (New York: John Wiley & Sons, Inc., 1958). The point above is taken from S. M. Miller and Elliot G. Mishler, "Social Class, Mental Illness, and American Psychiatry," *Milbank Memorial Fund Quarterly*, Vol. XXXVII (April, 1959), pp. 174-99.

class,[14] but the differences probably are variations upon the theme of the stable working-class pattern. While we think in terms of working-class sub-cultures, and, to some extent, lower-class subcultures, a key to understanding them, we believe, is likely to be the *stable* working-class subculture.

PHENOTYPES, GENOTYPES AND THE MIDDLE CLASS

Our analysis is aimed at developing *themes* in working-class life. Thus, we are interpreting the *meaning* of findings rather than reporting new findings. We have utilized the published materials commonly employed plus our own interviews and observations of working-class people.

A major inadequacy in explanations of the working-class life style has been the failure to explain behavior in terms of genotypes. For example, in attitudinal polls in which similar questions are asked of middle- and working-class people, many differences are revealed between the two groups. But what is the meaning of the replies? For example, if workers agree with the statement, "Communists should be imprisoned," does it mean that they are especially unaccepting of civil liberties or that they are punitive towards those whom they see as criminals, and that they consider punishment an effective deterrent and a just reward for wrongdoing? They may be wrong in all respects, but does their attitude reflect fundamentally a rejection of Bill of Rights thinking or a punitive attitude which has as one of its results in a specific situation, the denial of civil liberties? Emphasis on the phenotype, civil liberties, may obscure the basic dynamics of the attitude in stressing a Bill of Rights little known to workers.[15]

Another illustration of phenotypic analysis was the tendency of Davis and Havighurst to denote long breast-feeding as belonging in the cluster they termed permissive child care. This may have been accurate for the middle class, since long breast-feeding is associated there with the *ideology* of permissiveness: indulgence, reliance on love, child-centered, and so forth. It is not for the working class, because long breast-feeding is not related genotypically to the permissive child-rearing *ideology* in that class.[16]

A second major difficulty in explaining working-class life is the preoccupation with comparing it with the middle class.[17] The comparisons have perhaps

---

[14] Robert Blauner, in his thoughtful paper, "Industrial Differences in Work Attitudes and Work Institutions," points out important differences among workers in different industries. Bennett Berger, *Working Class Suburb* (Berkeley: University of California Press, 1960), believes there are differences in attitudes among workers of "Arkie" and "Okie" backgrounds, and workers of a nonrural background. A variety of studies show the importance of educational differences among workers, a factor with which we are very concerned. See Frank Riessman, *Workers' Attitudes Towards Participation and Leadership,* unpublished Ph.D. dissertation in social psychology, Columbia University, 1955.

[15] Cf. David Joseph Bordua, *Authoritarianism and Intolerance, A Study of High School Students,* unpublished Ph.D. thesis, Department of Social Relations, Harvard University, 1956, pp. 228, 237, 239.

[16] Evelyn Millis Duvall, "Conceptions of Parenthood," *American Journal of Sociology,* Vol. LII (November, 1946), pp. 193-203. Cf. Martha Wolfenstein, "The Emergence of Fun Morality," *Journal of Social Issues,* Vol. VII, No. 4 (1951), pp. 15-25.

[17] Hyman Rodman, *op. cit.*

The
Working-Class
Subculture:
A New
View

inevitably a pejorative tone so that, for example, at one time those critical of the middle class could charge it with having poor child care compared to the more spontaneous workers. It appears that some of the critics of this view have moved to the other pejorative extreme and are now critical of working-class child care and rather uncritically praising of the middle-class style of child care.[18]

A difficulty then in analyzing the working class has been this value shift to a more positive orientation towards the middle class and therefore a more critical view of the working class. As one class ascends in approval the other descends because the two classes are seen in a contrapuntal and judgmental relationship.

Another difficulty is that the middle class has apparently changed considerably in various ways so that comparisons involving the middle class are frequently of official norms rather than actual practices, of old norms rather than present norms. For example, it is frequently said that many working-class children of talent do not go on to college because they lack the ability to defer gratification, an ability the college-bound middle-class youth display. Is it really true today in the prosperous middle-class youth culture of the United States that most middle-class youth are deferring gratification when they go to college? More likely, many look upon it in anticipation and retrospect as coming closest in their total experiences to the realization of gratifications.[19] Frequently, it seems that the working class is compared with an inner-directed, economically marginal middle class of yore than with an "acting-out," "other-directed," "affluent" middle class of today. The shifts in the middle class, murky as they are, make it especially difficult and dubious to use it as a yardstick for elucidating (and frequently evaluating) working-class life.

BASIC THEMES

Before discussing a few of the themes which we think are basic in working-class life, we present a brief over-all picture of what we believe are the essential characteristics of the stable American worker today.

He is traditional, "old-fashioned," somewhat religious, and patriarchal.[20] The worker likes discipline, structure, order, organization and directive, defi-

---

[18] Cf. Urie Bronfenbrenner, "Socialization and Social Class through Time and Space," in E. E. Maccoby, T. M. Newcomb, and R. L. Hartley, eds., *Readings in Social Psychology* (New York: Holt, Rinehart & Winston, Inc., 1958).

[19] Some of us who have been through the mill of graduate school may feel, as suggested to us by Harold Wilensky, that we, at least, have deferred gratification! On the other hand, Allison Davis' discussion of "the graduate or medical student who is largely dependent upon his own earnings . . ." is certainly out-of-date for at least the medical student. Allison Davis, "Socialization and Adolescent Personality," in G. E. Swanson, T. M. Newcomb and E. L. Hartley, eds., *Readings in Social Psychology* (New York: Holt, Rinehart & Winston, Inc., 1952), p. 530.

[20] The cross-class F-scale uniformly shows that workers are more likely than middle-class individuals to support the statement that "the most important thing a child should learn is obedience to his parents." Maccoby and Gibbs have pointed out that workers strongly demand respect and obedience from their children. Eleanor E. Maccoby, Patricia K. Gibbs, *et al.*, "Methods of Child Rearing in Two Social Classes," in William E. Martin and Celia Burns Stendler, eds., *Readings in Child Development* (New York: Harcourt, Brace & World, Inc., 1954), pp. 380-96. Riessman's data indicate that not only parents but older people in general are to be obeyed and respected. See Frank Riessman, *op. cit.*, also Duvall, *op. cit.*

nite (strong) leadership, although he does not see such strong leadership in opposition to human, warm, informal, personal qualities.[21] Despite the inadequacy of his education, he is able to build abstractions, but he does so in a slow physical fashion.[22] He reads ineffectively, is poorly informed in many areas, and is often quite suggestible, although interestingly enough he is frequently suspicious of "talk" and "new fangled" ideas.

He is family centered; most of his relationships take place around the large, extended, fairly cooperative family.[23] Cooperation and mutual aid are among his most important characteristics.[24]

While desiring a good standard of living, he is not attracted to the middle-class style of life with its accompanying concern for status and prestige.[25]

He is not class conscious although aware of class differences. While he is somewhat radical on certain economic issues, he is quite illiberal on numerous matters, particularly civil liberties and foreign policy.[26]

The outstanding weakness of the worker is lack of education. Strongly desiring education for his children, he shows considerable concern about their school work, although he feels estranged and alienated from the teacher and the school, as he similarly feels alienated from many institutions in our society.[27] This alienation is expressed in a ready willingness to believe in the corruptness of leaders and a general negative feeling toward "big shots."

He is stubborn in his ways, concerned with strength and ruggedness, interested in mechanics, materialistic, superstitious, holds an "eye for an eye" psychology, and is largely uninterested in politics.

STABILITY AND SECURITY

We suspect that one of the central determinants in working-class life is the striving for stability and security.[28] External and internal factors promote instability and insecurity. Chief among the external factors is unemployment and layoff. Prosperity has of course barred the anguish of the prolonged de-

---

[21] Frank Riessman, *op. cit., passim.*

[22] For a review of the relevant literature, see Frank Riessman, *The Culturally Deprived Child* (New York: Harper & Row, Publishers, 1962).

[23] Floyd Dotson, "Patterns of Voluntary Association Among Urban Working Class Families," *American Sociological Review,* Vol. 16 (October, 1951), pp. 687-93. "In at least 15 of the 50 families, leisure time activities of the husbands and wives were completely dominated by the kin group. In another 28 families, regular visiting patterns with relatives constituted a major, although not exclusive, form of social activity." (P. 691.) Also see p. 693.

[24] August B. Hollingshead, "Class Differences in Family Stability," in Bendix and Lipset, *op. cit.,* p. 290. A similar point is made by Allison Davis, Burleigh B. Gardner, and Mary R. Gardner, *Deep South* (Chicago: University of Chicago Press, 1941), p. 111. Also see John Useem, Pierre Tangent, and Ruth Useem, "Stratification in a Prairie Town," *American Sociological Review,* Vol. 7 (June, 1942), p. 334.

[25] The relevant literature is discussed in Miller and Riessman, "Are Workers Middle Class?," *op. cit.*

[26] The Centers' findings can be interpreted to support the first sentence of the paragraph despite Centers' mode of analysis. Richard Centers, *The Psychology of Social Classes* (Princeton, N. J.: Princeton University Press, 1949). Cf. Ralf Dahrendorf, *Class and Class Conflict in Industrial Society* (Stanford: Stanford University Press, 1959), pp. 288-89. On civil liberties and foreign policy, see Lipset, *op. cit.*

[27] Riessman, *Education and the Culturally Deprived Child,* has a discussion of some of the relevant literature.

[28] Hollingshead, *op. cit.,* pp. 290-91.

pression of the 1930's, but the danger of occasional layoffs of some duration are not remote during the usually shaky prosperity conditions which are interlarded with episodes of recession, plant relocation, industry decline and strikes.[29]

Chief among the internal factors promoting instability are family discord, including divorce and desertion, intergenerational conflict, and the desire for excitement.

Coping with the instability threats becomes a dominant activity within the working-class family. Many practices, such as mutual aid and cooperation, extended family perspectives, are important as adjustive mechanisms. "Getting by" rather than "getting ahead" in the middle-class self-realization and advancement sense is likely to be dominant.[30] For example, the limited desire to become a foreman is partly a result of the economic insecurity resulting from the loss of job seniority in case of a layoff.[31]

Part of the ambivalence toward obtaining a college education reflects the same emphasis on security. Even a highly talented working-class youth is not sure what he can do with a college diploma, and he may fear the disruption of his familial, community and peer-group security.[32]

The poll data indicating the unwillingness of workers to take economic risks and their greater concern for jobs with security is part of the same pattern of a striving for stability.[33]

TRADITIONALISM

The American working class is primarily a migrant group; not only have people come from European farms and rural settlements to American factories but they also have migrated from America's rural life to the industrial scene.[34] Traditional practices, once thought to be infrequent in urbanized, industrialized, nuclear-oriented families, are very strong in working-class families.[35] The pattern is patriarchal, extended (with many relevant cousins, grandparents, and aunts and uncles) and delineated by sharply separated sex roles. The family is not child-centered (or child-dominant or dominating),

---

[29] Charles H. Hession, S. M. Miller and Curwen Stoddart, *The Dynamics of the American Economy* (New York: Alfred A. Knopf, Inc., 1956), Ch. 11.

[30] Joseph A. Kahl, *op. cit.*, pp. 205-10.

[31] Ely Chinoy, *op. cit.*, and Charles R. Walker, *Steeltown* (New York: Harper & Row, Publishers, 1950) have data showing the considerable reluctance of workers to become foremen.

[32] The initial attraction of many working-class youth to engineering is partly due to the apparently concrete and clear nature of the work and the presumed definiteness of the education for a particular type of job. Motivating working-class youth to go to college may require an expansion and sharpening of working-class children's interpretation of the job market.

[33] Centers, *op. cit.*, p. 62.

[34] Lloyd Reynolds, *Labor Economics and Labor Relations* (Englewood Cliffs, N.J.: Prentice-Hall, Inc., 1949), pp. 7-23.

[35] Recent literature, particularly Litwak and Axelrod, have pointed out that traditional practices are more widespread than previously thought in the middle class. The lack of differences between middle-class and working-class respondents reported in the studies may be due to the lack of sensitive instruments. While our analysis is not necessarily based on the notion of greater traditional and extended practices in working-class than in middle-class families, we believe that these practices assume a greater importance in the overall activities of the former.

but parent-centered and controlled. Traditional values of automatic obedience by children are expected to be the norm even if not always observed in practice.[36]

One probable consequence of this is that workers seem to be more authoritarian than they probably are. For, while on the F-scale type of test they tend to be "conventional," a characteristic of the authoritarian according to Adorno *et al.*, it is doubtful, as we have tried to argue elsewhere,[37] that this conventionalism means the same in both the middle and working class.

The worker also has a traditional attitude toward discipline which again may be confused with authoritarianism. All the child-rearing data indicate that workers utilize physical punishment as a basic discipline technique. In the eyes of the worker punishment discourages people from wrongdoing whether the punishment is inflicted upon them or upon others who serve as "examples." There is also a "rightness" about punishment for a misdeed, for punishment is the other side of responsibility for one's actions. Thus, for example, acceptance of the death penalty may not be the result of a sado-maschistic character structure but the product of a belief in the efficacy of punishment in deterring others from misdeeds and in the value of attaching responsibility to people's actions.[38] Workers consequently do not easily accept the notion that an individual is not responsible for his crimes because of his emotional state at the time of their occurrence.

INTENSITY

We believe that one of the most neglected themes in working-class life and one of the most difficult to understand and interpret is that of intensity. This intensity is expressed in a number of different ways. It is found in the areas in which workers have belief and emotional involvement. While there are numerous areas about which workers are confused, and lacking in opinion (for example, the high percentage of "No answer" and "Don't know" on public opinion polls), there are important spheres in which they have definite convictions and, indeed, are highly stubborn. Their beliefs about religion, morality, superstition, diet, punishment, custom, traditional education, the role of women, intellectuals, are illustrative here. Many of these attitudes are related to their traditional orientation, and they are held unquestioningly in the usual traditional manner. They are not readily open to reason and they are not flexible opinions.

Other possible sources of this intensity may be their physical (less symbolic) relation to life,[39] their person-centeredness (to be discussed below), and their lack of education.

---

[36] Duvall, *op. cit.*

[37] Miller and Riessman, "Working-Class Authoritarianism: A Critique of Lipset," *op. cit.* Also, our "Social Class, Education and Authoritarianism," a paper presented to the American Sociological Society, Washington, 1957.

[38] Cf. Bordua, *op. cit.*

[39] The discussion by Miller and Swanson on the "motoric" orientation of workers is one of the most suggestive in the literature. Daniel R. Miller and Guy E. Swanson, *Inner Conflict and Defense* (New York: Holt, Rinehart & Winston, Inc., 1960).

Threaded through much of working-class life is a person-centered theme. On one level this theme has an informal, human quality, of easy, comfortable relationship to people where the affectionate bite of humor is appreciated. The factory "horseplay," the ritualistic kidding, is part of this although by no means all of it. It is an expressive component of life.[40]

At another level, it is the importance of personal qualities. One learns more from people than from books, it is said. At a political level, the candidate as a decent, human person is more important than the platform.[41]

In the bureaucratic situation, the worker still tends to think of himself as relating to people, not to roles and invisible organizational structure. This orientation is an aspect of particularism, the reaction to persons and situations in terms of their personal qualities and relations to oneself rather than in terms of some universal characteristics of their social position. The neighbor or workmate who gets ahead is expected "not to put on airs"; he should like the "old gang" and accept them despite his new position. An individual is expected to transcend his office. A foreman is an s.o.b. not because he has stresses and demands on the job which force him to act strongly and harshly, but because of his personal qualities. Contrariwise, one of the top executives is frequently regarded as one who would help the rank-and-file workers if he had the chance, because *he* is a "nice guy"; putting him in the stresses of a new position would not force him to act as others in that position have acted.[42] It is the man not the job that makes for behavior; this attitude is not a class-conscious one, far from it. Another example of particularism is the juvenile delinquent who reacts positively to the social worker or therapist who seems to be interested in him beyond the call of professional duty.

PRAGMATISM AND ANTI-INTELLECTUALISM

With workers, it is the end-result of action rather than the planning of action or the preoccupation with means that counts. An action that goes astray is not liked for itself; it has to achieve the goal intended to be satisfactory.[43] It is results that pay off. While this orientation has an anti-intellectual dimension, it does somewhat reduce the reliance on personality (person-centered theme) by its emphasis on results. Workers like the specific action, the clear action, the understood result. What can be seen and felt is more likely to be real and true in the workers' perspectives, which are therefore likely to be limited. The pragmatic orientation of workers does not encourage them to see abstract ideas as useful. Education, for what it does for

---

[40] *Ibid.*

[41] Cf. Lipset, *op. cit.*, pp. 285-86.

[42] S. M. Miller, *Union Structure and Industrial Relations: A Case Study of a Local Labor Union,* unpublished Ph.D. thesis, Princeton University, 1951.

[43] Melvin L. Kohn, "Social Class and the Exercise of Parental Authority," *American Sociological Review,* Vol. 24 (June, 1959), pp. 364-65.

MILLER
RIESSMAN

one in terms of opportunities, may be desirable but abstract intellectual speculation, ideas which are not rooted in the realities of the present, are not useful, indeed may be harmful.

On the other hand, workers often have an exaggerated respect for the ability of the learned. A person with intellectual competence in one field is frequently thought to be a "brain" with ability in all fields; partly this is due to the general abstract nature of ideas regardless of field. If a real obstacle comes up, they may expect "the brain" to have a ready solution for it, even if they may not be willing to adopt it.

At first glance, the anti-words orientation may appear to be incompatible with the possible appeal of the charismatic. But it is not. For the charismatic are charismatic because they can be emotional and expressive, qualities not usually associated with abstract ideas. Also, the charismatic leader may promise "pie in the sky" but it is a very concrete, specific set of ingredients with a clear distribution of the pie.

—— EXCITEMENT

Another component in workers' lives is the appreciation of excitement, of moving out of the humdrum. News, gossip, new gadgets, and sports are consequently very attractive to workers. To some extent, the consumership of workers—the desire to have new goods, whether television sets or cars—is part of this excitement dimension. The excitement theme is often in contradiction with the traditional orientation.

It is worth noting that different subgroups within the working class may favor one theme rather than another. Thus younger groups, and especially juvenile delinquents, are probably much more attracted to the excitement theme, are more alienated and less traditional. On the other hand, workers with a more middle-class orientation are probably less alienated, more traditional and pragmatic.

—— PARSIMONY AND VARIATION

In the preceding remarks we have touched only very fleetingly on a few themes of working-class life and ignored other important themes, like cooperation and a physical orientation, almost completely. While we can sum up our analysis in a relatively few descriptive adjectives, such as person-centered, traditional, pragmatic, and so forth, we have been unable to develop a parsimonious conceptualization, such as a nondeferred gratification pattern, which attempts to explain by this single formulation or theme a vast array of behavior. Perhaps the simplest shorthand, if one wishes to use it, would be Parsons'; employing his criteria, we could say that workers are particularistic rather than universalistic, affective rather than neutral, ascriptive rather than achievement-minded, diffuse in definition of role rather than specific. But this summary may obscure more than it reveals.

Indeed, our analysis contains a number of themes which may, in part, be in opposition to each other. For example, traditionalism and alienation have

The
Working-Class
Subculture:
A New
View

certain conflicting features, as do pragmatism and person-centeredness, and the resulting strains and adjustive mechanisms are important to analyze.

Let us make just two points to indicate the general value of the orientation that we have only sketchily presented here: (1) It may be possible to understand other working-class and lower-class styles by looking for sources of variation from the stable working-class pattern. (2) The development of the stable working-class style among lower-class and working-class youth might be the goal of educational and other socializing and remedial forces rather than instilling the middle-class value structure.

VARIATIONS OF WORKING-CLASS CULTURE

By stating that we are describing the stable worker we imply that there are other worker subcultures. We feel that the stable worker has been relatively ignored in the emphasis on the "underprivileged," "lower-class," unskilled, irregular worker and the middle-class oriented worker. By understanding the stable worker, important leads are provided for understanding other subcultural variations.

The unskilled, irregular (read "lower-class") worker lacks the disciplined, structured and traditional approach of the stable worker and stresses the excitement theme. He does less to cope with insecurity and instability. In the large industrial and commercial centers today the lower-class style of life (as distinct from the stable working-class style) is found particularly among peoples relatively new to industrial and urban life: Negroes, Puerto Ricans, transplanted Southern whites. They have not been able so far to make the kind of adjustment that stable workers have. Frequently, they have special problems not only of discrimination but of fairly menial (service) jobs at low pay, extremely poor housing and considerable overcrowding. Some children of stable workers do not develop the stable pattern and assume the lower-class style. A few children of middle-class parents become lower class: they have unskilled jobs and adopt the lower-class style of life. But the bulk of individuals with the lower-class style come from those who are children of unskilled workers and of farmers, thus including many of the ethnic people of whom we spoke earlier.[44]

Another deviant group from the main working-class pattern are those workers who are very much concerned with achievement of success for children and for the symbols of success in consumership. In many cases the families are secure and stable and have been able to make a workable accommodation to the stresses of their lives. But this is not enough for the middle-class orientation; in many cases there is a vague opportunity and motivational factor present.

Those of working-class origins who do move into the middle class and into the middle-class style of life are likely to have a middle-class cross-pressure in that they more frequently than other working-class children have relatives

---

[44] The data to support this assertion can be computed from the two American studies detailed in the appendix to S. M. Miller, "Comparative Social Mobility," *Current Sociology,* Vol. IX, No. 1, 1960.

who were or are middle class. Their grandparents may have been middle class; their parents though in working-class occupations are likely to have more education than is typical in the working class and to have other attributes of middle-class life.[45] If we may give a literary example, in *Sons and Lovers,* the hero, brought up in a mining community, had a working-class father but his mother was a teacher and came from a middle-class community. Undoubtedly, the hero, whose life follows that of D. H. Lawrence, received motivation from her to move into literary activities and probably also some early direct help in reading and school. The motivational factor is important but it is likely linked to the background and experiential factor of grandparental and paternal activities.

We have discussed these two styles in different ways. The lower-class style is considered to be the inability to develop an adequate measure of coping with the environment so that some degree of security and stability ensues. The origin of the middle-class style would seem to emerge from the stable pattern. A working-class family would likely first go through a stable period of accommodation before it or the children developed middle-class orientations. *It is not intrinsic in the stable pattern that a middle-class orientation emerge but the stable stage would seem to be a necessary step in most cases for the development of a middle-class orientation.*

Other variations in the subculture of workers exist. Religious, ethnic, educational, and regional factors are important in producing deviations from the pattern we have described.

THE STABLE STYLE AS GOAL

Explicitly as well as implicitly, many agents of educational and other institutions that deal with working-class and lower-class youth attempt to "middle-classize" them. When any effort is extended toward the juvenile delinquent, it is usually with this orientation. Such endeavors are largely a failure because the middle-class outlook is alien to the experiences, prospects, and values of these youth. Possibly there is a better chance of emphasizing working-class values; for example, cooperation—as happens in group therapy— rather than vocational success in middle-class terms. We recognize that it is not easy to develop some of the working-class values but they are probably much easier to develop than the middle-class ones. In addition, emphasis on the former may develop a more favorable attitude on the part of the youth to both the institution and its agents than does the insistence on the middle-class values.

A basic value question is involved here: Do we attempt to make the middle-class style a model for all to follow? Or do we adopt a rigid cultural relativity position that the lower class has a right to its way of life regardless of the social effects? Or do we attempt to develop what appear to be the most positive elements, from the point of view of society and the individuals involved,

_____

[45] Cf. the remarks of Kaare Svalastoga in S. M. Miller's "Report of the Fifth Working Conference on Social Stratification and Social Mobility," International Sociological Association, 1960.

of the styles of life closest to them? While we have some doubts about the answer, the possibility of the stable working-class style as the goal adds a new dimension to a deep problem that deserves more forthright scrutiny than it has received.

Our attempts at interpreting working-class life will undoubtedly prove inadequate. But we are certain that without an attempt at analyzing the contexts and the genotypes of working-class behavior and attitude, the *description* (and there is faulty description) and interpretation of working-class life will remain a reflex of social scientists' changing attitudes toward the middle class.

Persistence and Change in Working-Class Life Style*

GERALD HANDEL

LEE RAINWATER

IN 1959 the United States Department of Labor issued a report entitled "How American Buying Habits Change," which stated: "The wage-earner's way of life is well-nigh indistinguishable from that of his salaried co-citizens." [1] By this means, the Labor Department heralded the near-achievement of a classless society in the United States. There is some evidence that this was welcome news not only to the Labor Department but to the business community as well. *Business Week* summarized the report in an article entitled "Worker Loses His Class Identity." [2]

The Labor Department report, written by economists, raises an issue which concerns sociologists seeking to understand the structure of American society. Berger's recent book[3] on a working-class suburb and Wilensky's review of it[4] serve to focus the issue: What changes have been taking place in the working class and how are they to be interpreted? Have the rise in working-class income in the postwar years and the movement of working-class people into suburbs been sufficient to transform working-class people into

---

* Presented to the 58th Annual Meeting of the American Sociological Association, August 29, 1963, Los Angeles, California, and published originally in *Sociology and Social Research*, Vol. XLVIII, No. 3 (April, 1964). Revised for use here.
    [1] "How American Buying Habits Change" (Washington: U. S. Department of Labor, 1959), p. 6.
    [2] "Worker Loses His Class Identity," *Business Week* (July 11, 1959), p. 90.
    [3] Bennett Berger, *Working-Class Suburb* (Berkeley and Los Angeles: University of California Press, 1960).
    [4] Harold L. Wilensky, Review of *Working-Class Suburb*, in *American Sociological Review* (April, 1961), pp. 310-12.

middle class—or, at least, to set in motion a strong process of transformatio[n] Berger says, "No." Wilensky says, "Maybe." The Labor Department says, "Yes." For it should be noted that the Labor Department report not only documents changes in working-class income and consumer behavior but states—without much documentation:

> The adoption of middle-class attitudes, the change in what workers have come to expect, even more than the greatly augmented real family income, points to this great revolution in class relations.[5]

Any social scientist who does research on working-class behavior and attitudes will almost certainly conclude that the obliteration of class lines asserted by the Labor Department report is a very considerable overstatement. The general question that remains is whether the working class has moved in the direction of becoming middle class and, if so, how far. This paper is one progress report on changes in working-class life style. Our view of the working class has much in common with that of Miller and Reissman, as expressed in that paper of theirs that immediately precedes ours in this book.[6] Rather than an over-all thematic analysis of working-class life style, however, we shall report some findings from a recent study.

We interviewed a sample of 298 working-class couples and 101 lower-middle-class couples—husbands and wives being interviewed separately—distributed in five cities: Camden, New Jersey; Gary, Indiana; Chicago, Illinois; Louisville, Kentucky; and Denver, Colorado. The working-class respondents were distributed by residence type: apartments, new and old houses in cities, old houses in suburbs, and new houses in new suburbs.

What we have to say here about the *working class* should be understood as referring to what Miller and Reissman have referred to as the stable worker. It excludes *both* the underprivileged worker and the worker specifically oriented to mobility into the middle class.

Three general conclusions seem warranted from our study:

(1) *Certain behaviors and attitudes increasingly found in the working class have a surface similarity to those in the middle class, but they have a different meaning for the working class than they do for the middle class.* These behaviors and attitudes are essentially adaptations to changes in the opportunity structure of American society rather than changes in the basic themes of the working-class outlooks. These changed attitudes and behaviors are occurring primarily in the areas of education and housing.

(2) *In the areas of family life and social participation, the working class seems to be dividing into two main groups, which might be characterized as traditional and modern. In these life areas, the modern working-class group begins to approximate lower-middle-class values and behaviors.*

(3) *In the area of consumer behavior, working-class behavior resembles middle-class behavior in spending for hard goods but not in other types of expenditure. This difference in expenditure pattern reflects persisting differences in working-class and middle-class life styles.*

---

[5] "How American Buying Habits Change," *op. cit.*, p. 7.
[6] S. M. Miller and Frank Reissman, "The Working Class Subculture: A New View." Presented at Annual Meeting of American Sociological Association, August 30, 1960. Published in *Social Problems*, Vol. IX (1960), 86-97, and reprinted in this book.

generalizations do not suggest a simple pattern of change. On the
ey indicate a complex pattern reflecting the interplay of many
what follows, we shall try to indicate how each of these generaliza-
es to specific life areas.

EDUCATION

cation is one of the life areas in which working-class expression of
attitudes appears increasingly to approximate those of the middle class.
Where once the working class could see little value in higher education, it is
now commonplace for working-class parents to express their educational
aspirations for their children in such terms as "I want them to go to college";
"I want them to go as far as they can"; "I want them to have all they can get."
A college education for their children is a widely expressed desideratum in
the working class today.

Yet, as soon as one penetrates beneath this statement of desire or hope, it
becomes clear that a college education tends to have quite different meanings
for working-class and middle-class people. To take only one indication of this,
working-class parents draw a sharp distinction between sons and daughters
with respect to the importance of college education. This is done quite explicitly. Not only do they seldom aspire to a college education for their
daughters, but they are likely to regard a daughter's stay in college as wasted
unless she both completes the course and applies what she has learned in an
occupation—school teaching being the occupation usually mentioned illustratively. Quite simply, education is regarded as preparation for a job, and a
better education is seen as leading to a better job and greater job security.
A higher education is perceived by working-class parents as desirable not only
because of the changing occupational structure but also because of the rising
educational standards set forth by employers. As one woman remarked, you
have to be a high school graduate nowadays even to get a job in a dime
store. Thus, education is conceived quite narrowly as vocational training and
a kind of entry card to an occupation, and this is in contrast to the middle-
class view.

While the importance of vocational preparation is by no means slighted
in the lower middle class, education is more broadly conceived. Such people
are likely to believe that education is valuable even if not put to direct use
in an occupation. They are likely to regard a year or two of college for a girl
as contributing to making her a more refined person rather than as a waste
of time and money.

The divergence of view between working and middle class is evident even
with regard to earlier schooling. When we ask women, "What should school
do for children? What should children get out of school?", we find that the
working-class women not only emphasize but tend to restrict their aims to the
teaching of basic skill subjects which will prepare the child for a job and
provide him (or her) with the necessary skills in reading, writing, and arithmetic that will enable him to meet the increasingly complex demands of
daily life.

In contrast, the lower-middle-class women not only emphasize these basic subjects but stress equally two larger goals. One goal is that the school should provide the child with what they refer to as a "foundation" for later learning. They regard schooling not only as preparation for a job but as a means for enabling the child to enjoy life more and to get more out of it. Second, they expect the school to teach the child "how to get along with other people."

It is interesting, in this connection, that both Miller and Reissman in their paper and Gans[7] in his recent book on the Italian working class in Boston describe the working class as "person-centered." Both authors indicate that interpersonal relationships are easy and informal. Perhaps this is one reason why working-class parents do not look to the school to provide preparation in interpersonal relationships. Middle-class parents, more attuned to symbolic manipulation, as well as more anxious about the management of impressions, as Goffman would say, expect the school to prepare their children for this kind of management.

HOUSING

Working-class people have been moving to new tract housing, both in suburbs and inside city limits. The attitudes that impel this move show certain differences from those of the middle class, although there are also similarities. One difference is that the working-class couple is more often prompted by a desire to flee from subordination to a landlord. Living in an apartment carries somewhat the same meanings as working for a boss: paying rent tends to be interpreted as serving his interests at the expense of one's own, while being a tenant means living in accord with a set of rules and regulations that are perceived as arbitrary. The landlord tells you to keep your children from playing in the halls of the apartment building, not to run any water after 10 P.M., not to be too noisy. Owning one's own home tends to mean to the working-class person escape from restriction, a rising above limitations—both those imposed by a landlord and those that come from being economically disadvantaged. To the middle-class person, owning a house tends to be perceived more as a validation of status; it is an assertion of one's rightful place in society. In buying a house, middle-class people do not conceive of themselves as fleeing from the superordination and economic exploitation of landlords.

In sum, the increasing esteem accorded education by the working class and the increased interest in homeowning—including owning a home in the suburbs—involve attitudes and behavior that superficially resemble those of the middle class but which have quite a different significance in the two classes.

FAMILY BEHAVIOR

In the area of family behavior, such changes are taking place that it seems useful to distinguish between a *traditional* and a *modern* pattern. The modern pattern is much more similar to that of the middle class than it is to the

---

[7] Herbert J. Gans, *The Urban Villagers* (New York: The Free Press of Glencoe, Inc., 1962).

traditional working class. The essential change is an increased importance given to the nuclear family with a corresponding decrease in importance given to the extended family. This change ramifies into such areas as occupation, residence, social participation and leisure time, and familial roles.

In the traditional working class, there is an intertwining of family relationships with economic relationships. For the working-class young man, this meant very often that the occupation he chose was one in which his father or uncle or some other relative was already working and could therefore enable him to be "taken on" in the same factory or to gain entry into the closely controlled union. In the modern working class, this link between family and occupation is broken; the young man is more likely to choose an occupation without reference to family. To an important extent, of course, this change is brought about by the contraction of older occupations and the development of new ones. But the change is also part of a more general loosening of extended kinship ties that characterizes the modern working-class outlook.

Another indication of this shift is that living near one's parents, sibs, or other relatives—which is highly valued in the traditional working class—is no longer important in the modern working class. This decrease in the importance of relatives affects social participation and use of leisure time as well. Numberous studies of working-class life, including the present one, have shown that working-class people are more likely than middle-class people to have most of their social participation with relatives. If for some reason they do not live near relatives, they are likely to spend vacations visiting them. The traditional working-class couple are not likely to have other couples as joint friends. In contrast, the modern working-class couple is more likely to have other couples as friends, and social participation with these friends is more important than participation with relatives. In the modern working-class couple, husband and wife have friends in common, and this is a shift from the traditional pattern.

All of these changes that are bound up in the shift of emphasis from the extended family to the nuclear family bespeak also a change in the role of the working-class wife. In the traditional working-class family, the wife thinks of herself in terms of what she does *for* her family. Her self-conception as a wife and mother centers around those situations in which she is separated from the other family members—cooking, doing the laundry, cleaning house. The traditional wife considers the kitchen the most important room in her house.

The modern working-class wife thinks of herself in terms of what she does *with* her family. Her self-conception is broadened from that of servant of the family's needs to that of sharer in family affairs. She considers the living room the most important room in her home, because that is the room in which the family relaxes together.

In sum, we see a difference, and we distinguish between a modern working class and a coexisting traditional working class, and we find that the difference lies in the relative importance given to the nuclear family as compared with the extended family.

HANDEL
RAINWATER

EXPENDITURE PATTERN

The prosperity which the working class has enjoyed in the postwar years has been expressed in behavior by increased purchase of houses, automobiles, and other consumer durables. At the same time, the American economy as a whole has been characterized by a rapid increase in expenditures for services. Working-class people's expenditures for service lag behind both their own expenditures for durables and behind middle-class expenditures for services. We can see several aspects of working-class life style which account for the relatively lower expenditures for services than is true in the middle class:

(1) Even though the proportion of working-class children going to college is rising, the proportion going is still lower than it is in the middle class. Further, working-class children going to college are far more likely to go to a publicly supported junior college or state university than to a privately supported institution whose fees are much higher. Thus, expenditures for education are likely to claim a smaller proportion of working-class than of middle-class income.

(2) Working-class men do a tremendous amount of work in fixing up their own homes—much more than do those of the middle class. Therefore, the expenditures for the services of carpenters, plumbers, electricians, and painters are likely to be less in working-class than in middle-class families.

(3) Working-class men are more likely to work on their own cars, so that expenditures for car repairs and car washing are likely to be less in working-class than in middle-class families.

(4) Working-class men buy suits of clothing quite infrequently. Thus, because of the way clothing fits into their life style, not only are their expenditures in this area much lower than in the middle class, but they are likely to spend proportionately less on drycleaning services than middle-class people do.

(5) Although some working-class people patronize coin-operated, self-service laundromats, they are much more likely to buy an automatic washer than to use a commercial laundry or diaper service.

(6) Working-class people are more likely to spend vacations either at home or visiting relatives. Their expenditures for hotel and motel rooms, as well as for transportation services, tend to be lower than is true for middle-class people.

(7) Working-class people do not eat in restaurants with any great frequency, although some working-class women say that they wish it were possible. Working-class meals away from home are more likely to be picnics in the park, dinner with relatives, or a stop at a drive-in than a restaurant meal.

In all of these areas, working-class attitudes and life style keep down expenditures for services, so that the great growth in the service sector of the economy is much more a middle-class phenomenon.

The changes in working-class life style do not allow for a simple "yes-or-no" answer to the question as to whether the working class is becoming indistinguishable from the lower middle class. In different life areas, change is proceeding at different rates and with different consequences. Still unanswered is the large question as to the factors that account for this complex pattern of change, including what seems to be a bifurcation of the working class.

Persistence and Change in Working-Class Life Style

The Behavior and Values
of Skilled Workers*

RICHARD F. HAMILTON

IN recent years it has been argued that, as a result of changes in the distribution of income in the United States, the best-off manual workers are in a position to maintain middle-class styles of life and behavior patterns. It has been argued, furthermore, that these workers have in fact taken advantage of this opportunity and have adopted or "converted" to middle-class standards. An example of this type of claim is to be found in Kurt Mayer's *Class and Society,* where he asserts that:

> . . . a large part of the working class shares a "white collar" style of life and accepts middle class values and beliefs. This is especially true of craftsmen, foremen, and skilled mechanics, whose high wages nowadays exceed the salaries of many lower middle class white collar employees and even of small businessmen. In many respects, therefore, the line which sets off the "aristocracy of skilled labor" from the bulk of semiskilled and unskilled manual laborers is more significant sociologically than the dividing line between skilled craftsmen and lower middle class white collar workers which has become increasingly blurred in recent years.[1]

If such a transformation has occurred, it deserves more study than it has hitherto received, since this does, after all, concern a change in the "most fundamental cleavage in American society." [2] If this is the case, works such as *Middletown* would now be obsolete and of historical interest only. The contemporary work of Lipset and Bendix would be limited in that it focuses on the "old" manual-nonmanual line and thus does not measure the most significant mobility step.

---

* This is a revised version of a paper presented at the Eastern Sociological Society meetings, April 6, 1963.
[1] Kurt B. Mayer, *Class and Society* (New York: Random House, 1955), pp. 41-42. The sentences immediately preceding this quotation read: ". . . there is ample evidence that the major class division in the United States, as in other Western countries, is that between the middle class as a whole and the lower or working class. This is largely a division between manual labor and white collar occupations . . ." Another quotation by the same author which argues that the major manual-nonmanual division is being shifted is found in his "Recent Changes in the Class Structure of the United States," *Transactions of the Third World Congress of Sociology,* Vol. III, p. 78.
[2] S. M. Lipset and Reinhard Bendix, "Social Mobility and Occupational Career Patterns: I. Stability of Jobholding," *American Journal of Sociology,* Vol. LVII (January, 1952) , pp. 366-74.

This paper will bring data to bear on the question of the assumed change and will explore the question of its causes. The two major concerns, therefore, are the following:

1. The Factual Question

Are the skilled workers closer to the white-collar or to the semiskilled workers in their outlooks and behavior? In other words, is the shift in class cleavage, which Mayer asserts, discernible in current behavior patterns?

Following general sociological assumptions, we would expect the major determinant of values to be the family, and, secondarily, the childhood peer groups and adult work groups. Given the fact that skilled workers tend to be the sons of manual workers or of farmers, it is reasonable to assume that their values will reflect these milieus. For this reason the major hypothesis of this paper is that *the values and behavior of the skilled workers will be similar to the semiskilled rather than to those of the white-collar workers.*[3]

This formulates the problem somewhat differently from Mayer's presentation. His basic statement that a "large part" of the working class shares or possesses traits which are frequently associated with the white-collar groups can scarcely be doubted. In a country which has a very high consensus on attitudes and values, there will obviously be little difference between *any* groups—occupational, ethnic, religious, regional, or otherwise. A "large part" of any group will share values and behavior possessed by most other groups. Thus, in part, the statement is a truism, and to formulate it in these terms is to put it in such a form as to make rejection of the hypothesis virtually impossible. The present formulation of the question allows us to determine the *degree* of difference between any two groups and to discover whether a shift in the basic line of class division has actually taken place.

2. The Question of Mechanisms

Mayer is ambiguous about the process whereby manual workers come to possess middle-class orientations. On the one hand, he suggests high income to be an "enabling" factor which allows the once-deprived to realize the middle-class ambitions they possessed even before affluence. The assumption here is that all persons share these aspirations; it is only their poverty which makes them different. If this were the case, we would have to raise the

[3] Data presented by S. M. Miller show that 80 per cent of the skilled are sons of manual workers (Richard Centers' study). This excludes those who are sons of farmers and also excludes nonwhites. The Survey Research Center's data (1956) presented by Miller show 88 per cent of the skilled as having fathers who were manual workers or farmers. If we take only those whose fathers were in the urban labor force, we find 82 per cent were the sons of manual workers. See S. M. Miller, "Comparative Social Mobility," *Current Sociology*, Vol. IX, No. 1 (1960), pp. 77-78; Natalie Rogoff's study of Indianapolis shows the same high percentage of skilled workers coming from manual or farm backgrounds. Seventy-nine per cent of the skilled in 1940 were the sons of manual workers or farmers. Taking the sons of fathers in the urban labor force only, the figure is 74 per cent who are second-generation manual workers. See her "Recent Trends in Urban Occupational Mobility," pp. 442-54 of Reinhard Bendix and S. M. Lipset, *Class, Status and Power* (New York: The Free Press of Glencoe, Inc., 1953). Per cents recalculated from Table 1, p. 445.

question as to the sources of this widespread value homogeneity.[4] On the whole, however, public-opinion data have shown no support for this view. On the other hand, a more realistic view and one which has been widely suggested is the aforementioned thesis of conversion. With income improvement, workers presumably for the first time acquire the new set of values.

Not mentioned by Mayer is a third possible explanation for the presence of "middle-class values" within the working class. This thesis involves no conversion process at all, but rather a "transfer" of these values as people shift from middle-class origins. Downward-mobile persons, in other words, may account for a considerable part of the middle-class values found within the manual occupations.[5]

These two processes are not likely to be mutually exclusive. Given the rootedness of values in social structure, we would predict that the majority of stable working-class populations are unchanged in their values. The transplants from urban middle-class origins, about 15 per cent of the manual total, we suspect to be largely unchanged in their values. The transplants from farm origins (about 40 per cent of the total), having a more ambiguous "class" position, are more likely to split, part of them "converting" to working-class identification and the rest remaining basically middle class in outlook.[6] If these assumptions are valid, then the converts to middle-class values would be the minor exception or deviant case.

Unfortunately, adequate data on the processes of change are not available; hence, for the most part, what is said on this point must remain on the level of speculation. On one point, however—the presumed income improvement— we do have evidence, data which cast doubt on the fact of income equality between skilled and lower white-collar groups. Furthermore, as we shall see, the best-off skilled workers are *least* like the middle class in attitudes and behavior.

Two subsidiary questions come up in the following materials stemming from findings not in accord with current definitions of the problem. The first has to do with the implicit model of class contained in the above quotation which suggests that the attitude differences associated with occupations are the result of income differences. In lieu of income, we have suggested that social pressures play the key role in value determination. Given this assumption, it is necessary to delineate the structure of these pressures. It may not be

---

[4] *Ad hoc* references to the "role of the mass media" are not sufficient as an answer. This point will be discussed below; see footnote 15.

[5] The terms "conversion" and "transplantation" are borrowed from the studies of suburban politics. These have shown, contrary to earlier speculation, that transplantation is the more important process in accounting for the Republican predominance in this setting. See Robert C. Wood, *Suburbia: Its People and Their Politics* (Boston: Houghton Mifflin Company, 1959), Ch. 5, and Roger H. Marz, *Voting Shifts in a Suburban Community: A Study of Migrants from Detroit* (East Lansing: unpublished Ph.D. dissertation, Michigan State University, 1960). Bennett M. Berger shows that a community with middle-class appearances but which at the same time recruits working-class transplants has an essentially working-class character. See his *Working Class Suburb* (Berkeley: University of California Press, 1960).

[6] Recalculated from data presented by S. M. Lipset and Reinhard Bendix, *Social Mobility in Industrial Society* (Berkeley: University of California Press, 1959), p. 21. Based on the Survey Research Center's 1952 data.

accurate to view the skilled workers as being midway on some continuum between the semiskilled and the white-collar workers merely because their typical income level lies on such a continuum. It is possible that what is operating are separate *sets* of pressures—which would mean that the imagery of a continuum is inappropriate. Some evidence presented below suggests support for this possibility.

A second problem is a definitional one and may be illustrated by the following quotation, which is also from Mayer:

> Certainly the American tradition of striving for success and upward mobility, so strongly embodied in the lower-middle-class way of life, extends its sway over many manual workers who share traditional middle class values. The style of life of many skilled and better-paid semi-skilled workers resembles that of the lower-middle class much more closely than that of the poorer semiskilled and unskilled manual laborers. The higher wages of recent years have enabled many working-men to buy their own houses and to furnish them much like those of white-collar people, whom they resemble by stressing respectability, sobriety, church member-ship, and mobility aspirations. Away from the job, they cannot be distinguished from the lower-middle-class white-collar workers.[7]

The question here is what constitutes a middle-class trait? Homeownership is listed as a middle-class characteristic; however, as we shall see, it appears to be much more of a skilled-worker trait than a white-collar one. In other cases, the differences in the distribution of the traits between the groups are so small that they can scarcely be considered in any sense an exclusive feature of any one class. In general, our procedure circumvents this problem by not making the definition central and merely asking where the greatest dif-ferentiation is to be found.

PROCEDURE

Our procedure involves a secondary analysis of two National Opinion Research Center nationwide surveys showing attitudes on issues and various types of behavior such as organizational membership, mass-media attention, and politics. In addition, data from other sources will be brought in where they are appropriate.[8]

For present purposes, we have taken the United States Census category "craftsmen, foremen and kindred" as equivalent to the skilled workers.

---

[7] *Op. cit.*, p. 47.

[8] The first, National Opinion Research Center study No. 367, is based on a national prob-ability sample of 2379 individuals and was used by Charles R. Wright and Herbert H. Hyman in their study, "Voluntary Association Memberships of American Adults: Evidence from National Sample Surveys," *American Sociological Review*, Vol. 23 (June, 1958), pp. 284-94. It was also used by Murray Hausknecht for his work, *The Joiners: A Sociological Description of Voluntary Association Membership in the United States* (New York: Bedminster Press, 1962). For details on the sample, see his Appendix A. The second, a quota sample within randomly selected areas, National Opinion Research Center study No. 399, was made avail-able by the Roper Public Opinion Research Center at Williams College, Williamstown, Mas-sachusetts. The author wishes to express his appreciation for the use of these decks. The date of the Mayer quotations is 1955. The date of NORC study No. 367 is 1955; that of No. 399 is 1956.

The Behavior
and Values
of Skilled
Workers

The category "operatives" are counted as semiskilled, and the clerical and sales as the lower white-collar group. Because there is a problem with the latter, many white-collar persons being women or young men with only a temporary or part-time job commitment, we have taken only married respondents and have classified them by the occupation of the head of the family. Basically, the frequency of appearance of traits in the skilled group will be compared with the frequencies among the white-collar (clerical and sales) workers and among the semiskilled.[9]

FINDINGS: THE FACTUAL QUESTION

Organizational Involvements

If the skilled workers have assimilated middle-class values and emulate middle-class behavior patterns, we should find a tendency to join and to be active in voluntary organizations, and these workers should be found in the same types of organizations as those joined by the middle-class groups. Previous studies have found a general pattern of greater joining among the skilled than is the case with other manual workers, but this level is well below the middle-class level and the types of organization joined are markedly different.[10] Our findings (NORC Survey No. 367) show the skilled workers to be closer to the operatives in the per cent belonging to formal organizations (Table 1). When we look at the type of organization joined, we find that the skilled are closer to the semiskilled in four of the five comparisons and match the clerical and sales personnel in only one, membership in patriotic organizations. This behavior pattern of the skilled indicates that the "traditional" pattern of cleavage is still the most important one.

Another organizational commitment not included among the foregoing groups is the trade-union membership. Here we find a marked difference between the white-collar and the blue-collar groups, with only 25 per cent of the former having a family member in a union as against 50 per cent of the skilled and 59 per cent of the semiskilled. Although it may be argued

---

[9] The linking of clerical and sales workers appears to be a convention which has a practical basis only, that is, an insufficient number of cases in any ordinary survey such as would allow separate consideration of each. There are important differences between the two with respect to education, income, and housing characteristics and probably in career lines. Unfortunately, these differences cannot be explored here, and we, too, shall follow the conventional procedure of combining the two and calling them "white-collar" workers.

[10] Komarovsky, for example, found that male skilled workers in New York City during the depression had almost as high a level of joining as did the low-paid clericals, although the type of organization joined was much different from those joined by the latter. In a later study and using a much better sample, Axelrod found that the craftsmen and foremen were identical with the operatives in their level of organizational affiliation and that both of these groups were more than 20 percentage points lower than the level of the clerical and sales workers. The discrepancy between Komarovsky's and Axelrod's findings is due to the former's inclusion of union memberships in her tabulations. See Mirra Komarovsky, "The Voluntary Associations of Urban Dwellers," *American Sociological Review*, Vol. 11 (December, 1946), 686-98, and Morris Axelrod, "Urban Structure and Social Participation," *American Sociological Review*, Vol. 21 (February, 1956), pp. 13-18.

that the union membership is not voluntary in the same sense as the other associations, the fact remains that they are affiliated—voluntarily, through the "press of circumstances," or forcibly—and as such, even though the influence may be a small one, it is still operating in their lives and is not typically present among the white-collar workers.[11] As compared with the union membership of the semiskilled worker, this is probably a more important influence, given the smaller, more stable, clublike or lodge-like locals in the craft unions. It will be noted below that the skilled workers tend to read the trade or the union magazines more so than is the case with the semiskilled. In general, this different pattern of organizational involvement and commitment would serve to insulate the skilled workers from the pressures or determinants which shape behavior in the mass society and thus provide some basis of support for a semi-independent subculture within the larger society.

A presumed middle-class characteristic mentioned by Mayer is church membership. Although neither NORC study asks for membership as such, No. 367 does ask questions on the regularity of church attendance and also whether the respondent considers religion important regardless of his institutional commitments. The over-all finding is that the percentage of skilled attending once a month or more frequently is identical with that of the semiskilled, and this "working class" level is below that of the white-collar persons.

Because the proportions of the three major faiths vary within these three occupational groups, the proportion of Protestants being highest among the skilled, it is necessary to control here because the low attendance may be due to this difference rather than to "class."[12] Within the Catholic faith, the evidence with respect to church attendance suggests support for Mayer. When we look at the sensed importance of religion, however, we find a different pattern; namely, that religion is more important to the Catholic skilled workers than to either the white-collar or the semiskilled groups. Among the Protestants, the skilled workers show a "working class" pattern in both attendance and estimate of the importance of religion. The pattern among the Protestant majority, then, shows no support for Mayer's thesis. It is likely

---

[11] In an unpublished paper on the future of white-collar unionism, Lipset shows with data that the unionized white-collar workers are likely to be of working-class origins. The process of social mobility transplants working-class traits into the middle class, as well as *vice versa*.

[12] The distribution is as follows: (NORC study No. 367)

	Occupation (Male main earners)		
Religion	Clerical, Sales	Craftsmen, Foremen	Operatives
Protestants	63%	75%	70%
Catholics	26	20	24
Jews	9	1	2
None, other	2	4	4
N =	(104)	(217)	(223)

Because of the number of cases involved, the following discussion considers only Protestants and Catholics.

that the pattern among the Catholic skilled workers reflects the cohesion of ethnic groups involved rather than any change in income.[13]

In summarizing the discussion of organizational membership patterns, the evidence shows little support for the assumption of a cleavage between the skilled and the semiskilled. The evidence suggests that the Mayer hypothesis about a shift in the location of the cleavage should be rejected.

Table 1

OCCUPATION AND ORGANIZATIONAL INVOLVEMENT*
(Husbands and wives, classed by husband's occupation)

	Occupation		
	Clerical, Sales	Craftsmen, Foremen	Operatives
Belongs to one or more organizations . . .	47%	32%	25%
N =	(176)	(405)	(405)
Type of organization:			
Veterans, military, patriotic	7%	7%	4%
Lodges, fraternal	15	11	9
Civic, service	19	10	7
Church, religious	10	6	7
Miscellaneous	17	11	8
N =	(177)	(408)	(408)
Attend church at least once a month	64%	55%	53%
N =	(168)	(396)	(391)
Catholics:			
Attend church	86%	81%	73%
N =	(45)	(88)	(88)
Religion "very important"	73%	84%	72%
N =	(44)	(91)	(92)
Protestants:			
Attend church	59%	50%	49%
N =	(110)	(290)	(286)
Religion "very important"	68%	63%	62%
N =	(115)	(290)	(287)

*NORC study No. 367.

---

[13] For evidence of the reduced saliency of "class" variables within cohesive subcommunities, see Bernard R. Berelson, Paul F. Lazarsfeld, and William N. McPhee, *Voting* (Chicago: University of Chicago Press, 1954), pp. 61-73, and Angus Campbell, Philip E. Converse, Warren E. Miller, and Donald E. Stokes, *The American Voter* (New York: John Wiley & Sons, Inc., 1960), Ch. 12.

Even in terms of the types of prejudice experienced, the skilled show a "working-class" pattern. For example, NORC study No. 399 asked: "Have you heard any criticism or talk against the Jews in the last six months?" The response follows:

	Occupation		
	Clerical, Sales	Craftsmen, Foremen	Operatives
Per cent "yes" (Catholics and Protestants only)	18%	8%	9%
N =	(126)	(229)	(194)

Media Behavior

If there is a trend toward picking up of middle-class values and behavior patterns, it should appear also in the attention paid the mass media by the skilled workers. Once again the evidence offers little support for the thesis. The pattern of book reading of the skilled workers is close to that of the semiskilled, and there is a large gap between these groups and the white-collar workers (Table 2). There is a similar gap in the frequency of magazine reading and in respect also to the kind of magazines read. Only with respect to attention paid the *Reader's Digest* do they exhibit a level which is closer to that of the white-collar workers than to the level of the unskilled.[14] Their pattern is not entirely an interstitial one, since, with respect to trade and farm magazines, they have a higher level of readership than either of the other two occupations. This would support the suggestion made above that the skilled form a relatively independent status group with interests separate from those in the rest of the society. Conceivably they have greater work satisfaction and greater interpersonal satisfactions and do not have the same need for the off-the-job gratifications associated with possession of the status symbols dramatized in the family and home magazines.[15]

We suggested earlier that the presence of middle-class values in the working class may be due to downward-mobile persons. In an attempt to take this possibility into account, we excluded the skilled workers with some college and those who were college graduates. The level of book reading and magazine reading among the remaining group was no different from that of the semiskilled workers.

Political Behavior

One other kind of behavior where evidence of a trend toward acquiring middle-class outlooks should appear is in the politics of the skilled workers. When we compare their political behavior with that of the clerical workers,

---

[14] A similar picture appears in the media studies; for example, Newsweek's *The Audiences of 5 Magazines* (New York: Newsweek, 1962); American Newspaper Publishers Association, *The Daily Newspaper and Its Reading Public* (ANPA, Bureau of Advertising, 1961).

[15] There is very little information about the impact of mass media on workers. This is especially surprising in view of the frequency of the claim that the media "convert" people to middle-class values. Such a claim is made by Lenski, for example, who says ". . . not only has the middle class been increasing in size relative to the working class, but its social standards are permeating the working class more and more with each passing year, thanks to the growing influence of the mass media. As a result, an ever increasing number of people who are objectively manual workers think and act like the middle class. This is especially true of the upper stratum of the working class: skilled and supervisory workers." See Gerhard Lenski, *The Religious Factor* (Garden City, N.Y.: Doubleday & Company, Inc., 1961), p. 44. Most of the available studies indicate the rootedness of values in primary groups and, hence, the likelihood that there are strong sources of resistance to such pressures. In addition, it should be noted that workers follow radio and television rather than the printed media, and that in these sources the major products advertised are soaps, tobacco products, drugs and cosmetics—not status symbols. For an extensive review of the impact of the mass media, see Joseph T. Klapper, *The Effects of Mass Communication* (New York: The Free Press of Glencoe, Inc., 1960).

however, we find once more no support for the thesis of a shift. They are four percentage points away from the semiskilled workers and are 15 from the white-collar workers in the per cent identifying as Democrats (Table 3). Essentially the same pattern appears with respect to the actual vote. The impact of affluence on the skilled workers will be considered below.

Attitude Toward Education

People have long since argued that education is a middle-class value. One source which asked an appropriate question—"How much schooling do most young men need these days to get along well in the world?"—found 65 per cent of the white-collar workers recommending college as against 53 per cent of the skilled and 49 per cent of the semiskilled. Thus, we see a fair-sized minority of the white-collar workers (35 per cent) not sharing the value and, at the same time, we see that, on the whole, the skilled workers

Table 2

OCCUPATION AND MEDIA BEHAVIOR*
(Husbands and wives, classed by husband's occupation)

	Occupation		
	Clerical, Sales	Craftsmen, Foremen	Operatives
During average week spends some time			
reading books	56%	46%	42%
N =	(176)	(404)	(404)
Reads three or more magazines			
regularly	42%	27%	21%
N =	(177)	(403)	(407)
Magazines read:			
Reader's Digest	29%	22%	14%
News, Business	12	4	3
Family, Home	54	38	33
Hobby, Technical, Trade, Union......	7	13	8
Farming	2	5	3
Miscellaneous	11	6	5
N =	(177)	(408)	(408)

*NORC study No. 367.

Table 3

OCCUPATION AND POLITICS
(Husbands and wives, classed by husband's occupation)

	Occupation		
	Clerical, Sales	Craftsmen, Foremen	Operatives
Identifies as Democrat (of the two			
parties)*...................	54%	69%	73%
N =	(140)	(301)	(301)
Per cent voting for Stevenson†	27%	42%	48%
N =	(105)	(172)	(117)

*NORC study No. 367 (1955).
†NORC study No. 399 (1956).

are much closer to the semiskilled in their attitude and consequent mobility orientations than to the white-collar group.[16]

Attitudes on Issues: Foreign Affairs

The skilled are like the semiskilled in eight of 19 comparisons on questions having to do with foreign affairs. In eight other comparisons, there are no differences between the three groups, and in only three comparisons are the skilled closer to the white-collar workers.

Another way of looking at this is to separate the issues into those which may be perceived as involving "costs" for the manual workers and those which affect all persons more or less equally. In the former category we may include issues of foreign aid and involvement, which many workers apparently perceive as an allocation of resources to others which could just as well be distributed domestically. It is reasonable to assume that the informal sources

Table 4

OCCUPATION AND FOREIGN AFFAIRS ISSUES*
(Husbands and wives, classed by husband's occupation)

Issues	Occupation		
	Clerical, Sales	Craftsmen, Foremen	Operatives
A. Skilled closer to semiskilled:			
1. Satisfied with program of UN . . .	74%	81%	79%
2. Favor artist-athlete exchange . . .	90	77	80
3. Favor aid to India	57	49	48
4. U. S. should be active in world affairs	86	71	70
5. Approve non-military assistance .	97	92	93
6. Stay out of Korea-type wars	20	25	27
7. Approve military aid to Europe . .	79	67	66
8. Can count on West German cooperation	92	82	83
B. No difference:			
9. Approve mutual defense arrangements	92	88	85
10. Should continue membership in UN	93	94	92
11. Approve work with allies (or drawback)	83	81	82
12. Approve economic aid to Poland .	60	59	57
13. Did all we could for Hungary	64	60	62
14. UN work rated "very useful" . . .	42	45	42
15. Can count on India	54	54	54
16. Can count on France	88	88	87
C. Skilled closer to white-colar:			
17. Expect war with Russia	20	22	33
18. Should halt H-bomb tests	44	43	51
19. Can count on England	93	91	86
N =	(129-139)	(216-240)	(167-196)

*NORC study No. 399.

[16] Herbert H. Hyman, "The Value Systems of Different Classes: A Social Psychological Contribution to the Analysis of Stratification," pp. 426-42 of Bendix and Lipset, *op. cit.*

The Behavior and Values of Skilled Workers

of information for most workers would support this viewpoint, and that the typical mass-media content picked up by workers would provide little influence to the contrary. On matters such as the imminence of war, the impact of fallout, and the attitudes of foreign nations toward us, it is reasonable to assume that there would be no strong class-linked position, since none of these concerns are central to the working-class or middle-class identifications.

When we examine those issues which we may consider "discriminatory" or which may be interpreted as such, we find that in six of nine such issues, the skilled hold a position similar to that of the semiskilled, and that on the other two there is no difference. The three issues on which the skilled are closer to the white-collar groups are ones which are nondiscriminatory.[17]

Attitudes on Issues: Domestic Affairs

An unsystematic selection of ten questions on domestic liberalism was done by the Roper Center for the author. This included questions on subjects such as attitudes toward big business and big labor, government spending for welfare, increased minimum wage, and so forth. On four of these questions, the results showed support for the hypothesis of the present paper. On five other questions, the skilled showed an independent pattern and only one supported Mayer. The greatest percentage differences were in support of our hypothesis.[18]

Style of Life

The assertion that homeowning is a middle-class characteristic is not supported by our data. The skilled workers are more likely than the clerical workers to own a home and, in fact, fall only a few percentage points below the level of the managers in this respect. This is the case even when we control for size of family and income. In some of these comparisons, the level of homeowning of the semiskilled comes very close to that of the white-collar group.[19] The likelihood is that homeowning is not a peculiar white-collar value but is more prevalent among the working class. Insofar as it is a middle-class value at all, it occurs rather among the "independents" or the old middle class.

The assertion that away from the job the workers are indistinguishable

---

[17] The questions which for this purpose were counted as "discriminatory" were 2-7, 9, 10, and 12. The skilled match the semiskilled in one other respect not shown in the table, namely, in the level of the "Don't know" or "No answer" response.

[18] The author intends to take up these issues in more detail in a forthcoming work.

[19] The data follow: Per cent owning their home: Professionals, 59 per cent; Managers, 69 per cent; Proprietors, 81 per cent; Clerical and sales, 58 per cent; Skilled, 63 per cent; Operatives, 53 per cent; Laborers, 44 per cent; Service, 54 per cent. The same basic findings occur in a study by John P. Dean, who reanalyzed a study of Steubenville, Ohio, (1950) and the Elmira, N. Y., voting survey of 1948. See his "The Ghosts of Home Ownership," *Journal of Social Issues*, Vol. VII (1951), pp. 59-68. A survey of French workers done in 1955 asked a separate question on the *desire* for homeownership, thus avoiding the obvious problem of ability to pay. This, too, showed that manual workers have a greater interest than white-collar workers or supervisors. This information is reported in the author's dissertation, "The Social Bases of French Working Class Politics" (Ph.D. dissertation, Columbia University, 1963).

from others gains only limited support in these data. Controlling for income, we find that the skilled homeowners show some tendency to own more valuable housing that the semiskilled, but they still fall short of the white-collar workers (Table 5). When we look at the renters, we find an extremely large division between the classes, the well-off skilled workers renting at prices which are even below those paid by the semiskilled.

Because these differences exist even where incomes are comparable, it seems reasonable to assume that a different use is made of income by these groups, that different values govern the consumption choices. This may not appear to be too remarkable an observation, but the fact remains that almost all social commentators have assumed common value orientations.[20]

THE FACTUAL QUESTION—CONCLUSIONS

The main conclusions thus far may be summarized as follows:

1. The hypothesis that the major line of class cleavage has shifted from the manual-nonmanual position to the skilled-semiskilled division does not appear to be supported. In the overwhelming majority of the comparisons made here, the skilled proved to be closer to the semiskilled in their attitudes and behavior. This was the case in (a) the level of organizational affiliation, (b) the types of organizations joined, (c) union membership, (d) religious involvement, (e) media behavior, (f) politics, (g) attitude toward education, (h) attitudes toward foreign affairs, (i) domestic liberalism attitudes, and (j) style of life.

2. Some of the comparisons show the skilled workers not fitting into the "interstitial" position which is predicted for them. On the contrary, they show a degree of independence in some respects which suggests that they may form a semiautonomous status group which is, in part, isolated from the rest of the population and can both set and enforce its own standards.

THE QUESTION OF MECHANISMS

The lack of support for the Mayer hypothesis may indicate merely an absence of the "enabling" earning power. If this were the case, then it might be merely a question of time before the transformation predicted by Mayer occurs. This possibility, however, meets with the immediate objection that the published data show the skilled earning *more* than the white-collar groups.

Our findings, on the other hand, show first, that the skilled in fact earn

---

[20] One of the few exceptions is in the work of S. M. Miller and Frank Riessman, "Are Workers Middle Class?" *Dissent* (Autumn, 1961), pp. 507-13. These authors cite sources which "demonstrate that at the same income level (even a relatively high one) wage-earners have different tastes, styles, and modes of reaction than middle-class people." A study by Otis and Beverly Duncan shows the skilled workers (in the Chicago Metropolitan Region) to be housed in outlying low-rent areas which would make them "distinguishable" from both clerical and sales workers and would distinguish the typical social pressures present in their neighborhood settings. See "Residential Distribution and Occupational Stratification," pp. 283-96 of Paul K. Hatt and Albert J. Reiss, Jr., *Cities and Society* (New York: The Free Press of Glencoe, Inc., 1957).

Table 5

OCCUPATION, INCOME, AND VALUE OF HOUSING*
(Husbands and wives, classed by husband's occupation)

| | Occupation | | |
Income	Clerical, Sales	Craftsmen, Foremen	Operatives
	Owners—Value estimated at more than $10,000		
$5,000 or less	45%	35%	27%
N =	(55)	(135)	(149)
More than $5,000	76%	66%	54%
N =	(52)	(115)	(61)
	Renters—Rent paid, $80 or more per month		
$5,000 or less	16%	4%	2%
N =	(44)	(105)	(141)
More than $5,000	33%	7.5%	15%
N =	(21)	(40)	(40)

*NORC study No. 367.

less than the clerical and sales groups, and second, that the best-off skilled tend to show the most pronounced working-class pattern.

Elsewhere it has been shown that for three reasons the gross figures on incomes misrepresent the cleavage between the white-collar and skilled-worker groups.[21] First, because of the inclusion of the relatively low-paid women heads of households who are disproportionately represented in the white-collar group, the medians for those occupations are pulled down. Second, the gross figures do not take into account career patterns. The data as given combine young and old, successes and failures, and do not make explicit the fact that a considerable portion of the white-collar workers are going to move up into occupations with higher incomes and considerably more prestige, namely, the manager-and-officials rank. Third, there is an inclusion of a well-paid nonmanual group within the category which is being counted as "workers," that is, the foremen. Even with this group included, we showed that, when we control for sex and age, there is no reversal indicated for the majority of the white-collar persons.

A more detailed examination of the data presented above shows that, within the skilled ranks, there is no relationship between affluence and values such as that predicted by Mayer. We noted, for example, in examining organizational memberships, that in one type the skilled matched the white-collar group in the level of affiliation. This exception does not indicate support for the Mayer hypothesis, because it is the skilled workers who *have not* experienced recent increased income who tend to belong to patriotic organizations. Those skilled workers reporting a current income

---

[21] See Richard F. Hamilton, "The Income Difference Between Skilled and White Collar Workers," forthcoming in the *British Journal of Sociology*.

"very much higher than ten years ago" proved to be closer to the semiskilled in all their memberships than were the nonaffluent skilled.[22]

In respect to politics we find that affluence, rather than creating Republicans, appears to have the opposite effect, because those skilled workers reporting incomes "very much higher" than ten years ago have the highest proportion of Democratic identification, whereas those whose incomes are the same or lower have the highest proportion of Republican identifiers.[23] These findings, once more, clearly reject Mayer's and support our hypothesis.

Because income is so unrelated to values (at least within the occupations in question), we must consider the alternative possible determinants. The most likely explanation for the presence of "middle-class" values, as explained above, is the transfer of these persons through downward mobility into this occupational group. None of the studies available to the writer at this time allow a test of this possibility. One published study in this country, however, as well as data from European settings, makes it quite clear that such mobility patterns constitute the most important single explanation for the existence of "Tory workers."[24]

As for the opposite phenomenon, the stable working-class commitment among those seemingly most vulnerable to the pressures in the direction of middle-class assimilation, the most likely explanation appears to be found in the special set of social conditions which effectively insulate them from the influences in the mass society.

We have suggested that the skilled workers form something of an autonomous status group with an organizational life and subcultural values which, in part at least, are independent of the dominant values of the larger society. Some of the evidence presented above shows support for this conclusion.

One indication of this independence was shown in the religious distribution of the occupations, wherein it appeared that the skilled escape from the "normal" processes of social mobility in our society. Presumably new immigrant groups enter at the "bottom" and gradually move "upward." Yet, as we saw, there was a higher percentage of Protestants in this group than in the white-collar or the semiskilled groups. A more detailed breakdown shows

---

[22] The percentages for this subgroup (matching the first six per cents in the middle column of Table 1) are 31, 5, 10, 10, 6, and 9.

[23] Lenski (op. cit., pp. 128, 139) has data showing that the upward-mobile children of Democratic working-class fathers in great measure retain their Democratic voting pattern and their "liberal" position on the level of governmental action with respect to unemployment, housing, and so forth. This result differs from the Lipset and Bendix finding, which shows most upward-mobile persons as Republicans. The discrepancy may well result from the fact that upward-mobile members of the working class are the children of parents who have "fallen" to this position; upward mobility is selective and involves those children whose parents brought middle-class mobility orientations with them into the working-class occupational setting. See Lipset and Bendix, op. cit., p. 67.

[24] See Harold L. Wilensky and Hugh Edwards, "The Skidder: Ideological Adjustments of Downward Mobile Workers," *American Sociological Review*, Vol. 24 (April, 1959), pp. 215-30, and Juan Linz, "The Social Bases of West German Politics" (Ph.D. dissertation, Columbia University, 1959), Ch. XIII. Linz shows that downward-mobile persons are less likely to be integrated in working-class social structures; they apparently isolate themselves within this setting.

that within the skilled group there is a predominance of Lutheran as well as Evangelical and Reformed Protestants, which fact would suggest that the skilled are in great measure of German origin. When we look for the birthplace of the respondents and their parents, we find that this group does in fact form something of an "old-immigrant enclave" within the larger society. It is quite conceivable that this stratum has for many decades formed an exclusive rank which excluded outsiders of different background and which, in great measure, passed these positions from father to sons through their knowledge of, and influence in, those places where apprenticeship training was available.

Contemporary evidence on social mobility also testifies to the likelihood of a semiautonomous subcommunity among the skilled. Lipset and Bendix have shown in their study of Oakland that there is a greater amount of generational continuity for the skilled than for most major occupational groupings, and that intragenerational continuity in these positions is second only to the stability of the professionals. There is some evidence that the downward-mobile persons "skip over" the skilled positions and fall into the semiskilled ranks.[25] It seems possible that movement in both directions bypasses the skilled positions. There is some evidence that the skilled, with the status satisfactions, relative job security, and traditional style of life, have little incentive to "try out" for another set of life goals.[26]

DISCUSSION

Because the evidence presented here can only be preliminary and ground-breaking in character, and because it depends on secondary analysis, it has been impossible to make all the controls and to follow up all the alternative hypotheses which might be of interest. As such, the conclusions presented here can only be taken as tentative. Some of the important follow-up questions suggested by our findings are these: (1) Is a change indicated in the attitudes and behavior of young skilled workers? (2) To what extent are the findings due to the effects of mass media? For all the speculation about the "role of television," there is precious little data showing its impact on workers and their values. (3) Because it appears likely that processes of transplantation are operating as well as conversion processes, it is important to assess the degree to which each is present. Future study should do more work separating those respondents who are in the same occupational stratum as their fathers and those who have changed, rather than simply comparing workers and middle class. Where "middle-class" values are found in working-class populations, it would be better to examine the origins of these workers, rather than invoke in the particular case the influence of the mass media

---

[25] Rogoff, *op. cit.*, Table II.

[26] Rogoff (*ibid.*) shows that the skilled are no more mobile into nonmanual positions than the semiskilled. The Survey Research Center study cited by Miller (*op. cit.*, p. 78) shows the same. A study by Gerald Gurin and others shows the skilled workers to have the greatest satisfaction in five areas of life different from those giving satisfaction in any of the major occupational groups. See *Americans View Their Mental Health: A Nationwide Interview Survey* (New York: Basic Books, Inc., 1960), p. 225.

HAMILTON

or of a "climate of opinion."[27] The same holds for the more rarely examined phenomenon, the presence of working-class values in the middle class.

It appears possible that consideration of the transplantation hypothesis may well account for a peculiarity that has long since been present in American sociology, namely, the fact that although "occupation" has been found to be the central variable in stratification studies, most research makes use of education, housing characteristics, socioeconomic-status indices, interviewer's judgments, and respondent's identification as the basic independent variables. The reason for this is simply that occupation has not served too well as a predictor of attitudes. Perhaps consideration of the father's occupation in conjunction with the respondent's may make it the predictor it "should be" on the basis of current sociological theory.

If these findings should gain support in further studies, then a number of theoretical orientations must be reconsidered. The Marxist "revisionism" which saw the skilled workers as having been "bought off" may well have been built on an imputation or on a faulty sample rather than on a fact. Similarly, the current speculation about the "end of ideology" may well be based on the same kind of error. If further research shows that the skilled workers have not been converted, then the most likely theoretical direction for explaining the end of radical politics is in the *leadership* of the left parties, and it would appear that Robert Michels is the most appropriate theorist.

The policy decisions in matters of economic development which see "national unity" and an end to radical left politics as the results of growth may, given the present findings, suffer as a result of the same erroneous factual assumption.

---

[27] This explanation is brought in continuously by Berelson, *et al.*, to account for findings. (*Op. cit.*, pp. 59, 61.) The relatively high level of Republican voting of the lower socio-economic-status groups has been accounted for as the product of the community "climate of opinion." Given the assumptions of this paper, an equally plausible hypothesis would be that the workers in Elmira, New York, are recruited from among the sons of farmers in upstate counties and were conservative even before they came into contact with this "climate." The question of the social origins, which is notable for its absence in American sociology, is frequently used in French sociology and proves to be a very useful variable. See, for example, Nicole de Maupeou, "Niveau d'aspiration, statut professionnel et revenu: Une étude sur de jeunes ouvriers parisiens," *Sociologie du Travail* (Janvier-mars, 1962), pp. 15-33; *L'actualité religieuse dans le monde*, "La pratique religieuse dans les grandes villes françaises," No. 52, 15 Mai 1955.

Part II

PARENT AND PROVIDER

WHAT sort of husband and father does a blue-collarite make, and how has his role changed over the years? How does his wife fare? How does his family evaluate his job? What does he shop for, and, in the case of the "new" working-class types, how well does he protect himself in the market place? These are the major concerns of the seven essays in this section, six of which were specially prepared for the section. Rodman challenges certain middle-class misconceptions about "new" working-class families, and illustrates his theses with the example of types of marital or quasi-marital relationships. Rainwater and Handel focus on the "old" or stable working-class group, and discuss both changes in family life and differences that persist between working-class and middle-class family styles. Patterson considers marketing behavior, and links up a general interpretation of working-class life with specific and frequently surprising examples of purchasing practices (such as the tendency of underprivileged "new" workers to buy "top of the line" models). Sexton looks next at the wife of the worker, and concludes that she, too, like the mass of men, lives a life of "quiet desperation." Dyer suggests, however, that, at least with respects to a steady job, blue-collar wives and children are "not generally frustrated, disturbed, disappointed and upset with their occupational situation." (He allows, nevertheless, for variation here according to type of job and community.) Hurvitz examines tensions and problems in blue-collar families, and, much like Sexton, finds evidence of a severe and mutually exploitative relationship between the spouses (see especially his closing portrait of "Jim" and "Mary Bluecollar"). Finally, Caplovitz discusses the "new" working-class consumer who engages in compensatory consumption and pays in exchange a very steep personal and material price.

Middle-Class Misconceptions About Lower-Class Families*

HYMAN RODMAN

HOW well can a middle-class person understand lower-class life? To what extent do his middle-class values lead him to misinterpret lower-class behavior? It is worth while asking these questions about any middle-class person—including social scientists and professional practitioners—who has ideas about members of the lower class. Whyte asked these questions a long time ago when he studied the structure of a lower-class Italian community in Boston,[1] and they have been asked many times since then by students of the lower class. But these questions have not usually been asked directly, nor have they been explored in much detail. For the most part, as in Whyte, they underlie the discussions about lower-class life. I therefore propose to focus upon these questions and to discuss their general implications. Although the discussion will be, for the most part, a general one, special attention will be paid to the area of lower-class family organization.

LOWER-CLASS AND NEGRO STEREOTYPES

If we consider the general attitudes of middle-class people toward the lower class, it is clear that there is a great deal of misunderstanding. The lower class is thought to be "immoral," "uncivilized," "promiscuous," "lazy," "obscene," "dirty," and "loud." Many different writers make it clear that this is the way the lower class is viewed within the United States[2] as well as within

---

*At the suggestion of the editors, I have drawn upon two previous publications in preparing this paper, while adding additional material. I am grateful for permission to use material from each of the following two publications: "On Understanding Lower-Class Behavior," *Social and Economic Studies*, Vol. 8 (December, 1959), and "Marital Relationships in a Trinidad Village," *Marriage and Family Living*, Vol. 23 (May, 1961).

[1] It is of interest that in the enlarged edition of *Street Corner Society*, published in 1955 by the University of Chicago Press, Whyte has added a section which deals with the difficulties he had in moving from a middle-class to a lower-class milieu.

[2] Herman R. Lantz, *People of Coal Town* (New York: Columbia University Press, 1958), pp. 227-28; Richard Centers, *The Psychology of Social Classes* (Princeton, N.J.: Princeton University Press, 1949), pp. 95-96; W. Lloyd Warner, *et al.*, *Democracy in Jonesville* (New York: Harper & Row, Publishers, 1949), pp. 249-50; August B. Hollingshead, *Elmtown's Youth* (New York: Wiley & Sons, Inc., 1949), pp. 110-11; St. Clair Drake and Horace R. Cayton, *Black Metropolis* (New York: Harcourt, Brace & World, Inc., 1945), pp. 559-63; James West, *Plainville, U.S.A.* (New York: Columbia University Press, 1945), p. 125; Allison Davis, Burleigh B. Gardner, and Mary R. Gardner, *Deep South* (Chicago: University of Chicago Press, 1941), p. 230.

many other countries.[3] The dominant characterization of the lower class is perhaps in terms of its "immorality," and this reflects the tendency on the part of the middle-class person to simply judge the lower-class person in terms of his own middle-class values.

Such social-class biases are extremely widespread and they appear to be found in most (if not all) stratified communities. For example, the same biases are found, as some of the above references have already shown, within Negro as well as white communities. Davis and Dollard state that "upper-class and middle-class Negroes often criticize lower-class Negroes for being loud, ignorant, black, or dirty persons."[4]

One result of the existence of these ready-made biases has been their extension to other than a narrowly defined lower-class group. For example, whites often characterize Negroes by the same stereotypes that middle-class people use in characterizing the lower class—"obscene," "dirty," "loud," "lazy," "promiscuous," "irresponsible," "happy." In presenting evidence that runs counter to the stereotype of the "happy poor," Alex Inkeles comments on the parallel stereotypes applied to the poor and to Negroes.[5] Copeland, similarly, writes as follows:

> It is obvious that these beliefs about Negroes are simply another form of those fictions almost universally applied to the lower classes of society. Wherever one social class looks down upon another as inferior, members of the latter are regarded as brutish in nature and vulgar. They are characterized superior in such animal qualities as strength and endurance, sexual potency, and the lack of sensitiveness to pain. They are thick-skulled, dull and unintelligent, primitive and childlike. Invariably these inferior classes who are regarded thus are also characterized as dirty and immoral, and contact with them is repugnant.[6]

Simpson and Yinger point out that it is not racial difference which leads to these prejudiced stereotypes—indeed, how can it be, when similar stereotypes are used toward white Protestant immigrants (from Arkansas and Oklahoma) to California, toward Polish workers in Germany in the late 1900's, and toward minority groups, racial groups, and lower-class groups generally?[7]

Part of the explanation for the extension of lower-class stereotypes to Negroes as a group lies in the often larger proportion of Negroes who are in the lower class and in the development of a racially competitive tradition in which Negroes are a physically distinguishable, and therefore vulnerable,

---

[3] For such views in the West Indies, for example, see: F. M. Henriques, *Family and Colour in Jamaica* (London: Eyre and Spottiswoode [Publishers], Ltd., 1953), p. 145; Lloyd Braithwaite, "Social Stratification in Trinidad," *Social and Economic Studies*, Vol. 2, Nos. 2 and 3, p. 126.

[4] Allison Davis and John Dollard, *Children of Bondage* (Washington: American Council on Education, 1940), p. 44.

[5] Alex Inkeles, "Industrial Man: The Relations of Status to Experience, Perception, and Value," *American Journal of Sociology*, Vol. LXVI (July, 1960), p. 14.

[6] Lewis C. Copeland, "The Negro as a Contrast Conception," in Edgar T. Thompson, ed., *Race Relations and the Race Problem* (Durham, N.C.: Duke University Press, 1939), p. 157.

[7] George E. Simpson and J. Milton Yinger, *Racial and Cultural Minorities* rev. ed. (New York: Harper & Row, Publishers, 1958), pp. 124, 167-68, *et passim*.

minority group.[8] By viewing and treating all Negroes as inferior, many whites were able to exploit the situation in both economic and emotional terms. Now that Negroes are united in a determined bid to make America a democracy at last, there are bound to be some fundamental changes in the traditional stereotypes. It is somewhat paradoxical, however, to hear white liberals talk about the "billions" our economy stands to gain through integration—the economic argument, as so often happens, is several paces ahead of the humanitarian argument.[9]

It is also paradoxical to hear white liberals decry nationalist groups such as the "Black Muslims"—a group that is, in a very healthy way under the present circumstances, opening up the following intriguing questions: Are whites superior to Negroes? Are whites and Negroes equally capable? Or are Negroes superior to whites? The importance of these questions does not so much rest upon empirical studies seeking answers to them (the evidence points, in general, to equal capacities), but upon the subjective states of mind that follow from having *three* such balanced questions vying in the market place of public opinion rather than *two* unbalanced questions. The white press has, on the whole, badly misinterpreted the Black Muslims by referring primarily to their alleged segregationist outlook, hatred of whites, and violent inclinations. It would be just as easy to refer to their interest in the dignity of the black man, his economic stability, and his moral behavior—including the important stress that they place upon a stable and responsible family.

THE SOCIAL SCIENTIST'S BIASES

It is also worth asking to what extent the social scientist who studies the lower class, and who is himself a member of the middle class, is influenced by his middle-class values.

The question on the bias of the social scientist is much more difficult to answer. Social scientists do not, for example, use labels such as "immoral" or "uncivilized" in writing about the lower class. They do, however, speak of the lower class as being less well socialized, "unintegrated," "immature," "pathological," and, much more commonly, as being "disorganized."[10] In many cases, the social scientist who uses these terms actually has a fairly good understanding of the effect of life's deprivations upon the lower class,

---

[8] It must also be remembered that the development of prejudiced stereotypes of Negroes, and the often accompanying discrimination, are largely responsible for the greater proportion of Negroes in the lower class. For a more detailed statement of the origins of prejudice toward Negroes, see: Simpson and Yinger, *op. cit.,* pp. 153-54, *et passim;* Gordon W. Allport, *The Nature of Prejudice* (Garden City, N. Y.: Doubleday & Company, Inc., 1958).

[9] See the superb analysis of English economic history and its relationship to Negro slavery in Eric Williams, *Capitalism and Slavery* (Chapel Hill: University of North Carolina Press, 1944).

[10] Davis and Dollard, *op. cit.,* p. 267; Madeline Kerr, *Personality and Conflict in Jamaica* (Liverpool: Liverpool University Press, 1952), p. 193; Madeline Kerr, *The People of Ship Street* (London: Routledge and Kegan Paul, Ltd., 1958), p. 156 *et passim;* Dom Basil Matthews, *Crisis of the West Indian Family* (Extra Mural Department, University of the West Indies, Trinidad, 1952), pp. xiii, 19, 125.

but, in applying such terms to the lower-class person or to the lower-class family, he is temporarily implying middle-class judgments. Why not speak of the total society as being pathological—if it is necessary to use this word—because this is what contributes to the lower-class behavior that we are concerned about? Davis and Dollard are clearly aware of this problem, and they make a similar point about social scientists:

> The most basic differences in habit formation between adjacent social classes are those between *lower class* and *lower-middle class*. The patterns of behavior in these two groups, in either the white or the Negro population, are so widely different that it is the common practice, even of sociologists, to speak of the lower class as "unsocialized," from their middle-class point of view.[11]

C. Wright Mills also notes this tendency, and he quotes the following passage from a book on social pathology:

> An individual who does not approximate these [socially approved] standards is said to be unadjusted. If he does not concern himself with living up to them, he is said to be demoralized or disorganized.[12]

Another technique that the social scientist sometimes uses is to describe the lower class by indirection. This is done by giving an account of lower-class behavior as it has been presented to the social scientist by middle-class informants. It is certainly significant that so many middle-class stories and quotations are used to characterize the lower class, and that very few lower-class statements are used to characterize the middle class. Preliminary results based upon a content analysis of books published about stratified communities support this.[13] At this point, data are available on only five books. In these books much more information is provided about the lower class by other classes than is provided about the middle class or upper class by other classes. The analysis is based upon the quotations of members of the community that are reported in the books. In one book, approximately 70 per cent of the material coded on the lower class consists of quotations from middle-class or upper-class respondents. The comparable mean figure for the middle class and upper class combined is approximately 25 per cent. These percentages for the remaining four books, comparing the lower-class figure to the mean figure for the middle class and upper class combined, are as follows: 61%, 0%; 20%, 7%; 36%, 35%; and 0%, 11%. In short, the results for one book run counter to our hypothesis, and in another book there is virtually no difference in the amount of material used from other-class informants about the lower class as compared with the middle and upper classes. It is nevertheless clear, from the remaining three books analyzed, that this indirect form of "bias" is very much in evidence and is employed (probably without the author's awareness) in a way that is ordinarily detrimental to the total image projected of the lower class.

It is perhaps also significant that even the sophisticated social scientist

---

[11] Davis and Dollard, *op. cit.*, pp. 264-65.

[12] C. Wright Mills, "The Professional Ideology of Social Pathologists," *American Journal of Sociology*, Vol. XLIX (September, 1942), p. 179.

[13] This investigation is supported in part by Public Health Service Grant MH 08249-01, from the National Institute of Mental Health.

may at times write about the lower class like the lay middle-class person. For example, Warner *et al.* indicate at a number of points that other classes look upon the lower class as being immoral, and so forth,[14] and they are clearly aware of these as stereotyped characterizations. At one point, however, they write as though they themselves have accepted these stereotypes of the lower class as matters of fact.

> The lower-lower class is characterized as a whole by its nonrespectability and immorality, and yet there are a few who may be quite respectable but, because of extreme poverty or living in undesirable neighborhoods, are associated with the nonrespectables.[15]

Is it too much to suggest that at times the social scientist's humanity—or shall we say inhumanity?—intrudes upon his scientifically antiseptic approach?

THE PROFESSIONAL PRACTITIONER'S BIASES

It is also of interest to ask to what extent the social worker (and the professional practitioner generally) is handicapped by his middle-class values in working with and understanding lower-class clients. This is a point that a number of social scientists have raised. For the most part, their opinions have been that social workers do a poor job in contacting or in meeting the needs of lower-class people. This is a position that has been stated by Koos, Whyte, and Spinley[16]—three social scientists who have themselves worked with the lower class. Historically, social workers started out with a moralistic approach to lower-class behavior, and it is only recently that they have become more psychiatric in their approach. This, of course, has paralleled the fact that more and more social workers are being professionally trained, especially within the United States. One of the most significant and promising approaches toward dealing with the lower class has been made by social workers within the past decade, and this is an approach that is beginning to spread to other practicing professions. The approach is best symbolized in the social work literature by such phrases as "hard-to-reach," "hard-core," and "multiproblem" families (or individuals or gangs). This approach recognizes the fact that many lower-class clients are difficult to work with, and it emphasizes the need to understand and accept lower-class families or delinquent gangs before making any attempts to reform them.

Social workers have not been alone in having difficulties with lower-class clients. This had been typical of all professional groups. Davis, Hollingshead, Sexton, and Riessman have referred to the cultural differences that underlie the difficulties that may be faced by teachers and their lower-class pupils,[17]

---

[14] W. Lloyd Warner, *et al., op. cit.*, pp. 33 and 249-50.

[15] *Ibid.*, p. 143.

[16] Earl Lomon Koos, *Families in Trouble* (New York: King's Crown Press, 1946), pp. 84-86; William F. Whyte, *Street Corner Society* (Chicago: University of Chicago Press, 1943), pp. 98-104; B. M. Spinley, *The Deprived and the Privileged* (London: Routledge and Kegan Paul, Ltd., 1953).

[17] Allison Davis, *Social Class Influences upon Learning* (Cambridge: Harvard University Press, 1952); August B. Hollingshead, *op. cit.*; Patricia Cayo Sexton, *Education and Income* (New York: The Viking Press, Inc., 1961); Frank Riessman, *The Culturally Deprived Child*, (New York: Harper & Row, Publishers, 1962).

and Hollingshead, Redlich, Overall, and Aronson, have done the same for psychiatrists and their lower-class patients.[18] They have pointed out, for example, that the lower-class patient frequently expects the psychiatrist to play an authoritarian role, and that this runs counter to the psychiatrist's therapeutic principles. Without really understanding the lower-class patient, the psychiatrist may then label the lower-class patient as being "unable to profit from therapy," or simply as "untreatable."

Ministers have had the same difficulty in working with their lower-class parishioners, and in many instances have abandoned their concern for members of the lower class as their own parishioners have risen in social status. A good deal of the history of sectarian development stems from the lack of satisfaction of lower-class individuals with the middle-class orientation of the established denominations and their ministers. Wynter, a novelist, highlights this middle-class ministerial attitude when she has Mrs. Brooke, the wife of an unsuccessful minister, say:

> Lady Harrington was right. The natives were created poor and wretched and damned. God had, for his own purpose, decreed it that way. There was really little that anyone could do to lighten their lot. The failure of her husband's mission . . . was therefore neither his fault nor hers.[19]

A fact of great significance, as I have already suggested, is that there has been a trend away from thinking of certain patients or clients as being "untreatable" toward thinking of them as being "resistive" and "hard to reach." This trend reflects a greater realization on the part of professionals that there is a two-way relationship between the professional person and his client, and that the professional shares in the responsibility of establishing a relationship that will be of help to his client. As we move away from talking of "untreatable" clients to talking of "resistive" or "hard-to-reach" ones, we are implying that the resistance *can* be overcome, and that the client *can* be reached. A very common saying within the United States, in reaction to the strong psychiatric orientation of social work, has been about the need to put the "social" back into social work. The current trend toward working hard in order to reach certain "hard-to-reach" clients is perhaps best referred to as putting the "work" back into social work.

A moral question underlies the work being done with members of the lower class, and it is a question that is not often asked because it concerns the morality of the professionals rather than their clients: Is it moral for the professional person who thinks his client is immoral to try to change his client? It is well known, or should be, that the lower-class person's behavior constitutes an adaptation to the conditions of his life, and it is conceivable that the professional who tries to help the lower-class person may only harm him. For example, pushing the lower-class person from a nonlegal union into a legal marriage may have unexpected and harmful effects; this has

---

[18] August B. Hollingshead and Frederick C. Redlich, *Social Class and Mental Illness* (New York: John Wiley & Sons, Inc., 1958); Betty Overall and H. Aronson, "Expectations of Psychotherapy in Patients of Lower Socioeconomic Class," *American Journal of Orthopsychiatry*, Vol. XXXIII (April, 1963).

[19] Sylvia Wynter, *The Hills of Hebron* (New York: Simon and Schuster, Inc., 1962), p. 180.

been referred to by Booth, Simey, and R. T. Smith.[20] The medicines administered to the lower-class person can, so to speak, make him ill for a long time
after he is made well. Not only the road to hell, but also the road of help,
can be paved with good intentions—and in order to prevent too much
overlap, it is necessary to proceed with caution and with knowledge when
setting out to help people. It is also well to bear in mind that in working
with the lower class, it may not be enough to take into account the "whole
person" and his family, but that it may also be necessary to deal with the
economic and perhaps social and political conditions of the society as a whole,
for these have a very great effect upon the shape of lower-class families and
lower-class individuals.

LOWER-CLASS FAMILY BEHAVIOR

It is lower-class family behavior that presents the greatest challenge to the
person who tries to understand lower-class life. The following have all been
considered as characteristic of the lower class: "promiscuous" sexual relationships; "illegitimate" children; "deserting" husbands and fathers; and "unmarried" mothers. These characteristics are frequently viewed in a gross
manner as, simply, *problems* of the lower class. My own feeling is that it
makes more sense to think of them as *solutions* of the lower class to problems
that they face in the social, economic, and perhaps legal and political
spheres of life.

How is it that lower-class behavior can so easily be misunderstood? That
a cross-eyed, middle-class view of lower-class behavior (uncorrected by lenses
designed to eliminate the "crossedness" and the middle-class values) can
lead to misunderstanding has already been pointed out. And one of the major
ways in which alien values become incorporated into one's view of the lower
class is through the use of middle-class terms to describe lower-class behavior.
It is little wonder that, if we describe the lower-class family in terms of
"promiscuous" sexual relationships, "illegitimate" children, "deserting" men,
and "unmarried" mothers, we are going to see the situation as disorganized
and chock-full of problems.

We therefore have to stress the fact that words like *promiscuity, illegitimacy,* and *desertion* are not part of the lower-class vocabulary, and that it is
inaccurate to describe lower-class behavior in this way. These words have
middle-class meanings and imply middle-class judgments, and it is precisely
because of this that we ought not to use them to describe lower-class behavior
—unless, of course, our intention is to judge this behavior in a middle-class
manner in order to bolster a sagging middle-class ego.

I am not saying—I want to be clear on this point—that demographers
should stop talking about rates of desertion or rates of illegitimacy. In a
strictly scientific sense, these rates have a clear enough meaning, and they
may be extremely important pieces of information for certain kinds of

---

[20] Charles Booth, *et al., Life and Labour of the People of London,* Final Volume (London:
Macmillan & Co., Ltd., 1902), pp. 41-42; T. S. Simey, *Welfare and Planning in the West
Indies* (London: Oxford University Press, 1946), pp. 183-84; Raymond T. Smith, *The Negro
Family in British Guiana* (London: Routledge and Kegan Paul, Ltd., 1953), pp. 178-79.

Middle-Class
Misconceptions
About
Lower-Class
Families

analyses. What I am saying is that these terms can also be used in a judgmental sense, and it is this judgmental use that I am cautioning against. I am also cautioning against the rather easy way in which a scientific stance on these matters can buckle under the weight of a middle-class morality. Consider the following example, in which the author rushes headlong into a fallacy that she apparently cannot see because of her middle-class blinders:

> In my opinion, it is indefensible to write off as "culturally acceptable" to a certain group poverty and its terrible hardships, personality disturbances and their painful results, or the pervasive effect of impaired relationships. How often we have heard that in a particular cultural group it's acceptable for a teen-age girl to have a baby out of wedlock. Whether or not this is a valid generalization is for the sociologist to study. The social worker, on the other hand, must be concerned about the loneliness a teen-age girl feels when she has no husband with whom to share her parenthood, when she cannot return to school, when her friends go out on dates while she stays at home to care for the baby, or when her friends get their first jobs and she must apply for public assistance.[21]

The social scientist who studies lower-class families should pay more attention to the language of the lower class than he does to the middle-class language. In a practical vein, this means that lower-class family patterns are usually best described in lower-class terms:

> The language problem is . . . involved in the terms used for the different forms of marital or quasi-marital relationships in the different parts of the West Indies. R. T. Smith has discussed some of the difficulties that develop when the observer sets up his own classification scheme for dealing with lower-class marital unions. In addition, the great variety of terms used by different observers for a marital union that is socially but not legally sanctioned, and the reasons they give for a particular usage, also suggest that the observer's terms may not be the most satisfactory ones. Henriques and R. T. Smith use common-law marriage; Clarke rejects the term "common law" because it suggests legal recognition, and uses concubinage; Stycos rejects "concubinage" and uses consensual union; Matthews, more simply and perhaps more sensibly, uses non-legal union. Although all of these writers recognize the distinctions between the legal and social aspects of the union, it seems to me that in using their own particular terms for the union, they may be causing unnecessary confusion. Would it not make better sense to use the terms that are used by the lower class itself to refer to these unions?[22]

Accordingly, in my own study of lower-class families in Coconut Village, Trinidad, I deal with three different kinds of marital or quasi-marital relationships—"friending," "living," and married. Through a consideration of some of the findings of this study we can come to a better understanding of what I regard as a major middle-class misconception of lower-class families—viewing certain patterns as *problems* when, in reality, they can as easily be viewed as *solutions*.

---

[21] Carol H. Meyer, "Individualizing the Multiproblem Family," *Social Casework*, Vol. XLIV (May, 1963), p. 269.

[22] Hyman Rodman, "On Understanding Lower-Class Behaviour," *Social and Economic Studies*, Vol. VIII (December, 1959) , p. 445. See original article for footnotes.

Although the few details that follow deal with lower-class marital relationships in Coconut Village, I believe that the essence of the description applies to lower-class families generically.[23] The "friending" relationship is one in which a man visits a woman at intervals for sexual intercourse, and in which he has certain limited obligations to the woman and to any children of his that she may bear. Although this relationship is not fully acceptable, it is the most frequent type of relationship, and it usually precedes one of the other relationships. The "living" relationship is one in which the man and woman live together under one roof, but in which they are not legally married. It is an acceptable marital relationship and it occurs more frequently than marriage. A married relationship is similar to a "living" relationship, but it involves a church marriage and a legal bond between the man and woman. It occurs least frequently within the lower class. From one point of view, these data represent a reluctance to take on responsibility, because a greater degree of marital responsibility is involved in the "living" than in the "friending," and in the married than in the "living" relationship.

One man put it this way when I asked him why the people were reluctant to marry: "Matrimony is a money that you can't spend." He explained this to mean that it was something you could not easily get rid of. Another man answered the same question this way: "You can buy a penny milk, so what you want with a cow, na?" Such comments are by no means unique to Coconut Villagers, but they do point out for us the reluctance of the villager to enter a strong marital alliance.

What are the reasons for this reluctance, especially on the man's part, to take on responsibilities within the marital relationship? Also, why is there a good deal of "marital shifting" within Coconut Village, such that most villagers in their lifetime will have gone through a great many "friending" relationships as well as three or more "living" relationships? Part of the answer to these questions must be sought in the relation of family life to the structure of the society as a whole, particularly to its economy.

All Coconut Villagers, with two or three exceptions, are members of the lower class of Trinidad society and face a series of economic deprivations. Although someone in approximately half the households of Coconut Village owns some land, not one household is able to earn its living from the land alone. The land is poor and the hoe and cutlass are the only tools used. Transportation is a severe problem because the lands are practically all at a considerable distance from the main road, so that the meager crops are difficult to market. Wage labor must therefore be relied upon by all households within Coconut Village, and here they share, with other members of the lower class, a situation in which wages are low, unemployment and

---

[23] See my forthcoming book on lower-class family organization. Cf. Lee Rainwater, Richard P. Coleman, and Gerald Handel, *Workingman's Wife* (New York: Oceana Publications, 1959); Lee Rainwater, *And the Poor Get Children* (Chicago: Quadrangle Books, 1960); Oscar Lewis, *Five Families* (New York: Basic Books, Inc., 1959); E. Franklin Frazier, *The Negro Family in the United States,* revised and abridged (New York: Citadel Press, 1948); Albert K. Cohen and Harold M. Hodges, "Characteristics of the Lower-Blue-Collar Class," *Social Problems,* Vol. 10 (Spring, 1963).

Middle-Class
Misconceptions
About
Lower-Class
Families

underemployment are high, and geographical mobility is at times necessary in order simply to find a job.[24]

It is the man who is responsible for the financial support of his wife and children. However, because the economic circumstances faced by the lower-class man often make it difficult or impossible for him to meet these responsibilities, it becomes clear why there is a reluctance to accept such responsibilities in the first place. We can therefore understand why "friending" occurs more frequently than "living," and "living" more frequently than marriage within lower-class communities. We can also understand why a marital relationship such as "living" becomes such an acceptable lower-class pattern, for it provides the lower-class person with a fluid marital bond.

In addition to the greater number of acceptable marital relationships the lower-class person can choose from, there is also a ready acceptance of a separation when economic circumstances make it necessary for the man to move in order to find employment.[25] In this way the man can later set up another marital relationship, when he is in a position to do so, while the woman may be able to set up a new marital relationship with a man who can support her.

Fluidity is therefore the essence of marital life. On the one hand there is fluidity with respect to the type of relationship a person enters into, and on the other hand there is fluidity with respect to the permanence of the marital bond, such that it is possible to shift from one marital partner to another. We can therefore see that the marital relationships that have developed are functional in that they provide the lower-class person with acceptable alternatives that permit him to live with both his conscience and his economic uncertainties.

This fluidity of the marital bond is, I believe, characteristic of lower-class families generally. Within the United States, the higher rates of divorce and desertion within the lower class, as well as of "common-law" unions and illegitimacy, are indicative of such fluidity. If, as I am suggesting, these lower-class patterns are responses to the deprivations of lower-class life, and if they are functional for lower-class individuals, then we can see the sense in which many of the lower-class family patterns that are often regarded as problems are actually solutions to other, more pressing, problems.

CONCLUDING REMARKS

We have seen that middle-class folk frequently are biased about the lower class, and that they tend to hold many misconceptions about lower-class family life. Social scientists and professional practitioners may share these biases. For example, the occasional use of a term like *profane* or *uncouth* by a social scientist to characterize the lower class suggests that a bias may very well be operating, and such a bias may have an important impact upon re-

---

[24] Geographic mobility is therefore not a good index of status mobility. For a brief discussion related to this point, see: Hyman Rodman, "The 'Achievement Syndrome' and Negro Americans," and Bernard C. Rosen, "Reply to Rodman," *American Sociological Review*, Vol. XXIV (October, 1959), pp. 691-92.

[25] Because a separation is easy under such conditions, it often takes place for personal as well as economic reasons.

search on the lower classes. Lest the reader believe that I am merely being finicky about the use of certain terms, I want to tell a story that I have heard. A social worker was presenting a paper that included case material about a lower-class client. She reported that her client's husband entered the room during one of her home visits, and she described him as a burly and taciturn man. One of her colleagues rose to object: "I beg your pardon. That's my husband you're talking about. He's not burly and taciturn. He's strong and silent!"

This recalls Merton's "engagingly simple formula of moral alchemy":

> For example, the proficient alchemist will at once know that the word "firm" is properly declined as follows:
>
> > I am firm,
> > Thou art obstinate,
> > He is pigheaded.
>
> There are some, unversed in the skills of this science, who will tell you that one and the same term should be applied to all three instances of identical behavior. Such unalchemical nonsense should simply be ignored.[26]

The moral of these stories is painfully obvious. If the middle classes are going to regard immorality as the special province of the lower classes and morality as the special province of the other classes, then middle-class people are not going to do a terribly good job in their relations with lower-class people—whether as researchers or as practitioners or in everyday discourse.

There are still many questions in the area of lower-class family relationships and values to which we do not have the answers. Are husbands or wives dominant? Are kinship ties stronger or weaker than in the middle class? Are values like or unlike the middle-class values? Or do we have a lower-class value stretch, in which members of the lower class have a wider range of values with a lesser degree of commitment to these stretched values?[27] Empirical data are needed in order to answer these questions. In addition, we need to be more specific in our questions—for example, exactly what do we mean by "the lower class"? And what exactly do we mean by "dominance," or "stronger kinship ties," or "like values"? And under what different conditions may we find different consequences? Additional variables that are cultural, historical, or psychological in nature may have an important bearing upon the patterns of lower-class behavior that develop.

With additional research we may eventually begin to get some answers to the many different questions that are being asked about lower-class families. In the meantime, additional research should at least help us to eliminate some of our biases about lower-class families. As Barbara Wootton has said, ". . . the first result of a demand for evidence which will stand up to rigorous scientific examination is the destruction of myths, and such destructive activity is likely for sometime to come to be the main preoccupation of the social sciences."[28]

[26] Robert K. Merton, *Social Theory and Social Structure* (New York: The Free Press of Glencoe, Inc., rev. and enl. ed., 1957), p. 428.

[27] See Hyman Rodman, "The Lower-Class Value Stretch," *Social Forces*, Vol. 42 (December, 1963).

[28] Barbara Wootton, *Social Science and Social Pathology* (London: George Allen and Unwin, 1959), p. 328.

Changing Family Roles
in the Working Class*

LEE RAINWATER

GERALD HANDEL

THE broad social trends operating in American society inevitably affect the several social classes in different as well as similar ways. We deal here with changes observable in the family roles of men and women of the upper portion of the working class. Our data come from three studies conducted during the last two years. The first was designed specifically to investigate changes in the life style of upper-lower-class families as a result of their increasing prosperity. That study involved interviews with about 300 working-class couples and 100 middle-class couples distributed in five cities across the country.[1] The second study was concerned with middle- and lower-class family-size norms and family-planning behavior, and involved interviews with 150 couples, most of whom lived in Chicago.[2] The third study was concerned with a broad range of family life and other aspects of the day-to-day life of Chicagoans, and involved interviews with 1000 men and women. We draw here upon the converging and overlapping findings of these three studies to outline some of the areas in which family roles in the upper working class seem to be changing, and to discuss the question of how working-class role orientations still differ from those of the middle class.

PROSPERITY AND THE BREAKUP OF THE
CLOSE-KNIT SOCIAL NETWORK

Two particular directions of change in the larger society seem of greatest importance in setting the context for family role changes in the working class. The first is the increased prosperity experienced by the group during the past 30 years and the greater economic security that by and large has gone with this greater prosperity.† Although upper-lower-class men and their wives

---

* Presented to the 58th Annual Meeting of the American Sociological Association, August 28, 1963, Los Angeles, California.

[1] Gerald Handel and Lee Rainwater, *Status of the Working Class in Changing American Society* (Chicago: Social Research, Inc., 1961).

[2] Lee Rainwater, *Family Design: Marital Sexuality, Family Planning and Family Limitation* (Chicago: Aldine Publishing Co., 1964).

† The lower lower class has not experienced this twin gain in economic status and security; instead, one effect of changes in the economic sphere has been to make their life situation even more unstable in that the lower-lower-class wage earners often find themselves in the position of earning high incomes for a short time followed by no income at all.

are often very much aware of the threat that automation poses to their new-found prosperity, their orientation tends to be more to the past and to how much better things are now, than to the future and how much worse their situation could become. The general tone of their morale, so to speak, is that "we never had it so good; and it should get better." [3]

The second direction of general change in the society that conditions the changes we observe in working-class family roles involves the increased spatial mobility of individuals and families with its effect of breaking up the close-knit social networks which observers of the working class have uniformly noted.[4] Not only do workers and their families move from community to community (in Chicago, this seems more characteristic of the lower lower class than of the upper lower class), but they move within the metropolitan area as their own neighborhoods are invaded by other ethnic groups or are torn down for redevelopment, as industry moves away, or simply as their desire for something better takes them away from the old neighborhood. The effect of these moves is to attenuate (both for the movers and for the stayers) the tight web of kin-based sociability that has traditionally characterized working-class life. It is important to note that the families involved are not always aware of the seriousness of their move; they may expect to retain the old ties, but find this incompatible with the ecology of their new settings.

THE INCREASING FOCUS ON THE NUCLEAR FAMILY

The most general effect of these two areas of change seems to be to focus the attention of the upper-lower-class couple more sharply on the nuclear family than has traditionally been the case. As their close-knit social network becomes denuded, husband and wife tend to fall back on each other and on their children for a sense of involvement and social worth. As they become more prosperous, their expenditures reflect the desire to build the family and the home into a more solid and gratifying enterprise. Money is turned into comfort for the family. Perhaps because resources are still limited, the emphasis tends to be on goods which seem to benefit the family as a whole and make its life more enjoyable. When the couple commits itself to a new home which will reflect its transition to the status of participant in the Good American Life, other investments in that home follow—the home is perfected

---

[3] Many of the effects of greater prosperity on working-class family life were anticipated by Allison Davis in his "Motivations of the Underprivileged Worker," in *Industry and Society,* ed. William F. Whyte, (New York: McGraw-Hill, Inc., 1946).

[4] We adopt Elizabeth Bott's concepts of social network and conjugal role-relationship in *Family and Social Network* (London: Tavistock Publications, 1957). Studies of working-class life which provide the base line for our discussion of change are: Bennett M. Berger, *Working Class Suburb* (Berkeley: University of California Press, 1960); Allison Davis, *Social Class Influences on Learning* (Cambridge: Harvard University Press, 1952); Allison Davis, Burleigh B. Gardner, and Mary R. Gardner, *Deep South* (Chicago: University of Chicago Press, 1941); Herbert J. Gans, *Urban Villagers* (New York: The Free Press of Glencoe, Inc., 1962); Lee Rainwater, Richard P. Coleman, and Gerald Handel, *Workingman's Wife* (New York: Oceana Publications, 1959).

as a place where the wife can work for her family without being weighed down physically, and where the whole family can enjoy the fruits of the husband's labor.

The focus on the nuclear family rather than on the close-knit networks of relatives, and long-time friends who become almost like kin, can be taken as the defining characteristics of a modern rather than traditional working-class life style. In this modern style, the nuclear family turns inward toward itself, rather than outward toward others, where a member's loyalties would effectively compete with loyalty to spouse and children.[5]

THE DECLINE OF HIGHLY SEGREGATED
CONJUGAL-ROLE ORGANIZATION

In terms of husband-wife relationship, there is a shift away from a pattern of highly segregated conjugal roles and toward more mutual involvement between the two. The husband does not define himself as an independent agent, as he traditionally tended to do. He is less likely to have his own friends and his wife, her separate set of friends. Instead, the couple tends to relate together as a couple. Within the family, the husband defines himself as a more involved person; he expects to participate more actively in family decision making and to leave fewer things up to his wife. Although he may not define himself as being as powerful as his traditional counterpart, he actually has more influence on what goes on at home because he is there more and because he expects to cooperate with his wife both in making decisions and in carrying them out. The wife, for her part, expects to consult her husband more actively; she is less likely to define herself as (by default or design) the person who must make all of the decisions around the house.

This departure from a traditional pattern of segregated conjugal roles is not always easy for working-class men and women (although, because it conforms to the wishes which working-class wives have always had, it may be more rewarding for the wife). The close-knit network of friends and relatives is often missed by both partners. We find, for example, that lower-class people are more likely than middle-class people to say that they wish they knew more people to visit and to invite to their homes. Husbands feel attracted to the old ways of staying out with "the boys," and the progress of the marriage is often one of the husband's gradually learning to settle down and stay at home, to give up "the boys" for his wife and children. Whatever temptations to be "disloyal" to his family the husband in less segregated role relationships may experience, he apparently does not give in to them very often, as compared with husbands in highly segregated relationships. For example, in our family-planning study, in 65 per cent of the couples having segregated relationships, at least one spouse comments that the husband spends too much time away from home with his friends, drinking, gambling, or playing around with other women, compared with only 20 per cent of couples having less segregated relationships. The children occupy a crucial role in this;

---

[5] Cf. Michael Young and Peter Willmott, *Family and Kinship in East London* (London: Routledge and Kegan Paul, Ltd., 1957).

RAINWATER
HANDEL

72

working-class husbands often seem most comfortable relating to their wives through their roles as fathers; they retain a good deal of uncomfortableness about just being husbands.

To the extent, then, that one can treat internal family role relationships as isolated from outside roles, the modern working-class pattern seems little different from the middle-class pattern of the home-centered *petit bourgeois* world. However, the middle class changes too, and one of the main directions of change seems to be for the lower-middle-class husband and wife to cultivate a greater interest in the outside world than has formerly been the case. These interests are part of the role conceptions that husbands and wives have of themselves and each other. Lower-middle-class men and women are more likely to talk of themselves and their spouses as socially active, as interested in informal socializing, as cultivating intellectual or artistic interests. Very few working-class people describe themselves or their spouses in this way. For the lower middle class, such interests are seen as enriching the conjugal relationship; in the working class, they are more likely to seem dangerous distractions, harbingers of conjugal segregation in a new guise.

Similarly, prosperity and greater job security do not seem to encourage working-class men or their wives to think of career advancement as they do middle-class people; instead, the focus on home as the locus of all good things continues in the emphasis they give to greater earnings (but not higher status) and to an earlier and better-financed retirement than was formerly enjoyed by men in their positions.

GREATER MUTUALITY IN SEXUAL RELATIONS

The movement of the working-class couple away from a high degree of segregation in the conjugal-role organization carries with it important changes in men's and women's roles as sexual partners. The traditional pattern of sexual relations in the lower class seems to have been one in which men regarded sex as for their own pleasure only, and their wives tended to agree. The husband expected to take sexual pleasure when he wanted it (and, to some extent, with whom he wanted); he did not expect to give pleasure in return, nor did his wife define herself as a person who might enjoy sex. She regarded participation in sexual relations as an onerous duty, a duty she accepted either stoically or with repugnance. Such a pattern seems quite characteristic of couples in highly segregated conjugal-role relationships, but not characteristic of couples in less segregated relationships. Indeed, the working-class couples in our family-planning study with less segregated conjugal-role relationships are indistinguishable from middle-class couples in their patterns of sexual relations, but are quite different from working-class couples who have highly segregated role relationships. For example, in 57 per cent of these more modern couples, both husband and wife speak of sexual relations as highly gratifying to them, compared with only 11 per cent of couples in the traditional role relationships of high segregation. In 75 per cent of the latter couples, the husband's interest in sexual relations is greater than his wife's, compared with only 36 per cent of the modern couples. It is of interest that, even with husbands, there is less likely to be very strong interest in sexual relations on the part of the more traditional men; only about 55 per cent of them indicate strong interest, compared with over three-quarters of the men in less segregated relationships. The latter are also more likely to mention spontaneously that they think it important for sexual relations to be mutually gratifying—74 per cent of them say so, compared with only 35 per cent of the husbands in highly segregated relationships. As might be expected, husbands' assessments of the degree of gratification their wives experience are more accurate for those in less segregated relationships—79 per cent of them make evaluations consistent with their wives' description of interest in sexual relations, compared with only 49 per cent of husbands in segregated relationships. Wives in segregated relationships are more likely to accuse their husbands of being inconsiderate of their feelings (by insisting on having sexual relations when the wife does not feel like it, or by not helping her enjoy sex); very few wives in less segregated relationships make this complaint. Finally, the more modern couples are most likely to emphasize the social and emotional gains from sexual relations (a sense of closeness, expression of love, sharing, giving, and so forth). Couples in more segregated relationships seldom mention these functions of sex, but speak only of the psycho-physiological gains of relief from tension and bodily need.[6]

We see, then, that shifts in the direction of greater cooperation and solidarity based on interpenetration of role activities in marriage carry with them an increased intimacy in the sexual sphere. This greater mutuality would seem both an expression of, and functional for, the increased self-sufficiency of a nuclear family in which husband and wife now rely less on outsiders for support and for a sense of primary-group membership and more on each other.

PARENTAL ROLES—THE EMPHASIS ON THE INDIVIDUAL CHILD

One of the notable differences between middle- and lower-class parents has been the psychic investment which the former make in the individual child, in contrast with the tendency of working-class parents to cathect their children as a group, a brood. There seems now to be a convergence of attitudes: middle-class parents believe that people want larger families, and lower-class parents believe that people want smaller families than traditionally. The practical effect of these shifts is to increase the consensus that the three- or four-child family is ideal. For working-class parents, within this ideal there seems to be a growth in interest in the individual child and in the desire to do well by him. The greater emphasis placed on education for the children is part of this, although more widespread is simply the desire to outfit children with the good things of life that the parents themselves missed. As the parents, and particularly the father, find their meaningful participation increasingly within the nuclear family, they tend to attach greater importance to their relations with the children, to spend with them the time formerly spent with relatives and friends. Fathers structure their relations with their children

---

[6] Cf. Lee Rainwater, *And The Poor Get Children* (Chicago: Quadrangle Books, Inc., 1960); and Lee Rainwater, "Marital Sexuality in Four Cultures of Poverty" (paper delivered at American Anthropological Association meetings, 1961).

around activities in which they can participate together—games, fishing, beach activities, and so forth—rather than taking brief fatherly pride at a distance between times of involvement in the more important outside activities they traditionally shared with their male companions. Mothers, for their part, seem to think of themselves less as servants of their families and more as participants *with* them in gratifying family activities. As noted earlier, the children become an important avenue by which the conjugal relationship is maintained, as well as a buffer to the rough edges that may exist in the relationship.

THE ISOLATED MODERN AND THE MASS MEDIA

Herbert Gans has nicely documented the resistance which traditional working-class people can bring to bear against the editorial and advertising messages communicated by the mass media.[7] The traditional working-class group, tightly bounded by a close-knit network of peers and expressing its solidarity through common values at variance with those of the larger society, discounts, selects, and molds mass communication in terms of its own social realities. With the more modern working-class couple, the situation is rather different. They do not participate in the same kind of close-knit peer-group society, and they are reaching out for the values of a Good American Life that they know is not centered in the traditional group. Their isolation from encompassing primary relations stimulates interest in the parasocial world that mass-media entertainment offers. Their search for a new and better life encourages receptivity to the social models embodied in the mass media and acceptance of the authority of the media as purveyors of the social, cultural, and material goods available to an American who "has made it." Their specific interest in enjoying a more comfortable and materially rewarding life stimulates a responsiveness to advertising and to the editorial material of home magazines, women's pages in the newspapers, and so forth, that their more traditional peers, whose consumer values are set and circumscribed by the peer-group society, do not have.

CONCLUSION

It is far beyond the scope of this paper to speculate about the reversibility of social change. To what extent are the adaptations modern working-class couples have made to the increased prosperity and the loosened ties of the peer-group society reversible if automation renders large numbers of them superfluous? Certainly it is unlikely that, under the impact of widespread unemployment of men in this group, there would be simply a reversion to the stable working-class patterns of an earlier time—not only because people have come to expect their better life, but also because, in the process of adapting to the lures of a more prosperous society, they have made consider-

---

[7] Cf. Gans, *op. cit.*, and Elihu Katz and Paul Lazarsfeld, *Personal Influence* (New York: The Free Press of Glencoe, Inc., 1955).

able progress in dismantling the old peer-group society; it would not be easy to reconstruct it. On the other hand, the tight little world of the nuclear family could not easily withstand the destruction of the kingpin of the Good Life that holds it together.

Marketing and the Working-Class Family

JAMES M. PATTERSON

ONE of the striking characteristics of the modern market is the basic similarity between the ways high-income families and low-income families distribute their expenditures over broad budget categories. Reference to Table I shows that, except for food and tobacco and, to a lesser extent, clothing, home furnishings and appliances, and automobiles, the high-income family and the low-income family handle their budget problems in much the same way. Consequently, income is no longer the important explanation of differences in family spending behavior that it once was. On the other hand, it must be remembered that, although the rich families and the poor families allocate their expenditures among broad budget categories in much the same way, this does not mean that the same specific products are always bought, or that, when the same specific products are purchased, they are similar in quality. The fact is that they are not. Still, it would be a mistake to assume that the high-income family invariably purchases the high-quality product and vice versa, for it simply is not true.

A striking example of how important it is to divide markets into segments along behavioral rather than along straight economic lines is found in the recent research on the "blue-collar" segment of the market. This is, of course, a very important market for most consumer goods, because it contains some

Table 1

WHERE THE MONEY GOES
(Percentage of all expenditures)

Expenditure Category	Under $3,000	$10,000 and Over
Food and Tobacco	35	24
Clothing	11	14
Home Operation	18	18
Home Furnishings & Appliances .	7	10
Medical and Personal Care	6	6
Automotive	12	15
Recreation and Other	11	13

Source: Life Study of Consumer Expenditures. Copyright, 1957, by Time, Inc.

25,000,000 families and in many specific markets represents up to 60 per cent of the market potential. (It is also the market segment that is most removed from the typical middle-class marketing executive's experience.) As a paradoxical segment in its marketing behavior, the "blue-collar" segment contains a great many surprises for the unwary observer who may try to understand it in terms of his middle-class values. Consider, for example, the following items from the trade press:[1]

- In 1961 52.2% of all outboards were sold to blue-collar families.

- The working class wife buys 40% of all *top-priced* refrigerators; 38% of the *most* expensive washing machines and 37% of the *best* sewing machines.

- In spite of a price differential between a premium coffee and other brands (private and national) working class families accounted for 20% more of the premium brand's sales than did white collar families in a special analysis based on reports from leading chains.

- In an analysis of sales of recent buyers of 20 different products and services, in 11 of the 20 categories, more sales were made to working class families than to Chicago's middle and upper class population.

There are many other examples that could be cited to demonstrate the unexpected facets of this great working-class market segment, but hopefully this list is enough to show that there is anything but a simple one-for-one relationship between social status and quality.

But why should this be so? The reasons, of course, are to be found in the underlying behavioral characteristics of the working-class family and in the ultimate ends they seek to achieve through their instrumental acts in the market place. Some of these characteristics seem to have a rather obvious relationship to market behavior, while others are much more subtle. In any case, all should be regarded as quite tentative. Given this caveat, let us now consider certain fairly well-established characteristics of the working-class family, and then we shall look at their implications for market behavior.

THE WORKING-CLASS WORLD[2]

The working-class world is a simple world. Meager education, routine and relatively simple workaday roles, limited information about diverse and remote events, coupled with the fact that close associates on and off the job are people very like themselves, apparently serve to foreshorten the working-class family's world view. Because both direct and vicarious experience with other or contrasting world views is limited and narrow, the working-class family's perspective is, in general, severely truncated and quite unsophisticated. Situations and alternatives typically are seen in black-and-white terms and people are classified as either "in" or "out" in "we" and "they" terms.

---

[1] Reported in *The New York Times,* December 20, 1961; March 7, 1962; and May 16, 1962.

[2] This section is based on the findings of: Albert K. Cohen and Harold M. Hodges, "Lower-Blue-Collar-Class Characteristics," *Social Problems,* Vol. X, No. 4 (Spring, 1963), pp. 303-34; Lee Rainwater, Richard P. Coleman, and Gerald Handel, *Workingman's Wife* (New York: Oceana Publications, Inc., 1959) ; and Bennett M. Berger, *Working-Class Suburb* (Berkeley: University of California Press, 1960).

Marketing and the Working-Class Family

This overly simplified world view, in turn, seems to produce certain other behavioral traits which characterize the working class. The first is a sense of fatefulness—a sense that the events that occur are caused by luck or chance. When the simple model of the situation fails to work (which is quite often), "fate"—not the model—is presumed to be the cause. This attitude, in turn, tends to create a sense of powerlessness and of insecurity. Furthermore, limited education and narrow social and cultural experience, combined with the absence of a rich and sophisticated variety of perspectives, seriously restrict the working-class member's ability to achieve his goals in the impersonal competitive sectors of society where it is "what you are" and "what you can do" that counts. Consequently, the working-class family tries to evolve a way of life that will both reduce its felt insecurity and allow it to achieve its goals in a personal and noncompetitive way. The general tendency is to seek out the routine and familiar and predictable and to avoid the uncertain. And because members of the working-class family frequently lack both the confidence and the ability to do and say the right thing in new situations, they try to avoid situations where new roles must be improvised and new relationships established. Furthermore, because they frequently are not able to compete effectively in the impersonal social world, they tend to fall back on an elaborate network of highly personal relationships with people similarly circumstanced—primarily, neighbors and kin who help each other in time of trouble. This heavy reliance on personal relationships as a means of goal achievement and security, in turn, means that the working-class family is overly concerned about what others think of them and, therefore, subjected to tremendous pressure to conform to accepted working-class norms and standards.

In sum, the working-class family tends to be a family of limited social activity and experience which emphasizes personal, noncompetitive bases of status and social identity. Typically, they don't know the middle-class Joneses, and, because there is always a chance that they will be socially downgraded, they seldom risk trying to keep up with them. Their world view is one of pervasive anxiety. They tend to prize the present, the known, the personal. They avoid the competitive, the impersonal, and the uncertain. They tend to indulge rather than invest—they are overly preoccupied with the stability of basic, human relationships and they are in large measure "other-directed." Furthermore, because most working-class families see themselves severely restricted in their ability to rise in social status, the "others" with whom they identify, that is, the frames of reference which govern their behavior, are largely chosen from within their own class. Perhaps more than in any other class, the working-class family looks horizontally for its norms and standards rather than outside or up to the next class.

IMPLICATIONS FOR THE WORKING-CLASS FAMILY'S

MARKETING BEHAVIOR

As we noted earlier, our interest in the behavioral characteristics of the working-class family was to use them as a basis for tentative explanation of the working-class family's paradoxical marketing behavior. There is, of course, a certain danger in trying to do this, because we may be reading more into the observed patterns of marketing behavior than they deserve; and after-the-fact middle-class rationalizations about the working class should always be regarded as suspect. Still, a number of possible relationships between behavioral characteristics and patterns of market behavior readily suggest themselves and are worthy of note.

1. The limited-experience world, limited in experiences both direct and vicarious, tends to cause working-class family expenditures to be concentrated into fewer categories of goods and services and more in terms of immediate consumption than is true of middle-class families, where the experience world is much broader.

2. The inordinate concern for enhancing their working-class position and stabilizing their interpersonal relations apparently causes the working-class family to avoid spending their money in ways that are not regarded as respectable or that are "out of place." Consequently, they merely seek to achieve the "common man's" level of recognition and respectability with their spending; they seldom try for more. They know that to try to keep up with the middle-class Joneses is doubly risky, because they typically are not very good at playing this game, and at the same time doing so might weaken or alienate certain important personal relationships which they had formed as a hedge against the proverbial "rainy day."

3. Given this much less ambitious goal of merely keeping up with the Cassidys rather than the Joneses—that is, to strive only for a "common man" level of recognition and respectability—certain contrasts with middle-class marketing behavior seem to take on a new meaning. For example, the emphasis on the contents of the house rather than the house itself. For the middle-class family, the house is the status symbol par excellence. Perhaps even more, it is a symbol of upward striving and of collective self. But for families whose upward mobility is restricted by limited social skills and perspectives, the house apparently symbolizes something much more practical and utilitarian. Consequently, working-class housing tastes run to "decent," "clean," "new," "safe," and the like. And, with the exception that they seek to avoid slums or checkerboard neighborhoods, the socially significant address has little or no meaning for them.

It is the contents rather than the house that becomes the center of spending interest for the working-class family. In fact, within the working class itself, there are striking differences between the dark-blue- and light-blue-collar families. Albert Cohen and Harold Hodges[3] recently found that the prevailing market value of the so-called "lower-lower class" family's car, TV, and basic appliances averages almost 20 per cent higher than the average value of equivalent "upper-lower"-class family's possessions, despite a median family income that is fully one-third lower. They would hold that this is due, in part at least, to the fact that the lower-lower-class member's basic pessimism causes him to spend in ways that promise immediate gratification. Also, because the lower-lower-class conjugal family is a precarious entity at best, its members

---

[3] Cohen and Hodges, op. cit., p. 330.

are apparently reluctant to invest heavily in a house whose principal function is to serve as a presentation of the "collective self" and to demonstrate the common identity of the conjugal family; their house serves other ends.

4. The observed tendency to buy an unexpected share of nationally advertised brands and top-of-the-line models can in part be explained as a consequence of the pervasive anxiety that characterizes the working class. Apparently the working-class family reduces its insecurity about value and quality when they buy a known brand or premium model. In fact, there seems to be a widespread feeling around working-class families that "you only get what you pay for."

5. The working-class family's tendency to "trade" along local, known, and friendship lines can perhaps be explained by their overriding concern with personal relationships.

6. And finally, the tendency of the working-class family to shop in certain stores and not in others can be explained in part by their reluctance to chance being socially downgraded by either the sales clerks or the middle-class customers whom they think they will find there. Also, this shopping pattern can perhaps be explained in part by their discomfort at being surrounded by a "foreign" symbol system. Thus, the advertisements, décor, location, type of sales personnel, and class of clientele all combine to give a store a class identification which is widely understood.

CONCLUSION

To the extent that these observed patterns of working-class market behavior and their suggested explanations are true, they have a number of important implications for the prediction of market behavior in general and for the design of a marketing strategy which will reach and appeal to this segment in particular. The working-class market is not only big and important; it is a different market. The working-class family has different goals and different problems and often a different view of the world from those of families in other market segments. Consequently the answers to "what" and "where" and "why" the working-class family buys is frequently quite different from those for other market segments.

Wife of the "Happy Worker"*

PATRICIA CAYO SEXTON

THE myth of the American woman casts her as a cheery *Saturday Evening Post* portrait, presiding over the succulent roast, with smiling offspring reaching for their portions while the husband watches benevolently from the head of the table. The myth is pleasant but totally false when applied to the wife of the average worker.

No more accurate is the European male-inspired myth of the American woman as super-privileged, pampered by luxury and attention, dominating her husband and family, and spending most of her day flitting through the cocktail-club circuit. This may be a faithful portrait of some strata of American womanhood, but not of the worker's wife.

Her day's circuit is rarely concentric with the club and social rounds traveled by her middle-class counterpart. Instead of the Junior League, her concern is mainly with Junior and his unceasing demands on her energies. Instead of presiding over a PTA meeting, arranging a charity ball at the local yacht club, entertaining week-end guests, or even collecting signatures for Adlai Stevenson, she is busy with Junior's whooping cough, the week's ironing, the plugged sink, the wet pants, the runny nose, the pay check that can't cover expenses, the kids who won't stop yelling and fighting—and the husband who offers little affection or attention in payment for her drudgery.

In observing that "the mass of men lead lives of quiet desperation," Thoreau used the traditional masculine gender to submerge the feminine. Today even those intellectuals who believe in the myth of the Happy Worker will have to admit that "quiet desperation" aptly describes the life of his wife.

The worker's wife belongs to one of the largest and (paradoxically, in view of its size) most neglected groups in our population. It is even larger than our Negro minority—about 18,300,000, compared with about 17,500,000 Negroes (many of whom can't even vote). But while the Negro's collective voice is coming through loud and clear these days, shaking up our whole pattern of society, the workingman's wife has no collective voice. Indeed, there is nothing "collective" about her; she is basically unorganized, a central quality of her life. She is neither a joiner—nor a participant. Though deeply religious, she is much less likely to attend church regularly than her middle-class counterpart, and still less likely to take a more than menial role in church affairs. Similarly, her PTA activity is relatively limited, and—most

---

* Reprinted by permission of the author and *The Nation*.

tragically—she is usually a stranger, sometimes suspicious and hostile, to her husband's union, the one organization that ought to have a natural interest in her potentialities.

She is, typically, a harried housewife, lonely, worried about everything from the diaper wash to world cataclysm; and—above all—she is virtually isolated from life outside the confines of her family and neighborhood. In the sociologist's language, she is a "primary" group person living in a "secondary" group society.

She does not have time or money for club life and "entertaining"; worse, she seems to lack the inner resources—the self-direction, the confidence, the assertiveness, the will—to move about freely in the larger world. Though deeply resourceful in organizing her own household with limited means, she usually doesn't have the impulse, much less the know-how, to go outside her home for help—to set up neighborhood nursery groups, for example, in order to reduce her work load. She is almost helplessly dependent on the neighborhood folkways and mores—what "other people would think" and, especially, her husband.

The middle- to upper-class American wife is perhaps the best-organized, the club-joiningest person around. Of the 11 million members of 15,000 women's clubs in this country, only a light sprinkling are the wives of workingmen. And, while the club woman may be vaguely dissatisfied with her life and may turn to the psychoanalyst's couch (or someone else's) for sufficient male attention, she at least has the resources to find occasional release from the confining grip of home and husband.

The lack of resources—financial, psychic and social—of the workingman's wife may account for the discovery recently made by a mental-hygiene survey (*Americans View Their Mental Health*) that she belongs to one of the two most discounted groups in our society—the other group being male clerks.

That the worker's wife is less than dutifully contented must be surprising information to many. Writers and scholars have done little to tip us off; while plotting almost every gesture of the club woman and the working woman, they have offered barely a footnote to the inconspicuous and undemanding workingman's wife. Like other observers, they seem to look right through and past her to those women who can be seen and heard, whose influence on the national scene is unmistakable.

A new study, *Workingman's Wife* (Rainwater, Coleman and Handel), is one of the few exceptions to the rule. Regrettably, the study is a product of market-research sociology and, as such, its central purpose is commercial rather than scholarly; adding to this deficiency is a total absence of statistics against which the reader may check conclusions. Still, the study offers some unique and illuminating insights into this unknown woman:

Vitally dependent on her husband, emotionally and financially, the workingman's wife is inclined to see him as "insensitive and inconsiderate, sometimes teasing, sometimes accusing, sometimes vulgar, always potentially withholding affection." In their sexual relations, she often feels he treats her as an "object for his own personal gratification without the kind of tenderness she so much wants."

SEXTON

Typically, the only recreation she enjoys are TV and visits with neighbors and relatives.

She is largely alien to her husband's life and interests. Often, when he goes off hunting and fishing with the boys, she will not even share his vacation. Unlike the middle-class woman, she tends to place "low priority on recreation and vacations as things on which to spend money." Restricted to the house, more than one out of three have "never learned to drive a car" and would be hard pressed to find recreational outlets away from home.

While the middle-class wife generally has intimate knowledge of her husband's job and working life, conceiving her main job to be that of hostess to his friends and business associates, the workingman's wife sometimes knows nothing about her husband's work—what he does or even where his job is located—and rarely thinks of herself as a means of advancing her husband's career through excellence as a hostess and "contact-maker."

The worker's wife is likely to view the world as chaotic and to feel she has no power to shape her own life or the course of civic or world events.

She is more emotional than the middle-class woman and has deep-seated fears of loneliness. She is also more altruistic: "pity and sympathy for the unfortunate are among the most readily experienced emotions." She is more willing to forgive others for the mistakes they make. "Doing for others— whether it be their own families or their friends—is a major motivation for the working-class woman."

She is much more discontented with her financial status than is the middle-class woman, and has little confidence in the economic future, believing that her family's fortunes are at the mercy of conditions which she cannot in any way control. "Working-class women manifest a clear case of depression phobia." She is very savings-conscious, and would, in an ideal budget, allot 40 per cent more to savings than would the middle-class woman.

She is firmly opposed to installment buying, but has no alternative. Two-thirds of those interviewed were in installment debt and feeling guilty about it.

Her taste runs to "modern" in everything; she values appliances and modern furniture more than a big house in a good neighborhood—"an expensive-looking house is vaguely frightening to these women"; many reject the idea of living near "substantial people" on the basis that they would feel uncomfortable around people who are "high toned" and "uppity."

In clothing, the middle-class woman prefers the "natural look" while the working-class woman's choice of accessories often gives her a kind of "dime-store appearance." Expenditures on her children, the study concludes, give the worker's wife greatest satisfaction; expenditures on clothing for themselves is the most satisfying to middle-class women.

Organized labor, the group that touches her life most closely, has been grossly neglectful of the worker's wife.

Frequently, all the worker's wife knows about her husband's union is that it takes up a lot of his time, if he's active, and that it occasionally threatens to deprive her of the family pay check. For her husband, the union can provide purpose and excitement; but while he is off attending a political-action caucus or a local, department or steering-committee meeting, she sits home, working and waiting, night after night, with only the TV, her kids, and perhaps *True* magazine for company.

Only during strikes, when her support is a life-and-death issue, is any real effort made to set up communications with her. In strikes at J. I. Case, Ford of Canada and elsewhere, the disgruntled housewife—unmoved by union *élan*, uninformed about strike issues and without money to run her house—has sparked back-to-work movements. These efforts, lacking leadership and spirit, have usually failed, but the undercover effect of the nonunion housewife on the holding power of her striking husband cannot be measured. Perhaps it is responsible for the settlement of many strikes short of victory.

Some union people feel that the worker's wife should be consulted before a strike is called; after all, the strike affects her just as deeply and depends as much on her for its success as it does on her husband. If her consent is needed to see the strike through, it should be solicited before the strike is called. Some women, of course, do not need selling; during almost every strike there are some eager union wives who serve in the soup kitchens and around the local hall without solicitation. For some of these women, the strike serves as an exciting relief from the monotony and the loneliness of their home routines.

Union men, it is said, do not recruit union wives because they are too busy with other things. This oversight, however, is more than a matter of preoccupation, for the union man all too frequently feels that a wife's place is at home, preferably in the kitchen, doing exactly what she *is* doing.

Except among younger union members, who are perhaps more enlightened and who have not yet fallen into a pattern of conflict with their wives, there is evidence of out-and-out resistance to efforts to recruit her support. To bring women into active union life represents an invasion of the workingman's last guarded treasure: the masculine world, the world of work, protest, rebellion—his only "social club" where some would, if they could, hang up a sign as in exclusive bars, For Men Only.

The workingman, the union man, is threatened by inexorable social forces over which even his powerful union has no direct control: automation, unemployment, layoffs. His own pleasures are few enough, and his fears are great and growing. Threatened to the saturation point, he will often, in anger and impotence, strike back at his wife.

In one of the most sensitive areas of his life—politics—the worker is as distrustful of the woman voter as he is of the woman driver. He still thinks "the women" put in Ike. The truth is that his wife votes the same ticket he does, with only fractional deviations. *When Labor Votes* (Kornhauser, Sheppard and Mayer) suggests that, among union members, more men than women voted for Ike (26 per cent of men and only 19 per cent of women in the sample).

The truth is also, however, that these women often fail to cast any ballots at all on election day, simply because their voting strength has not been mobilized.

When women's auxiliaries are organized in the local union (there are several hundred in the country), the union man will often complain about an invasion of jurisdiction. If the women work on political action, they are transgressing on the work of the union's political committee; if they delve into community problems, they are duplicating the function of the community-services committee. And so it goes.

In cases known to the writer, local officers have even insisted that successful political-action committees of union wives be broken up. Duplication of effort is the stated objection; the real explanations, perhaps, go deeper. Often when these women, with their bottled-up needs for expression, are let loose on an organization, they show an almost breathtaking eagerness for activity. Again, this kind of supercharged enthusiasm is threatening to men who have enough problems as it is.

These women, normally shy, even tongue-tied, in mixed meetings, very often lose all speech inhibitions in women's groups. On such occasions, they may even be more outspoken than their mates.

Also, because their approach to the labor union is less immediate, practical, job-centered than their husbands', they appear to be interested in a broader range of subjects. The underdeveloped nations, for example, are objects of real concern to the union wife—a product perhaps of her generous supply of "pity and sympathy for the unfortunate."

The final and most dangerous pitfall for the union wives' organizations is that, under pressure, these groups may become involved in local union elections. The result: headaches for the local and a misdirection of purpose for the wives.

None of these excuses are sufficient to justify the union's failure to mobilize the support and the enormous political potential of the union wife. The middle-class wife, through her frantic club activity, is an indispensable political support for her husband. Politically and otherwise, the workingman's wife is a cipher—a lonely, frightened, unhappy, frustrated cipher—and will remain so until the union, or some other group, decides that her potentials are worth exploiting.

On the political front, the Women's Activities Department of the AFL-CIO seems to be making some forward movement. On the research front, perhaps now that the market sociologists have begun to dig into the workingman's wife, other more disinterested scholars will continue the search.

Wife
of the
"Happy Worker"

Family Reactions
to the Father's Job*

WILLIAM G. DYER

HOW does the blue-collar wife feel about her husband's job, knowing that it has relatively little status and is often hard, dirty, and dangerous? What are the reactions of the children in the blue-collar family to this same set of occupational facts? How does the father feel about himself and his work, knowing the facts about his job, and knowing, too, that his family knows the same facts?

How the blue-collar family reacts to the father's job depends on a number of conditions to be explored in this essay; but, contrary to some commonly held middle-class notions, the blue-collar family is not generally frustrated, disturbed, disappointed, and upset with their occupational situation. Job conditions do create problems in the home for blue-collar families—as well as for families on all other occupational levels—but the data from my research and from other similar studies indicate that *most blue-collar families have a high level of acceptance of the occupational setting of the family, and job satisfaction is positive, although not as high as for white-collar families.*

Some men choose to deny any connection between their work and their family life, but research data indicate that their families display a keen perception of the work situation as it affects the father and the family, and, in fact, that there is a high correlation between the feelings of husband, wife, and children about the job.

In some cases, job satisfaction, or the lack of it, seems to be the factor of primary importance influencing the whole tenor of family life. In one family the father indicated deep dissatisfaction with his job. The children all felt this and mentioned that "Daddy is cranky all of the time. He used to take us to the movies, but now he doesn't any more."

The wife mentioned that her husband's dissatisfaction with his work was the major problem in the home. She was constantly trying to get him to change jobs, but fear that he would be unable to secure an equally well-paying and steady job kept him working in a situation he disliked. She said, "He is very unhappy with his job and it naturally reflects in his attitudes and conversa-

---

* This article is a summary of the author's research, more technical aspects of which may be found in the following: "A Comparison of Families of High and Low Job Satisfaction," *Marriage and Family Living*, Vol. XVIII, No. 1 (February, 1956); "The Interlocking of Work and Family Social Systems Among Lower Occupational Families," *Social Forces*, Vol. XXXIV, No. 3 (March, 1956); "Parental Influence on the Job Attitudes of Children," *Sociology and Social Research*, Vol. XLII, No. 3 (January-February, 1958).

DYER

tion at home. His naturally happy-go-lucky attitude is disappearing. The reasons he doesn't like his job are—he gets no paid vacation unless he threatens to quit, his job is dirty and hard, and he doesn't like the caliber of people he works with."

The above situation indicates a regular, common pattern. Blue-collar family members are aware of the lower prestige and status level of the father's job, and there are some negative feelings about this. But, when complaints about the job are mentioned, they are specific complaints about actual job conditions, and these are the conditions that affect the family. Although the job situation may be the spawning place of job dissatisfaction, the family may well be the incubation spot that nurses the grievances that result in job termination, transfer, absenteeism, work slowdown, and low morale. More research is needed to determine what factors are actually involved in a worker's decision to change jobs, to stay home, to get a transfer, or to work at minimum capacity.

COMMUNITY SETTING AND FAMILY REACTIONS

The type of community within which the blue-collar family resides seems to make a difference in the reactions of the family members to the father's job. My data were collected in a small Midwestern college town where the blue-collar workers were predominantly employed in small shops and businesses. Blue-collar families were not ecologically concentrated but lived interspersed with other occupational families. Social, school, and church life were a general mixture of occupational groups. This type of setting is quite different from that shown by the work of Rainwater, et al.,[1] who studied the blue-collar wife in larger cities—more urbanized and industrialized—or by that of Berger,[2] who investigated the patterns of blue-collar families who lived in a homogeneous working-class suburb. Gurin and his colleagues gathered data from blue-collar families from a general, more widespread survey.[3]

All of these studies indicate that blue-collar families are aware of their occupational status level; but, as mentioned before, a general feeling of acceptance and job satisfaction prevails. However, in the small Midwest community there appear to be more cases where family members are more directly aware of occupational differences and chafe against them. Some rationalize their position. As one wife said, "My husband could take some small white-collar job, but he prefers to work in construction and he meets a lot of fine people. Naturally, you feel that your husband could have a more important job, but we have had a wonderful life together."

Because of the dominance of the college in the community where my data were collected, most of the residents were sharply aware of educational differences. Children of lower-occupational workers went to public school and college with the children of college professors and other professional people,

[1] L. Rainwater, R. Coleman, and G. Handel, *Workingman's Wife* (New York: Oceana Publications, Inc., 1959).

[2] Bennett Berger, *Working-Class Suburb* (Berkeley: University of California Press, 1960).

[3] G. Gurin, J. Veroff, and S. Feld, *Americans View Their Mental Health* (New York: Basic Books, Inc., 1960).

Family
Reactions
to the
Father's Job

and comparisons were made between the occupations of their fathers. As the interviews with the children pointed out, those blue-collar children who had reference groups dominated by children of professional fathers tended to be dissatisfied with their father's occupation, for it was not a source of reward for them in these out-family relationships. A trend similar to that of the children was found among the women, where the wife also had reference groups outside the family composed of women with husbands of more prestigeful occupations.

In those communities where the blue-collar family members associate with reference groups that are more occupationally homogeneous, any negative feelings about the prestige level of the father's job remained rather vague and general, for the job is not as critical a source of contrast and upset in the reference group interactions.

Other characteristics of the community may also have a bearing on the responses of the families. Because of the lack of large industry in the Midwest situation, there were few union activities, and union influence was practically never mentioned in the responses of workers or their families. In more strongly unionized areas, the labor union might possibly have a more significant role in the family satisfactions with the job.

FAMILY AGE AND REACTIONS TO THE JOB

The data from most studies point out that older workers and their families are more satisfied with the job than are younger families. When the worker is older, it seems that prestige and other factors are often subordinate to the satisfaction of having a source of steady income. One older worker remarked, "The job I have is a good one for a man of my age. It is steady until retirement." His wife also commented, "The work is easy for a man of his age. The job is steady and he is always sure of his check. I can't think of anything particular I dislike because I think he has a good job for an elderly man."

Children's reactions to the job also vary with the ages of the children. When children are young, the jobs of fireman, policeman, cowboy, and others are romantic and desirable. Those jobs that young children can understand seem also to have appeal: mechanic, service-station attendant, truck driver, barber, and so forth, in contrast to such occupations as clerk, accountant, bookkeeper, and salesman. However, as children get older, they become more aware of other aspects of occupations, and the tendency is for older children to be less satisfied with their father's blue-collar job than is the case in younger children.

WIFE'S REACTIONS TO THE JOB

The data from my study are somewhat at variance with Rainwater, *et al.,* concerning the reactions of the wife to the husband's job and the influence these have on him. From my study, the wife appears to be the main source of influence on the husband, and in most cases the husband recognizes and admits her impact on his feelings about the job. Although many children—particularly the older children—have decided feelings about the job, neither they nor their fathers admit that they have any great influence on the father.

DYER

This is not to assume that such influences are not present, and it is possible that the feelings of the children are more important than are realized and admitted.

The Rainwater data show that the wives in their study seem to feel isolated and left out of the husband's job, and that they appear to feel that they have little influence or effect on the husband and his job. One wife in their study said, "I wish he'd let me take interest in his work, but he doesn't want to talk to me about it at all. He just grunts when I ask him about it. He never wants to discuss it with me." [4]

They also found that two-thirds of the wives, when asked how a woman could be helpful to her husband in his work, said, "By regarding the job as the man's concern and (the wife) should concentrate on caring for his needs, doing a good job of housekeeping, caring well for the children, and being a good respected woman herself." [5] In contrast, two-thirds of the middle-class women said that the most helpful thing for the wife was "taking an interest in the husband's work and being a good hostess."

Here again the difference between the two studies may be in the community setting and the type of blue-collar jobs. The Midwest community involved more blue-collar workers connected with work in small businesses or work stemming from a home-based operation. It would appear that the Rainwater study involved more workers from larger, more routinized, and mechanized job situations. This difference in the type of job and apparent family involvement is indicated by a statement from a machinist in the Midwest study. He said, "My family does not say much about my job as I don't discuss it with them very much. It is somewhat of a technical nature and most of it pertains to machinery and machines. Women, as a rule, are not too interested in mechanical apparatus." This type of statement would not be found in other types of blue-collar jobs.

As compared to the white-collar worker, my data show that there seems to be a greater awareness of the details of the father's job among blue-collar workers. The resultants of the job are more obvious. Father often comes home dirty and tired. He carries tools and may engage in his occupational activities at home, which allows greater familiarity with the job.

Again, the data show that, despite the verbalizations on the part of some husbands that the wife has no influence on his job feelings, when asked how he thinks his wife feels, the blue-collar husband has a very accurate perception of his wife's feelings. Communication at some level apparently is taking place, and he knows how she feels.

The studies generally agree that the wives feel that the husband should do something he likes. As one woman said, "The man should do the job he likes. The woman shouldn't push into his work. Some women ask me why I let him do such dirty work (auto mechanic) and come home looking like a grease monkey. Well, that's what he knows how to do and he likes it, so it's all right with me." [6]

---

[4] Rainwater, *op. cit.*, p. 76.

[5] *Ibid.*, p. 85.

[6] *Ibid.*, p. 85.

For the blue-collar family, the job is much more a source of livelihood, while for the white-collar family, the job is a source of prestige satisfaction, a source of gratification, and a more central life "theme" for the family. Rainwater concludes, "For the working class wife, the husband's job is a necessity. It takes him away from home to earn the money the family needs to keep going. She hopes that this job will not be too demanding, and that he will come home in good spirits. Preferably, they should live close enough to his work so he does not tire from traveling back and forth." [7]

JOB INFLUENCES ON THE CHILDREN

Out of the family reactions to the father's job comes the formation of attitudes in the children toward occupations. All of the studies are consistent in showing that the majority of blue-collar workers do not want their children to follow their line of work. The wives concur in this feeling, and it seems to be transmitted to the children, for all but a few of the children expressed a desire to follow an occupation different from that of the father. This is in contrast to the general trend for sons of most lower occupational workers to actually follow in their father's footsteps, particularly as to occupational level. Further study is needed to look at the problems of conflict between occupational preference, opportunity, and actual job location for blue-collar children.

The Midwest data show that the blue-collar teenager is aware of both the general prestige level of his father's job and the specific job conditions that affect the family. Both of these considerations influence his feelings about the job. More data are needed from blue-collar children in other types of community settings to see whether both of these sets of forces operate on the feelings of the children in the blue-collar family.

Compared with the father and the mother, the blue-collar child consistently has the lowest feelings of satisfaction with the father's job. The father's job satisfaction score is the highest, followed by the mother's, and then by the children's. It seems that the negative aspects of the father's job inject themselves most forcibly into the family system, are talked about in the family, and leave negative impressions on the children. Couple this with the tendency on the part of the parents to encourage their children to get into a different line of work from the father's, and the roots of the children's dissatisfaction are rather clear. The girls in the family are apparently encouraged, and they would like, to marry someone of a higher occupational level.

THE FATHER

From my data in the Midwest community, it is clear that the father knows how his wife and children feel about his job, and this does have some effect on his feelings about his work. He is aware that his job carries less prestige than other types of occupations, and knows that his family knows this, and this knowledge apparently has some effect. However, all family members mention specific job conditions as the most important factors influencing their feelings—

---

[7] *Ibid.,* p. 87.

such things as: salary, hours, working conditions, type of fellow employees, interesting work, amount of time away from home, degree of danger in the job, dirty or unpleasant work. It appears that if all of these conditions are favorable, the effect of the lower prestige of the job is minimized. Yet, the data also show that, even when these conditions are favorable, blue-collar workers and their families have lower job-satisfaction scores than white-collar workers. The most obvious explanation is the prestige level of the job.

SUMMARY

Blue-collar family members have to take into account the general effect of the father's job. The degree to which the job is a point of disruption and frustration to the family is apparently influenced by: (a) the type of community setting within which the family lives, (b) the age of the family, (c) the type of blue-collar work of the father, (d) the reference groups of the family members, (e) the specific job conditions that are satisfactory or unsatisfactory. More research is needed to systematically control the above variables.

The job is an important fact for all families, regardless of occupational level. The father's job is a point of assessment and evaluation for all family members, particularly in their contacts outside the home. However, despite the recognized lower prestige level of the blue-collar job, the blue-collar family is generally satisfied with the father's work if the specific job conditions are satisfactory to him, leaving him pleasant and happy when he comes home, and if the salary is adequate to the needs of the family.

Regardless of these factors—and, apparently, no matter how satisfied the father is with his job—the blue-collar boy is encouraged to seek an occupation at a higher level than the father and it is hoped that the girls will marry someone in a higher occupational position.

Marital Strain
in the Blue-Collar Family

NATHAN HURVITZ

THE blue-collar worker in Southern California who wears a sport shirt on his job, who drives to work in a comparatively late-model car which he parks alongside a comparable auto owned by a white-collar worker, and who returns to his neat tract house not far from the home of the white-collar worker, is a blue-collar worker nevertheless. And the fact that he is a blue-collar worker who cannot be distinguished from a white-collar worker means that he has special problems. For, although he presents the appearance of a comfortable middle-class white-collar worker, his feelings are different. He does not have the personal security and comfort that his observable prosperity might imply. He is not sure that he will perform his own roles correctly or that he will respond properly to the roles of others, and thus he is timid about venturing out of his family circle where he may expose his limitations to others. His fears are reflected in feelings of insecurity and insignificance which permeate all of his relationships, his marriage included. The present paper examines the sources of marital strain in the blue-collar family which are associated with the particular situation of the American worker who is precariously balanced between two styles of life.

The situation of the American worker is one in which he is most subject to the pressures of a capitalist economy. The productive relations of capitalist society affect the personal and family relations of all class members. In addition to the problems common to all members of the society, particular problems arise for individuals which are unique to their position in the class system and to their own personal histories. More specific information about the causal relationship between class position and personal and family disorder requires further research, but the worker, as the most exploited and the least secure member of the society, will reflect this exploitation and insecurity most sharply. Thus, we know from recent research that there is greater incidence of divorce and desertion in the lower-status groups, and that these groups are more prone to psychological disorders.[1]

---

[1] August B. Hollingshead and Frederick C. Redlich, *Social Class and Mental Illness* (New York: John Wiley & Sons, Inc., 1958); Jerome K. Myers and Bertram H. Roberts, *Family and Class Dynamics in Mental Illness* (New York: John Wiley & Sons, Inc., 1959); Gerald Gurin, *Americans View Their Mental Health* (New York: Basic Books, Inc., 1960); Leo Srole, *Mental Health in the Metropolis* (New York: McGraw-Hill Inc., 1962).

HURVITZ

Because the worker is the most exploited member of the community, both in his work setting and as a consumer in a profit economy, he may respond by withdrawing as completely as he can from those activities which may harm him. His family becomes very important to him, although he knows he cannot be dependent upon other family members, because their positions do not permit them to perform any real services for him. They may be helpful in times of need, but he does not face such a situation now—although he may get money to make a down payment on a house from his parents or in-laws. It therefore appears that it is primarily because of his feelings about himself that he remains close to his family. "He is family-centered; most of his relationships take place around the large extended, fairly cooperative family," and "cooperation and mutual aid are among his most important characteristics." [2] At the same time, his family is the setting in which he expresses the feelings which arise from his exploited and insecure status. Thus, "Coping with the instability threats becomes a dominant activity within the working-class family." [3] Although the mutually exploitive relationship between the spouses in the contemporary American family is demonstrated in several consistent ways in all classes, this mutual exploitation may be more severe in the working-class family, which is therefore subject to greater marital strain.

The present paper will analyze sources of marital strain in the blue-collar family, utilizing a method of measuring marital strain which is based upon the concept of role. "Role" refers to (1) units of conduct which by their recurrence stand out as regularities, and (2) which are oriented to the conduct of others. The recurrent interactions form patterns of mutually oriented conduct.[4] These units of conduct appear as role-sets on a Marital Roles Inventory; and the spouses are instructed to rank their own roles as they actully perform them and to rank the spouse's roles as they expect or prefer them to be performed. The difference between the rank order that a pair of spouses assigns to a

---

[2] S. M. Miller and Frank Riessman, "The Working Class Subculture: A New View," *Social Problems*, Vol. IX, No. 1 (Summer, 1961), pp. 90-91, and reprinted in this book. Miller and Riessman point out that there are important differences among workers in different industries, of rural and nonrural backgrounds, and of different educational levels (Note 14, p. 89). Such differences in the samples of blue-collar workers studied lead to differing and even conflicting conclusions. Thus, some of the findings presented in this paper are similar to those reported by some investigators while others are not. Different findings may be due to: (1) the definition of who is a blue-collar worker; (2) the characteristics of the sample studied; (3) the methods and instruments used; and (4) the point of view or emphasis of the investigator. Any combination of these factors may result in different findings. Finally, the size of the sample studied, the present one included, may be too small for the broad generalizations that are made.

Some of the differences between the findings reported here and those reported by Rainwater may be due to the following: Rainwater's sample consisted of lower-lower-class women; the present sample consists of upper-lower-class women who are moving toward middle-class identification. The Marital Roles Inventory utilized for the present study offers 11 different roles for each spouse to rank, although it appears that Rainwater offered four different roles for each spouse to rank. Lee Rainwater, *And the Poor Get Childen* (Chicago: Quadrangle Books, 1960). Some of the findings reported by Rainwater in *And the Poor Get Children* appear to differ from those reported by him in *Workingman's Wife*. Lee Rainwater, *Workingman's Wife* (New York: Oceana Publications, 1959).

[3] *Ibid.*, p. 91.

[4] Hans Gerth and C. Wright Mills, *Character and Social Structure* (New York: Harcourt, Brace & World, Inc., 1953), p. 14.

particular role-set, one as role performances and the other as role expectations, is called the Index of Strain.[5] The rankings of the role-sets by the sample of blue-collar husbands and wives studied for this paper are given in Tables 1 through 4.

The sample studied consists of 24 couples whose names were given to the writer by blue-collar couples known to him in the counseling setting. The sample couples are like the counseling couples in that they are people with whom the counseling couples socialize and are comfortable; and they are like them in occupation, place of residence, number of children, work setting, and income. However, unlike the counseling couples, they are couples without known marital problems. The sample couples were to be used to determine the differences in the rankings of the marital roles between couples who acknowledge marital problems and those who do not acknowledge marital problems. The modal rankings of the marital roles were determined from an analysis of the rankings of the Marital Roles Inventory by the 24 sample couples. The interpretation of their replies is based upon these rankings and subsequent discussion with the sample couples, and also upon the writer's intimate association with the counseling couples. It is the writer's assumption that there is no qualitative difference between the experiences, attitudes, and values of the sample couples and the counseling couples, and that both sets of couples have the same problems, but that the counseling couples have them to a greater degree, so that the strains have grown so great that it became necessary for them to go for help.[6]

THE SITUATION OF THE BLUE-COLLAR FAMILY

The following information about the sample is offered about an artificially created modal family. This modal blue-collar family is white and Christian and lives in its own tract house in the South Bay area of Los Angeles described by Rolf Meyersohn in "Changing Work and Leisure Routines."[7] The modal husband is between 28 and 33, the modal wife is between 24 and 29, and they have two children.[8] The husband is employed in an aircraft, missile, or aerospace plant. His salary may be as high as $600.00 a month, but his wages average between $100.00 and $125.00 a week and his take-home pay depends upon the number and kinds of deductions and whether he works overtime —although he has very little opportunity to do so now. The wife may have been employed as a general clerical worker or assembly-line worker, often in the same plant in which her husband was employed when they met, and she

---

[5] Nathan Hurvitz, "The Measurement of Marital Strain," *American Journal of Sociology*, Vol. XLV, No. 6 (May, 1960), pp. 610-15.

[6] The kind of relationship the writer has with the counseling couples leads him to some observations rather than others about the sample couples, and the findings presented here must be evaluated in this light.

[7] Rolf Meyersohn, "Changing Work and Leisure Routines," in Erwin O. Smigel, ed., *Work and Leisure* (New Haven: College and University Press, 1963), pp. 97-106.

[8] The fact that these couples have two children after some six to eight years of marriage indicates one difference from the sample studied by Rainwater. These couples are aware of and use contraceptive devices regularly, and they are not in conflict about this aspect of their sexual relationship. They are not resigned to fate or uncaring about additional pregnancies. Lee Rainwater, *And the Poor Get Children, op. cit.*

worked after her marriage until she quit to have their first child. Both spouses were born outside Southern California but came here before their marriage. Both completed high school and may have had a course or two in junior college, technical school, or business school. When asked, this couple regards itself as middle-class but modifies this in some way, such as "modest middle-class," or "young middle-class," indicating that the spouses do not feel that they have achieved comfortable or stable middle-class status.

This blue-collar family is neither lower-class, as might appear by objective criteria such as occupation, income, and educational level, nor middle-class, as it identifies itself. It is part of the stratum of the population which was born in the lower class—which it is leaving—and is moving into the middle class, although it has not yet arrived. Because its present prosperity has been thrust upon it—that is, the spouses did not make special efforts through education or training to achieve their prosperity—their value orientations and intra-family dynamics may be different from those of others who have achieved middle-class status by their own efforts. Sometimes the spouses regard their present prosperity as due to chance and believe that they will eventually return to their "usual" way of living. Therefore, they do not make efforts to create a middle-class way of life for their families. They accept a lower-class status and way of life even while they earn comparatively well. Sometimes, however, they attempt to and are successful in their efforts to move out of their lower-class status into a comfortable lower-middle-class identification with appropriate middle-class values, affiliations, and so forth. Most often, however, the spouses appear to experience some conflict about the class status that would be ascribed to them because of their appearance and possessions. They feel that somehow they are lying about themselves because their appearance does not reflect their self-evaluation. Even when they believe they could enjoy cultural activities, for instance, they may deny this for fear of exposing their ignorance. The problem is compounded when the spouses make different decisions regarding their class identification despite their common backgrounds.

Rainwater points out that the workingmen's wives' "whole previous lifetime training in most cases was built around a different conception of how to live," and so, despite their present prosperity, they "don't take on new habits automatically."[9] However, in the typical situation, the wife is more likely to develop middle-class values and attitudes faster than her husband. Although the husband's values come almost entirely from other blue-collar persons, such as his family, fellow workers, and friends, his wife has other sources in addition to these. The ubiquitous Dr. Spock has introduced the blue-collar wife to middle-class child-training methods. These are reinforced by the professionals whom she must consult and who counsel her about her children: the pediatrician, schoolteachers, P.T.A. speakers, and so forth. Daytime TV programs which present human relations experts, the Family or Women's section of the daily newspaper, with its special features for women, the magazines she reads, and so forth, all further establish and reinforce middle-class values and attitudes in the wife rather than in her husband. The

---

[9] Rainwater, *Workingman's Wife, op. cit.,* p. xi.

Marital
Strain
in the
Blue-Collar
Family

husband's traditional ways and the wife's changing ways, which will be called the spouses' *differential value system,* come into conflict in a number of family situations.

The present prosperous position of this blue-collar worker means certain special problems for him and his family. He believes he is fortunate to enjoy his present good and steady earnings, for he does not see these as something he has achieved by his own efforts. He regards himself as the victim of circumstances—not their creator—even though these circumstances are presently benign and are enabling him to prosper. He feels inadequate and self-deprecating, and describes himself as being less adequate than his material possessions. Despite his prosperity, his negative self-evaluation permeates his relationships with other people, his wife included. He is aware of his low status as a factory worker, despite his sport shirt, auto, and tract house. In fact, he has bought these, or he has been prevailed upon to buy these, to obliterate the observable status differences between himself and others in the plant. But he has experiences on the job, with professionals, with salesmen, and so forth, which reinforce his negative self-feelings. He knows his limitations, even though others may not, and he does not want to expose himself to them for fear that they will see through him and either reject him for what he is not or take advantage of him for what he is. The family and social dynamics which created feelings of self-deprecation which limited his advancement have now been replaced by his limited advancement, which reinforces the feelings of self-deprecation.

SPECIAL PROBLEMS OF THE BLUE-COLLAR WORKER

The earnings of the husbands in this sample are steady and good, and this fact has several implications. Although they are aware that their prosperity comes from a preparation-for-war economy, and that there may be subtle moral questions about their work, they do not appear to be concerned with these questions. At the same time, they are aware that they have joined the society they never felt part of, and they identify with it even though they feel that it has never really served them. They are concerned that "their" company get an aircraft or missile contract, regardless of how this is accomplished, so that their personal prosperity may be prolonged. Also, these men live in an area in which aggressive efforts are being made by Negro organizations to integrate new housing developments. These men acknowledge the Negroes' need for housing and the injustice of their being refused homes they can afford to buy, but they question why these efforts at integration have to be made so near where they live and would prefer that they be made elsewhere. There are no expressed issues of conscience about these situations, but it appears that they may be sources of family strain, because the wives are more likely to be disturbed and express their feelings to the husbands.

Although these men are aware that automation is replacing blue-collar workers in many industries, and they are aware of and anxious about automation in their own plants because they know that their skills can be readily replaced, they make little effort to upgrade their skills. Although each man wants to protect his position, he does not have the energy, after a day's work, to prepare himself for another job. He may feel that he got his job by chance and that it is not wise to reach for more than he has for fear of drawing attention to himself and thereby jeopardizing his present good situation. So he holds on to the job and makes the best of it, although he fears the eventual layoff which he is sure will come. And, with the loss of his job, he knows he will lose whatever status he presently has as a well-earning member of the community. Thus, each time rumors about layoffs circulate, fears and anxieties are aroused which are brought into his home.

The blue-collar worker feels a pervasive anxiety that his own and his family's security, which is based upon his carrying out his primary role to earn the livelihood and support the family, may be lost through his inadequacy or through damaging social changes. His feelings are matched by his wife's anxiety that she may fail in her primary role to care for the children and help them grow. And just as the blue-collar worker is most likely to feel this anxiety most sharply in relation to his role responsibilities, despite his relative prosperity, the blue-collar wife is most likely to feel this anxiety in relation to her role responsibilities even though the immediate material conditions of her life have also changed. Rainwater states, "The wives of workingclass men, being less well equipped educationally than their sisters in the upper middle class, experience these developments not only as rewards with increased incomes, leisure and other value experiences, but also . . . with a sense of inadequacy, and feel an inability to cope with new conditions that surround them and invade the privacies of their inner lives."[10] The blue-collar wife is aware of her husband's self-deprecating attitudes, and they are matched by her own. She is aware that she was chosen for marriage by the man her husband is and that she chose him because of the woman she is. Prior to marriage she had an opportunity to go to junior college and to date students there, but she did not care to go because continuing her education beyond high school was not part of her family experience nor part of her own ambition. When she worked, she dated white-collar employees and men who had the potential for getting ahead, but she did not feel comfortable with them: they weren't her kind. The man who is her kind is so because his self-deprecatory feelings are like her own, and her choice may be an expression of her own feelings of lack of self-worth. The feelings of a woman who has married a man who is not a success by the middle-class standards to which she is exposed and to which she would like to aspire create a special problem for the blue-collar wife.[11] She transfers her loyalty from her husband to her children almost as soon as they appear and she attempts to prove her worth as a person by her effectiveness as a mother.

---

[10] Rainwater, ibid., p. vii.

[11] Even those who seem most interested in understanding her apparently do so because they want to exploit and manipulate her as a "market." Burleigh B. Gardner, in his "Introduction" to Rainwater, ibid., states, "It is the purpose of this book to set forth in some detail the life style of the working class family, and to provide some clues regarding how best to reach these people with advertising and sales messages." (P. ix.) Rainwater himself states, "We believe this report represents one of the most fully documented motivation researches to date. We have given many excerpts from interviews and projective test protocols to illustrate . . . how these women actually think, and feel and behave, and as such should be of interest to people whose work involves these women as a 'market.'" (P. 24.)

On the basis of the foregoing analysis of the situation of the blue-collar worker and his wife, the following generalizations are proposed to guide the interpretation of their rankings of the role-sets on the Marital Roles Inventory and the investigation of the sources of marital strain in the blue-collar family: (1) blue-collar workers are of lower-class origin and are moving toward, but have not yet arrived, at middle-class identification; (2) they are aware of significant differences between themselves and middle- and upper-class members, despite their observable similarities; (3) these differences are due to the blue-collar worker's feelings about himself as the most exploited, the least secure, and the least significant person in the productive process; (4) these are feelings of self-deprecation and lack of self-worth; (5) these feelings are shared by both the husband and the wife; (6) the wife is more exposed to middle-class attitudes and values through the mass media; and, although her feelings about herself may remain the same, she is more likely to assume middle-class values and attitudes before her husband; (7) the spouses therefore have a differential value system.

MARITAL ROLES RELATIONSHIPS IN THE BLUE-COLLAR FAMILY

Research has shown that "for almost three out of every four industrial workers studied, work and the work place *are not* central life interests."[12] However, it is also true that work and the work place are central life requirements, and that it is through the husband's role as wage earner that the family is tied in with the process of production and the economy as a whole. Thus, although the family is no longer a production unit in itself, it is still an economic unit which is organized about the husband's function as the breadwinner. His job is the major consideration in intrafamily and interfamily decisions, and his career is the basis for long-term family planning. The family residence depends upon where the husband works; and whether or not his wife works is also largely dependent upon his job and earnings. The family status comes from the husband's job, and from this comes his authority in the home.

The family, in turn, is a unit which has as one of its primary purposes to facilitate the wage earner's effective functioning in his role as breadwinner. It is his family that helps the worker to compete in the labor market, to maintain his productivity, to resist the exploitive process, and to replenish and revitalize himself. It is also his family that requires him to maintain his function in the productive process when he feels he cannot compete, when he cannot maintain his productivity, when he cannot resist the exploitation, and when he cannot recoup his strength for another day, another week, another month on his job. It is because he maintains his role as breadwinner on his own job, in his own plant, and, through this, in the economy as a whole that he creates the wherewithal upon which his family functions and from which he gains his authority and status in the family. Thus, both the blue-collar husband and the blue-collar wife give first rank to his livelihood-earning role.

---

[12] Robert Dubin, "Industrial Workers' Worlds: A Study of the 'Central Life Interests' of Industrial Workers," in Erwin O. Smigel, *op. cit.,* pp. 53-72.

The blue-collar husband gives second rank to his companionship role, which is an indication of his dependence upon his wife. The very necessary and real services she performs for him enable him to carry out his primary role, and in response he appears to offer his companionship. Because of his feelings of self-deprecation and lack of self-worth, and because of his feeling that he may not be accepted by others for the person he wants to be, he withdraws from interaction with people outside his family and becomes more dependent upon his wife. However, there are few companionship activities in which the spouses participate together. Most of the husband's free time is taken up with doing his chores and repair work about the house, tinkering with the auto, building models, cleaning and repairing guns or fishing materials, and so forth; and the wife, when she is not busy with the children, is involved with her household chores. The only companionship activity they share alone together appears to be watching TV. Other activities, such as visiting one or the other's relatives, an occasional Sunday outing, or a drive-in movie, are performed with the children. Their companionship does not include exploration of each other's thoughts and sentiments or a probing for the feelings that are aroused by the important experiences each has. Thus, one doubts that the blue-collar husband performs this role as well as he ranks it high.

The wife's companionship role is less important to her, and she gives a higher rank to her roles relating to the children, because they need her more and also they offer more gratification. This difference in rankings may indicate a source of strain when the husband approaches his wife on a companion level whereas the wife regards it more important to participate with the children. Although she wants and needs her husband as a companion, she is aware of his limitations; and she is also aware that his general companionship gestures eventually become specifically sexual ones. Although she regards herself as a sex partner and does not reject their sexual relationship, she is disappointed in his behavior because it appears to be consistent and repetitive; and she avoids his sexual attention by not inviting his companionship interest and activity. The wife is also involved with the larger family to a greater extent than is her husband. She talks with her own family and with her in-laws daily or several times during the week, and one of the spouses' companionship activities is the discussion of the information she learned from her phone calls. The wife's phone calls to the larger family not only serve to exchange family and local gossip but are a source of information to verify rumors about layoffs, plant expansion, contracts awarded, new projects being planned, and so forth, which the family members share with each other to maintain a more effective position in the employment situation. The wife maintains a friendly relationship with their families because both spouses often feel that people outside the family will either exploit them or reject them; and they feel they can be friendly with people who demonstrate their concern. For the blue-collar husband, then, it appears that being a companion to his wife is more important to him than it is for his wife to be a companion to her husband; and it is more important for her to fulfill a companionship function for her husband than it is for her husband to fulfill a companionship function for her.

The wife ranks first her role to care for the children's everyday needs. Her children are her primary interest; and her husband is sometimes given the feeling that he was chosen as a means to serve her goal of motherhood. Although she spends more time and effort on her daily routine of homemaking chores, the children are much more significant to her, and she ranks this role higher. It is likely that the inadequacies which appear in her homemaking activities because of her involvement with the children may disturb her husband, although he also ranks his wife's child-caring role first. The wife, then, gives high rank to her role of helping the children grow, so her child-caring and child-guidance roles are ranked together; the husband separates them. He accepts that his wife must care for the children's everyday needs, but he believes that the homemaker, companionship, and sex-partner roles come before her role as the children's friend, teacher, and guide. This difference serves as a source of strain, and the blue-collar husband may complain that his wife "is always busy with the kids" when he wants her attention.

The spouses' differential value system is expressed in their conceptions of how to help the children grow. The husband believes that he helps his children grow by making them tough, by teaching them how to fight back, by training them for physical stamina and endurance, and by teaching them to get ahead because they fear him. This requires him to threaten and punish his children, to ridicule them for failure, to encourage aggression toward others. The mother rejects such training. She evaluates this training as offered by someone who did not get ahead himself, and compares it with training suggested by the human relations experts she is exposed to—whose present status indicates that they did get ahead. She is more likely to reason with the children, to comfort them, to teach them to fulfill her expectations for them because they love her, and to allow gratification of their wishes while the father inhibits them. Thus, the blue-collar wife characteristically complains that her husband is too severe with the children, whereas the husband characteristically complains that his wife is too lenient with them. In addition to the differences and conflicts that the spouses have between themselves on this issue, the children are more likely to identify with the supportive mother. The father is then left feeling superfluous in the family, despite his sincere efforts to help his children grow up in a way that he believes will enable them to compete in the harsh world he has come to know. These feelings of rejection in his own family further reinforce his feelings of self-deprecation and lack of self-worth and serve as a basis for continued irritations between himself and his wife.

Managing the family income and finances is an important role in the blue-collar family and a significant source of strain. Like other Americans, the blue-collar worker is induced to buy his own home and a new-model car. He is also pressured into buying the many wonderful machines that are available to perform household services. Because the blue-collar family cannot afford these purchases from current earnings, it must go into debt not only for such long-term projects as a home and auto, but also for many short-term expenditures, such as clothes, appliances, and so forth. Each expenditure must be carefully evaluated in relation to the family's existing indebtedness, and each decision about how the money is spent is an important issue in the blue-collar family. The responsibility for managing the income appears to be accepted by both spouses as the husband's, although the wife appears to be the one who carries it out. The wife not only buys the family food; she also buys the clothes for herself and the children, and she also buys most of her husband's clothes. She must also pay the vendors, such as the milkman and the breadman who deliver to her door. Because other expenses, such as the payments on the house and the car, for gas and electricity, to the credit union, to a loan company, and so forth, are fixed, no great authority is given to her when she is permitted to make out and sign the checks. Nevertheless, the blue-collar husband who feels his loss of authority in other aspects of his functioning may want to demonstrate the authority he has in relation to spending the money which he has earned in his primary role. Because everyone recognizes that he earns the livelihood, it is important for him to determine where the money will be spent. His wife regards other roles as more important, and she also challenges his authority when she ranks her expectation of this role so much lower than he ranks it himself.

More serious problems occur when there is not enough money to meet the family's needs. Then the question of how to manage the family income to assure the economic security of the family becomes a serious source of strain. The spouses transfer the responsibility for keeping their accounts from one spouse to the other; they keep a budget book to review where their money has gone; they earmark money for special purposes; they agree not to spend cash. But they cannot maintain a plan because they are too near the margin of financial disaster to be comfortable with any plan. A layoff for a month may mean using up their savings, converting the cash value of their insurance, the repossession of their appliances or furniture, or re-financing their auto and home. There is, therefore, considerable fear of unemployment, which, next to war, "is the most frightening, humiliating, and angry experience our society has to offer."[13]

Often the only savings in the family may be put aside for the children's education. Frank Marquart states, in his discussion of the auto worker, that "A small sum is set aside each pay day for the future education of his children. 'If I can help it, my kids are going to get a college education when they grow up. . . .' "[14] However, this money is also used in a crisis situation. In paying their bills, the wife wants to pay the physician whom she has to see, whereas her husband wants to pay the gas-station owner whom he has to see. Until one or the other is paid off, one of the spouses may be too embarrassed to go back for continuing services. If the situation becomes too tight, money may be borrowed from the credit union. This arouses anxiety about whether this money will be repaid in time to borrow again to meet a loan commitment, for Christmas, or for a needed repair.

For all men in our society, effective functioning as a sexual partner is important in the self-evaluation of their masculinity. The blue-collar husband, who has more reason to question his effectiveness as a man, may be more concerned with demonstrating his sexual capacity than the white-collar

---

[13] AFL-CIO, *What Everyone Should Know About Government Spending and Full Employment,* Publication No. 53, p. 4.

[14] Frank Marquart, "The Auto Worker," *Voices of Dissent* (New York: Grove Press, 1958).

101

husband. The husband ranks his sex-partner role comparatively high, whereas the wife ranks this role comparatively low; and it may therefore be expected that the spouses' interaction about this role may be a source of strain. The husband lives in a much more sexually stimulating setting than his wife. He has experiences which evoke sexual feelings toward her without stimulating concomitant friendly and affectionate feelings toward her. Many blue-collar wives learn that it is only in the sex-partner role that their husbands express affection toward them. Some wives accept this as the usual relationship; others reject such sexual advances. Because of the absence of the affectional element, the wives can be detached from the sexual relationship, and they learn to manipulate it to their own purposes to control the husband. Wives may participate in sexual intercourse to reward their husbands for favors granted or in exchange for favors expected.

The low rank given to this role by the wife may indicate that the sexual relationship, as such, is not as important to her as it is to her husband, although she is pleased at his concern about her gratification. This low rank also reflects the less sexually stimulating environment in which she functions compared with that of her husband. When the wife consistently rejects his sexual advances, or when she uses the sexual relationship in an exchange bargain, the husband experiences considerable strain. He not only feels the depersonalization and demasculinization that comes from being exploited, but, as his wife does not meet his erotic needs and expectations, he may also experience this demasculinization at home. Because the husband ranks his roles relating to the children following his sex-partner role, whereas his wife ranks her sex-partner role following her roles relating to the children, their different performances and expectations in regard to involvement with the children may disrupt their sex-partner roles.

Both spouses rank the sexual-partner roles high as an expectation of the other spouse, following their expectation of the spouse as a companion. This appears to indicate that both the husband and the wife expect the other spouse to perform the companion and sex-partner roles in close association, even though this is not the way the wife ranks her role performance. The wife's ranking of her role may represent her effort to separate her own companion and sex-partner roles, but her expectation is that her husband couple his companion and sex-partner roles toward her. This may indicate that she regards her own sexual feelings as less important than her husband's, and that she knows that considering his sex-partner role as more important than she does her own is less likely to lead to marital strain. The wife may rank her expectation of her husband as a sex partner as high as she does, not primarily because of the erotic aspect of the sexual relationship, but because of the affectional element in it.

It is only after his roles as breadwinner, manager of the family income, companion, and sex partner to his wife that the blue-collar husband ranks his two roles related to the children. To a considerable extent, the children appear to be a consequence of marriage and do not seem to play a significant part in his everyday activities and attitudes. He occasionally describes the things that are important to him without referring to the children. His wife, however, cannot do this. To her the children play an essential part in her life's activities. One wonders, therefore, what pleasures the blue-collar worker gets from his parental role. Although children represent to the wife the fulfillment of her childhood expectations and aspirations, children to the husband may represent the denial of his childhood expectations and aspirations. The blue-collar husband has a limited amount of interaction with his young children, for he has a couple of hours with them after work during the week and a few hours with them on the week-end. However, he customarily complains about being tired when he comes home from work. He wants to read the paper or have a beer while he watches the TV news. The children are therefore kept away from him during the week and he participates with them for only a limited time. The time with the children on the week-end often becomes disturbing because he eventually expresses his authoritarian attitude toward the children and a family hassle ensues. He is aware that his philosophy of child rearing is different from his wife's, and he feels that his philosophy—and he is as well—rejected when his wife permits behavior that he does not allow. Even if he insists that his philosophy of child rearing be respected and that his injunctions be followed while he is at home, he is aware that after he has gone to work, the mother's relationship with the children will revert to that which expresses her philosophy.

The husband knows that he is repeating with his own children his father's pattern in dealing with him, and that this pattern did not equip him for the accomplishments that others have achieved. He is therefore led to question whether his approach is as valid as he sometimes insists it is. He may want to be more involved with his children, but it has to be on his own terms—it is too difficult for him to accept them on their own terms. Their behavior is irritating, and, though he wants to be as permissive as his wife advises, this permissiveness is too great a burden for him. He is annoyed by the children's demands upon him and prefers that they be seen and not heard—as his father expected of him. (And he now identifies with his father and can relate to him.) The blue-collar worker is aware that his children's chances for achieving the good things of life are less than those of the children of the white-collar worker whom he sees in the community, and this again is a source of self-deprecation. Although he wants to see his children achieve the mobility that he did not, and he wants to see his children accept comfortably any status they might achieve, the blue-collar worker is aware that their achievement may remove them from comfortable interaction and communication with him. He thus faces the dilemma in which he wants to see his children achieve, knowing that if they do so, they will disrupt the kind of family pattern that he feels comfortable with in his relationship with his own parents.

Practicing the family religion or philosophy appears to be more important to the wife than to the husband in the blue-collar family, because she ranks this role sixth whereas the husband ranks it last. Such a significant difference between the rank each gives this role for himself may imply that this role is conceived or defined differently by husbands and wives. This is not only related to the fact that the wife participates in church activities more than her husband does. To her, practicing the family religion means more than going to a particular church. It means being a "good Christian," which

103

implies living by the Golden Rule, being fair, and so forth. Her husband tends to mock her unrealistic evaluation of the world in which they live —which serves as another source of strain.

The wife ranks together her roles to practice the family religion and to serve as a model of women, which may indicate that she recognizes some overlap in these roles. The wife apparently believes that as she practices the family religion or lives by her friendly philosophy, she serves as a model of women. The husband appears to believe that as she serves as a model of women offering warmth, comfort and support, and so forth, she practices the family religion. Thus, if the husband also perceives some overlap between the model role and the religious role, this may indicate that he identifies religion as the wife's function and therefore ranks it considerably lower for himself. To some extent religious identification and participation in organized church activities are expressions of a desire for some kind of affiliation with people who have like-minded attitudes and concerns. This may be the blue-collar family's one affiliation in the community, and participation in the church may also represent identification with their own parents, who urge such an affiliation upon them.

The blue-collar husband ranks his role to do the jobs around the house comparatively high. This is so not out of preference but out of necessity. Because of the cost, he is involved with the maintenance and improvement of his home. He mows the lawn, while his wife does the gardening, and he does the minor plumbing and electrical repair work. He has also learned to do repair work on his auto, and he spends considerable time shopping for auto parts, studying manuals, and checking with friends about how a particular job should be done. Although his chores leave little time for leisure or self-improvement, the work is necessary. To him it is more important than participating in religious activities or advancing his family in the community. He also does his wife's work around the house, although this is usually done only after some nagging on her part, unless a pattern of helping her has been established. However, he does not appear to resist doing her work in an emergency. Because the wife knows that pressure upon her husband causes strain, she asks him to help her as seldom as possible.

Although both spouses rank the decision-making role low, each spouse ranks this role higher for himself than he does as an expectation of the spouse. Several reasons may be given to explain this for the husband. The blue-collar worker's self-attitudes may modify the traditional authoritarian role of the husband and father. As he views his status, he may believe that his decision-making role cannot be important, for he is aware that he does not make decisions—they are imposed upon him. This is so even in the one role that he ranks high: managing the family income. He may not care to make decisions in some areas, such as about the children, for he knows that this is an area about which his wife has strong feelings. The wife's ranking of the decision-making role appears to reveal two different attitudes toward the traditional authoritarian role of the husband and father. On the one hand, she appears to regard her husband as dominant and controlling, and she accepts a subordinate position in relation to him as the wage earner. On the other hand, she resists this authority, particularly in regard to her child-

HURVITZ

caring role. She is aware that when decisions are made that do not suit her, she can manipulate her companion and sex-partner roles to gain her ends. In general, it appears that each of the spouses has an area of decision making that is more or less accepted by the other: the husband in regard to managing the income, and the wife in regard to caring for the children. In these areas, as well as in others, it appears that the decisions in the family are made passively and by default rather than actively and through interaction.

Because the wife regards as her primary roles to care for and to guide the children, she can separate these from her model role, which she ranks considerably lower. The husband ranks his guidance role and model role together. Although the blue-collar wife knows that she can perform her primary roles effectively, her self-feelings enter into her evaluation of her model role. Because she is married to a man who is not a success, and because their mutual choice may indicate her own inadequacy, she may not see herself as an effective model. Because of his rankings of his other roles and of his awareness of his inadequacy in relation to the children, the husband does not rank his model role high. The model role is an ambiguous one in that it has no specific components but is enacted as the spouses perform their other roles and in the attitudes and values which they foster in their children.[15] As indicated, the wife may identify this role with her practice of the family religion or philosophy, whatever her self-feelings may be. Because of his own self-attitudes and his awareness of his limitations, the husband does not have a consistent positive model to present, so his inadequacy makes him a lesser male model for his children, and this in turn reinforces his feelings of inadequacy.

The husband ranks last his roles to represent and advance his family in the community and to practice the family religion or philosophy. For self-protection, he withdraws from community involvement and finds his safest association with other family members. Although he may not prefer to continue his identification with lower-class members, he does feel more secure with these people. He knows that his relative prosperity has been achieved without his being a churchgoer, and he knows that whether he goes to church or not will not influence the forces which have created his prosperity. And, although he knows that he is exploited, he is not class-conscious in the Marxist sense, for this also implies a conscious effort to effect change, and so he does not take an active part in union affairs. Neither does he join many other groups, although he may participate in a fraternal order or in a bowling ·league or gun club. He is aware that, although he has made significant progress from his origins, he has not really made his family secure; he has not advanced it as well as he wants to from the kingdom of necessity to the kingdom of freedom, and therefore he ranks these as the lowest of his roles.

Both the blue-collar husband and the blue-collar wife rank last the wife's role to help earn the living. Because all the husbands in the sample are working and the families have young children, it is unlikely that the wives would work. Nevertheless, the wives talk about going to work even though they know that this is unrealistic in their present situation. To the husband,

---

[15] Nathan Hurvitz, "The Components of Marital Roles," *Sociology and Social Research*, Vol. XLV, No. 3 (April, 1961), pp. 301-9.

Marital
Strain
in the
Blue-Collar
Family

a working wife may represent his own inadequacy; and he can justify his wife's working and agree to it only because of a family crisis. To the wife, working means going back as an assembly-line worker in an electronics plant, as a general clerical worker in a huge office, for the telephone company, or as a waitress. Earnings for such unskilled work are low, and a baby sitter is expensive; hence, very little money may be left after a week's work. Because the working-class wife, unlike the middle-class wife, has never learned skills, the use of which could help her to fulfill herself as a person, she returns to work only if family economics require it. Some working-class wives may go to work to get away from an unpleasant home situation; the respite from the children and the camaraderie on the job with like-minded women are worth the low pay, the bad hours, and the pressure.

REVIEW AND SUMMARY CASE PRESENTATION

A review of the role relationships of the spouses is based upon two broad generalizations about the blue-collar worker and his wife. First, this man and woman have self-deprecatory feelings due to their origins and status. Second, the wife has assumed certain middle-class attitudes and values as a result of her greater exposure to these through the mass media. The spouses' self-deprecatory feelings determine attitudes and a style of life which are different from those which their middle-class possessions imply; and they are therefore alienated from the prevailing way of life of middle-class Americans. The wife's developing middle-class values draw her away from the spouses' accustomed ways and values and may be a source of conflict in the blue-collar family.

The blue-collar husband regards earning the livelihood as his primary role. Although he ranks his companionship and sex-partner roles high, he is concerned with his job and with managing the family income. Then come his involvement with his children, his activity about the house, his responsibility as a decision maker, and, finally, his participation in the community and in practicing the family religion. The wife's primary roles are to care for and guide the children. Then as homemaker and companion, she supports her husband in his breadwinner role. She also assumes responsibility for managing the family income and for directing the family's religious values and practices. She ranks low her roles as sex partner, decision maker, and participant in the community; and in final place she ranks her role to help earn the livelihood.

The spouses' self-feelings appear in their concerns about the husband's job: because of his limited skills, they are anxious about his continued employment. The complete destruction of the established balance of role performances and role expectations that occurs when he loses his job indicates how much their concern about his continued employment motivates their behavior. This concern is reflected in their differences about managing the family income. Both spouses believe they can do this more effectively then the other, but decisions are actually imposed upon them by the family's growing needs. The husband has expectations of his wife as a sex partner which she may not fulfill. Here we have the making of a relationship in which the husband exploits the wife by withholding money from her while the wife exploits the husband by withholding sex from him. The area of religious identification is left to the wife, although she may solicit her husband's help in defining and carrying out the required activity. But the husband's experiences take place in a setting which educate him to a set of values which require him to evaluate other people as adversaries, and he wants to teach his children to live by such a code. The wife rejects these values and wants to protect her children from them. She regards them as the values of people who have not succeeded as well as others who appear to be more permissive toward their children. This differential value system is most often expressed in the spouses' relationship with their children and is another significant source of strain.

A summary of the role relationships between working-class spouses may best be seen in the interaction of a hypothetical couple. Here, then, are Jim and Mary Bluecollar as each begins his day and reflects on his experiences of the day before:

Jim Bluecollar, wearing a bright sport shirt, drove to work in his 1960 Buick. Driving along on the Freeway, no one would know what he did; other drivers might even think that he was a project engineer. Jim worried about his job. He wondered whether the rumors about the cancellation of the job he was working on were true, and whether there really were machines that could replace 40 guys like him. Guys like him were a dime a dozen. If he only had something people really needed, then he wouldn't be scared all the time; he'd be a different person altogether. The auto—he bought the auto when he was working overtime, and now there wasn't any more overtime. He was also paying on the bedroom furniture Mary insisted on buying for the kids. The kids made him mad last night. They had on a stupid kids' show, and when he came home tired and switched the TV to a program about fishing, they started to yell. And Mary hollered at him! He tried to explain to her that she was always sticking up for the kids, that she babied them too much, but she kept busy in the kitchen. He tried to watch the kids' show, but the kids climbed on him. So he went out to mow the lawn just to get away. He came back in when Mary called him for supper. While they were eating, the kids raised hell and he yelled at them some more—even though he didn't want to. After dinner Mary got the kids off to bed, so he lay down on the sofa and fell asleep. When he got up, Mary was in her bedclothes. She had showered and looked relaxed and pretty. He tried to kiss her, but she turned away. When he asked her what was wrong, she started to tell him off about the kids—that he didn't play with them, that he always yelled at them. He tried to explain that he played with them and tried to toughen them up, but she complained he was too rough—that he'd hurt them. But she was the one who was making sissies out of them. He saw he wasn't getting anyplace, so he tried to get Mary off this kick. He tried to touch her, and although she let him, she didn't respond. He thought he got his message through to her and prepared for bed. When he came out of the bathroom, he heard the TV. He asked Mary to come to bed with him but she refused —she said there was a movie on she just had to see. Not again! He'd be damned if he'd get her that dishwasher. Let her ask him. If they didn't argue about the kids, it was about money—and then she held out on him. Damn! But maybe things would be different tonight. . . .

While her husband was driving to work, Mary Bluecollar cleaned up after breakfast. She always prepared breakfast for him—that's the way her mother did for her father. This morning she wanted to explain she was sorry she didn't come to bed with him as she knew he wanted. But she couldn't tell him because he was mad, and she couldn't cajole him out of his mad because the kids were around. There wasn't the chance. There was never a chance to tell him how she felt. But why did he always complain about the kids? Who was he to talk? He wasn't such a big success to tell her how to raise the kids. If they grew up his way, they'd end up in the shop like him. He treated the kids like grownups, like he came first. It was true, he worked hard. But if he had gone on in school or taken that class they offered him, he'd have a better job now. So he had no one to blame but himself. He wanted to do what was right, but sometimes he did such foolish things. Why did he have to get such an expensive car? To baby it all the time? Like that gadget for the motor bike he was building for the kids—and they were years too young to use it. They should save their money; build up a reserve; put some aside for the kids' schooling—he wanted it that way. And why did he always expect her to have sex with him just because he wanted it? He hardly spoke a dozen civil words to her and then he wanted to go to bed with her. Were all men like that? But he really felt bad when she turned him down. And he wanted her to enjoy sex, too—and sometimes she did. Sometimes she didn't believe he wanted her—why should he want her? She wasn't that pretty, nor that smart, nor sexy. She liked him. They could make a good family together. He really liked the kids, but he didn't know how to show it. He didn't know how to show her he liked her, if he did. She didn't want to turn him down, but it kept him in line. He knew she wanted him to save money for the kids' school. She wanted him to go to church, too. When he'd open the kids' account or when he'd come to church with her, they'd have a party. But was that all he needed her for—to keep his house and go to bed with him? Damn! But maybe tonight things would be different.

Maybe they would and maybe they wouldn't. . . .

Table 1

MODAL RANKING OF THE HUSBAND'S ROLES AS ROLE PERFORMANCES
BY THE SAMPLE OF BLUE-COLLAR HUSBANDS

I earn the living and support the family.
I am a companion to my wife.
I manage the family income and finances.
I am a sexual partner to my wife.
I help the children grow by being their friend, teacher, and guide.
I serve as the model of men for my children.
I do my jobs around the house.
I decide when the family is still divided after discussing something.
I do my wife's work around the house if my help is needed.
I represent and advance my family in the community.
I practice the family religion or philosophy.

Table 2

MODAL RANKING OF THE HUSBAND'S ROLES AS ROLE EXPECTATIONS BY THE SAMPLE OF BLUE-COLLAR WIVES

He earns the living and supports the family.
He helps the children grow by being their friend, teacher, and guide.
He is a companion to his wife.
He is a sexual partner to his wife.
He serves as the model of men for his children.
He does his jobs around the house.
He practices the family religion or philosophy.
He manages the family income and finances.
He represents and advances his family in the community.
He decides when the family is still divided after discussing something.
He does his wife's work around the house if his help is needed.

Table 3

MODAL RANKING OF THE WIFE'S ROLES AS ROLE PERFORMANCES BY THE SAMPLE OF BLUE-COLLAR WIVES

I care for the children's everyday needs.
I help the children grow by being their friend, teacher, and guide.
I am the homemaker.
I am a companion to my husband.
I manage the family income and finances.
I practice the family religion or philosophy.
I serve as the model of women for my children.
I am a sexual partner to my husband.
I decide when the family is still divided after discussing something.
I represent and advance my family socially and in the community.
I help earn the living when my husband needs my help or when the
    family needs more money.

Table 4

MODAL RANKING OF THE WIFE'S ROLES AS ROLE EXPECTATIONS BY THE SAMPLE OF BLUE-COLLAR HUSBANDS

She cares for the children's everyday needs.
She is the homemaker.
She is a companion to her husband.
She is a sexual partner to her husband.
She helps the children grow by being their friend, teacher, and guide.
She serves as the model of women for her children.
She practices the family religion or philosophy.
She manages the family income or finances.
She represents and advances her family socially and in the community.
She decides when the family is still divided after discussing something.
She helps earn the living when her husband needs her help or when the
    family needs more money.

The Problems
of Blue-Collar Consumers

DAVID CAPLOVITZ

THE consumption of goods takes on special significance for many working-class families, particularly the vast numbers of semiskilled and unskilled workers whose marginal existence more closely approximates the "old" rather than the affluent "new" working class. With little prospect of greatly improving their social status through occupational mobility, they often turn to consumption as the one sphere in which they can make some progress toward the American dream of success. In contrast to the conspicuous consumption of the upper strata observed by Veblen, the blue-collar classes today are apt to engage in *compensatory consumption.* Appliances, automobiles, and the dream of a home of their own can become compensations for blocked social mobility.[1]

The consumption opportunities of today's working class are greatly enlarged by that rapidly expanding American institution, the installment plan.[2] Through the mass media, Americans in all walks of life are bombarded with messages to buy durable goods while being reassured that the absence of cash is no obstacle to consumption. "Easy payments" and "no money down" are the advertising slogans that lure even the poorly paid lower reaches of the working class into the market place.

Although many observers have noted the growing affluence of the working class,[3] relatively little attention has been given to the ways in which its members meet their wants, particularly their use of installment credit and the social, psychological, and economic consequences of this method of buying.[4] Even less attention has been given to the consumption patterns of the

---

[1] The idea, if not the term, *compensatory consumption* has figured prominently in the writings of Robert S. Lynd. See *Middletown in Transition* (New York: Harcourt, Brace & World, Inc., 1937), pp. 26, 447-8; *Knowledge for What?* (Princeton, N. J.: Princeton University Press, 1939), pp. 91 and 198. Eli Chinoy also calls attention to the pattern of compensatory consumption in his study of automobile workers. See Eli Chinoy, "Aspirations of Automobile Workers," *American Journal of Sociology,* Vol. LVII, 1952, pp. 453-59.

[2] Outstanding installment debt increased from 14.7 billion dollars in 1950 to 52.7 billion dollars in 1963.

[3] See, for example, John K. Galbraith, *The Affluent Society* (Boston: Houghton Mifflin Company, 1958), Bennett Berger, *Working-Class Suburb* (Berkeley: University of California Press, 1960), and Ferdynand Zweig, *The Worker in an Affluent Society* (New York: The Free Press of Glencoe, Inc., 1961).

CAPLOVITZ

110

marginal members of the working class—those whose low wages place them in the "other America." The tacit assumption has been that these poorly paid workers, having little money, cannot possibly be consumers of costly durable goods.

A recent study of the consumption patterns of low-income families in New York City conducted by the Bureau of Applied Social Research of Columbia University shows that the facts of the matter are quite different.[5] Interviews were conducted with 464 families living in four low-income housing projects in Manhattan. Although the main emphasis of the research was on the consumers, the study did not ignore the merchants. Interviewers talked with some of the many furniture- and appliance-store merchants located in these neighborhoods in order to learn their views of the marketing situation.

The median income of the families interviewed was about $3,300 in 1960, the year of the study. Some 15 per cent were receiving welfare assistance. The families exhibited many of the characteristics associated with low income. Most of the family heads had unskilled or semiskilled jobs. The majority were members of racial or ethnic minorities (45 per cent were Puerto Rican, 30 per cent Negro, and 25 per cent white). Only 17 per cent were natives of the city; the rest were migrants, generally from the South or from Puerto Rico. The average family consisted of four persons, and more than 40 per cent had six or more members. Their educational level was quite low. Only 17 per cent of the family heads had completed high school, and about half did not continue their education beyond elementary school. Their place of origin, their ethnicity, and their low educational level all suggest that these consumers are products of traditionalistic cultures poorly trained in the ways of urban, bureaucratic society. As we shall see, this fact underlies many of their problems as consumers.

I shall first describe the main patterns of consumption that were found to exist among these families and then present a brief picture of the special system of marketing that has evolved in low-income sections of our cities in response to the distinctive needs of these consumers and the merchants who provide them with the goods they want. The final section of this paper considers the generality of the findings based on a New York City sample and points up some of the ramifications of credit buying for other areas of working-class life.

CONSUMER PRACTICES OF THE URBAN POOR

In spite of their poor economic position and shaky credit status, most of the families interviewed were consumers of major durable goods. For example:

[4] Some information on working-class patterns of consumption can be gleaned from the invaluable annual surveys of consumer finances conducted by the Survey Research Center of the University of Michigan under the direction of George Katona.

[5] This study was undertaken on behalf of three New York City settlement houses that had become quite alarmed by the installment debts besetting their neighbors. For a full account of this study, see David Caplovitz, *The Poor Pay More* (New York: The Free Press of Glencoe, Inc., 1963).

—Ninety-five per cent owned at least one television set (five per cent owned more than one).

—More than three in five owned a phonograph.

—More than two in five owned a sewing machine.

—More than two in five owned an automatic washing machine.

—More than a quarter owned a vacuum cleaner.

—One in seven owned an automobile.[6]

Most of the families had moved into public housing during the five-year period preceding the study, and most of them had bought a good deal of furniture in that period. The typical family bought sets of furniture for at least two rooms when they moved into the project and had spent approximately $500. Some 16 per cent had paid more than $1,000 for furniture bought at the time of the move. The overwhelming majority of these families purchased new rather than used durable goods. For example, 85 per cent bought only new furniture.

The prices they paid for appliances were quite high. Forty per cent, for example, paid more than $300 for their TV sets and 13 per cent paid more than $400. A number of families owned expensive combination television and phonograph sets, and one family reported paying $900 for such an appliance.

How are relatively large families with incomes averaging only $3,300 able to buy such expensive merchandise? The answer lies in the institution of credit and the special forms it takes in low-income areas. Approximately two-thirds of the appliances owned by these families were bought on credit, and 80 per cent of the families had used credit to buy at least some of their major durables.

This dependence on credit accounts in part for another fact about their consumer habits, their narrow scope of shopping. In their famous study of the unemployed of Marienthal, Jahoda, Lazarsfeld, and Zeisel discuss the "proletarian consumer."[7] They use the phrase "reduction in effective scope" to describe his shopping behavior. By this they mean that the blue-collar families limited their shopping to the immediate neighborhood; they were not particularly conscious of quality; they did not shop around before buying. These attributes characteristic of lower-class consumers in Marienthal in the early 1930's also apply to the low-income consumers in our study.

Hardly any of the families shopped for major durables in the downtown department stores and discount houses. They went instead to the local stores and to appliance chain stores that advertise "easy credit" plans.

Symbolic of their narrow shopping scope is a consumer practice that we found to be quite frequent in the sample, buying from door-to-door peddlers, the men with the traditional slogan of "a dollar down, a dollar a

---

[6] Although automobile ownership in this sample is far below the national average, it is probably not too different from the figures for Manhattan as a whole.

[7] Marie Jahoda, Paul F. Lazarsfeld, and Hans Zeisel, *Die Arbeitslosen von Marienthal* ("The Unemployed of Marienthal") (Allensback und Bonn, Germany: Verlag für Demoskopie, 1960).

week." These "customer peddlers," as they are called, were prevalent several generations ago when large numbers of European immigrants were arriving in this country, and they are still thriving today. In fact, the new housing projects may have stimulated their revival. Today's peddler need not climb the rickety stairs of dilapidated tenements; these projects, housing large numbers of potential customers, have elevators to carry him from floor to floor.

Fully half the families had made at least one credit purchase from these door-to-door salesmen, and more than a third had made repeated purchases. Most families regretted buying this way when they discovered that they were paying exorbitant prices for shoddy merchandise. But approximately 20 per cent have had continuing relationships with peddlers, regarding them almost as friends. The peddler serves as a purchasing agent for these families, getting them practically anything they need. Unlike most of the local merchants and the more bureaucratic stores that offer credit, most of the peddlers do not use installment contracts. The exceptions are outdoor salesmen for large firms that specialize in a particular commodity such as encyclopedias or pots and pans. These men are not interested in building up a clientele. Once the contract is signed, this kind of salesman gives the customer a coupon book with instructions for mailing monthly payments, and then he disappears. But the more usual peddler is the man in business for himself, hoping to establish permanent relationships with his customers. His credit is of a more traditional kind. When payments are late or are less than the specified amount, he does not add on service charges. This flexibility is appreciated by the customers and explains why some continue to buy from peddlers even though they know that they pay much more than they would at a store.

In view of the large amount of credit buying in this group, it comes as no surprise that the majority—more than 60 per cent—had outstanding consumer debts. Their precarious financial position is indicated by the fact that most had no savings at all to back up their debts. Only 27 per cent had at least $100 in savings.[8]

CONSUMER PROBLEMS

Their lack of shopping sophistication and their vulnerability to "easy credit" would suggest that many blue-collar families encounter serious difficulties as consumers. The study found this to be true. One in every five had experienced legal pressures because of missed payments. Their goods were repossessed, their salaries were garnisheed, or they were threatened with garnishments.[9] Many of the families in this position had heavy credit

---

[8] The proportion of families with installment debt in this sample was close to the national figures for spending units with comparable income. But these public-housing families in New York City were much less likely than comparable income groups in the nation to have liquid assets. See *1960 Survey of Consumer Finances* (Ann Arbor: Survey Research Center, University of Michigan, 1961).

[9] It is of some interest that none of the respondents had any difficulty understanding the word *garnishee*. This may well be one word that is better known by the poorly educated than by the better educated.

obligations that reached crisis proportions when their income was suddenly reduced through illness or unemployment. This account of a typical situation is given by a 27-year-old Negro husband:

> I first bought a bedroom set. I still owed money on it when I wanted a living room set. I went back to the store and bought the living room set on credit. *At that time I was working and making good money. That was two years ago. Six months ago I got sick and stopped working. And so I couldn't pay any more. . . .* When I got sick, I still owed $288. Last week they sent a summons saying I have to pay $440 not $288. We have to pay, but what I'm going to do is pay the $288, not the $440.

Like many of these consumers, this young man did not understand that he is liable for the interest on his debt as well as court costs and legal fees.

Inability to maintain payments was not the only problem these consumers encountered. The merchant's failure to live up to his obligations had created difficulties for a much larger proportion, some 40 per cent. This group includes families who were seduced by "bait advertising" and high-pressure salesmen into buying much more expensive merchandise than they had intended, families who were given erroneous information about the costs of their purchases, and families who were sold, as new merchandise, merchandise that had actually been reconditioned. The many incidents of "bait advertising" uncovered in the study can be illustrated with this typical experience of a 26-year-old Negro housewife:

> I saw a TV ad for a $29 sewing machine, so I wrote to the company and they sent down a salesman who demonstrated it for me. It shook the whole house, but I wanted to buy it anyway. But he kept saying it would disturb the neighbors by being so noisy and he went out into the hall and brought in another model costing $185. . . . I actually had to pay $220. He promised if I paid within a certain amount of time I would get $35 back. But since my husband was out of work, we couldn't pay within the time period, so I didn't get the refund. . . . I was taken in by the high-pressure sales talk.

Some unscrupulous salesmen disguise themselves as representatives of the housing authority and trick families into making purchases. Thus a number of families found themselves buying sink cabinets that they thought were being installed free of charge by the project's maintenance men. An extreme incident of this kind involved the sale of encyclopedias. A 37-year-old Puerto Rican woman told an interviewer:

> When I first moved in, a man who said he was the manager asked me to sign some papers. It turned out I signed for encyclopedias thinking I was signing some housing authority forms as a new tenant. I went to the Legal Aid Society to complain. The case is still in court. My husband was threatened with a garnishee by the encyclopedia company.

These two kinds of problems—legal difficulties resulting from missed payments and exploitation by merchants—are not necessarily independent of each other. Some families capable of maintaining payments stopped paying when they discovered that they had been cheated. But instead of gaining retribution, they were more often than not subjected to legal sanctions brought upon them by the merchant. This process can be seen in the experience of a 28-year-old Puerto Rican man:

> I bought a set of pots and pans from a door-to-door salesman. They were of very poor quality and I wanted to give them back but they wouldn't take them. *I stopped paying and told them to change them or take them back.* I refused to pay. . . . *They started bothering me at every job I had.* Then they wrote to my current job and my boss is taking $6 weekly from my pay and sending it to pay this.

It is not clear from his account whether he had lost some of his previous jobs because of the efforts to garnishee his salary; this does happen with some frequency. Many employers simply will not be bothered with garnishments and do not hesitate to fire workers whose salaries are attached.

As the previous incident suggests, the laws regulating installment sales unwittingly act in favor of such merchants, simply because these traditionalistic consumers have little understanding of their legal rights and how to exercise them. By taking matters into their own hands and stopping payments on faulty merchandise, they only bring additional troubles upon themselves.

There is another aspect to this unwitting result of the legal structure. The merchants who offer "easy credit" frequently sell their contracts at a discount to a finance company. Many low-income consumers do not understand this procedure. They mistakenly believe that the merchant has gone out of business and assume that nothing can be done about their problem. The practice of selling contracts to credit agencies thus often has the consequence of absolving the merchant of his responsibilities to the consumer, not because the law gives him this right, but because the consumer does not understand what has happened.

In keeping with their inadequacies as consumers in a bureaucratic society, most of these families had no idea what they could do about their financial problems. When asked directly where they would go for help if they found themselves being cheated by a merchant, some 64 per cent said they did not know. They could not name any of the community agencies equipped to deal with these problems, such as the Legal Aid Society, the State Banking and Finance Department, the Small Claims Court, and the Better Business Bureau. The Better Business Bureau was the agency most often cited by the minority who had some idea where they could go for professional help.

In presenting this picture of buying patterns among low-income families, I have said nothing about variations *within* this group. These consumers are by no means of a piece. Their shopping practices are affected by various social characteristics apart from income. For example, the most active consumers, those who rely most on credit, and those who experience the most consumer problems tend to be the Puerto Ricans and Negroes rather than the whites, the relatively large families, and the young families. The education of the household head is closely associated with scope of shopping and knowledge of community agencies. In contrast to the majority who did not finish high school, the minority who did complete high school were much more likely to shop in the large downtown stores and were much more aware of sources of professional help for consumer problems.

THE LOW-INCOME MARKETING SYSTEM

Looking at the marketing relationship from the side of the merchant, we can ask: how is it possible for the many furniture and appliance stores located in lower-class neighborhoods to extend credit to these relatively poor risks?

One way in which the merchants protect themselves is to have unusually high markups on their merchandise. In this special system of sales-and-credit, cheap goods are sold at prices that in the larger market place are commanded by high-quality merchandise. In East Harlem, one of the areas studied, the merchants use a number system to price their goods, referring to "one-number," "two-number," and "three-number" items. Each number stands for a 100 per cent markup over the wholesale price. For example, a TV set that costs the merchant $100 and is sold for $300 is a "two-number" item. According to a former bookkeeper in such a store, the merchandise in East Harlem is never sold for less than one number and is often sold for more. Another sign of an unusual pricing system in these stores is the absence of price tags, signifying that prices are not standardized; there are hardly any "one price" stores in low-income neighborhoods.

But the high markup does not in itself insure that the business will be profitable. No matter what he charges, the merchant can stay in business only if he receives payments from his customers. The assumptions of any credit system—the customer's intention and ability to pay—cannot be taken for granted in this market.

To some extent the merchant can count on legal controls over his customers. But these often prove inadequate, because many of the customers are employed only irregularly and others depend on welfare. Furthermore, the merchant who frequently resorts to legal controls is likely to lose good will in the neighborhood. For this reason, the merchants interviewed were reluctant to make extensive use of their right to sue defaulting customers.

Thus, in addition to formal controls, the merchants depend heavily on informal, personal controls over their customers. The merchants reported that they operate their credit business on a "fifteen-month year," anticipating that their customers will miss about one in every four payments. This is considered a normal part of the business, and the merchants take it into account when they compute the markup.

Many merchants adopt the methods of the customer peddlers, employing their own canvassers who visit the families in their homes, both to collect payments and to sell additional merchandise. As part of the informal system of control, the merchants encourage weekly payment plans with the customer bringing the payment to the store. This continuous contact enables the merchant to get to know his customer. He learns when the customer receives his pay check; when his rent is due; when job layoffs, illnesses, and other emergencies occur; in short, he gathers all kinds of information that allows him to interpret the reasons for a missed payment. Because the customer

CAPLOVITZ

116

comes to the store with his payments, the merchant is ready to make another sale when the first is almost paid for. As a result, many customers are continuously in debt to the merchant in a pattern reminiscent of the relationship between the sharecropper and the company store. We might almost call these traditionalistic consumers in our cities "urban sharecroppers."

Various informal devices are employed in this marketing system for sifting and sorting the consumers according to their risk and matching them with merchants willing to extend them credit. For example, when a merchant finds himself with a customer whom he considers to be too great a risk for him, he does not discourage the customer. Instead he directs him to a merchant with a less conservative credit policy. The peddlers also steer their customers to local merchants. When their customers request major appliances that they do not handle themselves, the peddlers will refer them to an appropriate merchant who is ready to extend them credit. The referring merchants and peddlers receive a commission for their service—another factor affecting the final sales price.

This marketing system is not only different from the more formal, bureaucratic market; it is in many respects a *deviant* system in which unethical (for example, bait advertising) and illegal practices (for example, the sale of used merchandise as new) are commonplace. And yet this system, with its obvious exploitative practices, is able to persist because it performs important social functions. In a society in which consumption is not only a matter of obtaining material conveniences, but also a means of gaining self-respect and winning the respect of others, this marketing system makes consumers of people who fail to meet the requirements of the more legitimate economy. Even the welfare family is able to consume in much the same manner as its social peers who happen not to be on welfare.

In addition to satisfying the wants of poor risks, the system makes the traditionalistic consumer, who is apt to be intimidated by the impersonality that pervades the large downtown stores, feel more at home. The local merchants are expert at personalizing their services. Many quickly establish a first-name relationship with their customers. In keeping with these practices, the local merchants now employ Puerto Rican salesmen in order better to serve the many Spanish-speaking migrants in these areas.

AREAS FOR FURTHER RESEARCH

Without systematic data on national samples of working-class families, we cannot know how accurately this portrait of low-income consumers in New York City describes the working class in general, particularly its more affluent members. What data exist from other studies, however, suggest that a number of these patterns are general throughout the working class. Thus, Rainwater and his colleagues found that working-class wives, in contrast to middle-class women, have "extremely narrow horizons in their choices of shopping places," preferring neighborhood stores to the downtown and suburban shopping centers.[10] This preference, they point out, stems from

---

[10] Lee Rainwater, Richard P. Coleman, and Gerald Handel, *Workingman's Wife* (New York: Oceana Publications, Inc., 1959), p. 163.

The Problems
of Blue-Collar
Consumers

the desire for more personalized relationships with merchants than those to be found in the bureaucratic market place. Apparently, then, traditionalistic behavior is rather pervasive among working-class consumers, presumably even among those who are not migrants from rural areas.

The Rainwater study also notes the widespread use of installment credit by working-class families. Two-thirds of their respondents had outstanding installment debts other than mortgages.[11] The *1962 Survey of Consumer Finances* showed that 46 per cent of the nation's households had installment debts early in 1962. Among spending units headed by blue-collar workers, the figures range from 56 to 58 per cent.[12] An important question for further research is the extent of excessive debt burdens among working-class families. Being overburdened with debt is by no means the exclusive province of the marginally employed, low-income families, such as those we interviewed. Vast numbers of the working class today (and, judging by the accounts of Suburbia, of the middle class as well) find themselves in this predicament. Some indication of their numbers is provided by the Survey Research Center's studies. In early 1962, 29 per cent of the nation's spending units were making annual debt payments amounting to 10 per cent or more of their income. This figure was lowest among those with very low income (below $2,000) and very high income (above $10,000), and highest among the income groups comprising most working-class families. About a third of the households in these groups were making installment payments amounting to 10 per cent or more of their income.[13] The increasing numbers of personal, as distinct from business, bankruptcies is even more telling evidence of debt problems. Personal bankruptcies have increased at a rapid rate over the past decade, from about 25,000 in 1950 to 132,000 in 1962.[14] National figures on garnishments and wage assignments are not available, but in the City of Chicago alone there were 59,000 garnishments entered in the Municipal Court in 1962, an increase of 20 per cent over the 1961 figure.[15] The number of workers in Chicago who had deductions made from their 1962 salaries to pay installment debts is still larger than this figure, because wage assignments, not processed in court, must also be counted.[16]

In view of these increasing signs of debt entanglement, the processes through which families become overextended in debt deserve to be explored.

---

[11] *Ibid.*, p. 156.

[12] George Katona, Charles A. Lininger, and Richard F. Kosobud, *1962 Survey of Consumer Finances* (Ann Arbor: University of Michigan Survey Research Center, 1963), p. 66.

[13] *Ibid.*, p. 71.

[14] *Annual Report of the Director of the Administrative Office of the United States Courts*, 1962, p. 171.

[15] A new Illinois law, which went into effect in 1961, extended the period of a single garnishment from one week to four weeks, thus reducing greatly the number of different garnishments involving the same debtor. As a consequence, most of the garnishments in 1961 and 1962 represent judgments against different consumers.

[16] Some idea of the frequency of wage deductions to pay installment debts is provided by figures assembled by Inland Steel's garnishment administrator, Mrs. Dorothy Lascoe. According to Mrs. Lascoe, in each bi-weekly pay period, such deductions are made from the wages of close to 1,000 of the 18,000 employees in Inland's plant in East Chicago, Indiana.

To what extent is the indebtedness a result of the consumer's poor management and irresponsibility, or of his eagerness to acquire worldly possessions in the pattern we have identified as "compensatory consumption"? And to what extent are debt burdens the outcome of the working-class consumer's vulnerability to shady sales practices and high-pressure salesmen? Our study uncovered a number of families who were heavily in debt, not because they were eager to buy, but because they were pressured into making purchases that they had had no intention of making. Ignorance, gullibility, and naïveté, rather than irresponsibility and eagerness to buy, lie behind their credit problems.

Apart from the reasons for excessive debt, we need to know much more about its consequences for working-class life. It is clear that consumer indebtedness can involve the job situation. Because many employers fire people who are garnisheed rather than submit to the nuisance of the necessary paper work, installment buying is a factor in job insecurity and turnover. Where the jobs of workers are protected by strong unions, as in the automobile and steel industries, management frequently finds it necessary to institute entire bookkeeping departments that do nothing more than handle the garnishments of employees.[17] The implications of this facet of the employer-employee relationship could be fruitfully studied. To what extent does the garnishment induce attitudes of dependency in the workers vis-à-vis management? Does the garnishment limit the worker's mobility in the job market? To what extent does management take on responsibilities for educating their employees as consumers and for protecting their legal rights?

Another sphere in which the ramifications of installment debt deserve study is the family life of blue-collar workers. It is not hard to imagine how the pressures of debt might contribute to marital tensions, but, guess-work aside, the extent to which consumer troubles lie behind the nation's divorce and separation rates should be studied in a systematic way. Finally, the psychological impact of indebtedness needs to be studied. That worry over debts may be an important factor in the mental health of blue-collar workers is suggested by the results of a study in progress at the National Opinion Research Center.[18] In two samples of white working-class urban dwellers, interviewed in 1963, the proportion who were worried about financial debts was 32 per cent in the first group and 39 per cent in the second. Some 55 per cent of a third sample—a group of working-class Negroes in one of these cities— were worried about their debts.

In the current national climate of buying now and paying later, excessive

---

[17] Even in these industries, many companies will fire employees with multiple garnishments. Instances of multiple garnishments are quite common. Mrs. Lascoe studied the records of Inland Steel's East Chicago plant for September, 1956 to September, 1957 and found that in that year 2500 employees were garnisheed at least once; more than 1,000 of these were subjected to three or more garnishments. Inland is more progressive than many companies in that it does not fire its workers for being garnisheed.

[18] This is a study of mental health-related behavior supported by a Grant from the National Institute of Mental Health.

indebtedness is fast becoming a recognized social problem.[19] Several popular books have recently appeared on the excesses of the credit boom in America.[20] There has been a rash of newspaper exposés of credit rackets, and considerable publicity has been given to the as-yet-unsuccessful efforts of Senator Paul Douglas to pass a "truth-in-interest" bill in Congress.[21] Educational programs for consumers are being instituted by welfare agencies, and pressure is mounting in various states to revise antiquated statutes governing consumer credit.

Undoubtedly, much can be done through legislation to reduce the abuses that now occur in the credit field. But efforts to change the quasi-traditional, "deviant" marketing system now catering to the wants of working- and lower-class families must take into account the aforementioned functions of that system. Society in effect now presents the poor credit risks with the unpalatable choice of not possessing major durables, thereby forfeiting whatever self-respect and comfort is to be derived from consumption, or being exploited in this marketing system. Until alternative institutions can be devised for providing poor risks with merchandise, it is doubtful that the system can be drastically altered. And until more legitimate merchants learn how to deal effectively with traditionalistic consumers, the system will also gain support from the many who *are* eligible for credit in the more reputable stores.

---

[19] For a discussion of what constitutes a social problem, see Robert K. Merton, "Social Problems and Sociological Theory," in Robert K. Merton and Robert A. Nisbet, eds., *Contemporary Social Problems* (New York: Harcourt, Brace & World, Inc., 1961), pp. 701ff.

[20] Hillel Black, *Buy Now and Pay Later* (New York: William Morrow & Co., Inc., 1961); Clyde Farnsworthy, *No Money Down* (New York: Macfadden Books, paperback, 1963).

[21] Aligned against the Douglas bill are the powerful lobbies of the financial industry, who argue that informing the consumer of the true annual interest he pays for credit would be harmful to the economy. This is a rather classic example of the resistance to making latent functions manifest. The world of consumer credit provides further examples of sociological oddities. The credit merchants are beginning to express alarm about the rising bankruptcy rate, publicly declaiming the decline in American morals that permits people to declare themselves bankrupt. This may lead merchants to exercise more caution in urging debt burdens upon their customers. But some of the more daring merchants are beginning to capitalize even on the bankrupts. Knowing that the law does not permit a person to declare bankruptcy more than once in seven years, they advertise their willingness to extend credit to bankrupts. In this fashion, the poor risk is converted into a good risk, a status-transition in no way contingent upon the consumer's earning power.

CAPLOVITZ

120

Part III

WORKING-CLASS ADOLESCENT

HANDICAPPED early in life, working-class boys and girls limit their aspirations and barely secure even their minimal goals. Miller examines the outlook of adolescents from both the "new" and the "old" working class in an attempt to explain this record. Among other things, he comments on the vocational plans of potential dropouts and the failure of schools to adequately advise these youngsters of their own aptitudes: "Society needs better mirrors and developers than we have now—and the largest reservoir of undeveloped talent is in the working classes." Morland documents failure with his report on the underdevelopment and underutilization of abilities in a mill-village area. Purcell looks at the displaced aspirations of Negro packinghouse workers who want prestige and power for their children, and finds in this a false idealization of the white-collar job and a false devaluation of the blue-collar job: "The thinking of these people lays bare the relative meaningless and apparent irrelevancy of much factory work to life in the American society." Davis considers the career plans of adolescent daughters of blue-collarites and finds, for example, that three-fourths of the 925 girls in her sample do not really expect to obtain the job they would most like to have. Karacki and Toby focus on the juvenile delinquent from the "old" or stable working class. The boys do not appear to be especially deprived, by either objective or subjective criteria, but they do suffer from a failure to develop commitments to adult roles and values. Friedenberg suggests that such failure may have its roots in working-class rejection of middle-class culture. Frankly pessimistic about our ability to reform our clumsy efforts to help alienated dropouts, he asks: "Can we—do we even really wish to—help them deal with their situation on their terms with our resources, while leaving our way of life aside till somebody asks for it?" Dansereau, in the concluding essay, ponders the likelihood that children of blue-collarites will have ample work opportunities in the near future, or that they will be equal to these opportunities. He counsels a new approach to vocational education, and warns that "dollars not invested in training most assuredly will join others in welfare programs of catastrophic size."

The Outlook of
Working-Class Youth*

S. M. MILLER

THE debate on whether or not a youth culture exists in the United States suggests a continuity, as well as a discontinuity, between the youth and adult worlds. Youth is a preparation for adult life, but it is not only that—it has a dynamic of its own, which may be little related to the adult world. Nevertheless, some see youth as little men. For example, Walter Miller, in an important series of articles, seems to picture juvenile delinquency as a normal manifestation of aggressive activity which he believes to be ubiquitous in lower-class structure. Consequently, he does not search for special factors which affect those lower-class youth who become delinquents.[1] On the other hand, although the child may be the father of the man, the resemblance may be minimal. I have been impressed, to cite a fairly common observation, with the difference between rough and tough working-class boys of 14 and their milder brothers of six. Realistic (or perhaps pessimistic) probation officers have told me that their success with many boys with whom they work is not due to professional expertise but results from the aging of boys into men— they marry, they find a job, and they give up criminal activities. Many delinquents develop fresh anchorages in the world which route them into a new life pattern quite different from that of their youth.

Obviously, the job is one of the chief anchorages of life; for many who have been in the prolonged interregnum of graduate studenthood, the feeling of being grown up occurs only when the first full-time job is achieved. For boys of working-class homes, a job may be equally important—but in quite a different context.

---

* This paper was originally presented at the Annual Meetings of the American Sociological Association, Washington, August 1962. I am indebted to the following for comments: Louis Kriesberg, Martin Rein, Seymour S. Bellin, Frank Riessman, Patricia Sexton, and Alice Chapin. The revision of this paper was partially supported by a grant from the Social Security Administration, United States Department of Health, Education, and Welfare.

[1] Walter B. Miller, "Lower Class Culture as a Generating Milieu of Gang Delinquency," *Journal of Social Issues,* Vol. XIV, No. 3 (1958), p. 6, footnote 3. In his penetrating analysis, Miller notes the existence of "subtypes of lower class culture" but does not pursue this point. Although his emphasis is on cultural characteristics, such as "female-based" household and "serial monogamy" mating patterns, he elsewhere employs educational, occupational, and income variables to define the lower class. See his "Implications of Urban Lower-Class Culture for Social Work," *Social Service Review,* Vol. XXXIII (September, 1959), pp. 229 ff. His major stress is on cultural or status characteristics as defining the lower-class culture.

Because my reference to delinquents may be misleading, and since "working class" has many varied meanings, let me immediately point out my loose usage of the term. I am taking as my bailiwick a large group: I am including all nonwhite-collar and nonfarm populations, so that urban low-income families without a wage earner are involved as well as manual families of varying skills and diverse income levels. In short, the analysis purports to apply to urban people who are not in the upper and middle classes (these two classes being defined by occupational categories). The main concern is with males who do not go on to college, whether high school graduates or dropouts.

We lack adequate information on the educational experience of working-class youth in the United States. The best estimate we have is that at present one-third of the youths of all social classes will never finish high school. Conflicting national data would place the percentage of dropouts in the working class as between 35 per cent and 55 per cent. If we take 40 per cent as a low working-class dropout rate, then of the 60 per cent who do graduate from high school, no more than 30 per cent go on to college. (About half of all high school graduates begin college.) The working-class college-going rate is lower than 50 per cent, so that 30 per cent is a high estimate. Thus, of all working-class youth, perhaps one-fifth (the range of estimates would be between three-tenths and one-sixth) will have some college. The class differences in percentage who graduate from college is undoubtedly greater, because working-class youth are more likely than middle-class youth to leave college without the diploma. The 20 per cent figure is a third of the over-all middle-class rate of college attendance.[2] I hasten to add that these estimates may have very large errors in them, and that I believe the percentages of working-class college-goers to be too high.

James Davis, on the basis of his analysis of census data, argues that the percentage of high school graduates who go on to college has varied relatively little in this century. It has stood in the range of 45 per cent to 50 per cent. The higher percentage of our population going to college today results from a higher percentage of high school graduates rather than from an increase in predispositions among high school graduates. One implication of these data is that, to increase the percentage of college students, the emphasis should be placed on getting more students to finish high school.[3]

---

[2] Charles B. Nam and James D. Cowhig, "Factors Related to College Attendance of Farm and Non-Farm High School Graduates: 1960," Series Census—ERS (p. 27), No. 32 (Washington, D.C.: United States Bureau of the Census, June 15, 1962), p. 14.

[3] James A. Davis, "The Role of Higher Education in Career Allocation," a paper presented at the annual meetings of the American Sociological Association, Washington, September, 1962. My analysis of United States Office of Education data generally supports Davis' contention. (S. M. Miller, "High-School Dropouts and Graduates: Some Long-Term Data," Syracuse University Youth Development Center, 1963.) The percentage of high school graduates entering college has been stable at 51 per cent to 53 per cent between 1954 and 1962.

It could be argued, in contradiction to the point that college attendance will be increased by expanding the number of high school graduates, that a greater number of high school graduates means lower-quality graduates who are not "college material." I do not agree. Every generation has its own definition and imagery of "the bottom of the barrel." It is a social, not a technical, definition. Many high school dropouts, I suspect, could do better if they skipped high school and were directly admitted to college!

The importance of education in affecting job possibilities is trumpeted currently by those seeking to discourage youth from dropping out of school. Clearly, the schools have become the occupational gatekeepers: the level of education affects the kind and level of job that can be attained. Those who have trouble with school—as do many working-class youth—are permanently disfavored.

The emphasis on education as the union card for jobs is unfortunate, I believe. We are increasingly living in a "credential society," where we evaluate people, not on the basis of performance ("He does a good job"), but on the basis of credentials ("He's a Harvard man"). Many of our presumably universalistic criteria for occupational advance are more guild-restrictive than achievement-based. People who have unusual ability—as Admiral Rickover pointed out in relation to teaching credentials—but who have not had certain courses or formal licensure-type qualifications cannot attain jobs (usually, higher-level jobs). Could a Richard Titmuss, Britain's premier social welfare expert, a holder of a chair at the London School of Economics, but a man without a bachelor's degree, have been able to secure a similar post in the United States if he were an American? Those from low-income backgrounds with limited educational advantages are particularly badly hit by credentialism. Consequently, the largest reservoir of undeveloped talent is in the working classes.

Schools are imperfect sifters, sorters, and *developers* of individuals, especially of working-class youth. Particularly shocking is the difficulty in gaining an accurate view of oneself, of one's talents and interests, through school. *For many, school does not operate as an effective mirror reflecting the self.* Particularly disturbing are the number of people who take, or want to take, aptitude tests and the frequency with which test results surprise the subject. Implicitly, many people are saying, "I don't know what I am good at; I'm not even sure what I am interested in." *Society needs better mirrors and developers than we have now.* Schools are increasingly relied on to provide these mirrors. Their failure is especially disabling for working-class youth, who have few other avenues through which they can learn of themselves and the larger world.

The ineffectiveness of schools with many working-class youth, especially those that are poorest, has grave consequences. Alternative routes to occupational advance are closing off, and the educational system provides the central avenue. Leaving school before graduation is looked upon as failure, and it compresses occupational possibilities for a lifetime.

INCOME DIFFERENTIALS BY EDUCATION

The general rise in the level of education has not reduced the importance of education; it has shifted upward the breaking point where education leads to high or low income. It is certainly better to be a high school graduate than a dropout, but it is much better to be a college graduate. As Vance Packard

Table 1

EDUCATION AND ANNUAL INCOME (OR EARNINGS)—MALES, 25 YEARS OF AGE
AND OVER

Years of School Completed	1939	1946	1949	1956	1958
Elementary:					
Total	$1,036	$2,041	$2,394	$3,107	$3,096
Less than 8 years	Not	1,738	2,062	2,613	2,551
8 years .... Available		2,327	2,829	3,732	3,769
High School:					
1 to 3 years	1,378	2,449	3,226	4,480	4,618
4 years	1,661	2,939	3,784	5,439	5,567
College:					
1 to 3 years	1,931	3,654	4,423	6,363	6,966
4 years or more	2,607	4,527	6,179	8,490	9,206

Source: Herman P. Miller, "Money Value of an Education," Occupational Outlook Quarterly, Vol. 5 (September, 1961), p. 4.

has pointed out, the "diploma elite" is clearly advantaged. The differences in annual income between the high school graduate and the high school dropout are less than those between the high school graduate and the college graduate. The gap between those with a high school diploma and those with a college diploma is increasing.

These results are indicative of what I believe to be a general tendency toward income and wealth inequality in the United States since the immediate post-World War II years. Increasingly we shall be concerned not only with poverty (living below a minimum standard of living) but also with inequality: the widening spread between the poor and new working classes on one hand, and the upper-middle and upper income classes and wealth recipients and holders on the other.

Both poverty, demarcated by an income level at which a person is unable to purchase a specified amount of goods and services, and inequality, the comparison of the varying incomes and wealth of different groups, have to be considered in viewing the prospects of dropouts and high school graduates.

THE DROPOUT

What will happen to the dropout? The first and perhaps most important thing to realize about dropouts (as perhaps of all groups) is how varied are the individuals who are funneled into this category. At the Syracuse University Youth Development Center, we have been surprised to learn that between 10 per cent ond 25 per cent of those who drop out of school go on to further education and training.[4] A sizable additional percentage probably get additional schooling in the form of on-the-job training. Perhaps as many as one-quarter move into higher-level skilled manual and lower-level white-collar jobs. Negroes have a more difficult time than whites do.

Not only do dropouts show considerable variations in their experience, but they come from different backgrounds—what has surprised us in studying

---

[4] Betty L. Saleem and S. M. Miller, "The Neglected Dropout: The Returnee," Syracuse University Youth Development Center, 1963.

The Outlook
of
Working-Class
Youth

Syracuse is that perhaps 25 per cent of all dropouts come from what might be called "nice neighborhoods." [5] What may be working here is a recessive mobility pattern. The boy whose father and grandfather were white-collar workers is less likely to drop out than a boy whose father is white-collar and whose grandfather was blue-collar. It may be that the downwardly mobile families differ in the level of their white-collar jobs or the security of these jobs, or they may have little expertise in helping their sons to finish school or be less interested or less able to motivate their children toward educational goals. Incidentally, the mobile boy of a manual family is probably more likely to have a white-collar grandparent than is a nonmobile manual son. Assuming that I am correct in stressing the three-generational connection, the social psychology of it would be worth examining. If we are interested in promoting upward occupational mobility for more individuals, perhaps we can find functional equivalents of a middle-class grandparent.

Clearly, then, dropouts are not a homogeneous grouping, and high school graduates, as we shall see, are even less homogeneous. But a sizable percentage (probably 40 per cent) of male and female dropouts (or the mates of the latter) will be confined to unskilled, low-level, irregular jobs or will be out of the labor force for lengthy periods. These occupational categories are not growing in the United States. The unskilled and semiskilled and service categories are not likely to absorb large numbers of people.[6] The outcome, unless we have some big economic changes, will be that a large number of people will be unable to obtain employment which is regular or will not be rewarded enough to support a family at a minimum decency level. (Fifty per cent of the poor families in the United States have heads who are employed.)

As many have begun to see, we are developing an urban poor that is likely to be considered "colored" (Negro, Puerto Rican, Spanish-speaking). A higher percentage of these disadvantaged people will be dropouts and a sizable percentage of dropouts will be doubly disadvantaged—by virtue of both educational and ethnic-group status. For many of the poor, almost every strand of their poverty has a multiplier effect, inducing greater poverty or restricting them to poverty.

One consequence is that social-assistance payments will have to be high to maintain families headed by marginal workers and by individuals who are not in the labor force. The Newburgh fight over welfare is the Shays' Rebellion of a declining economic community, and I would expect more conflict. The price of slow economic growth is the transfer of income (through taxation) to the poor, rather than the shifting of the poor into remunerative employment and higher income through economic expansion.

I would guess that, without significant economic changes, 20 per cent of

---

[5] S. M. Miller, Carolyn Comings, and Betty L. Saleem, *The School Dropout Problem—Syracuse* (Albany: New York State Division for Youth and the Syracuse University Youth Development Center, 1963).

[6] The "service" occupational category, popular opinion to the contrary, is not rapidly growing. What is growing is a more broadly defined set of activities which are called "service" industries, for example, banking, health, and professional services.

our population will continue to live in considerable poverty. At present, one out of 25 persons in this country obtains some kind of social-assistance help (not including Social Security benefits). This figure is likely to grow with increasing urbanization in the setting of economic sputtering.

Many, if not most, dropouts are not only likely to be living below the poverty line but also will be suffering from increasing inequality as the rest of society moves ahead more rapidly.

THE HIGH SCHOOL GRADUATE

The high school graduate picture is at least equally complex, with some attending college, others moving into relatively adequate jobs, and a number doing poorly.

It has been frequently pointed out that half of the gifted high school graduates do not go on to college at all. Many in this high-I.Q., noncollege-going group come from manual, low-income families. Insufficient attention is devoted to encouraging and facilitating the entry of low-income youth to college. The rate of college-going goes up where a college is near, so that community colleges can play an important part. Linking the last high school years to the community college might be important. Student subsidies and flexible arrangements are also necessary.

What happens to the noncollege-going high school graduate of the manual classes? Here we have to separate males and females, and I have restricted the discussion to males. My conclusion from a variety of studies is that it pays a working-class boy to finish high school, but not by an overwhelming amount. The best estimate that I can make from available census data is that 20 per cent more of white working-class sons who graduate from high school end up in white-collar jobs than do white nongraduating sons. For Negro males, it is a slightly smaller percentage. (For girls, contrariwise, high school graduation makes a big difference, since the diploma opens many clerical jobs.) Not all of these white-collar jobs offer higher pay, so that the occupational income advantage may be overstated here. It may be that the high school graduate advances more rapidly than do dropouts, but my inference from some limited data is that the differences do not increase over time.

The occupational differences between dropouts and graduates may be due less to their level of education than to their social-class background. As far as I know, there are no national published data which report occupational level by both level of education and occupation of parent. What I have done is to make the very arbitrary assumption that an approximation can be obtained by simply averaging the occupational levels of (1) all high school graduates who did not attend college (thus including some middle-class sons) and (2) nonwhite high school graduates (including a few who went to college). The rationale for this procedure is that working-class sons who graduated from high school did not fare as poorly as nonwhite high school graduates, nor as well as did all high school graduates, because many of the latter are middle-class sons. The average provides a crude idea of the level of occupa-

Table 2

OCCUPATIONAL DISTRIBUTION OF EMPLOYED MALE HIGH SCHOOL
GRADUATES 16 TO 24, NOT ENROLLED IN COLLEGE, GRADUATED
PRIOR TO 1958, IN OCTOBER, 1959

Major Occupational Group	(1) All Noncollege Attendees	(2) Nonwhite*	Estimate of Working-class Sons [Average of (1) and (2)]
Professional, technical	6.4%	3.4%	4.9%
Managerial	5.0	-	2.5
Clerical, etc.	12.7	15.5	14.1
Sales worker	5.7	1.7	3.7
Craftsmen, etc.	20.2	11.2	15.7
Operators, etc.	27.8	19.0	23.4
Service Workers, etc.	5.5	17.2	11.3
Farmers, etc.	6.1	3.4	4.8
Laborers, etc.	10.5	28.5	18.5

*Includes college graduates.

Source: Sophia Cooper, "Employment of June 1959 High School Graduates, October, 1959,"
U.S. Bureau of Labor Statistics, Special Labor Force Reports No. 5, May, 1960 (also in
Monthly Labor Review, May, 1960). Adapted from Table C.

tional achievement among working-class, noncollege-going high school graduates. In the absence of firm data, one has to make heroic assumptions if even
the crude magnitude of a problem is to be estimated.

Because working-class sons are likely to get poorer jobs than will middle-
class offspring, even in the same occupational category, I would guess that
at least one-quarter of high school graduating, working-class sons end up
in low-level, low-income jobs. This is the picture soon after graduation; it
undoubtedly improves in later years. Less than 10 per cent end up in fairly
high-level jobs soon after graduation. High school graduation helps the working-class boy, but the help may not be great or immediately apparent.

These results are in some conflict with the contention that it is much better
to be a high school graduate than a dropout. An extensive campaign is going
on to get youths to stay in school. It will have limited success, because, if we
could partial out family status in viewing the relation of graduating to occupation, I believe that we would find that graduation does not make a great
difference for the working-class boy. It is the linkage of graduation with prior
middle-class status that makes the major difference in the over-all results of the
relation of high school diplomas to occupations.[7] And I suspect that many
working-class boys have some awareness of these facts.

[7] In these dropout investigations at the Syracuse University Youth Development Center,
we have made one attempt to study this possibility, utilizing the Quincy, Illinois, data made
available by Bowman and Matthews from their study [Paul H. Bowman and Charles V.
Matthews, Motivations of Youth for Leaving School (Quincy, Illinois: Quincy Youth Development Project, University of Chicago, 1960)]. The reanalysis of their data does not support the
contention of the text. The difficulties of identifying parental and youths' occupations and
the smallness of the community may have been instrumental in producing these results. I
believe that studies of larger cities with more detailed occupational designations would
support my contention. The reanalysis is reported in George Freskos, "The Occupations of
Youth: The Impact of Education and Father's Occupation," Syracuse University Youth
Development Center, 1964.

Why do individuals end up in various occupational niches? Here, it is important to dispel what Martin Hamburger has termed "the myth of occupational choice," with its implication of conscious decision making. The complex process of desires, possibilities, and pressures that affects the kind of jobs which an individual has over his lifetime does not imply a simple choice event. What occurs is a recurring and frequently unpredictable series of events in which "choice" is frequently the obverse of necessity.

In the euphemisms of labor-market jargon, working-class youth's first full-time job is termed an "entry" job. This implies movement into a clear structure with demarcated lines of movement. As Harold Wilensky has pointed out, this is clearly not true in the case of many blue-collar jobs.[8] To talk about a "career" is misleading, he notes, because the orderly step-by-step upward movement implied in the concept of "career" frequently does not take place among blue-collar workers.[9]

The turning points and changes from job to job are usually outside the control of the worker. A short layoff may bring a worker from one skill level to another in the same plant; a more extensive layoff may lead to a similar job with a different employer; a still longer layoff may lead to a new kind of job. Some workers may attempt a small business for a while. It is not the more assured pattern of the white-collar worker, who is likely to move ahead or at least retain his job in his firm or one like it if he works hard and well. The lower the skill level, the less the control of work and the less the advantage to stay in a particular occupational activity. The blue-collar worker probably changes jobs to a great extent because he has to move. The occurrence of unemployment even during boom times means that a high percentage of American workers of all ages have suffered fairly prolonged unemployment during their working lives.[10] It is probably this circumstance of unemployment which is the most important reason for job changing.

The prospects are that some high school graduating working-class youth will go into white-collar and technical work. These jobs will be comparatively stable, but the holder of a high school diploma will soon hit the ceiling. Others will go into various production jobs. They will be part of the "stable working class" that is described elsewhere in this volume.[11] Changes in productivity ("automation"), in the location of industry, and in the demand for various products will make many of these production jobs insecure. A smaller group will drift into various lower-level jobs with low pay and low stability.

[8] Harold L. Wilensky, "Work, Careers, and Social Integration," *International Social Science Journal*, Vol. XII, 1960, pp. 543-60.

[9] Our preliminary analysis of dropouts' short-run employment histories tends to support this point. Betty L. Saleem and S. M. Miller, *The Dropout Two Years Later: The Employment Experience of Syracuse Dropouts*, Syracuse University Youth Development Center, 1964.

[10] James N. Morgan, *et al., Income and Welfare in the United States* (New York: McGraw-Hill, Inc., 1962).

[11] S. M. Miller and Frank Riessman, "The Working-Class Subculture: A New View," *Social Problems*, 1961.

The Outlook
of
Working-Class
Youth

The bulk of the high school graduating group is unlikely to fall below the poverty line for long periods. Some will, however, as automation and industrial relocation erode their jobs. The dominant experience of the non-college group will be a growing inequality—the widening of the gap between their group and the better-off groups in society.

In the next section, we turn from examining the job prospects of various groups of working-class youths to their relation to the educational system which has such a deep impact on their occupational futures.

THE MOTIVATION FOR DROPPING OUT

Why do many working-class youth drop out of school? One explanation is in terms of the rejection of school. Dropouts are said to find school, as at present conducted, a completely alien and negative experience. They actively want to get away from this negative, boring experience.

If the following four conditions did not exist, I would have more confidence that the essential problem of dropouts is that they dislike school.

First, most dropouts do not leave school as soon as they are legally eligible.

Second, many dropouts withdraw in the senior year.

Third, many dropouts assert that they were push-outs. Of a group of boys who have dropped out and were unable to get a job, most of them claimed that they did not voluntarily withdraw from school. They asserted that they were pushed out, and frequently in a fairly direct way.[12]

Fourth, our Syracuse unemployed dropouts, who should be likely candidates for the post of school critics, had a generally favorable attitude toward school: they asserted that they had a positive feeling about at least some teachers; they thought that teachers were generally fair, and they missed school because of its social aspects, such as meeting friends during the school day. This attitude may be a nostalgic glow for a past which appears in retrospect more attractive than a difficult present, but the absence of a deep, pervasive antipathy toward school is surprising in a group which had problems of "adjustment" in school and conducted itself or was conducted out of it.

The interrelations of dropout and school are intricate ones, with much ambivalence and misperception on *both* sides. The dropout has been studied from the perspective of the school authorities, and much has been lost in this one-sided analysis.

The practice of attributing to all dropouts the characteristics of the most troubled or troubling has frequently obscured the fact that most dropouts are neither isolated nor separated from their families. Another study in Syracuse shows that the overwhelming percentage of dropouts who were unmarried two years after dropping out lived with their families and were certainly involved in the family network.[13] This tie suggests that contact

---

[12] S. M. Miller and Ira Harrison, "Types of Dropouts: 'The Unemployables,' " published in this volume.

[13] Kenneth Baldwin, *et al., The Syracuse Dropout—Two Years Later,* unpublished group master's thesis, School of Social Work, Syracuse University, 1962. This study was supervised by Maurice Connery.

through the family may be important in affecting the educational and occupational activity of dropouts.

An alternative line of explanation of early school leaving, which is neglected but seems to me to be important, is the failure of working-class parents, youth, and school to mesh. Because education is seen instrumentally, working-class youth are not interested in school as such, and the school's inability to interest them compounds the problem. Survey data show that a high percentage (lower than for the middle class, but not much lower) of working-class parents wish their children to go to college. These results suggest that many working-class parents do not know how to translate their educational concerns for their children into operationally effective practices. Other aspects of the lives of the working-class youth do not further an interest in school as an arena of hope. Perhaps most important is the fact that schools fail to engage themselves effectively with low-income youth.[14]

ASPIRATIONS

I am suggesting that "low aspirations" are not the main cause of working-class youths' early school leaving. They are an element in it, but not the main one. Aspirations result from experience and expectations as well as influencing them.

Low-income Negroes are particularly interested in education. Many educators assert the reverse, but their ignorance of the outlook of Negroes is symptomatic of the failure to engage honestly with the poor in many of the widely heralded educational programs aimed at "the disadvantaged."

This indictment may be too strong because the survey and other data on aspirations, expectations, and behavior are bewildering. For example, Louis Kriesberg presents data which show that 21 per cent of children of low-educated fathers applied to college (an indicator of aspirations); 31 per cent of such children applied in 1955-1956. Despite this 10 per cent increase in applications (and, presumably, aspirations), only two per cent more of the offspring of low-educated fathers actually enrolled in college (from 18 per cent to 20 per cent).[15]

What does an aspiration reflect? Negroes at probably every income level have higher educational aspirations than whites, yet they have lower educational attainments. In the Higher Horizons program in Harlem, the aspirations of Negro youths rose markedly. A large percentage now said that they wanted to be physicians, lawyers, and the like. What does this mean? Awareness of only a limited number of middle-class occupations which are well known because of their high prestige? Or an indication of a rise in hopes but

---

[14] I have discussed this and other types of dropouts more fully in "Dropouts—A Political Problem," *Integrated Education*, August, 1963. The complete version of this paper will appears in Daniel Schreiber, ed., *The School Dropout*, National Education Association, 1964.

[15] Louis Kriesberg, "The Relationship between Socio-Economic Rank and Behavior," *Social Problems*, Vol. X (Spring, 1963), p. 341. Published in the Reprint Series of the Syracuse University Youth Development Center.

not of a specific dedication to the particular occupation mentioned? Or the translation of middle-class occupations of high prestige into "glamour" occupations, so that they become the legitimated equivalents of the common high-prestige occupations of lower-class children? Or is the high professional aspiration a specific desire for the specific occupation? We lack the knowledge to clarify the significance of aspirations.

Aspirations have some connection with behavior, but the relationship is a complicated and a two-way one. I think that in social research we have been too prone to accept at face value solicited answers to deceptively simple questions. We have been willing to utilize reliable, scalable items and have paid much less attention to the problems of validity. I do not believe that we understand enough about working-class people to use indiscriminately the questionnaire techniques that are so widespread. I am afraid that on this point of aspirations I must resort to the defense of the stubborn traditionalist, which is to criticize method and to avoid analyzing the implication of results. I just do not understand the results of aspiration studies, and I suspect them to be largely artifacts of sociological research production today.

THE JOB WORLD OF THE DROPOUT

Pay and security are central items in the low-level dropouts' evaluation of jobs. Job knowledge is limited and pretty much restricted to jobs with which there is some fairly direct contact. The concern in not with a "big" job, but with a job they can get and which pays a "reasonable" amount of money ($60 or $70 a week is considered good pay by many low-level young dropouts).

The unmarried young male dropout still does not have work as a central life concern; he is disturbed if unemployed, but he is caught up in his peer-group activities. There is little talk about work; his family would like him to get more education and a better job, but they do not know how to move him in this direction—"He's a big boy now." The dropout recognizes that he is limited occupationally, but he seems to reduce his potential frustration by adjusting his concept of what is a necessary income level.

Dropouts who are steadily employed at better jobs and working-class high school graduates are probably somewhat different, but we do not have good information on them. Some dropouts are undoubtedly "career-oriented," seeing a path to economic advance and concerned about it; others see a mode of advance, but it is not a very central concern; and for still others, there is little self-aware concern with the job except for its stability.

For girls, the job involvement is even more limited. Many working-class girls, willy-nilly, will work for a good part of their lives, as have their mothers. Yet they do not define the job world as a concern, nor do they think in terms of work. Marriage is thought of as an alternative to work, even though for many it will not be. Are these girls denying something they do not like, or are they hoping that things will be better for them than it was for their mothers, although they are willing to cope with the vicissitudes of economic strain when they emerge? Or is ignorance or a wish for a magical solution involved?[16]

The job world, for young and unmarried working-class youth, is still a shadowy phenomenon. Perhaps it is only the shock of marriage, with its new ménage and economic responsibilities, which forces the male to confront the job world as a permanent and major slice of life; not a few, of course, attempt to avoid this realization.

CONCLUSION

I have written much more boldly than the data permit. Considerable variation exists from study to study. The "working class" is differently defined in many investigations. Conditions vary tremendously from community to community, affecting the employment and job prospects of dropouts and other youth: although New York is not America, neither is Muncie. My references to studies should not obscure the fact that I use them illustratively rather than being able to formulate generalizations from a flowing band of information. We know little. Nevertheless, I shall conclude in this outspoken way.

The current campaign to encourage youth to stay in school can be successful only if it is partially unsuccessful. For, if all potential dropouts stayed in school and graduated, there would not be enough "appropriate" jobs for them. This campaign may boomerang by convincing some dropouts that their chances are even worse than they are, that it is not worthwhile to try to do anything to improve their employment chances, and that they are pretty inadequate people.

The emphasis on educational and occupational mobility obscures the likelihood that a variety of low-paying, low-skill jobs will remain in the economy. What will happen to people in these jobs? Do we not have to improve the conditions of these low-level jobs as well as to encourage people to get better-paid, more productive positions? In our emphasis on mobility, we seem frequently to forget those left behind.

Is obtaining a high school diploma a guarantee of a secure, well-paid job? I have tried to show that today many young high school graduates are not doing well. The likelihood is that a growing percentage will not. And, if we are concerned with inequality as well as with poverty, high school graduation will not be solving our problems.

We are going to continue to have a sizable number of poor and near-poor people in America. Some attribute our difficulties to the "culture of poverty," which perpetuates poverty by preventing the emergence of motivation to overcome the pressures of one's environment. I think this position is misleading and ill-based. A raising of motivational level and personal action today can reduce the extent of poverty, although not by a tremendous amount. The

---

[16] Maurice Connery has alerted me to the outlook of female dropouts and has influenced this paragraph.

jobs have to be there. Over the long haul, occupational outlooks are going to have an intimate relationship with occupational possibilities. There is an educational escape-hatch for a sizable number of working-class youth, but its width can be widened only by economic expansion.

Kent Revisited:
Blue-Collar Aspirations and
Achievements

J. KENNETH MORLAND

IN the heart of the textile manufacturing area of the Piedmont South lies the town of "Kent," a community of some 5,000, about one-third of whom live and work in its mill-village sections. The author made an intensive study of the blue-collar mill workers in these sections during 1948, living with the workers and their families for a year and recording their way of life.[1] Ten years later he returned to find out what had happened to the mill people in the interval.[2] He was specifically concerned with whether or not the mill-villagers continued to form an hereditary occupational group, as they had in 1948.

The earlier study had revealed that mill-village areas and the blue-collar workers who lived in them were separated socially and geographically from the rest of the community. Mill people made up the lowest class of whites in the Kent social structure, and they had very limited contact with upper-class whites in the "town" sections. Most of the workers lived in company-owned houses, attended their own churches and clubs, married other mill workers, and were immersed in kinship-centered activities. A majority of their children did not finish high school, dropping out to take jobs in the cotton mills. Mill-villagers formed a tightly knit in-group, united by occupation, extensive

---

[1] Published as *Millways of Kent* (Chapel Hill: University of North Carolina Press, 1958). The other two divisions of the town were also studied. Hylan Lewis did the research on the Negro sections, published as *Blackways of Kent* (Chapel Hill: University of North Carolina Press, 1955), and Ralph Patrick studied the "town" sections. These studies gave perspective to the social-class position of the mill people.

[2] The full report, "A Follow-Up Study of the Mill-Village Sections of Kent," is on file in the Institute for Research in Social Science at the University of North Carolina.

kinship relations, and social-class position. They formed what might be termed an "enclave." [3]

To find out what had happened in the enclave, the author conducted interviews with over 100 Kentians, including most of the heads of 96 mill families studied in detail in 1948. These families had been chosen at random and were representative of the 290 families in the village sections. The interviews were designed to find out if there had been changes in the jobs and residences of the family heads, how much schooling children in these families had received, and what jobs they had entered during the ten-year period. Finally, responses to a questionnaire on educational and occupational aspirations were secured from pupils, including mill children, then attending the Kent junior and senior high schools. Information from the interviews and questionnaires could show to what extent the enclave had persisted and what factors were involved in persistence or change, particularly the parts that social milieu, schooling, and aspiration played. Although limited to the study of blue-collar workers in one industry and in one community, this study has advantages that come with follow-up research in a town previously analyzed intensively. Furthermore, generalizations about the persistence of enclaves can be derived only from the study of specific enclaves. In this way, knowledge of the blue-collar mill-villagers of Kent can help to throw light on the future of other comparable enclaves of mill workers throughout the Piedmont South.

THE FAMILY HEADS

A large majority of the heads of the 96 families were found to have remained in their mill jobs and in the mill villages. Almost 92 per cent had continued as mill operatives or had retired or died without entering other occupations. The few who left the mill entered other blue-collar jobs, with the exception of one, who became a Church of God minister. This high degree of continuity in mill work supported a conclusion of the earlier study, namely, that *once entered into, blue-collar textile work was usually followed for life.*

Only 5.2 per cent of the heads of the families had changed their county of residence during the ten-year period and could therefore be termed "migrants" as defined by the United States Bureau of the Census. For the nation as a whole, census figures show that, for each of the ten years in question, the percentage of the population changing county of residence ranged from 5.8 to 7.1 per cent, with an average of 6.4 per cent per year. Thus, the residential migration rate of the mill family heads was lower in *ten* years than

---

[3] Thus, as a social-class division, the mill people formed a social *group* rather than a statistical stratum. They were, then, different from the class divisions Lenski found in Danielson, Conn., reported in "American Social Classes: Statistical Strata or Social Groups?" *American Journal of Sociology*, Vol. LVIII (September, 1952), pp. 139-44, and from those found by Lasswell, reported in "Citrus City," in "A Study of Social Stratification Using an Area Sample of Raters," *American Sociological Review*, Vol. 19 (1954), pp. 310-13. It was Lasswell who suggested that the mill people be called an "enclave," in a review of *Millways of Kent* in *Sociology and Social Research*, Vol. 43 (1958), pp. 61-62.

Kent
Revisited:
Blue-Collar
Aspirations
and
Achievements

the rate for the entire population of the nation was in any *one* of the ten years. So far as the heads of the family were concerned, then, *the enclave persisted.*

Several factors were identified as contributing to this relative stability of occupation and residence. (1) First, there were no noticeable alterations in the operation of the textile mills themselves, nor did the industry as a whole change significantly. Obviously, a necessary condition for this hereditary occupational enclave to persist is the continuation of the mills which provide the occupation. The administration of the Kent mills was still in the hands of paternalistic owners, and labor unions had made little headway. A few minor alterations in the technique of manufacturing had occurred, but they had not affected the utilization of the labor force in an observable way.

(2) Manifest personality traits, nourished by the mill-village way of life and described in detail in the earlier study, were those that would tend to promote continuity in textile work. Workers had been found to be more passive than aggressive, more ready to accept their social conditions than to try to change them, more dependent than independent, and comparatively low in self-confidence. In their jobs, they had been shown to be dependable, loyal, cooperative, and hard-working. These traits made it unlikely for them to strike out on their own as long as the mills afforded a reasonably secure living.

(3) The pull of the enclave itself remained strong, particularly in view of the lack of acceptance outside. Most workers had many relatives in the villages, and extended kindred groups were an important part of the social structure there. Within the villages, mill people were accepted warmly, without reservation; they belonged. But outside the confines of the village sections lived upper-class Kentians who did not look upon them as social equals and Negroes whom mill people did not accept socially. The risk in trying to move out into less friendly and less familiar circles was great, and, besides, it was unnecessary. In spite of the fact that mill people themselves still tended to accept the town's low evaluation of blue-collar textile work, most of them were content to remain where they were.

MILL CHILDREN OUT OF SCHOOL

Between 1948 and 1958, 132 children in 58 of the 96 families either graduated from high school or dropped out of elementary or high school. Table 1 summarizes the jobs these children held in 1958. It shows that more than half, 51.5 per cent, had become blue-collar textile workers. Because it is likely that some of the 22 children having temporary duty in the armed services or not employed at the time of the study will go into mill work, the percentage of children in textiles will probably increase. And, as already noted, if past trends continue, it is probable that those who have entered cotton mills as operatives will remain in such work until their retirement.

When the intergenerational mobility rate of the Kent mill workers during 1948-1958 is compared with data on the United States as a whole, the mill-village mobility rate is found to be low. For example, Lenski reports that, for a representative sample of males in the United States in 1952, about one-

Table 1

OCCUPATION IN 1958 OF 132 KENT MILL CHILDREN WHO COMPLETED HIGH SCHOOL
OR DROPPED OUT OF ELEMENTARY OR HIGH SCHOOL BETWEEN 1948 AND 1958,
BY SEX

Occupation	Male (N = 64) (Per Cent)	Female* (N = 68) (Per Cent)	Total (N = 132) (Per Cent)
Textile Operative	48.4	54.4	51.5
Carpentry, Painting	12.5	11.8	12.1
Armed Forces: Draft Duty ...	12.5	8.8	10.6
Clerical, Sales	6.3	8.8	7.6
Never Employed	9.4	0.0	4.5
Attending College	7.8	1.5	4.5
Farming	3.1	5.9	4.5
Nursing	0.0	4.4	2.3
Other†	0.0	4.4	2.3

*If married and not employed outside of the home, occupation of husband is given.
†One was a beautician; one was married to a Church of God minister; one was married to a mill superintendent in another state.

third of those who had fathers in blue-collar jobs had entered white-collar jobs.[4] In other words, he found that about one-third of the sons of blue-collar workers became white-collar workers. In contrast, only 15.6 per cent (10 of the 64) of the Kent mill boys can be said to have become white-collar or potential white-collar workers.[5] Among the mill girls, 19.1 per cent either became white-collar workers themselves or married white-collar workers. This percentage of mill girls moving upward into white-collar work did not differ significantly from that of the boys.[6]

This comparatively low intergenerational occupational mobility rate of Kent mill workers can be more readily understood when viewed in the mill-village setting. As had been true in 1948, Kent mill children continued to be the chief source of labor for the Kent mills, and they were still given first consideration when openings occurred in the mills in which their parents worked. Superintendents, parents, and children felt that such special consideration was "right," for the mill child "deserved" preferential treatment. Mill work still offered a form of occupational security for the mill child—even an inducement to leave school as soon as he reached the minimum age. It is of interest to note that a majority of the 132 children became textile workers in spite of the fact that mill children in school in 1948 had expressed desires to enter other occupations, for at that time only 3.5 per cent said that they wished to become mill workers. Although mill work was not something to which the mill children aspired, it was something on which they could fall back in the event their aspirations did not materialize.

The amount of schooling received by the mill children can throw further light on their low occupational-mobility rate. When we compare the actual years of schooling received by the children and those received by their parents,

---

[4] Gerhard E. Lenski, "Trends in Inter-Generational Occupational Mobility in the United States," *American Sociological Review*, Vol. 23 (October, 1958), pp. 514-23.

[5] These include the three in sales, six attending college, and one in the armed services who graduated from college. Because the other seven in the armed services did not finish high school or go beyond it, they will be likely to enter blue-collar work.

[6] Chi square = 0.28, 1 d.f., $P > .50$.

Kent Revisited: Blue-Collar Aspirations and Achievements

Table 2

YEARS OF SCHOOLING OF MILL CHILD COMPARED WITH YEARS OF
SCHOOLING OF PARENT,* BY OCCUPATIONAL RANK OF CHILD

Years of Schooling	Child in Blue-Collar Job (N = 109) (Per Cent)	Child in White-Collar Job (N = 23) (Per Cent)
Child More Years than Parent	81.6	87.0
Child Same Number of Years as Parent. . .	14.7	13.0
Child Fewer Years than Parent	3.7	0.0

*The parent with the greater number of years of schooling.
Chi square (with "Child Same Number of Years as Parent" combined with
"Child Fewer Years than Parent") = 0.366; 1 d.f.; $P > .50$.

we find that 82.6 per cent of the children received more schooling than either of their parents. However, having more years of schooling than their parents was not significantly different for children entering blue-collar jobs than it was for those entering white-collar jobs, as Table 2 shows.

When we relate differences between generations in *level* of schooling attained with occupational rank of the children, however, we obtain a different result. By "level of schooling" we refer to the following categories: less than elementary school (eight grades); elementary only; high school attendance, without graduation; high school graduation only; beyond high school (special training in nursing, secretarial work, business, and so forth, or entrance into college). Table 3 shows that a significantly greater number of mill children reached white-collar positions if they attained a higher level of schooling than did their parents. It was the level of schooling, then, and not the number of years as such, that appeared to be crucial in the upward occupational mobility of the mill children.[7]

Further interpretation of the relation between level of schooling and occupational mobility is suggested from interviews with children, parents, and mill superintendents. Graduation from high school continued to be con-

---

[7] It is of interest to compare these findings with those from a study in Puerto Rico. This study suggests a pivotal year-level in schooling which leads to a breakthrough for the effects of education itself. It is the level that is crucial. See M. M. Tumin and A. S. Feldman, "Status, Perspective and Achievement: Education and Class Structure in Puerto Rico," *American Sociological Review*, Vol. 21 (August, 1956), pp. 464-72, esp. p. 470.

Table 3

LEVEL* OF SCHOOLING OF MILL CHILD COMPARED WITH LEVEL OF
SCHOOLING OF PARENT,† BY OCCUPATIONAL RANK OF CHILD

Level of Schooling	Child in Blue-Collar Job (N = 109) (Per Cent)	Child in White-Collar Job (N = 23) (Per Cent)
Child Higher Level than Parent	56.9	87.0
Child Same Level as Parent	41.3	13.0
Child Lower Level than Parent	1.8	0.0

*Levels include: Less than Elementary; Elementary Only; High School Attendance, Without Graduation; High School Graduation Only; Beyond High School.
†The parent with the higher level of schooling.
Chi square (with "Child Same Level as Parent" combined with "Child Lower Level than Parent") = 9.84; 1 d.f.; $P = < .01$.

sidered the normal goal of schooling by most of those living in the village sections. Thus, when asking how far a mill child had gone in school, the author received a reply almost invariably expressed in the following way: "He finished" (meaning that he completed high school) or, "He quit" (meaning that he stopped before graduating from high school). Although high school graduation was the goal, less than half (44.7 per cent) of the 132 children reached it. Of those who did not graduate from high school, only one boy (1.4 per cent of the total number of nongraduates) became a white-collar worker. High school graduation in itself, however, did not assure a mill child of becoming a white-collar worker, for only 15.9 per cent of the children stopping with graduation entered white-collar work. At the same time, all 15 who went beyond high school became white-collar or potential white-collar workers. Again, the level of schooling appeared to play a vitally important part in upward mobility.

Conversations with teachers and mill officials suggest that a decision about occupation was made prior to the one about education. Teachers and officials reported that mill children would often ask if they should drop out of school to take a job in the mill. Those asked stated that they reminded the children that once they stopped school and entered the mill, they were in such work for life. The mill child's decision (provided he had done well enough in school to be able to make a decision) to drop out or to go further in school rested, then, on a decision about what occupation he wished to enter. Stated in another way, it was not more schooling that led the mill child into white-collar work. Rather, it was the decision to try for white-collar work that led to more schooling. C. Arnold Anderson, in a study of the relation between vertical mobility and education, concludes that ability and motivation operate independently of schooling in generating upward mobility.[8] This does not appear to be the case with the mill children, however. Ability and motivation can lead to higher levels of schooling; but, unless the higher level of schooling is reached, upward mobility of the mill child is highly unlikely.

MILL CHILDREN IN SCHOOL[9]

Aspirations of mill children in school at the time of the restudy give further insight into the factors involved in the stability of the enclave. On the questionnaire administered to all pupils in the Kent junior and senior high schools was the question, "How much more schooling would you like to have?" Of the 290 mill children responding, all but 2.4 per cent stated that they wished to complete high school at least, and more than one-fourth of them wanted to finish four years of college. Although this level of aspiration was significantly lower than that for upper-class "town" children,[10] it still appeared unrealistically high in view of the past accomplishments of mill children. And the mill children responding evidently realized this, for they

[8] C. Arnold Anderson, "A Skeptical Note on the Relation of Vertical Mobility to Education," *American Journal of Sociology*, Vol. LXVI (May, 1961), pp. 560-70.

[9] Portions of the data in this section are derived from J. Kenneth Morland, "Educational and Occupational Aspirations of Mill and Town School Children in a Southern Community," *Social Forces*, Vol. 39 (December, 1960), pp. 169-75.

[10] Chi square = 70.59; 3 d.f.; $P<.001$.

Kent
Revisited:
Blue-Collar
Aspirations
and
Achievements

Table 4

REPLIES OF 290 MILL CHILDREN IN GRADES 7 THROUGH 12 OF THE KENT
SCHOOLS IN 1958 TO THE QUESTIONS: "HOW MUCH MORE SCHOOLING WOULD
YOU LIKE TO HAVE?" AND "HOW MUCH MORE SCHOOLING DO YOU THINK YOU
WILL ACTUALLY BE ABLE TO GET?"

Amount of Schooling	Would Like To Have (Per Cent)	Will Be Able To Get (Per Cent)
Not beyond high school	37.2	54.8
High school, plus special training* . . .	37.6	29.7
College, four years	22.4	13.4
College, plus professional training . . .	2.8	2.1

*Refers to training in business, nursing, and trade schools.
Chi square = 19.24; 3 d.f.; $P < .001$.

modified their aspirations significantly when asked, "How much more school-ing do you think you will *actually* be able to get?", as Table 4 shows.[11]

The Kent school children were also asked, "What kind of work would you like to do when you finish your schooling?" The most frequent replies of the mill and town boys were much the same, with "engineer" the most popular preference for both. When the answers were categorized in levels of aspiration according to the Warner-Meeker-Eels Revised Scale for Rating Occupation,[12] it was found that there was no significant difference in levels of aspiration between mill and town boys, as is seen in Table 5.

Mill and town girls likewise showed similarities in their occupational preferences, because secretarial work and nursing were the two top prefer-ences of both. The level of aspiration of mill girls, however, tended to be lower than that of town girls, with a difference that was statistically significant at the .02 level of confidence, also seen in Table 5.

Following the question on occupational preference was one which asked, "What kind of work do you think you will *actually* do when you finish your schooling?" The percentage of mill children (63.3 per cent) who thought they would enter the occupation of their choice was lower than that of the town children (75.0 per cent), the difference being statistically significant at the .02 level of confidence.[13] The majority of mill children who gave explanations for not entering the occupation of their choice stated that they would prob-ably go into mill work. Among the explanations were these: (from an eighth-grade boy who wanted to become a lawyer) "Most likely I will get a job in a mill. Well, my father and mother have both worked in mills and I figure I will, too"; (from a tenth-grade girl who wished to become a stenographer) "I guess I'll go into textiles, because you have to have money to get anywhere these days"; (from an eighth-grade boy who wished to become a professional baseball player) "I will work in a mill if I don't get a pro offer"; (from a

[11] Replies of town children to these two questions did not differ significantly; that is, the town children thought they would actually get as much schooling as they wanted.

[12] W. L. Warner, M. Meeker, and K. Eels, *Social Class in America* (Chicago: Science Re-search Associates, 1949), pp. 140-41.

[13] Replies were grouped into three categories: "Same as occupational preference," "Different from occupational preference," "Not sure." Chi square = 8.19; 2 d.f.; $P < .02$.

Table 5

OCCUPATIONAL ASPIRATIONS OF MILL AND TOWN CHILDREN* IN GRADES
7 THROUGH 12 OF THE KENT SCHOOLS IN 1958, BY SEX

	Boys		Girls	
Level of Aspiration†	Mill (N = 120) (Per Cent)	Town (N = 82) (Per Cent)	Mill (N = 152) (Per Cent)	Town (N = 82) (Per Cent)
High	49.2	63.4	38.2	58.0
Medium	20.8	19.5	48.0	32.1
Low	30.0	17.1	13.8	9.9

*Does not include those who were undecided.
†According to the Revised Scale for Rating Occupation, from W. L. Warner, M. Meeker, and K. Eels, Social Class in America (Chicago: Science Research Associates, 1949), pp. 140-41. "High" comprises ratings 1 and 2 of the Revised Scale; "Medium" comprises ratings 3 and 4; "Low" comprises ratings 5 and 6.

Chi square for boys = 5.21; 2 d.f.; $P > .05$.
Chi square for girls = 8.50; 2 d.f.; $P < .02$.

twelfth-grade girl who wished to become a secretary) "I think I have an office job waiting for me when I graduate—at least, I was promised one. If I don't get it, I guess I'll go to work in a cotton mill."

The comments of the mill school children and the remarks of their parents indicated that mill people themselves did not have high regard for mill work. (This was also a conclusion from the earlier study.) They seemed to feel that it was all right to work in a cotton mill if there was nothing else available, but that many other jobs were preferable. An eighth-grade mill girl expressed this attitude when she wrote that she wanted to become a nurse, "because I wish to make something of myself and not work in any mill." Although mill parents did not object to their children becoming cotton mill workers, neither was there any encouragement. They felt that children should have full freedom in deciding their occupation and that they should go into something that they liked. It is logical to assume that this attitude toward mill work could help to account for its rarity as an occupational preference. Children who were not encouraged to aim explicitly at mill work as an occupation were not likely to state it as a preference. This low evaluation of mill work could also be used to explain the relatively higher aspiration of mill children in occupation than in schooling, because most other types of occupation would rank higher in the Warner-Meeker-Eels scale than blue-collar cotton-mill work. It is also possible that the mill children were not aware of the relationship between the amount of schooling received and the possibility of entering white-collar occupations.[14]

Two questions that related to educational and occupational aspirations were: "Do you think anyone can go to college if he really wants to?" and "Do you think everyone in Kent has about the same chance to get ahead?" Re-

---

[14] A. O. Haller and W. H. Sewell in "Farm Residence and Levels of Educational and Occupational Aspiration," American Journal of Sociology, Vol. 62 (January, 1957), pp. 407-11, drew this conclusion about farm and nonfarm high school seniors studied in Wisconsin. The farm boys had significantly lower educational but not occupational aspirations than nonfarm boys.

Kent
Revisited:
Blue-Collar
Aspirations
and
Achievements

141

plies to these questions can help to explain the mill children's relatively high level of aspiration, when compared with the levels reached by their parents.[15] A large majority of the mill children replied in the affirmative to both questions, and they were not significantly different from the upper-class town children in their responses. Mill children tended to express American ideals by saying: "Where there's a will, there's a way"; "If only a person tries hard enough, he can do anything"; "You are what you make of yourself." But mill children who replied negatively to the questions did so with much more feeling than did the town children who disagreed. The latter stated in a matter-of-fact way that there were unambitious and inferior people who could not go to college or get ahead. However, mill children thought that injustice and discrimination were involved: "Some people have to go to work when they finish high school because they don't have the money for college"; "You have to live in the upper part of town to be recognized, let alone get ahead"; "When you go to try to get a job, people don't go by your qualifications, but by the family you have—I know lots of cases like that"; "We may have the same chance to get ahead, but there is no place for us to go."

Although these reservations appeared in a few cases, the great majority of mill children expressed belief that getting ahead in Kent was a matter of individual desire and effort. They demonstrated through their own aspirations that they shared the American dream of moving upward. In spite of their low-class position and the sharply limited economic and educational resources of their families, the mill children had acquired the conviction that all Americans have equal opportunity and treatment.

If these aspirations were realized, they would, of course, take the younger generation of mill children out of the mill villages and doom the enclave. But in view of the discrepancy between the aspirations of the mill children in 1948 and their outcome ten years later, we must assume that *there is little relation between aspiration and fulfillment among children of the enclave.* Growing up in the mill villages does not provide the training or the resources that would enable mill children to move ahead.[16] Mill parents themselves have had little schooling and are not equipped to offer help and direction to their children. Mill houses are too small for quiet study, and they have few encyclopedias or dictionaries or other study aids. The wages of mill workers tend to be comparatively low and irregular. On the other hand, the mills offer a quick road to an independent income, and life in the village section gives security that comes with being among one's own.

---

[15] LaMar T. Empey in "Social Class and Occupational Ambition: a Comparison of Absolute and Relative Measures," *American Sociological Review,* Vol. 21 (December, 1956), pp. 703-9, points out the necessity of distinguishing between "relative" and "absolute" aspirations. In a study of male high school seniors in Washington State, he found that lower-class respondents had lower aspirations than upper-class respondents (that is, lower absolute aspirations). However, relative to their social status, their aspirations were no lower than those of upper-class respondents.

[16] The disadvantages faced by the mill child in schooling are similar to those met by the lower-class child reported by Jackson Toby, "Orientation to Education as a Factor in School Maladjustment of Lower-Class Children," *Social Forces,* Vol. 35 (March, 1957), pp. 259-66.

CONCLUSION

The ten-year follow-up study of the Kent blue-collar mill workers shows that the enclave of village sections has persisted. Almost all of the heads of families in the villages had continued as blue-collar operatives in the Kent mills, and most of their children who entered work during this period had become mill workers. This hereditary occupational class continued in spite of the fact that these children went to school longer than their parents and in spite of their lack of desire to enter mill work. This persistence of the enclave occurred, then, not because of a lack of ambition of mill children to move upward, but primarily because of nonpersonal factors. The cotton-textile plants offered a ready occupation to mill children in a setting where kindred and friends gave warm acceptance. At the same time, mill-village life did not provide the kind of training in knowledge and personality that would enable most mill children to compete successfully outside the village sections.

Although mill children in school at the time of the follow-up study expressed educational and occupational aspirations far beyond the levels reached by their parents and siblings, doubt was cast, even by the children themselves, on the actual fulfillment of these aspirations. Again, it is not so much the lack of high aspiration that makes it probable that these children will become mill workers; rather, this probability is related to the stability of the cotton-textile industry, the "pull" of the enclave, and barriers present in the Kent social-class system.

These findings showing the persistence of the Kent mill-village enclave raise a number of questions: At a time in America when far-reaching technological and economic changes, along with ready accessibility of transportation, are making for extensive mobility, are there other types of blue-collar enclaves that still persist? If so, are factors making for stability in these enclaves similar to those that make for the persistence of the Kent village sections? In the recent past, what enclaves have broken up, and what social forces helped to bring about their demise? To what extent are the abilities of the members of enclaves, in Kent and elsewhere, being underdeveloped and underutilized? To what extent are aspirations being frustrated and at what cost to the nation and to the individuals involved? Research designed to answer these and related questions can broaden our understanding of the nature, the effects, and the future of enclaves of blue-collar workers in America.

Kent
Revisited:
Blue-Collar
Aspirations
and
Achievements

143

The Hopes of Negro Workers for Their Children

THEODORE V. PURCELL

THE American Negro revolution of the 1960's has been long a-building. A small part of the story behind it will come out in this chapter. Our story is primarily the story of Negro packinghouse workers and their hopes for their children—people from two border cities, East St. Louis and Kansas City. This is part of a research project[1] begun in 1950, largely completed in 1960, and now brought up to date. Cutting across both space and time, the purpose was to make a depth study of the thoughts and feelings of the packinghouse workers in three major plants of Swift & Company, the meatpacker, and in the three competing unions of the industry, the United Packinghouse Workers, the Amalgamated Meat Cutters, and the National Brotherhood of Packinghouse Workers.

To get the story of these blue-collar people, I spent many months living in their neighborhoods, in Goose Hill of East St. Louis and in Kansas City with the Croatians on Strawberry Hill and the Mexicans in Armourdale. I interviewed over 790 workers and had countless conversations with them over coffee or beer, at home or at work. Only the Negro workers will be quoted here.

Let us begin by taking a look at the neighborhoods, plants, and unions that so much influence the lives and hopes of these Negro people.

Missouri was once a "slave state," while Kansas and Illinois were always free. Kansas City is really a "border city," as is East St. Louis. The half-defined racial patterns of border cities often make interracial relations more complex and unpredictable than in cities of the deep South or the North. Perhaps as a result, the Negro people of Kansas City seem less aggressive than Negroes of such Northern cities as Chicago, New York, and Detroit. They appear more conservative, more depressed. They have not had the professional and leadership groups such as we find in Chicago's Bronzeville.

East St. Louis is a dismal industrial city of about 100,000 people in Illinois, across the Mississippi from St. Louis. Going about East St. Louis, one gets the impression of arrested growth. One sees inadequate zoning, unbuilt sidewalks, a vacant lot, a big tank, or a boarded-up tenement next to a neat row

---

[1] Reported in *The Worker Speaks His Mind* (Cambridge: Harvard University Press, 1953), and *Blue Collar Man* (Cambridge: Harvard University Press, 1960), by Theodore V. Purcell.

of houses like the Gompers Project. One sees a city of trucks, gas stations, throaty Diesel locomotives, and grim factories. Crime, poverty, and unemployment beset East St. Louis. The city has been unable to attract new industry. Indeed, it has been losing industry. In August, 1959, the big Armour plant closed down, putting many hundreds of Negroes out of work. Incidentally, 61 per cent of the Negroes were unable to find jobs a year later, as opposed to 36 per cent of the whites.[2] Facts like this will help explain the attitudes we find.

Local 78 is the East St. Louis Swift local of the Amalgamated Meat Cutters and Butcher Workmen. The international Amalgamated is an old, well-financed union found mostly in retail stores and fur, leather, and poultry houses and also having important locals in the meatpacking industry. Local 78 is a secure, conservative organization favorable to Swift but aggressively pro-union.

Local 12 in Kansas City is quite different. It is a key local of the National Brotherhood of Packinghouse Workers, Independent. The AFL-CIO United Packinghouse Workers' militant efforts to win over the Brotherhood workers have helped make Local 12's leaders both aggressive and progressive. The two unions in this study differ greatly in age, strategy, leadership, and policies. Local 12 is less secure than local 78 and less affluent. At times it is more aggressive regarding grievances, but much less aggressive in bargaining.

The Kansas City and the East St. Louis Swift plants are both old, multi-storied plants with the full range of packinghouse operations. However, there are important differences in interracial patterns. At Kansas City Swift, Negro men have been hired for many years, and Negro women also were hired after World War II. The Negro men work in almost all the operating departments, ranging from 100 per cent Negro in the Tank House (a difficult job) to about 1 per cent in the Auto Departments. Although there were no Negroes in the office force or Standards Department, a few Negroes were in first-line supervision. Past segregation conditions in the use of plant facilities such as dressing rooms and cafeterias had been corrected many years ago. As for Local 12, it is an integrated local, but it sedulously avoids social activities where problems of mixing the races might occur.

At Swift East St. Louis, until recently, integration has been less advanced than at the Kansas City plant. Negro women had not been hired for many years. Negro men have about the same spread of jobs as at Kansas City, with the exception of supervision. However, Swift is now trying to get Negro foremen, and has already hired Negro wage-incentive men. The work forces of both plants are nearly half Negro. Until recently the big employees' cafeteria at East St. Louis was segregated. In addition, the East St. Louis plant had two autonomous but partially company-supported employees' social organizations, the New Frontier Club and the Arrow-S Club. The latter was all-white and the former was all-Negro. However, in the summer of 1963,

---

[2] *Progress Report, Automation Committee,* Armour and Company and United Packinghouse, Food and Allied Workers, AFL-CIO, and Amalgamated Meat Cutters and Butcher Workmen of North America, AFL-CIO (Chicago: June 19, 1961), p. 4. See also Richard C. Wilcock and Walter H. Franke, *Unwanted Workers* (New York: The Free Press of Glencoe, Inc., 1963), pp. 49, 50, and *passim.*

Swift insisted that either the clubs must integrate or the company would withdraw its support. The clubs did not integrate, and they have been practically disbanded. Local 78 has not taken as militant a stand regarding civil rights as Local 12 has taken.

Between the two plants we see considerable differences in racial opportunities. Paradoxically, the East St. Louis Negroes, with less racial equality (until recently) than was found at Kansas City, are more favorable to their opportunities. We shall see the reasons for this below.

But, differences apart, we see clearly in both plants the strong seeds of Negro discontent. It is true that these people are generally satisfied with their pay, working conditions, foremen, and so forth. Most have allegiance to both company and union. But they are definitely not satisfied with their advancement and racial oportunities. This fact must be remembered when we look now at their aspirations for their children.

In a workingman's wishes for his children we have a valuable "nondirective" attitude that can tell us something not only about the worker's children but about himself. Will the blue-collar man have a double standard, one for himself and one for his children? We know in advance that most American parents obviously want their children to "do better" than themselves. But is there an important aspect of this question that is hidden and not so obvious at all?

The sentiments we report refer to having one's children come to work in the plant itself, in the packinghouse. We are not referring to office work. Yet our findings must be related to this fact: both Swift plants are actually intertwined with many family relationships, cutting across lines from hourly paid to salaried and from union to management.

Our over-all findings are reported in the accompanying table.

The principal finding in the table is that the *majority of the packinghouse workers, both Negro and white, want their children to work elsewhere than in the packinghouse.* Only 26 per cent of the Kansas City people wanted their children to follow them into the plant, although 47 per cent of the East St. Louis workers agreed.

ATTITUDES TOWARD HAVING THEIR CHILDREN WORK AT THE PACKINGHOUSE
Random sample of workers in two Swift plants; Kansas City—121; East St. Louis—152, stratified by service, sex, and race; including union leaders and foremen
(In per cent)

Group	Favorable		Neutral		Unfavorable	
	K.C.	E.S.L.	K.C.	E.S.L.	K.C.	E.S.L.
All workers, weighted totals . . .	26	47	8	7	66	46
Colored men.	14	57	6	6	80	37
White men	31	45	6	11	63	44
Foremen	36	32	19	8	45	60
Local 12 union leaders*	17		17		66	
Local 12 union stewards	17		0		83	
(CIO leaders)	0		0		100	
Local 78 union leaders		50		33		17
Local 78 union stewards		20		0		80

*Estimated.

We see a big difference between Kansas City and East St. Louis, with the latter more favorable to having their children work in the plant. There is a difference between the white men of the two respective plants. But there is a much bigger difference between the colored men of the two plants. The East St. Louis Negroes are more favorable to having their children follow them into the plant, in good part because they are more favorable to their equal opportunities for advancement. Reasons for the more critical views at Kansas City Swift are two: First, the militancy of the raiding UPWA group at Kansas City makes the Kansas City Negroes more conscious of their rights. Second, the significantly greater number of Southern-born Negroes in East St. Louis (73 per cent, as opposed to 57 per cent at Kansas City) tends to make these people more conservative and content with their lot. In fact, practically all our results (most not reported in this chapter) find the East St. Louis Negro workers more satisfied.

Incidentally, as for length of service, we find that the younger workers in both plants tend to be less favorable to having their children come into the plants. Doubtless, just because they are younger, they are more ambitious for their children.

Let us listen to some of these blue-collar people now to see what they desire for their children and why.

First, Bruce McCauley.[3] McCauley is not a very satisfied employee, yet he has a moderate degree of company allegiance. He is a Negro who is quite concerned about the lack of equal opportunity as he sees it. This affects his thoughts about his children coming to the plant.

INTERVIEWER: How about your kids; do you figure on getting them in here to work?

McCAULEY: I wouldn't want a kid of mine to ever have a job like this. I'll try to educate 'em, I wouldn't want them to even *live* around here. [He laughs.] If I can ever get them through high school, you know, and through college—I'll try my best to send 'em on farther up, you know. Because anything they can do, I want 'em to do it. Because—I see right around here—I know a pretty girl that's a stenographer. Well, she never will get a chance to do it unless she takes a job with a legal judge or somethin'—not a judge, you know, a J.P., Justice of the Peace or somethin' like that. She might work in his office. But otherwise, I'd never want to see any child of mine, not even a boy. No sir. Not to work here.

Some Negroes are favorable, however, especially in East St. Louis. For example, John Adams, 45 years old although with Swift for only one year, says about his son, if he had one:

Well, you know, if he wanted to work, you know, I feel like, you know, he couldn't get a better job nowhere than a place like this, you know. Where he could learn a whole lot workin'. They'd learn him how to do a lot of things, how to butcher, cut up meat, doing things.

INTERVIEWER: So you think you might bring him here, huh?

ADAMS: Yes sir, if I had one.

---

[3] All names used here are fictitious, and the interviews are disguised.

The Hopes
of Negro Workers
for Their
Children

Jacob Jarrow, age 33, with two girls and a boy, says:

> No. Try to keep 'em out. I'd rather for 'em to go somewhere else. Any place besides a packin' house. Because—this place, when they get you once used to bein' a sucker, why you can't hardly get away from it. They press you down an' arthuritis or a cold. I have pleurisy myself. You don't be the same when you go out of here. I hope they will (do better elsewhere).

Two more Negro workers, both veterans and both with Swift about ten years, give different reasons for not wanting their children here. A semiskilled butcher, Wilson Brown has eight children. About them, he says:

> No, I hope I can give 'em an education. . . . I think they can get a better job than here. I'm going to try my level best to give 'em some school. . . . Give 'em a chance to get another job.

Robert Greene, like Brown, is a war veteran. He sees no opportunity:

> No. Not especially. No good. . . . Well, as far as colored people are, there's no future here for 'em. Any place would be better than a packin' house.

Old-timer, Warren Moore, a semiskilled meat trimmer, rated very highly by his foreman, has this to say about his son:

> He did come in to work awhile, but he looked over there and seen how I was workin'. So he come out there one day an' tol' me, he says,—first time he ever did get back at me—. "Old man," he says, "Swift's making a fool outa you. They ain't gonna make no fool out of me!" [Moore laughs heartily, but a bit self-consciously.]

> INTERVIEWER: Ain't going to make a fool out of me?

> MOORE: That's what he says. [*Laughing*] Yeah, I mean he quit, too! . . . He don't like *no* part of the stockyards.

> INTERVIEWER: What's the trouble with it, do you figure?

> MOORE: Well, he says, they work me too hard.

Irving Harding, only 20 years old, has one daughter and is expecting another child. A very quiet and youthful worker, he seems fairly well satisfied. His foreman rates him as a good worker, but not too smart. He would prefer a nice home to buying a car.

> INTERVIEWER: Well, if you get a boy and he grows up, would you expect to bring him in here to work?

> HARDING: No.

> INTERVIEWER: No?

> HARDING: No! . . . I'd like fer him to be a teacher, or a doctor or somep'n like that. I'd try to make him the *best one* in the world!

As for his own future in working in the plant, his comments are revealing:

> HARDING: Well, I really don't see no future in workin', you know, alla time. So that's about all I know is workin'. . . .

This identification of "working" with unskilled or semiskilled work is common enough. "Working" to Harding and to many other workers means work that is unskilled, unimportant, not very highly valued by the community, with little future.

> HARDING: So that's about all I know is workin'. 'Cause I didn't get no higher'n the tenth grade in school. . . . And you know you haveta, *nowadays* ya haveta have a college education. And so about all I know how to do is work. Beside, I was a athalete. . . . The 220. I ran relay.

I had some long interviews with two key union leaders from one of the plants, George McComb and Theodore Stillman. This interview was in Mr. Stillman's very comfortable home. Stillman is tall and lean with smiling lines at the corners of his eyes. McComb is shorter, stocky, with gray hair. Both are strong unionists, but dissident. At one point we got talking about aspirations for their children.

> INTERVIEWER: If you had a son, George, would you want him to come into the packinghouse and start him out on a job? How would you feel about that?

> McComb: At one time, I could answer you like this: At one time the management of that plant, when I was fighting to get more Negro women in the plant—uh, that was back in 'forty-three, 'forty-four—they offered, uh, to try to console me, or try to appease me one way or the other, to satisfy me. They told me, uh, "Is your wife workin'?" I says, "No, she's not workin'." And he says, "Well, why don't you bring your wife down? We can give her a job."

> INTERVIEWER: They offered that, huh? The employment office?

> McComb: Yeah, that is . . . no. That was the general superintendent. See, I was fightin' with the superintendent. And I wouldn't have my wife or any relatives of mine do, that is, to work in that plant under these conditions. I wouldn't come and get 'em here to work in there, brother or sister, or wife, or anything like that. And work on those production lines. Because it just, well I just don't. I detest that setup down there so badly you know, because of the way that they treat people in there, you know? First thing I know, when they was hired in there, they wouldn't get the equal breaks that any other person that would be hired in there. I guess you know about more or less the screening process of women when they are hired in there, you know? They got to have certain characters. And then get put on the roughest job in there. So those are the conditions, that's the reason that I wouldn't. No.

> INTERVIEWER: How about you, Ted—if you had a son, would you want him to . . . would you bring him in the packinghouse?

> STILLMAN: Well, to be perfectly frank about the idea, no. For the simple reason is this. If I had a son—which I do have two step-daughters, now—we spent quite a bit of money on trying to get those kids an education. Of course, they have been through college, both of 'em. And uh, well one of them at one time did ask me "How about me comin' down to Swift and getting a job?" I said, "No, your mother has spent considerable money on you to prepare you for other work, which I think is much more pleasant work, and I think you should use that now, as a matter of fact." And for that reason I don't think, in fact, I know, that if I had the say as to whether or not they go in there, I'd say no. Because of the preparations that we have made for them to get something better. If the thing was set up different, if they had the opportunity of anybody else when they went in there, it would make a different picture.

Now they are capable of running these dictaphones and so forth and so on, teletype machines. Well, if they had such openings there, I believe that they can qualify for it. And if they had the opportunity to get such jobs, or even if they

The Hopes
of Negro Workers
for Their
Children

had the opportunity to go into a plant and work on a job until they had an opening to get an advancement, or go into the departmental offices as clerks, like the other people has the chance to advance, under those conditions I wouldn't hesitate.

Although we are concerned with Negroes here, we can do well to hear at least a few representatives of another minority group, the Mexican-Americans. Julio Contreras is a newer employee at the Kansas City Swift plant. I asked him about bringing his children into the plant:

CONTRERAS: No. I hope not, Father. . . . Packinghouse work is for the people that don't have enough sense to work anywhere else, mostly. . . . They don't have no chance. . . .

INTERVIEWER: Yes?

CONTRERAS: I couldn't go—even if I worked twenty years, I couldn't be an electrician. I couldn't be a painter. I couldn't be a—We [Mexicans] have no other choice, Father. [He laughs.]

One other Mexican view reinforces Contreras, but for a somewhat different reason. Paula McLane, in spite of her name, is Mexican-American. As for bringing her son into the East St. Louis plant, she says:

Well, if he was gonna be a supervisor, if he was gonna hold an office. But if I had a son, and he wanted to work in the gang, 'specially on that killing floor, I wouldn't have him. No, I wouldn't. 'Cause I think that there is—there is uh, what my husband says—there is a race difference in there. They treat the colored people better'n they do the white man in there.

INTERVIEWER: Do they?

PAULA McLANE: Yeah. Now, if he was gonna work in the office like the rest of these young fellas do, B-checkers and all those, why they got it nice. That's all right. It's all right. I mean there's nothing wrong with the packinghouse. It's good. Swift & Company's a good company. They just don't know what's goin' on.

Dex Briggs is a new man with the company. He is 27 and is doing unskilled labor. He says he wants to work for a few years and then get into the real estate business. He has already been in and out of many packinghouses in Chicago and East St. Louis. From many cues in the interview it was clear that he was a somewhat confused person with emotional troubles and neurotic tendencies. Apparently he picked up some jargon from previous dealings with his Army psychiatrist. He has one young son, whom he does not want to come into the plant. Mr. Briggs is not at all typical, because of his background. He wants his son to study psychiatry or psychology.

INTERVIEWER: . . . Do you expect to get him in here to work someday?

BRIGGS: I doubt it very seriously, I don't have any intentions of him doin' too much manual labor whatsoever. . . . And then, too, with conditions the way they are, you know, with people of proletarian status, you understand, if a person has a minimized amount of intelligence you can more or less direct the child's future, you know. . . .

Well, frankly speakin', if it was in that profession, you understand, I'd like for him to be tops, you know. Say, for instance, in the field of psychiatry or psychology or some place in that, you know. But a local physician or local surgeon, I don't think I would go for that too much. . . . Well, the reason I say that, you understand, I've taken quite a survey of myself, you know. And, seein' as though that I like doin' the work in a man's mind. And a, just bein' presumptuous that he's similar to me in any relations whatsoever, you know, I just hope he'll be directed in that channel.

Pat Lindberg is a meat worker, eight years with Swift. Mrs. Lindberg is quite satisfied with conditions in the plant for herself. She has dual allegiance to both company and union. But in discussing whether or not she might wish her children to come in to work in the Kansas City plant, she says:

If I can help it, definitely not. . . . My daughter wants to be a nurse. [And Mrs. Lindberg hopes her son will be a doctor.] . . . In fact, that's what helps 'em [her children] as a whole; because bein' in public is like, you know, bein' a nurse— and that's somethin'. That's tangible and somethin'. That's ah, it's not as common as workin' down here. *I mean, I don't mind workin' down here myself. I don't figure they're any better than I am. But I just wouldn't want them to come down here if they can get somethin' better.*

Union steward, Major Rice, an old-timer with the company, concludes with the common theme of *education* as a reason for not wanting his children to come to Swift:

Well, no, I wouldn't want my boys to start where I did. They started with a good *education;* went to the Army. Married now. He's doin' good, and he's makin' a good salary from the government. He's got a steady job, and buyin' his own home. Wouldn't never want him to come here. The young fellow I got at the house now—I wouldn't want him to come here . . .

I always wanted to be a chemister. We had a large family to work from. Seven boys and two girls. That's the family I come from.

In short, our data find both Negroes and whites thinking very much alike. In aspirations for their children, both races are together. Both races, on the whole, want their children to avoid the packinghouse like the plague.

We can gather the reasons for this into three areas: First, there are difficult working conditions present in many packinghouse departments, although not in all. Second, there is often a lack of advancement opportunities, owing in part to the meat industry's great contraction in manpower during the last 15 years. Third, the workers want their children to get a better education that will fit them for white-collar or professional work.

But let us go deeper than these verbalized reasons. These people want prestige and power for their children. The community's lower evaluation of factory work, especially packinghouse work, leads these people to look for such prestige and power in white-collar jobs and in the professions. The workers have a double standard, one for themselves and a different one for their children.

These findings have been reinforced by other researchers, such as Chinoy[4] among the auto workers, Blum among the packinghouse workers,[5] and Seidman *et al.*[6] among steelworkers, textile workers, plumbers, and metal

[4] Ely Chinoy, *Automobile Workers and the American Dream* (New York: Doubleday & Company, Inc., 1955).

[5] Fred H. Blum, *Toward a Democratic Work Process* (New York: Harper & Row, Publishers, 1953).

[6] Joel Seidman, Jack London, Bernard Karsh, and Daisy Tagliacozzo, *The Worker Views His Union* (Chicago: University of Chicago Press, 1958).

workers. Berger,[7] studying auto workers in a new California suburb, finds that "None . . . hoped his children would follow in his occupational footsteps. . . . An overwhelming majority of the sample say they want college educations for their sons."

Antonovsky and Lerner,[8] studying the occupational aspirations of lower-class Negro and white youth, came up with similar findings and a good analysis of some of the reasons. They find that these young people also stress the professions and white-collar jobs as ideals. They find that Negroes' ambitions are higher than the whites'. They give two reasons for this: First, because the Negroes tend to come from more disorganized home life, they have come to believe that there are only two kinds of American Negroes, the exceptional and the masses. "To succeed can only mean to achieve highest status." There is no in-between. Second, these Negroes know well that skilled trades, small business, and corporation jobs are often closed to them. Another poignant reason is: "The acute problem of lack of self-esteem which besets the members of a minority group which has psychologically accepted its inferior status." They also note significantly: "The high stated aspirations of these Negro youngsters have large components of unrealism."

The small city of upper New York State in this study is quite different from East St. Louis or Kansas City. Yet this analysis makes sense when applied to these border-city Negro workers. There is one difference: we find little difference between the Negro and white packinghouse workers in their desire for professional jobs.

The *Newsweek* study of 1963,[9] conducted by public-opinion analyst Louis Harris, polling over 1,250 Negroes nationally and interviewing 100 Negro leaders, give us additional clues to Negroes' aspirations for their children. The study finds that, of its sample, "A whopping 97 per cent want their children to complete high school." But the study also finds "one out of five Negro families had a child drop out of high school."

The study also raises the issue of unrealism. "The *Newsweek* poll shows that Negroes aspire to almost unrealistic heights. Fully 30 per cent of the rank and file think they are qualified to rise to the professions or white-collar business, which is considerably more than the national average of 24 per cent." The study also finds that some Negroes are well aware that, because of their long subjugation, some of their race may not yet be qualified for better jobs. Here, of course, we run right into the vicious-circle problem.

As for the packinghouse workers, *clearly the hopes of all these parents, both Negro and white, cannot be realized.* Many of their children will not go to college either because they are not qualified or because they have too little money. Furthermore, there will always be blue-collar work. In spite of accelerated automation, there will be many service jobs and semiskilled jobs remaining in the meatpacking industry. Who will man these jobs in the future?

---

[7] Bennett M. Berger, *Working-Class Suburb* (Berkeley: University of California Press, 1960), pp. 20-21.

[8] Aaron Antonovsky and Melvin J. Lerner, "Occupational Aspirations of Lower Class Negro and White Youth," *Social Problems* Vol. 9, No. 2 (Fall, 1959), pp. 132-38, esp. pp. 133 and 135.

[9] *Newsweek*, July 29, 1963, pp. 15-36, esp. pp. 18 and 20.

Some of the blue-collar workers' aspirations for their children are the obvious, normal, and healthy ambitions of parents raised on the American Dream of upward mobility. Indeed, for the Negro workers, their aspirations for themselves and especially for their children can best be gathered up in just a few human words—but to some white people, startling and threatening—the words of James Baldwin:[10] *"Negroes want to be treated like men: a perfectly straightforward statement containing only seven words."*

But there is another aspect to our findings that is by no means obvious. Unions and managements rarely discuss it. Workers seem hardly aware of it. In my opinion, this aspect is unrealistic and disturbing: many packinghouse workers, both Negro and white (and Negro perhaps more than white) seem to have a false idealization of the white-collar job and a false devaluation of the blue-collar job—of its dignity, its potential satisfactions, of its considerable skills and responsibilities. The thinking of these people lays bare the relative meaninglessness and apparent irrelevancy of much factory work to life in the American society.

What are the implications of all this for the future? The problem of the meaningfulness of work is complex and difficult. The engineer, the economist, the industrial psychologist and sociologist, management and union leaders —these people can help. But the values of our society regarding both the meaning of work and the meaning of leisure—these are more elusive. In my opinion, the philosopher and the theologian will need to become more involved. What I am saying is that the meaninglessness of work in American society is closely related to the meaninglessness of life to many American workers. Working toward the solution of this problem is no small challenge.

BIBLIOGRAPHY

Antonovsky, Aaron, and Melvin J. Lerner, "Occupational Aspirations of Lower Class Negro and White Youth," *Social Problems,* Vol. 9, No. 2 (Fall 1959).

Armour and Company, United Packinghouse, Food and Allied Workers, AFL-CIO, and Amalgamated Meat Cutters and Butcher Workmen of North America, AFL-CIO, *Progress Report, Automation Committee.*

Baldwin, James, *Nobody Knows My Name.* New York: The Dial Press, Inc., 1961.

Buckley, Louis F., "Discriminatory Aspects of the Labor Market of the 60's," *Review of Social Economy,* Vol. XIX, No. 1 (March, 1961).

Ginzberg, Eli, *The Negro Potential.* New York: Columbia University Press, 1956.

Greer, Scott, *Last Man In.* New York: The Free Press of Glencoe, Inc., 1959.

Hope, John, II, *Equality of Opportunity.* Washington: Public Affairs Press, 1956.

Morrow, J. J., "American Negroes—A Wasted Resource," *Harvard Business Review,* Vol. 35, No. 1 (January-February, 1957), pp. 65-74.

Norgren, P. H., A. N. Webster, R. D. Borgeson, and M. B. Patten, *Employing the Negro in American Industry.* New York: Industrial Relations Counselors, Inc., 1959.

Purcell, Theodore V., *Blue Collar Man.* Cambridge: Harvard University Press, 1960.

---

[10] James Baldwin, *Nobody Knows My Name* (New York: The Dial Press, Inc., 1961), p. 67.

————, "Management Versus Jim Crow," *Management of Personnel Quarterly*. University of Michigan, Vol. 1, No. 4 (Summer, 1962).

————, *The Worker Speaks His Mind*. Cambridge: Harvard University Press, 1953.

Wilcock, Richard C., and Walter H. Franke, *Unwanted Workers*. New York: The Free Press of Glencoe, Inc., 1963.

Careers as Concerns of Blue-Collar Girls

ETHELYN DAVIS

CAREER concerns of blue-collar girls may be related to their social position both as women and as members of working-class families. By adolescence the young girl is well aware of the different role expectations for men and women, and at least to some extent realizes that the entire range of occupational choices might wisely be narrowed to those considered appropriate for women. For the young girl in a blue-collar family, the range of occupational choices may be narrowed further. The occupational aspirations of parents and friends, the amount of education she expects to be able to obtain, as well as the attitudes she foresees that her future husband will hold regarding her work, may reduce the possibilities from which a blue-collar girl may realistically make her selection.

Students of all family backgrounds are introduced to similar occupational information through school sources. Movies and television make certain positions more visible to all viewers. In childhood fantasy, the blue-collar girl may have seen herself occupying any of these positions. However, by adolescence, and especially by the last years of high school, the reality of work is near enough for her selections to be relatively practical and possible for her personally.

Friedan traces the developments of the past ten years in American society by which the interest of women in "careers" has been greatly reduced and emphasis has been placed almost wholly on home, husband, and children.[1] Under these circumstances, occupational ambition would scarcely be appropriate for the woman worker. In studying working-class wives, Rainwater found that they conceived of their role as centering in the care of husband and children, and that they expected their satisfactions to come from concerns for others rather than any personal achievement outside the home.[2] To

---

[1] Betty Friedan, *The Feminine Mystique* (New York: W. W. Norton & Company, Inc., 1963), pp. 15-16.
[2] Lee Rainwater, Richard Coleman, and Gerald Handel, *Workingman's Wife* (New York: Oceana Publications, Inc., 1959), p. 26.

what extent does the adolescent blue-collar girl reflect these trends as she talks of her occupational choices?

This study explores the goals, ambitions, and interests of the adolescent daughter of the blue-collar worker in relation to her probable work experience in later life. The information has been obtained from questionnaires completed by 4,760 students in the seventh through the twelfth grades in 70 communities in Texas and near-by states during December, 1961 and in 1962.[3] The 2,549 girls, who represent 54 per cent of the total, have been the main object of this study, although boys' answers have been included for comparative purposes. The major portion of the analysis is based upon responses of 925 girls who are daughters of blue-collar workers and represent 42 per cent of the total sample of girls.[4]

OCCUPATIONAL GOALS

According to Friedan, the "feminine mystique" has returned women to the home and created a sense of guilt in those who are gainfully employed, especially if they enjoy working. She finds that the popular women's magazines have contributed greatly to this new feminine image by limiting articles to those concerning home and family and refusing to admit that women have any interest in outside affairs.[5] Adolescent daughters, as well as their mothers, are exposed to the views in these magazines, and they may accept the feminine role as centered entirely in husband and children with no place for career. Marriage and family are clearly in the minds of the girls in this study, and their replies indicate this as one of their major concerns for the future. Nevertheless, when asked the type of job they hope to obtain when they finish school, most of them state some occupation outside the home. Forty-two of the 925 blue-collar girls give "housewife" only, indicating that they do not intend to work elsewhere, although eight give a combination with housewife first, and one wants to be a missionary or housewife.

The girls state significantly more frequently than the boys that they have given much thought to the type of work they should enter when they finish school. This may reflect the girl's reaction to the prospect of a dual role as housewife and worker, which the boy does not need to consider, as well as to the limitations which are placed upon her choices. In American society it may no longer be fashionable for women to speak of "careers," but 60 per cent of the blue-collar girls believe that most women would like to have a job some day in addition to a home and children. This proportion is significantly higher than for girls whose fathers are in other than blue-collar occupations and is also greater than the response of the boys. Boys more frequently believe that girls should not work unless it is absolutely necessary, and thus they reflect the traditional male attitude toward women who work.

---

[3] The research reported in this paper is a portion of a study in the sociology of youth which has been partially supported by a grant from the Hogg Foundation for Mental Health of the University of Texas.

[4] The blue-collar girls in this study include the daughters of skilled, semiskilled, and unskilled or service workers.

[5] Friedan, *op. cit.*, pp. 33-68.

Thirty-six per cent of the girls feel that it is all right for the wife to work even though it may not be absolutely necessary, which again would indicate that they are not fully convinced that the wife should limit herself entirely to being a homemaker.

How much awareness the adolescent girl may have of the fact that women workers tend to be concentrated in a few occupations is unknown, but over half of these girls select one of the four categories of secretary, teacher, nurse, and beautician. "Secretary" far outnumbers any other and is over twice as frequent as "teacher," the nearest to it (see Table 1). Occupational choices for the blue-collar and other girls are similar, except in the areas of secretarial work, teaching, and certain other professions. More blue-collar girls wish to be secretaries, and fewer of them express an interest in teaching or others of the professions. Airline stewardess, doctor, model, laboratory technician, and commercial artist are chosen with some frequency, although 47 other types of work are mentioned by one or more of the 925 blue-collar girls.

The older girls show less interest in nursing and more interest in secretarial work, perhaps reflecting the trend from fantasy to reality with the approach of specific job preparation. The recognition that certain occupations require not only more education, but also better academic standing is reflected in the greater desire among those of higher scholastic averages to be doctors, teachers, and other professionals. Beautician, model, and various jobs that do not require special training are mentioned more often by those whose scholastic achievement is below average. Those with average scholastic records more frequently mention nurse, secretary, and stewardess. The various types of nurses and secretaries, and the different levels of preparation required of them, are seldom indicated by mention of a specific type of nurse or secretary.

Although some of the students do not foresee anything to prevent them from attaining the position they desire, the majority recognize that some obstacles may affect the achievement of these goals. *Only one-fourth of the blue-collar girls really expect someday to obtain the job they would most like to have.* Many factors could be responsible for this, but a large proportion

Table 1

OCCUPATIONS DESIRED BY 925 BLUE-COLLAR GIRLS

Occupation	Number	Occupation	Number
Secretary	240	Interior Decorator	10
Teacher	122	Lawyer	10
Nurse	101	Saleswoman	9
Beautician	63	Fashion Designer	8
Housewife	51	Church work	8
Airline Stewardess	31	Business	8
Doctor	18	Scientist	6
Model	18	Armed Services	6
Laboratory Technician	14	Rancher	6
Clerical Work	13	Other Professional	24
Commercial Artist	12	Other White-Collar	11
IBM Operator	12	Miscellaneous	24
Entertainer	11	Undecided	41
Social Worker	11	No Answer	37

state a desired occupation and then give "housewife" as the occupation they expect to obtain. Marriage is seen as the most possible obstacle to the achievement of the desired occupation, and 41 per cent foresee marriage as preventing them from securing the employment they most desire. Marriage may make it impossible for the girl to work outside the home or may simply mean choosing a less desired job. Boys do not expect marriage to affect their chosen careers as do the girls. The possibility of their career being affected by marriage does not show a relationship to any particular occupational choice nor is there any difference between the blue-collar and other girls. All girls are exposed to the current ideas regarding the feminine role, and they appear to be aware of its demands and expectations.

A lack of education is another possible obstacle, and those who desire to be teachers and other professionals are most aware of this possibility. A lack of education is mentioned more than twice as often by the blue-collar girls as compared with the daughters of professionals and managers. This difference in educational goals is reflected in the differing attitude toward college. While 86 per cent of the daughters of professionals and managers would like to attend college, only 44 per cent of the blue-collar girls so desire. Those who wish to be doctors, teachers, and other professionals are especially concerned about college, whereas those wishing to be beauticians, secretaries, or housewives with no outside occupation are much less interested. One-fourth of the positions desired by the blue-collar girls would definitely require college preparation, and the girls wishing these occupations are realistic in their interest in higher education. One-third of the blue-collar girls think that teen-agers are more interested in working than in going to school, as compared with only 13 per cent of the other girls. The difference in educational goals of blue-collar families and middle-class families is often noted in sociological literature, and Rainwater's study of working-class mothers found that, even though they might speak of the child's obtaining a college education, they seldom took organized action toward such goals.[6]

Two occupations, although quite different in qualifications and duties, may seem equally attractive to an adolescent who is attempting to make a definite decision. A number of the 925 girls are not sufficiently certain to state any preference. With the more glamorous characteristics of some jobs portrayed through television, movies, Career Day programs, and other sources, a choice may become increasingly difficult. Two or more jobs are mentioned by 43 of the 925 blue-collar girls. The most frequent combinations are (1) teacher or secretary, (2) doctor or nurse, (3) teacher or nurse, (4) teacher or beautician, and (5) nurse or secretary. These are occupations which have frequently been chosen by other girls and do not represent an ambivalence between a girl's unusual and customary choice. They also represent the selection of an alternative if the first choice cannot be accomplished. The girl who knows she could not finish medical school may be able to complete a course in nursing. A job as secretary, vocational nurse, or beautician will require less preparation than a position as teacher.

---

[6] Rainwater, *op. cit.*, p. 102.

Careers as Concerns of Blue-Collar Girls

Certain occupations in our culture have traditionally been reserved for women. Many others have been barred to women even though women might qualify for them. Women are increasingly being permitted to enter the labor force at higher levels.[7] During the prosperity of the past 20 years, the labor reserve has been the married women.[8] When more workers are needed in certain types of positions, an appeal is made to women workers. Girls are being encouraged to enter the fields of engineering, science, and mathematics, even though these are traditionally men's occupations. Only one of these 925 blue-collar girls wishes to be an engineer, six would like to be scientists, and none mentions mathematician. Although there has been a large increase in the proportion of women employed as clerical and sales workers, the professional and technical workers have shown a slight decline in recent years. Most American families still appear to accept an ideology holding that, if the wife is gainfully employed, her position should be lower than her husband's in the occupational hierarchy and should yield a smaller portion of the family income.[9] The old image of the career woman is fading, and the adolescent girl today is exposed to a different view of the woman worker. She does not, therefore, seem to aspire to positions which require intense competition with men or which men wish to consider their province.

The occupational choices of these girls may also be a reflection of their class-linked acceptance of society's traditional definition of appropriate positions for women. The choices also show the selection of an occupation which may be available anywhere the husband may locate, because his position will probably determine the community in which the family will live. They also may be related to the anticipated satisfactions from doing this type of work.

It must be noted that there are traditional women's occupations which are mentioned rarely by these girls. Only one girl wants to be a waitress, one a cook, one an elevator operator, one a seamstress, and four telephone operators. None mentions a desire to be a maid. The proportion of women employed as household workers has shown a particularly large decline in recent years. Paid employment for women has tended to become less physically tiring and to have more status than formerly.[10] This lack of interest in certain occupations may simply be a reflection of this trend.

The lack of interest in particular jobs may also indicate that work is seen as a ladder of social mobility rather than a lateral move. Empey's study of high school boys found that the level of aspiration was higher for middle-class boys when measured by absolute standards, but that the relative occupational-status aspirations of the working-class boys were significantly higher than the occupational statuses of their fathers. When working-class boys aspired to get ahead, they chose occupations at different status levels

---

[7] Ruel Denney, "American Youth Today," *Daedalus* (Winter, 1962), p. 136.

[8] "Change and Choice for the College Woman," *AAUW Journal*, Vol. 55 (May, 1962), p. 276.

[9] F. Ivan Nye and Lois W. Hoffman, *The Employed Mother in America* (Chicago: Rand McNally & Co., 1963), p 5.

[10] *Ibid.*, p. 11.

from those of the higher strata.[11] Although these girls do not aspire as often to positions in teaching and other professions, their level of aspiration is largely beyond that of their parents.

Many studies have asked for prestige rankings of occupations, but these often are concerned with the positions most common to men. The listing from this questionnaire included a number of occupations common for women. When the prestige ranking of the blue-collar girls is compared with the frequency with which each of these occupations is chosen by the girls, it is found that, although "doctor" ranks first in prestige, it is seventh in frequency of self-choice; "nurse" is second in prestige and third in choice; "teacher" is fourth in prestige and third in frequency of desirability; "secretary" is fifth in prestige and first in frequency; "beautician" is eight in prestige and fourth in frequency of choice. Frequency of choice as an occupation ranks above prestige for "secretary," "teacher," "beautician," and "housewife." It would seem that a high prestige ranking of the occupation is not an important factor to the selection of the occupation. These rankings are very similar to those given by the daughters of professionals and managers. The selection of the occupation, then, appears to be realistic whereas the rankings reflect the absorption of middle-class standards. Occupations such as waitress, cook, and elevator operator, which were seldom chosen, were not included in the listing, and the extent to which prestige might be related to a lack of interest in these positions is not known from this study. Several students refused to rank the occupations because they felt that all jobs should have the same prestige.

BASES FOR SELECTION OF OCCUPATIONS

In explaining the basis for their choice of occupation, the blue-collar girls say most frequently that this has been their own choice. The most important influence from others has come from parents, but there seems to be little difference in the choice of an occupation according to parents' suggestions. Regardless of social class, they do not feel that their parents have tried to guide them into particular occupations.

Table 2

OCCUPATIONS RANKED BY PRESTIGE AND FREQUENCY
OF CHOICE BY BLUE-COLLAR GIRLS

Rank by Prestige	Occupation	Rank by Frequency of Choice
1	Doctor	6
2	Nurse	3
3	Teacher	2
4	Lawyer	8
5	Secretary	1
6	Housewife	5
7	Social Worker	7
8	Beautician	4

[11] LaMar T. Empey, "Social Class and Occupational Aspiration: A Comparison of Absolute and Relative Measurement," *American Sociological Review*, Vol. 21 (December 1956), p. 708.

Careers
as Concerns
of Blue-Collar
Girls

The second most important influence they feel has come from reading about the job. This would include ideas obtained incidentally in fiction as well as from articles intended to explain the job. Reading has been particularly influential for those who wish to be stewardesses, nurses, models, and the more unusual professional selections, such as psychiatrist and occupational therapist.

Knowing someone engaged in the work they are selecting has influenced particularly those who desire to be teachers, nurses, secretaries, and beauticians. Those choosing other professions and white-collar jobs have been influenced little by acquaintances, and none of those interested in becoming an airline stewardess has been affected by knowing someone engaged in this occupation. More blue-collar girls feel that their friends have influenced them than do the other girls. This has been especially true for those desiring to be beauticians, housewives, and teachers, and has had little effect upon those wishing to be nurses or to engage in other professions. Friends would not be expected to broaden the range of desired occupations, since their knowledge of work opportunities is probably not very extensive.

Teachers, counselors, Career Day programs, and other school personnel are considered to have contributed only a small part toward the selection of their occupation, and this part has consisted largely in creating an interest in teaching and other professions. A knowledge of possible careers has been broadened through these contacts, but the middle-class bias of these programs may be responsible for the smaller influence they have had on the actual choice.

The girls who wish to be nurses and secretaries especially note the influence of movies and television. Both of these occupations have been dramatized in popular television programs. Blue-collar girls who belong to fewer clubs and have fewer other extracurricular activities perhaps devote more time to watching television and would be exposed to these suggestions.

A lack of sufficient knowledge about possible occupations is acknowledged by many of the girls, and three-fourths are quite positive that they would like more information about different types of work and job requirements and opportunities. One reason for the concentration of choices in such a few occupations may be a lack of knowledge about other possibilities. Schools have attempted to assist students through vocational counseling and Career Day programs. The wide variety of occupations available today makes it difficult to present an over-all view of job opportunities and descriptions. Beauticians are invited to Career Day programs, but the majority of occupations discussed at these meetings are college-centered and of greater interest to middle-class students.

The choice of occupation of the daughter might be related to the work in which her mother is engaged. Two-thirds of the mothers of both blue-collar and other girls are not working outside the home. This proportion is considered typical for women as a whole in the United States.[12] When they are employed, the mothers of the blue-collar girls are less frequently engaged in professional occupations. Only 6 per cent of the blue-collar girls

---

[12] Nye and Hoffman, *op. cit.*, p. 7.

wish to enter the occupation of their mothers. Most of these are secretaries, although there are a few teachers, salesclerks, and nurses. The number of mothers employed as waitresses, salesclerks, seamstresses, and maids and in factory work far exceeds the number of daughters who wish such occupations. The mothers may serve as "models of disassociation" and so lead the daughters to desire other occupations. Rainwater found that working-class wives considered their lives dull and monotonous, and even those who worked did not feel that their lives were any more interesting.[13] These daughters may be seeking occupations which will help keep their lives from following the same pattern.

Many factors may influence the desirability of a position, and these may vary from one person to another. What makes a job seem attractive to one person may not appeal to another. The majority of the blue-collar girls say they have selected their occupation because it sounds interesting and because they think they would enjoy this type of work or some special aspect of it. Those who want to be teachers often say that they like children, whereas those interested in being airline stewardesses feel it will offer something exciting and different. A large proportion of the blue-collar girls say they have chosen the type of occupation mentioned because they want to help others. Boys' reasons are that the work sounds interesting, it pays well, and they think they will enjoy it. Girls say that they want a job where they can deal with people, whereas boys prefer to be their own boss or are less concerned about working with others. Forty per cent of the boys feel that the most important feature of a job is for it to pay well, while only 24 per cent of the girls agree with this statement.

The blue-collar girls who have chosen their occupation because it offers a chance to help others have selected especially to be teachers and nurses, and so would seem to be realistic in their choice. This desire to help others may be related to the girls' acceptance of the feminine role based upon a subordination of individualistic goals to those of the family as a group.[14] A much smaller number of the girls have selected a position they think will provide an opportunity to get ahead, and none of these wishes to be a teacher or nurse. A strong desire to get ahead would not be consistent with the new feminine role.

ANTICIPATED WORK SATISFACTIONS

As to the most important features of working on any job, the blue-collar girls rank enjoyment of the work itself as first; the chance to help others is second; working with nice people is third; security of steady work is fourth. High pay is ranked fifth and the opportunity for rapid rise is sixth. The emphasis upon relationships with other people rather than upon getting ahead may be noted, as it is compared with the difference in the role of the wife and husband in the family situation.

Married women who are employed give money as their chief reason for

---

[13] Rainwater, *op. cit.,* pp. 33-40.

[14] Florence Kluckhohn, "The American Woman's Role," *AAUW Journal,* Vol. 55 (May, 1962), p. 207.

working, and the pay which the job brings is important to them. Whether it is the real reason or whether they consider it an acceptable reason, they seem to be consistent in this reply.[15] The adolescent daughters do not reflect the same attitude, for they consistently rank high pay as a minor consideration in selecting or holding a job. This desire to help others, which is so frequently expressed by the adolescents, may be satisfied among the employed mothers in their care for husbands and children. A job, to them, would have more appeal through other characteristics. However, the adolescent girl appears to have been socialized to feel that the woman's role is that of helper to others, and she sees this in both work and her future home.

Ambition, then, is not an important consideration for these girls. The way in which this seems to be accepted is demonstrated in several types of replies. Forty-nine per cent of the boys want people to think of them as ambitious; 33 per cent of the girls feel this way. Half of the blue-collar girls feel that ambition is far more important for a boy than for a girl, reflecting some of the difference between the working-class wife and the professional wife. Although 81 per cent of the girls think it is as important for a girl to graduate from high school as it is for a boy, the blue-collar girls reply significantly less often than do the other girls. Their belief in the value of high school graduation as the means to a better job is greater than that of the other girls. The fact that the occupations selected by blue-collar girls less frequently require college education would emphasize more strongly the importance of high school graduation, because this achievement will probably terminate their schooling. The blue-collar girls, then, state that an education is important because it helps get a better job, and a better job is defined as one they will enjoy and one where they can help others. This attitude toward education appears to coincide with working-class adult ideas regarding education.

WORK EXPERIENCE

One of the difficulties of adolescents today is the lack of opportunity for work experience in an urban-industrial society. This seems to be especially true for girls. Work experience in adolescence could help smooth the transition to the world of work and afford an opportunity to assume

Table 3

MOST IMPORTANT FEATURES OF A JOB AS RANKED
BY GIRLS AND BOYS

	Rank	
Work Satisfaction	Girls	Boys
Enjoyment of the work itself	1	1
Chance to help others	2	6
Working with nice people	3	5
Security of steady work	4	3
High pay	5	2
Opportunity for advancement and promotion . . .	6	4

[15] Nye and Hoffman, *op. cit.*, pp. 23-25.

responsibility gradually.[16] Twenty-seven per cent of the blue-collar girls work after school or on Saturdays, and this does not differ significantly from the daughters of fathers who are engaged in other than blue-collar occupations. Over half of the girls who work are baby sitters; 20 per cent are clerks in stores; the others are distributed between waitresses, receptionists, hospital workers, and a few miscellaneous types of jobs. Both groups of girls agree wholeheartedly that it is good for teen-agers to work while in high school and that they should have some work experience by the time they complete high school. The lack of work during high school makes decisions regarding employment reflect the orientation of others in American society more than personal convictions based upon real-life experiences.

SUMMARY AND CONCLUSIONS

The blue-collar girl sees her role as one of demonstrating the qualities of friendliness, good appearance, kindness, consideration, and concern for other people. She expects her satisfactions to come from these characteristics, whether they derive from caring for a husband and children or from an occupation outside the home. She is aware of the importance of femininity in the woman's role. However, she is not completely convinced that woman's only place is in the home and that work should not be considered. She has thought seriously about what her future role will be, and she thinks that girls often want to work in addition to caring for their families.

The selection of an occupation is limited largely to the few best-known women's occupations. Her absolute level of aspiration is not as high as that of the white-collar girl, but it is well beyond that of her parents. Her mother's occupation appears to hold little interest for her. The occupation which she selects show a certain amount of mobility in the difference between her choice and her mother's current position, although not so much as might be possible if she were to desire a professional position. She feels a lack of sufficient information about jobs and would certainly like more help in making her decision. Nevertheless, she displays a certain amount of knowledge about types of work in her selections in relation to the education she expects to obtain, the academic record needed, and the satisfactions to be expected from different types of jobs. Prestige ranking appears to have little influence on her choice, but the fact none of the less desired positions, which would probably have low prestige in her ranking, were included in this question might have affected this response. Had jobs such as maid, elevator operator, or waitress been included in the listing, the result might appear to be different.

The blue-collar girl is quite similar to the girl from other occupational categories in the basis for selecting a job, in the work satisfactions she expects to derive, and in work experience. She differs in occupational goals in having less desire to be a teacher and more to be a secretary, and in having less interest in other professional positions. She feels to a greater extent that the man's role is still predominant, in being of the opinion that he should

---

[16] H. Kirk Dansereau, "Work and the Teen-Ager," *Annals of the American Academy of Political and Social Science,* Vol. 338 (November, 1961), p. 50.

be more ambitious, that it is more important for him to complete high school, and that women should not work after marriage unless it is necessary.

The recognition of obstacles to prevent the achievement of her desired role is quite realistic, with marriage and lack of sufficient education as the chief deterrents to the desired goal. This is especially important to the blue-collar girl, who is more likely to marry younger and receive less education than the white-collar daughter. The selection of an occupation has been influenced especially by sources nearest to her, such as parents and friends, and by outside resources which are available to all, such as reading and television. School influences have been less important, perhaps owing to their middle-class bias.

Major work satisfaction is not to come from advancement in a position, from ambition, or from high pay, but rather from service to others. This expectation reinforces society's treatment of the woman worker and helps keep a distinction between the work world of the man and the woman. Expecting satisfactions of a different nature from those of the boy may relieve the girl of some of the frustrations which might otherwise come from the differential treatment of men and women employees and may keep her, as a wife, from being a competitor with her husband. The occupations which she chooses are most frequently those which offer the opportunity to derive satisfactions from service to others. They are also traditional women's occupations, and she shows little interest in pioneering into the man's work world or in competing with him. Some of the difficulty in interesting girls in fields in which there is a shortage of workers may be accounted for in this way. Traditional blue-collar conservatism may also reduce her interest in entering these work areas.

Despite the realism involved in many of her decisions and explanations, she also displays a certain amount of idealism regarding work. Her own lack of actual job experience, as well as her youth, may contribute to her idealistic view that work is to be enjoyable, interesting, and helpful to others, even though the parents' work is frequently lacking in these qualities. Work, to her, is not just for pay to support a family or to help buy extra luxuries, or the means to recognition and distinction through ambition and striving, but is a way of achieveing certain desired personal and socially acceptable goals and satisfactions which are to come through assistance to others.

The Uncommitted Adolescent: Candidate for Gang Socialization*

LARRY KARACKI

JACKSON TOBY

SEVERAL influential theories trace gang delinquency to social and economic deprivations experienced by segments of the adolescent male population.[1] Residence in central-city slum districts, low socioeconomic background, or membership in a disadvantaged racial group predispose a youngster to failure in competition for the goals of American life: status, power, money. The experiencing of this failure or its anticipation creates a "problem of adjustment" for which membership in the delinquent gang may become the "solution."

This paper describes a gang (to be called the Dukes) which does not seem accounted for by deprivation—even by *relative* deprivation. While the Dukes manifested the familiar pattern of poor academic and work performance, on the one hand, and street-corner violence and petty theft, on the other, the members did not appear especially deprived either by objective or subjective criteria. A more plausible explanation seems to be that their academic failures, their disinterest in conventional occupational roles, and their emergence as a delinquent gang were all attributable to the same underlying factor: a failure to develop commitments to adult roles and values.

The Dukes used a small park as a hangout—as well as the locus of card games and athletic events. During the summer of 1960, when we did most of our field work, there were about 33 members, the majority 18 years of age or older. Although there is a substantial Negro minority in the large Midwestern city where the Dukes live (about a quarter of the city's population in 1960), there were no Negro members in the gang. This is not surprising; the Hamilton Park neighborhood had only one nonwhite resident in 1950 out of a total population for the census tract of 4485. Hamilton Park is a predominantly Catholic neighborhood, and all of the Dukes except one were Catholic. And, except for one member who was born in Ireland, all members were native-born of Irish, Italian, and German extraction.

* The field work on which this paper is based was supported by the Youth Development Program of the Ford Foundation. Reprinted from *Sociological Inquiry*, Vol. XXXII, No. 2 (Spring 1962). The paper is reprinted by permission of the authors and *Sociological Inquiry*.

[1] Albert K. Cohen, *Delinquent Boys* (New York: The Free Press of Glencoe, Inc., 1955); Richard A. Cloward and Lloyd E. Ohlin, *Delinquency and Opportunity* (New York: The Free Press of Glencoe, Inc., 1960); Clifford R. Shaw and Henry D. McKay, *Juvenile Delinquency and Urban Areas* (Chicago: University of Chicago Press, 1942).

The
Uncommitted
Adolescent:
Candidate
for Gang
Socialization

The Dukes organized during the summer of 1955 with an initial member-ship of about 20. There was an election of officers and the establishment of a club treasury. At the insistence of their first and only president, they chose the name "Mafia," because it stood for "organization" and because he thought it meant "the upper hand, top dog" in gangsterdom. However, when several parents objected to this name, it was changed to the "Dukes." Ostensibly, the purpose of the club was to hold parties at the homes of the various members. From 1955 to 1958, however, social activities took second place to delinquency. The Dukes, individually and collectively, were involved in a series of brawls which ultimately gained them city-wide notoriety. For some, this was a continuation of earlier behavior since they already had histories of delinquency. And there is a real possibility, as in the case of their president, that some joined the Dukes with this end in mind. For others, however, membership in the Dukes brought with it their first experience with serious lawbreaking.

Initially, their delinquencies were confined mainly to petty thefts from neighborhood stores. Gradually they moved on to more serious larcenies so that a partial listing of things they stole would include food and drink, cigarettes, clothing, toilet articles, prophylactics, athletic equipment, portable radios, records, automobiles and parts, tools, and money. A few Dukes were involved in armed robberies. Nearly all the Dukes engaged in sexual inter-course with promiscuous dates and prostitutes. Several were put on probation on a rape charge, and one was reported to have fathered a child by a mentally retarded girl. A few "played the queers," both for "kicks" and for money payments. Added to this, there were numerous minor offenses such as malicious mischief, drinking under age, and traffic violations.

Despite a diversity of offenses which seemed to stop only at drug using, the major preoccupation of the gang was street brawls. The Dukes saw themselves as a fighting gang with a deserved reputation for being the toughest in town. This emphasis upon fighting reflected the status hierachy within the group; the best fighters tended to occupy positions of esteem and leadership. However, the Dukes were not completely emancipated from the norms of their families and their neighborhood. They rationalized their brawls as self-defense, maintaining that they had never started a fight. Instead, their fights had always been provoked by "wise guys," "punks," and others who, unlike the Dukes, did not realize that fighting was "stupid." Viewed in this manner, they could maintain that it is wrong to start a fight and at the same time justify defending themselves with whatever means were available. As one member put it, "Everybody knows that fighting is stupid so there's no sense in giving [their enemies] a chance." Thus, they took pride in their reputation as a fighting gang for, although they claimed not to have sought such a reputation, it was, after all, a just and fitting reward for teaching their provokers a lesson. This rationalization was so effective that the con-demnations of the police, school officials, clergymen, and, in some instances, their parents did not seem to bother them.

Their fights ranged from impromptu scuffles involving one or two Dukes to well-planned "rumbles" in which almost the entire membership participated. Many took place at Hamilton Park (their "turf"), but fights also occurred at schools, taverns, restaurants, parties and on the street. The *number* of fights was considerable and undoubtedly contributed to their reputation, but their brutal, almost savage behavior during some fights was even more important. For instance, on one occasion a Duke hospitalized two opponents with a blow from behind with an aluminum crutch. At another time, the stomping administered to an opponent was such [as] to require hospitalization for several weeks. Moreover, the stomping did not stop until the forcible removal of the assaulting Duke. On other occasions, opponents received broken noses or arms or similar injuries. Through all of this, the Dukes claimed to be blameless. As the crutch-wielder put it, "I never started a fight. I can really say that."

By 1960, the Dukes were changing back into a social club. Partly because the members had reached the age when gangs spontaneously disintegrate, partly because the Recreation Department had assigned a part-time detached worker to the group, it had taken on the title and appearance of a social-athletic club. The members engaged in informal athletic events and held dances on a fairly regular basis. The change to more conventional activities split the Dukes into two large cliques which, while capable of concerted action, were characterized by separate and often opposing interests. The members of one clique expressed no further interest in brawling or stealing; in the other, delinquency persisted, but its frequency appeared considerably reduced as compared with the past. Despite this change, the fact remains that the Dukes had been a delinquent gang, yet it did not seem to fit the deprivation theories of gang formation.

INADEQUACIES OF DEPRIVATION THEORY
TO ACCOUNT FOR THE DUKES

We have two reasons for considering deprivation theories inadequate to account for the emergence of the Dukes: (1) The socioeconomic background of the members seemed at least average, and (2) The nondelinquent adjustments made by most members in 1960 and 1961 suggested that major obstacles did not exist to their participation in the educational and occupational life of the community. Let us first consider their socioeconomic origins. They definitely were not slum dwellers: they resided in an area at the periphery of the city which, according to census tract data for 1950, compare[s] quite favorably with the city as a whole. In 1950, 89 per cent of the dwelling units in the census tract including Hamilton Park were built in 1920 or later, while the city figure was 35 per cent. (See Table 1.) The median value of single-unit dwellings for sale within the tract was $11,974 versus $10,027 for the city as a whole. There was a marked difference between resident-owners in the tract and the city as a whole, 75 per cent and 42 per cent, respectively.

There were fewer male unemployed in the Hamilton Park area than in the city (3% vs. 6%) and a higher proportion of workers in white-collar and skilled-labor occupations. Moreover, median family income was $4,237, a figure far in excess of the $3,153 city median and bettered by only 10 of the

The Uncommitted Adolescent: Candidate for Gang Socialization

190 city census tracts reporting this information. Only when educational background is considered do city figures closely approximate the Hamilton Park area. In both instances, the median school year completed was 9.4. It would seem, then, that the Hamilton Park area was far from a slum area. Using occupation as our measure, the best characterization of the area in terms of socioeconomic class would seem to be that it was mainly an upper working-class and lower middle-class neighborhood. Indicative of this, the four occupational categories generally regarded as white-collar comprised 35.6 per cent of the total male employed while the craftsmen and foremen category was 31.5 per cent of this total.

The Dukes seemed to be a representative sample of the Hamilton Park population. Most of their parents were homeowners who had resided in the area for a number of years and whose occupations (see Table 2) were primarily upper working and lower middle class. From this description, we would not maintain that their background was devoid of deprivation. Our impression, however, is that it would be stretching deprivation theory beyond its intended limits and beyond possible empirical validation to argue that the disadvantaged position of the residents of such a neighborhood is enough to provide the etiological force for subcultural delinquency.

It is true that the Dukes tended to have poor school and work records, and such histories are often taken as indicants of alienation and deprivation. For example, eight of the seventeen for whom official school records were obtained had withdrawn from high school, and interview data for the others showed a comparable degree of early school-leaving. Moreover, of the nine recorded graduates, none ranked above the third decile in his graduating class while six were in the last three deciles. This poor performance is even worse than it appears to be; the Dukes who graduated usually did so at vocational school or, if they remained at an academic high school, concentrated upon mechanical and shop courses. One, for example, obtained 120 of his 240 passing credits in shop or closely related courses. Consider further that several of those who graduated had to remain additional semesters, attend summer school, or in other ways make up credits for "flunked" courses. Their work histories present a similar pattern of maladjustment. The majority either had never worked or had held only one or two brief jobs before reaching eighteen. Those with longer work histories often were fired or quit jobs knowing that discharge was imminent. Several turned their jobs into opportunities to commit thefts. Only a few can be said to have approached the norm for a good employee.

These performances are consistent with deprivation theories of alienation and gang formation. What is crucial to know, however, is not merely that the Dukes were poor students and employees, but also the reasons for their inadequacies. And here the indication is that they were not so much unable as unwilling to devote themselves to school or work. Thus, the scores obtained by members of the Dukes on vocational and aptitude tests administered by the detached worker, a trained vocational guidance counselor, indicated in most cases that they had performed far below potentialities. There is, however, more direct evidence: the types of adjustments made by Dukes who at the

Table 1

COMPARATIVE POPULATION AND HOUSING CHARACTERISTICS
OF THE HAMILTON PARK CENSUS TRACT AND THE CITY AS A WHOLE,
1950 CENSUS DATA

Population and Housing Characteristics	Hamilton Park	Total City
A. Population characteristics*		
1. Race:		
White	100.0	83.7
Nonwhite	–	16.3
2. Families and unrelated individuals:		
Families.	92.0	76.0
Unrelated individuals.	8.0	24.0
3. Years of school completed:		
Elementary school or less	47.1	46.1
Finished one year high school or more. . .	51.9	51.0
School years not reported.	1.0	2.9
Median school years completed.	9.4	9.4
4. Income in 1949:		
$4,999 or less	62.0	76.6
$5,000 or more.	34.4	18.2
Income not reported	3.6	5.2
Median income.	$4,237	$3,153
5. Male labor force:		
Employed	97.1	94.1
Unemployed.	2.9	5.9
6. Occupation of male employed:		
Prof., technical and kindred	8.1	6.2
Managers, officials and prop.	8.7	7.7
Clerical and kindred	11.7	9.1
Sales workers	7.1	5.5
Craftsmen, foremen, and kindred	31.5	24.5
Operatives and kindred	21.2	28.4
Private household workers.	–	.1
Service workers.	6.5	7.5
Laborers	4.9	10.1
Occupation not reported.	.3	.9
B. Housing characteristics:		
1. Occupancy:		
Owner occupied	74.8	41.9
Renter occupied	24.2	56.3
Other	1.0	1.8
Median value.	$11,974	$10,027
Median rent	$43.75	$35.23
2. Per cent with indicated substandard conditions:		
No private bath or dilapidated	1.1	13.7
No running water or dilapidated.	.3	5.4
1.01 or more persons per room.	5.0	10.1
3. Year built:		
1919 or earlier.	11.0	65.1
1920 to 1929.	72.2	23.7
1930 or later	16.8	11.2

*Unless otherwise specified, figures are given as percentages.

time of our investigation were (in their words) in the process of "settling down." A number of them had returned to school either to finish high school or to begin college. Of those entering college, one had made a 3.6 average of a possible 4.0 while several others had achieved creditable records. Of those

The Uncommitted Adolescent: Candidate for Gang Socialization

169

who returned to high school, two had done well enough to give serious thought to continuing their education at the college level. In these instances, the return to school was financed by steady employment as illustrated by a Duke who, while attending evening college, was employed at two jobs during the day in order to finance college on a full-time basis. For others, jobs were ends in themselves rather than means for financing further education, for example, a Duke who was completing his plumber's apprenticeship and another who, as a member of the Air Force, was assigned to work at a physics research laboratory.

It should be pointed out that not all the Dukes had made nondelinquent adjustments at school or work at the time of our investigation. Nor would we suggest that all of them were capable of this. But enough had done so to suggest that their early maladjustments at school and on jobs did not derive from an inability to achieve along conventional lines since, if anything, their later accomplishments had to overcome the handicap of early failures. We think that what is needed is an explanation which takes into account what was conspicuously lacking in the Dukes in early adolescence: the motivation to achieve along conventional lines.

Table 2

OCCUPATIONS OF THE FATHERS OF MEMBERS OF THE DUKES

Club Member	Father's Occupation
1. Robert J.	Engineer
2. Harold W.	Manager, parking lot
3. Richard S.	Tavern owner
4. William A.	(Father deceased) Formerly tavern owner
5. William H.	Oreboat captain
6. James E.	Teamster union official
7. Roger M.	Barber
8. Ronald M.	Barber
9. Terrance M.	Fireman; Salesman part time
10. Joseph G.	Fireman
11. Thomas H.	Fireman
12. James C.	Police ambulance driver
13. James B.	Policeman
14. Gerald O.	Plasterer
15. Edward M.	Iron worker
16. Melvin L.	Iron worker
17. Kenneth Y.	Auto mechanic
18. Gerald C.	Factory foreman
19. Edward S.	Factory foreman
20. John L.	Factory foreman
21. Henry G.	Tool and die man
22. John F.	Tool and die man
23. Robert D.	Railroad yardman (retired)
24. William C.	City employee
25. Carmon C.	Construction foreman
26. John A.	Construction laborer
27. Joseph D.	Truck driver
28. Gerald K.	Truck driver
29. Neil I.	Furnace operator (Stepfather)
30. Frank L.	Shirt cutter (Foster father)
31. Donald L.	(Father deceased) Mother cafeteria employee
32. John E.	(Father deceased) Children support mother
33. Richard K.	Unknown

AN ALTERNATIVE EXPLANATION:
LACK OF ADULT COMMITMENTS

Bennett Berger has suggested that the "youth culture" with its emphasis upon such values as irresponsibility, hedonism, and expressive behavior is an "expression of a social system's functional ability to cope with its inevitable failure to achieve perfect socialization." [2] Within this context we think the Dukes can best be understood. For it is our impression that the Dukes failed to develop early in adolescence commitments to adult roles and values which would have mobilized their interests and energies and which would have served to relate them to school and work. In lieu of this, they drew instead upon the youth culture for meaning and purpose, and out of this emerged a delinquent gang.

Some support for this interpretation is to be found in the remarks the Dukes made about high school. One, for example, summed up his academic experience with the comment, "It was something to do in the afternoon." Another remarked, "School was all right, but it didn't appeal to me." Their attitude toward courses was expressed by a Duke who said, "I didn't want to take nothing hard. I wanted to take the easy stuff to get through." And homework drew this rather typical response, "I knew I couldn't sit down most of the time and read. I liked to go out."

Of far greater importance to them was their involvement in the youth culture. Thus one Duke, explaining his lack of concern for school commented, "I wanted fun more than I wanted to go to school." Another, presently in college, accounted for this poor performance during his first years of high school by saying:

> "I guess I tried until the eighth grade. I started slumping then. Other things were more important to me, I guess. I started hanging around [the park] at nights. . . . I guess I was kind of wild when I was a freshman and sophomore. Things seemed so far away that I didn't care."

This involvement in the youth culture was incompatible with diligent performance in school. School was not viewed by the Dukes as an opportunity to prepare for adult occupations or for college. Nor did they select their courses or pursue grades with the future in mind. Instead, they regarded school within the framework of their adolescent interests. Thus, a Duke who made the honor roll in his junior year explained this not by a desire to attend college but as an attempt to make an impression on a girl. Another, noting that he had taken algebra and biology, explained his choice of academic over shop courses by the fact that he could then get out of school earlier. Thus, it was possible for a Duke who had flunked out to express a liking for school while one who had graduated gave the opposite response, the difference appearing to be their differing ability to enjoy themselves at school.

---

[2] Bennett M. Berger, "On the Youthfulness of Youth Cultures" (Mimeographed), p. 3.

FLUNK OUT: "I liked [school] except for homework. I had a big ball. Most of the teachers liked me. They tried to get me out for football and wrestling. I played before, but I just quit. I was too lazy. I wasn't dumb or nothing because, if I study, I could pass. (Did you try to do well in high school?) No, I was just too lazy. If I didn't have fun, I didn't like it. I'm surprised I got as far as I did."

GRADUATE: "I didn't like [school]. I could have had a lot of fun if it wasn't for homework. I figure you go to school all day. They should give it to you then. When you go home, it should be your time. I'd do it sometimes; sometimes not. I'd rather be outside."

Work was also regarded by the Dukes in light of their adolescent interests rather than as a career. Although an imposition, work could provide funds to buy cars or clothes or for dates. As a result, it was not uncommon for a Duke to be employed long enough to purchase, say, a car and then to quit and remain idle until he was again in need of a substantial sum of money.

In addition to explaining their attitude toward school and work, the orientation of the Dukes to youth culture value underlay other aspects of their behavior. It was, for example, a basis by which they distinguished between adolescents whom they considered "normal guys" and pathological creatures they called "Sids":

NORMAL GUYS: "One of our clique."

SIDS: "For Sidney. What do you imagine he'd be like with a name like that? That's a kid that stays by himself or another guy. He's all books. . . . We do what we want to and have a good time. They stay home—they're mamas' boys—while we're out playing ball. (Why do you play ball while a "Sid" will stay home?) Maybe he wants to stay home. (And you?) I'd just rather be out with the guys having a good time. (But why this difference?) Maybe his ideas are different. Maybe his idea of a good time is staying home watching TV. My idea is out with the guys having a good time."

Besides this initial distinction, their attitude toward other adolescents was in part determined by whether they were regarded as being "scholars" or "tough guys" or, in other words, as being oriented to school values or, like themselves, to the youth culture. Thus, "tough guys," by seeking the same reputations as the Dukes, were viewed as rivals or allies depending upon how the Dukes got along with them and were described in such terms as "chicken," "punk," or "member of a brother gang." "Scholars," on the other hand, were not after a tough reputation but good grades, something to which the Dukes were indifferent. Consequently, the Dukes felt neither animosity nor affinity toward them, their attitude being pity for the fun they were missing.

Lastly, it appears that much of their delinquent behavior was an expression of three "youth culture" values: (1) desire for immediate gratification, (2) loyalty to peers, and (3) assertion of masculinity through physical aggression. Their desire for immediate gratification was expressed in a wide range of delinquent and quasi-delinquent activities, such as joy rides through the countryside, beer and wine parties at the park, escapades with homosexuals, and occasional acts of vandalism. Hedonism was also involved on the many occasions when stealing became a game to see who could steal the most as well as in response to a particularly challenging situation, as when the Dukes decided to steal the gumball machine from a particular drugstore. While

KARACKI
TOBY

172

these activities were often rewarding in terms of material benefits, the context in which they occurred suggests that the diversions they provided in what might otherwise have been dull evenings were more important. Apropos of this point, the Dukes reported giving up planned thefts on several occasions upon learning of a party. Lack of "things to do" was their greatest complaint about the Hamilton Park neighborhood.

The importance attached to peer loyalty by the Dukes is best seen in the explanation given by one of them of what "going all out for a guy" meant:

> "If a guy called up and needed help, no matter when he was calling, you'd be willing to give help. Also, if he needed money, you would lend it. And if he was in a fight, you'd be willing to stand by him and get beat up if it meant that. You wouldn't let him down in a tight spot."

Undoubtedly, this motivation contributed to the willingness of the Dukes to fight for each other and for the reputation of the gang. Indicative of this, the reason given for the break-up of the "brother gang" of the Dukes shortly after accepting new members was that a number of the *old* members did not feel that they knew the *new* members well enough to go "all out" for them. Nonetheless, there were instances when Dukes fought or committed thefts as favors for non-Duke friends.

While immediate gratification and peer loyalty were values shared by all the Dukes, the assertion of masculinity through physical aggression was more characteristic of some than others. The best and most active fighters among the Dukes were weight lifters or boxers. (See Table 3.) Those who were "tough guys" tended to be the high-status members of the gang, but it is not clear whether toughness was a prerequisite for high status or whether personalities with strong masculinity needs also sought power over others.

We do not think that this similarity between values expressed by the Dukes in delinquent behavior and those expressed in other areas of life such as school and work was a mere coincidence. On the contrary, we hypothesize that the emergence of the Dukes as a delinquent gang and their involvement in the "youth culture" were two sides of the same coin. In support of this hypothesis, we note that the shift to non-delinquent behavior on the part of many Dukes by 1960 and 1961 had been accompanied by a shift in personal orientation from the youth culture to adult roles and values. That is to say, the nondelinquents tended to be the Dukes who had

Table 3

RELATIONSHIP AMONG FIGHTING PROWESS, INTEREST IN BOXING AND
WEIGHT LIFTING, AND STATUS WITHIN DUKES

Status		High		Medium		Low		
Boxer or Weight Lifter		Yes	No	Yes	No	Yes	No	Total
Fighting Prowess: Superior		3	1	3	4	1	1	13
Good				3				3
Poor or avoided fights ...					4		5	9
Total		3	1	6	8	1	6	25*

*Eight Dukes are omitted for lack of information. Fighting-prowess rankings were supplied by the club president and verified, as well as was possible, by the field researcher. Ratings as to status are estimated on the basis of interview information and personal observation.

The Uncommitted Adolescent: Candidate for Gang Socialization

successfully returned to school or who appeared to have begun to establish work careers. (See Table 4.) Moreover, a number had steady girls and were planning to marry. Several could no longer be considered active members of the Dukes since they made but rare appearances at the Park or other hangouts. They were, as they saw themselves, the less adventuresome, more mature element within the Dukes, and their behavior appeared to bear out their self-conception.

This shift in orientation also was expressed in the comments the Dukes made about themselves. Thus, a Duke who had done poorly in high school but who was currently taking college courses at night and working by day contrasted his high school days with his present situation:

HIGH SCHOOL: "I got C's and D's because I didn't apply myself. I couldn't get myself to study. Something was always coming up. I got by on as little as I could."

PRESENTLY: "I'm a little bored now. I think I would have wanted to go to college. I think I could have gone had I saved. But I think I'm all right now. The way I see it, I'm making an effort to get through. It may take a long time but I'm trying."

Table 4

OCCUPATIONAL AND EDUCATIONAL ACTIVITIES OF THE DUKES AND PARTICIPATION IN DELINQUENT ACTIVITIES AS OF APRIL, 1961*

Continued Delinquency:
 1. Edward M.: Presently in Army.
 2. Henry G.: Recent inductee into Army after year as part-time handy man for city.
 3. Roger M.: Recent inductee into Army after nearly two years unemployed.
 4. Ronald M.: Unemployed nearly two years.
 5. Kenneth Y.: Completing trade school, one year behind class.
 6. William C.: Completing day high school, one year behind class.
 7. Terrance M.: Employed part time as a wall washer.
 8. Richard S.: Employed at government motor pool, seventh job in past year.
 9. Melvin L.: Drop out from college, presently unemployed.
 10. Donald L.: Plumber's apprentice past six months.

Doubtful Delinquency:
 1. Robert D.: In Army.
 2. Gerald K.: In Army.
 3. James B.: Completing first year of college.
 4. Harold W.: Completing second year of college.

Nondelinquent:
 1. William A.: In Army.
 2. John L.: In Army.
 3. John F.: Recent inductee into Army. Had been employed as a machine operator.
 4. Joseph G.: In Army, preparing to become an auto mechanic.
 5. John A.: In Air Force. Assigned to college physics research lab.
 6. Carmon C.: Recently returned from Army. Formerly head copy boy for a local newspaper.
 7. William H.: In Army. Attending night school to receive high school diploma.
 8. Robert J.: Unemployed. Attending night school to obtain high school diploma.
 9. David S.: Salesman in children's store.
 10. Gerald C.: Head chef at local outlet of a national restaurant chain.
 11. Gerald O.: Near completion of plumber's apprenticeship.
 12. Frank L.: Truck driver-handy man for plumbing concern. Attending night school to receive high school diploma. Plans to continue in college.
 13. Neil I.: Machine operator. Attending night school to obtain high school diploma. Plans to continue in college.
 14. Joseph D.: Milkman. Attending night college.
 15. Thomas H.: Full-time timekeeper plus part-time work. Attending night college while saving to attend full time.
 16. James C.: Full-time park employee plus part-time work cleaning a tavern. Attending evening college while saving to attend full time.
 17. John E.: Completing first year of college. B average.

KARACKI
TOBY   *Two Dukes omitted for lack of information.

174

Another who had also been too busy to study during high school spoke first of present disappointments and then of fears for the future:

DISAPPOINTED IN SELF: "Yes, in the fact that I didn't go to college as soon as I got out of school. The fact that I didn't graduate with my class. The fact that I didn't use my *knowledge in high school and do my best. . . .*"

FUTURE FEARS: "The only thing I'd be afraid of would be being a failure in life; not being able to get a steady job and to settle down and raise a good family."

Still another, different from the rest in that he began to "settle down" sooner than most of the others, could find no disappointment in his present situation, his reason being:

"I got a good job. I'll be out of the (plumber's) apprenticeship pretty soon. I think I'm better off than most of the fellows. I look ahead. If you don't start when you're younger and start at the bottom, you got no time. Before you'll know it, you'll be thirty. So I figured right after high school, I'd get my trade and waste no time."

These examples show an emergence of commitments to adult goals and values. In contrast, no change in orientation occurred with Dukes who in 1960 were still involved in brawls and thefts. These Dukes were still oriented to the youth culture; to being weight lifters, boxers, "lovers," "agitators," and "tough-guys." They were the Dukes who were most frequently found at Hamilton Park and who seemed most intent upon having a good time and maintaining their teen-age reputations. Of the delinquents, only a few held steady jobs, the others remaining unemployed for long periods of time or shifting from one job to another, as, for example, one boy who had held seven jobs in a year's time. As to school, a few delinquents had returned but none for very long for, as one of them put it, school "seemed to take up too much of my night."

CONCLUSIONS AND IMPLICATIONS

Our investigation of the Dukes raised questions about the sociocultural conditions making for adolescent gang formation. We suspect that objective deprivations in the economic or political senses are not necessary to produce alienated youth and that "relative deprivation" may conceal circular reasoning, namely, the inference of previous deprivation from existing alienation instead of proof that deprivation was indeed antecedent to alienation. Perhaps the trouble has been that too much delinquency research is done in deprived neighborhoods. In such neighborhoods socioeconomic deprivations and adolescent alienation are found side by side, and the relationship between them is thereby confounded. Perhaps it is more difficult for deprived youngsters to develop commitments to legitimate social structures like the school but not impossible. Yet such commitments (or the lack of them) may be what make gang membership attractive or unattractive. Put another way, objective deprivation may produce a striving to succeed instead of alienation if there are positive commitments to the educational system or the occupational world.[3]

---

[3] Jackson Toby, "Hoodlum or Business Man: An American Dilemma," Marshall Sklare, ed., *The Jews* (New York: The Free Press of Glencoe, Inc., 1958), pp. 542-50.

Modern industrial societies are differentiated societies, not only in the sense of the division of labor but also in the sense of the structural independence of institutions. The individual is ideally supposed to pass through stages of successive commitment, first to the family of orientation, then to the school and to the peer group, and ultimately to the occupational system and to the family of procreation. The adolescent stage is one in which the individual (and particularly the boy) is expected to choose among alternatives in a sense quite different from anything that has gone before. Thus, a boy *has* parents and siblings, but he *decides* on course of study and a job. (The range of choice is probably greater for lower-class boys than for middle-class boys.) Thus, Durkheim's analysis of egoism in an increasingly differentiated society becomes especially pertinent to the situation of adolescents.[4] Gang delinquency may be part of the price industrial societies pay for giving adolescents the freedom to choose among competing commitments.

An Ideology of School Withdrawal*

EDGAR Z. FRIEDENBERG

IN talking about the youngsters who drop out, I am not going to start with the assumption that they ought to be retained. My hunch is that a large proportion of the dropouts may be doing what is best for themselves under the atrocious circumstances that exist. But I do want to analyze those circumstances, and see why the schools have so little to offer these youngsters. For the ambitious middle-class student it has evolved to fit, the public high school and junior high school curriculum serves, I believe, a primarily liturgical function. This is not so true of elementary school, because the basic skills really work. If you read as you are taught there, you will understand at least the words; if you write, your words will be understood; if you follow the rules of arithmetic, your calculations will check out and your books will balance, although you may never have the remotest conception of mathematics.

High school, however, is another matter. What would happen to the businessman, or just citizen, who attempted to apply what he was taught in high school civics to the actual power structure of his community or his country? Who learns to love reading, or to find the kind of reading he can love among the classics and the bitty anthologies of the high school English course? High school history, by and large, is not even propaganda, because nobody is ex-

---

[4] Joseph Neyer, "Individualism and Socialism in Durkheim," Kurt H. Wolff, ed., *Emile Durkheim 1858–1917* (Columbus: The Ohio State University Press, 1960), pp. 32-76.

* "This essay has been adapted from a paper read by the author at the Symposium on School Dropouts held in December, 1962, in Washington under the auspices of the National Education Association and subsequently published in *Commentary*, in June, 1963." The paper is used here with the permission of *Commentary*.

pected to believe it or to be moved by it; it is received as official myth. We tell youngsters that the Pilgrims came to New England searching for religious freedom not in order to give them an understanding of the actual root values of Colonial New England, but in order to provide them with the relevant cliché about the relation of church and state in America, and to let them know that a good middle-class American thinks of "my religious affiliation" or "the faith of my choice." This keeps the youngsters from getting hung up on religion, like an Italian peasant or rural Southerner. As for high school science, it has, since Sputnik, increased its work load enormously and often tries to duplicate the content of college science courses. But essentially, it serves not as an introduction to science but to legitimate the American middle-class epistemology; science proves that Truth is an aggregate of general principles induced from empirical data that observers can agree on. The function of science is to protect people from odd-balls by setting up the rules so that subjective feeling is discounted. The scientific method, then, becomes a way of separating ends and means. When we want to win an election, or spy on the Soviet Union, or redevelop a slum, we go about it scientifically—that is, by defining what we are trying to do as a technical problem. Naturally, we care about the feelings of the people affected; people's emotions are a very important factor. That's why we have psychologists on our team.

It is even truer than the progressives have always maintained that there is no valid distinction between the curriculum and the extra-curriculum. What counts is the total experience of the student, and what he learns in both the classroom and the playing field is a posture, a pattern of anxieties and a pattern of responses for dealing with it. There is seldom any pleasure in scholarship or ideas as such; the classroom and the playing field alike are places where you try to make it, and learn the techniques for making it that alienate you least from your peers. The over-all rules are the same in both: learn the ropes; don't get hung up; always be friendly, sincere, and creative. And win!

The important thing about his familiar picture is that it is a picture of a totally instrumental institution. Nothing about the institution is meant to be valuable, here and now, for its own sake. I don't mean that high school students don't have any fun. Of course they do; in the suburbs, at least, the high school is a "fun place." But this sort of fun is a part of the social pattern to be learned; being "fun" helps you to make it as well or better than anything, and it takes a great deal of social skill which American adolescents, notably, do learn.

We have never had much interest in what education means and feels like to the youngsters who are subjected to it; only in what it might help them to make of themselves. Even the Supreme Court, in its decision against segregation, could not rest on the moral obloquy and insult that segregation imposes on Negro children; that was not enough. It had to support its position further by pointing out that a major reason why separate schools could not be equal even if they were identical was that the Negro students couldn't make the same contacts there that white students could in their school, and that this was what people really go to school for.

So it is: the Court has done our motives no discredit, but merely reaffirmed our tradition. The public school gives poor boys a chance to develop

An Ideology
of School
Withdrawal

177

their potentialities, both by formal education and by providing an opportunity to mingle with and learn from their social superordinates. The commonwealth is then the richer for the skills they later contribute, which would otherwise have been forever lost. This is exactly the opportunity our dropouts need, and which they ought presumably to welcome. So what has gone wrong?

What has gone wrong is pretty complicated; but basically I think one might locate it in the schools' perennial assumptions about the nature of what they have had to offer the children of the poor. These assumptions were probably never valid; but both the school and the poor once believed them. Now, only the school continues to assert them, though no longer with much conviction.

The schools assumed that in order to get ahead in America the student had to learn not only a body of skills, but also a set of social conventions, increasingly subtle and refined as he climbed up the ladder. In school he was taught techniques for handling things and manners for getting along with people. The teachers were the transmitters of an alien culture—alien to them, too. Social mobility was a process like preparing to get a job as a rice farmer in China or a coffee-grower in Brazil. There was a strange language to be learned—from instructors who didn't speak it too well themselves; a strange body of techniques to be mastered—from teachers who had never practiced them at first hand. It would all have to be learned over again when he got there; but at the time it seemed relevant, and made the student feel that he was well on his way.

Now, there are three important ways in which this situation differs from the condition in the high school today. In the first place, the problem of dropouts did not then exist. Most of the students who drop out today would never have been in high school fifty years ago; the school-leaving age has risen irregularly over the past decades, and a more rigid and self-confident school policy would not have hesitated to keep students in grade school until they reached it, whatever it was, if they did not pass. A good many of these dropped out and took unskilled jobs, which existed; and that was the last anyone thought of them till election day six or seven years later. They weren't a dropout problem; they were the working class.

But those who didn't drop out, even though they came from a working-class background, did not feel at the time that they were losing their identity. This happened later, after they had made it, in the classical discovery of the loneliness of the long-distance runner. In school you were still you: *striving* didn't separate you from other poor, immigrant boys; it was exactly what poor, immigrant boys were supposed to do. There was no intimation at the time that you were leaving yourself behind. It wasn't that you were becoming a different person; the old *you* was learning new tricks. Education was instrumental, all right—it has always been that in America—but the instruments were thought to be in the curriculum. The student didn't have to learn to think of *himself* as one.

And finally, nobody doubted what the norms were. It seemed very clear that the people in the next stratum up were the ones who knew what the student had to learn; he had to be able to do what they did. This wouldn't make them accept him willingly; but it would allow him to work his way in even if they didn't.

FRIEDENBERG

178

I don't mean to imply that the school actually delivered the social mobility it promised; sometimes it did, more often it didn't. But this was the way it was supposed to work, and why there was so little controversy over whether compulsory school attendance was good for the individual as well as for the commonwealth. As long as the students who stayed in school believed in education naïvely, it served—much better than religion could have in this heterogeneous country—as the opiate of the people. And opium vendors don't have dropout problems.

Apparently, however—to judge by the present situation—they can: the American poor are getting over their addiction.* It takes more and more education every year to invoke the same dream; and reality breaks through too often, leaving them sick, mean, and edgy. The educational establishment, fearful of losing popular support, is naturally much concerned with the possibilities of a *rapprochement,* of which two have already been tried. The simplest of these is an effort to beef up the traditional, but paradoxically faltering, economic appeal of education. Students are reminded over and over that today, more than ever, you need a high school diploma to get any sort of job and a college degree to get a good one. They are given the statistics on the fabulous return education, as an investment, brings in over a lifetime in increments of annual income. The unemployment data on adolescents and unskilled labor are stressed so that the youngsters will understand how hopeless things will be for them if they drop out of school. If they and their teacher are sophisticated enough, the demographic shift in job-type may be explained: how unskilled and blue-collar work has fallen off, while service and white-collar jobs, demanding a higher level of school achievement, have enormously increased in proportion.

All this is true enough; but the implication is false. It does not follow that most of the students now dropping out would have a better chance, even economically, if they stayed in school. As S. M. Miller and Frank Riessman have pointed out in a recent WBAI broadcast, the illusory success of some of these school-retention efforts in leading students to better jobs is based on the fact that they made hardly a dent in the number of school dropouts; if the programs had been successful in reaching the students, they would inevitably have failed in delivering the jobs. In our economy, the demonstrable economic value of an education is partly a consequence of its scarcity. The blue-collar-white-collar figures are relative, and one loses sight of how much smaller the white-collar one was to begin with. The absolute increase in white-collar opportunity does not compensate for the absolute loss in blue-collar jobs—a discrepancy which is rapidly increasing in magnitude as automation proceeds.

---

* Thus, in her recent study of the schools in Big City, Patricia Sexton reports dropout rates even in *elementary school* of 15.5 per 10,000 children from families earning from $3,000–5,000 annually, falling to 3 children per 10,000 for families earning $5,000–7,000. For families making more than $9,000, the rate was less than 1 child per 10,000. In high schools, of course, the rate is enormously greater, but follows the same pattern. There is no high school in Big City whose median family income is less than $5,000. For schools with median family incomes ranging from $5,000–5,999, Sexton found a dropout rate of 19.2 per cent of the total registration per year, falling to 7.9 per cent for schools whose students had a median family income of $7,000–7,999, and to 3.6 per cent for the school whose students came from families having median incomes above $9,000. [*Education and Income* (New York: The Viking Press, Inc., 1961), pp. 97 and 202.]

Today's dropouts are, perhaps fortunately, pretty skeptical kids; if they all believed that the school could deliver them to a brighter economic future we would soon have unemployed IBM operators and technicians hanging around the way India and Africa have lawyers.

The other, and more sophisticated, *rapprochement* is represented by the Higher Horizons Program, about which I wish I could bring myself to be less doubtful, for it is a program that seems to me characterized by much intelligence, ingenuity, enthusiasm, and sheer good will. Its appeal, moreover, is not purely economic. I understand it to be an attempt to convey to students that middle-class culture, *in toto,* is not beyond their grasp. It can be theirs, if only they do their work. As the title implies, the Higher Horizons approach seeks to make education appear more worthwhile to the student, and encourages him to remain in school to develop his potentialities, by raising his level of aspiration not just economically but culturally. As the boy lifts himself to gaze beyond the slum, there comes into view the Museum of Modern Art.

It is heartening to find the middle class so generously willing to share its resources and, for once, apparently confident of their value. It is also obvious that if the middle class cannot somehow make public education acceptable to the poor on its terms rather than theirs, middle-class dominance of public education—a long-established fact of American life—is doomed. But if the effort is successful, it will remind me of a story that a very intelligent, very British, very working-class hospital orderly used to tell, in a sensitive effort to ease his middle-class patients' embarrassment at the services he was obliged to perform for them. This story concerned a small pharmaceutical firm that was facing bankruptcy. It had an established reputation as Britain's most reputable manufacturer of suppositories. But respect for craftsmanship, as is well known, was declining; their customers, apparently, were turning to other sources for satisfaction. Things looked black. Then the firm consulted one of Madison Avenue's most resourceful advertising agencies. And the agency, after much brainstorming, came up with a slogan that at once opened vast markets to the company by motivating the very segment of the population which had hitherto most successfully resisted its appeal. The slogan was, very simply, "If you don't like our suppositories, you know what you can do with them!"

The dropouts, by and large, don't like middle-class culture, and they know quite well what we can do with it. Dropping out is one way of telling us, and it is about time we turned our attention to the things about the school that are bugging them. The school is the arena in which these youngsters encounter middle-class life; this is where the dropouts fight the ten-year ideological war that ends in their defeat and rout. In this warfare the core values of their culture and the values the school represents are at issue, and any one that we start by considering will lead to the others. I think the most fruitful might be the familiar question of deferred gratification, or impulse control, which is the source of so much conflict with the school authorities.

We all know the school's side of the question; and know that lower-class youngsters act out their conflicts. Retention programs try to face up to this by helping the youngsters learn more self-control and giving them some valid experience of being rewarded for it, so that they will discover for themselves that certain very desirable goals exist that can only be achieved by people who plan, save, and give a soft answer to wrath-provoking circumstances. In this way the kids learn that there may be more desirable rewards than the immediate pleasure of blowing up and shooting your bolt. "Now, Dionysus, let's think about what we're really trying to get done here," friendly Apollo is always urging; and of course he is right. The difficulty lies in getting Dionysus to listen.

I think the youngsters who drop out are probably, in many ways, a more promising moral resource than those who stay in, and I think they are driven out in part by moral revulsion from the middle-class life of the school. They could never, themselves, identify their feelings as moral repugnance because they view morality as being on the side of the enemy and therefore square; they imagine they dislike morality and have never been allowed to realize that they have morals of their own. They don't have a complete moral system, because they are not systematic; they are unprincipled in their behavior, because principles are too abstract for them to handle. But in a concrete situation they can be trusted more safely than their middle-class peers who are trying to make it.

If we are to grow anything better, the dropouts are the kids to start with, for they have come part way on their own, against heavy opposition, already. They are ill-disciplined. They have no basic skills. They are so sore that any place you touch them hurts, and when they are hurt they hurt back. They are extremely parochial, limited in their experience of the world to a few city blocks of desolate slum, and therefore both gullible and suspicious about anything beyond it. They are sometimes homeless, and never have any quiet place to study and think. They are inconveniently aware of their own sexuality and inconveniently skilled at bringing it to the attention of others. They live, their teachers sometimes say, like animals; and as they say it, a ghost sobs, harshly. But if these youngsters are trapped, it is not in their apprehensions of pseudo-events. They are not alienated from themselves. They still have access to their sense-data, and, on their own terms, they are accustomed to fidelity.

These are the qualities that, I believe, we hoped to preserve and continually renew by building an open society in which a sensitive, compulsively masculine boy could become an Ernest Hemingway and a poor but beautiful waif a Marilyn Monroe. But at this juncture, less fatal alternatives to mediocrity are needed. Can a school geared to success and social mobility help formulate them? Its traditions are against it, its staff is against it, its relationship to the community power structure is against it.

To reach the dropouts and give them a reason for staying, the school would have to start by accepting their *raison d'être*. It would have to take lower-class life seriously as a condition and a pattern of experience—not just as a contemptible and humiliating set of circumstances that every decent boy or girl is anxious to escape from. It would have to accept their language, and their dress, and their values as a point of departure for disciplined exploration, to be understood, not as a trick for luring them into the middle class, but as a way of helping them to explore the meaning of their own lives. This is the way to encourage and nurture potentialities from whatever social class. Talent, and genius, when real, are expressions of individual experience and

An Ideology of School Withdrawal

181

the inner life. But success and higher status are not the first goal to which talent or genius is devoted—though they are sometimes the last.

I do not mean to imply that I accept Sitwell's Fallacy: that the poor are happier in their station in life and should be left to enjoy it. Most lower-class people of whatever age hate lower-class life, I am sure: the noise, and the filth, and the crowding, and the vulnerability to the police and illness; never feeling quite well or quite rested. Worst of all, perhaps, is the constant din of the mass media—including the school—telling them that if they were any good at all they would be middle-class like everybody else, and live in loveliness in Larchmont. But the fact that they have reason to hate their life of fear and deprivation does not give us the right to force ours on them as the only acceptable alternative to it. This is something they must work out for themselves, and the school's job is to help them understand most fully the meaning and nature of what they have to work with. Basically, the problem of reaching the dropout is analogous to that faced by the Peace Corps in reaching the peoples of underdeveloped countries. Can we—do we even really wish to—help them deal with their situation on their terms with our resources, while leaving our way of life aside till somebody asks for it?

Frankly, I doubt it. This is not how the teachers I know approach lower-status youngsters. They are afraid of them, for one thing. The principal is afraid of disorder which looks bad in his record and in the records of his teachers, and they each have their careers to think of, too. So they learn early to keep the kids in line; this comes first. Order is helpful to learning, but it doesn't come first, it grows out of the common task; and teachers who put it first are not enthusiastic allies in keeping disorderly youngsters in school till a basis for order can be created. Order is not, to be sure, the central issue, but it will serve to symbolize the sharpness of the issue between those whose security depends on the suppression of impulse, and those who depend on its expression.

In the urban public school today, the former predominate, and I don't think they can be easily changed, within the limits of personality and bureaucracy that characterize the school. If they can be, there is no fundamental reason why the kinds of youngsters who now drop out may not be well served. But this is a big if, for the public school, as it is, is profoundly expressive of our culture. And the fate of the "dropouts" is just one more expression of their actual status in our democracy.

Work
and the Teen-Age Blue-Collarite

H. KIRK DANSEREAU

IN AMERICAN society today we face a dilemma in trying to provide employment for the two extremes in the labor force, the teen-ager and the older worker. Individuals in these two classifications appear to be in competition for the available jobs, a situation which would not exist under conditions of full employment. However, the persistence of relatively sluggish economic growth indicates that stress on this competition is likely to continue. The older worker views the youngster's entrance into the labor force as a threat to his own job security, particularly in the less skilled occupations. The young workers no doubt feel that they are being blocked from many jobs which they could hold, blocked frequently from the training which they could otherwise obtain, for example, limited apprenticeship programs, limited on-the-job-training, and limited vocational training in the schools. These factors may soon lead to an even more serious shortage of skilled craftsmen by the end of this decade.

Work is still a man's world; the young are readily admitted to it only in time of war. Even the legislation which is ostensibly intended to protect the young at times prevents them from getting the work experience necessary for them to become meaningful additions to the labor force. Part of the problem lies in society's failure to prepare youth for a smooth transition from adolescence to adulthood and its related work roles. Millions of the young have not been well prepared for work life; but often even the well-prepared find discrimination related to age, for example, lower pay, less responsibility, less job security. These work conditions hold for most young people as they enter the world of work but are virtually a foregone conclusion for the child of the blue-collarite. Frequently he brings with him low aspirations and expectations not greatly at odds with what he gets. He may find that his blue-collar background, as well as his age, conditions the employer's evaluation of his abilities.

Today the American labor force is larger than ever before. More people than ever are working, but we are also faced with a relatively large and enduring unemployment. Increasing automation, at least in the short run, will have no salutary effect on the unemployment rate. Automation, with its demands for technical competence, can now offer little place for the blue-collar child, who is less likely to have the necessary qualifications; moreover, it is he who is probably most unaware of the opportunities in that field. Limited knowledge of opportunities is related not solely to gaps in formal channels of communication but also to the informal influences of family and peers. That is, a limited range of perspectives can result from one's contacts with others and with what the latter believe to be the worthwhile or even the available jobs.

ASPIRATIONS

There is considerable literature dealing with the aspirations of American youth. Broadly speaking, one could begin with the materials on the ranking of occupations. Rankings made by the youngsters most certainly reflect the influence of adults; and it can be generally assumed that, given free rein, youth tend to list and rank those occupations with which they feel somewhat familiar and in the order of their own preferences for holding such jobs. Other research and writings deal specifically with aspirations, both educational and vocational; and for purposes of analysis, distinctions frequently are made between aspirations and plans or expectations conditioned by economic or social reality. Regardless of the terminology, it is known that very often actual plans or expectations fall below the youngsters' expressed goals which they would like to attain.

In Williamsport, Pennsylvania, ninth- and twelfth-grade students and persons in the age group 18 to 24 years were asked about their job preferences.[1] The respondents were then asked to be as realistic as possible and to list the jobs they thought they would get. "Over 50 per cent of them listed expectations or attainments different from their aspirations." "An interesting finding of this study is the decline of expectations as age increased and the realities of the near future became more apparent." "Approximately half of the ninth and twelfth graders who aspired to professional positions expected to attain them. Fewer of the 18-to-24-year-olds aspired to the professions, but only 7 per cent of this group had attained these positions." Further, the younger persons expected to continue on to college; but those beyond high school age had more often gone directly to work. Girls in their senior year of high school appear to have been more realistic than were the boys. The female students' expectations more closely approached the actual attainments of the 18-to-24-year-old women.

For a number of years Buck has been engaged in a longitudinal study of Pennsylvania youth.[2] His findings offer some insight into who among the youngsters is likely to acquire the education necessary to attain the higher occupational goals. Farm youth, as is well known, were less likely to continue their educations than were those of other residential backgrounds; and many teen-agers, even though intellectually qualified, discontinued for financial reasons. Eighty-four per cent gave reasons other than academic difficulty. Of these, almost "one-fifth of the total group mentioned the necessity for aiding the family as a reason for dropping out of school and slightly over one-fifth

---

[1] M. E. John and Kathleen Moyer, *Adolescents: Their Interests, Aspirations, and Models*, The Pennsylvania State University, Agricultural Experiment Station Bulletin 695 (June, 1962), pp. 6, 8, 9.

[2] Roy C. Buck and Bond L. Bible, *Educational Attainment Among Pennsylvania Rural Youth*, The Pennsylvania State University, Agricultural Experiment Station Bulletin 686 (November, 1961), pp. 14, 17.

mentioned taking a job." High school dropouts were found to have come from homes where the father's education was low. These fathers were for the most part blue-collar workers employed as operatives, for example, "truck driver, worker in industry below the rank of foreman, and similar blue-collar occupations not considered to be crafts." The study also found that those who had gone on to college to attain their professional and business employment aspirations had had these goals since the sophomore year in high school. Blue-collar aspirations, no doubt tempered by realism, were found to be characteristic of the high school dropouts.

Andrew's 1957 study of over 15,000 Arkansas high school seniors shows a high interest in education beyond high school.[3] He found that nearly 45 per cent had plans to attend college, and an additional 34 per cent planned other programs, such as trade school, business school, or military service. Of those who thought of getting a job immediately, the largest percentages of expected occupations were those of laborers and skilled craftsmen for the boys and office work for over one-third of the girls.

Previously Berdie had studied nearly 25,000 students.[4] Over one-third expressed plans to attend college, and the same proportion planned to enter work life. The largest percentages of those planning for immediate jobs had fathers who were skilled tradesmen or factory workers. In these cases the fathers themselves had a modal education of eight years.

A study of the aspirations and plans of 1,000 ninth-graders was undertaken by Stephenson.[5] He found both aspirations and plans becoming progressively lower as the socioeconomic ladder, determined by the father's occupation, was descended. The gap between aspirations and plans increased toward the bottom of the ranking. Aspirations seem to have been more consistent but invariably higher than were the plans. Plans were made in accordance with position. Stephenson reported:

> Thus, the mobility orientation pattern suggested is one in which aspirations are relatively unaffected by class and, hence, reflect the general cultural emphasis upon high goal orientations, while plans or expectations are more definitely class based and, hence, may reflect class differences in opportunity and general life chances.

Stephenson also pointed out that lower-echelon respondents have been found to seek job security, to attempt to avoid risk, to place less value on education, and to expect lower occupations and incomes.

Cohen reaches somewhat similar conclusions.[6] For example, he argues that the lower blue-collar class has had little experience in a variety of social and cultural worlds; its work roles are less complex; its life is beset by insecurity. The member of this class thus prefers the familiar, routine, and predictable. When his parents express an interest in higher education for him, the

---

[3] D. C. Andrew and Francis Stroup, "Plans of Arkansas High School Seniors," *Personnel and Guidance Journal*, Vol. XXXIX, No. 3 (November, 1960), p. 300.

[4] Ralph F. Berdie, *After High School—What?* (Minneapolis, Minnesota: University of Minnesota Press, 1954), pp. 125, 127, 128.

[5] Richard M. Stephenson, "Mobility Orientation and Stratification," *American Sociological Review*, Vol. 22, No. 2 (April, 1957), pp. 207, 212, 205.

[6] Albert K. Cohen and Harold M. Hodges, Jr., "Characteristics of the Lower-Blue-Collar-Class," *Social Problems*, Vol. 10, No. 4 (Spring, 1963), pp. 305, 307, 316, 318, 322, 323.

emphasis is primarily upon the practical and financial aspects of that education. Cohen believes the lower stratum to be pessimistic, cynical, and distrustful. These characteristics are undoubtedly related to the insecurity and uncertainty of their day-to-day existence.

That differences in educational and occupational aspirations and plans are not limited to our immediate culture is evidenced by the findings of a recent thesis dealing with Puerto Rican high school seniors.[7] Silva found that a lower percentage of the children of blue-collarites planned to attend college; yet, a majority did have such plans; and the lower percentage is in large measure explained by the parents' dependence upon financial aid from the children rather than by negative attitudes toward higher education. Over all, however, she found that the aspirations and plans of the lower-class youth were much more modest than were those of youth of the higher strata. Here, too, in keeping with Stephenson's results, she found a wider gap between aspirations and plans in the families of the lower occupational ranks. Middle-class youth were pressed to make definite occupational plans, usually for attaining upper-level positions.

As the above studies indicate, some children with blue-collar backgrounds do aspire both to further education and to occupations above the parental level. Simpson has delved into an explanation.[8] His idea was that a relationship exists between parental influence and mobility aspiration among working-class boys, that parental advice is a better predictor of high ambition than is the boy's social-class background. His findings bear out this contention. In addition, he suggested that the boy's associates influenced his aspirations. The latter idea was also confirmed. He stated:

> It is thus apparent that parental advice and middle-class peer-group influence were both related to ambition and mobility aspiration among middle-class and working-class boys in the two schools; and that in parental influence, peer-group membership, and extracurricular activities, the mobile working-class boys resembled the ambitious middle-class boys more than the unambitious middle-class boys did.

Simpson reached the conclusion that parental influence was the more strongly related to aspiration; but he went on to say:

> A working-class boy was most likely to aspire to a high-ranking occupation if he had been influenced in this direction by both parents and peers, and least likely to be a high-aspirer if he had been subjected to neither of these influences.

With regard to the aspirations and expectations oriented toward the education necessary to attain the higher occupational goals, a recent paper by Rehberg discusses the relevance of parental pressure.[9] In an economically de-

---

[7] Ruth M. Silva, "Occupational Plans and Aspirations: Puerto Rican and American High School Seniors Compared" (unpublished Master's thesis, Department of Sociology and Anthropology, The Pennsylvania State University, 1963).

[8] Richard L. Simpson, "Parental Influence, Anticipatory Socialization, and Social Mobility," *American Sociological Review,* Vol. 27, No. 4 (August, 1962), pp. 519, 520, 521, 522.

[9] Richard A. Rehberg and others, "The Occupational and Educational Expectations and Aspirations of Tenth Grade High School Youth" (unpublished paper, Departments of Sociology and Educational Services, The Pennsylvania State University), pp. 31, 32, 33, cited by permission of Richard A. Rehberg.

pressed Pennsylvania community, he found that students' educational aspirations and expectations were higher when parental pressure was high. Among students from the lower socioeconomic stratum, when paternal pressure to do so was high, 70 per cent aspired to continue beyond a high school education. Only 52 per cent had such aspirations when paternal pressure was low. The percentages for expectations were 51 per cent and 19 per cent, respectively. In the upper stratum, 92 per cent aspired to higher education when paternal pressure was high and 73 per cent when paternal pressure was low. Here the percentages for expectations fall to 83 per cent and 64 per cent, respectively. Findings for maternal pressure were similar. Rehberg's work also reiterates the discrepancy between aspirations and expectations.

Obviously, the studies cited above are only a few of those conducted; but they provide ample evidence for the conviction that *aspirations and expectations vary by social class,* that *neither is likely to be very high for the blue-collar child,* and that *parental influence is important.* While there is some evidence to support the notion that those with high aspirations are more likely to fill the higher positions, some will not make it. On the other hand, those with low aspirations seem irrevocably doomed to comparable job levels. Haller has discussed the limitations of the knowledge which the lower-level children have about upper-level occupations.[10] Their parents are likewise limited in their knowledge. He emphasizes the near-futility for the working-class child:

> In any community, there are a few youngsters who plan at, say 10 years of age, to enter a certain occupation and who at age 30 are really in that occupation. Except for a few who plan to enter their fathers' occupations, practically all of these are from the middle or upper class.

Although the obstacles to blue-collar youth appear formidable, it is surely safe to say that *those who do not aspire most certainly are unlikely to achieve.* The relationship between educational and occupational levels is obvious. These youth must be made aware of their need for some kind of training. Cowhig's report for the end of the 1950's is illustrative of this fact.[11] Very few who had failed to finish high school ever found work as professional or managerial workers; 7 per cent held white-collar jobs, and unemployment among them was nearly double that for those with diplomas. By way of contrast, 85 per cent of the male college students had found white-collar positions; 47 per cent were employed as professional, technical, and kindred workers.

JOB OPPORTUNITIES

With our largest labor force ever and with more than ever employed, although many on part time, there is also a persistent unemployment of some 5,000,000 would-be workers. The expression "chronic and persistent labor

[10] Archibald O. Haller, Lee G. Burchinal, and Marvin J. Taves, *Rural Youth Need Help in Choosing Occupations,* Michigan State University, Agricultural Experiment Station Circular Bulletin 235 (1963), p. 6.

[11] James D. Cowhig and Charles B. Nam, *Educational Status, College Plans, and Occupational Status of Farm and Nonfarm Youths: October 1959,* U. S. Department of Commerce, Bureau of the Census, U. S. Department of Agriculture, Economic Research Service (August, 1961), p. 11.

Work
and the
Teen-Age
Blue-Collarite

surplus" does little to soften the blow. No occupational category escapes the impact of unemployment, but it is well known that unemployment strikes hardest at the lower occupational levels. There are also area and industrial differences. Secretary of Labor Wirtz recently commented that a number of industries have shown no growth in the number of jobs.[12]

In answer to the question, "What industries are those?", he responded:

> Among major industries, since 1957 alone, manufacturing employment has declined by over 400,000, transportation by over 300,000, contract construction by over 200,000 and mining by 180,000. And, of course, agricultural employment has continued to drop at an average rate of 200,000 a year.
>
> In some industries this reflects a decline in demand. But in others we have been getting increases in production with decreases in the number of workers.

It can easily be seen that these are among the jobs which might have been filled by the working-class children who concluded their formal training after high school or even before. To take care of the new entrants to the labor force, the Secretary has estimated a need to create 50,000 or more jobs per week. This cannot occur at our present rate of economic growth. The resulting gap in jobs wanted and jobs available could be an expanding, if not devastating, unemployment, particularly for the younger workers. Blue-collar youngsters would contribute even more heavily to the unemployment rolls, for they contribute comparably to the school dropouts. *The Manpower Report of the President* provides some interesting facts and projections.[13] The percentages of persons in the labor force completing high school and completing college rose from 1952 to 1962. The percentage with less than five years of education declined. Skilled workers averaged three years of high school; only farm workers, laborers, and private household workers still averaged only an eighth-grade education. In recent years, laborers have exhibited highest unemployment, followed by operatives and kindred semiskilled workers and service workers. The report projects a labor force of 93,000,000 by 1970, and it is expected that 7,500,000 of the teen-agers will be high school dropouts. These youth have a dual problem: many jobs are already unavailable to them because of age; additionally, the lack of formal education or other training will deny them equal competition for the jobs available.

Feldman's report serves to warn that an effort to solve the problem of unemployed youth cannot be postponed.[14] Three and one-half million high school graduates will attempt to enter the labor force during 1963, 1964, and 1965. During these same years, 2,000,000 dropouts will do the same. During 1961, 12,000,000 children under age 18 were in families with incomes below $3,000. Many of these were obliged to leave school to aid their families. In

---

[12] From a copyrighted interview in *U. S. News & World Report* (April 1, 1963), p. 66.

[13] President of the United States (John F. Kennedy), *Manpower Report of the President and A Report on Manpower Requirements, Resources, Utilization, and Training*, U. S. Department of Labor (March, 1963), pp. 12-13, 90.

[14] Lloyd Feldman and Michael R. Peevey, *Young Workers: Their Special Training Needs*, U. S. Department of Labor, Manpower Research Bulletin No. 3 (May, 1963), pp. 1, 9.

such cases their fathers often had not gone beyond the eighth grade. These blue-collar children have little hope at present. Their plight, along with that of others who drop out for any reason, must be perceived in the light of Zeisel's statement:[15]

> Thus, virtually all the occupations providing expanding employment opportunities in the post-war years have been those requiring relatively long periods of education and formal training. Many of the jobs requiring little or no training which were available in past decades to workers disemployed in contracting areas of the economy are disappearing.

Such statements and the rather ominous statistics lead one to wonder whether there really are job opportunities for any of the newcomers. Some believe there are, emphasizing the training needs of those who seek work.

Numerous reports show the growth of the upper-level, white-collar jobs, a shift from goods-producing to service-type industries.[16] Jobs in construction and finance-insurance-real estate are expected to increase at a rate above that of the "increase in total employment anticipated by 1970." Trade, service, and government will also exceed the average growth. Manufacturing is expected to hold its own. Although below the average, even transportation, public utilities, and mining are expected to provide additional jobs. In addition, education, distribution, business, and personal services have shown recent increases, and the trends are expected to continue.[17] The world of work must adjust to the changing age structure of the society. "Significantly, nearly half the increase in the labor force will be under 25 years of age," that is, by 1970. We shall need more technicians, skilled craftsmen, and clerical workers; a high school education or the equivalent will be required. Even though recently one-fourth of the young people between the ages of 16 and 21 were out of work, it was reported: "Jobs were going begging for machinists, tool and die makers, dental technicians, sheet metal workers, electricians, nurses, auto mechanics, dietitians." Beyond these, many professional jobs—mathematician, physicist, teacher, engineer, and so forth—were waiting to be filled.

In the past, former Secretaries of Labor Mitchell and Goldberg have pointed up the coming need for skilled craftsmen in the 1960's. Had these warnings been taken seriously, many of our youth would not be unemployed. It is fact that the majority of our dropouts have the intellectual capacity to complete the training necessary to fill most of the available work positions.

Many ideas concerning the employment of youth have been put forth. Among these are a youth corps, training under the Manpower Development and Training Act and the Area Redevelopment Act, apprenticeship programs, and on-the-job training. Except for the first, youth will be hard pressed in the

---

[15] Joseph S. Zeisel, *Manpower and Training: Trends, Outlook, Programs,* U. S. Department of Labor, Manpower Research Bulletin No. 2 (March, 1963), p. 7.

[16] U. S. Department of Labor, Bureau of Employment Security, *Job Guide for Young Workers . . . 1963-1964 Edition,* pp. 13, 15.

[17] U. S. Department of Labor, Bureau of Labor Standards, *Design for Community Action,* Bulletin 248, pp. 2, 3.

Work
and the
Teen-Age
Blue-Collarite

189

competition with adults. As of a year ago, fewer than 16 per cent of the trainees in the ARA program were under 20 years of age;[18] and even more recently the Manpower Development and Training Act accounted for no more than 60,000 trainees. Older workers feel they have first call in such programs and likewise hold the line on apprenticeship and on-the-job training.

Much of the blame for the present unemployment situation is laid to the youngsters who "just don't have the perseverance of our generation," or who "just don't know what it is to work." Teachers and employers are blamed for their shortcomings; also blamed is the older worker who "won't give the kids a chance." Frequently, however, technological change is billed as the villain.

AUTOMATION

In a sense, automation is a paradox: it both takes and provides jobs. Although incomplete in development and coverage, it has made its mark in the automotive industry, the mine, the railroad, and steel. It will increase in these and in other walks of life—the office, laboratory, and government. Wherever automation occurs, there will be some joblessness; but its impact will be felt most immediately by the blue-collar children—the same youngsters, and those yet to follow, who cannot now qualify for the vacancies which do exist. Other industries are rapidly being closed to them;[19] these include metalworking, engineering and product development, chemicals, petroleum, and electrical goods.

For those who are prepared, automation could open the door to employment. As DuBridge has said:[20]

> It is, however, in our primary and secondary schools that our more serious problems lie. I have mentioned that it is here that high talent in every field needs to be discovered, encouraged, and challenged. But here, too, must all types and levels of abilities and interests be recognized and guided. A research engineer may be needed to develop a new automation device for industry; but a dozen competent electronic technicians must be available to keep it working.

Yet the United Steelworkers of America, countering the argument that layoffs brought on by automation are rare, make a cogent point:[21]

> Granting that layoffs are rare, one still is faced with the question of how to employ the new members of the work force if the purpose of using automatic equipment is to prevent or remove the necessity of hiring more men. . . . The unemployed are those who were not hired in the first place. A person who is unable to find his first job is just as unemployed as the person who has been dismissed.

---

[18] U. S. Department of Labor, Office of Manpower, Automation and Training, *Training for Jobs in Redevelopment Areas* (A report of occupational training and related activities under the Area Redevelopment Act, for the fiscal year ending June 30, 1962), p. 11.

[19] Edgar Weinberg, "An Inquiry into the Effects of Automation," in *Impact of Automation*, U. S. Department of Labor Bulletin No. 1287 (November, 1960), pp. 21 and 22.

[20] Lee A. DuBridge, "Educational and Social Consequences," in The American Assembly, *Automation and Technological Change*, © 1962 by The American Assembly, Columbia University. Reprinted by permission of Prentice-Hall, Inc., publisher.

DANSEREAU   [21] United Steelworkers of America, *Shorter Work Week*, Booklet No. PR-137, p. 31.

Obviously, no economy can operate without a labor force; there will always be jobs, and the problems we face are, What jobs? and How many? What knowledge is needed, and how can it be acquired? My own informal surveys of steelworkers indicate that the vast majority, at least of local union leadership, do not want their children in the mills; they do, however, want them employed. They will battle endlessly to attain that goal. The AFL-CIO, speaking for the bulk of organized labor, has suggested steps toward the solution of the consequences of automation.[22] It has recommended federal responsibility for the broad problem of economic growth, technological survey, and continuing review. It has also suggested federal-state-local cooperation with regard to training and retraining and concern for distress areas and older workers. Further, the organization has called for the encouragement of free collective bargaining as a solution to some of the specific problems. There is little question but that widespread joint effort toward solution is necessary.

CONCLUDING STATEMENT

The problem of providing work for the teen-ager or young adult is far from simple. This is particularly true for the child of the blue-collarite, for he is least likely to be prepared to handle the jobs of the future, as is his case with regard to many of the vacancies of today. The impact of automation only accentuates his unprepared state. A joint labor-management committee reported:[23]

> Only through a coordinated approach in which public policy and private action mutually reinforce one another can the employment problems of technological change be met.

The committee endorsed a bill recommending relocation and training benefits; it recommended improved employment services and a study of integrated public-private pension systems. Similar provisions can perhaps be provided for those at the initial phase of work life.

Statistics show the greater security of the educated worker, and educators have argued the need for a smooth transition from school to work life. The desired transition cannot occur without access to a reasonably worthwhile job, and the preparation for that job cannot occur unless the training is available and able to hold the student's interest. Archaic legislation regarding vocational training must be updated to provide funds for the training necessary to meet the nation's needs, to serve the majority of our future workers. If we are to mollify the blow of unemployment for the blue-collar child, we must learn his capabilities and guide his aspirations and plans accordingly. *This task must start early and stay late;* home, school, church, government, and mass media, each has its part to play.

The blue-collar child has untapped talents which are vital to our remain-

---

[22] AFL-CIO, "The Impact of Automation—A Challenge to America" in *The American Federationist*, Vol. 68, No. 8 (August, 1961), pp. 13-17.

[23] Ewan Clague, *Social and Economic Aspects of Automation*, A paper prepared for the Joint Automatic Control Conference, University of Colorado (June 28, 1961), p. 17.

Work and the Teen-Age Blue-Collarite

ing in a place of world leadership regarding standard of living and human dignity. We have already allowed too many to become "lost." The problem of releasing those talents will not come with mere shouts—"There oughta be a law!" or "You gotta educate 'em!" The solution can come with joint effort; mistakes will be made, and money will be spent. Successful programs will reflect imagination and ingenuity. As to the financial cost, dollars not invested in training most assuredly will join others in welfare programs of catastrophic size.

Part IV

THE COMMUNITY

OUR concern here is with the worker as friend, neighbor, newcomer to the city, long-time urban resident, participant in urban renewal, and the like. Hausknecht discusses workers as members of voluntary associations, and suggests that the low level of participation is part of a self-regulating cycle, one which cripples the capacity of the working class to cope with the environment and to seize the opportunity that participation offers. Spinrad raises the question of the impact of the suburban life style on blue-collar participation in trade unions. He finds evidence of diminished interest in unions on the part of many such suburbanites, but notes the steadfastness of an influential core of rank-and-file leaders. Blum looks generally at variations in primary-group experience by social class, and Cousens looks more specifically at interaction within lower-class organizations (the block club and the school club). Leggett offers clues to an understanding of blue-collar behavior with his analysis of sources of working-class consciousness and points up some significant differences among types of workers. The working class, he concludes, "is heterogeneous, both in terms of social background and class views." Rubin focuses sharply on the reactions of particular types of workers to an urban renewal program, and notes that such programs have generated leadership among blue-collar workers, at least at the block level. He speculates, finally, about the effect of urban rehabilitation on the class mixture in the racial ghetto. Both Powles and Stamler turn attention to the new urban arrival (members of the "new" working class). In the first case this is the "country boy" of the Southern Appalachian Region; in the second case, it is the Southern Negro worker who has moved to Chicago. Powles uses two case histories to illustrate both successful and marginal urbanization. Stamler discusses the urbanization of Negro blue-collarites and contrasts new and longer-established samples of Negro urbanites with one another and with samples of white blue-collarites. Her data call attention to the provocative notion that there may be a relatively permanent conflict between increased urban aspirations and the failure to realize them, a conflict that means stress long after urbanization is achieved. In the final essay, Miller recommends certain strategies of reform designed to help alleviate one or another of the various problems brought up in the preceding essays. "We may not have a good chance to succeed in changing America," he concludes, "but the linking of the new working class to those who are affluent but concerned with the quality of life offers our best hope in the stalemate society."

Social Structure, Social Class, and Participation in Primary Relationships*

ALAN F. BLUM

I. INTRODUCTION

THIS essay offers a theoretic framework to encompass much of the recent sociological research on variations in primary-group experience by social class. Class-linked attributes of individuals help condition and set limits upon types of personal relationships. Despite this fact, very little empirical research in sociology has been addressed to this problem. Within the scope of a review of this sort, our discussion will be organized around interrelated substantive problems which appear to have the greatest relevance for such an inquiry.

We have three major goals: to review relevant contemporary research on social-class differences in primary relationships; to do this from the perspective of a coherent and systematic theoretical framework, one which identifies the crucial variables in this area of inquiry; and finally, to facilitate an examination of some sociological conceptions concerning the involvement of the working classes in primary relationships. In this way, we hope to identify certain suggestive substantive problems and promising research areas in the study of primary relationships.

The nature of our problem implicates us in at least two traditions of literature. On the one hand, the systematic study of social stratification in modern, complex societies has been little informed by empirical research directed toward an examination of class-based variations in patterns of social interaction. Despite the richness of material provided by the classic studies in this area—a derivative of the fact that the observers were, in many cases, participants in the phenomena under study—and the careful and intimate descriptions which they provided of primary relationships in the working classes, the fact remains that these studies were conducted at an earlier period

---

* This is a condensed and considerably revised version of a much longer and more detailed review of the literature entitled *Social Class Variations in the Patterning of Personal Relationships*. I would like to thank Earnest Lilienstien and Mayer Zald, of the University of Chicago, for critical comments on the first draft.

195

in the development of the social sciences and have a limited usefulness today.[1] A general ambivalence underlies these monographs: on the one hand, they portray the meanness, the impoverishment, the insecurity, and the apathy characteristic of working-class primary relationships; on the other hand, these studies are rich with suggestions of the spontaneity, the direct and immediate delights and gratifications which the working classes derive from participating in primary relationships. This question of the differing levels of gratification experienced by members of the social classes through participation in primary relations is one of the problems which we shall consider.

The second major tradition of literature from which we borrow has focused upon the functioning of primary groups within large-scale social systems. The line of inquiry, initiated by Simmel and Durkheim and continued by Shils,[2] has focused upon the ways in which primary relationships serve to bring people together in close, voluntary alliances by enfusing their encounters with some permanence, structure, and supportiveness. This tradition has been notable for its attempts to link the functioning of primary groups to the operation of the larger social system, and for its recognition of the relationship between societal complexity and primary relationships. However, its most important contribution has been in its proclivity to isolate for study the qualitative properties of different types of primary relationships. This had led to an increased understanding of face-to-face interaction within diverse primary contexts. Despite these typological contributions, this macrostructural tradition—in its zeal to reconstruct the processes by which primary structures are linked to larger structures—has ignored the problem of class variations in the organization of primary relationships. Thus, this brings us around full circle to the problem of class-based differences in the quality and types of primary relationships. Such a consideration, one left untouched by the macrostructural tradition of inquiry, constitutes an important point of concern in the present paper.

II. ASSUMPTIONS OF THE REVIEW, PROBLEMS OF CONCEPTUALIZATION, AND THE IDENTIFICATION OF RELEVANT LITERATURE

Before entering into our review of the literature, we shall indicate certain conceptual problems in selecting material to discuss. Our focus is upon primary relationships rather than primary groups. We consider primary relationships as relatively intimate, face-to-face personal encounters of varying

---

[1] By the "classic" studies we mean the survey tradition of Le Play and Booth, the European studies of Hawlbuachs and Bednarik, and the various American monographs such as the *Middletown* books, *Elmtown's Youth, Street Corner Society*, and the like.

[2] See the various relevant essays by Simmel in K. Wolff (ed.), *The Sociology of Georg Simmel* (New York: The Free Press of Glencoe, Inc., 1950); G. Simmel, *Conflict, and the Web of Group Affiliation* (New York: The Free Press of Glencoe, Inc., 1955) (*Conflict* translated by K. Wolff; *Web of Groups Affiliation* translated by R. Bendix). E. Durkheim, *Suicide* (New York: The Free Press of Glencoe, Inc., 1951); E. A. Shils, "The Primary Group," in H. Lasswell and D. Lerner (eds.), *The Policy Sciences* (Stanford: Stanford University Press, 1951); E. A. Shils, "Primordial, Personal, Civil and Sacred Ties," *British Journal of Sociology*, Vol. 8 (1957).

degrees of permanency and structure. On the other hand, primary groups are relatively structured and enduring associations of more than two individuals, united by a sense of their common fate, whose motivations and activities are organized in the service of certain instrumental goals. Although primary relationships are often transformed into groups, this is not a necessary component. Such relationships may be transient and relatively unstructured contacts just as long as they are regularized and personal.[3] This definition is primarily a policy decision which gives us some leverage in selecting or excluding materials for review. Thus, despite its many suggestive insights, we omit the small, diffuse literature on ideological primary groups.[4] Our orientation also permits concentration upon the social relationship as a unit of analysis rather than on the structural properties of small groups.

There are certain other basic assumptions which underlie our selection of material for inclusion. First, our concern is with industrial laborers rather than with agricultural workers. Second, we ignore the literature on primary relationships formed at work, because it has been reviewed in other places. Third, we shall for the most part, ignore the older literature in the area, although at points we shall use brief summaries to initiate discussion. Fourth, our focus upon primary relationships enables us to exclude the literature on participation in voluntary associations and other similar types of organizations. Fifth, by using material derived from observation of natural contacts and groups, we shall tend to ignore experimental research on small groups. Finally, this review samples from representative findings and makes no claim for exhaustive coverage.

III. SOCIAL-STRUCTURAL DETERMINANTS
OF PRIMARY INVOLVEMENT

In an incisive analysis of social networks, Elizabeth Bott has distinguished between "close knit networks" in which the friends, neighbors, and relatives known by a married couple tend to interact with and to know one another, and "loose knit networks" in which all of these people known by the married couple do not know one another.[5] She finds that the type of sex-role specialization developed by spouses is related to the structure of the social network.

---

[3] The primary relationship can be conceptualized as an episode of interaction, usually between two (but sometimes more) participants, that is personal, reciprocal, and intimate and tends to recur with some periodicity. Goffman is probably the major theorist in the study of primary relationships as distinct from the study of primary groups. He has recently introduced the concept of "situated activity systems" to suggest something of this distinction, although it is not exactly what we have in mind. See E. Goffman, *Encounters* (Indianapolis: Bobbs-Merrill Company, Inc.,); perhaps the various studies produced by Riesman, Watson, and Potter from their sociability project are closer to our conception of the primary relationship. See J. Watson, "A Formal Analysis of Sociable Interaction," *Sociometry*, Vol. 21, No. 4 (December, 1958), pp. 269-80.

[4] Shils, "Primordial . . . ," *op. cit.*; also, G. Almond, *The Appeals of Communism* (Princeton, N. J.: Princeton University Press, 1954).

[5] E. Bott, *Family and Social Network* (London: Tavistock Publications, 1957); parts are reprinted in N. Bell and E. Vogel (eds.), *A Modern Introduction to the Family* (New York: The Free Press of Glencoe, Inc., 1960), pp. 248-57. Bott's book is one of the neglected classics of modern sociology.

This relationship occurs in the following way: the more connected the social network, the greater the degree of segregation between the roles of husband and wife; the less connected the social network, the less the degree of segregation between the roles of husband and wife. Thus, the degree of segregation in the role relationship of husband and wife varies directly with the connectedness of the family's social network. Furthermore, she found that the degree to which marital roles were segregated was largely a function of the husband's occupation.

> Husbands who had the most segregated role relationships with their wives had manual occupations, and the husbands who had the most joint role relationships with their wives were professional or semi-professional people.[6]

In a study of suicide and homicide, Henry and Short introduced the concepts of "external restraint" and "relational system."[7] The strength of external restraints refers to the degree to which behavior is required to conform to the demands and expectations of other persons. The strength of the relational system refers to the degree of involvement in social or cathectic relationships with other persons.[8] The lower-class male, for example, is typically involved in a close-knit social network, one which is characterized by the high degree of external restraint which it exerts upon his behavior. That is, his behavior is oriented to conform to the demands and expectations of a community of interrelated alters. These others, by acting in concert, subject him to a greater degree of control than that to which the middle-class male is subjected. In the same sense, the close-knit social network forms a stronger relational system. This is so because of the greater degree of control exercised over the lower-class male, and also because of the fact that the various alters acting concertedly serve as a stable and continuous source of interpersonal gratification. Henry and Short state that "the strength of external restraint to which behavior is subjected varies positively with the strength of the relational system and inversely with position in the status hierarchy."[9] Thus, the working classes are involved in stronger relational systems and are subjected to stronger external restraints. Both of these conditions seem to describe the operation of close-knit rather than loose-knit social networks.

How adequately does this conceptual orientation account for certain crucial images of working-class involvement in primary relationships? Although we cannot reach a verdict on the empirical status of many of these issues, we may enumerate them as follows:

1. The working classes appear to maintain old friendships longer, and to be more resistant to new friendships than the middle classes;
2. The working classes are less likely to derive personal friendships from their work contexts;

---

[6] Bell and Vogel, p. 251. Bott does make the point, though, that there is no simple correlation between social class and kin network.

[7] A. Henry and J. Short, *Suicide and Homicide* (New York: The Free Press of Glencoe, Inc., 1954).

[8] Henry and Short, pp. 16-17.

[9] Henry and Short, p. 17.

3. The working classes are less likely to become involved as active participants in voluntary associations and in other types of community organizations;

4. The working classes are less likely to produce innovative behavior, such as occupational or geographic mobility;

5. The working classes experience more tension in their marital relationships, but are still less likely to become divorced as compared to the middle classes.

IV. PATTERNS OF FRIENDSHIP

Our first expectation that the working classes should be more likely to cultivate and maintain old friendships is partially supported by unpublished data collected by Hess and Davis.[10] Three sources of friendship are grammar school, high school, and the old neighborhood: when middle- and working-class persons identify the number of friendships which they still maintain from each of these contexts, the data show little difference between the two classes in the maintenance of old school friendships but a sharp tendency for working-class persons to maintain more relationships from their former neighborhoods.

A report by Norman Bradburn on the distribution of "happiness" in four communities in southern Illinois presents evidence in support of our expectation that middle-class persons will be more likely to create new friendships than will working-class people.[11] Sixty-nine per cent of the high-status respondents reported meeting new people during the previous week (prior to the interview), as compared to only 51 per cent of the low-status subjects. What is not accounted for in these data is the source, intensity, and intimacy of these new relationships—are they really primary relationships, or merely casual encounters, and what are the conditions under which they are formed?

The conventional sociological interpretation of the supposed working-class preference for old friendships and their resistance to involvement in new relationships has usually been accompanied by the hypothesizing of an intervening psychological disposition. This disposition has been described in terms of a generalized working-class suspiciousness toward new relationships and a fear of engaging in new contacts. We would suggest, however, that any advantage enjoyed by middle-class individuals in the number of new friendships which they create is most likely a function of the interpersonal richness of their occupational environments, rather than a function of their "openness" or greater psychological flexibility.

These comments lead naturally into our second expectation, that middle-class persons will derive more of their friendships from work than will lower-class individuals. Data from a number of sources tend to support this generalization: Reiss finds that middle-class persons spend more of their time

---

[10] These unpublished data are currently being analyzed by J. Gerasimo, of the Committee of Human Development at the University of Chicago, and were gathered on a project directed by Robert Hess and Allison Davis. For a representative study derived from this project, see R. Hess, "High School Antecedents of Young Adult Achievement," in R. E. Grinder (ed.), *Studies in Adolescence* (New York: The Macmillan Company, 1963), pp. 401-14. I want to thank Messrs. Gerasimo, Hess, and Davis for providing me with these raw data from which I made my computations. They should not be held responsible for my use of the material.

[11] N. M. Bradburn, *In Pursuit of Happiness*, National Opinion Research Center; University of Chicago, May, 1963, Report No. 92, p. 53, Table 2.23D.

than the working-class persons do in relationships with "clients" derived from the job context.[12] Hess and Davis' data show that 36 per cent of the middle-class respondents in their sample, as compared with 22 per cent of the working-class respondents, identify friends from work. Litwak's data indicate that men in bureaucratic occupations are much more likely than are manual workers to be involved in team relationships on the job and to have jobs where talking things over with colleagues is characteristic (the differences between entre-preneurial and manual occupations is slight, however).[13] Gans has discussed the working-class lack of identification with the world of work as a derivative of their generalized antipathy toward the larger society:[14] this type of psycho-logical set is certainly not conducive to a vigorous search in one's occupation for new interpersonal gratifications.

V. STRUCTURAL DIFFERENTIATION AND
WITHDRAWAL FROM PRIMARY INVOLVEMENT

At this point we shall attempt to indicate the way in which the structure of working-class social networks specifically mitigate against both working-class participation in voluntary associations and the manifestation of other behavior which we normally classify as innovative and mobile. These issues are represented by our third and fourth expectations.

Vernon Dibble has noted that people whose status sets bring them into recurrent and varied association with others similar to themselves tend to be more isolated than individuals whose status sets bring them into contact with a variety of people different from themselves.[15] Presumably, the status set of the working-class person is much more likely to minimize his contacts with different others and to increase his isolation from other types of relationships. An individual's membership in a close-knit social network is actually an in-volvement in a structurally undifferentiated group.

The degree of structural differentiation in a group is one component of group structure which has important implications for the extent of member involvement in other relationships external to the group. The degree of struc-tural differentiation refers to the number of different statuses existing in the group and the degree of difference between them. In structurally undifferen-tiated groups, there is little difference in the authority of members, the diffu-sion of responsibility is more widespread, and any given member is capable of invoking the norms of the system against another member.

Cross pressures are most usually generated in situations where the in-dividual is exposed to the conflicting directives of two undifferentiated groups to which he is affiliated, or of one undifferentiated and one differentiated

---

[12] A. J. Reiss, Jr., "Rural-Urban and Status Differences in Interpersonal Contacts," *The American Journal of Sociology*, Vol. LXV, No. 2 (September, 1959), pp. 188, 189, Table 3.
[13] P. Fellin and E. Litwak, "Neighborhood Cohesion Under Conditions of Mobility," *American Sociological Review*, Vol. 28, No. 3 (June, 1963), p. 369.
[14] Herbert J. Gans, *The Urban Villagers* (New York: The Free Press of Glencoe, Inc., 1962), see Ch. 6, pp. 120-42.
[15] I lean heavily here upon an unpublished and untitled paper by Vernon Dibble, of Columbia University, which is a most valuable contribution to the study of social structure.

group. The individual involved tends to minimize these inconsistencies by dissociating himself from the group which prescribe norms that conflict with those prescribed by the more highly valued group. The working-class person's affiliation with his relatively undifferentiated close-knit social network automatically makes him more vulnerable to cross pressures than are the middle-class members of loose networks. Thus, his attempts to minimize normative conflict by avoiding contact with other groups of less salience to him should result in his more active withdrawal from primary contacts with colleagues and from participation in other types of associations. These less salient groups threaten to undermine the normative consistency which he derives from his close-knit social network. By assuming in this way that close-knit social networks are essentially undifferentiated social systems, as compared with loose-knit social networks, we imply that the working classes are more susceptible to cross-pressuring situations and, in their efforts to avoid these situations, are more likely to withdraw from other types of primary relationships. In this way, we might account for the insulation of working-class families and for their isolation from other personal relationships and associations.[16]

VI. THE IMPACT OF THE SOCIAL NETWORK
UPON THE MARITAL RELATIONSHIP

What of the relationship between a person's involvement in his social network and the degree of gratification which he derives from his marriage? In the sense that the working-class individual is involved in a close-knit network, he has attachments to two undifferentiated systems: his social network and his dyadic marital relationship. Bott has recognized that one's commitment to a close-knit network can serve to undermine conjugal solidarity. However, the network can also function as a resource by freeing spouses from total dependence upon one another—they invest more of their affect in relationships outside of the conjugal unit—and they are also provided with assistance and support in performing certain domestic tasks. However, a major effect of this increasing involvement in the gratifying close-knit social network seems to be a growing distance between the spouses and, possibly, an increasing hostility. Gans finds

> the marriage partners are much less "close" than those in the middle class. They take their troubles less to each other than to brothers, sisters, other relatives, or friends.[17]

The link between conjugal-role segregation and the connectedness of the social network then suggests a dilemma: as the close-knit network increasingly comes to serve as a source of gratification for working-class spouses, their own interpersonal relationships deteriorate and suffer. Thus, although we expect working-class marriages to exhibit greater degrees of tension and discontent

---

[16] There is a large literature which documents the greater participation of the middle classes in voluntary associations.

[17] Gans, *op. cit.*, p. 51.

Social Structure, Social Class, and Participation in Primary Relationships

on the part of the spouses, we also anticipate a lesser likelihood of divorce because of the high levels of normative control exerted by the social network.[18]

We shall now recapitulate our description of class differences in certain areas of primary involvement:

1. The working-class married male is subjected to a stronger set of sanctions and normative controls than the middle-class married male because close-knit social networks exert greater degrees of control over behavior.

2. The greater the degree of control to which a person is subject, the less variability he exhibits in his behavior.

From these basic assumptions, we derived the following propositions specifying class differences in various aspects of primary involvement:

3. Structural undifferentiation is more characteristic of close-knit than of loose-knit networks, and the more undifferentiated a social system, the more effectively it mobilizes the loyalties of members.

4. Individuals who have attachments with undifferentiated groups are more vulnerable to cross-pressuring situations, which can be avoided only through their withdrawal from participation in other types of groups whose normative directives are inconsistent with the directives issued by their highly valued undifferentiated systems.

5. The working classes should be less likely to make new friendships at the primary level than the middle classes, because such friendships must be incorporated into their social networks. In close-knit networks, such incorporation requires the tacit assent of a community of others, thereby reducing the control which the individual exercises in his selection of new friends.

6. The working classes are less likely to become involved in primary relationships with co-workers and others, because such relationships serve as potential sources of normative conflict with their social networks.

7. The working classes are less likely to innovate in terms of occupational or geographic mobility, because such innovations constitute threats to the solidarity of the close-knit network.

8. The working classes are more likely to be isolated from activities, issues, and associations at the level of the community and larger society because their close-knit networks minimize their contacts with others different from themselves, and prevent the cultivation of loyalties to other social systems.

9. The working classes are more likely than the middle classes to experience dissatisfaction with their marriages because the close-knit network increasingly becomes their primary source of gratifications.

The theoretic orientation which we identify in this paper, focusing upon the relationships between social class and the structure of social networks, aids us in developing systematic explanations for the differences between the classes in their experiences with primary relationships. At this point we

---

[18] For levels of marital dissatisfaction by social class, see Bradburn, *op. cit.*, p. 50, Table 2.22c . . . : "At every level of marital tension, low SES men are more dissatisfied with their marriages than are high SES men." Also, R. O. Blood and D. M. Wolfe, *Husbands and Wives* (New York: The Free Press of Glencoe, Inc., 1960), Table 123 on p. 254, and Table 113 on p. 228.

would like to move a step further. We shall now apply this orientation to a discussion of two classic problems in the analysis of class variations in primary involvement: In the first place, there has been a persistent tendency to describe working-class primary relationships as essentially familistic, as compared with middle-class interaction. Second, it has usually been assumed that low status operates as a precondition of withdrawal from primary involvement, and that working-class people tend to be alienated from primary contact to a greater extent than do middle-class persons. These two problems are stated most clearly in Genevieve Knupfer's classic article in which she summarizes older research findings in this area. In terms of the alienation of the working classes, Knupfer reports

> . . . Evidence indicates that even in face-to-face contacts (lower status) people are more limited. Informal social activities, such as visiting friends, are more infrequent among them.[19]

Furthermore,

> . . . What friendship contacts there are among (lower class) people are apt to be confined to a narrower area.[20]

It is our intention now to examine the two classic problems from a perspective that is based upon more recent evidence. Is it true that the working classes are to a greater extent than the middle classes alienated from primary contact? Are working-class primary relationships more restricted and narrower in scope in the sense that they tend to draw upon family members as interaction partners to a greater extent than middle-class relationships?

VII. THE PROBLEM OF WORKING-CLASS FAMILISM

It has long been assumed in sociological circles that the general insecurity of working-class people, their provincialism, and their distrust of strangers force upon them a greater reliance on kinsmen as sources of interpersonal gratification. At first glance, the evidence which is available to bring to bear upon the issue is supportive of this contention. From their data collected in a study of two British communities, Young and Willmott find that manual workers have twice as many average contacts per year with their siblings as do clerical and professional people.[21] However, they suggest that the fact that the higher-status people live further away from their siblings than the lower-status subjects do may account for the findings. In the same vein, Berger finds that the subjects in his working-class sample maintain frequent contacts with their kinsmen. However, Berger lacks a middle-class standard for comparison.[22] A constant theme running through the Rainwater, Coleman,

---

[19] G. Knupfer, "Portrait of the Underdog," in *Class, Status, and Power,* eds. R. Bendix and S. M. Lipset (New York: The Free Press of Glencoe, Inc., 1953), p. 257.

[20] Knupfer, *ibid.,* p. 258.

[21] M. Young and P. Willmott, *Family and Kinship in East London,* rev. ed. (New York: Pelican Books, 1962), p. 171, Table 16.

[22] Bennett M. Berger, *Working Class Suburb* (Berkeley: University of California Press, 1960), Ch. 5, pp. 54-79.

and Handel book on working-class wives concerns their preference for familial contact and their withdrawal from interaction with nonrelatives. These dispositions are interpreted as a function of the insecurity of the working-class wife.[23]

None of these data are compelling enough for us to accept the image of working-class familism at this time. In the previously cited study, Bradburn presents data on the percentages of persons of high and low status who had varying degrees of contact with relatives during the week prior to the interview.[24] Surprisingly, these data show a relationship in the direction opposite from what we might be led to expect. That is, people of higher socioeconomic status (SES) tend to interact with more relatives than do low SES individuals. Furthermore, we suspect that many of the traditional expectations which we harbor concerning the greater involvement of working-class people in primordial relationships at the family level can be explained as an artifact of geographical propinquity and of the effects of social mobility. These expectations were developed from research comparisons between mobile middle-class people and stationary members of the working class. When mobility is controlled, Young and Willmott find radical reductions in the frequency of working-class contact with their kin.[25] Litwak finds that the working classes see their relatives more than the middle classes do only when the kin of the middle-class respondents do not live in the same city, and his controls for mobility tend to eliminate these differences.[26]

The concept of the "peer-group society" which Gans uses in his analysis of one segment of the urban working classes is similar to the notion of the close-knit social network which we have liberally adapted from Bott.[27] Gans' concept represents an advance, however, in the sense that he distinguishes sharply between primordial relationships that are familistic and those that are personal: the peer-group society is a network of friends, peers of the same sex, and relatives of the same age; involvement in the peer-group society does not imply intense personal attachments to parents and senior relatives.

---

[23] Lee Rainwater, Richard P. Coleman, and Gerald Handel, *Workingman's Wife* (New York: Oceana Publications, Inc., 1959), esp. pp. 103-14. One of the reasons which they adduce for this withdrawal from contact with nonrelatives is a tendency for working-class wives ". . . to remain strongly attached to their own fathers," a fact noted on page 105, which is not systematically explained and appears to fly directly in the face of a substantial body of literature on socialization and the family. Reading this book is like reading a revised and updated version of the classic analysis of the radio soap opera written by Lloyd Warner and William Henry some twenty years ago.

[24] Bradburn, p. 53, Table 2.23D.

[25] Young and Willmott, *op. cit.*, p. 131.

[26] E. Litwak, "Occupational Mobility and Extended Family Cohesion," *American Sociological Review*, Vol. 25, No. 1 (February, 1960), pp. 15-16, Tables 2-4. Although Litwak's theoretical interests are somewhat different from our concerns, his data are probably the most useful: he presents strong evidence in this paper for the position that higher-status people are likely to be involved in a greater number of family contacts than the stationary manual classes; see Table 7, p. 14.

[27] The Gans book is probably the most useful study we have found for the purposes of this paper. Although it came to our attention after the major details of the theoretic orientation had been evolved, and thus had no role in the development of our conceptual scheme, it lends strong support to our argument.

> The mainstay of the adult-peer society is the family circle . . . the circle is made up of collateral kin: in-laws, siblings, and cousins predominantly. Not all family members are eligible for the peer group, but the rules of selection—which are informal and unstated—are based less on a closeness of kinship ties than on compatability.[28]

Thus, although primordial attachments delineate the boundaries of the relationship and implicitly define the field of eligibles, personal criteria ultimately set the standards for the inclusion of new members.

VIII. THE PROBLEM OF ALIENATION

The question of the alienation of man in individual society has often been formulated in terms of the prevailing disengagement of individuals from intimate, personal, face-to-face contacts. A major assumption has been that low levels of activity and participation in primary relationships outside of the immediate domestic sphere are correlates of low status in these societies. The evaluation of such an issue requires data on the differences between the social classes in the amounts of time which they respectively allocate to primary relationships. Although a few relevant studies exist, they are only rarely couched in research formats which will permit testing the hypotheses in which we are interested. This is so because, in most cases, the data were collected in studies designed for other purposes and emerge only as a side effect of the research operation.[29]

In general, then, the data which we might bring to bear upon the question of social-class variations in the frequency of primary contact are not conclusive. If the working class is truly the alienated stratum, we suggest that it is possibly not an alienation manifested in their infrequent primary contact, or in their unwillingness to participate in a number of personal relationships. Rather, it appears as a type of alienation imposed by the structure of the working-class social network. Participation in the close-knit network does not necessarily imply a greater *frequency* of contact with friends. However, it does suggest that the person's primary relationships are regulated and controlled to a greater extent by a highly structured system of normative restraints which are imposed by a community of interlocking alters. Alienation from certain relationships results to the extent that the individual becomes absorbed by his close-knit social network and his commitments to other relationships become undermined. The paradox is that this alienation is a function of intense primary involvement within one's network of affiliates. Thus, the working-class person is alienated from a wider range of interpersonal contacts as he becomes increasingly involved in more intense and intimate personal relationships with his homogeneous community of friends.

---

[28] Gans, *op. cit.*, p. 39.

[29] The most relevant material which we located on social-class differences in the frequency of primary contact were found in the following sources: S. Graham, "Social Correlates of Adult Leisure Time Behavior," in *Community Structure and Analysis*, ed. M. Sussman, (New York: Thomas Y. Crowell Company, 1959), p. 348, Table 26; D. L. Meier and W. Bell, "Anomia and the Achievement of Life Goals," *American Sociological Review*, Vol. 24, No. 2 (April, 1959), p. 195, Table 61; A. J. Reiss, Jr., *op. cit.*

Social
Structure,
Social Class,
and
Participation
in Primary
Relationships

205

IX. A NOTE ON THE QUALITY OF WORKING-CLASS INTERACTION

Although we cannot offer a firm judgment on the quality of working-class interaction, we might suggest the following considerations: Relationships within close-knit networks are likely to be more personal and intimate than contacts in loose-knit networks. This phenomenon is primarily a function of the solidarity prevailing within undifferentiated close-knit networks. An individual in such a network is less free to cultivate his repertoire of role skills, or to sustain alternative definitions of self in diverse role context. This is so because his performances are visible and public to an interrelated network of audiences who all tend to develop a common, standardized set of images and expectations concerning his behavior. Intimacy tends to be a natural derivative of situations where the individual can no longer sustain different roles in public settings because the people in his environment simultaneously observe him in all of these contexts. If distance crystalizes in settings productive of high degrees of segregation in an individual's role set, intimacy should characterize the social relationships in the close-knit networks.

X. DISCUSSION AND IMPLICATIONS

We have attempted, with reference to empirical research, to sustain a promising theoretical orientation to the problem of social-class differences in the patterning of personal attachments. In most cases, this has been rendered difficult because the research which we reviewed was not designed in the most appropriate way for our purposes. For example, investigators have failed to develop standardized measures of primary involvement: most of the previous studies have used some attribute of persons, such as their membership in certain groups, or a characteristic of their behavior, such as the number of personal visits or meetings attended, as measures of personal contact and participation. Primary involvement can be conceptualized in various ways: in terms of the amounts of time a person invests in his relationships, in terms of the number of interactions he sustains over a specified period of time, or in terms of the number of close friends that he identifies. It is obvious that subsequent research in this area requires the development of more sensitive indices of primary involvement which will make use of all of the relevant information. It is risky to attempt additional speculation on the basis of the existent evidence. The theoretical orientation which we have introduced has aimed to identify crucial variables by sensitizing social scientists to the kinds of information necessary if such an enterprise is to be profitable.

XI. CONCLUSION

In this paper we have used a basic set of concepts to attempt a provisional clarification of certain interrelations between social structure, social class, and the patterning of personal relationships. In this vein, we have attempted

BLUM

206

to specify the crucial structural mechanisms which account for social-class variations in primary relationships. We have used this schema—revolving around the concept of social network—to account for many of the commonly accepted generalizations concerning class differences in primary involvement. We have also attempted to shed some light upon certain conventional sociological conceptions concerning working-class familism and working-class alienation by examining these problems from the perspective of the social-network conceptualization. Although we have not intended to offer a "theory" of primary relationships, our desire has been to sensitize sociologists to important substantive problems and areas of inquiry in the study of such relationships.

The Blue-Collar Joiner

MURRAY HAUSKNECHT

THE extent to which any segment of a society's population belongs to voluntary associations is important, because associations are means through which individuals cope with their environment. In terms of the society as a whole, the number and strength of associations have an important bearing on problems of social stability and social change.

In a modern, large-scale, democratic society, voluntary associations are means for furthering the political and economic interests of individuals. This implies that political effectiveness demands that the individual participate in the political processes as a member of an organization. His organizational membership, therefore, serves the further function of helping him transcend his routinized day-to-day activities on the job and in the family by establishing linkages with the broader community and society. By mediating between the individual and the state, associations protect the individual from the unrestrained exercise of power and, by the same token, serve to protect the "elites" who control and exercise this power.

The latter are particularly vulnerable to "direct action" by "masses" not tied to the political system through associations, that is, action organized on the basis of ideologies subversive of the institutions underpinning the positions of the "elites" and feeding on anxieties of alienated individuals living under conditions of social crisis. From the perspective of the democratic system as a whole, then, voluntary associations are key structural elements. On the one hand, the associations represent sources of countervailing power vis-à-vis the state, and so help insure the conditions for a "pluralistic" society. On the other hand, by mediating between citizenry and "elites," the associations act as stabilizing forces preserving democratic institutions. The absence of associations or a low membership rate presents a favorable ground for the

207

rise of totalitarian ideologies and parties. Associations have other functions, as we shall see; but the ones briefly outlined here have been the main concern of social theory from De Tocqueville to the contemporary theorists of mass society.[1]

Numerous studies of association membership rates have been made of samples drawn from communities and from the entire nation. Although some parts of the picture which emerges are foggy and vague, one part stands out sharply and clearly: *The working class does not join associations in any great numbers.*

In 1954 and 1955, two surveys of national samples collected information about the memberships of respondents. (7.)[2] Both surveys showed the same pattern of results: When income and education are used as indices of class, the blue-collar population has fewer association members than does the middle class. The relation of membership and socioeconomic status may be seen in the statistics on membership by occupation given in Table 1. This relationship holds, regardless of size of community.

The statistics for the mid-1950's are consistent with earlier findings in specific communities, for example, the Lynds' in Middletown of the 1920's (14); Warner's in Yankee City of the 1930's (20); and Komarovsky's in New York of the 1940's (11). Among the recent researches, Cohen and Hodges report in 1963 that their survey of 2,600 respondents in three California counties shows blue-collar people joining associations in fewer numbers than middle-class individuals. (3.) A study of a California working-class suburb states that "70 per cent of our respondents belong to no clubs, organizations, or associations at all; only 8 per cent belong to more than one." (2, p. 59.) Nor is this a peculiarity of the American working class; sociological studies in England report similar results. For example, Dobriner cites a recent research, still

Table 1

MEMBERSHIP IN VOLUNTARY ASSOCIATIONS BY OCCUPATION*

| Occupation | Per Cent Who Belong to | | | |
	None	One	Two or More	Total
Professional	47%	24%	29%	100% (259)
Proprietors, Managers, Officials . . .	47	24	29	100 (294)
Farm Owners	58	28	14	100 (265)
Clerical and Sales	59	21	20	100 (240)
Skilled Labor	68	19	13	100 (447)
Semiskilled Labor	77	14	9	100 (492)
Service	73	18	9	100 (142)
Nonfarm Labor	79	16	5	100 (155)
Farm Labor	87	13	0	100 (54)
Retired, Unemployed	77	11	12	100 (35)

*(7, p. 25)

Source: National Opinion Research Center, Survey 367, 1955.

---

[1] For an elaboration of this view of associations, see Kornhauser (12), upon whose work this summary relies heavily.

[2] Numbers in parentheses refer to the numbered entries in the bibliography at the end of this article.

unpublished, of an English working-class suburb in which 82 per cent of the population belongs to no associations. (4, p. 54.)

The consistency with which this pattern is found points to the necessity of examining the social and cultural situation of the class for its causes.

The working class lives in a relatively encapsulated and circumscribed physical and social environment in which the emphasis is on the specific and concrete rather than the general and abstract characteristics of events, persons, and social relationships. When compared with those of the middle class, blue-collar beliefs, attitudes, and behavior represent not so much a subculture as a "counter-culture."

The central focus of working-class life is the home and family; the strongest, most intimate, and enduring relationships are with kin. (3; 5; 9; 10; 23.) Although the individual is part of an informal local network of friends and neighbors to a greater extent than is the middle-class individual, he is less likely to be invited into the home than are the friends and neighbors of the latter. (3; 5; 18; 23.) The model for all social relationships is the family; that is, social interaction with others tends to be on a highly personal or primary basis. There is a shallow and minimum commitment to the more impersonal or secondary relationships demanded in most spheres of a complex society. (3; 16; 19.) This is reminiscent of an earlier, rural, non-industrial community, as is the blue-collar individual's strong attachment to his immediate locality. (10; 18; 23.) The home and the immediate neighborhood represent the "real world"; the journey to work represents a daily sortie into an alien world.

The spheres beyond the neighborhood, the peer group, and the family remain alien partly because the individual does not understand them; the deficiencies of his education and the consequent restrictions of his experiences put him at an intellectual disadvantage. (5; 15.) Therefore, the larger community and society appear as arenas of uncontrollable forces, and the people inhabiting them are viewed with suspicion and hostility. (3; 5; 13; 15.) The misanthropic and intolerant perception of others is extended even to those who live within the immediate locality. (5; 10; 18.) These perceptions and attitudes are reinforced by the empirical experiences of the individual: it is, indeed, too often a world in which he finds himself grasping the short end of the stick. Yet his dominant reaction to the situation is "fatalistic" —nothing can be done to change this alien world in which he is forced to exist. (3; 5; 15.)

This orientation is related to the individual's preference for the familiar and routine as well as to a high level of "anti-intellectualism," although there is much respect for those with "brains" or those who are "smart" enough to "beat the system" and escape the onerous tasks of life. (13; 15; 17.) But the desire for the routine and familiar is not a preference for the serene and placid. In fugue-like fashion another theme runs through this subculture, one emphasizing "masculine" values and a search for "thrills," "risks," and "excitement." (17.) Gans talks of this as "action-seeking" in contrast to "routine-seeking" (5), whereas Miller describes it as a "rhythm of life [that] fluctuates between periods of relatively routine or repetitive activity and sought situations of great emotional activity." (17, p. 10f.)

The low rate of association membership in the working class is part of a self-perpetuating cycle. The rate means an absence of a cultural expectation or norm of membership, leading, in turn, to a cultural inexperience with this form of behavior and reinforcing an opposite expectation. But the rate is also a result of other elements of the subculture, just as these elements are themselves partially determined by the inexperience with voluntary associations.

One model of an association, the political party or economic-interest group, has as its smallest possible focus as an organization the community as a whole. Because it demands that the membership maintain the same focus, it presumes that the rank and file is able to grasp the relationship between experiences in their immediate environment and the broader social system. In a complex society, this is often exceedingly difficult under the best of circumstances, but it is an almost impossible demand for a population tightly bound, by intellectual disabilities and social relationships, to the specific, concrete immediate experience and locale.

An association brings together individuals who are strangers to one another in more or less impersonal, secondary relationships; their common bond is a specific interest. This requires of the individual a capacity to inhibit suspicion and hostility toward others, and maintaining this attitude represents a severe strain on the tolerance of blue-collar persons. If the sphere in which the association is active is highly complex, for example, influencing the local power structure, there is a tendency for the organization to become bureaucratic, and for impersonal social relationships to become the dominant mode. In any organization it is possible to establish primary relationships; indeed, this opportunity represents one of the main functions of associations. However, the more "formal" the organization becomes, the more irrelevant do these primary relationships become; the "businesslike" atmosphere of the pragmatic and efficient organization does not nourish primary relations. Once an organization takes on this cast, it creates a difficult situation for the blue-collar individual oriented to the kind of interaction found in the family and the peer group.

Secondary relationships are founded upon norms which restrict behavior based on the unique and personal characteristics of individuals. In such situations those who construe the world in highly personal, particularistic terms have difficulty coping with authority. The politician, for example, is defined as having obligations to those who granted him the "favor" of voting for him, and he is accused of betraying them and "selling them out" when, constrained by the impersonal norms of a democratic system, he cannot meet their demands. (5.) In the context of an association, this attitude stirs the never too-latent suspicion of strangers. The inability to understand and deal with this normative system—the dominant one in our society—reinforces the feeling that the world is "alien" and beyond control, and this feeling is itself a major barrier to joining associations: "Why attempt the impossible?" This, to bring our explanation full circle, is an unanswerable question for a stratum whose experience with associations is minimal.

But, despite all this, some do join: what of them?

There is an alternative model of a voluntary association, for example, social and athletic clubs, fraternal societies, and the sedate middle-class sewing, gardening, and literary circles. Although there is some overlap between organizations of this sort and the other model, they differ from it by being primarily arenas for satisfying the "expressive" interests of individuals. It is in this kind of association, where the dominant mode of relationship is personal, that we find the blue-collar joiner.

A national survey found the working-class joiner in "church-related," "fraternal," and "social and recreational" organizations. The most characteristic organizations to which the middle class belonged were "civic and service." (7.) A similar pattern is true of the New York metropolitan area, and Berger notes that in a working-class suburb only one person belonged to the "civic improvement club . . . which, presumably, it would be to everybody's interest to join." (11; 2, p. 61.) In a Boston slum area, residents belong "only to those organizations which offer opportunities for peer-group activity which are not available elsewhere. For example, the Holy Name Society of the parish church gave the men an opportunity to take communion together, and to bowl together." (5, p. 106.) A recent survey of Negro neighborhoods in Lincoln, Nebraska reports a relatively high rate of membership, but "while persons in our sample belong to such groups as the National Association for the Advancement of Colored People, they were far more likely to belong to expressive associations (for example, Birthday Club, North Side Squires, Saturday Nighters Society . . . and so forth)." (1, p. 653.)

The blue-collar joiner behaves in a manner as consistent with his subculture as the nonjoiner. He tends to select organizations which can be structured in terms of primary relationships, and those which have roots in the immediate locality with little or no connection with the larger society; that is, the member of the "North Side Squires" is more encapsulated than is the member of the NAACP. Another kind of congruence with the subculture can be seen in the names of the Nebraska Negro organizations: the "Saturday Nighters Society" vividly captures the theme of "excitement" and "action-seeking."

The preference for personal relationships and "action" probably plays a role in determining the behavior of those who belong to "instrumental" associations. Because those joining such types of associations may be expected to resist attempts to "formalize" the organization, they may represent an internal source of strain. Second, and more important, they will tend to resist orderly, routinized, "rational" courses of action and be prone to programs which promise "excitement" and "action." Thus, in labor unions the wildcat strike or the rejection of contracts negotiated by leaders may not be so much the result of a "radical" membership in revolt against a "conservative" leadership as an example of the blue-collar rank and file succumbing to the lure of "action."

Data on *who* the working-class joiners are is scarce, and one must speculate and extrapolate from scattered fragments of evidence. In a Boston slum neighborhood, it is reported that participants in community activities are individuals who are marginal because of upward mobility or for other reasons. (5.) In a California working-class suburb, women who were not working had a higher rate of membership since their move to the suburb than did their husbands. (2.) In a further analysis of a national survey containing information on membership, Richard Hamilton finds some evidence suggesting that downwardly mobile individuals have a higher rate of membership than the nonmobile blue-collar group. (6.) An English sociologist, comparing an old working-class area and a new "housing estate" in Oxford, reports that in the latter there is "a readiness to join formal organizations" in contrast with the older area and its "widespread lack of desire to be identified with a particular group, almost amounting to an inability to enter any obligation that looks like a contract." (18, p. 113.) In their research on English working-class children who had passed their "eleven plus" examinations and gone on to a university education, Jackson and Marsden found that about one-third of the families of the children were of "the sunken middle class . . . submerged wings of middle-class families thrusting their way upwards through education." (8, p. 56.) Many of the families lived in areas in which the social classes were mixed, and thus the children had access to resources and facilities normally absent in working-class neighborhoods. Finally, a significant number of the parents were active in voluntary associations.

The evidence suggests that the blue-collar joiner is marginal in two respects: he is not well integrated into the informal relationships of his area, as a result of mobility in the class system or as a result of residential mobility independent of social mobility. The latter situation obtains in the American suburb and the Oxford "housing estate." Physical relocation breaks ties to kin and peer groups, and association membership may offer an opportunity to establish new personal relationships. If the new area is one in which the middle class is "visible," then we may expect that it will serve as a model or reference group for part of the blue-collar stratum. Thus, a high valuation on education is a typical middle-class norm, and the Jackson and Marsden finding seems to imply that mixture of the social classes may begin to affect working-class behavior. The work of Willmott and Young offers some support for this hypothesis. In a London suburb containing populations of both classes, they discovered a shift in the working class toward middle-class patterns of social relationships and away from those typical of a traditional London slum area. (22; 23.)

Turning to the socially mobile individuals, it is obvious that the aspiring blue-collar person will be highly motivated to join associations. Of more interest, though, are speculations about the downwardly mobile joiner. Wilensky and Edwards' examination of the beliefs and attitudes of these "skidders" discloses that "the skidder reaches not in the direction of his fall, but back up the structure. The values and beliefs of the middle-class family retain their force despite later status loss." (21.) This is in line with the discovery that it is children from the "sunken middle class" who are most apt to use the new English educational opportunities. The downwardly mobile individual attempts to maintain distance between himself and the life situation he finds himself in, and what better way to retain his middle-class self-image than by maintaining his association membership or joining for the first time? It can be further hypothesized that the skidder living in a working-class neighborhood is also residentially mobile and so marginal in both senses. If he attempts to retain his middle-class residential location, then

HAUSKNECHT

212

the surrounding environment facilitates his retention of membership. Finally, it will be the aspiring and downwardly mobile persons who will most probably be found in the "instrumental" organizations.

In sum, a significant segment of working-class joiners may be composed of two streams of individuals moving in opposite directions within the class system.

The nature of the working-class subculture which accounts for associational membership rates also helps explain why the working class is susceptible to mass movements. (12.) If we recall what has been said about the organizing principles and structure of associations, the basis of the attraction of mass movements becomes apparent.

The mass movement tends to be all-inclusive; that is, where the association appeals to segmental interests primarily either of an "instrumental" or "expressive" nature, the mass movement's structure allows for both these interests to be satisfied within its confines. As long as "expressive" interests are subordinated to the political—the politicalization of all life—they are not defined as irrelevant. The inclusiveness of mass movements is a result, in part, of their rejection of "rationality"; action is not constrained by the institutionalized procedures of a democratic political system. One symbol of this rejection is that the structure of a mass movement is based on a charismatic leader. This structure, like the greater freedom for "expressive" interests, is highly congruent with the subcultural emphasis on the personal and a rejection of impersonal norms.

The "irrationality" of the mass movement has other functions as well. It is based on the assumption of the thorough rottenness of the existent society; a premise in accord with the suspicion and hostility prevalent in the subculture. The rejection of democratic norms of political behavior obviates the necessity for a type of discipline and intellectual grasp of the social processes of the kind demanded by associations. An illustration from contemporary America may clarify what is at issue. The member of the National Association for the Advancement of Colored People and the member of the Congress of Racial Equality, despite apparent differences in the methods of these organizations, are required to exercise a great deal of self discipline. The NAACP member has to restrain his resentment and bitterness while the legal machinery majestically grinds its way to a decision; and the CORE member, dedicated to nonviolence, must restrain himself in the face of the direct aggression of others. Both organizations, each in its own way, accept fundamental values of the society and adopt courses of action which are congruent with middle-class cultural patterns.

The mass movement, however, puts no severe strain on the capacities of its followers: it does not ask them, as the NAACP does of its members, to see the relationship between the immediate situation of deprivation and a complex legal tactic executed in that remote "alien world" full of strangers; nor does it, like CORE, ask them to forgo "masculine" behavior. To be sure, there are organizational structures within a mass movement which do require a tight discipline; however, the discipline of the Storm Trooper, for example, did not forbid "direct action" on the streets as a means of

The Blue-Collar Joiner

213

political behavior. Here is an example of the alternating rhythm of the "repetitive" and the occasions for "excitement." In short, a major attraction of mass movements is their embodiment of a major theme of the working-class subculture, "excitement" and "action-seeking."

The irony of the working-class attraction to mass movements is that, when they are successful, the likelihood is that the position of the stratum will not be improved and may perhaps even be worsened.

Summary

The situation of the working class in our society is a far cry from that conjured up by the old radical slogan of the "downtrodden masses." But it is an equally far cry from the image implicit in the slogans of "affluence" and "the end of ideology." One of the implications of this discussion of blue-collar association membership is that the situation of the class can be likened to that of a disabled person. An association of citizens is a means of effective political participation, a means of influencing the decisions affecting one's life. The inability of the working class to use this instrument cripples its capacity for coping with the environment and seizing the opportunities it offers.

BIBLIOGRAPHY

1. Babchuk, Nicholas, and Ralph V. Thompson, "The Voluntary Associations of Negroes," *American Sociological Review,* Vol. 27 (1962), pp. 647-55.

2. Berger, Bennett M., *Working Class Suburb.* Berkeley: University of California Press, 1960.

3. Cohen, Albert K., and Harold M. Hodges, Jr., "Characteristics of the Lower Blue Collar Class," *Social Problems,* Vol. 10 (1963), pp. 303-34.

4. Dobriner, William M., *Class in Suburbia.* Englewood Cliffs, N. J.: Prentice-Hall, Inc., 1963.

5. Gans, Herbert J., *The Urban Villagers.* New York: The Free Press of Glencoe, Inc., 1962.

6. Hamilton, Richard, "The Behavior and Values of Skilled Workers," 1963. (Unpublished)

7. Hausknecht, Murray, *The Joiners.* Totowa, N. J.: The Bedminster Press, 1962.

8. Jackson, Brian, and Dennis Marsden, *Education and the Working Class.* New York: Monthly Review Press, 1962.

9. Kahl, Joseph A., *The American Class Structure.* New York: Holt, Rinehart & Winston, Inc., 1957.

10. Kerr, Madeline, *The People of Ship Street.* London: Routledge and Kegan Paul, Ltd., 1958.

11. Komarovsky, Mirra, "The Voluntary Associations of Urban Dwellers," in *Sociological Analysis,* eds. Logan Wilson and William L. Kolb. New York: Harcourt, Brace & World, Inc., 1949, pp. 378-91.

12. Kornhauser, William, *The Politics of Mass Society.* New York: The Free Press of Glencoe, Inc., 1959.

13. Lipset, Seymour M., *Political Man.* Garden City, N. Y.: Doubleday & Company, Inc., 1960.

14. Lynd, Robert S., and Helen M. Lynd, *Middletown*. New York: Harcourt, Brace & World, Inc., 1929.

15. Miller, S. M., and Frank Riessman, "The Working Class Subculture: A New View," *Social Problems*, Vol. 9 (1961), pp. 86-97.

16. _____, "Are Workers Middle Class?" *Dissent*, Vol. 8 (1961), pp. 507-13.

17. Miller, Walter, "Lower Class Culture as a Generating Milieu of Gang Delinquency," *Journal of Social Issues*, Vol. 14 (1958), pp. 5-19.

18. Mogey, J. M., *Family and Neighborhood*. Oxford: Oxford University Press, 1956.

19. Purcell, Theodore V., *Blue Collar Man*. Cambridge: Harvard University Press, 1960.

20. Warner, W. Lloyd, and Paul S. Lunt, *The Social Life of a Modern Community*. New Haven: Yale University Press, 1941.

21. Wilensky, Harold L., and Hugh Edwards, "The Skidder: Ideological Adjustments of Downward Mobile Workers," *American Sociological Review*, Vol. 24 (1959), pp. 215-31.

22. Willmott, Peter, and Michael Young, *Family and Class in a London Suburb*. London: Routledge and Kegan Paul, Ltd., 1959.

23. Young, Michael, and Peter Willmott, *Family and Kinship in East London*. New York: Free Press of Glencoe, Inc., 1957.

Blue-Collar Workers as City and Suburban Residents— Effects on Union Membership

WILLIAM SPINRAD

INTRODUCTION

TO some observers, the recent growth of suburban communities is seen as a vast population shift from the mass anonymity of the metropolitan center to the intimacy of the quasi-small town. Socially, the result is presumed to be more genuine social integration as opposed to the peripheral attachments characteristic of the large city. Politically, it is supposed to imply more direct involvement in civic affairs by more of the citizenry. To others, the suburbs are simply an extension of urbanism to formerly rural areas. However, some commentators would go further. In terms of one specific set of social relations and civic involvements, suburbanization may actually represent the extreme of urbanization. Attachment to one's occupational group may be more severely attenuated. This may be particularly true of the organized body of occupational colleagues of industrial workers, the trade union.

The suburban life style is at the opposite end of the continuum from that of the medieval-guild city, where, to quote Lewis Mumford, "the workshop was a family" permeated by the "intimate union of domesticity and labor."[1] The typical suburbanite's daily life is severed into two physically and psychologically distinct sections, respectively located in the work world and the home-leisure setting, each with its distinct concerns and its different milieus. Problems that confront the suburban resident—real-estate taxes, zoning, resources for the volunteer fire department—are completely irrelevant to the types of issues with which union locals are traditionally involved. Furthermore, the suburban ethos is predicated on the alienated character of work experiences, as in the words of C. Wright Mills, "unsatisfactory means to ulterior ends lying somewhere in the sphere of leisure."[2] With this orientation, the entire work setting can become a necessary but tangential part of existence. Because the trade union is part of that setting, the tendency to regard it as a useful bureaucratic service agency rather than a community of fellow citizens may be enhanced by residential dispersion.

Of course, this is most characteristic of the commuter to the city. But other suburbanites, with few exceptions, work in geographic environs which are, by design, quite different from the "residential" areas in which they live. The distinction is probably not so dramatic for most city residents, although they, too, are obviously far from the medieval-city pattern. The suburb is thus like the contemporary city, but "much more so."

Another typical feature of suburban communities may foster decreased attachment to one's trade union. Although the dichotomization of work and home worlds is common to most commuting suburbanites, the split is particularly sharp for industrial workers. Their home lives are spent in environs containing more middle-class residents than are usually found in city neighborhoods where industrial workers typically live.[3] The suburbanite's home community will thus contain many neighbors who are sociologically quite different from his work group. Not only will he regularly be exposing himself to personal influences which are openly anti-union, or at least non-union, but he will be part of a middle-class milieu which encourages acceptance of values potentially inimical to unionism: an inordinate concern for status and for consumption display as an expression thereof; an insistence that disputes, including industrial disputes, can best be solved by discussion and conciliation rather than aggressive action; an orientation toward individual initiative rather than collective activity for solving job problems; a possible political conservatism, reflected in voting patterns.

---

[1] Lewis Mumford, *The Culture of Cities* (New York: Harcourt, Brace & World, Inc., 1938), p. 35.

[2] C. Wright Mills, *White Collar* (New York: Oxford University Press, 1951), p. 237.

[3] Concepts about "classes" are often very loose and careless. Our distinctions are based entirely on *occupation*. "Working class" thus means "blue-collar" workers; "middle class" refers to "white-collar" workers of various types. The question of income and consumption patterns is not immediately pertinent. Therefore, the popular notion of an income homogeneity in suburban neighborhoods is of a different order from the occupational heterogeneity to which we refer.

SPINRAD

216

Such a diminution of involvement in and loyalty to the union need not, of course, be the path of every unionist who moves to the suburb. There are several hypothesized conditions which will result in continued attachment. He may maintain his orientation toward his work group and/or avoid involvement in the suburban community. His ideological commitment to unionism may be sufficient to counteract other influences. He may achieve the suburban ideal and actually live in two separate worlds with compartmentalized values.

SUMMARY OF THE LITERATURE

Systematic research on suburban living is, despite the widespread attention to the subject, rather sparse. The one study that is, ostensibly, most pertinent to our theme, deals with automobile workers living in a "tract" community near San Jose, California.[4] The major conclusion was that there was little evidence of a "suburban life style." However, one may question whether the author was actually dealing with a "suburb" in the more conventional usage. The auto workers lived in a fairly homogeneous community, composed primarily of their work colleagues, with the plant only a short distance away. Except for the architecture and the recency of development, the place he investigated seems more akin to a traditional small industrial town.

Otherwise, research findings tend to support our contentions about suburbia, especially the emphasis on family and leisure in the suburban value scheme. Compared with city residents, suburbanites are more oriented toward family; cityites are oriented more toward career.[5] The move to suburbia is, above all, seen as an opportunity to provide a better environment for children.[6] Suburban status may be measured as much by participation in leisure activities as by occupation or income.[7] In an extreme interpretation of these findings and more impressionistic observations, David Riesman concluded that, in residential suburbs, "men treat their work as delinquents treat school."[8] Another of our emphases, the gap between the suburban quasi-small town vista and the macroscopic issues, is expounded in an extensive account of suburban politics.[9] There is some support for the belief that typical residential suburbs, unlike the deviant working-class "suburb" already mentioned, tend to be heavily white-collar or occupationally heterogeneous in composition.[10] But whether the result is an absorption of "middle-class

---

[4] Bennett M. Berger, *Working Class Suburb* (Berkeley: University of California Press, 1960).

[5] Wendell Bell, "Social Choice, Life Styles, and Suburban Residence," in *The Suburban Community*, ed. William Dobriner (New York: G. P. Putnam's Sons, 1958) pp. 225-42.

[6] *Ibid.;* also, Walter T. Martin, *The Rural-Urban Fringe* (Eugene, Oregon: University of Oregon Press, 1953), p. 37.

[7] Rolf Meyersohn and Robin Jackson, "Gardening in Suburbia," in Dobriner, *op. cit.*, pp. 271-86; and Philip H. Ennis, "Leisure in the Suburbs," in Dobriner, *op. cit.*, pp. 248-70.

[8] David Riesman, "The Suburban Sadness," in Dobriner, *op. cit.*, p. 379.

[9] Robert C. Wood, *Suburbia, Its People and Their Politics* (Boston: Houghton Mifflin Company, 1959).

[10] Ernest R. Mowrer, "The Family in Suburbia," in Dobriner, *op. cit.*, pp. 147-64; Harold Wattel, "Levittown: A Suburban Community," in Dobriner, *op. cit.*, pp. 287-313; William Dobriner, *Class in Suburbia* (Englewood Cliffs, N. J.: Prentice-Hall, Inc., 1963), pp. 97-99.

values" by working-class suburbanites is still to be tested. One reason why this may not occur is suggested by the observation that many commuters continue to be immersed in their city work worlds.[11]

THE STUDY

As a possible test of some of the aforementioned hypotheses, the Institute of Management and Labor Relations of Rutgers University conducted a study which sought to compare union members who were city and suburban residents. The inquiry consisted of intensive interviews with 46 male members of two locals of the United Automobile Workers, AFL-CIO. The plants of each local are located in or adjacent to the city of Newark, New Jersey. One of the companies involved manufactures die-castings; the other, various precious-metal products. Neither is associated with any national company.[12] The sample included a representation of Newark residents and those who live in residential suburbs, as well as a significant proportion of skilled and semi-skilled workers in each plant. All but one of the respondents had been working in his plant for more than a year.

It would be presumptuous to claim that this small sample, although selected by random choice and the additional ingredient of availability, was, in any statistical sense, representative of the workers in the two plants —much less of industrial workers in the United States generally. Our interpretations must, thus, be accepted as suggestive rather than valid. Because our interviews were intensive, lasting an hour and a half and generally tape-recorded, we were more interested in the dynamics of the relation between residential community and union involvement and attitudes rather than the typicality of the respondents interviewed. To what extent the findings can be extended to other workers is a matter for subsequent research.

The choice of "extreme" cases is, therefore, quite appropriate. The suburbanites lived in clearly defined residential suburbs.[13] The cityites lived in one of the most clearly defined urban centers of the country, in which both cityites and suburbanites worked.[14] Of course, a myriad of other residence-work setting patterns are possible; these may well represent more blue-collar workers than those investigated. How our findings could be applied to them is hardly self-evident.

---

[11] Walter T. Martin, "The Structuring of Social Relations Engendered by Suburban Residence," *American Sociological Review*, Vol. 21 (August, 1956), pp. 446-53; D. M. Pappenfort, "Metropolitan Dominance and Suburban Social Structure" (unpublished Master's Essay, University of Missouri, 1951).

[12] The two factories and the two union locals were quite different. There was widespread resentment among the die-casting workers about the job, the company, fellow workers, the local, and the local officers. Attendance at union meetings was usually poor. The metal-processing workers reported a high job morale, satisfaction with the company, approval of the local, and large attendance at meetings. These differences, however, had little bearing on the findings to be reported.

[13] In all cases, the number of people gainfully employed in the community was very small.

[14] An unofficial estimate places the number of people who work in Newark as four times the number of gainfully employed who live there.

SPINRAD

218

The residential community variable should be further spelled out. As indicated in the interviews, the occupational composition of the suburbanites' neighborhoods was either heterogeneous or dominantly middle-class. The one deviant who lived in a predominantly working-class area gave responses which were typically "cityite." The city residents lived in traditional city-type neighborhoods. These were "all-purpose" areas, with business, recreation, social facilities, and so forth, all very close by. Many had a distinctive "ethnic" character, with a dominant proportion of one or more ethnic groups and "ethnic" stores, organizations, extended family ties, and so forth. Almost all were overwhelmingly working-class in composition. The one significant deviant, who lived on the outskirts of Newark in an area "suburban" in every way except for the accident of political boundary, responded more like a "suburbanite."

Because statistical statements would be inappropriate, the material will be presented in terms of a series of *modal* types of respondents. The typology utilized is based upon the *independent variable*—city or suburban residence—and the *dependent variable*—union attitudes and involvement. To make the typology more descriptive and to elaborate the findings, several *intervening variables* were examined. These included such factors as: involvement in the residential community and the work setting, the physical and psychological separation from work place and meeting hall, type of job and job aspirations, and the status emphasis and political conservatism deemed characteristic of suburbanites.

DEPENDENT VARIABLE—UNION INVOLVEMENT AND ATTITUDE

The independent variable has already been described. The extent of union *involvement* was determined by the number of regular local meetings attended. Those who attended at least four out of ten meetings in the past year were classified as "active"; those who attended fewer were "inactive."

The significant *attitude* variables were, in line with the study design, those concerned with *individual* versus *collective* action and *conciliation* versus *aggressiveness* in solving shop and personal problems. Larger union questions-opinions about the union international, the labor movement, political values, and so forth, proved generally irrelevant and unrelated to the above attitude dimensions. A few examples may illustrate the bases for the classifications.

Individual Action

This category comprised those responses which overemphasized one's own personal problems or those of a specific subgroup rather than problems of the shop workers generally, which implied that the respondent did not personally need the union and that, in fact, the union might prevent some workers from "getting ahead." Some examples were: "I never needed the union to get me more money"; ". . . would have made more money if I had not spent so much time with the union."

Blue-Collar Workers as City and Suburban Residents— Effects on Union Membership

219

Collective Action

An important feature of this orientation was an emphasis on the "solidarizing" function of unionism, namely, "if there were no union, we would be bucking each other"; ". . . a good union man is not just out for himself"; criticism of those who "don't back each other up."

Conciliation

This included those responses which favored a less aggressive approach in collective bargaining (whether they praised or criticized the union along these lines), which were against demands for higher wages in negotiations, which were generally opposed to extensive contract demands, and which expressed a belief that "unions get out of hand."

Aggressiveness

Included were responses which approved the vigorous stand of local officers toward management or criticized them for "being too much on management's side," which approved the idea of strikes (however qualified the approval), or which emphasized that a major union function was protection against managerial arbitrariness.

Combining these two dimensions, it was possible to classify every respondent as relatively "loyal" or "non-loyal" to basic unionist principles.[15] Combining this distinction with the "activism" criterion should logically permit a fourfold categorization. As might be expected, however, no "activists" were "non-loyal."

CITY AND SUBURBAN RESIDENTS

In comparing city and suburban residents, the first significant finding was that a similar proportion from each group were "active" or "inactive," that is, attended meetings fairly regularly. But the activists represented two disparate types.[16] Almost all the suburban activists had been officials in some local union, were informed and articulate about union matters, and, in most cases, took the floor at meetings. Few city activists had held any union position, and several were uninformed about union matters and had never spoken at union meetings. The participation index thus required the addition of dimensions such as knowledge, articulateness, actual involvement when attending meetings, and previous union activity.

Among the "inactive" members, city and suburban residents differed markedly in their typical attitudes along the lines already indicated. The city nonactivist, even though he did not always act on his convictions, tended to advocate worker solidarity and militancy. The suburban nonactivist seemed

---

[15] The implications of this classification should not be misconstrued. Only one respondent was actually "anti-union." The others accepted the value, necessity, and legitimacy of unions in general and their own in particular.

[16] Some of these findings were reported in William Spinrad and Bernard Goldstein, "The Influence of City and Suburban Residence on Union Membership," paper delivered at meetings of American Sociological Society, New York City, August 29, 1960.

to have absorbed the middle-class values of personal achievement and adjustment of disputes. He was thus "disloyal" to some basic principles of unionism.

At least two other city-suburban differences were apparent. Some suburban activists, although identifiable among the local leadership cadre and generally loyal to unionist principles, did indicate some deviation, as in their opposition to strikes and skepticism about having a "union shop." Some of the suburban nonactivists were formerly active in this or other locals; this was not true of any city nonactivists.

Therefore, six possible types of participation-attitude portraits were indicated:

    I.   Activist—informed, articulate, speaks at meetings, loyal to union principles.
    II.   Activist—same as "I" except for some deviation from union principles.
    III.   Activist—uninformed, inarticulate, doesn't speak at meetings, never an official, loyal to union principles.
    IV.   Nonactivist—belief in aggressiveness and solidarity.
    V.   Nonactivist—belief in conciliation and individualism, formerly active.
    VI.   Nonactivist—same as "V," but never active.

Table I, systematizing what has been outlined, locates each type as characteristic of Newark or suburban residents. There was little overlapping among the respondents, and none is indicated in the table. Cityites were typically either III- or IV-type unionists: active-uninformed or nonactive but favoring aggressiveness and solidarity. Suburbanites were generally in one of the other categories.

REFINING THE VARIABLES

Classification among city and suburban residents compelled an elaboration of the independent variable. As an introductory statement, one of the hypothesized intervening variables was the nature of interpersonal contacts in the respective residential milieus—working-class in the city, more middle-class in the suburbs. The responses generally supported this conjecture. This

Table 1

TYPE OF UNION MEMBER, BY RESIDENCE

City Residents		Suburban Residents	
TYPE III	Activist, uninformed, inarticulate, does not speak at meetings, never holds office, loyal to all union principles	TYPE I	Activist, informed, articulate, speaks at meetings, has held office, loyal to all union principles
TYPE IV	Nonactivist; belief in agressiveness and solidarity	TYPE II	Activist, same as Type I, except for some deviation from union principles
		TYPE V	Nonactivist; belief in conciliation and individualism; may have been active
		TYPE VI	Nonactivist; same as Type V, but was never active

Blue-Collar Workers as City and Suburban Residents— Effects on Union Membership

221

suggested, as an additional dimension, the degree of integration in the neighborhood and community, resulting in exposure or lack of exposure to the expected interpersonal influences. Because all respondents were in a working-class setting on the job, providing a possible countervalence to other influences, the third possible dimension was the extent of orientation to the work group. Combining these three dimensions—type of community, integration into that community, and orientation toward the work group—yields a 16-fold typology. Table II sets up this typology and locates types of union members listed in Table I within one or more of the categories.

A few crucial relationships emerge from the findings, as illustrated in the table. Among suburbanites, union activists were characterized by some immersion in and orientation toward the work group. Work-mates were friends and leisure associates, people from whom they would borrow money, forming, in fact, a generic reference group. This is true whether or not they were involved in their suburban communities. Suburban nonactivists lacked such contacts with an orientation toward their work group.

Within the suburban nonactivist sample, the factor of community integration did have some bearing. Those whose responses showed some evidence of *decline* in union participation and loyalty were involved in neighborhood and community life, including suburban organizations. Those for whom both the community and the work group had little meaning had never been active; suburban residence had, for them, meant a retreat to an isolated "cottage castle," a correlate of their individualistic approach to shop problems.

Because very few of the city residents were oriented toward their work group, this was not a factor which distinguished between activists and nonactivists among them. Activists' integration into their largely working-class neighborhoods, plus association with working-class contacts elsewhere, provided their most salient interpersonal influences.[17] The city nonactivist tended to be a social isolate, although his few contacts were usually working-class.

The unionism of the modal city and suburban residents thus present different patterns. The cityite's unionism tends to be an "instinctive" out-

Table 2

TYPE OF UNION MEMBER, BY RESIDENCE AND INTERVENING VARIABLES

	City Residents		Suburban Residents	
	Integrated in Community	Not Integrated in Community	Integrated in Community	Not Integrated in Community
Work-Group Oriented..	—	—	TYPE I OR II	TYPE I OR II
Not Work-Group Oriented	TYPE III	TYPE IV	TYPE V OR VI	TYPE VII

---

[17] This included the likely effects of membership in neighborhood, ethnic, and family associations—largely working-class in composition. In fact, there is some evidence that membership in a religious organization, like the Holy Name Society, may provide for a significantly different interpersonal milieu in a working-class city neighborhood or a heterogeneous suburban area.

growth of the working-class milieu in which he has spent most of his life. If his immersion in that setting is more intense, he will be relatively active in his union, although with few formulated ideas and no leadership role. The suburbanite's unionism seems more of a deliberate choice and is correlated with the extent of work-group orientation and apparent ideological commitment to unionism. The choice for him is between articulate unionism with some assumptiom of leadership or "lukewarmness" to basic union principles.

OTHER FINDINGS

The question of type of job had meaning particularly in the die-casting plant group. In the metal-processing plant, city and suburban residents were equally likely to be skilled or semiskilled, and the job variable, furthermore, seemed generally unrelated to any indexes of union involvement and attitudes. In the die-casting plant, skilled workers, many of them highly paid tool and die makers, comprised most of the suburban activists, but also most of the Type V nonactivists—those with evidence of a decline in union activity and, in most cases, of involvement in the local community. The latter, therefore, seemed best to represent the hypothesized suburbanization effect. The Type VI respondents—the suburbanites who had never been active in any union—were most likely to be semiskilled.

The "job aspirations" findings may be somewhat surprising. With the presumed emphasis on middle-class status in the suburbs, it might be assumed that suburbanites would be more oriented toward "upward" job mobility. On the other hand, the suburban life style emphasizes consumption rather than work, and this should be true of status strivings likewise. Our data support the latter emphasis. None of Type V or VI suburbanites, those who are lukewarm to some union principles, indicated any aspirations for white-collar or small-business positions. Many of them, especially the highly skilled, well-paid workers, felt that they had already "arrived." They believed that they had attained a satisfactory status, as revealed by their suburban addresses, their homes, and their consumption goods equal to those of their middle-class neighbors. In contrast, many semiskilled city workers were actively seeking clerical, semiprofessional, and small-business positions.

Other information gathered can only be summarized very briefly. There was little evidence of a greater tendency to general political conservatism among suburbanites, as indicated either by vote choice or attitudes toward national political issues. There was thus no direct connection between values in the microscopic shop society and those of the macroscopic "great society." However, suburban residence did, as expected, imply a "parochial" orientation toward community and neighborhood problems. City residents emphasized issues of concern to progressive trade unionists—housing, race relations, and crime. Suburbanites mentioned things like real-estate taxes—where the union stand is often contrary to those of homeowners—keeping trucks off the road, building a bridge over a brook, and preventing the construction of a public swimming pool.

Expectations about attitudes towards traveling to the shop and to union meetings were also borne out. Suburban residents were more likely than city residents to complain that the trip was too long, even though the actual travel time was approximately the same. Furthermore, suburban activists tended to give a lower estimate than nonactivists of the time it took to get to work and to meetings when both came from approximately adjacent areas. The dramatic physical contrast between city and suburb seemed to make the trip to work and union meetings appear a greater chore among the suburban nonactivists.

Finally, the length of time in the suburbs seemed to be less important than was anticipated. When the suburban sample was divided into those who had lived in the suburbs five years or more and those who had moved there recently, the two groups contained about an equal proportion of activists and nonactivists. Similarly, there was no indication of greater political conservatism among the old-time suburbanites. Several interviews did imply a possible diminishing of unionist values over time among the Type V group—the former activists. But in the absence of a longitudinal or careful retrospective study, the implication is that the impact of suburbia occurs very early and is, to a great extent, a result of respective "susceptibilities."

CONCLUSIONS

On the basis of a suggestive study of particular groups of blue-collar workers, suburbanization does appear to have some effect on their unionism. Few become anti-union or more politically conservative. Some may become less active in their unions. Many will begin to prefer individualistic and conciliatory methods for solving shop problems. The accompanying and conditioning features of these changes include: a sense of status achievement; an overemphasis on consumption and leisure; a feeling of extreme psychic separation from work place and meeting hall; a lack of interest in work-mates; a concern with the special issues of suburban communities which are outside the scope of union affairs; a removal from a working-class milieu and, for some, immersion in a more middle-class environment.

But all suburban blue-collar workers do not follow this trend. Those who remain close to their work groups, for whom the leisure-consumption orientation is not all-pervasive, remain active in their unions and, despite a few deviations, generally loyal to union principles. These, in fact, constitute the most concerned and involved union members.

What does this portend for the future? The increased suburban trend will probably accentuate the frequently observed tendency toward diminished union activity and militancy. The data, however, do not suggest any decline in acceptance of unions and little conscious—much less aggressive—anti-unionism. As long as the rank-and-file leadership cadre remains relatively active, these attitudes may be enough to maintain the ongoing union position in American society.

Of course, this is not meant as a prediction about the future of unions in the United States. There are obviously too many other factors involved.

SPINRAD The consumption-leisure emphasis, of which suburbanization is both a reflection and a cause, has been partially responsible for the diminished vigor of the American labor movement. But, although the change in residential community of many blue-collar workers does affect their unionism, it does not alter the basic functions of unions, which almost all the respondents in the study in some manner accepted.

Indigenous Leadership in Two Lower-Class Neighborhood Organizations*

F. R. COUSENS

INTRODUCTION

IT is well known to sociologists that the last century has witnessed a vast proliferation of voluntary associations in American society. The changing structure of our society and the growth of great urban centers in this period, and the division of labor and increasing specialization which contributed to depersonalization on the job, concurrently with the anonymity of urban living resulting from personal fragmentation in secondary-group relationships, have all provided fertile soil for the emergence of associations and the opportunity for more primary types of interaction.

However, the various social strata in our society are not equally represented in these voluntary associations. Research on the correlation between social class and patterns of membership and participation demonstrates, rather conclusively, that individuals of lower socioeconomic status tend to have, on the average, fewer affiliations.

There are several reasons for this: persons in the middle class belong to more associations and those of a more diverse nature by virtue of their higher educational levels, occupations which yield higher incomes and afford more leisure, and, generally, a style of life characterized by less preoccupation with economic security. Their life style not only involves a higher and more secure income, earned with less physical energy; it also includes degrees of experience with ideas and not so exclusively with things or people. This makes it relatively easier for middle-class individuals to identify with abstract concepts and social issues. Furthermore, their greater access to more segments of the total society provides them with skills which their lower-class counter-

* The study was conducted while the author was Director of Research for the Michigan Fair Employment Practices Commission. The views expressed herein do not necessarily represent those of the Commission.

parts lack entirely or possess to a lesser degree, and these skills can be acquired only through experience. Many voluntary associations have goals which are intangible and abstract—a type of activity less likely to attract lower-class individuals. Knupfer believes that this is "a manifestation of lack of effort to control the environment and may spring from deeply ingrained habits of doing what one is told."[1]

Lower-status individuals knowing less about abstract matters also display less interest in and less desire for changing things. Because the latter is the most common single feature of the voluntary association, it is not surprising that those of lower status have lower incidence of participation than their higher-status contemporaries. The current study adds an additional dimension, namely, that such individuals belong to different types of organizations as well.

The corollary of understanding such lack of motivation is the recognition that, if you wish to attract lower-class individuals to a voluntary association, its aims must be defined and interpreted to have more direct and personal bearing. Riessman's study of working-class participation shows that individuals at this stratum do not generally participate for reasons of status aspirations or because of a sense of civic responsibility, but only when they see the necessity for doing so. "They must be shown the practical value of participation, i.e., the direct benefits deriving from it."[2]

This study was designed to analyze, in detail, the block and school clubs in a particular working-class area, these associations having been selected for a number of reasons. Because the emphasis and focus are on *indigenous* community participation, it was felt that organizations whose objectives are oriented to the local community and seek, therefore, to recruit their memberships from a limited geographical area would better serve the goals of the study. Furthermore, both organizations are directed toward tangible goals which are of more direct interest and concern to local residents. For all these reasons, participation in either or both of these organizations would provide more accurate criteria with which to evaluate the degree of identification with the community and with some of the agencies and institutions within it.

THE AREA

The geographic area covered by this study is one of the oldest sections in the City of Detroit and is characterized by many and varied social and economic problems. Despite urban renewal and clearance, it remains among the most densely populated sections of the city. The average age of its population is slightly lower than that for the city, reflecting the higher proportion of children who are of school age or younger.

Demographic analysis shows income, education, and occupational level of this population to be significantly lower than the average for either the city or the metropolitan area. The housing, like the residents, reflects lower

---

[1] Genevieve Knupfer, "Portrait of the Underdog," *Public Opinion Quarterly*, Vol. II (Spring, 1947), pp. 103-14.

[2] Frank Riessman, *Workers' Attitudes Toward Participation and Leadership* (unpublished Ph.D. dissertation, Columbia University, 1955), p. 155.

socioeconomic status than most other sections of Detroit and all the suburban areas. The study area is rated lowest on a five-point scale measuring average family income, value of homes, and monthly rent, and at the highest point in substandard homes, overcrowding, dependency, unemployment, tuberculosis, mortality, adult crime, and juvenile delinquency.

The entire area can be subdivided into two neighborhoods or sub-communities which coincide with the respective service areas of two settlement houses: Franklin and Sophie Wright. That served by the Franklin Settlement is older, has been predominantly Negro for a longer time, and is lower in economic status. A total of 214 completed interviews in both subcommunities show these respondents to be, on the average, more stable and to have slightly higher levels of income and education than the total population of the area. It might be more accurate, therefore, to regard them as members of the blue-collar working class rather than the lower class, according to the typology formulated by Miller and Riessman.[3]

That they are atypical for the lower class is also manifested by the pattern of their affiliation with formal associations. Although almost half of the respondents belong to only one organization, and the mean for the entire group is less than two, they nevertheless show more organizational activity than the average for their status group in the typical urban population.

The *types* of organizational affiliations of this sample, however, are more similar to what might be anticipated from individuals in their stratum of society. Most are to be found in the block clubs and/or the school clubs; if they belong to a third organization, it is most likely to be church-affiliated, fraternal, or social, in that order. Political organizations, on the contrary, seem unimportant to this group, since only 15 of the 214 indicate such an affiliation.

In keeping with the findings of Cohen and Hodges,[4] these respondents have most of their social contacts in the immediate neighborhood, with socializing taking place in their homes, the clubs, churches, stores, settlements, and the school, in that order.

From the foregoing, it would be expected that respondents would express a generally positive attitude and identification with their neighborhood; however, such was not established. Despite affirmative responses to questions probing such attitudes—that is, considering the area a good place to live—it is significant that most of the respondents would not want their children to continue living there after they are married.

THE BLOCK CLUBS

Experience with block clubs makes possible some theoretical assumptions: (1) their goals are concrete, and thus more easily interpreted to individuals with relatively little education; (2) their aim is to protect property values, which is of importance to families of low income for whom the acquisition

---

[3] S. M. Miller and Frank Riessman, "The Working Class Subculture: A New View," *Social Problems*, Vol. 9 (Summer, 1961), p. 88, and available in this book.

[4] Albert K. Cohen and Harold M. Hodges, Jr., "Characteristics of the Lower-Blue-Collar Class," *Social Problems*, Vol. 10 (Spring, 1963), pp. 313-14.

of a home requires a financial sacrifice; (3) they provide opportunities for informal social activity, which can be important in achieving greater racial harmony in an interracial neighborhood; (4) as a group, they can apply the pressure necessary to achieve improvements for their neighborhood which they could not do as individuals.

For these reasons, it is to be expected that most of the members of the block clubs will be, as Ravitz predicts, "first home-owners, lower-middle-class Negroes, who are conscious of common problems around which they can organize." [5] To say that these are the characteristics most common among members of block clubs is not to say, however, that residents who possess these characteristics are, to a significant extent, members of block clubs. It helps to delineate the potential universe but does not imply how many from this universe will, with any degree of probability, become members. Using the above characteristics as "tests of membership," it is found that only a small proportion of those eligible actually belong. The data do not indicate what the potential is, but community leaders agree that the membership in the block clubs represents a small minority of the residents.

The question then must be asked: when an association is organized and focused on the bases which are most meaningful to lower- or working-class people, why do so relatively few choose to identify with them, provide leadership, and otherwise help to support and achieve the objectives for which they were created and for which there is apparently a strong interest and desire?

For a long time it was assumed that "habits of submission, low levels of aspiration, and lack of information," which typify the lower-class individual, serve as permanent and serious deterrents to such people in any attempt to modify their environment.[6] Furthermore, "reality factors," such as longer working hours and more strenuous occupations, leave little time and energy for participation; also, the financial cost of belonging and attending meetings all combine to deter affiliation and activity on the part of lower-class individuals. The Richards and Polansky study, for one, shows that such reality factors "apparently do not account for very much of the difference in level of participation between classes." [7]

In the present study, not a single respondent gave lack of time, energy, or money as the reason for not having joined. Most of the nonmembers simply stated that no one has ever asked them to join; some felt that the block club would interfere with their activity in other associations, whereas others did not like some of the people who belonged there or did not approve of the club's objectives. These reasons cannot be considered unique to the lower class, since they resemble, in great measure, those given by nonmembers in a study of middle-class respondents.[8]

---

[5] Mel J. Ravitz, "Sociology of the Block Club," speech, November 20, 1959.

[6] Genevieve Knupfer, "Portrait of the Underdog," in Bendix and Lipset, *Class, Status, and Power* (New York: The Free Press of Glencoe, Inc., 1953), p. 257.

[7] Catherine V. Richards and Norman A. Polansky, "Reaching Working-Class Youth Leaders," *Social Work*, October, 1959, pp. 31-39.

[8] Frances R. Cousens, *Americans for Democratic Action: A Study in Middle Class Political Behavior* (Unpublished thesis: Wayne State University, Detroit, Michigan, 1951).

School clubs have practically no limits on membership; anyone living within the area served by a particular school and sympathetic to the aims of the school can join the Parent-Teacher Association or other type of parents' organization within that school. As a practical matter, however, appeals are directed only to parents of the children who attend there. Even within these limitations, the potential is enormous. The nine elementary schools studied have a combined total of approximately 8,000 children. Estimating two children per family allows for a potential of 4,000 if only one parent joined. The available data show that the parents' organizations in all the nine schools had, as of September, 1961, a combined membership of less than 700,[9] or 17.5 per cent of those who might join, and this is a conservative estimate.

What are some of the reasons for this very poor response to an organization which has as its aim better relationships and cooperation between the home and the school?

In addition to the long history and tradition of parents' organizations in the public schools, there has been a recent trend to new and stronger community orientation on the part of educators. Educational literature is replete with remonstrances that American schools can be most effective only when they are aware of the need for cooperation with the communities which they serve. Moreover, there is an awareness that the school must assume the initiative and provide the leadership in establishing such cooperative relationships. Manifestation of such orientation may be seen in the Detroit school system, where special and permanent citizens' advisory committees are formed and urged to participate in every major facet of the school program: building sites and plans, curriculum development, financing, minority-group relations, personnel, and the like. There is also provision for professional staff assistance in the formation of parents' organizations and guidance in their program activities. Within the last two years, a comprehensive plan of parent-teacher conferences has been established and appears to be functioning successfully. All these efforts on the part of the administration and its staff have one major aim, namely, better liaison between the school and the home, and the consensus of those who are close to the Detroit schools is that this goal is being served.[10] Our impression is that all these efforts represent a trend in the proper direction—one that merits the commendation of all who recognize the need for closer cooperation between the two most important and most universal agencies in the socialization of the child.

Careful and studious observation reveals, however, that despite these efforts, there remains a lag in translating this orientation and program into more effective organized interaction between parents and educators, such as is rep-

---

[9] Personal interview with Laurentine Collins, Department of School and Community Relations, Detroit Public Schools, Detroit, Michigan.

[10] Personal interviews with Miss Collins and Dr. Drachler of the Department of School and Community Relations, and Mr. Roy Stephens, Board Member of the Detroit Public Schools.

Indigenous Leadership in Two Lower-Class Neighborhood Organizations

resented by the parents' clubs within the school. Perhaps the most elusive quality surrounding such interaction is the fact that it is accorded general recognition and approval by all educators, including the principals interviewed for this study. All agree, verbally at least, that the interests of the children, the teachers, and the parents can be well served through the medium of such organization. Where, then, does the fault lie for the seeming failure in bringing about successful organization in lower- or working-class areas?

There is sufficient evidence in the present study and others cited that, regardless of social status and economic class, all normal parents want what is best for their children. Within this concept, education assumes an even greater importance for parents who themselves have little education. Riessman points to the fact that, when his working-class respondents were asked, "What is the thing you've missed in life you'd most want a child of yours to have?" they named education as often as did the middle-class person without a college education.[11]

The parents interviewed in this study display the same strong emphasis on education, with almost half of them indicating that they want their children to have a professional career, and an additional 27 per cent saying, more generally, that they want a "good education" for their children. They seem not only to appreciate the intrinsic value of education, but they display sharp understanding of what it would mean for their children's future, for example, better jobs and, generally, a better life for them. They feel also that, by and large, the school and its staff are doing a good job to provide educational opportunities for their children.

With such positive attitudes toward the school on the part of these parents, combined with a newly strengthened orientation of schools toward parental participation as a positive factor, why, then, do not these factors combine to create an effective parents' organization in the schools of this lower- and working-class area?

The findings in the present study would indicate that the reasons are to be sought on both sides of the school-home relationship. Working- and lower-class parents may desire to participate in the school clubs but do not do so for a number of reasons:

(1) Because of their own limited education, they are unable to translate, without help, their concern, interest, and aspirations for their children into the type of abstract program and activity provided by the school clubs;

(2) Because of their limited exposure and experience with formal associations, they are reluctant or inadequate to assume the initiative in seeking out the school club in order to become a member;

(3) Attendance at school meetings may be frustrating and unrewarding if the program is above their level of understanding or if they are not received with much warmth, interest, or cordiality at the school;

(4) The club leadership may be inadequate in meeting the needs of the membership through the activities which are sponsored.

The above list is not meant to be exhaustive, but merely an indication of the most typical reasons for lack of enthusiasm or participation on the part

[11] Frank Riessman, *op. cit.*

of rank-and-file members in formal associations. It should be pointed out, also, that they did not emerge from the data but have been extrapolated for the reason that, most often, individuals are not conscious of the subjective factors operative in their lack of participation. Rather, the members tend to emphasize superficial factors of which they are cognizant, for example, lack of time and energy, not having been asked to participate more fully, and so forth, when the real reason, particularly in the case of lower-class people, is lack of incentive.

It would be self-defeating to conclude, from the foregoing, that it is simply not possible to provide incentives which are sufficient for those in the working or lower classes to participate in community associations of the type under investigation in this study. From what is already known about the correlation between types of participation and social-class membership, the following conclusion can be drawn: organizations which are oriented to the local community and function to cope with community problems, which are sufficiently uncomplicated, are the ones which will be most attractive and appealing to lower-class individuals. Such people cannot be expected to undertake the solution of abstract, global problems. These must be left to people with much more education and power, since they usually have greater access to the total society and have the skills to deal with such considerations. Lower-status people can be helped to generate interest and enthusiasm and to assume responsibility for problem solving at the local-neighborhood level.

Having thus answered the question of what types of activity offer the greater potential for involvement of lower-class individuals, the question which follows is, How can this best be done? The findings from this study would indicate that:

(1) In a lower-class neighborhood, a distinction must be made between residents who display a significant degree of personal, financial, and residential stability. Not all residents of such neighborhoods are equally disadvantaged by irregular employment and little education nor do they exhibit the same degree of social and personal disorganization. To locate potential indigenous leadership, the more stable elements of the community must be found in order to enlist their aid in promoting the objectives of an organization or movement with which they can identify.

(2) Although individuals in the lower strata of our society do not generally exhibit the extent of formal affiliations found among individuals of a higher socioeconomic status, many can be found who already belong to one or more voluntary associations; these can be interested in additional affiliations.

(3) When lower-lass individuals affiliate, it is with different types of associations from those favored by their middle-class counterparts; the former respond mostly to appeals which are direct and concrete and which can be more easily internalized.

(4) In order to reach lower-class individuals for the purpose of recruiting them into an association with less direct goals, the goals must be defined and interpreted for them in personal and specific terms.

(5) Because organizational skills are acquired only through direct experience, lower-class individuals, because of their limited response to associational activity, therefore, have few such skills and are, therefore, more reluctant to assume positions of leadership and responsibility in the organizations

Indigenous
Leadership
in Two
Lower-Class
Neighborhood
Organizations

they do join. Also, because indigenous leadership is usually more effective than that of professional outsiders, it is especially important to cultivate such leadership.

(6) The pervasive confusion between race and social class has given rise to a persistent, but erroneous, stereotype about the degree of identification possible among Negroes. The data in this study were collected primarily from Negroes and indicate that race by itself is not a valid criterion or determinant of community life.

(7) Detroit, like other Northern urban areas, provides Negroes with more opportunities for the acquisition of organizational experience and skills than does the milieu of the rural Southern areas where many of the residents in lower-class communities originated. Therefore, length of tenure in the Detroit area is positively correlated with degree of identification and level of participation possible in voluntary associations.

(8) Assistance from professionals and agencies either outside or within the community is necessary and important in locating potential members and in training them for participation and leadership. It cannot, however, serve as a substitute for such grass-roots involvement and commitment, nor should it be taken as a criterion of the effectiveness of lower-class community organizations. Far too often, when the professional assistance is withdrawn, the organization tends to retrogress.

SIMILARITIES AND DIFFERENCES BETWEEN THE
BLOCK AND SCHOOL CLUBS IN THIS AREA

The situation in each of the types of organizations analyzed in this study is both similar and different. Both exhibit characteristics of prolonged dependency. Unlike middle-class organizations, these cannot be organized and then left to their own devices; instead of attaining autonomy and independence, the chances are that they will wither. Agencies which plan on initiating such activities should also plan on providing them with professional staff assistance until such time as indigenous leadership can be found, recruited, trained, and depended upon to replace the professional. If sufficient staff is not available to provide the necessary service for the required time, it would be better to start fewer organizations or none at all, because withdrawal of professional assistance may result in the loss of the entire investment to that point.

The settlements should approach the block clubs in precisely the same way as they do clubs which function within the settlement. There, each is sponsored and served by a staff member who is sensitive to the needs of the membership and who plans activities commensurate with those needs and the abilities they possess. There is little expectation that these clubs will achieve sufficient autonomy and self-direction in a short period and thus be able to continue independently.

On the contrary, the expectations set for the block clubs appear to have been unrealistic, because they are composed of unskilled individuals who are inadequate to carry on alone after the initial stimulus provided by the settlement. It would have been better, probably, to start fewer clubs but to remain with each for the time necessary for it to develop its own direction and leadership.

COUSENS

The school clubs present a somewhat different situation. Their tradition is not only much older than but also different from that of the block clubs. The school and its professional personnel have always performed a significant role in their organization and expect to continue in such a service capacity. For this reason, school clubs may not develop indigenous leadership for precisely the opposite reason, namely, that professional help was provided for too *long* a period.

Another serious difference between the two types of associations is that the settlements display much stronger motivation for the block clubs than many principals and teachers seem to manifest with respect to the school clubs. Despite a half-century-old tradition of home-school cooperation, the real impetus for involving parents in the schools is of recent origin, and many educators feel bound by both the old tradition and the new impetus but with little genuine conviction about the efficacy of these organizations. Thus, a halfhearted attempt is often made to assemble parents with little intelligent planning to keep them organized or to cater to their needs and abilities. In a middle-class area, the potential for indigenous leadership is greatly magnified, and the school can delegate much of its responsibility to the club members. In lower-class areas, the school must provide not only the motivation but the training for leadership skills as well. It is at this level that principals seem to be inadequate to the task. Among the nine elementary-school administrators interviewed for this study, some stated that they welcome parents into the school and are disappointed that so few have joined the parents' club, but one gets the impression that this represents lip service more than conviction. Others spoke in glowing terms of the parents' club in their school but went on to deprecate the ability of the members to do anything but the most mundane tasks. Still others seem to regard parents in the same way as they regard the children, with patient tolerance but little respect. It is not difficult to deduce why such principals do not have more successful clubs in their schools. Their conscious and subconscious attitudes permeate the teaching staff, who, in turn, regard parents either inside or outside the school as necessary evils to be tolerated or ignored.

On the other hand, there were among the nine principals some who, by word and deed, exuded respect and confidence in parents as adult, mature human beings. Nevertheless, they did not ignore the fact that these adults lacked many of the skills necessary for effective participation and leadership; therefore, they provided them with all the help which the school could offer. Parents were encouraged to attend training sessions in order to assume increasingly more responsibility in and for their organization. Cooperation was acknowledged with gratitude, and help was offered when needed, without implying that the parents were inferior because they needed help. In such a relationship, the attitude of these lower-class people was transformed from one of apprehensiveness and hostility to a feeling of being a partner, with the school, in the process of developing in the children positive attitudes toward the school.

Schools, by themselves, cannot be expected to make any appreciable changes in community life except over a relatively long period. Most of the problems in lower-class areas are inherited by the school, which can only

Indigenous
Leadership
in Two
Lower-Class
Neighborhood
Organizations

attempt to modify them. What teachers and administrators can do is understand and teach with understanding of the child's out-of-school problems. As with most human problems, these can be considered as problems or as a challenge, depending largely on the attitudes and capabilities of the professionals who deal with them. Working with lower-class parents can be fully as rewarding as working with their children, and it requires the same kind of understanding, patience, and creative skill.

Establishing a parents' club in the school is only the first step toward building a positive relationship on a permanent basis. Parents must be encouraged to come, and must be welcomed into the school as partners in helping their child to achieve—not as interlopers storming a closed domain. In this respect, an important lesson may be learned from the program for adults which has been established as part of the Great Cities Project. The professional staff in the Project schools are receptive to new ideas and anxious to experiment with new methods; those who are not are permitted to transfer elsewhere. In their work with children and parents, they are building a sound relationship between the school and home which should be widely emulated.[12]

Much research remains to be done in this general area of lower-class community participation, particularly as it affects the school and the home. Evaluation of methods employed in the Great Cities Project should contribute important insights. Other studies of an experimental nature should be made to evaluate various types of approaches used by schools in working with parents and other community residents. More funds must be allocated for concentrated efforts in lower-class school areas, and these efforts must be followed up by careful analysis and evaluation.

As the central cities of our metropolitan regions become increasingly more nonwhite, more lower-middle-class and lower-class, many changes will result, requiring changes in community relations as well as in curriculum and teaching methods. Such an investment for the future may be well compensated by a lower incidence of social and personal disorganization. It is our firm belief that the urban schools must assume the initiative in such an investment in order to be more effective in performing their primary function, namely, socialization of each new generation of American children.

---

[12] Personal interview with Dr. Carl Marburger, Director of the Great Cities Project for the Detroit Public Schools System.

Sources and Consequences of Working-Class Consciousness*

JOHN C. LEGGETT

THE FOCUS

THOSE interested in the sources of working-class consciousness in an industrial community should distinguish between its apparent and less evident origins. Historically, contrasts in wealth, dips in employment, and the activities of aggressive unions have been both visible and significant as generators of militancy. Certainly, in the last 30 years many social scientists and laymen alike have attempted to relate the growth of consciousness to increases in economic insecurity and the protests of unions, particularly the industrial variety located in heavy manufacturing such as steel, rubber, and automobile. During the Great Depression of the 1930's, many workers who were found in these unions and industries became quite militant and thereby confirmed the expectations of not a few observers.[2] Now, however, it would seem that conditions are conducive to acceptance of the class order, and labor unions in general are no longer aggressive. Consequently, many of us have concluded that the entire working class is without class consciousness and have inferred that the latter is without political consequence—other than indifference to class questions or commitment to the existing political situation.[3] These conclusions rest on shaky premises, for they unwisely overlook the *less* conspicuous origins of verbal militancy, consequently disregard its incidence, and con-

* I am deeply indebted to the Social Science Research Council, the Horace H. Rackham School of Graduate Studies, the Department of Sociology of the University of Michigan, and the Department of Political Science of Wayne State University for their assistance. In addition, I would like to thank Gerhard Lenski, David Aberle, Herbert Blumer, Morris Janowitz, Daniel Katz, Werner Landecker, and Robert Mowitz for their provocative criticisms and suggestions.

[2] Classical studies on working-class radicalism in the 1930's include Alfred W. Jones, *Life, Liberty, and Property* (Philadelphia: J. B. Lippincott Co., 1941), and Robert F. Brooks, *When Labor Organizes* (New Haven: Yale University Press, 1942).

[3] The old stress on class has been replaced by emphasis on status. Many writers treated the American scene during the 1950's as if it had been one of general prosperity, deemphasized the importance of class, and stressed the relevance of status. Illustrative was a series of essays edited by Daniel Bell, *The New American Right* (New York: Criterion Books, 1955).

sistently neglect its political potential. This paper will attempt to compare the impact of the more obvious with the less noticeable sources of working-class consciousness and to comment briefly on its political importance. In so doing, we may be able to shed some new light on several old questions.

MARX'S CONTRIBUTION

Marx delineated what he judged to be the roots of working-class consciousness. In so doing, he helped to make them visible. Indeed, Marx's treatment of consciousness has traditionally provided us with a limited but useful set of ideas for dealing with its origins, content, and consequences. Clearly, Marx made at least three important contributions to its study. First, he specified several of its interrelated sources, such as an increase in economic insecurity, the development of vivid contrasts in wealth, the growth in concentration of workmen in factories, the related intensification of communication among them, and the consequent development of unionization. Second, he presented a sketchy but provocative description of what he meant by "class consciousness." Third, he related it to the political world, and in so doing he indicated the structural conditions under which consciousness would have its greatest political impact.[4] In his day, Marx's observations revolutionized the thoughts of not a few people. Today, many of his notions still appear insightful but seldom surprising. In any event, Marx has alerted us to the relevance of many conditions about us.

Yet, Marx's treatment of the social sources of class consciousness proved to be wanting in at least two important respects. First, he slighted the theoretical salience of ethnic-group membership, even though he briefly noted how racial differences divided the labor movement in the United States.[5] Second, Marx erred in his analysis of the political role of workers reared in

---

[4] Marx's comments on the origins of consciousness can be found scattered throughout his writings. See, for example, "The Communist Manifesto," in *Capital, The Communist Manifesto, and Other Writings,* edited by Max Eastman (New York: The Modern Library, 1932), pp. 329-33; "Wage, Labor, and Capital," in *Selected Works, Vol. I* (New York: International Publishers, 1933), pp. 268-69; "The Eighteenth Brumaire of Louis Bonaparte," in Karl Marx, *Selected Writings in Sociology and Social Philosophy,* eds. T. B. Bottomore and Maximilien Rubel (London: Watts and Co., 1956), pp. 188-89; "Capital, Vol. I," in Dwight Macdonald, *The Root is Man* (Alhambra, California: The Cunningham Press, 1953), p. 23.

Marx's references to the content of class consciousness appear in a variety of sources, including Karl Marx, *The German Ideology,* Parts I and III (New York: International Publishers, 1947); "Preface to *A Contribution to the Critique of Political Economy,"* in Karl Marx, *Selected Writings in Sociology and Social Philosophy, op. cit.,* p. 52; "Poverty of Philosophy," *ibid.,* pp. 186-88.

Some of Marx's ideas on the political consequences of working-class consciousness can be found in "The German Ideology," *ibid.,* p. 65; "Preface to *A Contribution to the Critique of Political Economy,"* *ibid.,* p. 52. Also see Engels' incisive remarks on consciousness and politics within a parliamentary framework, in "English Fabian Socialism," Karl Marx and Friedrich Engels, *Basic Writings on Politics and Philosophy,* ed. Lewis S. Feuer (Garden City, N.Y.: Doubleday and Company, Inc., 1959), pp. 446-48; "Why There Is No Socialist Party in America," *ibid.,* pp. 457-59.

[5] Karl Marx and Friedrich Engels, *The Civil War in the United States* (New York: The Citadel Press, 1961), pp. xlv, 280-81.

agrarian regions and relocated in industrial towns. He concluded that workmen who had but recently migrated from rural areas would hold a lower degree of class consciousness than those seasoned throughout their lives to the harsh realities of industrial capitalism. Largely because of this assumption, Marx held that revolutionary enthusiasm would seize the working class of industrialized Germany before a working-class revolution could occur in largely agrarian countries such as Russia. Of course, Marx did not say that an embryonic working class would express a low degree of class *élan*. For example, he was well aware of the Chartists and even more militant British working-class movements that existed at the time. Yet, he viewed these collectivities as immature expressions of a working class *less* class conscious than a proletariat steeled for several generations through exposure to industrialization and the agitational activities of labor unions.[6]

Of these two oversights, the latter has proved most interesting to social scientists. G. D. H. Cole,[7] Adam Ulam,[8] Alfred Jones,[9] Harold Wilensky and Charles Lebeaux,[10] and a host of others[11] have indicated that on the whole the most aggressive workers are those driven from backward rural areas. An awareness of these developments has led me to focus my attention on the class consciousness of the uprooted.

PROCEDURE

The Sample

In order to weigh the importance of uprootedness, ethnicity, and more apparent considerations, 375 male blue-collar residents of the city of Detroit were interviewed in the spring and early summer of 1960. These respondents were selected from seven districts of high ethnic concentration, that is, residential districts known to be highly homogeneous in terms of ethnic social organization. A list-random-sample procedure was used to select respondents from these districts, three of which were predominantly Negro, three Polish,

---

[6] Karl Marx, "Communist Manifesto," in *Selected Writings in Sociology and Social Philosophy, op. cit.*, pp. 184-85.

[7] Cole's analysis of the embryonic and mature British working class can be found in *A Short History of the British Working Class* (London: George Allen and Unwin, 1952).

[8] See Adam Ulam, *The Unfinished Revolution* (Cambridge, Mass.: Harvard University Press, 1960), pp. 58-90.

[9] Alfred W. Jones, *op. cit.*, pp. 61-66.

[10] Harold Wilensky and Charles N. Lebeaux, *Industrial Society and Social Welfare* (New York: Russell Sage Foundation, 1958), pp. 27-132.

[11] Lipset and Kornhauser have presented information on the differential tempos of industrial development and the incidence of political extremism in Scandinavia. Their findings support the contentions of Cole and the others mentioned. See Seymour M. Lipset, *Political Man* (Garden City, N.Y.: Doubleday & Company, 1960), pp. 68-71; and William Kornhauser, *The Politics of Mass Society* (New York: The Free Press of Glencoe, Inc., 1959), pp. 150-55. In the United States, Liston Pope has found that many of the workers who took part in the bitter 1929 textile strike in Gastonia, North Carolina, were also recent immigrants from rural areas. See his *Millhands and Preachers* (New Haven, Conn.: Yale University Press, 1942), pp. 213-306.

and one northwest European. Only male Negro, Polish, Ukrainian, German, and British (non-Southern-born) workers were interviewed.[12]

The sample was selected and most of the interviews were conducted during the late spring and early summer of 1960, a period of relative economic prosperity for the community as a whole, although its economic structure was obviously not up to par. The 1957-1958 recession had ended and the percentage of unemployed had dropped from 20 per cent of the total labor force to six per cent in April and May of 1960. However, even though unemployment had declined considerably, many men laid off during the 1957-1958 recession had failed to find work after the automobile industry had recovered. The study, then, drew its sample from a population of workmen many of whom had faced considerable economic insecurity during the late 1950's. A large proportion of this category, it might be added, were Negro immigrants from the southern United States.[13]

Less Apparent Yet Potential Sources

The sample thereby selected workmen who might be classified into three types of ethnic groups: proletarian, industrial, and affluent. Proletarian ethnic-group members share low status and fill primarily semiskilled and unskilled work roles. Negroes in Detroit would be an example. The industrial ethnic group consists primarily of semiskilled and skilled workers, although a significant proportion of its members may be found in clerical and retail occupations. Members of the Polish minority group in many large Northern industrial towns would constitute one current historical counterpart of this category. It should be noted that the industrial ethnic group maintains more prestige than the proletarian entity, but less than the affluent collectivity. The latter includes a disproportionately large number of middle-class members, most of whom are professionals, businessmen, and executives. However, it should be mentioned that a large number of affluent ethnic-group members are skilled workmen. German and British nationality groups located in Detroit correspond to this ideal type.[14]

---

[12] A very high proportion of those interviewed consisted of semiskilled auto workers, such as body assemblers, welders, painters, inspectors, and body sanders. In addition, the sample included many skilled factory workers; for example, tool and die as well as pattern makers. The building construction trades and teamsters were also represented, although they constituted a distinct minority.

[13] The impact of widespread economic deprivation on Detroit Negroes during the late 1950's has been described by David Street and John C. Leggett in "Economic Deprivation and Extremism: A Study of Unemployed Negroes," *American Journal of Sociology*, Vol. LXVII (July, 1961), pp. 53-57.

[14] Information gathered in a 1958 random sample of the Greater Detroit adult population revealed the following occupational distribution by ethnic group: Negro, 88 per cent blue-collar (BC), 12 per cent white-collar (WC); Poles, 69 per cent BC, 31 per cent WC; Germans, 52 per cent BC, 48 per cent WC; Britons (non-Southern English, Scotch, Welsh, and mixture), 45 per cent BC, 55 per cent WC. The ethnic prestige of each group proved to be directly related to percentage white-collar (of course, no causal relationship is implied). See John C. Leggett, *Working-Class Consciousness in an Industrial Community* (Ph.D. dissertation, University of Michigan, 1962), pp. 144-53.

Uprooted workers include all workmen born in agrarian regions and re-settled in Detroit. For the purposes of this paper, they refer to Southern-born Negroes and European-born Poles. By contrast, prepared workmen are born and raised within industrial regions and include Northern-born Negroes and Poles.[15]

Degree of Working-Class Consciousness

Working-class consciousness can be defined as a cumulative series of mental states, running from class verbalization through skepticism and militancy to egalitarianism. *Class verbalization* denotes the tendency of working-class individuals to discuss topics in class terms. They need not do so consistently. In fact, only the occasional use of class symbols designates one as having some facility in their usage. *Skepticism* occurs when an individual believes that wealth is allocated within the community to benefit primarily the middle class. *Militancy* refers to a predisposition to engage aggressively in action to advance the interests of one's class. *Egalitarianism* has reference to favoring a redistribution of wealth so that each individual within the community would have (1) the same amount and (2) the material basis thereby for the full development of his natural talents.

In order to measure *class verbalization,* the first aspect of class consciousness considered, a battery of eight unstructured questions was used. Each question deliberately made no reference to class, in order not to prejudice the answers of the respondent. He was asked whom he had voted for in the last election and why, who was his favorite president and why, and so forth. If the worker used class terms in just one of these instances, his comments constituted class verbalization.

Skepticism was weighed through the use of the following question: "When business booms in Detroit, who gets the profits?" If the respondent used categories such as "rich people," "upper class," "big business," and similar class references, he was treated as class-conscious in this regard.

Militancy was measured by asking the interviewee to project himself into a situation in which workers were about to take action against a landlord, and to indicate whether or not he would join the group in a series of activities, including picketing. If he would take part in the latter, the study classified him as militant.

---

[15] A distinction can be made between agrarian and industrial regions. The former refers to one in which (1) industry creates relatively little wealth, and (2) the population maintains agrarian forms of social organization and values. An industrial region exists where the population depends almost entirely upon an industrial base for its sustenance, and where agricultural endeavors supply only a fraction of the population with its livelihood. See John C. Leggett, "Uprootedness and Working-Class Consciousness," *American Journal of Sociology,* Vol. LXVIII (May, 1963), pp. 684-85.

It should be noted that categorizing foreign-born Germans and Britons as either uprooted or prepared proved to be impossible, because the study's data did not indicate whether they were born in agrarian or industrial regions. However, had data on region of birth been available, no doubt most of them would have been treated as prepared, given the industrialized character of most of Britain and Germany just prior to World War I, the period when most of the foreign-born in the sample were growing up.

Egalitarianism was determined to exist when the worker agreed with the notion that the wealth of our country should be divided up equally so that people would have an equal chance to get ahead.[16]

These various aspects of class consciousness were linked to one another so as to measure the degree to which each worker had developed class consciousness. Ideally, workers thereby fell into one of the following five categories: militant egalitarians, militant radicals, skeptics, class verbalizers, and class indifferents. Figure 1 indicates how workmen were typed.

It should be noted that approximately three-quarters of the respondents held opinions that corresponded either exactly or consistently with this model. Only one-fourth of the workers maintained a point of view that was inconsistent with this configuration. Although they were clearly "error types,"[17] they nevertheless were categorized, as were the rest, on the basis of a point system suggested by Guttman.[18] Thus, a total of 375 workers were classified.

Figure 1

IDEAL CLASSIFICATION OF RESPONDENTS—FOUR ASPECTS OF CLASS CONSCIOUSNESS

Individuals Typed According to Class Perspective	Egalitarianism	Militancy	Skepticism	Class Verbalization
Militant Egalitarians	+*	+	+	+
Militant Radicals . .	−†	+	+	+
Skeptics	−	−	+	+
Class Verbalizers . .	−	−	−	+
Class Indifferents . .	−	−	−	−

*"+" refers to class-conscious.
†"−" refers to non-class-conscious.

---

[16] This treatment of class consciousness, although original, rests on several formulations found in sociological literature. Not only the ideas of Marx and Guttman, but those of Manis and Meltzer, as well as Alfred Jones, have been used to define the various aspects of class consciousness. Marx has pointed to the utility of thinking in terms of degree of class consciousness, while Guttman has suggested a suitable measurement technique. Manis and Meltzer have wisely suggested that class consciousness can be treated in terms of its many aspects, whereas the findings of Jones, in his study of Akron sit-down strikers, have warned the researcher against ignoring its militant forms. Clearly, then, this definition is a synthesis of several important writings. Guttman's presentation of a useful measurement technique can be found in Samuel Stouffer, *et al., Studies in Social Psychology in World War II*, Vol. IV (Princeton, N. J.: Princeton University Press, 1950), pp. 3-90, 172-212. Also see Jerome G. Manis and Bernard N. Meltzer, "Attitudes of Workers to Class Structure," *American Journal of Sociology*, Vol. LX (1954), pp. 30-55; and Alfred W. Jones, *op. cit.*, pp. 250-80.

[17] "Error types" refer to those patterns of response which are inconsistent with those presented in Figure 1. For example, workers who scored "plus" on class verbalization, "minus" on skepticism, and "plus" on both militancy and egalitarianism would constitute error types. Again, workmen who answered positively on verbalization and skepticism, "minus" on militancy, but affirmatively on egalitarianism would also be counted as error types.

Perhaps these and other unusual patterns of response occurred because the respondents did not understand the questions posed by the interviewer. However, this was certainly not always the case. Indeed, the existence of inconsistent answers suggests a lack of consensus among workmen on the question of degree of militancy. For some, picketing would be more extreme than favoring equality. These workers might therefore value the latter but eschew personal participation in picketing demonstrations. On the other hand, evidence collected in the study indicates that most workmen viewed picketing landlords as less extreme than favoring equality.

[18] For further information on the construction of these types, see John C. Leggett, *Working-Class Consciousness in an Industrial Community, op. cit.*, pp. 73-135.

Of these, 38 qualified as militant egalitarians, 87 as militant radicals, 114 as skeptics, 98 as class verbalizers, and 38 as class indifferents. We shall now relate these types to forces potentially associated with militancy.

THE IMPORTANCE OF ETHNICITY AND UPROOTEDNESS

The less apparent sources of consciousness differentiate class opinions more clearly than considerations traditionally linked with working-class militancy (see Figure 2). It should be noted that 59 per cent of the proletarian, 29 per cent of the industrial, and 14 per cent of the affluent workmen proved to be militants, although, at the other extreme, the distribution of nonmilitants fell into the expected pattern: proletarian, 13 per cent; industrial, 38 per cent; and affluent, 54 per cent. Much as expected, the uprooted outdistanced the prepared to a highly significant degree.[19] On the other hand, union membership, skill level, employment status, and especially personal income had less of an impact than one might expect, although several of these considerations continued to be of some importance. Perhaps most noticeable in this regard was skill level. Here, however, the small number of unskilled workmen prevented generalization. Two of the other more visible forces—employment status and union membership—were of some significance, especially when they were combined with ethnicity and uprootedness. Noteworthy in this regard was union membership, which served to accentuate the militancy of the proletarian ethnic-group members and the uprooted.[20] Perhaps most surprising was the inability of personal income to sharply differentiate workmen. This particular finding and several others deserve interpretive comment.

INTERPRETIVE REMARKS

The Proletarian Ethnic Group

Conflict with employers contributes to the class consciousness of workmen found within the proletarian ethnic group. A disproportionately large number of its working-class members can be found in occupational positions characterized by economic insecurity—a source of antagonism between employers and employees located in modern industrial communities. Perhaps more important, the low prestige of the collectivity results in discrimination against these workmen in employment, promotion, and retention, thereby heightening their insecurity, increasing conflict between employers and employees, and consequently accentuating militancy. Coupled with employer discrimination is another consequence of low ethnic prestige: unequal treatment at the hands of those who command the distribution of many goods and services. Members of the business community repeatedly deny these workmen equal access to residential, educational, and other consumer resources largely allocated by

---

[19] Theodore Purcell's study of Chicago packinghouse workers supports my findings. He repeatedly demonstrated that Negroes were more militant than whites. See Theodore Purcell, *The Worker Speaks His Mind on Company and Union* (Cambridge: Harvard University Press, 1953).

[20] John C. Leggett, "Uprootedness and Working-Class Consciousness," *op. cit.*, p. 690.

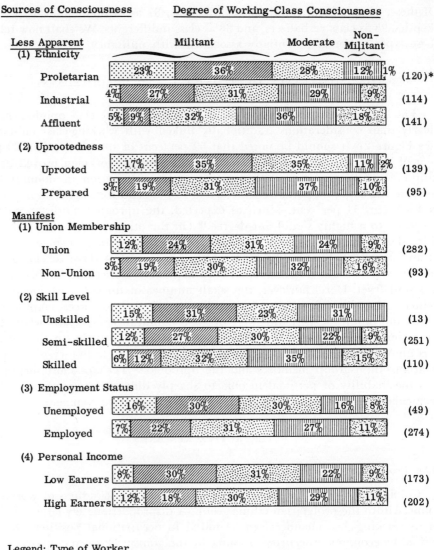

Figure 2

SOURCES AND DEGREE OF WORKING-CLASS CONSCIOUSNESS—A COMPARISON

private business interests. Their behavior constitutes a source of considerable unrest, partially because it occurs within a community where supposedly ability and not ascribed status should be crucial in determining one's life chances.

The same workers who are subject to discriminatory policies pursued by employers are isolated from them socially, a condition which facilitates the development of class consciousness. Intimate and friendly relations between these two groups are prohibited by conflict rooted in the issues mentioned and by institutions concerned with the maintenance of segregation. Under these circumstances, these workmen can choose verbal solutions that are consistent with their class and ethnic interests and certainly *not* in keeping with the desires of the business community.[21]

Many of the workers located within the proletarian and industrial ethnic groups share not only a common ethnic background but an uprooted status position as well. These workers expressed an extremely high level of class consciousness.[22] Why uprootedness should have this impact will now be considered.

Uprootedness

The uprooted—in comparison to the prepared—bring with them fewer skills and experiences which might help them to deal effectively with their new environment. Consequently, they are readily exploited during part, if not all, of their work lives. This exploitation, coupled with insufficient skills, effectively limits their chances to obtain secure working-class positions or to move into the middle class. Marginal economic position, linked to blocked mobility, in turn creates grievances and sometimes engenders collective protests demanding an alteration of their condition. The situation of the uprooted has these consequences, in part, because workmen are able to compare their present economically insecure positions with (1) their original optimistic expectations developed prior to movement to the industrial community and (2) the relatively high standard of living maintained by the middle class and much of the working class as well.

A host of other considerations no doubt contribute to the class consciousness of the uprooted. One factor deserves particular attention. The uprooted presumably develop an antipathy toward the supraordinate (higher-ranked) classes in general because the latter, in both agrarian and industrial regions, have exploited them. In agrarian regions (such as much of the southern

---

[21] On the other hand, many of the conditions common to the affluent ethnic group favor the weakening of their militancy. It should not be forgotten that discriminatory practices operate in their favor, at least in some respects. For example, employment opportunities denied to minority groups become available to them, and job promotion and retention in the firm operate in the same way. Furthermore, public and private rewards are distributed so as to give the "affluents" occupational positions which are relatively secure. Consequently, these working-class elements face fewer problems in employment; and, when they are so confronted, they can frequently count on the aid of friends who are helpful and employers who are biased—in their favor.

One more point: It might be argued that businessmen are not the only ones who discriminate, particularly in the job arena. This is certainly the case, because many Americans unions also discriminate on the basis of race. However, it should be noted that these particular unions contain a minority of the unionized workers in the community studied. The overwhelming majority of workmen belonged to the major industrial unions, which in turn led in the fight for civil rights during the 1940's and 1950's.

[22] Worthy of our attention is the finding that uprootedness has an impact even when one takes ethnicity into account. See John C. Leggett, *ibid.*, pp. 687, 691. Furthermore, uprootedness does not upset the relationship between ethnicity and working-class consciousness. Southern-born Negroes are more militant than foreign-born Poles, and Northern-born Negroes hold more class-conscious views than do their Polish counterparts. In addition, it should be noted that the latter were more militant than workmen of German and British background.

United States and Poland prior to World War II), upward mobility and improvement of status among the lower classes are generally impossible. Rigid norms and legal structures, backed by the landowning aristocracy, control them, to the extent that the subordinate classes find it difficult to express their grievances without being severely repressed by the upper class or its representatives. For this reason, those so adversely affected develop a marked dislike for this particular supraordinate class. This attitude is later generalized to include all supraordinate classes when the dominant class in the industrial community also acts with little regard for their economic and social welfare.

The impact of past membership in a society where there is a high degree of class rigidity should not be overestimated, however. One cannot say that subordinate-class membership within an agrarian region is the sole source of working-class consciousness for the uprooted. Rather, it would seem that an exploited position in an industrial community, when coupled with past membership in an agrarian community, contributes to militancy.

The uprooted differ markedly from the prepared in previous experiences. The latter are natives of an industrial region and are thus in a much better position to acquire the occupational skills and urban values so useful in adapting successfully to the demands of the industrial community. Because of their greater sophistication, they are subject to less economic exploitation, blocked mobility, and economic insecurity. In addition, the prepared do not carry with them the strong dislike of ruling groups found in preindustrial society, for, after all, they were never members of this form of social organization. Partially because of these differences in past experiences, the prepared develop a lower degree of class consciousness than do the uprooted.[23]

TRADITIONAL CONSIDERATIONS

Social forces traditionally associated with class consciousness have less impact than one might expect, partially because many union members and insecure (less-skilled and/or unemployed) workers can be found among affluent ethnic groups and prepared workmen. Those found in the latter two categories can depend upon preferential treatment based upon prestige and/or skills. These workmen constitute a more fortunate segment of the working class.

Interestingly, amount of personal income is minimally correlated with working-class consciousness, since earnings fail to correspond with economic

---

[23] Werner Landecker has developed a quite similar interpretation of the sources of class consciousness. His explanation both achieves a higher degree of generality than the one advanced in this study and presents a point of view consistent with my own:

"It seems then that in one form or another a large proportion of the population perceive their present social positions as stepping stones to higher levels. Under such conditions, one will tend to view oneself or one's family as being potentially above the transitional level occupied at the present time. Only if prospects for up-mobility seem to be dim, do people come to think of themselves as being in the same boat with others of similar status and as being part of a distinct class. It seems then that the frequency of up-mobility which is assumed to occur stands in an inverse relation to the prevalent degree of class consciousness. *The higher the apparent frequency of up-mobility is, the lower the degree of class consciousness will tend to be.*" (Emphasis my own.) See Ronald Freedman, *et al., Principles of Sociology* (New York: Holt, Rinehart, & Winston, Inc., 1952), p. 462.

security. Indeed, not a few workmen in an advanced industrial community earn low, steady, and predictable incomes, which, if anything, abate the development of militancy.[24]

AN ADDITIONAL CONSIDERATION: IMPACT OF CONSCIOUSNESS ON VOTING CHOICE

So far, we have considered several sources of consciousness but have not referred to its impact on the political preferences of Detroit workers. Because this problem has been treated in detail elsewhere,[25] a condensed analysis should suffice. In an election in which Detroit workers gave their overwhelming support to a pro-labor candidate (G. Mennen Williams) for governor (the 1958 gubernatorial race), 76 per cent of the militant workmen supported him. At the same time, workers who expressed either a moderate or a low degree of consciousness behaved as expected: 70 per cent of the moderates and 50 per cent of the nonmilitants cast their vote for this reform politician. *Among voters only,* 95 per cent of the militants, 88 per cent of the moderates, and 69 per cent of the nonmilitants voted for Williams.

Perhaps of more interest than the figures just presented are the workers' justifications for their choices. Apparently, class considerations assumed paramount importance for many of them:

"I like his platform. It was for the workingman."

"I think he's doing a good job for the poor people. I think he's 100 per cent for the workingman."

"I thought he was a good governor. He's a staunch supporter for working-class people."

"He seemed to do fairly well as far as politics go. He's for the workingman. That's probably keeping him out of the presidential race."

"As I told you before, I'm strictly Democratic. Williams is number one. He's for labor. He's for the workingman."

"He did a pretty good job. He was for the working people."

"He was giving the workingman a fair shake, where Bagwell wasn't giving us anything."

"I didn't vote, but I liked Williams. (Why?) Oh, I don't know. He seems to be a fair guy. He's honest. If he can do something for the worker, he does it."

"Williams is more for the working class."

"He's a good man. He always helped the workingman and was the workingman's choice."

As interesting as the figures and quotes may be, they do not take into account the independent impact of racial-group membership. This factor has proven to be especially important in the community studied, where, for the

---

[24] See Seymour M. Lipset, *op. cit.,* pp. 231-37.
[25] John C. Leggett, "Working-Class Consciousness, Race, and Political Choice," *American Journal of Sociology,* Vol. LXIX, (September, 1963), pp. 171-76.

past several decades, the vast majority of Negroes (irrespective of gradations of working-class consciousness within the group) have voted in favor of politicians committed to strong civil rights programs. Such was also the case in this election. Of those Negro workers who voted, almost 100 per cent of the militants cast their votes for Williams; but what is more interesting, over 90 per cent of the *nonmilitant* types did so as well. As these percentages indicate, a low degree of class consciousness had little effect on the political choices of these Negro voters. However, if one examines the impact of consciousness within the white category, the information gathered more clearly sustains our expectations. Seventy-four per cent of the militants, 67 per cent of the moderates, and only 47 per cent of the nonmilitants voted for the candidate.

The hard core of Williams support among whites could be found among militants who belonged to the unions. While unionized workers voted disproportionately in favor of the pro-labor politician, perhaps of more interest was the combined impact of union membership and class consciousness. An analysis of the entire sample of white workers revealed a predictable pattern of voting support for Williams: (1) militant unionists, 80 per cent; (2) moderate unionists, 72 per cent; (3) nonmilitant unionists, 52 per cent; (4) militant nonunionists, ($N = 5$); (5) moderate nonunionists, 50 per cent; (6) nonmilitant nonunionists, 38 per cent. Clearly, then, the combination of a high degree of consciousness plus union membership created a block preference, while, at the other extreme, nonunion types who were less militant voted as expected.[26]

CONCLUDING REMARKS

Workmen who are uprooted or members of the proletarian ethnic group prove to be the most militant—a tendency which is accentuated by membership in labor unions. Such membership, along with economic insecurity, helps to generate consciousness of their class, but less than one might expect. Perhaps of most interest is the double impact of unionization and class consciousness on the political choices made by white workers.

We can now reject the current stereotype of American workmen as a homogeneous population unable to develop class standards or to vote in a manner consistent with their interests. Many of them are militant, and their class views have predictable political consequences. On the other hand, it is clear that a very sizable proportion of workers resident in industrial communities like Detroit are anything but aggressive in their class opinions. If any-

---

[26] On the other hand, even if the measure of consciousness does point effectively to political choice, one might still question the data itself, for, after all, the items used to measure working-class consciousness do not make any reference to class identification, perhaps the most popular measure of class consciousness. This objection is reasonable. However, a close-ended measure of awareness of class position, when substituted for class verbalization and linked to other measures of consciousness, can be related to political preference. When this is done, the evidence proves to be almost identical with information presented on race, union, consciousness, and voting choice. Clearly, then, the substitution does not change the findings.

Other objections might also be raised. For example, it might be noted that no attempt was made to relate objective positions of workmen to *anti*-working-class *or* middle-class consciousness. Such an effort should prove to be worthwhile, but this task I leave to future research.

thing, they *do* approximate the present and popular image of American workmen. To sum up, *the working class is heterogeneous, in terms of both social background and class views.*

Social scientists should continue to focus on these differences. However, it might be rewarding to pay particular attention to the more militant workmen and their adversaries. Observers so oriented during the decade ahead might profitably study the mechanisms of persuasion used by the principal contenders—working-class Negroes and the white business community.

Resident Response to Urban Rehabilitation in a Negro Working-Class Neighborhood

MORTON RUBIN

I

"YOU ask me if living in this neighborhood has contributed to my realizing the things that are most important to me and my family? . . . In a way it has, ... It has shown me how other people live. . . . It has shown me that there are better ways to live."

The above represents a typical response of a portion of 100 residents of "Middle Roxbury" who were interviewed by me during the summer of 1963. Evaluation of neighborhood living relative to the important things of life was the final question in a survey which itself culminated six years of surveys and participant observation in a blighted working-class Negro neighborhood, a neighborhood that had once been mixed race-ethnic and in the minds of its older residents had once been a wonderful place in which to live.[1]

---

[1] The 1963 survey consisted of a 20 per cent sample drawn at random and by intervals from the Boston City Directory in the Dale Neighborhood Association area and a 10 per cent sample drawn in similar fashion from adjacent contrasting blocks. As far as possible, a proportion of the group represented a reinterview of a 1958 sample in Middle Roxbury. Results of the earlier study are reported in Morton Rubin, "The Negro Wish to Move: The Boston Case," *Journal of Social Issues*, Vol. 15 (1960), pp. 4-13. Participant observation study of the neighborhood association, leadership, and urban renewal has been supported variously by Northeastern University Basic Research Fund, the Social Science Research Council, and the National Institute of Mental Health.

In the 1963 survey, some 44 per cent of the sample gave a positive response to the evaluation of the neighborhood as a contributing factor in attaining life satisfactions. Outright negative responses were given by 21 per cent of the sample, and 17 per cent had mixed feelings, mainly nostalgic for the past and negative about the present. The statement cited in the text was held by 18 per cent of the sample, and might be considered negative.

The bulldozers were clearing out the worst streets of the neighborhood during the summer of 1963. Abandoned automobiles were littering the vacant lots where the city had finally begun to raze burned-out houses. Other abandoned houses were responding to active adolescents who frolicked therein, sometimes setting fires and often making pocket change by selling abandoned fixtures.

Urban renewal had just come to Washington Park, Roxbury, and this was the nadir of its existence. Everyone noted the tearing down; everyone awaited the building up. Foundations for middle-income rental housing were being dug at the Notre Dame Academy site, recently exchanged by the Roman Catholic archdiocese for a suburban move. Renewal officials and community organizers were meeting with owners to discuss plans for reha- bilitation, for this was to be a program of Urban Rehabilitation despite the current impact of spot clearance. The last families were being relocated from houses in Early Land Acquisition areas, to make way for further construction of homes and shopping and recreational facilities. A new boulevard was being prepared to transect the neighborhood, to draw traffic away from the narrow, zigzagging side streets of the neighborhood.

What can be said of the satisfactions with and loyalty toward a neighbor- hood that is so reduced at present yet presents promise in the future? To what extent are race-ethnic and class factors significant in attitude formation? How do the residents act and react to forces of an economic and political nature that surround the neighborhood, yet affect local life from day to day and beyond?

Researches on an Italian-American blue-collar neighborhood in the old West End of Boston by Lindemann, Fried, Gans, Ryan, and others suggest that forced dislocation of "urban villagers" by urban development may lead to increased mental illness and related phenomena akin to bereavement for a lost home.[2] It is also suggested that the stable working-class neighborhood has positive functions for its members in a society that is admittedly middle- class, metropolitan, and perhaps suburban.

Middle Roxbury in the Washington Park renewal area of Boston differs from the Italian old West End or the North End or the Irish Charlestown neighborhoods of Boston in several respects. Italian or Irish blue-collar workers are often such workers by choice. Their neighborhood residence into the third generation is also often by choice. Their older neighborhoods are often located near the core of the city, giving the property enhanced market value and making the journey to work minimal. The blue-collar residents either have relatives who live in the suburbs, or they themselves may have summer places along the seashore. Relatives may come to the core city to shop and to visit in an atmosphere of nostalgia and often historicity.

In contrast with this, the urban Negro at present is more transient than the other blue-collar ethnics. He has limited choice of neighborhood irrespec- tive of occupation and income. The Roxbury section of Boston is beyond the

---

[2] See articles by Lindemann, Fried, Ryan, and Gans in *The Urban Condition,* ed. Leonard J. Duhl (New York: The Free Press of Glencoe, Inc., 1962).

core, having become urban only after the coming of the streetcar.[3] Commuting to jobs downtown from Roxbury is excellent, but job decentralization makes an automobile imperative. While Boston's Negro history dates from the Boston Massacre (1770), its Negro impact is a post-World War II phenomenon.

The Irish, Italians, and Jews were ultimately absorbed into Boston's textile and leather factories, construction work, state and municipal government posts, small businesses, and the free professions. The textile factories have gone South and have been replaced by electronics, which requires higher skills and is located on peripheral highway 128. Hospitals, schools, and other institutions still need unskilled and service workers, but the construction industry is dominated by ethnic, guild-like unions. Retail business opportunities require greater amounts of capital, and the professions tend to be associated with large organizations or bureaucracies. Boston Negroes have concentrated in the low-paying unskilled or service occupations or in some professions. Unlike the heavy industrial centers of the Midwest or the Middle Atlantic States, New England offers little to those who seek semiskilled jobs with high hourly pay rates. This is one explanation for Boston's Negro population being only 65,000, although it represents 10 per cent of the total and reflects an increase of 65 per cent for the 1950-1960 decade.

The Washington Park renewal area and Middle Roxbury represent the fourth Negro neighborhood in Boston's Negro history, after the West End, South End, and Lower Roxbury. A fifth neighborhood for Negro blue-collar workers is emerging in Dorchester. Middle and Upper Roxbury were settled by Negroes during and immediately after World War II (Upper Roxbury is middle-class). The Dorchester move has been triggered by demolition in Lower Roxbury, renewal in the South End and Washington Park, and by the generally expanding numbers of Negroes in the city. Negroes tend to move into Jewish neighborhoods, because Jews offer less physical resistance than other groups, and the Irish and Italian blue-collar neighborhoods continue to be populated by members of the third generation (Jews are more mobile).

Admittedly, most of Boston's blue-collar neighborhoods are in need of rehabilitation or conservation, because the three-decker wooden houses, brick cold-water flats, and converted single-to-duplexes are tired with age and outmoded in appurtenances.[4] The low morale of the populace, likened to alienation, parallels the physical state of the city.[5] Urban renewal is designed to remedy the latter; "people renewal" concerns itself with the human factors.[6]

---

[3] See Sam B. Warner, Jr., *Streetcar Suburbs* (Cambridge: Harvard University Press and M.I.T. Press, 1962).

[4] See Chester Rapkin and Associates, *The Washington Park Urban Renewal Area* (Multilithed for the Boston Redevelopment Authority, 1961).

[5] See Murray B. Levin, *The Alienated Voter: Politics in Boston* (New York: Holt, Rinehart & Winston, Inc., 1960); also Edward C. Banfield and associates, *A Report on the Politics of Boston* (Mimeographed by the Joint Center for Urban Studies of M.I.T. and Harvard University, 1960), esp. Part VI-C, by Ralph Otwell, "The Negro in Boston."

[6] During 1961, Action for Boston Community Development (A.B.C.D.) gathered together task forces on specific problem areas associated with urban renewal. See Rheable M. Edwards, Laura B. Morris, Robert M. Coard, and associates, *The Negro in Boston* (Mimeographed for A.B.C.D., 1961).

Resident
Response
to Urban
Rehabilitation
in a
Negro
Working-Class
Neighborhood

A typical exchange during the Middle Roxbury survey might go as follows:

> ... "Who is responsible for urban renewal in Roxbury? . . . I suppose the city
> officials and the planners. . . . After all, anyone can see how run-down this
> neighborhood is . . . But then the people have been asking for this for a long
> time, the crowd at Freedom House, the Roxbury Community Council, the War-
> ren and Munroe and Dale Street Improvement Associations. They have put
> pressure on the officials." [7]

If there is a priority system for urban renewal, one would expect core city
neighborhoods to be redeveloped first, and the "grey area" neighborhoods,
the "streetcar suburbs," to be rehabilitated later. In a city such as Boston,
which is almost completely dominated by the Irish, and where Negroes constitute such an ineffectual minority, one might wonder at the selection of
Washington Park, Middle Roxbury, as the first urban rehabilitation project
in the city, and one of the first in the nation. Some say that it derives from
the pressure of the civic groups, the nostalgia of Mayor John F. Collins for
his home neighborhood, the supreme challenge of the project to Boston Redevelopment Authority Administrator Edward J. Logue. More sinister responses include, "Let's keep the colored happy and they'll stay in Roxbury,"
and "They're driving out the poor Negroes and building new housing to
bring back the whites." Blue-collar whites and blue-collar Negroes, respectively, make the above comments on the selection of Washington Park for
urban rehabilitation.

In any event, Irish Charlestown's blue-collar workers turned down urban
rehabilitation, at least temporarily. The demise of the Italian West End keeps
the Italians of the North End on guard against similar proposals. The Irish
of South Boston and the Italians of East Boston feel that their blue-collar
neighborhoods are sufficiently stable, whereas the Irish and Jews of Dorchester
would just as soon raise a cordon of high prices to block Negro entry and
call this "conservation" of neighborhood status. The alternative plan in Dorchester is invasion-and-succession of Negroes at inflated prices for scarce
housing.

II

The more stable blue-collar residents of Middle Roxbury perceive the
neighborhood as its side streets, bordered by main streets. Housing antedates
World War I and consists of single-family wooden buildings and brick apart-

---

[7] Middle Roxbury survey results showed 37 per cent of the sample felt that officials were
most responsible for bringing renewal to Roxbury; 25 per cent felt that citizens and civic
groups were most responsible; 16 per cent cited a combination of officials and civic groups;
9 per cent mentioned businessmen or developers; and 13 per cent had vague impressions.

The genesis of the neighborhood association movement and urban renewal in Boston is
to be found in William C. Loring, Jr., Frank L. Sweetser, and Charles F. Ernst, *Community
Organization for Citizen Participation in Urban Renewal* (Boston: Housing Association of
Metropolitan Boston and the Massachusetts Department of Commerce, 1957). For comparative
studies, see Martin Millspaugh and Gurney Breckenfeld, *The Human Side of Urban Renewal*
(New York: Ives, Washburn, Inc., 1960); Julia Abrahamson, *A Neighborhood Finds Itself*
(New York: Harper & Row, Publishers, 1959); Peter H. Rossi and Robert A. Dentler, *The
Politics of Urban Renewal* (New York: The Free Press of Glencoe, Inc., 1961).

ments, predominantly on the main streets. There are a few mansions, attesting to the "suburban period" of a century ago, yet dilapidated and dangerous monstrosities in the contemporary environment.

The neighborhood has been predominantly Negro since World War II. Those whites who continue to live here neighbor with the older Negro property owners, sharing the Protestant churches and increasingly noticing the attraction for Negroes of the Roman Catholic church and parochial schools. The Negroes divide themselves into long-term, small property owners and tenants, and more recent tenants. The former groups are older in age and higher in status. Rental collections are an important form of income for blue-collar landlords whose occupations may be service or unskilled or who may be widowed or near retirement age.

Nonresident (absentee) landlords form another important group. They may be either former white small property owners who moved to the suburbs while retaining their former dwelling, or else they are large-scale, nonlocal white owners ("slum landlords"). Both groups of nonresident landlords are blamed for the blight and for the introduction of undesirable lower-class tenants. The blame is partially justified, but this is the group that offers moderate rental housing for which there is a high demand. Renewal seeks to curb the excesses of slum-landlordism, but it has not yet replaced the low-rental housing which it has demolished.

Continuing to look at the neighborhood from the inside out, there are several shops on the main streets, servicing local needs. There are also larger, heavy industrial-commercial or warehouse-type structures that are nonlocal and are considered to be blighting influences. Renewal seeks to consolidate the former into small shopping centers and to relocate the latter along industrial belts.

Good public transportation—both surface lines and rapid-transit elevated —run along the two main streets to a juncture at Dudley Square. But the side streets are unsafe for pedestrians after dark and the elevated structure is a major blighting factor in the larger neighborhood district. The local renewal program cannot cope with the removal of the elevated structure until federal mass-transit and highway programs can be coordinated to suit local needs.

The people have demanded that the city provide better street lighting and street patrols. They feel that the parks and open spaces invite further danger rather than provide relief from tension. Fear for safety has increased out-migration and has led to the use of taxis and numerous noisy police dogs in a neighborhood already cluttered with transient and abandoned trucks and passenger cars of every vintage. Residents have mixed feelings about off-street parking lots, proposed by renewal authorities. Both the car parked in the street below and the child playing in the street below are felt to receive greater surveillance than when the car is located on a parking lot and the child is playing in a playground or tot-lot.[8]

There are two elementary schools and a junior high school in the neighbor-

Resident
Response
to Urban
Rehabilitation
in a
Negro
Working-Class
Neighborhood

---

[8] For theories about surveillance, see Jane Jacobs, *The Death and Life of Great American Cities* (New York: Random House, 1961).

hood, dating from the pre-World War I period and almost completely Negro in patronage. The high school at the edge of the neighborhood was converted from local use to citywide technical specialization because of decreased enrollment and local sentiment against *de facto* racial segregation. Local Negroes are now disturbed that so few of their youths are able to qualify for entry into the technical high school because of inadequate background in the junior high and elementary schools of the neighborhood. Many Negroes are sending their children to elementary Roman Catholic parochial schools on the periphery of the neighborhood because they feel that the quality of instruction in such schools is higher. They are dispersing high school students and are considering dispersal for junior high school groups. Renewal will add several new elementary schools within the neighborhood and will build a junior high school on the periphery. *De facto* segregation is likely to remain in the elementary schools, but hopefully the junior high school will be integrated.

Local Negro residents appear more concerned with quality of schooling and discipline than with issues of segregation. Organizational civil rights leaders, the clergy, and youth groups have linked school integration with the struggle for quality. During an organized demonstration by "leaders" and youth in June, 1963, several adult informants said that they opposed NAACP demonstrations that utilized youths. They felt that youths were sufficiently uncontrollable, and that adults should do their own negotiating for civil rights. To the blue-collar workers, quality education appears to mean discipline of the student and his ability to qualify for the next stage in education or job placement. Boston schools are found wanting on both counts by most Negroes. Action for Boston Community Development is supposed to program intensively for culturally disadvantaged groups in the schools, formalizing the sporadic attempts by civic and church groups.

There are two high-status Protestant churches in the neighborhood and several other Protestant and Roman Catholic churches on the periphery. Store-front churches are increasing in number as they move from demolished Lower Roxbury or else open their doors to the newer settlers. The established Protestant and Roman Catholic churches that were once white are either integrating or else have become missionary types of churches. The all-Negro established churches cater to the stable blue-collar and white-collar owners and tenants.

Renewal will permit a few churches that wish to expand to do so, especially with respect to their educational and social service facilities. St. Marks Congregational Church, a high-status Negro group, is expanding its facilities and is also participating in the construction of moderate-income housing. Charles Street A.M.E. Church, an old group with mass support, is also planning local housing development. (Academy Homes is sponsored by the Building Service Employees International Union.)

Nonresidential land use is rounded out by a proliferation of taverns, barber and beauty parlors, eating places, drugstores, phonograph record shops, and other enterprises that are both legitimate and at the same time act as hang-outs for nonlegitimate activities, such as gambling, prostitution, excessive drinking, and so forth. Alleyways, abandoned lots, and abandoned buildings provide even more intensive impetus to such behavior. The trend has been

RUBIN

from the main streets to the interior side streets, increasing with fires and vandalism, and posing major threats to the life as well as to the property of the residents.

Urban renewal has promised to help the residents who supported it by Early Land Acquisition of the worst through streets and sections of the main streets for the highway, new housing units, shopping centers, schools, and recreational centers. Local long-term owners and tenants have supported their blue-collar leaders and white-collar "organizational leaders" through neighborhood associations, district councils, and the churches, on a promise of clearing out the "worst element" and despite higher costs for rehabilitating the rest.

The test of rehabilitation is the city's replacement of vice and neglect with new enterprise and higher-quality facilities. During the 1963 summer survey in the neighborhood, there was a two-to-one feeling of optimism about what renewal would do for the neighborhood. What lingering doubts there were had to do with rising costs and the dislocation of the poor. Others felt that the city had failed to enforce its codes in the past, and they doubted that renewal would make a difference in the future. Major concern appeared to be with "people renewal," as expressed in association meetings.

The hostility between small property owners and stable tenants on the one hand and transient tenants and absentee owners on the other appears to be fundamental to an understanding of the neighborhood's problems and prospects. Stable middle-class and blue-collar groups are opposed to what they consider to be the lower class. The fact of Negro segregation and the proximity of the small Negro middle class to the blue-collar group heightens contacts among several class groups. It charges the middle class with leadership obligations and opportunities while at the same time creating a feeling of status anxiety among them.

The lower class has not participated in renewal plans and it has tended to drift to adjacent neighborhoods, wherever families can afford to pay the rents. Renewal officials try to secure sound housing, either public or private, for them, but they are faced with major problems arising from large numbers of children and from the bad image of the Aid to Dependent Children (A.D.C.) welfare family (with absent male head of household).

Yet it is questionable whether the children of A.D.C. mothers cause as much difficulty as the children from families where neither parent exercises control. Large numbers of mothers as well as fathers work during the daytime, leaving children to care for one another. Other parents work a night shift and sleep in the daytime, often ignoring the needs of their children. Although we have no proof that working mothers lead to delinquent offspring, there is adequate evidence that Negro family life in the working class is disorganized.[9] Many informants felt that families would meet the higher costs of renewal and rehabilitation by increasing their hours of work. It remains to be seen to what extent enforcement of density codes will curb the prevalence of "doubling-up" of families in the neighborhood.

---

[9] See, for example, E. Franklin Frazier, *The Negro in the United States*, rev. ed. (New York: The Macmillan Company, 1957). For Boston data, see Walter B. Miller, "Implications of Urban Lower-Class Culture for Social Work," *Social Service Review*, Vol. 33 (1959), pp. 219-36, and subsequent articles on this theme.

Resident
Response
to Urban
Rehabilitation
in a
Negro
Working-Class
Neighborhood

Renewed strength for the neighborhood must consist of attracting younger persons as property owners or as stable tenants. After World War II, the G.I. Bill helped some Negro veterans acquire property (albeit at inflated prices) from white families ready to move to the suburbs. These blue-collar veterans had sufficient know-how to maintain their property, and their children provided a stable element in the local schools. Many have aspired to middle class through the generation reared and educated in Boston, thus following the patterns of Jewish, Italian, and Irish antecedents. But we have already noted the criticism of the schools, whose student body has been influenced by the influx of new migrants. Peer-group culture tends to cater to the culture of the latter group. In desperation, some parents seek housing in other Boston neighborhoods or in the suburbs, but they are limited primarily by income, if not by race. Informants in the 1963 summer survey felt that single-family homeownership in other neighborhoods or the suburbs was financially beyond their means.

Yet renewal is causing a small dispersal of owners, dislocated but compensated at fair appraisal prices. Several such persons feel that renewal is an opportunity for them to leave an undesirable situation. There is no bereavement for a lost home. Evidence still has to be gathered on the results of relocating lower-income families from the Early Land Acquisition areas. Rumors during the summer of 1963 were mixed. Some felt that the lower-income persons were being bettered by relocation in public housing and sound private housing. Others noted the discrimination against such families and the rise in costs.

Other owners said that they would participate in rehabilitation, hoping that the mortgage refinancing would keep costs in line. Tenants in such homes felt that quality would justify small increases in rents. The city tax rate has recently been stabilized after several years of major rise. Other owners implied that they might, themselves, move to the suburbs and recoup costs through renting to more tenant families. The effect of extended absentee-landlordism, this time by Negroes, would probably vitiate the renewal program, which emphasizes an increase in owner-occupied dwellings.

III

My research has been concerned with the function of local leadership and civic associations in the renewal process. Urban renewal is a bureaucratic-political process with implications for big-business and middle-class interests. Blue-collar-worker neighborhoods have been suspicious of the major political and economic forces at work in urban renewal. Negroes have been particularly concerned that in many cities urban renewal is called "Negro removal."

In Boston the West End urban development, or clearance, affected Italian groups more than it did Negroes. Yet the New York Streets redevelopment project in the South End was held responsible for attracting some lower-class Negroes into Middle Roxbury. The spot-clearance features of the Washington Park Urban Rehabilitation project have caused fear on the part of low-income

Negroes. It is the middle-class and the stable blue-collar-worker groups that wish to rid the neighborhood of the lower-class group through renewal.

To this extent the neighborhood associations, church meetings, and the formal leadership represent the blue-collar small property owner and long-term tenant whose orientations to the middle class have succeeded through their children, who have been educated, have grown up, and have moved away. Stable blue-collar workers among these Negroes appreciate the need for adequate educational, recreational, and safety facilities in a rehabilitated neighborhood. They are not urban villagers. Their eye is on a future with civil rights rather than on the past. They are more like the generations of European migrants who preceded them to the city than they are like the present blue-collar remnant. The Jews serve as a model for many of these Negroes, who feel that the schools are better in Jewish neighborhoods. At the same time, they resent felt economic exploitation by Jewish landlords and merchants.

The civic-association movement in Roxbury has been helped by Freedom House, which grew out of Negro-Jewish potential conflict, by the Roxbury Community Council, and by organized social-welfare attempts to curb delinquency. Local Protestant churches have served as major centers for civic efforts, with moral support from Roman Catholic groups. More recently the situation of police protection has brought forth mass rallies on the part of Negroes. Local groups, sparked by the NAACP and CORE, have moved on school and job issues, paralleling national civil rights efforts. Voter-registration drives are also under way.

The many years of "bootstrap operation" by local persons has led to the emergence of effective blue-collar leadership with a voice at the public works department at city hall and down at the police station. Community organizers at Freedom House, the Roxbury Community Council, and now the Boston Redevelopment Authority and Action for Boston Community Development, have come to rely on the old stalwarts while at the same time encouraging new leadership.

Participation in civic associations has meant long hours at night meetings in all seasons and extremes of weather. But some persons have gained in social status, and others have entered well-paying jobs with "the Establishment." Urban renewal does not merely request citizen participation; it finds numerous positions in community organization, relocation work, and other clerical pursuits. Welfare and philanthropic funds have flowed to the Roxbury Community Council, Action for Boston Community Development, and Freedom House. Local realtors, lawyers, and architects are finding new *raisons d'être* through urban renewal. It is finally the turn of blue-collar workers to agitate for local construction jobs. The NAACP is conferring with government, management, and the unions on Negro concern with job opportunities.

There is still a general attitude of skepticism on the part of local persons—owners and tenants, blue-collar and white-collar—toward the ultimate accomplishments of urban renewal in the neighborhood. Renewal is supported as an act of desperation. Negroes, especially, feel that they need federal aid to make their place in Boston. They feel that they want their share of funds and jobs, for they realize that renewal is big business. Small property owners view renewal as a last measure for recouping property investments. Younger families view renewal as a means of revitalizing the city's decrepit facilities.

It is the long history of municipal neglect that is at the root of the skepticism. It is the fact of limited income and racial disability that is at the base of whatever localistic orientation exists. Other neighborhoods in Boston (other than Dorchester, which is tipping) are too hostile to Negro entry. The suburbs offer for sale mainly single-family houses, which are too expensive for blue-collar workers to maintain as compared with multifamily units within the city. Moreover, most unskilled and service jobs, especially those for women, are still downtown, and commuting from the suburbs would be difficult and expensive.

It is probable that the Boston-reared generation with middle-class orientations will move to the suburbs in due course. A rehabilitated blue-collar neighborhood like Washington Park, Middle Roxbury, will appeal to older blue-collar workers and to younger, stable in-migrants to the city. Renewal in Middle Roxbury is unlikely to change the patterns of ethnic segregation in Boston, but it will separate the lower-class Negroes from the stable blue-collar and white-collar groups. *The problem of the lower class is not really being solved by urban renewal, and neither is that of race.*[10]

IV

This analysis of resident response to urban rehabilitation in a Negro working-class neighborhood illustrates how the dynamics of residence, race, and class are interlocking. The urban renewal program was designed to provide "decent, safe, and sanitary" housing for the people, and at the same time it was proposed to make urban neighborhood life more rewarding, both financially and socially. Yet urban renewal has opened a Pandora's box wherever it has come.

Renewal has become involved in class conflict. It has been accused of driving out lower-income groups in favor of middle- and upper-income groups.[11] Its relocation procedures may raise the quality of housing for those who cooperate, but large numbers do not cooperate because they are hostile to bureaucracy or because they are so localistic that they resist a move to some different or distant environment. There is a limited supply of public housing, and the reputation of existing projects makes them unattractive to many who are eligible for them.

Renewal has alternately been accused of causing Negro removal or else continuing racial segregation. There is little evidence that renewal has

---

[10] This author is collaborating with Lawrence K. Northwood and others in a volume on *Race and Renewal: Studies in Community Organization, Policy and Planning.* (Write to The School of Social Work, University of Washington, Seattle, for details.)

[11] See Herbert J. Gans, "The Human Implications of Current Redevelopment and Relocation Planning," *Journal of the American Institute of Planners,* Vol. 25 (1959), pp. 15-25.

coped with the issue of integration.[12] The Negro group provides an intensive example of class conflict. The majority are blue-collar workers, living near a small middle class and threatened by an invading lower class. On the positive side, renewal has given status and some career opportunities to middle-class Negro leaders. It has generated leadership among blue-collar workers, at least at the block level.

Urban rehabilitation has forced the physical planner and the architect to become politically adept. They have had to go among the people as well. Often they find themselves in a cross-fire between aroused citizens and their officials. Planners have become educated in the frustrations and aspirations of working-class and minority people. They have come to know the middle-class "organizational leaders" at numerous meetings, and they have also come to know working people, both at meetings and in their homes during survey inspections and appraisals. Rehabilitation has involved planners and people for a longer period than redevelopment has. It is more difficult to motivate the best to stay and to participate.

We await the effect of urban rehabilitation on the class mixture in the racial ghetto. The lower class is likely to be removed, because the worst housing is experiencing spot clearance. The working class will receive better-quality used housing, and perhaps some new housing if costs can be controlled. It is uncertain at this point to what extent middle-class Negroes will remain in such a rehabilitation area as owners or as renters.[13] Many will consider moving to the suburbs as open occupancy begins to prevail. Others might move to the suburbs and become absentee landlords, using rental income to support single-family residence. Yet there are many who find social status and career satisfactions in the ethnic neighborhood, and renewal would like to motivate these families to stay, to lend stability and continued leadership.

We await the success of urban renewal's housing and density code enforcement, because it is most likely to affect continued middle- and stable blue-collar working-class residence in the neighborhood. If the middle class leaves, to what extent will the working class provide neighborhood leadership? Or will it continue to rely on such middle-class representatives as clergymen, social workers, small businessmen, and politicians (who may be lawyers or insurance or real-estate brokers)? To what extent will renewal relieve the problems of the lower class by generating new forms of public housing that are less institutional and more generous in the encouragement of upwardly mobile types?

The social ills that existed before renewal have been brought to the surface. There is now governmental and philanthropic foundation support for "people renewal." The planning, social work, and education professions are gaining greater support as businessmen and politicians find themselves

---

[12] See Lawrence K. Northwood, "The Threat and Potential of Urban Renewal: A Workable Program for Better Race Relations," *Journal of Intergroup Relations*, Vol. 2 (1961), pp. 101-14.

[13] Howard E. Freeman and Lewis Watts (Florence Heller Graduate School of Social Welfare, Brandeis University, Waltham, Mass.) are currently conducting research in Washington Park on "Housing Needs and Mobility among Middle Class Negro Families in an Area Undergoing Urban Renewal."

Resident Response to Urban Rehabilitation in a Negro Working-Class Neighborhood

enmeshed in class and ethnic conflicts hitherto reserved for private discussion. Citizen participation in urban renewal is bringing to the urban scene those professional techniques that have been so well demonstrated in rural areas both in the United States and overseas. In the wake of social-action programs enters the social scientist. There appears to be a place for social research in urban renewal, too.[14]

Resignation, Industrialization, and the Problem of Social Change: A Case History of a Coal-Mining Community

HERMAN R. LANTZ

INTRODUCTION

IN a society such as ours, with its traditional emphasis on mobility, individual effort, and initiative, there has been a tendency to forget that *a large number of persons do not subscribe to these values*. Indeed, such groups represent organized subcultures with a value system antagonistic to change. Such groups are of significance sociologically, but their very existence has profound implications for social policy as well. Because they are unable to sustain themselves, they constitute a serious economic burden for the country. We shall be concerned with the social and economic significance of these communities in this paper.

The material for this report is an outgrowth of the author's observations of small, depressed communities and the life therein, as well as of an intensive study of one particular community, published under the title of *People of Coal Town*.[1] With respect to the first point, I wish to say that the observations of depressed and economically impoverished communities resulted in several insights. To begin with, although economic impoverishment was clearly manifest, a search of the deeper processes and ethos of community life revealed other more serious problems. There appeared to be a marked

---

[14] Panel discussions on the Role of the Sociologist in Urban Renewal have been conducted by the author and his colleagues at the 1962 annual meetings of the Society for the Study of Social Problems and at the 1963 annual meetings of the Eastern Sociological Society. Synopses are available through the Sociology Department, Northeastern University, Boston 15, Massachusetts.

[1] Herman R. Lantz, *People of Coal Town* (New York: Columbia University Press, 1958).

apathy and hopelessness about change and about making life different or better. The youth growing up in these communities were unconcerned for the future and were willing to settle for much less than one might expect. One could not help but believe that within these communities there was a tremendous waste of potential talent which would never be realized and considerable energy employed in the service of maintaining apathy and hopelessness. Thus, although these communities were economically depressed and were in dire need of assistance, there were equally serious problems at the social-psychological level. When one makes observations such as these, there is the temptation to look for economic rehabilitation as the solution for both the economic and social-psychological problems which confront people in depressed communities.

It soon becomes apparent, however, that much of the difficulty cannot be changed simply by revitalizing the economy of the community. This is so largely owing to the fact that, once started, many social or psychological processes are not reversible in any simple way, that is, by removing the causative agents. Neurotic insecurity is not reversed simply because the conditions which produced the insecurity are removed. Juvenile delinquency, which in part may be related to poverty, slums, or inadequate family relationships, is not easily reversed when these kinds of conditions are changed. Why? It seems to me that in both illustrations we are dealing with processes which, when evoked, represent a way of viewing life which has its own logic, frames of reference, and energy investments. Once started, these neurotic or delinquent processes take on functions of their own and can operate independently of the original causative agents. Thus, one may remove those factors initially causative only to discover that the social processes, which may have been at one point in time related to these causes, operate autonomously because they have developed functions of their own.[2]

In turning our attention to the analysis of the community, let us assume that a series of economic and social disasters results in patterns of resignation. Once patterns of resignation are initiated and become functional, they probably will not be removed in any simple way by the introduction of a new economic base. Indeed, patterns of resignation may be so antithetical to change as to operate in a way that creates a hostile environment for industrial innovations. *The essence of the resigned community is to be found in the way in which it deals with social change. Resignation functions to minimize change.*

Although resignation implies apathy, it is an apathy in the face of change. The resigned community can react with considerable hostility when its value system is under attack and the normative codes violated. Moreover, the resigned community can persist in imposing its value system to the point of demoralization of the protagonists. These are salient features to be considered in dealing with resignation.

No better illustration of the points made in this introduction is found than in the case history of Coal Town which follows. Here we shall examine

---

[2] Alvin W. Gouldner, "Reciprocity and Autonomy in Functional Theory," in *Symposium on Sociological Theory,* ed. Llewellyn Gross (New York: Harper & Row, Publishers, 1959), pp. 248-51.

Resignation,
Industrialization,
and the Problem
of Social
Change:
A
Case History
of a Coal-Mining
Community

the reaction of a resigned community to industrialization and observe the ways in which it attempted to come to terms with industrialization.

The material for this case history is derived from research in Coal Town, some of which has already been published, as previously noted. Briefly, for those who are unfamiliar with the study, *People of Coal Town*, the following should be pointed out. Coal Town, as the name implies, is a mining community of about 2300 people. It has gone through the typical socioeconomic cycles of growth, depression, and decline which characterize many American communities of this type.

The material I am about to present focuses on the natives who settled in Coal Town, since their culture best illustrates the processes described in this report. The European immigrants who comprised the other group in the community are significant in the present discussion only insofar as they represented other value systems which differed from those of the natives. As a result, the conflict over positions in the mine was highlighted.

THE NATIVE GROUP—PREINDUSTRIAL PHASE

The historical backgrounds of the people who settled in the Coal Town area originally are not altogether clear, but it is generally believed that they were descendants of the Scotch-Irish who moved west through Pennsylvania during the eighteenth century. From here they moved gradually down the valleys and gaps to the back country of Virginia, the Carolinas, and Georgia. By the time of the Revolution, the stream began to flow into Kentucky and Tennessee. During the early part of the nineteenth century, these people moved into the Coal Town area.[3]

An analysis of the people who settled in the Coal Town region suggests certain characteristics and problems which have historically plagued them. These difficulties have to do with a marked inability to adapt to the demands imposed by social change, especially when this involved some basic reorientation of their way of life. They were traditionally the onlookers, never really part of the changes that took place around them; and, as a matter of fact, they were somewhat fearful of changes. Their basic mode of adjustment was to retreat and move on whenever life became too difficult or too complicated. As a group, they sought the simple, casual existence. They were satisfied with little and made few demands on others, expecting few to be made on them.[4]

Why do we find these people in such a setting? Historians allude to the answer, but the problem has never been dealt with systematically, although, indeed, it is most significant. In order to understand adequately the native who settled in Coal Town, it becomes necessary to examine his ancestry and the sociohistorical circumstances which gave rise to his way of life. Here it is essential to examine the experiences in the European situation as well as the American scene. The ancestors of the Coal Town native were part

---

[3] See Leyburn on the Scotch-Irish for a definitive treatment of this problem. James Leyburn, *The Scotch Irish in America* (Chapel Hill: University of North Carolina Press, 1962).
[4] Carl Bridenbaugh examines the role of the Scotch-Irish on the frontier. See Carl Bridenbaugh, *Myths and Realities* (Baton Rouge: Louisiana State University Press, 1952).

of the large Scotch-Irish migration from Northern Ireland in the seventeenth and eighteenth centuries. Few of these people were wealthy, and a good many were underprivileged. Toward the end of the seventeenth century, the discrimnatory legislation of the English Parliament severely curbed Ulster wool growing and cloth manufacturing; those clinging to the Presbyterian faith were forbidden to hold public office; conditions were further aggravated by rising rents and the famine which occurred in 1740.[5] Many of these people were able to establish themselves in various occupations and professions when they came to America. A large segment of these people, however, were less successful. They were victimized by slave labor from the plantation system, and they became part of the large mass of poor whites in the South. What land they could afford was usually the eroded soil released by the cotton growers, who had already exploited the land for what could be had. Thus, for the most part, the newcomers operated small submarginal farms and supplemented this operation with hunting and fishing. Their general situation was aggravated by visitations of malaria, typhoid, and hookworm.

These are the kinds of people who resided in the area of Coal Town prior to industrialization. They were essentially resigned and wanted to be left alone without the complications of social change, and they might well have had their wish had not coal been discovered.

THE REACTION TO INDUSTRIALIZATION[6]

Coal mining was initiated without active interest or support from natives in the area. It was developed with outside capital by persons from another region. There is no evidence to suggest that innovations were sought or encouraged by these people.

From the first, the natives looked on industrialization as an attack on their way of life. This view of mining was manifest in several ways. To begin with, they resented the changes which mining brought. They resented the noise, the smoke, having the land torn up, and the general disturbance created by these changes. The mines themselves frightened these people. They feared the darkness, the unknown, the new and different sounds under ground.[7] A native reported:

> The natives were not really attracted to the coal mines. The farmers were afraid to go underground so the company was forced to import laborers. My father hated working in them mines. He used to say, "I never lost nothing in them mines and I ain't goin' down to find it."

All of this was upsetting, especially because no opportunity was made by management to orient the inhabitants to mining or industrialization. For

---

[5] Leyburn, *op. cit.*

[6] The first mine was sunk in 1900; actual mining commenced in 1904. The processes about to be described commenced with the date 1900; the remaining dates are approximate ones designed to help orient the reader with respect to the sequence of processes.

[7] The author does not wish to imply that all isolated people must react to industrialization this way. See Herbert Blumer, "Early Industrialization and the Laboring Class," paper read at the Annual Meeting, American Sociological Society, Sept. 1959, Chicago, Ill., also published in *Sociological Quarterly*, Vol. 1 (January 1960).

those who could overcome the fear of mining itself, there were other doubts. Mining, to be sure, brought with it very real economic benefits. Although wages at the outset were not very high, they were far in excess of what one might earn as a hired hand on a farm or as an operator of a small, submarginal farm. Nevertheless, although the opportunity for better income and the opportunities for new material possessions opened up new horizons, these also created additional conflicts. For to receive the economic benefits meant also to give up a way of life. This involved relinquishing the simple and casual existence, engaging in hard labor, and adjusting to industrial routines.

Indeed, the means for reaching economic goals (hard work and adjustment to industrial routines) were foreign to the native and could be realized only at the expense of a considerable amount of social stress. What was available—their own institutionalized patterns of work, characterized by casualness and indifference—constituted a serious obstacle to success in the industrial milieu. One observer said this:

> Bird-hunting was a pleasurable pursuit in this community and I believe that it contributed much to labor disputes. For instance, when someone would want to go bird-hunting, why he would either not show up on the job or else he was looking for something so that he could get out of work, and was more apt to pick a fight or look for some grievance that could be brought against the Company. It was said here that a man would give his wife anything except his bird dog. The bird dogs were much more important than the wives and there were many dogs here. I'll tell you that.

NATIVE EFFORTS TO DEAL WITH NORMS OF INDUSTRIALIZATION

The natives rejected the norms of the mine managers and hoped that the economic rewards of industrialization could still be realized within the framework of their traditional way of life. Thus they hoped to substitute their institutionalized patterns of work for the norms of industrialization. Rejection of the norms of industrialization was manifest in high absenteeism, in the ignoring of working schedules and mining routine, and in opposing other innovations which worked at cross-purposes with their way of life, their preferred casual existence, and their individualism. Because wages were relatively high, the amount of work necessary to earn a good wage in the natives' terms was minimal.

Nevertheless, although the amount of money they earned may have been satisfactory at first, their desire for greater economic rewards increased. Because they were still unwilling to change their orientation to work, the value conflicts between the desire for economic reward and the means for its achievement became more acute. Demands for higher wages per unit of coal produced became a source of constant irritation between the natives and mining management. Little progress was made by the natives with respect to obtaining higher wages until they joined the labor union.

UNIONIZATION

I do not wish to imply that the rise of labor unions among these native working-class people in Coal Town can be explained simply on the basis of

LANTZ

262

their wish to receive greater economic reward without concomitant effort. Obviously, there were many facets to this problem, for the miner did have genuine grievances against mining management, such as safety conditions in the mine. I think it is true, however, that these particular natives saw in labor unions an opportunity to deal effectively with mining management. These native blue-collar workers failed to realize, of course, that in time union affiliation would also mean a commitment to production schedules, to routines, and to other facets of industrialization which were at odds with their way of life. Management fought acceptance of the union for several years; and during this period, violence was quite pronounced. Initially, Negroes were introduced by management (1909) in an effort to combat the union. The Negroes were soon discouraged from remaining by native miners who intimidated them and reportedly used violence frequently.

Following displacement of the Negro the management accepted the union. Although such acceptance was a victory for the native, mining management was distressed, particularly since the production schedule in the mine was constantly upset by the native patterns of indifference and high absenteeism. It was out of these circumstances that mining management imported European immigrants, who appeared in large numbers around 1910. Although the natives were suspicious of the immigrants from the first, they accepted immigrants as members of the union, because the natives saw the growth of union members as a powerful weapon to be used against management.

The introduction of immigrants, however, ushered in a conflict of tremendous proportions in the natives' efforts to realize the benefits of industrialization without a basic change in their way of life. For the immigrants possessed the real assets in terms of success in the industrial milieu. They worked hard, adjusted well to schedules, were dependable, and were productive. Mining management recognized these patterns from the first, and, with the exception of supervisory positions, held by English-speaking immigrants, the central and southern Europeans were soon preferred to natives, especially for work in the pits. An observer pointed this out:

> The immigrant was more dependable because he would always show up for work. The Company could not depend upon the native miner because there was so much absenteeism. The immigrant was preferable because of the amount of coal that he would dig with a pick.

Under these circumstances, the conflict between the desire for benefits of industrialization and the natives' means for achieving their economic goals increased. Either the natives had to change their manner of dealing with industrialization or they would be displaced by the immigrant. Not only were the natives losing out to the immigrant with respect to jobs in the mines, but they were irritated additionally by the immigrants' ability to derive more benefits from the fruits of their labor. For example, the natives had little experience with, or interest in, the budgeting of salaries. Many, having been removed recently from a barter economy, had neither the knowledge nor the interest required to save. They were prone to be impulsive in their

Resignation, Industrialization, and the Problem of Social Change:

A Case History of a Coal-Mining Community

buying habits, purchasing things whether they could afford them or not; they were frequently in debt. The immigrants, on the other hand, were traditionally frugal; they saved and knew how to budget, and, although they were careful about what they purchased, they were able to own comparatively more than the natives.

Thus, the natives found themselves confused and bewildered. Their land was invaded by what seemed to them to be strange and contemptible people with peculiar working habits, languages, food customs, and dress. In the natives' eyes, the immigrants were the inferiors. Yet these inferiors were more successful in obtaining and holding mining positions. Further, these inferiors managed their economic affairs so well that they were able to save.

> A NATIVE: The foreigners here really knew how to save that money. Here they got ahead of the Americans, I think. You see, the Americans blowed in their money, and I guess that's why I don't have any today myself.

> THE SON OF AN IMMIGRANT: There was a tremendous amount of jealousy and envy for those who lived better than they (the natives) did, you see.

The conflict at this stage for the native was not only one which concerned itself with economic goals and the means for their attainment, but it represented a basic internal conflict of values with respect to their traditional way of life. These natives saw in the immigrants' orientation to life a refutation of their own value system; such refutation precipitated ambivalence, doubts, and confusion.

During the period of World War I, much of the potential conflict between the native and the immigrant was held in abeyance. Work was plentiful, labor was in demand, and mining management was in no position to fight with the native. Following World War I, with rising unemployment and mechanization of mining, the conflict between native and immigrant recommenced. This period ushered in an era of considerable lawlessness and violence which at times bordered on anomie and took the form of open conflict. The natives berated the immigrants in interpersonal relations so that the immigrants would conform to the natives' norms regarding productivity.

> A NATIVE: The foreigners had been depressed so long that they tried to overdo themselves when they got to this country. They didn't know what a day's work was. They were greedy. After they got more Americanized, they knew that there was another day's work coming but most of them didn't realize at first that there was any future so they worked like hell every day. The natives did not try to keep up with them because if they did they would kill themselves. No American would work as hard as they did because the foreigners didn't have any sense. Americans would have more sense than to work that hard.

Outside the mine, the natives reacted against the immigrants by focusing on their differences with hostility which was expressed toward the immigrants' way of life, patterns of food, language, and work. The native employed whatever means was possible to help make the immigrant become discouraged and demoralized.

LANTZ

UNION PRESSURE ON MINING MANAGEMENT

At this point the natives, who had always been in control of the union, began to exert pressure on mining management to replace immigrants with natives whenever possible. There were also attempts to dismiss immigrants from the union for the slightest infraction of the rules. The natives' efforts to eliminate the immigrants from the mine, and the immigrants' efforts to resist, accentuated an already existent anomic condition within the mine and in the community.

The conflict within the community and the attempt to eliminate the immigrants from the union continued until the late 1920's. The immigrants, realizing what was happening, were instrumental in introducing a rival union into the community in an effort to preserve the mining positions they held. At this point a jurisdictional dispute between the union controlled by the native and the one introduced by the immigrant emerged. The real issue here was control of the mines and the personnel, native or immigrant, who would be employed in them. This was a very bloody struggle that continued for several years until the early 1930's; it often turned family against family and made traitors of previously honest people.

The immigrants' union lost; with limited financial and legal backing, and with accusations of radicalism, their cause suffered. The native union, presumably because of national power, as well as strong financial and legal backing, was able to win. Although mining management would have preferred the immigrant for work in the pits, they chose not to become involved in this struggle. Following their defeat, the immigrants found it virtually impossible to find employment in mining. On the other hand, although the natives had finally won, what they won was hardly worth the struggle; for the amount of work, owing to the depression and mine mechanization, was so limited that the natives found themselves struggling with other natives for the few jobs that were left. The community settled into a state of pronounced economic deterioration from which it has never really recovered, although conditions were relatively better during the World War II period.

LIFE IN COAL TOWN TODAY: DIMENSIONS OF RESIGNATION

The sociohistoric experiences of the natives are particularly pertinent in understanding the way of life which characterizes them today. As the reader will recall, these people had a tradition of resignation—of being at the periphery of social change. Their experiences with industrialization were both frustrating and, in the final analysis, disappointing. Theirs is a history of community failure, one in which they were unable to deal effectively with the confrontations of social change. Not only was the value system disturbed and relationships upset, but the benefits of industrialization were minimal and did not last. These experiences as blue-collar workers were compounded with the indifference and impersonality of mining management. The net

Resignation, Industrialization, and the Problem of Social Change: A Case History of a Coal-Mining Community

265

effect of these experiences tended to entrench a fear of industrial change as well as a feeling of inadequacy in regard to coping with its complications. These effects are significant for understanding the dimensions of resignation to be discussed.[8]

A look at life in Coal Town today suggests that patterns of resignation are quite pronounced. They are essentially characteristic of the native element and of some of the children of the immigrants who remained in Coal Town; the immigrants themselves, now quite elderly, seem largely to have avoided the resigned syndrome, clinging to their own value system instead.

In this final section of the paper, therefore, I wish to deal with the basic dimensions of resignation and to point out the significance of this factor for understanding the problems of social change which beset this community.

An intensive analysis of the depth interviews taken, plus many hours of observation of the Coal Town people on the part of the research team, suggest the following basic characteristics of a major segment of the native population. No claim is made that the resigned syndrome characterizes all members of the native population in Coal Town. The exact extent of resignation among this population is still dependent on a more refined analysis. The data suggest that resignation is less prevalent as one ascends the educational ladder, and it is also generally less common among women.

BASIC CHARACTERISTICS OF RESIGNATION

1. *Detachment from others.* In Coal Town one dominant characteristic among the natives centers in their detachment from others. Emotional involvements with others and concern for others are at a minimum. There is also a marked detachment and separation from any positive identification with the community.

2. *Absence of serious striving.* In Coal Town a second dominant characteristic among the natives is found in minimizing individual abilities and capacities. Active discouragement of personal abilities is pronounced.

3. *Aversion to effort.* In Coal Town a third dominant characteristic among the natives centers around their attitudes toward work. Tasks which require effort and concentration are to be ridiculed, shunned, and disvalued.

4. *Restriction of wishes.* In Coal Town a fourth dominant characteristic among the natives centers around minimizing the wish for new or better things. Such wishes are considered to be unrealistic and are likely to invite scorn from others.

FUNCTIONAL RELATIONSHIP OF RESIGNATION TO SOCIAL CHANGE

What functions do patterns of resignation serve? It becomes very clear that the dimensions of resignation which have been described are functional in controlling social change by manifesting themselves to minimize change. With detachment and taboos on wishes, persons in the community are blocked with

---

[8] See H. M. Caudill, *Night Comes to the Cumberlands: A Biography of a Depressed Area* (Boston: Little, Brown & Co., 1963), for an excellent analysis of some of these problems.

respect to new possibilities either for themselves or for others. If by chance an innovation does attract some members of the community, the community's lack of serious purpose and aversion to effort soon defeat the likelihood that anything will change. It is difficult for the people to maintain consistent interest in almost any enterprise, since they have serious doubts about things turning out well for them. For example, in spite of overt pronouncements about helping their community, the people in this community are largely not interested in examining the possibility of changes.

On the basis of resigned values, there is considerable inertia when it comes to serious consideration of new industries; but even if some industries were interested, they would be confronted with obstacles which would make it difficult to reach a positive decision about locating in this community. Industries of any stature and stability are concerned with the nature of the community in which their plant is to be located. With resigned values, the community develops a deteriorated quality; industry is generally quite reluctant to locate in deteriorated areas unless there are significant compensations to be obtained. Here there are few compensations. To locate a plant in the area is to invite difficulties at the executive and semiexecutive level; the community's problems create difficulties for personnel and their families. Schools and service facilities are inadequate. The general manner of living in the resigned community, which is stifling and anti-intellectual, is hardly an incentive for the bright, alert executive.

An examination of the labor supply in a community of this variety reveals other discouraging problems. What might responsible industry desire in a labor supply? Such industry would wish to find a labor supply that would be predictable and dependable, as well as having a distribution of various kinds of skills. Responsible industry would probably find little of this in the present scheme of things. Skills and crafts are at a minimum. Now, the lack of skills and crafts is due to a variety of causes; but one of the principal reasons is that resignation creates a way of life in which the development of new skills and crafts is minimized. Even in the skills and crafts present, resignation is manifest, for workmanship and performance are considered poor and below what one might expect elsewhere; there is a general attitude of indifference toward the quality of work. Further, these people have not given up trying to control those elements in the industrial process which are at odds with their still casual, simple, preferred way of life. It is easy for them to become provoked at management. There is still a tendency to disrupt work through absenteeism and, in some instances, strikes.

If industry could overcome all of the obstacles which have been pointed out, it would still be necessary for them virtually to assure the community that certain important patterns of life would not be disturbed. The introduction of alien groups is identified with change and disruption. These people would want some assurance that the basic patterns of relations with respect to Negroes would not be disturbed; Negroes could not be brought into the community. The attitude toward Negroes in this instance arises out of the fear and hopelessness which the natives have with respect to economic competition.

It is clear that the dimensions of resignation become manifest in conditions which impose serious obstacles on responsible industries which are looking for a community in which to locate. Thus, significant and stable industry has never developed an interest in this community, and the factories that Coal Town has been able to attract are small and without interest in or commitment to the community.

We have focused on how resignation is functional in minimizing industrial innovation, and on the changes which might be associated with it. The patterns of resignation are perhaps functional in still another, and perhaps even a more significant, way. They are responsible for maintaining the integration of the social and psychological structure of members of the community. To be sure, it is integration at what some may consider to be a high price. Nevertheless, by minimizing innovations, the patterns of resignation control shifts in status and role, as well as shifts in wealth and social class; thus, the social structure remains pretty much intact without internal disruption.

Insofar as resignation limits social change, it also results in the ultimate decline of the community. Resignation results in restricted economic opportunities with little opportunity for change. With a reduction in economic opportunities, other services become restricted. The youth who might in a sense rescue the community leave if they are capable of warding off the values of resignation. Those who remain are in no position, either agewise or personalitywise, to change things. The economy of the community is largely dependent on miners' pensions, Social Security, and public assistance. Because employment in the area is seasonal and spasmodic, precise income figures are difficult to compile. Living on what is termed "rocking-chair money" is part of the normative value system and is acceptable for the most part, although there are some deviants from this pattern who have higher aspirations.

As a result of the processes described, the observer who looks at this community sees what appear to him to be the signs of peace and tranquillity. In comparison with the dynamic and mobile life in the urban center, the resigned community gives the superficial appearance of a community without psychic disturbances. *Such a conclusion would be misleading indeed.* Although the social and economic difficulties are serious in themselves, the effects of resignation on personality are equally serious. My own view is that there is much potential talent and creativity buried in the resigned community. At this point, what creative energies are present become burdened with and are buried in the resigned process.

THE PROBLEM OF REHABILITATION

Efforts at rehabilitation of the resigned community are numerous. There are always some who see the solution of the resigned community's problems in terms of economic change, of attracting industry. Moreover, most federal and state aid programs see the rehabilitation of the chronically depressed area largely in economic terms. Thus, operating with the classical model of the economic, rational, self-seeking man, the assumption is made that if what we have described as resignation is a response to chronic economic depression, then economic rehabilitation can reverse the process of resignation. Such a

LANTZ

268

view, as noted earlier in this paper, seems to me a gross oversimplification of the problem. The autonomy of subsystems which take on functions different from those intended precludes any reversal of resignation in any simple way. Moreover, I doubt that the classical economic model has much application for resigned communities.

Patterns of resignation are functional; and any program attempting change will have to come to grips with how and why these patterns are satisfying in the present. For example, the minimizing of change in the resigned community is intimately related to interactional patterns in which destructive behavior is leveled against persons wishing for new things. There are value and pride, as well as status arrangements, associated with ridicule for those who wish to break out of the pattern of resignation, and these people change slowly. Informants pointed this out:

> You see, I remember when I had my boy here and I wanted him to take music lessons because I like music a great deal. Well, when I suggested this to him everybody laughed at the idea. You see, if you did anything like this, if you wanted to improve yourself or wanted to take piano lessons, you were a sissy.

> If you showed any intellectual ability, you were a misfit. Any ability that you might have was played down. These I refer to as environmental cripples in this area. These are the persons who had the ability but who were forced to forget or were not encouraged to go on and develop their intellectual capacities.

Because rehabilitation of the resigned community is often synonymous with introducing industry, it is interesting to note, as previously suggested, that these communities have been bypassed by the values of industrialization and by the virtues of the Protestant ethic—particularly those involving self-discipline and the capacity for and interest in hard labor. Possessing neither the basic skills nor the necessary value orientation, such communities have tried to deal with the industrialization on their own terms. The result is that which is often termed "plant failure." Frequently there is plant mobility. Basically these results arise from the resigned community's inability to integrate the industry and from the industry's lack of knowledge about the community into which it moves.

Industrialization has been minimal in these communities. But let us assume that suddenly the resigned areas become industrialized—what then? Given the conditions I have described, the skills and basic discipline necessary for industrialization would be lacking, and large numbers of workers would probably have to be imported, making of the resigned native a minority group in his own community, with all the resultant antagonisms and potential for deviant behavior. In a sense, the basic history of the experience with mining may be repeated. Thus, one compounds the probability of frustration for the local population—not to mention the wasting of large sums of money, public and private—and the energies of those involved.

These remarks are not designed to suggest that the problem of resignation cannot be dealt with, but it does mean that there are exceedingly complex facets of the resigned community that must be understood. *The resigned community is a common phenomenon in American society today.* Although not all depressed communities are necessarily resigned, many are. Maximum return for public funds will be realized when we understand the needs of the resigned community to avoid change. For these are in conflict with the efforts of policy makers to produce change. Basic research into the nature of resigned social structures is a must; whether such research is consistent with the orientation of policy makers is something else again.

BIBLIOGRAPHY

Boewe, Charles, *Prairie Albion*. Carbondale: Southern Illinois University Press, 1962.

Bridenbaugh, Carl, *Myths and Realities*. Baton Rouge: Louisiana State University Press, 1952.

Caudill, Harry M., *Night Comes to the Cumberlands: A Biography of a Depressed Area*. Boston: Little, Brown & Co., 1963.

Hughes, Charles C., and others, *People of Cove and Woodlot*. New York: Basic Books, Inc., 1960.

Lantz, Herman R., *People of Coal Town*. New York: Columbia University Press, 1958.

Lazarsfeld, Paul, and Hans Zeisel, *Workers of Marienthal*. Vienna, Austria: Socio-Economic Institute, 1933.

Wilcock, Richard, and Walter Franke, *Unwanted Workers*. New York: Free Press of Glencoe, Inc., 1963.

The Southern Appalachian Migrant: Country Boy Turned Blue-Collarite*

WILLIAM E. POWLES

INTRODUCTION TO THE SUBJECT

A steady flow of young people (and some older ones) is in progress all over the country, a flow from country to city. Education, self-betterment, and economic opportunity are among the forces which pull; the declining profit of the family farm and the surplus of family members are influences which propel. The

* This report is based on findings, readings, and discussions associated with the course of a research project on preventive mental health measures in different industrial and occupational settings. This project is financed by the National Institute of Mental Health, under research grant MH287. Based in the College of Medicine, University of Cincinnati, its director is Professor W. Donald Ross. The author, who co-directs clinical aspects of the project, is indebted to others on the team, particularly its sociological consultants, James S. Brown, Ph.D., and the late Roscoe Giffin, Ph.D. Many of their ideas have been incorporated, although the ultimate formulations lie with the author. E. Russell Porter, M.P.H., contributed a critical reading of the manuscript, with helpful comments, besides taking part in research discussions.

particular focus in this chapter is the character of the industrial laborer who has migrated and metamorphosed from the "country boy" of the Southern Appalachian region, particularly of the farming and mining counties of southeast Kentucky. This new blue-collarite is now found in substantial communities in the cities of the industrial North, from Pittsburgh to Chicago, where his habituation has been fraught with stress and upheaval as well as conspicuous success and satisfaction. Haunted always by a culture of chronic depression, the people of the Southern Appalachian highland have lost an important source of income with the increasing mechanization, followed by the closing down, of the soft-coal industry. Its folk, previously held in their geographic and social isolation by the warmth of familiarity and tradition and a fatalistic stoicism, have been pushed out into the stream of the "greater society" by the Great Depression, governmental relief measures, and military service, and pulled to the cities by the lure of jobs and dollars in the industrial boom of the two World Wars and the Cold War. Their own energetic pioneering spirit, dormant for a hundred years, has them on the move again.

This paper will be an attempt at a composite sketch of the life and philosophy of the "Southern Appalachian Migrant" workingman as seen in a mental-health research project in a Midwestern industrial city. The research team, including psychiatrists, psychologists, a social caseworker, anthropologists, and an economist, has examined a complex of data on some 300 working people; among these were 60 men who were born in the Southern Appalachian region; and among the latter, we got to know 20 more personally and clinically by direct contact and interviews. Besides attempting to sketch some general features of the background, adjustment, and current values of these men, we shall give two case histories (disguised in essential details) to illustrate both successful and marginal urbanization.

The composite generalizations given are, of course, faulty insofar as they give the impression that there is *one* Appalachian region or *one* type of Appalachian *émigré*. The reader must bear in mind that people and places are diversified everywhere. Nevertheless, we believe that some general processes and characteristics are worthy of delineation. Two poles of thinking are evident in the literature available on the Southern Appalachian people.[1] On the one hand, they are pictured as strange, intriguing, almost other-worldly, comprehensible to the "outsider" only through the medium of literary caricature or scientific exposition. On the other hand, the better they are known, the more they seem like other Americans, with each of the traits they bear being visible in some form anywhere in the "greater society." The truth is that they *are* Americans, rural, Southern, Caucasian, Protestant, English-speaking, drivers of cars, and viewers of television, *and also* that they cope with their lives in a variety of ways which have some special flavor not met in other rural Americans. The reader may well wonder: "Well, what is so special about the men described in this paper?" He is right. He may also muse: "How interesting, how distinctive, these men are!" He is right again!

_____

[1] This kind of dichotomy has been particularly well pointed out in a discussion of the nature of the Puritans and Puritanism, to which the author turned to understand the basic Puritan philosophy of the Appalachian people: R. B. Perry, *Puritanism and Democracy* (New York: Vanguard Press, 1944).

The Southern Appalachian Migrant: Country Boy Turned Blue-Collarite

The Appalachian region, stretched to its possible limits, can be imagined to extend from the rocky fjords and isolated fishing coves of Labrador and Newfoundland, through Nova Scotia and New England, through the Appalachian Mountains proper and their foothills, to the equally isolated creek valleys of the hills of Arkansas and Oklahoma. Isolation and the struggle for subsistence have been the key forces shaping the life of the people throughout this belt. Isolation, the interaction with forbidding nature, the dogged fight for a living, and the loss of continuing contact with the ongoing stream of the "greater society" have led[2] to the retention and special development of unusual dialects and social patterns, some truly archaic and others arising out of local conditions.

The outside world claims that the people of Appalachia "look odd," "talk funny," "act stupid." They are lampooned as "Newfies," "Arkies," "brier-hoppers," "hillbillies," "poor white trash," fit only for the hills or the slums. No doubt a minority may have gone under and stayed under, stupefied, demoralized, debauched, debased, inbred, reverted over generations to the status of near-savages, without (so it is broadly hinted by their detractors) even the incest-taboo of most respectable savages. But the majority, despite their lack of emphasis on formal learning and their shyness of the great, busy city world, are warm, friendly, intelligent people, loving their land, creating a folk music both cheerful and sad, and, when transplanted to the city, coping with characteristic vigor with that forbidding world. Their misfortune is that the stable and successful evoke little notice. Only the minority come to the attention of social agencies, the law, and the press. In the city, this minority probably amounts to no more than 10 per cent.[3] And among this minority, difficulties in understanding the social machinery of the city are of far more importance than *any defect* of character or intelligence.

The *"Southern Appalachian"* region has been variously defined and surveyed by governmental agencies, religious and welfare groups, and social scientists, because it has long been regarded as a socially and economically distressed section of the United States. This region stretches from Virginia and West Virginia to the northeast corner of Alabama, comprising portions of seven states.[4] It embraces the Blue Ridge Mountains along the southeast; a broad intervening valley, which was the pathway of settlers in the eighteenth and early nineteenth centuries; and the Allegheny and Cumberland Plateaux on the northwest.

---

[2] A. Toynbee, *A Study of History* (As abridged by D. C. Somervell) (London: Oxford University Press, 1947).

[3] This type of estimate is a difficult one to establish. See E. R. Porter, "When Cultures Meet—Mountain and Urban," *Nursing Outlook*, Vol. II (June 1963), pp. 418-20.

[4] This is the definition followed in the most recent definitive study of the region; the following work discusses other definitions and studies, and is a major reference source:

T. R. Ford (ed.), *The Southern Appalachian Region: a Survey* (Lexington: University of Kentucky Press, 1962).

POWLES

The Kentucky portion of the region seems to have known the greatest concentration of distress and the highest emigration rates. It is also the country from which the majority of Appalachians in our mental health study came. The magnitude of the migration from Kentucky is suggested by figures such as these: In each of the decades 1940-1950 and 1950-1960, Kentucky lost 13 per cent of its people by migration. In 1950-1955, about one-fifteenth of the state's population of three million left home, and in 1940-1950 an estimated 372,988.[5] We are therefore basing our descriptions primarily on the ex-Kentuckian seen in city industries, as if he were a "type" for the region generally and as a particularly vivid example of the urbanization of rural people generally.

MIGRATION, NORTHWARD AND UPWARD

Migration is a word of many connotations. The Appalachian migrant follows a kind of flyway, like the defined and predictable paths of migratory birds: he heads north, perhaps on sheer impulse, beckoned by some cousin or brother or friend, or by an inviting Appalachian community within or on the outskirts of a big city, as well as by rumor or actual prospects of a cash-paying job. If he settles down, the same flyway takes him back repeatedly to his real home on weekends and vacations. Count the cars heading south and east along the main highways of Kentucky on a Friday night, or north and west on Sunday night or Monday morning!

Arrived in the city, to various degrees bewildered and disoriented, the Appalachian migrant is likely to make his first rough nest in a slum where his folks may have arrived a short time before, where life is informal and housing cheap: tenements often charge rent weekly, an apparent economy to the untutored. Such districts in a Midwestern city (ghettoes, they might be called) are unkempt and disorderly, not merely because of poverty and social instability, but because such city amenities as garbage collection are unknown and unpracticed "down home." The lucky or more enterprising migrants soon find a job. They move to a more settled lower-class district, renting an apartment, and hoping ultimately for something better. Migrants, if "successful," rise through apartment-renting to home-owning in a lower-middle-class section, still in the congenial neighborhood of other Appalachians but with an increasing participation in city middle-class ways, such as membership in a regular community organization or a formally structured church. The highest ambition of many is to own an acre or two of land in the suburbs or true

---

[5] See the "Ford Study" noted in footnote 4.

Also, R. Giffin, "When Families Move from Cinder Hollow to Cincinnati," in *Mountain Life and Work* (Quarterly of the Council of the Southern Mountains, Berea, Kentucky), Fall issue, 1956. This article provides key summaries on a number of issues.

Also, J. S. Brown and R. J. Ramsey, "The Changing Kentucky Population: a summary of population data for counties," *Progress Report No. 67*, Kentucky Agricultural Experiment Station, Lexington, September 1958.

Also, E. R. Porter (footnote 3).

The Southern
Appalachian
Migrant:
Country Boy
Turned
Blue-Collarite

farm country, where one may till one's own ground and reap its fruits and do some trucking or squirrel-hunting and fishing in time away from work. Some remain settled on the various rungs of this migratory "ladder." A few never even make it out of the slums.

CHARACTERISTICS AND CONFLICTS

Who is this Appalachian rural dweller turned industrial laborer? City folks call him "brier" or "hillbilly": he is content to call himself "country boy," a term full of pride, though outwardly self-effacing and apologetic. He is an energetic, independent, warm, proud man under his drawling, socially rough exterior, a fighter and an avenger if need be. One gets the feeling that he has never been able, or never been allowed, to cry as a child, and that the expression of any sad, lonely, or anxious feeling is taboo for him. Physical pain, maybe: spiritual pain, no. Such stoicism, born of generations of hardship, may not always help him, although it is always admirable. He may needlessly put up with chronic malnutrition or ill health without doing something about it, even when help is freely available.

The Puritan ideal of industry and uprightness, and the devil take the hindmost, seems literally embodied in his life style. Within this life style, of course, are many types: the admired leader, the equally admired rough guy, the gentle, conscientious martyr, and, of course, the handful of maladjusted laggards, whom the devil seems to be gaining—and others.

Individualism in personal life and personal responsibility in interpersonal relations are ideals for the Appalachian man. Although his woman is often strong, forceful, and sustaining, she remains in the home, and his world is something of a man's world, where a man is supposed to get his way and to lean on no one. The idea of leaning on the community may be a doubly foreign one to him. For one thing, the idea of community itself is almost nonexistent for the citizen of an isolated hillside farming or mining hamlet. The idea that some nebulous entity called "the city" imposes law and justice and demands allegiance, or will in turn give help and support, is simply incomprehensible and incredible to the Appalachian newcomer. As an example, the idea that one may not beat one's own wife or take personal vengeance for a theft or affront may come as an insulting attack on one's personal integrity.

In the city, the traditional relationship of husband and wife becomes shaken up, with resultant confusion, anxiety, and anger. For example, in the city, wives are expected to be more outgoing (literally), and city wives are often active at church or PTA, in addition to managing the home's relation to the community, doing the shopping, and answering door calls of salesmen or social workers. This disruption in the traditional balance of power includes practical consequences. For example, the Appalachian workingman will be highly suspicious at first of any community agency which deals with his wife "behind his back" while he is at work; yet he probably will have neither the time nor the inclination to enter such dealings himself. A recurrent problem for such agencies is getting the father—the breadwinner and traditional boss—involved.

POWLES

274

Recent years seem to have seen some softening of this stance of individualism.[6] The Appalachian "down home" has received, and welcomed, relief money; he has joined the army with distinction; he has joined labor unions, amid strife, and appreciated the significant social and medical benefits they have provided; and he becomes a good union man in the city. It is as if he can join a group which fights battles, and fights outside of the family circle, within which he is a peaceable man.[7] Perhaps it is just such a fighter who comes to the cities, leaving his more passive counterpart "down home."

HOME, FAMILY, AND RELIGION

The Appalachian workingman is, almost above everything else, a family man, to whom "home" and "folks" have a particularly deep significance. "Home"—the creek valleys of Appalachia (sometimes roadless), the coal mines, the hillside farms, the small, strung-out hamlets—is never seen by the traveler along the busy highways. Unknowing outsiders type it as the forbidding world of a primitive, suspicious people who may shoot the stranger on sight, and in any case certainly not worth entering. But home to the Appalachian migrant is the affectively real world, the world of solid contact with the earth, with nature and fresh, unpolluted air, the world of family ties and friends and familiar language, where time clocks and traffic lights do not artificially hem one in.

To this blessed land he returns whenever he can, on weekends and vacations and at times of crisis, to visit his father, and brothers, and his wife's sisters and their husbands and children. He knows it is a poor, ungiving land, and while he hopes he can retire here in his old age, he knows and dreads that he cannot. He finds he knows fewer and fewer people at home, for his peers, like himself, have almost all up and moved to the city; the children have growed up; the older folks have passed on. But he can sit and talk, or just sit. He can go out with his rifle-gun or spinning rod to hunt or fish up the holler, or just tramp.

He keeps his soul alive for many years, perhaps all his life, by his contacts with the homeland. He is not, of course, much of a letter writer.

The family of people into which the Appalachian workingman was born retains a particularly intense meaning for him throughout his life, emotionally sustaining him, but also in a special way being a piece of social machinery of great personal assistance. As well as the home circle which brought him up, he has "folks," the wider circle of kin to whom he literally feels as to parents, brothers, and sisters, and within which he probably does not choose a wife.[8] This wider or "extended" family is not a vital part of most city-dwellers' experience. But for the Appalachian migrant, its strengths, resources, and ramifications play a crucial role. Almost invariably, he came to the city on a family "flyway," to visit, or to look into news from a weekend homecomer that some jobs were open in his cousin's plant. He works his way into city

---

[6] See particularly the opinion surveys conducted in the "Ford Study."
[7] See Giffin (footnote 5) for the concept of "conflict-oriented groups."
[8] See J. S. Brown, "The Conjugal Family and the Extended Family Group," *American Sociological Review*, Vol. 17, No. 3 (June, 1952), pp. 297-306.

The Southern Appalachian Migrant: Country Boy Turned Blue-Collarite

life via kinfolk who have already a toe hold, however precarious, in the community. He negates his family ties only in one special case. This occurs when he begins to feel contempt for, and to cut himself off from, kinfolk whom he has bypassed on the urbanization ladder, who have gone to the devil, failed to make it, remained trash in the slums. Conversely, those who don't make it may fail because they lack a family organization to help them. The kin system in his plant, or adopted brothers from the Appalachian region, very often play a similar sustaining function for him: a father, a brother-in-law, a bunch of fellows from "down home," with whom he can fraternize at noon break or pass time in the car pool or the tavern across the road. (Some plants literally do their hiring through a kinship network, a system eminently satisfactory to both management and employees.)

His wife, too, is part of an interlocking network of kin and friends on her side, in which he may participate actively, or which he may accept as wholly right while leaving them strictly alone.

Of the institutions and ties which sustain him, religion plays an important but a peculiarly shaky part. Strongly religious by nature, a Puritan and a fundamentalist by tradition, he is neither a theologian, a "joiner," nor a believer in ecclesiasticism or the social gospel. The other-worldly sects to which he feels attracted have little or no formal structure. The "upper class" have belonged to a Baptist or Methodist group at home and look down on the Holiness and Pentecostal "lower class" with their purported loose morals and religious excesses;[9] but even the relatively settled churches have in the city no firm counterpart to which any formal transfer of membership is possible or which can go seeking out newcomers. The church "down home" has preached a religion of future reward for poverty and suffering on earth and has not fitted its members to adapt to a complex new society, much less to a changing society. However, just as his most important social contacts in the new city surroundings may be in the corner tavern, the Appalachian migrant may find an important transitional rallying point in the store-front church, that rough, informal, evanescent congregation to which he can commit himself without too many questions being asked, where fancy clothes are not worn, where a spirit of comradeship exists but none of the puzzling and frightening organizational paraphernalia of the city, where he can sing hill music to a guitar or accordion and pour out in emotional release the feelings his usually stoical bearing hides. Probably nothing could be more forbidding for him (if he ever got there, which he doesn't) than the big city church with its highfalutin ways, its formal music, and its organized worship; this place of sanctuary for others could give the Appalachian only a feeling of unwantedness and inferiority. Later, as he works up the ladder of urbanization, he may be drawn to and feel safe in a formal city congregation. But he may be left at loose ends, vaguely feeling he wants to, and should, go to church but also feeling unwanted and shy at reaching out to join.[10]

---

[9] See J. S. Brown, "Social Class, Intermarriage, and Church Membership in a Kentucky Community," *American Journal of Sociology*, Vol. 57, No. 3 (November, 1951), pp. 232-42.

[10] See also three articles in the *Catholic Telegraph-Register*, April 22 and 29 and May 6, 1960.

POWLES

EDUCATION

A final note on education. The average educational attainment of Appalachian workingmen is low; for someone to have had the motivation, or luck, to stick with schooling through high school is exceptional. The problem of illiteracy or near-illiteracy in otherwise bright men is common and highlights their essential resourcefulness. Our study uncovered one illiterate foreman! Although most migrant men want their children to receive a much better education than they did, their attitude is a conflicted one. They are unable to supervise their children's schoolwork. The community of Appalachians in which they live may tend to impede regular school attendance. Their own pride in being self-made though poorly educated may set a rather negative example. Impressionistically, we may say that the Appalachian workingman is both ashamed and proud of his formal ignorance, as of his origin. He admires the formally ignorant preacher whose only use for education is to comb the Bible. Accordingly, his lack of education spurs him to have his children do better in the city, but his pride spurs him to deny his own deficiencies and to avoid taking advantage of educational opportunties himself. Undoubtedly, formal education will be the bridge by which his children may reach out and rise in the "greater society." [11]

TWO CASE HISTORIES

The following two descriptions of workingmen need some explanation. Their identity is disguised through altering some crucial details but, hopefully, without blurring some of the color or the contradiction of what has been learned about them. Both men have been selected because they have been in the city for many years, are relatively typical workingmen, and can immediately be identified by their speech and their own self-definition as Southern Appalachians. Perhaps it is chiefly at this point that the reader will ask: "What is different here from any other workingman of any other origin?" The second sketch illustrates the small minority of Appalachian migrants who are in some constant social difficulty. But even here it should be noted that this man has held a job, with a relatively good wage, for a relatively long time.

Virgil Stevens, aged 40, has been a maintenance pipefitter in a cement factory for 13 years. His manly, somewhat chubby, pink face, his warm brown eyes, his tousled, wavy blond hair, now gray-streaked, and his quiet, sincere manner quickly engage one's friendly interest. At work he is a busy man who mostly works unsupervised, having charge of miscellaneous maintenance of a main building as well as pipefitting work. He keeps track of repairs as they are needed, from his own cruising and observation as well as from work orders. He works best under medium pressure: when many back orders are piled up,

---

[11] See E. G. Youmans, *The Educational Attainment and Future Plans of Kentucky Rural Youths,* Kentucky Agriculture Experiment Station Bulletin No. 664, Lexington, January, 1959.

The Southern
Appalachian
Migrant:
Country Boy
Turned
Blue-Collarite

he gets harassed and his efficiency goes down; he is even more uncomfortable if there is nothing to do, and has actually punched the clock and gone home, without pay, at such times.

He is thoroughly liked by his peers, although they are a bit awed by his conscientiousness. His foreman wonders if he is always working up to his true ability, and mentions occasional outbursts of temper and smashing things. These episodes occur when he is over- or underworked. Unlike most hourly paid employees, he plans time off well ahead with his foreman, never letting the company down and offering to make up any work he leaves unfinished. These times off are taken because he is an ordained Baptist minister and occasionally is asked to preach or to lead a revival out of town.

Stevens was born in a small coal-mining town in West Virginia. Outsiders have considered this a rough town, but Stevens laughs at such an idea: he is very fond of his home and visits regularly, one weekend a month, and in summer vacations, "to see his father" (his mother is alive, but he doesn't mention her). His father was a miner all his life and seems a hearty old man at 80 years of age; he married rather late. The son followed his father into mining, after somehow keeping in school to completion of grade 10. He picked up machine work, was a petty officer machinist in the navy, and, with a G-I Bill vocational course, emerged as a qualified tradesman. A brother and several cousins preceded him to the city during the war; one works in his plant, but he somewhat proudly points out that he got his own job without the offices of his cousin.

The Stevens live in a rather settled lower-middle-class municipality in an industrial metropolis. Mrs. Stevens, aged 26, looks after their four children, aged 3 to 8, carefully and helps to save money for their future education and the purchase of a house, although they also give heavily to their church. She occasionally takes in sewing or does part-time store work in the Christmas rush. Mrs. Stevens comes from the same home town as her husband; she is the baby sister of his old-time school friend. She came to the city to visit her brother and to seek work, but married very soon and has been homemaking ever since. Mr. Stevens remains on very friendly terms with his wife's folks, who are active in his church and admire him greatly. The Stevens' social life revolves around their church, a small Missionary Baptist congregation. Mrs. Stevens persuaded her husband shortly after their marriage to come to church; he experienced a religious conversion, studied assiduously, and was ordained. He was the chief minister of the congregation for a while, but felt he was not doing the best job; so he is now assistant minister, sings in the choir with his wife, preaches once a month, and visits other churches in the city and "back home" when invited.

Their health is good. There are hints that both husband and wife suppress some fears and nervous feelings; but on the whole they cope with life actively and happily and contribute constructively to both work and community.

Porter Winters has been for 18 years a semiskilled operator in a sewage and fertilizer treatment plant. Aged 45, a huge, gaunt, lean, hawk-faced man, he wears a constant expression of worry and suspicion, his hands shake a little all the time, and his drawling voice has a complaining, breathless quality—one might say that he gives one the feeling of being haunted by some unseen ghost. This appearance is related to a constant vicious circle of tension, heavy drinking, shakiness, and more heavy drinking, an activity which is social as well as self-medicating, for he finds pleasure in the company of boys from down home.

Winters has had a hard row to hoe. Born on a small farm in Tennessee, losing both parents when he was eight, farmed out (at least, in his own view) as an indentured laborer to various families from that age on, wandering to various farm jobs in his teens and early adult life from Virginia to Arkansas, with an occasional stint in the coal mines, he is unable to call any one spot his home. He does, however, fraternize with a bunch of fellows from Southeast Kentucky at the neighborhood tavern, where he spends almost every evening and weekend. Here he has been in occasional fracases, twice having had to be off work for lengthy periods with knife wounds.

Mrs. Winters is a "mountain gal," also from Southeast Kentucky, whom Winters met shortly after coming to the city, and who was a waitress at a restaurant he frequented. She sees little of her husband, blaming his drinking for this. Mr. Winters, on the other hand, blames her for never being at home, as she chooses to work for rather low wages in a restaurant, washing dishes. Mrs. Winters says she never sees a cent of her husband's pay. They seem to speak little, except to quarrel. They rent an apartment in a small business section of the city, better than slums but an unsettled area where many Appalachians are congregating. One son, aged 20, has left the home to get married, his father not being quite sure to whom, because he does not want to know or mix with her folk. They are somewhere in town. Another, aged 17, has quit school and is bumming around somewhere about the country, there being some suspicion that the police are after him. Winters deplores the unsettled, disobedient ways of modern youth, and feels that he has given much to his sons without receiving either respect or satisfaction in return. He is extremely fond of his high-school-aged (15-year-old) daughter, who is at home when his wife is not. His wife suspects an incestuous relationship between them; whatever this daughter is receiving emotionally, she appears by far the most settled person in the family, keeps things smoothed out at home, and is attending school fairly regularly, hoping eventually to be a practical nurse.

Winters is quite popular at work. The other men consider him a conscientious workman, driving himself and giving everything to his job, but something of an unpredictable character whom one does not approach closely for fear of raising tensions or tempers. His foreman and the personnel department also rate him well and seem genuinely unaware of his rather frequent absences from work, his fairly numerous accidents, and his evident functioning below maximum efficiency on Monday mornings and around pay times. He moves slowly but is always accomplishing something. Much of the time he is aware of a gnawing upper-abdominal pain, which he mostly laughs

The Southern
Appalachian
Migrant:
Country Boy
Turned
Blue-Collarite

279

off but for which he occasionally visits the medical clinic for some medicine and a chat with the nurse or doctor. Seven years ago, following an injury to his lower abdomen at work, he suffered a serious nervous breakdown, was in a mental hospital three months, and failed to keep up his follow-up treatment; he now experiences a mixture of fear and dislike toward psychiatrists.

Winters has been asked several times if he would do something about his drinking. This makes him angry, as he feels he is a moderate drinker and just enjoys being with the down-home boys. He has also been offered social casework to straighten things out at home more to his satisfaction, but he says nothing can be done until his wife and boys shape up, and he remains stuck in a rut of grumbling and complaining about how hard life is treating him.

Obviously, these two men differ in their basic childhood formative experiences and basic personal make-up. But might one have made it better, or the other worse, if some present realities had been different?

Winters has no home and no family; his brothers and sisters are hardly known to him, and his foster homes are put well behind him. He gets some feeling of family at work and at the tavern, but little or none with his wife or across town or down south where he still visits some acquaintances. Stevens had a stable family life, came to town along a family "flyway," and has a three-dimensional family experience: at work, at church, and "down home."

Stevens has a stable church. Drawn into attendance by his wife, and in respectful obedience to his mother's teachings, he has a crucially important avocation which in his eyes claims more than any other loyalty. Winters feels that everyone should go to church, but he doesn't, as people would look down on him. Maybe one of these days . . .

Winters is almost illiterate—a great handicap, though also a distinction, in the city. He has no vocational training, only his innate resourcefulness and tenacity holding him in a semiskilled job. Stevens reads well, especially the Bible, and puts a high premium on obtaining a better education for his children.

Stevens is a law-abiding man, although sometimes a frustrated and explosive one. He understands personal morality vividly, but probably has a limited concept of social justice or group morality. Winters instinctively feels the law to be his enemy and persecutor; after all, he was imprisoned for stealing food for his foster family from a freight car during the depression. He cannot understand why one must carry insurance on one's automobile: is it not one's own business?

Perhaps Winters' one sustaining institution is his tavern. Stevens, of course, is a teetotaler. Although Stevens has never been approached by a social agency, and has no social problems, Winters exhibits a strong suspicion of the meddling of social workers, who have approached both him and his wife from psychiatric hospital, juvenile court, and research project. He seems unable to visualize the community, in the guise of a hospital, agency, or university, wanting to help with his family difficulties: he is cognizant only of the shame and danger of leaning on, or being scrutinized by, strangers.

POWLES

280

IN SUMMARY

Hill folks from the Southern Appalachian region have been pouring into the North's industrial cities (and the South's) in a stream which can be called torrential for the past 20 years. A minority of them create social problems. The great majority, although undergoing all the stresses which any immigrant experiences, make it successfully and unobtrusively in the city. Their men have entered the labor force as a significant new population, fitting in as good workmen and union members on the whole, and retaining some of the cultural features of language, life, and philosophy in which they grew up. Individualism, Puritanism, and stoicism are said to be their common traits. They love their home land and, nourishing themselves by frequent visits "down home," sustain their spirit in the complex and impersonal city. So, too, their own families and wider kin relationships supply them with key satisfactions as well as important help in obtaining city jobs and steadying their feet on the rungs of the long climb up from the slums to the settled residential districts or semiagricultural suburbs.

Many questions have been raised as to how to help this stream of migrants. They do not understand or reach out for help easily, because of their lack of understanding of community agencies, coupled with their Puritan values of self-help. Nevertheless, they are evidently capable of group relationship and action, whether in feuding, military service, labor unionism, the tavern, or the store-front church. Perhaps the most significant person to help them will be from among themselves: the social scientist, the community worker, the minister, the union leader, or the personnel officer, *who is one of them,* and can feel and speak with them, value their values, know their land and folks. Certainly, research and action programs are further needed

1. To understand these folk better, and to dispel the many hostile and contemptuous stereotypes applied to them.
2. To facilitate their learning of the complex social machinery of the city—for they are quick learners, resourceful in coping with the physical environment.
3. To help them maintain their identity and warm culture, while fitting into industrial urban society.

The Southern
Appalachian
Migrant:
Country Boy
Turned
Blue-Collarite

Acculturation and
Negro Blue-Collar Workers

ROSE STAMLER

"ACCULTURATION" is usually defined as the adoption, by a group entering a new cultural environment, of the dominant values, attitudes, and behavior of the "host" group (2).* Sometimes it is the "host" who is expected to do the changing and it is the guest, often uninvited, whose culture becomes dominant—for example, when the American Indian was "host" and the white European settler the "guest." The huge waves of immigration of the nineteenth and early twentieth centuries, mainly from Europe, hurled millions of individuals into the acculturation process, as part of their integration into American life. Every major United States city, and many a farm area, was the scene of this often painful drama. But with the ending of large-scale European immigration in the 1920's, a new phase of this drama has unfolded. In 1940, two-thirds of the Negro population of our country lived in the rural South. By 1960, two-thirds were living in the urban centers—one-third in the North and one-third in the cities of the South. This tremendous shift in population— from rural to urban, and in large numbers, from South to North—has again swept millions into new cultural settings.

The stresses and strains of this process hold more than an academic interest. In 1963, the drama is a compelling one and, accompanied by greater social upheaval than our country has witnessed in perhaps a century, has its repercussions in all aspects of our social life—communities, churches, schools, industry, and government.

It would be an oversimplification to state that the core problem is acculturation alone. Certainly the level and form of social conflict mark today's events as different from the problems surrounding the European migration. But there is a great need to know as much about today's drama as can be learned, for it is being enacted over so widespread an area of the country and is penetrating into so many aspects of our social life, that more and more are being drawn in as participants rather than merely as observers. Perhaps the study described below can add some knowledge, at least in regard to acculturation, as *part* of the larger picture.

---

* Numbers in parentheses refer to numbered items in the bibliography at the end of the chapter.

In late 1960 and 1961, as part of a public health program both of service and research, an opportunity arose to study some aspects of acculturation among low-income middle-aged Negro men in the city of Chicago.

One of the methods that medical research uses to probe both acute contagious and chronic noninfectious disease is *epidemiology*. This method seeks to find clues to the causation of these diseases by examining the differing rates of occurrence among different population groups, and by uncovering characteristics that may be associated with higher or lower rates. Increasingly, areas which are part of the "staked claim" of sociology have been considered fair exploration ground in these population studies. It is in this territory— where medical and sociological curiosity share a joint tenancy—that the investigation described in this article arose.

In an earlier study (1958), an important medical difference in two particular population groups was noted (4). Blood samples collected from several hundred low-income Negro men had been analyzed for the level of the substance serum cholesterol. The mean level in this group was found to be significantly lower than that of white men of a similar age. Since low serum cholesterol levels have been associated with lower rates of occurrence of coronary heart disease, this finding excited interest and stimulated further work to account for the difference.

Racial factors seemed unlikely as the explanation, for data showed that Negro men of *higher* income had a mean cholesterol level midway between that of the low-income Negro and the higher-income white. One likely factor might have been *diet,* which is known to play a part in determining blood cholesterol level. It was hypothesized that the diet of low-income Negroes in Chicago might vary in important ways from the typical Northern urban diet and might resemble more the diet of low-income Southerners, particularly that of Negroes of the rural South.

MEDICAL-SOCIOLOGICAL COMMON GROUND

But diet is known to be an element in a *larger* cultural complex, and it could be hypothesized than in this case dietary differences would go along with other sociological variables related to *acculturation.*

Many low-income Negro men in Chicago have at least childhood and some adult roots in the culture of the rural South. Simple observation revealed that here was a group segregated, in many ways, from the main stream of urban life. To what degree had this separation, both caste and class, prevented this group from becoming acculturated? To what degree were attitudes and ideas dominant in the urban culture reflected in the cultural pattern of those at the bottom of the urban socioeconomic ladder?

Most studies of modern urban life characterize the dominant ideas of the city (that is, the main socially approved, "most acceptable" ideas) as those of

Acculturation
and Negro
Blue-Collar
Workers

the *middle class*. A crude capsule classification of such ideas would place them in the general category of "planning ahead." Over and over again, this concept has been described almost as a red thread running through the stated value patterns of the urban middle class (1, 5). Self-reliance, preparing for participation in the urban world, and taking a measure of responsibility and initiative for one's own success—these ideas have been noted as almost ever-present in the modern middle-class credo.

Making these generalities more specific, the middle class has been found to favor such things as:

> The maximum amount of education possible for their children
> Planning and limiting family size, in order to guarantee education and other desirables
> Reliance, not on luck or fate, but on personal efforts, for success

How would a sample of Negro working-class men feel about these values? Were these values so pervasive in the urban culture that they would be evidenced not only on the main avenues but also on the back streets of that culture? Or were the barriers so high that the culture of the rural past, both recent past and that of childhood, would predominate?

It was proposed to look into these questions as part of a combined medical, nutritional, and sociological investigation. Before reporting on the findings and their possible meaning, it is necessary to present a brief description of the sample and the method used in the study.

SAMPLE

The sample included 175 married men, aged 30 to 49 years. They were volunteers for a thorough medical examination and were encountered in locations most likely to yield those of low income. Either the men themselves or their wives were approached,[1] at such places as the Board of Health free Pre-Natal Stations or when accompanying their youngsters during the free school health examinations provided for the children of the medically indigent. (A very high percentage of the population in the low-income areas took advantage of these free school examinations, to help meet the legal requirement that the children have an examination prior to first and fifth grades.)

Although income figures were not asked directly, data on such items as unemployment status (there were 22.9 per cent unemployed in the sample) and subjective interviewer observation of the housing location of respondents satisfied us that we were, in reality, dealing with a low-income group. At least 90 per cent of the final sample were engaged in (or had skills limited to) blue-collar occupations. As many as 49 per cent ended their formal education before the ninth grade. The vast majority (85 per cent) were migrants, and about one-fifth had spent all their childhood and most of their adulthood in the South. Among the migrants, two-thirds had spent at least their childhood in the *rural* South.

---

[1] About 55 per cent of those asked to participate actually completed the examination and the interview. The most frequent reason given for declining was the recency of a previous medical examination.

Trained interviewers accompanied physicians into the homes of those couples who were to receive the medical examination. Interviewers were Negro women, in an effort not to add ethnic barriers to any respondent-interviewer barriers. While the physician carried out his tasks with one of the parents, the interviewer was occupied with the other. Interviewers attempted to conduct their work in the family kitchen, to increase accuracy of the dietary data. Although both men and women were given the medical examination and the dietary interview, the men were the only subjects of the sociological interview, owing to the focus of the study—heart disease in the middle-aged male and possible associations with sociological factors.

The fact that respondents were obtaining the benefits of an extensive diagnostic examination helped get the cooperation needed to gather important dietary and sociological data.[2]

The dietary information was of two types—a recall of food eaten in the previous 24 hours and a listing of those foods considered by the respondent to be his "favorites." Although both methods of obtaining dietary data have definite limitations, particularly for drawing conclusions about *individuals,* the data for the *group* are meaningful as a description of the over-all pattern.

The sociological variables were covered in a questionnaire which focused on expressed attitudes, demographic background, and, to a lesser degree, behavior. The remainder of this report centers on our findings on these sociological variables and, in a later section, on the possible medical implications of these findings.

ATTITUDES

It should be noted that respondents' attitudes were judged at their face value. The investigators had no way to gauge "sincerity," nor was any effort made to do so. The contact between an interviewer and the subject was usually too brief and too narrow for the interviewer to be able to decide, "Now did he *really* mean that?" Whether a respondent gave a "middle-class answer" because these actually were his values or because he knew that they were the values at a premium in our culture was immaterial to the interests of this study. In *either* case, the response constituted *some* measure of the impact of middle-class ideas and values on these working-class men.

Education

The men were asked:

> Supposing you had a boy who was graduating from the eighth grade. How much more schooling do you think he should have before he stops and goes to work?

---

[2] When the diagnosis and reports from laboratory tests were complete, written summaries of the medical results were given to all examinees for follow-up care.

Acculturation
and Negro
Blue-Collar
Workers

Responses fell into three categories—"high school," "college," and in fifteen cases, "as much as he can get" or "as much as possible." (It was not completely clear whether the latter response really meant college or not, but it is likely that this *was* its meaning, in view of the words added on the value of education.)

It is noteworthy that, although 49 per cent of the men themselves had had from zero to eight years of formal learning, not a single one of the 175 respondents in any way suggested that eight years of education was enough for his son:

Table 1

ADDITIONAL SCHOOLING DESIRABLE FOR EIGHTH-GRADE BOY

Desirable Amount	Number	Per Cent
High School	49	28.0
"As much as possible"	15	8.6
College or More	111	63.4
	175	100.0
"As much as possible" plus College or More	126	72.0

From approximately two-thirds to three-fourths of the men, therefore, responded in a highly acculturated fashion. This result contrasts sharply with results of an earlier study conducted by the National Opinion Research Center (3). In the year 1947, N.O.R.C. asked an almost identical question of a sample (predominantly white) of middle-aged men. They reported that less than 40 per cent of the working-class sample recommended college education as important for young men, whereas almost 70 per cent of the upper class did so.

Perhaps the key factor to explain the difference is the 13 years that elapsed between the 1947 N.O.R.C. study and 1960, when we repeated the question to a group of Negro workers. These years were ones of a stepped-up shift to urban residence, and it is likely that awareness of the part that education plays in advancement in the urban setting has increased considerably. Likewise, this has been the decade where education for Negroes has been a focus of national attention, starting with the Supreme Court decisions on desegregation and heightened by the large-scale direct actions of Negro students, particularly in the South.

However, it should be noted that the highly acculturated response on education was not an isolated phenomenon. Other items asked received a very similar type of response.

Planning and Limiting the Size of the Family

The men were asked:

> Do you think parents should try to have large families, or do you think they should try to limit the size of the family, or should they just let nature take its course?

They were also asked:

> If a couple was starting out today in married life, about how many children do you think would make the ideal or best-size family?

A very large percentage answered in favor of limiting family size (80 per cent), and almost two-thirds (64 per cent) felt that three children or less was the ideal size:

Table 2

FAMILY PLANNING AND IDEAL FAMILY SIZE

	Number	Percent
Planning:		
Favors Limiting	137	79.7
Leave to Nature	34	19.8
Large Families Best	1	0.6
	172*	100.0
Ideal Size		
0-3	106	64.2
4 or more	59	35.8
	165*	100.0

*Excludes noncommittal respondents.

The responses on these two related items do not differ very much from what would be expected from urbanized middle-class subjects. If it is recalled that, in practice, the median number of children in middle-class United States families is approximately three, then our respondents resembled them, in *stated attitude,* to quite a high degree.

Role of Luck in Life

This question was put as:

Do you think that how well life works out for a person depends mostly on luck?

If the respondent answered "No," or "Partly," he was asked, "What other things do you think count?" In some cases, those answering that luck did not count most attributed decisive influence to "fate" or "God's will." Such responses were grouped together with those who felt that luck counted most. The other two categories, presented in Table 3 below, are for those who said that education, hard work, self-help, and so forth, were what counted and that luck counted only in part or hardly at all:

Table 3

ROLE OF LUCK IN LIFE

Factor That Counts Most	Number	Per Cent
Luck, Fate, etc.	44	25.3
Partly Personal Effort	68	39.1
Personal Effort	62	35.6
	174	100.0

As can be seen, two-thirds of the respondents restated the middle-class allegiance to personal effort and self-reliance.

Another item that reflected the same general attitude, but to an even greater degree, was represented in a question on what to do with a sudden windfall of money. Respondents were asked:

> Suppose a friend of yours won a couple of weeks' pay (for example, in a pool at his factory). Suppose he was trying to decide what to do with the money. If he couldn't make up his mind about it, what would your advice to him be?

Over 90 per cent of the men gave answers fully in line with what could be expected from a sample of the middle class: save it, invest it, buy something worthwhile. Only seven individuals (four per cent) proposed something like "have a blowout."

On all attitude variables described thus far, a high percentage of the men gave what could be considered strongly middle-class responses. We come now to two items in which this was *not* the case.

The first was reflected in answers to the question:

> What do you think are the most important things parents should teach their children?

Had these men responded in a middle-class fashion, the majority would probably have answered in terms essentially of the Protestant ethic, brought up to date. Responses could be expected such as "Work hard," "Get an education," "Make something of themselves," "Self-respect," and "Respect the rights of others." This type of response was labeled "nonauthoritarian" or "nontraditional." The non-middle-class approach was labeled "authoritarian and/or traditional"; this category would include such responses as "Obey their parents," "Behave themselves," "Respect their elders," "Keep out of trouble," "Be mannerly," "Religion and the Bible," and "Go to church."

Since the men may have given not just *one* but several parental precepts, they had to be scored on their answers, and they were then grouped into four types of response patterns:

> Entirely authoritarian/traditional
> Mainly authoritarian/traditional (with *some* nontraditional responses)
> Equally authoritarian and nonauthoritarian (half and half)
> Mainly or entirely nonauthoritarian

Almost one-half of the respondents were scored as *entirely* authoritarian and traditional:

Table 4

PARENTAL PRECEPTS

Authoritarian-Traditional Orientation of Precepts	Number	Per Cent
Entirely	82	47.1
Mainly	38	21.8
Half and Half	31	17.8
Little or None	23	13.2
	174	99.9

In seeking a hypothesis that might help explain the difference between this response and all other attitudes so far examined, attention was directed to findings on the question of *reference group*. The men had been asked, after they had stated their opinions on each attitude, how they thought *others* felt on these matters. Did they think, for instance, that their parents would have agreed with their answers? Would their neighbors agree? Would Negro businessmen and professionals have the same views? Would white people? In other words, whom did these men think they were like, or whom did they *want* to be like?

One subgroup was thus identified (39 men) who had the Negro middle class and whites as their reference groups, and who held their neighbors as a *negative* reference group; that is, they tried to disassociate themselves from the attitudes and values of their neighbors. As could be expected, this subgroup of men negative to their neighbors had an even higher percentage favoring college, family planning, smaller-size families, and reliance on self-help than had the rest of the sample. This group of people, who indicated strong desires for upward mobility, gave the most acculturated responses *except* in regard to parental precepts. They were even *more* authoritarian-traditional than the others. Over 80 per cent of those "negative to neighbors" gave entirely or mainly authoritarian responses, as compared with 65 per cent of the others in the sample. Major stress was on "behaving" and "obedience."

Perhaps, then, this type of response on parental precepts is given by different groups who are found at two distinct points on a hypothetical acculturation scale. First, it could be given by those *least* influenced by the middle-class ethic, and whose experience has made them feel that authoritarian parent-child relationships are necessary to management and/or survival in difficult, often hostile surroundings. And second, this response could be given by those with strong aspirations toward upward mobility and who consider that "behaving" by their children (managed through authoritarian relationships) is a necessary prerequisite both for protection and for achieving these aspirations.

One further factor may help explain the *non*-middle-class response on parental precepts, against the somewhat unexpected background of the high percentages with "middle-class" answers on other items. Parent-child relationships are lived every day. They are less vague and distant than decisions that have to be made about future education, ultimate family size, luck and its importance, and so forth. They may more closely mirror the influence of objective social position—its hazards and its difficulties. If low-income Negro families (and especially migrants) are not, in fact, integrated in the main stream of urban life, then this may be more clearly reflected in the daily practices and in expressed ideas *about* these practices than in the more peripheral spheres of life.

This latter explanation may also shed some light on responses to another question aimed at assessing acculturation.

"Guest Meal"

How familiar were these men with middle-class concepts and practices in regard to "entertaining"? What was their idea of the most suitable "company meal"? How much of the Southern dietary tradition or pattern had lingered? The question was put in the following way:

Suppose you and your wife could invite some people over for a big dinner, and you had as much to spend on the meal as you would want to. If your wife asked what you wanted to have her fix, what would you ask her to serve? (Start from the beginning of the meal and go all the way through, please.)

Analysis of the responses was done by a panel of judges who made independent estimates of the type of meal suggested. Consensus of the three judges was used to score the meals as "mainly Southern," "mainly Northern," or "mixed." They used as guides the presence or absence of traditionally Southern food items, and the degree to which the traditionally Northern urban course-pattern appeared, as well as other individual criteria.[3] (An interesting point was that at least two of the three judges agreed in their characterizations in over 85 per cent of the cases.)

Once again, a small minority gave responses that were characterized as mainly Northern urban. Only 15 per cent of the men suggested a guest meal judged to be more typically Northern-urban than Southern:

Table 5

GUEST MEAL

Type	Number	Per Cent
Declined to Suggest Meal	37	21.5
Mainly Southern	57	33.1
Mixed	52	30.2
Mainly Northern	26	15.1
	172	99.9

Here, again, the small percentage recommending the Northern urban pattern may well reflect the actual daily practices and experiences, and may be a more down-to-earth measure of the real degree of integration into middle-class-oriented urban life. As a matter of fact, there is a high correlation between the type of *company* meal suggested and the respondents' *own* dietary practices. This becomes evident when one compares, for example, the 24-hour food-recall and the list of respondent's favorite foods with the guest meal that the respondent suggests. Although 65 per cent of those having many Southern items in their own diets suggested a guest meal judged to be Southern, those with *no* Southern items in their own diets recommended Southern guest meals in only 31 per cent of the cases ($p = <.02$).

Summary on Attitudes

In concluding this section on attitudes, it can be said that the group *does* reflect the impact of middle-class values—to an unexpectedly high degree. If in fact, as will be reported in a later section, this group differs from whites—especially middle-class whites—in diet and cholesterol level, this difference between the groups is not carried through on *expressed attitudes*. On most attitude items, the response is largely "middle-class."

The channels by which these middle-class values are imparted were not systematically investigated, and only impressions can be reported. It may be relevant, for example, that over 95 per cent of the respondents had television sets in their homes.

Other data, both behavioral and demographic, shed limited light on what the chief influences toward acculturation are, for this group. It is

---

[3] The judges were not connected in any other way with the study, nor were they nutritionists. They were volunteers familiar with food patterns in both parts of the country. All three were white-collar; two were Negroes; one was white.

unlikely that formal organizations that this group shared with the middle class presented such a channel, since only 16 per cent of the men belonged to *any* organization aside from church and union. It is interesting, however, that 50 per cent of the men *did* belong to unions. Although such organizations cannot be characterized as middle-class (especially since they were predominantly industrial unions of the unskilled), they *can* be considered to be at least an *urbanizing* influence.

Other factors, such as level of education and work skill, are not clearly correlated, in this study, with more acculturated attitude responses. It may be that the homogeneity in the group makes it impossible to evaluate these factors adequately. For example, only two respondents completed a part of college training, and less than one-quarter completed high school; thus, intra-group differences in level of education are slight. Similarly, when only 19 of the 175 respondents have white-collar skills, a fair estimate of the weight of "white-collar versus blue-collar" in influencing atttitude is not feasible.

One demographic item where differences do become apparent concerns birthplace. On almost all attitude questions, those born in Chicago more often are those responding in the most acculturated fashion. Being born and raised in the South, particularly in the rural South, does seem to make a difference in the degree of absorption of the urban middle-class values.

It should be remembered that not *all* attitudes examined reflect what we have called *high acculturation*. It would seem likely that the closer the attitude expressed is to the test of daily practice, the more likely it is that it will reflect the objective non-middle-class social position of the respondents.

BEHAVIOR

Space does not permit a full report on the behavior variables that were looked into. They are introduced briefly here only in order to give a summary answer to the question: Do more middle-class ideas lead to more middle-class behavior?

It must be realized that some doors to middle-class or urbanized behavior were open to this group, some were slightly ajar, and some were shut tight. Where the doors were open, a fairly high percentage of respondents went through these doors. This is evidenced by the degree to which they joined the urban organizations available to them—church and union. Approximately one-third of the men belonged to churches that could be described as established Protestant or Catholic churches of the urban type and, as cited above, one-half belonged to a union.

The relatively few other formal organizations within the immediate Negro community, and the barriers to their joining other, predominantly white organizations *outside* their community, may help account for the low percentage found to be members of other formal organizations.

On the other hand, when one looks at the medical practices of the group, these *are* highly acculturated. Over 65 per cent of the men had sought some form of medical care within the year prior to our interview. Although obtaining medical care by those of low income remains a problem, the existence, in a city the size of Chicago, of hospital clinics, Veterans Hospitals, and a

Acculturation and Negro Blue-Collar Workers

panel of physicians supplied by the Department of Welfare does open the doors to getting care when the patient is so motivated. (This is especially true when the medical complaint is acute illness or advanced chronic illness.)

However, not all doors that appear to be open *are* gone through. There are inconsistencies in the attitude-behavior relationship that cannot be explained on the basis of which doors are open. The failure of approximately 75 per cent of the respondents to report for an X-ray, as part of the examination, is one such inconsistency. Another is the disparity between "recommended" and actual number of children born to the respondents.

But the lag between stated ideals and actual practices is a phenomenon shared by all groups, and is a subject much studied in itself.

DIET

One form of behavior is dietary habit. A detailed analysis is not possible here, but a few points of interest should be noted. A comparison with 100 middle-income white men showed similarities in mean level but differences in distribution pattern for several variables. For example, the mean daily caloric intake of the Negro men was 2,354 calories, while for the white men it was 2,510. However, there was a larger group of the Negro men at the *low* end of the caloric range—21 per cent had less than 1,600 calories daily, as against 13 per cent of the white men. The same type of comparison was made on intake of saturated fats, a nutrient known to raise serum cholesterol level. Although the mean of the two groups differed little (43 grams versus 46 grams daily), 54 per cent of the Negro men consumed less than 40 grams daily whereas 40 per cent of the white men were so reported. The extremely low subgroup consuming less than 20 grams daily included 13 per cent of the Negro men but only eight per cent of the white men. Some differences were also shown in consumption of particular food groups. The Negro men ate less meat (especially less beef, veal, and lamb), less dairy products, and less butter than did the white men. They ate more pork and bacon and more margarine than did the white men. Those giving more middle-class answers tended to have less distinctly Southern items in their daily diets and lists of favorite foods.

Thus, there *were* differences in diet, but the data of the study do not permit a statement on whether these are sufficient, by themselves, to account for the previously noted differences in serum cholesterol level. Further examination is needed, for example, on long-term effect of a lower caloric intake on serum cholesterol level. Other characteristics of life pattern, related to dietary habits, may also provide important clues to the cholesterol differences. For example, although the Negro men in the group exhibited characteristic American obesity, it was somewhat less frequent than among whites. In a group of 1,000 age-matched white men in a local utility company, 56 per cent were 15 per cent or more overweight,[4] while 44 per cent of the Negro men in the study were

---

[4] The standard for desirable weight (for a given height) was taken from the recommendations of the Metropolitan Life Insurance Company. These tables are derived from actuarial computations based on mortality rates.

in that category. Greater physical activity by the Negro men is likely, since 90 per cent of them were in blue-collar occupations. This may also mean that some of the "extra weight" can be attributed to greater musculature rather than fat. Furthermore, there is some evidence that exercise may have a tendency to lower serum cholesterol.

The study confirmed that low-income Negro men do, in fact, have lower serum cholesterol levels. The white men in the utility company, aged 30 to 39, had a mean level of 215 milligrams per 100 ml. of serum, whereas the Negro men had a mean of 198. For those aged 40 to 49, the white men had a mean level of 237 and the Negro men had a mean of 208.

It would seem that several characteristics of the life pattern have to be considered in trying to account for these medically important differences. Diet, obesity, and physical activity should certainly be among them.

HYPERTENSION AND SOCIOLOGICAL FACTORS

As stated in the introduction, the investigators examined acculturation and urbanization for what could be learned about differential risk factors connected with coronary heart disease. When urban ideas appeared much more frequently than expected, the possibility arose that the data might shed light on *another* population difference in heart-disease rates.

The two major forms of adult heart disease are coronary heart disease (discussed above) and *hypertensive* heart disease. The latter often develops, over time, among those suffering from hypertension—high blood pressure.[5] National mortality data on hypertensive heart disease show that, among whites, this occurs more frequently among *urban* dwellers than among those in rural surroundings. There is little analysis of any data on urban-rural differences among *Negroes* in death from hypertensive heart disease. But the data *do* show that everywhere, urban and rural, Negroes are more likely than whites to have *hypertension,* the precursor of hypertensive heart disease.

Hypertension is a major chronic disease that afflicts a high proportion of the adult Negro population. In the sample used in this study, fully one-quarter were hypertensive.

There are many contemporary hypotheses on the causes of high blood pressure. One hypothesis states that hypertension is a disease of the central nervous system at the highest level, involving both unconscious and conscious psychological factors. These factors are not at all simple to study objectively, and this fact may help account for both the tentative nature of explanatory theories and the paucity of data on the subject.

It is suggested, however, that individuals who find their life situations filled with frustration and uncertainty, and who develop long-term hostility and suppression of rage or other negative emotions, might be predisposed to hypertension. It could be hypothesized that when high blood pressure becomes a *group* phenomenon, this could be related to the *group's* situation. It is possible that common negative social experiences could underlie the greater

---

[5] Hypertensive heart disease is an entity distinct from *coronary* heart disease, although those with hypertension are more likely also to develop coronary disease.

prevalence of this disease among Negroes. Was there anything in the data that might be used to explore this further? Detailed psychological questions were not built into the study originally. The line of investigation centered on attitudes, other measures of urbanization, and demographic data on the respondents. Could it be that stress, uncertainty, and frustration found expression in these data and might have something to do with the higher rate of hypertension?

Middle-Class Attitudes and Hypertension

What are the effects on blood pressure of the potentially stressful situation for men who are all dressed up, attitudinally, with no place to go? What happens when absorption of the middle-class values and ideas paints an attractive picture of "what life *could* be like," and yet life remains what it *is*—at the bottom of the socioeconomic ladder? If this should lead to greater frustration, and if, in fact, such psychological pressure increases the chances of having hypertension, then those who expressed more middle-class attitudes should have the highest percentage with hypertension.

Earlier, it was shown that those who had aspirations to upward mobility, and who were negative to their neighbors, gave middle-class answers more often than did the others.[6] Looking at the rate of hypertension in this group, it is found that, in fact, they did have a somewhat higher rate of high blood pressure:

Table 6

HYPERTENSION AND NEGATIVITY TOWARD NEIGHBORS

Attitude toward Neighbors	Number Hypertensive[7]	Per Cent Hypertensive
Negative ($N = 39$) . .	14	35.9
Not negative ($N = 135$)	31	23.0
		($p = > .10$)

The evidence, however, is inconclusive, when answers of the whole sample to *individual* attitude items are cross-tabulated with rates of hypertension. In some cases, those with the middle-class answer had a higher rate; in some cases, virtually the same rate, or even a lower rate of hypertension:

Individual-attitude responses, therefore, cannot be considered as confirming the hypothesis. When they are grouped, however, as in the case of those negative to neighbors, they are suggestive of an association between idea pattern and a somewhat higher prevalence of the disease. But in both single items and grouped ones, the numbers and differences are small.

Other Measures of Urbanization, and Hypertension

Aside from expressed attitude, other aspects of urbanization were reflected in the data. If increased urbanization is associated with increased rates of hypertension in this group (against the special background of remaining at

---

[6] The exception was on parental precepts, where this group gave more authoritarian-traditional responses. It is possible, as discussed earlier, that this may not be in conflict with, but actually be a part of upward-mobility aspirations, in the particular social context of this group.

Table 7

HYPERTENSION AND INDIVIDUAL ATTITUDE ITEMS

Attitude	Number Responding	Number Hypertensive	Per Cent Hypertensive
Desirable Schooling:			
College or "As Much as Possible" ..	126	32	25.6
High School	49	13	26.5
Role of Luck in Life:			
Doesn't Count—Self-Reliance Counts			
Most......................	61	17	27.9
Counts in Part—Partly Self-Reliance .	68	20	29.4
Luck Counts Most, or All	44	8	18.2
Ideal Number of Children:			
0-3	106	24	22.6
4 or More	59	18	30.5
Family Planning:			
Limit	137	33	24.1
Leave to Nature	34	11	32.4

the bottom of the urban ladder), then the longer the migrant has lived in Chicago, the greater should be the rate of high blood pressure. This is not to deny that the newcomer may experience considerable stress during his first months of dealing with an unfamiliar environment, but it is possible that, although this source of stress would decline over time, there may be a more permanent conflict between increased urban aspirations and the failure to realize them.

Table 8, below, indicates that, in fact, the longer the migrant's residence, the more likely the hypertension. This cannot, by the way, be attributed to the age differential, because, in the group studied, the prevalence rate of high blood pressure was virtually the same in the age groups 30 to 39 and 40 to 49:

Table 8

HYPERTENSION AND THE NUMBER OF ADULT YEARS LIVED IN CHICAGO

Adult Years in Chicago[8]	Number in Group	Number Hypertensive	Per Cent Hypertensive
Migrants:			
Less than 10 years	56	10	17.9
10-15 Years	49	13	26.5
16 or More Years	43	15	34.9
Chicago-Born	27	7	25.9

The data contain no clues as to why longer-term migrant residents have higher rates of hypertension than do the more urbanized native-born Chicagoans. Again, the small numbers in individual categories may be in part responsible. But the step-wise progression of hypertension rates with years lived in the city is a suggestive finding ($p = <.10$ in comparing hypertension rates for newcomers with those for the migrants here longest).

---

[7] In this study, "hypertension" includes "definite hypertension," a diastolic pressure of 95 or more millimeters of mercury as the lowest of three readings, plus "borderline hypertension"—a similar reading in the range 90-94 mm. Hg.

[8] Since 18 years of age.

Acculturation and Negro Blue-Collar Workers

Another possible measure of urbanization, aside from the demographic data above, concerns the familiarity of the respondent with the financial institutions characteristic of the city. The men were asked to indicate which of four possible financial items they had had experience with, including bank loans, insurance (life and other), and savings accounts. There was a marked rise in hypertension rate for the subgroups with greater financial experience:

Table 9

HYPERTENSION AND FINANCIAL EXPERIENCE

Number of Financial Items Respondent Used	Number in Group	Number Hypertensive	Per Cent Hypertensive
0 or 1	27	2	7.4
2 or 3	123	31	25.2
All 4	25	12	48.0

The small number in the extreme categories requires considerable caution in interpretation of the results, but the fact that the "most experienced" had six times as much hypertension as the "least experienced" is again at least suggestive ($p = <.01$).

Uncertainty and Hypertension

One element that might be included in the psychological pattern loosely denoted as "stress" is that of uncertainty—and particularly uncertainty in the context of an unsatisfactory situation.

The overwhelming majority of the respondents lived in poor housing, in overcrowded, badly maintained buildings, and surrounded by houses in similar condition. Respondents had been asked about their attitude toward their present location—whether they would like to stay where they were or move—and if the response was "move," they were then asked what they thought their chances were of doing so within the next year or two. If uncertainty and dissatisfaction had any association with the disease entity now being looked at, then the more dissatisfied would have higher rates of hypertension, and those who combined dissatisfaction with uncertainty would have the highest rates. Table 10 below seems to indicate this trend. Those wishing to move but unsure of their chances had the highest rate of hypertension:

Table 10

HYPERTENSION AND ATTITUDE TOWARD HOUSING LOCATION

Attitude to Housing Location	Number in Group	Number Hypertensive	Per Cent Hypertensive
Wants to Move	92	25	27.2
Thinks No Chance	24	5	20.8
Thinks Good Chance . . .	30	8	25.6
Not Sure if Chance	38	12	32.1
Wants to Stay	81	19	23.5

$\left. \begin{array}{c} \\ \\ \end{array} \right\} p => .10$

It was thought that examination of *longer-term* dissatisfaction and uncertainty might yield a similar trend, so that attitude toward migration decision was now evaluated in terms of possible association with differing rates of hypertension. The men had been asked whether, if they had it to do over again, they would leave the South, and, if so, whether they would come to Chicago again. Table 11 below suggests that those who were not happy with Chicago and also did not find the South acceptable were somewhat higher in hypertension rate than either those who preferred Chicago or those who preferred the South (there was almost no difference between the latter two groups):

Table 11

HYPERTENSION AND MIGRATION DECISION

Migration Decision	Number in Group	Number Hypertensive	Per Cent Hypertensive
Would Not Migrate Again	20	4	20.0
Would Migrate Again to Chicago . . .	92	21	22.8
Would Migrate But Not to Chicago . .	29	10	34.5

$p => .10$ (for the last two groups)

Summary on Hypertension and Sociological Factors

The association suggested in the data between the social situation of the group and their higher rates of hypertension presents both problems and challenges.

The first problem centers about the difficulty of measuring, objectively, the effects on individuals of potentially stressful group situations. Is what is stressful to one person in the group necessarily stressful to others? How can individual capacity to deal with potentially stressful situations be assessed? These and many similar questions pose themselves as soon as one enters the realm of sociopsychological factors and their association with medical variables.

Another problem results from the fact that these associations appeared during a "second look" at data originally gathered to help elucidate *other* medical-sociological relationships. Questions that could have made for more precision in evaluation were not asked. For example, did those with hypertension bring it *with* them from the South, or did they develop it during their Chicago experience? At what stage in their experience did the disease develop? What was the precise social situation these individuals faced in the South, and what were their reactions to it?

There must be particular concern with whether the associations appearing in the data are merely, or by and large, chance—resulting from the small numbers in the study.

But the challenge in the data cannot be ignored. If a subgroup of the Negro population can be identified whose psychological reaction to their group's social situation leads to higher rates of hypertension than does that of the rest of their group, this may have import for greater knowledge and, ultimately, greater control of this disease. It may help account, at least in part, for the Negro-white difference in hypertension rates. It may implicate psychological factors as important contributors to development of high blood pressure and, therefore, be of theoretical as well as practical significance. It may help point to social change as one necessary path to reducing high blood pressure.

Acculturation and Negro Blue-Collar Workers

For all these reasons, the suggestive material in this and other studies may prove productive if explored on a larger scale and in greater depth.

BIBLIOGRAPHY

1. Cohen, A. K., *Delinquent Boys* (New York: The Free Press of Glencoe, Inc., 1955).
2. Herskovits, M. J., *The Study of Culture Contact* (Gloucester, Mass.: Peter Smith, Publisher, 1958).
3. Hyman, H. H., "The Value Systems of Different Classes: A Social-Psychological Contribution to the Analysis of Stratification," in R. Bendix and S. M. Lipset, eds., *Class, Status and Power* (New York: The Free Press of Glencoe, Inc., 1953).
4. Stamler, J., D. M. Berkson, H. A. Lindberg, W. Miller, and Y. Hall, "Racial Patterns of Coronary Heart Disease. Blood Pressure, Body Weight and Serum Cholesterol in Whites and Negroes," *Geriatrics,* Vol. 16 (1961), p. 382.
5. Strodtbeck, F. L., "Family Interaction, Values and Achievement," in D. C. McClelland, *et al.*, eds., *Talent and Society* (Princeton, N. J.: D. Van Nostrand Co., Inc., 1958).

Some Thoughts on Reform *

S. M. MILLER

SOCIAL problems today are increasingly complicated by the upgraded skill requirements of our complex industrial machinery. High economic growth does not automatically assure jobs for people who are unskilled; it does not guarantee that any kind of labor will be employed in a rising economic market. And some of the poor, especially the aged, are unlikely to work regardless of the demand for labor. All this is true, but it should still be recognized that a high level of employment will increase opportunities for the poor. It may be that high production will not draw untrained people into those industries requiring high skill, but it may provide increased demand in service and other industries which do not require high labor skills.

Moreover, we should not take the nature of the demand for certain kinds of labor as a "given." If it is discovered that over time there is a scarcity of certain kinds of labor, it may well turn out that industries and government

* This essay is part of a larger chapter entitled "Poverty, Race and Politics" in Irving L. Horowitz, ed., *The New Sociology: Essays on Social Values and Social Theory in Honor of C. Wright Mills* (New York: Oxford University Press, 1964). The support of the Louis M. Rabinowitz Foundation is gratefully acknowledged.

can adapt technology which permits the utilization of relatively few skilled laborers and a greater number of unskilled laborers. The results of technology can be achieved in a variety of ways, and it may eventually be that producers will have to pay more attention to the supply and quality of labor than was formerly true.[1]

Again, a high sustained demand for labor will probably encourage many more youths to stay in school to obtain the kind of training which will fit them for more high-skilled jobs. In situations where jobs are scarce, where it is unsure what kind of skill will be necessary, it is unlikely that we will find many youths taking the risk of preparing themselves for the unknown. Willingness to be an adventurer grows when confidence in the outcome appears somewhat realistic. With rapid technological change and low economic growth, the value of further training is frequently problematic.

ECONOMIC CHOICES

The economic binding of the various groups of the poor is their common need for decent employment and decent social services. The achievement of these goals requires political action, for economic issues are political issues today. The economic choice before us is obvious: either we have a sustained, widespread economic growth or we will have to have a shift in the distribution of income. A sustained economic growth will mean what it has meant before—that disadvantaged groups will be able to get more of the goods of society; rising levels of production and employment will draw into the labor force large numbers of people presently unemployed and those classified as "unemployable."[2] Employed workers will shift into better-paying jobs and industries. If, however, the economy fails to grow at an adequate level, and if the benefits of growth are not widely distributed, then it will become increasingly necessary to have a redistribution of income.

In our country, the redistribution of income takes place to a large extent in transfer payments of welfare and social assistance. In an economy that is expanding with a great growth in the level of national income, it is relatively easy to transfer some of the income to the poor by collecting taxes and paying out "welfare." But, with limited economic activity, transfer payments become a heavier burden. Thus, "heating up" the economy reduces the numbers who require direct transfer aid and makes transfer payments relatively smaller as the total national product expands. Although special services and supports have to be built around high-level economic activity, the core is a strong economy.

---

[1] S. M. Miller, "The Meaning of Work," *Proceedings, Allenberry Conference on Mental Health in Industry* (Harrisburg: Pennsylvania Department of Mental Health, 1961), pp. 2-13. Marcia Friedman has a similar theme in her draft document, *Basic Issues Affecting Youth Employment,* Youth-Work Program Review, National Committee on Employment of Youth, February 28, 1964.

[2] Even with a growth in jobs, services would have to be expanded to extend adequate aid to those who cannot work for one reason or another.

THE NEWBURGH INCIDENT

I suspect that the meaning of the Newburgh incident[3] is that economically declining communities will not easily suffer a high level of taxation in order to maintain the poor. (I recognize that the facts of Newburgh were other than what was contended by the city manager; I refer to the symbolic character of the series of events connected with Newburgh.) Newburgh, I fear, reflects the wave of the future: the unwillingness of a local community to maintain its poor. Newburgh-type crises will increase as many communities find themselves increasingly disadvantaged economically and facing the need of aiding a large percentage of poor. Localities will strive to reduce the number of poor supported by welfare.

We are reluctant to support those who suffer from economic development and change. As Schumpeter pointed out a generation ago, the price of economic progress is social dislocation.[4] A society which is oriented toward justice and equity is willing to pay this price. It aids those disadvantaged by the growth of an economy, which improves the conditions of a large but still limited number of people. Our society is undergoing economic change but limited economic growth. The consequence is that many communities are not improving at all while the problems of many communities are worsening. In such a society, it is likely that there will be increased outcries against the sustenance of the poor. Social services, therefore, are increasingly political issues, frequently arousing the new working class to action.

SOCIAL SERVICES

We are beginning to get the thoughtful, analytical, and detailed appraisal of our social services that Titmuss and his students have provided in England.[5] One consequence is the beginning of an improvement in services. The following is an incomplete listing of current problems in our social services:

1. The inadequacy of existing services and facilities is disturbing—whether in terms of allowances or the availability of decent housing.
2. We have a crazy hodgepodge of private and public services with very little coordination among them. Private agencies are relied on to an extent unknown in any other contemporary society. "Hard-to-reach" clients are frequently the product of "hard-to-reach" agencies; "multiproblem families" may be a reflection of "single-purpose agencies."

---

[3] In Newburgh, New York, the new city manager was said to have inaugurated a campaign in 1961 to harass welfare recipients in order to drive them from the welfare rolls. Newburgh, a declining Hudson River city, had had a sizable increase in the number of its Negro residents. Welfare recipients were "mugged" (photographed) at police headquarters and treated as disreputables.

[4] Joseph A. Schumpeter, *Capitalism, Socialism and Democracy* (London: George Allen and Unwin, 1950).

[5] Richard Titmuss and his associates have been paid little attention by American sociologists. Of particular importance is his *Income Distribution and Social Change* (Toronto: University of Toronto Press, 1962) and *Essays on the Welfare State* (New Haven: Yale University Press, 1959).

MILLER

300

3. Many agencies, despite their avowed goals, have not been primarily oriented to the poor. As Cloward has indicated, the private agencies have sought a new clientele in the middle class.[6]

4. The orientation of many of our social services is remedial and policing rather than preventive. Until recently, welfare departments did almost nothing to increase the employment possibilities of their clientele. Frequently, they performed a police function with the poor. The concern has been with the morality of welfare and with the danger of people receiving it who are not legally eligible for it. Behind it all is a feeling that those who receive welfare are somehow touched by immorality. Welfare serves as a substitute policing system for low-income areas. In order to check on the poor, the welfare worker becomes an investigator, as she (or, less frequently, he) is called in New York City. Her purpose is to check periodically on the behavior of those who are receiving "alms" from the government. This police function permits the poor person little legitimate initiative, as the approval of welfare investigators is required for many actions. Consequently, the poor, thought of as being ignorant, illiterate, and unimaginative, have developed a variety of ways of coping with the welfare worker. Evasion is frequent as recipients become "welfare-wise." A great deal of police and control efforts are exerted on one side and a considerable amount of matching efforts at evasion on the other. The stalemate that is reached is one where frequently there is repugnance on the part of the authorities and lack of respect on the part of the recipients.

5. Routinization and bureaucratization characterize many services, private as well as public. The emphasis on the fiscal and moral side of social services had led to the requirement that welfare workers devote a great percentage of their time to filling out forms to determine which budget—federal, state or local—should be charged for the funds spent on clients. Little individualized attention is given to those who, to some extent, perform the function of serving as the clientele of the social agencies.

6. The personnel of many agencies are frequently not adequate for dealing with the problems of the poor. The more highly trained often are oriented to a psychoanalytic framework which has not been shaped for the specific problems of the poor. The less trained frequently do not see themselves (or are not permitted to see themselves) as more than clerks and bookkeepers.

7. A private government with limited checks has developed in many communities. Private agencies, soliciting funds on a mass basis from the community, often substitute for the government in providing services. These agencies, run as they are by self-perpetuating boards of the Community Chests, United Funds, and the like, tend to be undemocratic and unrepresentative of low-income areas in which they operate. The "tax base" of these agencies is regressive, since those at the lower end of the income scale tend to contribute a greater percentage of their income to community fund-raising drives than do those with higher incomes.

The maintenance of an oligarchic private government of charity means that the community as a whole, and particularly the new working class, have limited impact upon the decisions which are made, especially the distribution of funds. Increasingly, Community Chest funds go to agencies which are not primarily oriented to the poor, even though many contributors to the fund believe this is the purpose of their contribution.

Moreover, the agencies frequently operate in the form of colonial administrators to the "natives" living in the poor areas of the large cities. "Natives" have a minor role. They have little part in making the basic

---

[6] Richard A. Cloward and Irwin Epstein, "Private Family Agencies and the Poor," delivered at the Conference on Low-Income Culture, New York State Division for Youth, New York, June, 1963.

decisions. This is true even when, for political reasons, a few of the more acceptable "colored natives" are brought into the lower levels of administration or are sprinkled through the board of directors.

Strongly put, social agencies "cool out the mark" by providing enough services to keep the "natives" from becoming too distressed by events they see around them.[7]

Social services—their financing, their control, and their distribution—will increasingly be recognized as the political problems they are, for fundamental questions of who gets what, and how this is determined, are involved.

8. Comparatively little attention is directed at helping communities of the poor to move to self-action and self-help. Most social agencies are more concerned with using established community organizations than with building social action among the people who live in an area.

Concrete political results are the crucial aspects of social action. But the process of social action is also important. The experience of poverty, especially if prolonged, does not produce confidence in one's capacities or experiences which develop them. Emphasis on chance and luck—rather than on one's own steering as determining fate—grows under these circumstances. Frequently, among those who see no way out, a feeling prevails of being an object acted upon rather than a subject directing and channeling forces. Welfare assistance in its present form tends to encourage dependence, withdrawal, diffused hostility, indifference, ennui.[8]

In the course of pressing for the extension of citizenship rights where individuals feel that they have a right to demand things and are organizing to do so, the new working class may see itself more as actors. Members of the new working class should be encouraged to demand and act themselves for change and improvement in their conditions rather than to look to others to produce change for them. This kind of political mobilization will change the self-image and the psychology of the new working class toward feelings of control and power.

THE ORGANIZATION OF COMMUNITIES

Shying away from the political implications and dangers of trying to move Negro and other new working-class communities into action, most social agencies have not tried to produce pervasive change among the poor in metropolitan America today. What we must look for increasingly is not just the extension of social services, but the kind of situations in which the poor will tend to try to do something about their own plight. Saul Alinsky, Preston Willcox, and others have shown that such action is possible among the poor.[9]

---

[7] Erving Goffman, "On Cooling the Mark Out: Some Aspects of Adaptation to Failure," reprinted in *Human Behavior and Social Processes: An Interactionist Approach,* ed. Arnold Rose (Boston: Houghton Miffling Company, 1962), pp. 482-505.

[8] Warren C. Haggstrom explores these and other issues in two memoranda: "A Preliminary Report on Social Action Programs," Syracuse University Youth Development Center, February, 1963; and "The Power of the Poor," Syracuse University Youth Development Center, September, 1963.

[9] Unfortunately, the exciting and important work of these social actionists has been inadequately reported and codified. Haggstrom's work, listed in the preceding footnote, is the major effort to have an independent observation and appraisal of such programs. The lack of attention to these programs has accentuated the prevailing negative imagery of the poor—culminating in Harrington's notion of an impregnable culture of poverty—among social scientists. I have criticized this view of the poor in "Poverty and Inequality in America: Implications for the Social Services," *Child Welfare,* November, 1963.

MILLER

The need for developing indigenous leadership in the areas of poverty in the large city is often mentioned. Undoubtedly this is an important move. Perhaps, as Ben Zimmerman, executive director of the Mayor's Commission for Youth of Syracuse, New York, has pointed out, the thing that can be done most effectively by outsiders—noncolored, nonpoor—coming into the impoverished areas is to try to develop the kinds of issues, crises, and situations which permit, encourage, and engender the emergence of indigenous leadership. The aim should *not* be to select those who on the basis of friendship connections or personality seem to have leadership capabilities. Rather, the aim should be to help produce the kinds of situations which temper individuals, develop leadership capacities, and clarify the directions toward which the residents of the community want to move.

The situation is not, of course, an easy one. In many communities of the new working class, the likelihood of directed, concerted action toward political or any other kind of goals is extremely unlikely. These are communities which have a power vacuum with little internal dynamics of control and no real momentum. Areas which serve as "ports of entry" for migrants to the city are frequently of this type. Other communities of the poor are controlled largely by the police or organized criminal groups to the extent that one can talk about power and control in these areas. These areas are ones in which a countermovement can be particularly likely. Finally, in other areas local control is a strong possibility and even, to a limited degree, already existing.

The important thing to recognize is that, as Richard Brotman notes, one should not overgeneralize about the communities of the new working class. Some have remote possibilities of movement, but others may have considerably greater chances. The "gripes" of low-income neighborhood—whether about unemployment, the conduct of the welfare department, the regulations of public housing, or the behavior of the police—are political issues and will emerge as such if the new working class is politicized. We cannot recount here the incidents of action and mobilization among Negroes and others of the new working class, but the growing number of such cases underlines the possibilities.

One difficulty of organization for social action is that the initial issues have to be local and immediate, directly affecting the new working class. But many of the problems facing the new working class cannot be resolved at local levels; they need national action for effective policies and programs. Linking local actions to broader national concerns and building an orientation to the national political scene is one of the most difficult and important tasks facing social actionists.[10]

These remarks do not suggest that a powerful movement already exists in the Negro and other new working-class communities. Rather, it is my contention that there is a growing *potential* for political mobilization. Whether this potential is realized will depend to a large extent on what labor unions do. For, if unions fail to be concerned about the new working class, the likelihood

---

[10] This and other inadequacies of the social-action approach are explored in my memorandum, "Social Action Programs: Some Questions," Syracuse University Youth Development Center, April, 1963.

is that economic issues will not bind together the various groupings of the poor against cross-cutting ethnic and racial ties.

THE ROLE OF THE UNION

Of great importance, especially for Negroes, would be the opening up of the Jim Crow craft occupations and unionization of the low-paid, unorganized service industries. The trends in the labor force seem to be clear: we are developing a new working class which is largely "colored." At the present time, this new working class is largely outside of the unions which have not been effectively organizing old, nonunionized industry or the new or expanded industries. Indeed, in many unions, particularly those of a craft nature, there has been an exceeding reluctance to accept Negroes into membership. We are consequently moving into a situation where we have, to a large extent, a white union movement declining in terms of its coverage of the labor force, and the emergence of a new "colored" labor force, highly exploited economically and outside of the unions and the main economic structure of the United States.

If there is no concerted effort to bring Negroes into unions, whether in terms of organizing new industries which are at present unorganized or opening up existing industries and unions to Negroes and other minority-group members, the result may well be the demise of unions as a strong force in the United States with a moral base in the representation of the under-represented. A move toward the new, unskilled minority worker will have important implications for unions. It would propel them to examine new issues in American political life by providing a broad class base for unions. This base is now lacking: increasing income differentiation is advantaging those union members who are well paid while the low-paid improve their conditions at a slower pace. Problems of poverty, urban redevelopment, discrimination, and political representation—issues which are central to the problems of the new working class today in American society—will again come to the political fore if unions move toward this group.

Effective relations with the new working class depends on the development of new practices on the part of unions. The effort to organize Negro and other minority-group members of the labor force into unions may require intensive work in many communities to overcome a generalized distrust of unions. Such distrust has occurred because of discrimination and corruption in the unions with which the new working class has had some contact.

Once in unions, it may be important to have closer relations between their unions and their communities than is common. If I may draw an example from a union beyond the pale, the St. Louis local of the Teamsters, directed by Harold Gibbons, later to become Hoffa's right-hand man, tried the innovation of having community stewards as well as shop stewards.[11] The community stewards served to help members living in neighborhoods to organize with others to do something about their problems. For example, rat

[11] I do not have first-hand knowledge of the program but have relied on official union handouts and conversations with Local personnel. This local was studied by Arnold Rose in his *Union Solidarity* (Minneapolis: University of Minnesota Press, 1952).

infestation in certain areas was a great problem; community stewards organized to exert pressure on City Hall to provide services to reduce the danger. Other unions have had community involvement in a variety of ways, but the community emphasis has to be deepened and broadened. The rank-and-file member has to be brought into increasing importance in both the community and union. The useful activities of the community services division of the AFL-CIO are limited because the emphasis is to a considerable extent on securing representation on community chests and the like, without a clear-cut commitment to changing chest services so that they involve and benefit both the new and the old working class.

Many members of the new working class may become staunch, active, and useful union members. Many Negroes and other minority individuals are already effective union members. If their numbers grow and they feel accepted, the talented but discriminated against individuals who have not been educated into high-level occupations, as is increasingly happening among the old working class and their offspring, could serve as a reservoir of union leadership talent.

If the unions do not move in the direction of reaching out toward the new working class, there is a likelihood of a further attrition and atrophy of what has been a dynamic and significant force in American economic and political life. The more farsighted union leaders and staff have rightly emphasized the importance of organizing the nonunion and rapidly growing white-collar workers, especially professionals and technical workers. Such organization might have a dynamic for unions in increasing membership and in providing new kinds of people for union leadership. The reluctance of labor leaders to organize white-collar workers is pronounced, however, and may be due to their fear of this kind of well-educated union member as well as to jurisdictional problems. In any case, the organization of the new working class would have a greater dynamic. Not only are these people probably easier to organize than professionals and technicals, but their problems, concerns, and needs would force unions to address themselves further to basic issues in American life.

The best hope for revitalizing the stalemate society is that Negroes will move together with other new and old working-class groups and with some middle-class groups, regardless of color, to fight for common economic, social, and political interests. The labor unions of the 1930's played the role of fighting for legislation and social action which benefited great numbers of people beyond those then in trade unions. Negroes today, if they move together with other working-class groups to fight for common interests, can play this same role. Issues of economic growth, unemployment, income distribution, urban redevelopment, equality, education, welfare, police, and the increasingly important tax system would come to the fore at both local and national levels.

To a large extent, whether these developments take place depends upon the behavior of government, political parties, labor unions, and social agencies in making direct efforts to reach out to, to provide services to, and to demonstrate interest in the plight of the new working class.

The hope for the elimination of poverty rests in the movement toward political activity to instigate the deepening of economic and social rights. Poverty, like most other economic questions, is now a political issue. It is an issue of what level of economic product we shall be attaining and how it will be distributed. These are all crucial political questions. The raising of the problems of poverty to the political level and the encouragement of the new working class to do something about the situations which they face are the bases of a revived liberalism in the 1960's.

Part V

MORAL PERSPECTIVES
AND RELIGION

THE moral rectitude and religious piety of the working- and lower-class man has been the subject of social comment from his first emergence in history. The early English industrialist endowed him with a disproportionate share of original sin and laziness. In contrast, the early Social Reformers saw in him all of the virtues of natural man, distorted and put upon by exploitation. The pendulum has swung to and fro, telling more about the observer than about his subject. We can hardly claim exemption from these prejudices for ourselves, and we ask the reader to examine his own predilection before passing judgment on our observers.

Elsewhere in this book, Caplovitz points out the many ways in which the blue-collarite is victimized in the market place; Hurvitz discusses how the worker carries the negative influence of an exploitive job situation into his family life; and Miller and Reissman note the deep-set nature of the worker's suspicion and mistrust of others. Endleman, in the first of two original essays in this section, examines the blue-collarite's judgment of the behavior of others (including market-place and work-place "exploiters"). He also considers the blue-collarite's inclination to follow either heart's desire or the voice of conscience in situations involving moral decisions. Working initially with a typology of four types (Righteous, Don't-Get-Caught, Easy-Going, and Merciful-Just), Endleman concludes with a composite portrait of the dominant blue-collar moral orientation as it contrasts with white-collar perspectives.

Again, in earlier sections of the book various essayists commented on the religious values and behavior of blue-collarites, and especially on the traditional element, intense commitment, and low-level participation common in the matter (Sexton, for example, noted that while the blue-collar wife is "deeply religious, she is much less likely to attend church regularly than her middle-class counterpart, and still less likely to take a more than menial role in church affairs"). Vernon's essay in this section helps explain this behavior, as well as blue-collar preferences for particular religions. The essay goes even farther and raises the provocative question: ". . . do religious creeds and programs which are essentially under the control and direction of white-collarites provide the blue-collarite with what he wants in religion?"

Moral Perspectives
of Blue-Collar Workers

ROBERT ENDLEMAN

DO blue-collar workers differ from white-collar workers in their moral perspectives on the world? Do they make different kinds of judgments on the morality of others' behavior and on that of their own? Do they act differently in reference to moral codes?

Popular soothsayers keep discovering that modern man is in some kind of moral crisis: witness low goings-on in high places, TV quiz-show chicanery, school-exam cheating, "loose" sexual behavior, and so forth. Actually, little is systematically known of how many such transgressions go on, of what kinds, by whom they are committed, or, indeed, of who regards what behavior how.

To plot some terrain: people's moral perspectives vary. One dimension is "moral evaluation": one's judgments of others' moral behavior, the kinds of codes (stated or implicit) one uses and how one applies them. A second is "moral action:" what one himself does in situations involving "moral" decisions—where he decides whether to follow heart's desire or conscience's voice, to abet an erring friend or to thwart him in the name of "law" and "right."

Moral evaluation can range between the poles of Punitive and Tolerant. *Punitive* involves "toughness" toward criminals, delinquents, and other deviants; favoring the death penalty; retributive justice ("eye for an eye"); moralistic condemnation; rigid, absolutist judgments of the morality of others; for example, "If my kid steals, I beat the hell out of him!" and "Let's stop mollycoddling the criminals." *Tolerant* is, by contrast, more open-minded and relativistic: "Everyone cheats on income tax—why the fuss?" "Rigged TV shows are just entertainment, anyway—who was hurt?" It involves humane understanding toward deviants and violators: "Let's try to understand these kids—not just beat them down." It stresses restitution, not punishment. "If my kid steals, first I see he brings it back." Tolerant involves relativistic perspectives, recognition of ambiguities, opposition to the death penalty, concern with persons rather than rules. The Punitive wants justice to punish the violator; the Tolerant, to right a wrong, to protect the weak. Punitive stands for the most rigid interpretation of the laws or the mores; Tolerant sees these as flexible and modifiable. Punitive has official law and morality on his side; Tolerant, the sympathies of the "advanced, enlightened" behavioral sciences, from the relativism of anthropology to the perplexities of depth psychology.

The *moral action* dimension has as its poles Conscientious and Evading toward accepted moral codes. *Conscientious* means putting adherence to a code ahead of immediate personal gain, advantage, or enjoyment, and ahead of sympathies toward friend or kin involved in questionable pursuits. *Evading* involves the opposite, breaking codes in favor of personal gains or loyalties.

Even common codes may be felt differently, in both judgment and action dimensions, by people differently situated in a social world; and the codes themselves may vary from one social scene to another. Hence the need for a differentiated moral geography of the modern world. Our present coordinate is socioeconomic class, seen in its occupational dimension: "working class" (blue-collar workers, manual workers) versus "middle class"—here used as a catch-all for "all others, white-collar and up."

The two morality dimensions, cross-cutting, give four "ideal types" of moral perspective: *Righteous, Don't-Get-Caught, Easy-Going,* and *Merciful-Just*.[1] The *Righteous* are indignant and punitive toward others as violators of moral rules and conscientious about their own moral conduct. The *Don't-Get-Caught* are morally flexible about their own conduct, freely evading moral rules when it serves their needs, but punitive toward others who do the same and get caught. The *Easy-Going* are tolerant and relativistic toward both their own and others' moral conduct. The *Merciful-Just* are firmly conscientious in their own conduct, but mercifully tolerant toward others who violate.

Abundant evidence (see other essays in this volume) suggests that the blue-collar world should differ appreciably in moral perspectives, as in other ways, from the middle-class world. Let us see if and how it does.

The study reported here draws on intensive life-history interviews with over 100 New York metropolitan-area men. For technical reasons[2] the systematic

---

[1] Details of these types and some of their psychodynamic connections were worked out in an earlier study: Robert Endleman: *Four Moralities: Reactions to Murder.* (1956. Unpublished.) (Revision of Ph.D. Dissertation, "Value-conflict, Authority and Aggression." Harvard University, Department of Social Relations, 1955.)

[2] Usable interviews were obtained from 122 men: all gainfully employed, and hence all classifiable in terms of current occupation; age range, 28-60; occupation range, the whole gamut from lowest-skill-level laborer to highest-skill-level professional or executive. By occupation, 42 are manual laborers ("blue-collar," "working-class"), 30 are middle-class men who are sons of working-class fathers; 50 are other middle- and upper-class men. (For convenience, throughout this paper, "middle" means "middle and upper" without distinction.) The aggregate of 122 do not constitute technically a sample; nor does their distribution closely mirror the occupational, religious, ethnic, and similar distributions of the New York metropolitan area. Ethnically, they include Italians disproportionately in the working class and Jews disproportionately in the middle classes. In morality type, the Italians, disregarding class, are disproportionately *Righteous*. Religiously, Christians generally are more than ordinarily *Righteous*. Ethnically, Jews are more Tolerant (disregarding class); Christians are more Punitive; Agnostics are overrepresented in the *Merciful-Just* type. Working-class cases include a disproportionate number of Roman Catholics. Thus, in ethnic and religious terms, to use the 122 cases, classified by occupation and mobility, without some kind of control for ethnicity and religion, might produce very distorting results. Age might also be a factor, as the three subgroups are slightly different in age distribution. To introduce the element of control for age, ethnicity, and religion, we adopted the expedient of selecting three matched sets of 20 cases each: working-class; middle-class sons of working-class fathers; and middle-class sons of middle-class origin. Each set of 20 has the same proportions of the different ethnic groups, of the different religious affiliations, and of the different age levels. The two different middle-class sets were selected for further analyses involving mobility. In almost all the comparisons between the working-class group and the two middle-class groups, the differences are more pronounced between working class and upward-mobile middle class. For a preliminary report on the mobility findings, see: Robert Endleman, "Social Mobility and Moral Perspectives" (Paper presented at the meetings of the American Sociological Association, August, 1963).

comparisons are among three matched groups of 20 each: working-class, middle-class of working-class origin, and middle-class of middle-class origin. What did we find?

First, negatively: we found *no* significant differences between the working-class men and either of the middle-class groups on the *Moral Action* dimension taken alone. That is, workers, compared with middle-class men, were neither more Conscientious nor more Evading in their reported or reported-hypothetical moral conduct. One was as likely as the other either to support or to completely condemn a close friend scheming to "borrow" funds from a union or professional association which both belonged to or involved in another scheme skirting the boundaries of the law. (Practically all, of both classes, refused to go in on the hypothetical scheme with the friend. But they varied on how far they would go to protect or to expose the morally questionable friends; and the variation was no different for blue-collar than for white-collar.) Similarly, in their tendencies to escape or to give oneself up after having committed an understandable major offense; or to go along with an income-tax evasion scheme; or to participate in a TV quiz-show fraud, or in reports of actual offenses which they spontaneously mention having committed, there is no significant difference by class.

Second, the working class do not differ from the middle classes in the proportion showing a *Righteous* moral perspective—that is, Punitive toward others as violators of moral rules and Conscientious toward one's own moral conduct.

The blue-collar workers *do* differ systematically from the white-collars in the following respects. They are more punitive in moral evaluation of others' offenses, especially more so than middle-class men of working-class origin.[3] In over-all morality type, they are far more likely to espouse the *Don't-Get-Caught* morality[4]—punitive toward others' violations, but tending toward violations in their own moral conduct, a combination which suggests the rationale: the crime is not in doing it, but in getting caught.

Only one man of all the 42 blue-collar workers (in the total aggregate of cases) shows a *Merciful-Just* moral orientation: Tolerant toward other violators but Conscientious in one's own moral conduct.[5]

In detailed aspects of the Moral Evaluation dimension, we find the blue-collar workers systematically different from their middle-class counterparts in a number of other ways which illuminate a whole moral syndrome: they are far less likely to believe that the death penalty is never justifiable under any circumstances;[6] they are far more given to expressing a repressive or retributive justice (for vengeance, or to punish the offenders) as contrasted with justice

---

[3] Workers, Punitive: 17 out of 19; Mobile Middles, Punitive: 11 out of 20; Other Middles, Punitive: 12 out of 20. Taking all cases: Workers, Punitive: 36 out of 41; Middles, Punitive: 42 out of 79.

[4] Workers, *Don't-Get-Caught:* 10 out of 18; Middles, 11 out of 40. Taking all cases: Workers, *Don't Get-Caught:* 18 out of 38; Middles, 17 out of 76.

[5] By contrast, 18 out of 76 for the middle-class men. In the 20-man samples: Workers, *Merciful-Just:* 1 out of 20; Middles, 10 out of 40.

[6] Completely oppose death penalty: Workers, 1 out of 20; Mobile Middles, 9 out of 20; Other Middles, 5 out of 20.

ENDLEMAN

310

seen as a restitutive system (to right a wrong, restore an imbalance, rehabilitate an offender).[7] The kind of justification they give for their own moral-conduct choices also differs systematically from that of the middle classes: whether the conduct is itself Conscientious or Evading, the blue-collars are more likely to give an *expedient* reason for it, as contrasted to a principled one.[8] For example, they would say: "I wouldn't go in on any such scheme; I'd be afraid of getting caught," or: "I would try to escape, because I want to live!" or "I take all I can in deductions on income tax; I've got to look out for number one." (By contrast, a principled response would be: "I'd refuse to go on such a TV show; it's against my code to present myself as something I'm not"; or: "I'd help protect my friend, even though I disapproved his action, because my code of loyalty to friends comes ahead of my general respect for law.")

An empathic and insightful reading of the entire interview in context, probing to intuit some over-all "measure of the man," reveals a series of further distinctions by which the blue-collars differ—although not as sharply as they do in the matters already discussed—from the middle class. For one thing, generally, the whole texture of the blue-collar's moral judgments is much less *differentiated* than we find in the middle-class respondents. Opinions about either juvenile or adult offenders, for example, are likely to be rather crude, one-dimensional, dogmatic, across-the-board—especially seen in blanket condemnations, lumping together a great variety of types and severity of offenses, coalescing minor peccadilloes with such things as gang-fight knifings; demands to "get tough" with *all* of the "juvenile delinquents" regardless of differences among them; a common stereotyped response to all of the subtly different hypothetical conflict situations.

By contrast, middle-class men, especially the more highly educated, are more likely to pose distinctions in moral issues according to the severity of the offense, the types of values that are challenged, to make subtle, often legalistic distinctions (for example, "padding an insurance claim is necessary in order to get a fair deal, because the rates are set on these assumptions, but fraud on a cement contract for a public school is something else again"). Generally the middle-class are better able to think in terms of general principles (again, most likely, a function of higher education) and to deal with specific cases in relation to such general ideas, whereas the worker tends to be more concrete and more limited to the special details of the particular case, and also, correspondingly, tends to *personalize* moral issues.[9] Although not many of even the middle-class men see the electrical companies' price-fixing case as a problem of *institutional* arrangements rather than of personal morality, more of them than of the blue-collars see it that way. Blue-collars are more likely to assimilate that complex economic-moral issue to a simple picture of a businessman over-charging his customers out of personal greed—if, indeed, they have any perceptions of the case at all.

---

[7] Repressive justice: Workers, 15 out of 18. Mobile Middles, 7 out of 18.
[8] Expedient: Workers, 10 out of 12; Middles, 14 out of 31.
[9] Cf. Herbert Gans, *The Urban Villagers* (New York: The Free Press of Glencoe, Inc., 1962).

Another interesting difference is this: more of the blue-collars than of the white-collars show a pattern which can be called an "externalized conscience."[10] For example: "I wouldn't feel I was doing anything wrong if they told me it was my job to do this" (in reference to TV quiz-fraud temptation); or, "I don't take any moral position about this: it's wrong if the law says so—if I get caught, I'm wrong" (in reference to going in on a "shady" deal in real estate); or, in comment about someone else: "It had to be wrong, 'cause he [Van Doren] got into a lot of trouble about it." The implication is that only by exposure by an outside force is the fact of having done something morally wrong openly recognized. This, of course, is an element in the syndrome of the *Don't-Get-Caught* morality. There the capacity *not* to face moral implications of one's own transgressions is combined with punitiveness toward others who commit similar or even more trivial offenses, but who are known, exposed—"caught."

Most of the men of all classes we talked to are disapproving, if not actually punitive, toward the hypothetical close friend engaged in a deal involving use of union funds, or a "shady deal in real estate, just on the borderline of the law." But, pressed as to what they would do about this friend, besides refusing to go into the deal with him, some carry this disapproval to the universalistic logical extreme of saying they would make it their business to expose this friend—usually on the principled ground that what he is doing is simply wrong, and he should be stopped. Others indicate that the claim of friendship-loyalty is stronger than this universalistic notion of law and right, and would either actively protect the friend—in spite of disapproving his action (for example, by even lying under oath to conceal one's own knowledge of the friend's transgression)—or at least passively do so by not volunteering information against the friend (giving it only under oath, and only if necessary).

The latter syndrome—disapproval of the friend's morality combined with tacit support of him as a friend—appears no more often in the blue-collar men than in their white-collar counterparts. However, the universalistic extreme of going out of one's way to expose the "friend" appears *more* often in the upward-mobile middle-class men than in the working-class men.[11] Thus, on this scanty evidence, we find the workers less universalistic in their moralizing judgments on close friends. This tends to indicate that the code for the working class is not adherence to an abstract general principle of justice—and this indication ties in with the tendencies to concretize and personalize moral issues and to stay close to the immediate practical details of a situation.

A concomitant of authoritarian punitiveness in more of the blue-collar workers than of the middle-class men is a pattern of identification with the aggressor—that is, approval of harsh authoritarian controls that have been imposed upon oneself, particularly in childhood. For example, one worker documents in great detail the rigid and extensive controls he underwent in a parochial orphanage through nine years of his childhood, their extensive system of punishments, and how they broke his rebellious will—then comments that he is glad they were so strict and deplores the greater laxness he found in the same institution on a recent revisit. In another case, it was the worker's father

---

[10] Workers, 7 out of 15; Middles, 3 out of 16.

ENDLEMAN [11] Workers, 5 out of 17; Middles, 9 out of 17.

who was brutally disciplinarian, physically punishing the boy, almost as routine: "I'm glad he was so strict: I didn't go wrong. Kids today should have such discipline."

The *content* of the focus of moral concerns differs importantly from workingmen to middle-class men. We classified the focal points of moral concern into these five categories: Ascetic (concern with body pleasures, hedonism, impulsiveness); Authority (concerned with respect, deference, hierarchy, propriety); Integrity (concerned with honesty, truth to oneself, violation of trust); Property; and Person (concern with violation of the human person, by violence or sex). We find that the working class, compared with the middle class, show *more* concern with *ascetic* rules and with *property* rules, and *less* concern with rules about *personal integrity*. There were no differences in extent of concern with *authority* and with *person* (violation of the person). The persistence of an *ascetic* kind of moralism as a dominant keynote of working-class morality is an important differentiation of our society. As in many other respects, the middle classes express more "modern," "enlightened," or "emancipated" views about sexual morality and about related themes of self-expression. Although a phobic reaction to narcotics is a very common phenomenon in *all* of these interviews, it seems to be more prevalent in the working-class cases; and I classify this concern here with *ascetic* preoccupations: the general configuration is an obsessive concern for control against impulsiveness, against any forms of Dionysian expression, especially boundary-annihilating experiences: alcohol, drugs, gambling, and, in some forms, sex. Such asceticism is congruent with strict authoritarian self-controls, rooted in identifications with (unconsciously) hated and feared aggressors who represent authority. The instability of such controls—hence, the obsessive need to reinforce them—is suggested by the coexistence in the working class of such asceticism and of the *Don't-Get-Caught* morality, with its ominous lynch-law potentialities. On the opposite side, the scarcity of Integrity as the basic focal concern in morality in the working-class subjects, fits in with the asceticism, the externalization of conscience, the identification with the aggressor, and the double face that permits and rationalizes one's own transgressions while punitively condemning others who do the same and get caught.

My earlier impression was that the authoritarianism, the asceticism, and the externalizing that we find more commonly in the working class than in the middle class derived from the high proportion of Catholics, and specifically of Italian Catholics, in the working-class cases as compared with the middle-class cases. However, the matched samples of 20 each eliminated this disproportion: each class set has the same number of Catholics and of Italians—and still the relationship persists. Therefore, we can feel more confident that this is a class —rather than, or rather than *only*, a religious or ethnic phenomenon.

PORTRAIT

We are ready, then, to paint a composite portrait of the dominant blue-collar moral orientation as it contrasts with white-collar perspectives, especially those of people who have risen from working-class origins.

Our representative blue-collarite is a skilled or unskilled worker, of limited

313

formal education, and of rather limited sophistication in outlook on the world. He admits to a few youthful transgressions and fewer adult ones, of a minor nature, in a way that hints at more that has been concealed. What he does tell about—such as siphoning gas out of other people's cars in his late adolescence— is rationalized by any combination of the common "techniques of neutralization"[12]—"everyone was doing it"; "I needed it more than they did"; "I didn't realize it was wrong," and so forth. For lack of opportunity, his adult violations have not included any elaborate or large-scale income-tax evasions, but one guesses they would have had he had the chance. With respect to ambiguous moral situations, he leaves it to outside forces to determine the rightness or wrongness of certain lines of conduct, especially if he can define something as only part of his job: "*They* say to do this, so it must be all right." Conversely, if someone else got into trouble for doing that, it must be wrong. He might take a chance on a shady deal in real estate if he can be convinced that it's within the law; or he might refuse to go along for expedient reasons—too much danger. If he declined to go himself, and disapproved his friend doing so, he would *not* make it a principled point to expose his friend: let someone else, whose job it is, get the evidence on him—though he might also not go so far as to lie under oath to protect his friend. Much would depend on the expediencies of the situation.

For example, in the case of "borrowed" union funds, his disapproval of his friend derives not from abstract principle so much as from his conflicting loyalty to the union. He is concrete and personal about these things, especially where they affect him personally. The lure of huge amounts of money could easily lead him to participate in a TV quiz-show fraud, especially if "they" (sponsors and directors) can convince him it's all O.K. At the same time, he is outraged that someone like Van Doren put over such a fraud on *him*—making him "feel like a dope." (Unlike some of the middle-class respondents, his concern is *not* for Van Doren's having violated his own personal integrity.) He has some sympathy for the man in the story who in desperation killed another man who was blackmailing him—and would recommend a lenient form of punishment: here he finds an outlet for his punitiveness by dealing it out to the blackmailer: the rat deserved to be killed. If he himself had done such a killing, he would try to get away with it—not on principle, but as an expedient out of sheer will to live.

In his own childhood, he was often brutally beaten by his bully father, without principle or gradation. He tells about this in a matter-of-fact, almost affectless way; then adds, "I'm glad my father was so strict: see, I didn't go wrong." Delinquency he suggests, would be less today if all children were so treated. If he caught his own teen-age son stealing, he'd "beat hell out of him." He is greatly concerned about current sexual violations: the worst offense he judges to be rape. His concern about rape is less about the violation of the girl than about a more generalized feeling of atrocity about sex; alternatively, the most terrible voluntary act is narcotics (no sharp line between user and pusher). He is outraged that "they lose all control—it takes over." Prodded

[12] Gresham Sykes and David Matza, "Techniques of Neutralization: A Theory of Delinquency," *American Sociological Review*, Vol. 22 (December, 1957), pp. 664-70.

ENDLEMAN

to the user-pusher distinction, he waxes almost apopletic about the pushers, thinks they should be punished to the limit—the death penalty, even. He has no hesitation about the death penalty—for that, or for rape, or for murder—and readily invokes *lex talionis*: an eye for an eye.

In spite of his own teen-age offenses, he is convinced that teen-agers are worse today—and, of course, it's because they don't get enough discipline and restrictions from their parents, the schools, the police, and the courts: all these are not tough enough. No hint of attempt at understanding the violators or deviants, or even of some of the rebellious things he himself did as a youngster —rather, an unthinking assertion of authority and need for punishment, almost mechanically applied: retribution, not restitution. The moral judgments are basically undifferentiated, unempathetic, and uncompassionate; the assumptions about human behavior are crude and mechanical. Difficulties are met by simple formulae: "I break them or they break me. They broke me; I'm glad—it's good to be strict." "Someone gets out of line: punish him, never mind explanations." Exception: "My close friend: I won't cheat on him, let others prove he did wrong." Exception: "Me on a job: they ask me to do something; I don't have to think, is this wrong? *They* are the boss."

By contrast, the middle-class men, especially those up from the working class, tend toward the opposite poles on most of these variables: They are more tolerant of others as deviants or violators; more often they tend to combine such tolerance with conscientiousness toward their own moral conduct: *Merciful-Just*. They more often act or judge on principle—may even sacrifice personal loyalties to such a principle, an abstraction. Their moral judgments of others and themselves are more complex, more differentiated, more relativistic, often more confused (as contrasted with uncomplicated dogmatism common in working class), except that they may be dogmatic on one issue: opposition to the death penalty. Their conscience tends more to operate in terms of tough internal pressures and is less swayed by immediate externalities, while at the same time their perceptions of the world are open to the kaleidoscopic flux of the modern, ever-changing society—a paradox which is probably functionally related to their success in upward mobility compared with their more close-minded childhood peers.[13] They focus on restitutive justice and personal integrity—"to thine own self be true," rather than on retributive justice, ascetic rules, and property concerns. They tend *not* to identify with the aggressor.

A lot of these differences are related to the opposed polarities of funda-mentalist versus emancipated.[14] Much of the *content* of the moral judgments made by the punitive and the tolerant, respectively, tends to fall toward one or another set of stereotypes: the former, to the narrowest, most philistine phrasing of conventional and authoritative moral codes, particularly those of Puritan Christianity—but it can coexist with a tinge of modernity in the action di-mension: expediency, cynicism, looking out for Number One: in short: the *Don't-Get-Caught* morality. The Tolerant represents emancipation, being up to

[13] Robert Endleman, "Social Mobility and Moral Perspectives," paper presented at meet-ings of the American Sociological Association, Los Angeles, California, August, 1963.
[14] Talcott Parsons, "Certain Primary Sources and Patterns of Aggression in the Social Structure of the Western World," in Talcott Parsons, *Essays in Sociological Theory*, rev. ed. (New York: The Free Press of Glencoe, Inc., 1954), pp. 323-35.

date on the newest views of man, adapting them (often vulgarizing) to the complex moral exigencies of the day, tolerating—even enjoying—ambiguity. This is one broad stream of contemporary life, one shared by the more favored of the educated. The *Conscientious* pursuit leads one into a paradox of positions the opposite of the conflict of the Don't-Get-Caught: here exceptionalism means higher standards for oneself than for others, grappling with ambiguities where the test has to do with personal integrity rather than authoritarian submission to old goals.

Working-class Punitive Evaders, espousing a *Don't-Get-Caught* morality, condemning others and breaking the rules themselves; and the middle-class (especially the mobile) Tolerant Conscientious *(Merciful-Just)*, understanding others and demanding much of themselves, are each responding by an internally conflicting pattern to the tensions and difficulties of a world of ambiguity.

Religion and the Blue-Collarite

GLENN M. VERNON

MANY distinguishing characteristics of the blue-collarite have been identified in the chapters which have preceded this one. With these differences in mind, it is appropriate to raise the question as to whether similar distinctions obtain with reference to his religious behavior. The major premise of this essay is that such differences do exist and may, in fact, be more extensive than some have believed. Such relationships raise many theoretical and practical considerations, only a few of which can here be taken into account.

Religious differences are, of course, extensive. Actually, there is as much variability in the realm of religion as in any other dimension of living, in part because religion is not restricted to the empirical world but, rather, takes into account a dimension believed to be supernatural or superempirical. Any number of different explanations can be advanced to explain these differences, and any number of different reactions thereto are possible. Our concern in this essay will of necessity consider only limited aspects of the whole configuration. We shall not, for instance, concern ourselves with any value questions involved —whether, for instance, such patterns are good or bad. Neither shall we concern ourselves with questions concerning the involvement of the supernatural realm in these differences. We shall, in fact, be only indirectly concerned with etiology. Our major concern is to identify particular religious patterns and to relate them to other social variables—particularly, membership in the blue-collar group.

Study of the influence of religion in the life of man in general as well as the blue-collarite specifically has been somewhat neglected by the social scientist, although early writings in the area by Weber and Durkheim are now considered to be classics. If anything, the social scientist has generally tended to ignore

VERNON

316

the religious factor in his efforts to provide a social interpretation of human behavior. Increasing attention being given to this area has led to increased awareness to the fact that religion is a *social* phenomenon (whatever its other-worldly or supernatural characteristics may be) that is, intimately involved in the behavior of man. The following conclusion by Lenski in his Detroit Area study suggests the likelihood of continued attention to the area:

> Socio-religious group membership is a variable comparable in importance to class, both with respect to its potency and with respect to the range or extent of its influence.[1]

If this is true, serious question is raised as to the validity of any one-factor interpretation of man's behavior, such as a strict economic interpretation. Economic variables are not "in the driver's seat," dictating all other aspects of living. Man is an economic being, to be sure, but he is more than this! Even the terminology used most frequently in this book—"the blue-collarite"—could lead to the conclusion that the behavior of such individuals stems primarily from occupational or economic characteristics. This essay, however, leads to the conclusion that the economic factors influence religious factors; but, in like manner, the religious dimension (along with many others) influences the economic. Economic determinism is not an adequate explanation of man's behavior.

Answers to questions such as the following permit one to document such statements and to see more clearly just what some of these interrelationships are:

1. Are blue-collarites more likely to endorse certain types of religious beliefs than others? If so, what are they?
2. Are blue-collarites more likely to belong to certain religious groups than to others?
3. Conversely, are members of particular religious groups more likely to be blue-collarites than white-collarites?
4. How do church-attendance patterns of blue-collarites and white-collarites compare?
5. Do the church-membership and -activity patterns of the blue-collarite have anything to do with his chances of realizing the American dream of "bettering himself," and if he does, in fact, become upwardly mobile, what is likely to happen to his religious convictions and practices in the process?
6. If a flourishing new religious group were to be established today, would the individuals converted to the group more likely be blue- or white-collarites?

Let us, then, turn our attention to some of the evidence which has a bearing upon these and other such questions. The picture of the religious behavior of the blue-collar group is somewhat hazy and incomplete in some respects, but definite patterns have been identified. It should be made clear, at the outset, however, that, in the realm of religious behavior, the patterns we shall be discussing are only *more characteristic* of the blue-collarite than of other groups —they are not necessarily descriptive of *all* such individuals.

---

[1] Gerhard Lenski, *The Religious Factor* (Garden City, N. Y.: Doubleday & Company, 1961), p. 295.

Different religious groups obviously differ to some degree in their religious beliefs. One way, then, to distinguish between configurations of beliefs is to pay attention to religious affiliation. The significant question here is, "Do blue-collarites have a higher concentration of their numbers in particular religious groups than, say, white-collar individuals?" The answer is "Yes." While members from all socioeconomic levels are found in all of the *major* religious groups, the percentages from given socioeconomic levels do vary. This is shown by the results of four polls taken by the American Institute of Public Opinion in 1946 and 1947[2] with reference to the following groups: Baptist, Congregational, Episcopal, Jewish, Lutheran, Methodist, Presbyterian, and Roman Catholic. It was found that, of these groups, Baptists and Roman Catholics had the highest per cent of lower-class members and the lowest per cent of upper-class members. The groups with the highest per cent of upper-class members were the Episcopal, Congregational, and Presbyterian. When these groups are arranged roughly in order of decreasing percentage of upper-class members and increasing percentage of lower-class members, the pattern which emerges is: Episcopal, Congregational, Presbyterian, Jewish, Methodist, Lutheran, Baptist, and Roman Catholic. Had other smaller and more recently established groups been included, particularly those which the sociologist would classify as sects, the per cent of lower-class members therein would have greatly exceeded that of these major groups, which the sociologist classifies as "denominations." More recent research of the relationship between religious affiliation and specific variables such as educational level, occupation, union membership, and being listed in *Who's Who* indicate that this is a fairly stable pattern.

From this evidence it follows that the blue-collar individual, although he may belong to any of these groups, is more likely to be a member of the Baptist or the Roman Catholic groups than of the Episcopal, Congregational, or Presbyterian groups. And, conversely, the membership of the Roman Catholic and the Baptist churches is more likely to be composed primarily of blue-collar rather than white-collar workers.

These and other substantiating findings also indicate that a pattern of long standing in America still obtains with reference to Catholic-Protestant patterns. In colonial America, Protestantism was, in general, the religion of the ruling and advantaged white-collar classes. This still tends to be true, although there are indications that the Roman Catholic class composition is changing, with an increasing proportion of members now falling within the higher class levels. "Protestantism" is, of course, a very broad category, including thereunder individuals from all class levels. Certain Protestant groups are, accordingly, more likely than others to include within their midst the leading citizens of the community.

The apparent affinity of Roman Catholicism and the blue-collarite reflects, from the available evidence, something more than the fact that American Roman Catholics are relatively recent immigrants who entered our class structure at a

---

[2] For a more extensive discussion, see Glenn M. Vernon, *Sociology of Religion* (New York: McGraw-Hill Book Company, 1962), Ch. 19.

fairly low level. Lenski, for instance, in his study of the Detroit area, found, when he compared white Protestants and Catholics who began life at the *same point* in the class system, that the Protestants rose to or stayed in the ranks of the upper-middle class more often than did Roman Catholics. Catholics wound up in the lower half of the working class (these would, of course, be blue-collarites) more often than Protestants three out of four times, and the difference was particularly marked among sons of middle-class men and farmers. His findings are supported by other research. Those with Jewish affiliation were, as a group, more successful than the Protestants.

This broad conclusion reflects a series of other differences. From an analysis of several specific attitudes, Lenski concludes that, as a general rule, commitment to the "spirit of capitalism" or endorsement of value premises upon which capitalism is founded is especially frequent among white Protestants and Jews, and is much less frequent among Roman Catholic and Negro Protestants, even when position in the existing class structure is held constant. For instance, he asked which of the following five characteristics was considered the most important feature of a man's job: (1) high income, (2) no danger of being fired, (3) working hours short with lots of free time, (4) changes for advancement, and (5) the work is important and gives a feeling of accomplishment. "Opportunity for advancement" was given highest ranking by the Jews, and then, in order, by white Protestants, Roman Catholics, and Negro Protestants, although the differences on this particular question were not great.

Protestantism, in general, has further tended to view work by itself somewhat differently than Catholicism. Historically, Protestantism has, for several reasons, viewed work as a "calling." Luther, for instance, emphasized that all worthwhile occupations were equally important in the sight of God and told his followers that, when one was actively engaged in his occupation, he was at the same time serving his God and building his character. Catholic teaching, on the contrary, has frequently emphasized that work was primarily a necessary evil, which followed from the "fall" of Adam and was, consequently, a punishment or a penalty for sin.

Continued influence of these doctrinal positions is suggested by the finding in the Detroit study that, whereas the Jewish males were most likely to define work positively and by far the least likely to do so negatively, the white Protestants defined work in more positive degree than did Catholics or Negro Protestants. Further, it was found by Lenski that Protestants and Jews, as compared with Roman Catholics, tend to:

1. Be more "business-oriented"
2. Be less labor-union-oriented
3. View self-employment more positively
4. Be more inclined to believe that sons of workingmen have good chances for advancement
5. More frequently express great confidence in the value of ability
6. Be most likely to perceive of God as desiring to see men get ahead (difference not great, however)
7. Disapprove of installment buying
8. Be a bit less likely to keep detailed family budgets

319

Lenski concludes that, on the vast majority of the variables which he studied,

> . . . either Jewish or white Protestants have ranked first with the other ranking second, the Catholics have usually ranked third and the Negro Protestant 4th. With considerable regularity the Jews and white Protestants have identified themselves with the individualistic, competitive patterns of thought and action linked with the middle class, and historically associated with the Protestant Ethic or its secular counterpart the spirit of capitalism. By contrast, Catholics and Negro Protestants have more often been associated with the collectivistic, security-oriented working class patterns of thought and action historically opposed to the Protestant Ethic and the spirit of capitalism.[3]

He further reports that, from his evidence, Americanization and urbanization appear to increase rather than decrease these Protestant-Catholic differences.

Unpublished research by the author on the reactions of Mormon students at Brigham Young University to some of Lenski's questions has found them to be more like the Protestants than the Catholics.

The Catholic, then, appears to have certain experiences within his church and in his association with fellow Catholics which encourage his membership in the blue-collar group.

Greater understanding of the whole configuration, however, would be possible if differences on these variables between the various Protestant groups had been identified and analyzed. Protestantism is such a broad category that it includes thereunder many groups and individuals with drastically different characteristics with respect to many variables.

Not only do blue-collar individuals differ from non-blue-collarites in beliefs of a religious nature, but in their more overt religious behavior as well. The blue-collarite and his family do not, as a rule, participate in *formal* religious activities as often as does his white-collar brother. Rainwater, and associates,[4] in a study of the wives of blue-collar workers, to cite but one piece of research, concluded that despite the fact that working-class women are deeply religious and strongly hold or endorse religious beliefs which give them peace of mind and help when they are faced with problems, they are not as active in *formal* church activities as their middle-class counterparts. Less than half of all the wives in the study went to church as often as two times a month. The typical working-class wife attended church occasionally, maybe once a month or on important occasions, whereas the middle-class wives were more likely to be "regular" attenders.

Lenski found some interesting relationships between formal religious activity and economic behavior, which suggest some results of these attendance patterns. He found, for instance, that the men who were upwardly mobile, and thus more likely to move out of the blue-collar group, were more likely to be regular church attenders than the nonmobile men. However, from his evidence this is not a one-way causal relationship, but rather a reciprocal one. Church participation evidently facilitates upward mobility, while at the same time upward mobility is conducive to religious activity. In this respect he found further

---

[3] Lenski, *op cit.*, pp. 100-101.
[4] Lee Rainwater, Richard P. Coleman and Gerald Handel, *Workingman's Wife* (New York: Oceana Publications, Inc., 1959), p. 121.

Catholic-Protestant differences, and concluded that involvement in the Catholic Church does not have the same consequences as involvement in white Protestant churches.

The likelihood of being involved in the establishment of a new religious group, either as a leader in the movement or as a participant therein, is also related to one's position on the class continuum. The term "sect" is generally used to refer to new groups, wherein the members reject some or maybe all of the established religious groups and, likewise, define the secular world as being wicked and evil and therefore to be avoided or changed. Such groups are generally small in size, with the religious group itself, as well as the individual members thereof, being of limited financial resources. The clergy, which is usually part-time, is generally unspecialized, with little if any professional religious training. Services are not highly ritualized and, consequently, usually include an emotional emphasis wherein efforts are made to recapture the conversion thrill. They generally involve extensive audience participation. Such groups usually rely upon a somewhat literal interpretation of their scriptures and place emphasis upon other-worldly, as contrasted with worldly, rewards.

This configuration of characteristics is completed by adding the fact that membership for such groups comes primarily, although not exclusively, from the blue-collar group.

The blue-collar group has limited wealth, is more receptive to the message of a nonprofessional leader who is more "like us" than toward someone with an advanced academic degree, who may accordingly be seen as distorting religious "truth" with "worldly" learning. An emotional appeal is more attractive to the blue-collar individual than the more formal, intellectual approach used in the denomination. Individuals who have but limited access to the material rewards of society are more likely to be attracted to a religious interpretation which emphasizes the importance of other-worldly rewards, or an interpretation which in effect proclaims that the first shall be last and the last shall be first and in one way or another indicates that it is as difficult for a rich white-collar man to get into heaven as it is for a camel to go through the eye of a needle.

Concomitant with this, individuals with limited worldly resources are more likely than those with greater resources to be discontented with "the world" which has not bounteously rewarded their efforts, and are the ones who would most benefit from a reorganization of one type or another. They are at least somewhat "at war" with "the world." They are looking for change—if not in the world itself, at least in their position in the world. Thus, as Benton Johnson[5] has indicated, many sects incorporate in their beliefs an orientation toward the world which directly or indirectly encourages success therein. This is reflected in the statement of a minister of such a group that people "ought to desire to excel in their work." Inasmuch as such groups provide religious rewards for such behavior patterns as industriousness, frugality, deferred gratification, and so forth, they encourage those qualities which will bring economic success in a capitalistic economic structure.

When such behavior on the part of the blue-collarite does in fact result in

---

[5] Benton Johnson, "The Holiness Sects as Agents of Socialization in Dominant Values," paper presented at the Pacific Sociological Association meetings in Spokane, Washington, 1960.

Religion and the Blue-Collarite

a change of economic position, an interesting sequence of events is initiated. As economic change takes place, corresponding religious changes are likewise set in motion, and, as religious changes occur, related economic changes are facilitated. It is sociologically naïve to suppose that a blue-collarite can move into the white-collar group and maintain his old religious patterns completely intact. He may, to be sure, maintain membership in the same religious group, but his interpretation of the theology of his group, and his participation in the activities of his group, will undergo change, which may be subtle at first but over a period of years will be noticeable to those whom he has "left behind" in his "advancement." Change of religious affiliation may, of course, take place.

Such change should not, however, be viewed as necessarily "opportunistic." A more realistic interpretation is that religious beliefs and rituals which once were rewarding and satisfying to the blue-collarite no longer have the same effect. The conversion may be a very sincere one which permits the individual involved to more adequately (according to his standards) adjust to his new position in life.

This point can be expanded into a broad generalization about religion in general which applies to the blue-collarite, the white-collarite, and a representative of any other group which has distinctive characteristics. The point is that religious behavior is functionally related to the nonreligious behavior of the group and the individual and thus tends to harmonize therewith. Hoult calls this the principle of sociocultural compatibility.[6] Certain aspects of religion may, to be sure, be "out of kilter," but in such cases efforts are usually made to achieve greater harmony—a goal, which again, is not always fully realized.

The blue-collarite today lives in a world of rapid change and is constantly faced with problems and uncertainties, with little evidence that peace of mind and pocketbook is just around the corner. In the light of religion's functional utility, it is interesting to ask the following questions concerning the involvement of existing religions in the life of the blue-collarite:

> From whom does the blue-collarite expect the greatest help in his efforts to reach his goals? To whom does he turn most fervently and frequently for help—his labor union, his government, or his church? Where do his greatest loyalties lie, particularly when a conflict of interest arises?

The crucial question in broad terms is, *Do existing religious creeds and programs, which are essentially under the control and direction of white-collarites, provide the blue-collarite with what he wants in religion?* Are his "religious needs" being adequately met? If not, it would appear to be a safe prediction that new patterns will be developed, and the most fertile ground from which new prophets arise is the blue-collar group.

"The laborer deserves his wages"[7] is capable of more than one interpretation.

---

[6] Thomas Ford Hoult, *The Sociology of Religion* (New York: Holt, Rinehart & Winston, Inc., 1958).

[7] Luke 10:7 (Revised Standard version).

Part VI

PHYSICAL HEALTH

FOR reasons that are explored at length in this section, the blue-collarite appears more willing to remain physically ill than to seek and receive aid from available private and public resources. Suchman and Rosenblatt explore this phenomenon and point out in explanation that blue-collar workers are less informed about illness, are more skeptical of medical care, are more dependent when ill, and experience great difficulty in internalizing the "sick role." They call for the development of organizational means to deal with the values of blue-collarites. Rosengren focuses more sharply on class differences in playing the sick role and, after considering the attitudes and behavior of expectant mothers from the working and the middle classes, concludes that "the blue-collar fashion of meeting a personal crisis is no more fictional than that of the middle class." Rosenblatt and Suchman ask in the third essay, however, if this fashion might not be directed closer to public health objectives, and they accordingly discuss various attempts to alter the blue-collarite's underutilization of medical care. Zola pursues the question of utilization even farther, and relates it to ethnic differences in health and illness attitudes. Like the others, he, too, outlines a program of reform and future research, the potential gains of which "seem well worth the effort."

Blue-Collar Attitudes and Information Toward Health and Illness

DANIEL ROSENBLATT

EDWARD A. SUCHMAN

INTRODUCTION

DURING the twentieth century, medicine has become increasingly specialized and highly organized. We have witnessed the creation of enormous hospital complexes, highly technical research, specialization, and the trend toward group practice. The private family physician has often been replaced with a much more imposing bureaucracy of aides, nurses, ancillary therapists, technicians, and highly qualified specialists. Similarly, the office of the local general practitioner and the small neighborhood dispensary have tended to be replaced by specialty clinics, group insurance plans, outpatient departments, and other more impersonal arrangements for the provision of medical care.[1]

As medical care reaches out to all classes of society, it becomes important to learn what the effect of these organizational changes will be on blue-collar workers. Blue-collar workers in large industrial centers for the most part have been recruited from the poorer, relatively uneducated segments of the population and have to a high degree close ties to their original ethnic source. In the past, such medical care as they received tended to take place within the intimate, traditional confines of their own environment (with the exception of the health care provided them while at work). In other words, there was a more consistent framework between their values and such care as they received, whether charity or private.

Today the situation has altered, and if blue-collar workers are to benefit to the largest extent from the changes in the organization of medical care, it is necessary to evaluate the degree to which their attitudes differ from those of "rational" modern medicine. That is, it becomes important to learn whether or not the highly organized and rational, bureaucratic practice of modern medicine in itself becomes a further barrier to the blue-collar workers whose

---

[1] See in this connection Eliot Freidson, "The Organization of Medical Practice," in *The Handbook of Medical Sociology*, edited by Howard E. Freeman, Sol Levine, and Leo G. Reeder (Englewood Cliffs, N. J.: Prentice-Hall, Inc., 1963); Richard H. Shryock, *The Development of Modern Medicine* (New York: Alfred A. Knopf, Inc., 1947); and Henry N. Sigerist, *A History of Medicine* (New York: Oxford University Press, 1951).

social needs are geared to a more immediate personal, familistic, or even folk type of social structure.[2] For this reason, in the following study, we concentrate our attention on such sociomedical factors as knowledge of illness and preventive medical procedures and attitudes toward medical care and to selected dimensions of the sick role among blue-collar workers. In order to clarify our findings, we shall briefly present material on sociocultural variations within our blue-collar group as these relate to the sociomedical factors.

This report represents one major focus of a four-year study of the Washington Heights Health District of New York City,[3] which concentrates on the knowledge and attitudes of the residents with regard to health and illness. The purpose of this particular report is to determine the degree to which blue-collar workers differ in their responses to health and illness. It is our contention that blue-collar workers in New York City, on the basis of their norms, value orientations, and patterns of behavior, will define illness and patient status in characteristic ways, and, furthermore, that they will interpret the meaning of illness and patient status in ways which are conditioned by their membership within their blue-collar group. The organization of this report is (a) to describe blue-collar workers according to their knowledge, attitudes, and responses to illness; and (b) to analyze these sociomedical factors with reference to sociocultural orientations.

METHOD OF PROCEDURE

Data were obtained from a probability sample of 5,340 persons comprising some 2,215 families, by means of personal household interviews conducted during late 1960 and early 1961. The first interview was conducted with an adult member of the family, usually the female head of the household. This interview obtained the basic demographic data for all members of the household, an inventory of all chronic conditions and impairments, and a record of all medically attended illnesses experienced by any family member during the past year, together with an account of all medical care and the sequence in

---

[2] See H. Ashley Weeks, *Family Spending Patterns and Health Care* (Cambridge: Harvard University Press, 1961); Eliot Freidson, *The Public Looks at Hospitals*, Research Series No. 4, N. Y. Health Information Foundation, 1958; also Freidson's *Patient's View of Medical Practice—A Study of Subscribers to a Pre-Paid Medical Plan in the Bronx, N. Y.*, Russell Sage Foundation, 1961; and Paul B. Sheatsley, "Public Attitudes Toward Hospitals," *Hospitals*, May 16, 1957.

[3] This investigation was supported in whole by Public Health Service Grant No. CH 00010-05 from the Division of Community Health Services. Field work was aided by a grant from the Health Research Council of the City of New York, No. U-1053.

The Washington Heights Health District roughly covers the northern end of Manhattan. The total population is just under 300,000, based on the 1950 census. Ethnically the group is very mixed: population is about one-quarter Negro, 10 per cent Puerto Rican, one-quarter foreign-born (largely Russian and German Jews), with only 9 per cent white Protestants. However, in large measure, the various ethnic groups tend to have fairly distinct neighborhoods, so that contacts between groups may be at a minimum. Indeed, the leaders of the community do not think of it as cohesive, either in the sense of a small town or even a tightly knit neighborhood in an urban area. The group is similarly mixed with regard to our data on socioeconomic status. According to our index of socioeconomic status (based on a combination of education, occupation of head of household, and total family income), our sample contains 13 per cent with high SES, 67 per cent medium SES, 15 per cent low SES, and for 5 per cent, SES, information could not be ascertained.

Blue-Collar
Attitudes
and
Information
Toward Health
and Illness

which such care was received. All adult members of this initial sample were then listed and a random sample of 1,883 respondents was selected for a more detailed interview on symptoms of illness and related medical knowledge, attitudes, and behavior. This is the sample upon which the current report is based.

In classifying the sample according to occupation, we asked the following questions of all employed persons or those "looking for work": "What kind of work do you usually do?" and "In what kind of business or industry is this work done?" The answers were then classified according to the 1950 Census, "Detailed Occupation of Employed Persons."[4]

From these we have selected the four following major occupational groups, two blue-collar and two white-collar:

1. *White-Collar A.* Professional, managers, officials, proprietors, etc. ($N = 215$).
2. *White-Collar B.* Clerical and kindred workers (bank tellers, bookkeepers, cashiers) and sales workers (auctioneers, demonstrators, insurance agents, real estate agents, etc.) ($N = 365$).
3. *Blue-Collar A.* Operatives and kindred workers (apprentices, bus drivers, conductors, deliverymen, dressmakers and seamstresses, laundry and dry cleaning, meat cutters, milliners, taxicab drivers, truck drivers, weavers, textile and apparel operatives, etc. ($N = 286$).
4. *Blue-Collar B.* Private household workers, service workers (attendants, barbers, bartenders, beauticians, bootblacks, charwomen, cooks, fountain workers, elevator operators, porters, garage car washers, and general unskilled labor in manufacturing, etc. ($N = 260$).

Because of the small number of craftsmen in our sample and their placement midway between the blue- and white-collar continuum, we omitted them from this analysis.

SOCIOMEDICAL CHARACTERISTICS OF BLUE-COLLAR WORKERS

Theoretically, our hypotheses with regard to the patterns of medical care for the blue-collar workers can be simply stated: because of their placement as the more disadvantaged group of the urban society of which they are a part, their information and attitudes regarding health and illness will reflect simply another dimension along which they express their general alienation from the larger social norms. More specifically, with regard to our *measures of knowledge and preventive medical procedures,* we shall expect the blue-collars to be least informed about disease and least prevention-oriented, and not merely as a result of their poorer education.[5]

With regard to *attitudes* toward medical care, we measured two dimensions: *skepticism toward medical care* and *perception of physician's interest in patient's welfare.* We predict more skepticism on the part of the blue-collar

---

[4] Table 282, *Statistical Abstract of the United States, 1960, 81st Annual Edition,* United States Department of Commerce, pp. 218-21.

[5] See Edward A. Suchman, *Social Patterns of Health and Medical Care,* paper presented to the Annual Meeting of the American Sociological Association, Los Angeles, August, 1963, p. 15.

workers toward the established medical-care system, as well as a feeling of lack of interest on the part of the physician.

We also measured the blue-collar response to taking the sick role. Here we looked at two indices: the *acceptance of the sick role* as measured by an individual's willingness to go to bed and remain there as long as he is ill, and *dependency in illness*, based upon the individual's need for and acceptance of help from others when he is ill. Here we would predict that the blue-collar workers would find it more difficult to accept the sick role, because it would mean so many practical disadvantages, such as reduced pay check, need for greater contact with the generalized medical-care system, and so forth. The situation with regard to dependency in illness is just the opposite. We hypothesize that the more an individual's social roles tend to put him in a position of dominance, the more difficult it will be for him to accept his dependence in illness. Thus, we shall expect that blue-collar workers, as the less prominent occupational groups with less social power or influence, will more readily accept their dependence in illness. Dependence is for them a general response to the social order, and illness represents only another specific instance.

Let us now look at our findings (see Table I).

(a) *Knowledge of Illness*

The respondents were asked a series of factual questions dealing with various diseases in order to determine their general information level in regard to disease and its treatment.[6] Blue-collar A and blue-collar B workers have less knowledge of illness (36.3 per cent and 37.5 per cent) than white-collar A and white-collar B workers (who have 20.2 per cent and 20.7 per cent). In similar vein, the respondents were asked about their behavior in regard to a series of preventive health measures, such as polio immunization, periodical medical checkups, and balanced diet. The aim was to see how important the "rational" element of planning was distributed among the respondents. Here again our findings are consistent with the general theoretical position: blue-collar A and B workers tend to be lower in terms of preventive medical

Table 1*

RELATIONSHIP BETWEEN OCCUPATION AND SOCIOMEDICAL FACTORS

	Occupation			
Sociomedical Factors	Blue-Collar A	Blue-Collar B	White-Collar A	White-Collar B
1. % Low Knowledge of Illness	36.5	37.5	20.2	20.7
2. % Low Preventive Medical Behavior	18.9	15.3	12.7	12.1
3. % High Skepticism of Medical Care	28.3	28.1	20.0	14.8
4. % Low Physician Interest in Patient's Welfare	15.0	12.7	29.8	20.0
5. % High Acceptance of Sick Role	18.9	25.0	29.3	32.6
6. % High Dependency in Illness	38.5	30.0	14.4	16.2

*All of the numbers in each cell represent more than 25 cases.

[6] Details of the sampling, questionnaires, and index construction may be found in E. A. Suchman, *Socio-Cultural Variations in Illness and Medical Care*, New York City Department of Health, July 1, 1963, mimeographed.

Blue-Collar
Attitudes
and
Information
Toward Health
and Illness

behavior (18.9 per cent and 15.3 per cent, respectively) as opposed to the white-collar A's and B's (12.7 per cent and 12.1 per cent). Nor is this difference simply to be explained in terms of differences in educational background or ethnic background. Thus, the blue-collar workers, as other studies have shown, who are least apt to vote, to take part in community activities such as membership in formal organizations, and to be informed on issues of public information, are also less apt to have a high knowledge of illness or to have taken preventive medical behavior.

(b) *Attitudes toward Medical Care*

Scale analysis of a series of items indicative of attitudes toward medical care revealed two separate dimensions—"skepticism of medical care" and "physician's interest in patient's welfare." The first scale was composed of agreement or disagreement with the following statements: "I believe in trying out different doctors to find which one I think will give me the best care"; "When I am ill, I demand to know all the details of what is being done to me"; and "I have my doubts about some things doctors say they can do for you." Answers to the first scale are consistent with our hypothesis: blue-collar A and B workers are higher with regard to skepticism of medical care (28.3 per cent and 28.1 per cent), whereas white-collar A and B workers are lower (20.0 per cent and 14.8 per cent, respectively). The first of these statements on which the scale is based involves "shopping around" and the third is a frank statement of doubt. The second is a more ambiguous demand for information, with a strong suggestion of suspicion and distrust. This lack of confidence—doubt and distrust—is consistent with regard to the general situation of the blue-collar worker in the larger community.

There is another factor which may be at work here. If the blue-collar workers share the strong parochial and "folk" orientation of other less educated groups, then the traditional belief system may account in part for the greater skepticism toward modern "scientific" medical care. Finally, since their contact with the medical-care system is often through the more impersonal clinics and outpatient departments, as opposed to family and private physicians, then again we can readily understand greater skepticism toward medical care.

The scale of Physician's Interest in Patient's Welfare (Table II) was based on answers to the following statements: "Most doctors charge too much money" and "Most doctors are more interested in the welfare of their patients than in anything else." Here we find a strong reversal of our hypothesis: the blue-collar A and B workers evidence relatively less negative attitudes toward physician interest in patient's welfare (15.0 per cent and 12.7 per cent), than white-collar A and B workers (29.8 per cent and 20.0 per cent). It may be that the white-collar A's, who pay more for their care, are therefore more readily in agreement with the statement, "Most doctors charge too much money." Similarly, as fellow professionals and peers of the physicians, they may be in a better position to judge the accuracy of the idealized conception of the doctor as being more interested in the patient's welfare than in anything else. It appears that the white-collar workers have a greater degree of faith in the system itself than in its individual practitioners, especially along these two dimensions, and that the blue-collar workers are more skeptical of the system itself but have faith in the individual practitioner. Perhaps his inferior social position makes it less easy for the blue-collar worker to challenge the authority of the physician, especially because the blue-collar worker is apt to experience from his own parochial position a greater need for personal interest on the part of his healer.

(c) *Response to Illness*

One of the major sociological variables that has been hypothesized as affecting the way an individual responds to illness relates to the "sick role." Sick-role incumbents, according to Parsons, are exempted from normal social responsibilities, are not held morally responsible for their condition, but are obligated to get well as quickly as possible.[7]

Our index of Acceptance of the Sick Role is based on answers to two statements: "I find it very hard to give in and go to bed when I am sick," and "I usually try to get up too soon after I have been sick." Our hypothesis is borne out by the findings: both blue-collar A's and B's find it more difficult to accept the sick role (18.9 per cent and 25.0 per cent) than do the white-collar A's and B's (29.3 per cent and 32.6 per cent high acceptance). As we hypothesized, low acceptance of the sick role should be more difficult objectively for those individuals with fewer financial resources, as well as for those individuals who are less flexible in their ability to adapt to appropriate shifts in social roles.

"Dependency in Illness" is based on answers to two statements: "When I think I am getting sick, I find it comforting to talk to someone about it"; and "When a person starts getting well, it is hard to give up having people do things for him." These two questions tap one specific dimension of general dependence. For this reason we hypothesize that the more dominant members of the society, occupationally and otherwise, would report lower dependency in illness, and, further, that the blue-collar workers would be characterized as higher in dependence. Our findings confirm this hypothesis: blue-collar A and B workers score higher (38.5 per cent and 30.0 per cent) in dependency in illness than white-coller A and B workers (14.4 per cent and 16.2 per cent). In other words, there appears to be less dissonance for the blue-collar workers to depend on others than for the higher-status occupational groups.

SOCIOCULTURE FACTORS IN RELATION TO SOCIOMEDICAL CHARACTERISTICS OF BLUE-COLLAR WORKERS

Our original position held that blue-collar workers are more alienated than white-collar workers from the large-scale modern medical care system. Almost all of the findings presented above are consistent with this formulation. It now becomes necessary to learn whether or not those blue-collar workers who are more generally oriented toward "sophistication" and are more liberated from their primary groups also differ in their attitudes and informa-

---

[7] Talcott Parsons, *The Social System* (New York: The Free Press of Glencoe, Inc., 1951).

tion toward the sociomedical factors previously discussed. Our hypothesis is that the more "cosmopolitan" blue-collar workers will score more positively on the sociomedical factors than will the more "parochial" blue-collar workers. Similarly, we expect that the blue-collar workers will score higher on a measure of parochialism and that white-collar workers will score higher on a measure of cosmopolitanism.

Thus, in order to examine further the meaning of blue-collar responses to the previous sociomedical items, we first constructed an index of Cosmopolitanism-Parochialism and then noted their distribution along it. This scale was prepared by summarizing the respondents according to their rankings on the following five attitude indices: Family Orientation to Tradition and Authority, Family Togetherness, Religious Attendance, Reliance on Friends, and Friendship Solidarity.[8]

In general, the blue-collar A and B workers are significantly higher in their parochialism (38.1 per cent and 31.2 per cent) than the white-collar A's and B's (23.3 per cent and 20.8 per cent). This finding is not unexpected, since the blue-collar groups tend to have more limited experience with regard to education and travel, and to be drawn in large measure from ethnic groups who still retain a high degree of visibility, cohesiveness, and relatively greater reliance on the traditional forms as a means of organizing life. The more libertarian, emancipated, and independent groups are more apt to be found among professional and white-collar workers.

In the following analysis, we are concerned with learning the degree to which the response of the A and B blue-collar workers to our sociomedical data is in part a function of the more generalized sociocultural factor of cosmopolitanism-parochialism.

On the whole, we find that, for blue-collar workers, differences with regard to sociomedical data tend to become sharper once we introduce the factor of cosmopolitanism-parochialism. This is true for five of the six sociomedical indices dealt with earlier, and only in the case of the response to Preventive Medical Behavior is the finding obscured. (See Table II.)

With regard to Knowledge About Disease, blue-collar workers who are high on parochialism have less knowledge (40.4 per cent and 49.4 per cent) than white-collar workers who are also high on parochialism (34.0 per cent

---

[8] These scales were derived from answers to the following statements and questions:
Family
My family usually doesn't do things together; most of the time each goes his own way.
Everybody in my family usually does what the head of the house says without question.
My family usually waits until the head of the house is present before we have dinner.
In my family we think the old-time customs and traditions are important.
Friends
Almost all my friends are people I grew up with.
Most of my close friends are also friends with each other.
Most of my friends have the same religion as I do.
Most of my friends come from families who know each other well.
Community Integration
The parents of most of my friends come from the same country as my parents come from.
I prefer to deal in stores where clerks are the same kind of people as we are.
Religious Attendance
Did you attend religious services last week?
How often do you attend religious services during the year?

Table 2*

RELATIONSHIP BETWEEN OCCUPATION AND SOCIOMEDICAL CHARACTERISTICS
ACCORDING TO COSMOPOLITAN-PAROCHIALISM

	Occupation			
	Blue- Collar A	Blue- Collar B	White- Collar A	White- Collar B
Per Cent Low Knowledge About Disease				
Cosmopolitan-Parochialism:				
Cosmopolitan	29.9	34.7	14.3	16.0
Mixed	37.5	30.2	18.1	17.9
Parochial	40.4	49.4	34.0	35.6
Per Cent Low Preventive Medical Behavior				
Cosmopolitan	16.3	8.7	8.7	11.6
Mixed	24.1	17.9	23.3	10.8
Parochial	16.8	17.5	4.2	15.9
Per Cent High Skepticism of Medical Care				
Cosmopolitan	20.7	23.6	14.1	14.6
Mixed	23.3	20.6	26.0	14.2
Parochial	38.5	42.0	22.0	16.4
Per Cent Low Physician Interest in Patient's Welfare				
Cosmopolitan	20.7	20.8	27.2	21.2
Mixed	16.7	12.1	37.0	18.4
Parochial	9.2	6.2	24.0	20.5
Per Cent High Acceptance of Sick Role				
Cosmopolitan	28.7	27.8	26.1	32.5
Mixed	14.4	22.4	38.4	38.3
Parochial	14.7	25.9	22.0	21.9
Per Cent High Dependency in Illness				
Cosmopolitan	29.9	20.8	8.7	13.2
Mixed	37.8	28.0	17.8	17.0
Parochial	45.9	40.7	20.0	20.5

*Each number in every cell represents more than 25 cases.

and 35.6 per cent). Similarly, among the more cosmopolitan blue-collar workers, the same tendency remains for them to score higher on low knowledge about disease (29.9 per cent and 34.7 per cent) than for cosmopolitan white-collar workers (14.3 per cent and 16.0 per cent). The same is true with regard to the degree of Skepticism of Medical Care. Blue-collar workers who are more parochial tend to be more skeptical about medical care (38.5 per cent and 42.0 per cent) than more parochial white-collar workers (22.0 per cent and 16.4 per cent). This greater skepticism is equally true for cosmopolitan blue-collar workers (20.7 per cent and 23.6 per cent), in contrast with the cosmopolitan white-collar workers (14.1 per cent and 14.6 per cent).

Similarly with regard to the degree of Physician Interest in Patient's Welfare, the more parochial blue-collar workers report the smallest percentages (9.2 per cent and 6.2 per cent). The more parochial white-collar workers, however, show a much higher percentage of low physician interest in patient's welfare (24.0 per cent and 20.5 per cent). The same relationship exists for the more cosmopolitan blue-collar and white-coller workers, but on a much smaller scale.

The findings on Acceptance of Sick Role are not as clear-cut as the others. In 10 of 12 cells, there is a general tendency for blue-collar workers to show

Social Class
and
Becoming
"Ill"

a smaller degree of Acceptance of the Sick Role (see Table II). This is true when we compare the more parochial blue-collar workers with the more parochial white-collar workers and the more cosmopolitan blue-collar workers with the more cosmopolitan white-collar workers, with only the following two exceptions: the more parochial blue-collar B workers and the more cosmopolitan white-collar A workers.

The last item, Dependency in Illness, indicates very strongly that the more parochial blue-collar workers score twice as high (45.9 per cent and 40.7 per cent) as the more parochial white-collar workers (20.0 per cent and 20.5 per cent). The same trend holds for the more cosmopolitan blue-collar worker to be more dependent in illness (29.9 per cent and 20.8 per cent) than for the more cosmopolitan white-collar worker (8.7 per cent and 3.2 per cent).

Within the blue-collar group itself, the differences between cosmopolitan-ism-parochialism simply heighten five of the six sociomedical scales. Only on the Preventive Medical Behavior scale is there a lack of relationship among blue-collar A's, and even then it is not a reversal of the general picture but simply no difference.

Thus, an analysis of the relationship between blue-collar workers and sociomedical characteristics according to the dimension of cosmopolitanism-parochialism in almost every instance tallies with the findings of our previous data. For the most part, this addition of the cosmopolitanism-parochialism index only serves to heighten the differences between the blue-collar workers and the white-collar workers with regard to their information and attitudes toward medical care.

CONCLUSION

It is quite clear from our findings that, as compared with white-collar workers, blue-collar workers are less informed about illness, are more skeptical of medical care, are more dependent when ill, and experience greater difficulty in internalizing the sick role. This trend becomes even more striking for those blue-collar workers who are also more parochial and traditional in their general value orientation.

Clearly we see here a picture of a group which is not in step with present standards of good medical care and a situation that is not likely to change in the near future. Medical care will not become more parochial or less special-ized. This means that, if these social barriers are to be overcome, organizational means will have to be found to deal with these values on the part of the blue-collar workers.

More experimental demonstration projects, which are designed to offer more organic groupings for the provision of medical care, are needed. For example, the New York City Health Department is cooperating on a number of projects which offer care to all of the members of a housing project, thereby effecting somewhat of a return to the small neighborhood dispensary. Simi-larly, by opening family-centered clinics which are satellites to a large hospital, there is an attempt to return to a smaller, more personal form of care. At the same time, the attempt is being made to see if the values of the traditional, more closed society can be tied in with modern medical practice. In this regard, the New York City Health Department is experimenting with an adaptation of the health visitor so that local neighborhood people can be trained for para-medical functions which relate to health. However, the degree to which even these innovations will succeed in affecting the hard core of hard-to-reach blue-collar workers with regard to medical care remains doubtful, and, for this group, more imaginative solutions will have to be found.

Social Class and Becoming "Ill"

WILLIAM R. ROSENGREN

All women ought to know that invalidism, speaking generally, is a carefully cultivated condition. . . . Pain is ordained by God. . . . How can a mother love her child without suffering for it? . . . Be careful and guarded as to your society demands, lest they steal your time and strength and you be unfitted for the real duties of your home. . . . The sedentary life of many men renders them a prey to the gratification of their lower natures. . . . Look at beautiful pictures, study perfect pieces of statuary, forbid as far as possible, the contemplation of unsightly and imperfect models. . . . Above all, keep croaking companions away.[1]

SUCH was the character of advice offered to pregnant women in a handbook for "young wives" which sold over a million copies in English alone at the end of the last century. The daughters and granddaughters of the "young wives" to which this early document was addressed are given the following advice in an equally popular book published in 1956 and in reference to an obstetrical case taking place less than twenty years after the publication of the older book:

One of my earliest private patients was a dancer in a night club. She first consulted me when she had successfully completed three months of pregnancy. In taking the history and discovering her occupation, I was curious to see just how much dancing she did. Not only did she twirl, pirouette, and leap in the air, but two strong-muscled gentlemen tossed her back and forth between them like football ends warming up before the game. . . . Difficult labor is uncommon today, and the likelihood of being so penalized is small. . . . Don't become a stay-at-home introvert. . . . Sexual intercourse is permissible, desirable, and safe. . . . We now realize that pregnancy is a normal, simple, physiologic state.[2]

Although these contrasting images of pregnant women may well correspond to more basic changes in the definition of proper ladylike conduct during the

---

[1] Emma F. Angell Drake, *What a Young Wife Ought to Know* (London: Vir Publishing Co., 1902).

[2] Alan Guttmacher, *Pregnancy and Birth* (New York: New American Library of World Literature, 1956).

past half-century—from the fragile Victorian lady-in-waiting to the blasé sophisticate of the present day—still the "role of the sick" remains as a legitimate conduct alternative for persons who are incapacitated or who otherwise regard themselves as faced with a crisis situation which not only prevents them from following their usual round of life but also obliges them to retire into the exempt, dependent, and self-transforming status of the "sick." In American society, at least, illness has this joint physiological and social character about it.[3] Illness has physiological imperatives about it, as well as socially motivated roots and personally satisfying consequences.

Persons tend to enact the "role of the sick" under at least three different circumstances. First, one may enact the role of the sick because of being physically incapable of doing anything else—although even one bedridden in a plaster cast may be cantankerous about it. Second, one may play the sick role because it is perceived as personally obligatory as a consequence of interaction with significant other persons whose demeanor suggests that one "ought to" act sick—one's parents, a respected physician, and the like. Third, one may behave as if one were ill because the round of life in which one engages defines "illness" as being more reasonable and satisfying than some other form of conduct. It is with this latter possibility that social factors arise as the principal motivating and rewarding force and in which the condition of pregnancy stands as an optimum example of physiological ambivalence. Here the person has available the role model of the Victorian lady-in-waiting—to be exempted from her normal responsibilities, to be taken care of, and to be regarded by others as one who is "ill." Or, she may legitimately turn to the role model of the "pirouetting dancer"—to regard her condition as normal and not incapacitating, to continue with her usual round of life, and to regard medical care for her condition as routine rather than as problematic.

The study summarized and elaborated in this chapter is intended to shed some light on the social conditions under which pregnancy comes to be regarded as a personal crisis obligating the expectant mother to enact the "role of the sick." It is the main purpose of this chapter to discuss the part that social-class position seems to play in motivating one to play the "ill" role, and to suggest some of the rewards that stem from it, in the face of a physiological condition which others regard as normal and routine.[4]

---

[3] See Talcott Parsons and Renee Fox, "Illness, Therapy, and the Modern Urban Family," *The Journal of Social Issues* (1952) , pp. 2-3; 31-44; and Parsons, *The Social System* (New York: The Free Press of Glencoe, Inc., 1951). Ch. X.

[4] The study summarized here was supported by a grant from the Association for the Aid of Crippled Children, New York. Space limitations preclude an adequate discussion of methods and findings. The reader is referred to the following publications by this author: "Social Sources of Pregnancy as Illness or Normality," *Social Forces* (March, 1961), pp. 260-67; "Some Social Psychological Aspects of Delivery Room Difficulties," *Journal of Nervous and Mental Disease* (June, 1961), pp. 515-21; "Social Instability and Attitudes Toward Pregnancy as a Social Role," *Social Problems* (Spring, 1962), pp. 371-78; "Social Status, Attitudes Toward Pregnancy, and Child-Rearing Attitudes," *Social Forces* (December, 1962), pp. 127-34; (with S. DeVault), "The Sociology of Time and Space in an Obstetrical Hospital," in *The Hospital in Modern Society* edited by E. Freidson (New York: The Free Press of Glencoe, Inc., 1963).

STUDY SETTING AND RESEARCH PROCEDURES

This study was conducted in an Eastern metropolitan community and involved the interviewing of 115 obstetrical patients in a large lying-in hospital clinic and 60 patients of obstetricians in private practice. The clinic patients tended to be of lower socioeconomic status than were the private patients, although there was some overlap between the two groups. Focused as the study was upon relations between perception of self as "ill" and resulting behavior, a major task was to devise indicators of what might be regarded as social factors likely to move one to act as if one were ill.

In this sense, the most fundamental factor was social-class position, as indicated by education, income, and occupation. Simply, women of lower social status were less likely than middle-class women to have access to the valued goals of the society, and, as a consequence of this perhaps, were more likely to seek the dependence, support, and deference inherent in the role of the sick, and at the same time were more likely to perceive pregnancy as a personal crisis. In addition, account was taken of both inter- and intragenerational social mobility—the extent to which the woman and her family had experienced either a recent rise or decline in social-class position.

A third indicator was the kinds of social aspirations which the women expressed—how they saw themselves as striving toward the future in both the long and the short run. It was expected that those women who saw the future in essentially negative terms—as an avenue of escape from present difficulties and predicaments—would be more likely to seek the solace of the role of the sick than would women who saw their future as a means of positive goal-achievement. Conflicts in cultural values were also considered insofar as the woman expressed a commitment to values not commonly found among most women of her class position. Hence, it was expected that lower-class women who expressed many typically middle-class values—a crude indicator of alienation, if you will—and middle-class women who expressed many typically lower-class values would be more likely to become "ill" than would women who expressed values more consistent with their social-class position.

Further, self-image was tapped by asking each woman to judge herself as "higher" or "lower" than significant other persons in her round of life on the criteria of social, cultural, economic, and intellectual standing and physical attractiveness. It was anticipated that women with a low self-image would be more likely to enact the role of the sick than would women with a high self-image.

Account was also taken of the relation between each woman and her attending physician, and each situation was classified as either a role-conflict or a role-convergence situation. The first class comprised those in which the patient regarded her condition as an "illness" whereas the doctor did not— or vice versa. The second included those in which both doctor and patient conceived of pregnancy in an essentially similar fashion. It was thought that those patients in "conflict" with their doctor would be most likely to be those

Social Class
and
Becoming
"Ill"

335

who considered pregnancy as an illness and who, in turn, would most likely be women of lower social-class position.

Finally, the extent of each woman's belief in a series of common folk superstitions about nonnaturalistic and magical forces influencing pregnancy and childbirth was assessed. This included such ideas as "if a husband and wife quarrel, their baby will be ugly," "the absence of morning sickness is a sign the baby will be a boy," "the baby might die if you rock his cradle before it is born," "if a mother craves sweets, it is a sign the baby will be a girl," "shocking experiences to the mother tend to leave birth marks," and "morning sickness is a sign of a strong and healthy baby." We expected to find that lower-class women would be more committed to such forms of magical thought and would, at the same time, be more likely to regard themselves as "ill."

Three indicators of physiological problems were used. Length of labor time was drawn from the hospital records, as were indicators of gross difficulties during labor and delivery. Finally, the number of psychosomatic complaints which each patient had brought to the attention of her doctor was drawn from the records kept routinely in the examination room. It was anticipated that women who regarded themselves as "ill" during pregnancy would make many more psychosomatic complaints, have longer periods of active labor, and experience more gross problems and difficulties during the course of childbearing.

SUMMARY OF FINDINGS

Women of blue-collar status tended to regard themselves as more "sick" during pregnancy than did women of middle- or upper-middle-class status. Moreover, women who viewed the future—and, hence, the present—in negativistic and escapist terms were more drawn to the role of the "sick" than were others. In addition, those women who held to cultural values which were inconsistent with their objective social-class position were more prone to enact the role of the sick than were women whose value commitments were not of the alienated variety. Also, women with low self-images regarded themselves as more "ill" than did women with more positive self-esteem. And those women who were socially mobile—either upward or downward— were more likely to act the role of the sick than were those whose class position had remained relatively more stable. In addition, those women who were most likely to stand in a role-conflict situation with their doctor were those who regarded themselves as most "sick," which means, in turn, that the typical orientation of the physicians was that which viewed pregnancy as a normal, rather routine, and nonexempting event. Furthermore, those women whose prenatal care took place in the hospital clinic were not only more likely to stand in a role conflict with their physicians than were the privately cared-for women but also more likely to regard themselves as "ill" during the course of their lying-in. Finally, there was some evidence that women who regarded themselves as most sick were in fact those who subsequently experienced more gross difficulties and complications during labor and delivery—a near-classic example of the old dictum, "if a situation is defined as real, it is real in its consequences."

More important, however, was the consistent pattern with which blue-collar women were not only more prone to enact the role of the "ill" but also more likely to be characterized by other factors which were associated with high regard for self as sick. In comparison with the middle-class women, the blue-collar women were more likely to view the future in negativistic and grim terms, more likely to show a pattern of alienation in terms of attachment to values not normally in keeping with their social status, more likely to have a negative or otherwise inadequate self-image, more likely to have experienced recent upward or downward social mobility, more likely to have been confronted in the treatment setting by a physician who viewed pregnancy in different terms than they did, and more likely to have been treated in the hospital clinic with all the "illness"-invoking symbolism inherent in such establishments. It is not surprising, then, that it was the lower-class women who had, by and large, the longer lengths of labor time and more other difficulties during childbearing. In short, the physiological "facts" of illness were more pronounced among the blue-collar women, and likewise those social situations in which becoming "ill" seemed appropriate in terms of perceived expectations, and those factors and processes which were most likely to move one to seek the dependent role of the sick as a matter of reasonable alternative.

ENACTMENT OF THE ROLE OF THE SICK

The Middle Class and Psychosomatics:
the Blue-collar Class and Magical Thought

Just as there were many blue-collar women who regarded themselves as ill, so, too, there were a number of middle-class women who so thought of themselves. However, the ways in which each group expressed the fact of their having become "ill" were quite different. These middle-class women who saw themselves as sick tended to express such an attitude in the context of the medical-treatment setting by complaining to their doctor about a wide variety of body complaints and problems from which they said they had been suffering—each complaining about such things as earaches, headaches, nausea, dizziness, and the like. In short, they expressed their perception of self as sick in ways with which the medical professional could deal on his own medical terms. The blue-collar women who regarded themselves as sick, however, expressed remarkably few psychosomatic complaints. Rather, they resorted to a belief in the folklore of pregnancy and childbirth, which involved non-naturalistic explanations of cause and effect and which lay beyond the pale of modern medical science.

Thus, in general, four contrasting patterns existed among the middle-class women, on the one hand, and the blue-collar women on the other. The middle-class women were less likely than the blue-collars to regard themselves as sick. They were less often involved in those social situations in which becoming "ill" was a likely alternative. They were less often plagued by lengthy labor and complications in giving birth to their offspring. Finally, in those cases in which they did regard themselves as sick, they expressed such an attitude in the context of the medical-treatment setting and in terms which had both meaning and sense for the professional healer. The blue-collar women, however, were more likely to conceive of themselves as "ill." They were more often involved in patterns of life and situations likely to lead to the acceptance of the role of the sick. They were more often beset with actual physiological problems during labor and delivery. And, insofar as they did regard themselves as "ill," they eschewed the enactment of the sick role in medical terms and turned instead to folklore and magical thought.

"Illness" as a Personal Crisis

If relatively high educational attainment and greater exposure to the inroads that the "great tradition" of modern science makes upon the "lay traditions" of a people be considered perhaps as particularly important, it might be expected that middle-class women would be sensitized to the more currently popular professional images of sickness and health, as well as that they would be much more knowledgeable concerning the objective medical contingencies of childbirth in terms of physiology and morphology. Combine this with the middle-class woman's very real better chances for the survival of herself and her baby, and the pattern of low sick-role expectations among the middle-class women becomes not at all surprising. As one physician put it, "When a middle-class woman wants to try natural childbirth, it is usually because she wants to experience the whole affair of having a baby; when a lower-class woman wants to try, it is usually because she doesn't want to go under anaesthesia because she is afraid she won't wake up."

Consider the blue-collar woman[5]: the relative personal and social isolation in which she lives—isolated, at least, from the personal contacts and formal experiences by which one assimilates the meaning and significance of professional ministrations—the relatively minimal education she has achieved, and the life milieu in which she lives, where illness, incapacitation, and the like abound; and also the very real, heightened chances that either she or her baby may encounter either insult or accident during pregnancy—all of these factors and others combine to make the pattern of high sick-role expectations among this group particularly understandable. Considering also that the blue-collar woman is likely to be cared for in a clinic setting rather than by a private doctor, it is easy to see why she might regard herself as "ill." The middle-class woman choses her own physician—normally, on the basis of word-of-mouth advice from friends and relatives. She appears for her prenatal care in a treatment setting which has little of the symbolism of sickness—a

---

[5] There have been many characterizations of the life milieu of the lower class. The comments made in this paper are in debt to the following, among others: Donald E. Muir and E. A. Weinstein, "The Social Debt: An Investigation of Lower-Class and Middle-Class Norms of Social Obligation," *American Sociological Review* (August, 1962), pp. 532-39; S. M. Miller and F. Riessman, "The Working Class Subculture: A New View," *Social Problems* (Summer, 1961), pp. 86-97; Joseph A. Kahl, *The American Class Structure* (New York: Holt, Rinehart & Winston, Inc., 1953); Albert K. Cohen and H. M. Hodges, "Characteristics of the Lower-Blue-Collar-Class," *Social Problems* (Spring, 1963), pp. 303-34.

quite "living-room-like" waiting room, perhaps occupied by a nurse without a uniform. This is in dramatic contrast to the clinic-attending woman who experiences her treatment within the confines of a hospital, with ambulances going to and fro, with uniformed nurses and interns scurrying about, sometimes in apparent anxiety, with stainless steel, tile walls, and medicinal odors intermixed with medical machinery and equipment. Not only, then, does the life milieu and its attendant contingencies conspire to move the blue-collar woman toward the enactment of the role of the sick, but so, too, does the peculiar character of her obstetric-treatment episode.

The pattern of high psychosomatic complaints among the comparatively few high-sick-role middle-class women might be understood in something like the following fashion: For whatever reason the middle-class woman regards herself as "ill," it seems understandable that this should be expressed in psychosomatic terms in the context of the doctor-patient relationship. Given over as she is to the ultimately "normal" nature of pregnancy, and in view of what is sometimes regarded as the middle-class pattern of internalization of anxieties and conflicts, one might expect that the manifestation of concern about perceived illness should be expressed in covert psychosomatic terms. Considering also her greater knowledgeability about modern medical terms and practices, it seems natural that she should bring her complaints and worries to the attention of her doctor rather than to nonmedical persons to whom she might otherwise turn.

The enactment of the role of the sick by the lower-class woman, however, must be understood in somewhat different terms. Alienated as she is from the main stream of medical knowledge, more prone to externalizing her difficulties rather than internalizing them, standing in a position of great social distance from her educated and urbane physician, it seems unlikely that she will seek solace in psychosomatic or quasi-medical terms. And in further consideration of her low social-class position—with a lack of formal education and with extended kinship ties with grandmothers and great-aunts as lifelong agents of socialization—it seems more than reasonable that she should act out the anxiety she has over her "illness," not in the context of the doctor-patient relationship, but rather within the framework of her own lower-class subculture. Part of that subculture consists of a body of lore and superstition to which persons turn in the face of personal crises—not unlike the ways in which groups sometimes turn to bizarre and incredible ideologies which also deny the "real world" when faced with a perceived collective calamity. Pregnancy may be a personal crisis for a variety of reasons for either the lower- or the middle-class woman. But it is reasonable that the middle-class woman will turn to modern medical practice and the expression of bodily complaints within the medical-treatment setting in order to confront and deal with her crisis. But the blue-collar woman is more likely to eschew that alternative and face *her* personal crisis by means of a resort to that body of lore and belief which is an indigenous part of the subculture from which she comes and its associated constrained round of life.

Returning once again to the two contrasting images of the expectant mother, both of which are still current and available in American society: the trend appears to favor the "pirouetting dancer" above that which would "keep croaking companions away." If, indeed, there has been a very real change in the more appropriate model of conduct for expecting ladies, the material from this study would indicate that the blue-collar woman more often aspires to a form of conduct which has largely disappeared from the repertoire of conduct alternatives of the middle class. The blue-collar woman, in short, reflects a pattern of cultural lag in this respect. Students of collective behavior have taught us for many years that the circuit of fads and fashions is from the upper reaches of the system of social stratification to the lower. And if we include as fad and fashion all those patterns of behavior which are learned, which have symbolic meaning for persons, and which have sources within an identifiable social structure, then it seems particularly fitting to find that the blue-collar women in this study patterned their illness conduct upon a model which was "fashionable" among the middle class perhaps a generation or two ago.

Briefly, social-class position seems to be a basic component in defining the conditions—social, psychological, and medical—under which women come to regard themselves as "ill" and in molding the processes by which persons attempt to confront those situations which they regard as critical.

In regard to the first, a cogent statement by Jacobson is relevant:[6]

> Almost everyone is susceptible to the wiles of Dame Rumor. For nearly all possess an immodest twinge of avarice, vanity, provincialism, prejudice, partisanship, or escapism. These prevent the truth from entering the mind, allowing each to listen to whatever he desires to hear, believe what he wants to believe—to hear Dame Rumor's voice through the haze of error. Her words are irresistible. Indeed, they are maddening.

And relative to the second, Bockoven has said:[7]

> One lesson which can be derived from the history of institutional care . . . is that human beings are molded by whatever authority they respect and that ideas about human beings of authoritative origin eventually influence human behavior in the direction which confirms the authoritative idea.

Thus, "Dame Rumor," as a lyrical reference to all those collective ways by which persons embrace models for conduct, would tell us that the blue-collar fashion of meeting a personal crisis is no more fictional than that of the middle class. And, similarly, the self-fullfilling prophetic nature of "authoritative ideas" is illustrated in the fact that the blue-collar women who resorted to lore and magical thought experienced subsequent labor during childbirth which was no longer (nor apparently any more difficult) than was that of the middle-class women who enacted their crisis by means of psychosomatic complaints.

---

[6] David J. Jacobson, *The Affairs of Dame Rumor* (New York: Holt, Rinehart & Winston, Inc.,) p. 16.

[7] J. Sanbournce Bockoven, "Moral Treatment in American Psychiatry," *Journal of Nervous and Mental Disease* (August, 1956), p. 112.

The Underutilization of Medical-Care Services by Blue-Collarites

DANIEL ROSENBLATT
EDWARD A. SUCHMAN

INTRODUCTION

ONE of the characteristics of growth of the modern urban metropolis has been the need for a cheap source of unskilled labor. The technology of mass production until most recently has demanded the services of large numbers of "hands" to serve and tend the machines, or to perform simple operations which can later be assembled into more complex patterns.

Ideally, the concentration of large numbers of unskilled workers should need successive replacements as the unskilled workers either through greater training or experience (or, in the case of their children, through education) move up the occupational ladder. To some extent, this has been true, and New York has witnessed successive waves of migrations of indigent populations seeking jobs and a chance to rise in the occupational and class structure. On the other hand, sociological analysis indicates that, for many of the working class, the expectation is that they will continue to remain within the same class limits. The result over generations has been the creation of a genuine class system with its own expectations, values, and ways of living, often at variance with dominant middle-class orientations.

Traditionally, those segments of the working class who have been most divergent from middle-class standards have been characterized by the following traits: a high rate of unemployment, language problems, racial and ethnic diversity, high turnover of residence, low rate of upward mobility, and poor initiation into urban living. Ordinarily such people congregate in urban slum areas. The characteristics of slum dwelling have long been documented by sociologists, notably of the Chicago school: high rates of disease and mental illness, high rates of homicide, criminal and juvenile delinquency, high rates of alcoholism, drug addiction, prostitution, desertion, illegitimacy, and venereal disease, high rate of people on home relief, high rate of dropouts from school, low rate of belonging to voluntary associations, and so forth. In sum, all of the standard patterns of social disorganization are present as an obbligato to the theme of urban poverty.

Because these rates of social pathology and disorganization are relatively stable over time, it is clear that these problems of the urban slum are not transient but are deeply ingrained characteristics of metropolitan life. Seen in this context, health is only one of the areas of daily living where these people have unmet needs, and in some ways it does not represent their most salient needs. Official representatives of the New York City Health Department have been aware of this problem. For example, in planning a Public Health Practice Research Center, Deputy Commissioner Paul Densen states,

> The problem of the most effective way of getting the Health Department's services to the people who need them is a perennial one. That the establishment of clinics where people may avail themselves of their services is not enough is indicated by such things as the proportion of the population still unimmunized against poliomyelitis, by the proportion of women with little or no prenatal care, by the magnitude of the tuberculosis problem in certain areas of the City, and so forth. New kinds of "reaching out" devices need to be found to make further *strides* towards solving these problems.[1]

In similar fashion, in discussing the needs of a specific area of the city, Bedford-Stuyvesant, the notes from the Interdepartmental Health Council of June 26, 1962 states:

> Not only does it have enormous economic, health, housing, educational and other social problems, but it is seriously lacking in local leadership and organized services. . . . There was consensus that the complexity of the area's problems calls for a clear assessment of its needs and for a massive multi-service approach which will require a major outlay of funds. Piece-meal or emergent planning will accomplish little.[2]

In a slightly different emphasis, Dr. Leona Baumgartner, Commissioner of Health of New York, in a recent speech delivered at the 150th Anniversary Convocation of the Massachusetts General Hospital, addressed herself to the need for "radical changes . . . in the ways in which health and medical care services are organized and delivered."[3] The following report attempts to indicate the complexity of the general problem, *the underutilization of medical care,* by focusing on currently identifiable issues in the situation of New York City blue-collarites, and then goes on to mention some first attempts to introduce changes which will help modify this pattern.

RECENT DEMOGRAPHIC SHIFTS

During the last 15 years, there has been a dramatic redistribution of the population of New York City. Roughly one million New Yorkers have moved to the suburbs, while at the same time roughly another million nonwhites (Negroes and Puerto Ricans) have migrated to New York. Thus, although the number of inhabitants has remained approximately the same, the internal

---

[1] *Proposal for a Public Health Practice Research Center,* 1961, typed manuscript, p. 9.

[2] Minutes of IHC Meetings, June 26, 1962, typed manuscript, footnote pp. 1-2.

[3] *The Hospital, the Community and the Tragedy of Unused Medical Knowledge,* mimeographed speech, delivered Boston, Massachusetts, February 1, 1961, p. 2.

nature of the shift in subgroups of the population has great significance for the operation of all public health agencies. As a result of this fairly massive population movement, the urban blue-collar slum has grown within the core of the city, and, as the relative failure of the standard operation of the provision of health care becomes more apparent, new techniques of organization, administration, and the provision of medical and health services must be developed. The direction of some of these changes is highlighted by an understanding of the meaning of the population shift. Yet this simply represents the newer version of the old problem of the urban slum. One can perhaps best comprehend the significance of the shift in population by taking a look at the difference in economic and sociocultural groupings.

ECONOMIC AND CULTURAL FACTORS

On the economic level, the move to the suburbs meant that a largely middle-income or higher-income group, with its patterns of utilizing primarily private practitioners and voluntary hospitals, has departed from the city. In contrast with this, the new blue-collar migrants represent largely the lower part of the occupational ladder, with a consequent decrease in income level. Their patterns of utilization of medical care are constricted on the one hand by the lack of available funds and, perhaps more importantly, by the lack of sophistication in dealing with metropolitan private and public agencies offering services for the ill and indigent. Perhaps even more significant are the differences in sociocultural background between the two groups and the implications of these differences for the utilization of medical-care resources.

The Puerto Rican migrants represent a Spanish-speaking group with the patterns typical of Spanish colonial culture. Thus, in addition to the language barrier, Puerto Rican migrants to New York City, who have largely been blue-collar members of the lower socioeconomic and occupational strata, have had little contact with the highly organized and stratified structure of medical care in our metropolitan area. Moreover, their own concepts of disease and illness, of the seeking of medical care, and of treatment and rehabilitation differ from those of the American middle-class white-collar citizen. Similarly, the rural Negro who moves to New York from the South is also largely unacquainted with the elaborate patterning of medical-care services offered in urban settings, and he too shares different lay traditions and images of medical practice, the meaning of disease, illness, treatment, rehabilitation, and so forth.

TREATMENT BY PROFESSIONALS—AGENTS OF MEDICAL CARE

One special aspect of this problem that has important implications for the New York City Health Department is that many of the blue-collar urban poor and the new blue-collar migrants have had so little contact with professional members of medical-care specialties that, even though there may be an overt outbreak of symptomatology which is recognized as such by the individuals, their first recourse is to the lay referral network of immediate friends and relatives. This "lay referral system," in Eliot Freidson's terms, often consists of pseudo- and para-medical healers, such as fortunetellers, mediums, or makers of home remedies.[4] Later it may include semiprofessionals, such as the chiropractor, the faith healer, and so on. Only after a series of successive failures at treatment may one find such individuals coming to the official agencies for treatment. In other words, it is not a part of the tradition of medical care for the new groups to seek competent professional medical care at an early stage of illness. In part this may be due to high medical costs, lack of familiarity with modern medical practice, a general alienation from all official agencies, and so forth. Nonetheless, means of changing attitudes and behavior of this group in this regard must be developed.

PREVENTIVE BEHAVIOR

The concept of preventive medical care is largely a development of the middle-class culture of Western societies, most especially in Northern Europe and the United States. It is only within these groups that one finds a fairly elaborated structure of routine prenatal and postnatal care, of pediatric services with immunizations, of detection of caries, and screening for TB, cancer, diabetes, and so forth. Among the urban poor and the newer migrants to New York City, preventive care is frequently nonexistent, even for immunizations. Prenatal care, for example, is usually limited to the last trimester. Some research has indicated that this failure to use preventive facilities is not due to a lack of awareness of the existence of the facilities of the Health Department, but that instead one must look to an understanding of other factors and patterns in order to understand and then change this behavior.

For example, it is possible that in some measure the lack of preventive health orientation is another dimension of a general lack of future orientation that characterizes blue-collar workers. The problem is not wholly financial, although it may be aggravated by it. For example, regular checkups of automobiles to detect incipient repairs are not in the general value system of blue-collarites. In similar fashion, household objects are often worn out and discarded rather than repaired at an early stage of disintegration.

The body can be seen as simply another class of objects to be worn out but not repaired. Thus, teeth are left without dental care, and later there is often small interest in dentures, whether free or not. In any event, false teeth may be little used. Corrective eye examinations, even for those people who wear glasses, is often neglected, regardless of clinic facilities. It is as though the white-collar class thinks of the body as a machine to be preserved and kept in perfect functioning condition, whether through prosthetic devices, rehabilitation, cosmetic surgery, or perpetual treatment, whereas blue-collar groups think of the body as having a limited span of utility: to be enjoyed in youth and then to suffer with and to endure stoically with age and decrepitude. It may be that a more damaged self-image makes more acceptable a more damaged physical adjustment.

In this connection, concepts of illness differ for the two groups. For the blue-collar workers, with their greater distance from the whole medical-care

[4] Eliot Freidson, "Client Control and Medical Practice," *American Journal of Sociology,* Vol. 65 (1960), p. 377.

system, illness is related to dysfunction in work, primarily related to incapacitating symptoms. Symptoms which do not incapacitate are often ignored. For the white-collar groups, illness will also relate to conditions which do not incapacitate but simply by their existence call forth medical attention.

EDUCATION AND BELIEF IN RATIONALITY

In all cultures, the individual who suffers from illness is exposed to the anxieties which being sick engenders. Members of a sophisticated technological society ordinarily counter this tendency toward anxiety in part by relying on their educational backgrounds and exhibiting faith in the ability of modern medical science to help solve problems. This belief in rational scientific processes in the face of overwhelming anxiety is usually characteristic of more highly educated groups than it is of poorly educated groups.

Here, once again, one may contrast the difference between the blue-collar urban poor and the newer blue-collar migrants to New York on the one hand with the group which has left for the suburbs on the other hand. The Negroes and Puerto Ricans, as members of groups which are not as highly educated as the average New Yorker, are not as "rational" in their attitudes toward health and in the seeking of medical care when faced with illness and misfortune. In part, the problem becomes one of influencing the elements of culture which will facilitate the newer migrants' and the urban poor's taking part in the rational health services offered by the agencies within metropolitan New York.

PREJUDICE

Although good medical care explicitly excludes a prejudiced response on the part of practitioners toward members of other races, religions, or ethnic groups, it would be näive to assume that this proscription pervades the actions of *all* personnel. In the previous sections, we have discussed the necessity of understanding the special points at which the psychological and social background of the blue-collar urban poor and the newer blue-collar migrants affects their behavior in adjusting to medical care as found in New York. At the same time, it is necessary to be sure that the personnel of New York agencies are aware of the different attitudes of the blue-collar urban poor and the newer blue-collar migrants, and that every effort is made to reduce any prejudice which may exist on the part of personnel. In this connection, one might note that, when such prejudice exists on the part of current personnel, they not only succeed in making it difficult for the blue-collarites to seek medical care, but they also discourage them from even beginning to approach agencies and facilities. If any agency acquires a lay reputation as not wanting Negroes and Puerto Ricans to apply for help, it will soon find itself with a reduced caseload from these groups, regardless of the truth of the rumor. The groups in question are sensitive to their status of so-called second-class citizenship and, even in the case of serious illness, will hesitate to utilize agencies or facilities which they perceive as unsympathetic or unfriendly.

As the area of prejudice is a particularly sensitive one in the field of medical care, it is one that especially needs further investigation.

ANOMIE

Finally, one may recognize that the summation of all of these threats to personal and social integration may often result in what sociologists have called "anomie," a condition of normlessness, characterized by an excessive withdrawal from the social fabric, isolation, self-estrangement, a feeling of powerlessness and meaninglessness. In the context of anomie, it is not enough for the public-spirited official merely to provide services for these groups. The provision of such services takes place within the framework outlined in the early pages of this report, and unless something is done to alter that context, one may safely predict the continued underutilization of health services for this type of individual and community.

IMPERSONALITY, BUREAUCRATIZATION, AFFECTIVE NEUTRALITY, AND ACHIEVEMENT

Certain of the values of the blue-collar urban poor and the newer blue-collar migrants to New York contrast with those of dominant middle-class citizens. At the same time, certain of the expectations toward the setting and provision of medical services are also different. The white member of the middle class may not like it, but he is accustomed to accepting the fact that his hospital will be a large and complex organization in which he as a patient becomes separated from his family, is expected to become fairly passive, and is relatively helpless about looking after his own needs. He expects to be a tiny cog in a big, fairly impersonal structure, and he knows that, in many instances, the doctor and nurse will be more interested in his chart, or his temperature, than they are in him. On the one hand, his own unique qualities as a person are lost, or, as Erving Goffman might say, his self becomes reduced at the same time that he becomes subject to the rules and regulations of a large-scale, rationalized, bureaucratic organization.[5] Because he has been raised within this system, the white middle-class American has certain adjustive mechanisms for coping with these aspects of medical care.

The blue-collar urban poor and the newer blue-collar migrants to New York, however, come from backgrounds where the organization of medical care has not been so fully elaborated in terms of its bureaucratic hierarchy and complexity, where the individual is not submitted to the same degree of impersonal care once he decides to submit himself for clinic treatment or hospitalization.

Here, once more, one notes the need for adjusting the values and expectations of the newer blue-collar migrants and urban blue-collar poor to the practice of modern medical care, as well as for the exploration of techniques for modifying that practice for the benefit of all New Yorkers.

ROSENBLATT
SUCHMAN

[5] See, in this connection, the chapter "On the Characteristics of Total Institutions," in *Asylums* (Chicago: Aldine Publishing Company, 1961), pp. 3-124.

Another problem arises because of the traditional means of organizing medical care. Until very recently, the organization of medical care was oriented toward specialization of function. Patients were referred by specialized agencies to specialists in specialty clinics. The result was often that, although a specific organ or condition might receive excellent care, the patient as a whole tended to become fragmented in his medical care among the various agencies, clinics, specialists, and records. For this reason, in the last few years, there has been a persistent attempt to initiate demonstration research projects designed to offer comprehensive medical care on an integrated interagency basis. The New York City Health Department has been an active leader in this movement, and several of the following studies have been initiated as a direct attempt to find new ways of dealing with the organization of medical care for largely medically indigent groups. The first projects mentioned below deal with only welfare recipients, the next deal with special populations—the needy aged and the young adult—whereas the last one deals with a special ethnic group.

The Cornell Medical Welfare Demonstration Project is based on a fairly wide geographic area: the Welfare District. Instead of offering comprehensive medical care to this whole population, the Cornell Project has limited itself to a study of 1,000 families who are actively encouraged to seek their medical care from the New York Hospital. The aim of the project is to deal with the health needs of a special group of a much larger population, a sample of welfare families within a given district. An additional aim is to concentrate on initiating changes within the medical care that is provided, such as having, insofar as possible, a "family" physician. But it is limited with regard to social care, for the most part limiting itself to referrals to other social agencies, or, sometimes, coordinating interagency contacts. The attempt is made to reduce intrahospital fragmentation.

Briefly, the Cornell Project offers *comprehensive medical care* to a *representative sample* of a particular segment of a *large urban area* (a whole Welfare District), with little concern for social work and agency referrals. This project is now in its fourth year of operation and has been successful in maintaining contact with the majority of its 1,000 families. In so doing, it is managing to change the utilization patterns from over-reliance on home visits to more office visits on an appointment basis.

Persons eligible for the *St. Vincent's Medical Care Project* are those who live in the hospital service area and are on the rolls of the District Welfare Center. Because it was felt desirable to start slowly, the program is currently available only to those welfare clients who present themselves at the hospital for one or another reason.

When a patient is thus taken into the project, members of his family living in the same household also become project members—arrangements to see family members being made as indicated.

After certain personal data on the patient and his family are obtained and

The
Underutilization
of
Medical-Care
Services
by
Blue-Collarites

347

an initial medical evaluation is completed, patients are placed under the general supervision of the project's managing physician. They are referred as needed to specialty clinics for consultation, except where the best interests of the patient suggest that immediate management may best be carried out in the specialty clinic. In either case, the over-all care of the patient continues to be the responsibility of the project physician.

Home visiting, home care, and nursing-home liaison are planned for as part of the project.

Although similar to the Cornell Project, the St. Vincent's Project is building more slowly. In both there is an attempt to introduce loyalty to both the hospital and the physician in conjunction with offering comprehensive medical care and new dignity to the welfare client.

The Health Insurance Plan of Greater New York is also providing comprehensive medical care on a prepaid basis to a large segment of persons receiving Old Age Assistance and Medical Aid to the Aged in New York City. Under this program, about 13,000 of the 40,000 indigent aged will be brought into the main stream of medical-care services now being received by the 640 thousand H.I.P. members. This constitutes a basic change in the method and type of medical care to be obtained by these aged persons. The present fragmented approach to medical care is to be replaced by an integrated-group-practice system which stresses continuity of medical care. Much of the care will be offered at regular H.I.P. centers.

Essentially, this plan focuses on an element of medically indigent clients— the aged—and offers them an opportunity to receive the same medical services as other members of H.I.P., with government agencies underwriting the premium. The next program designs a special service restricted to the local needs of a similar group of aged persons.

These three projects—*New York Hospital, St. Vincent's,* and *H.I.P.*—all deal with persons on the rolls of the Welfare Department.

The Queensbridge Health Maintenance Service is primarily designed to demonstrate the practicality of offering comprehensive medical care to a group of elderly individuals of low income, all of whom are resident within a specific housing project. The health station is located within the housing project and is thus convenient to the group being offered services. At the same time, the Health Center offers the advantage of familiar surroundings and, for many of the patients, a long history of minimal contact—at least, with the housing project's central office. As part of its program of medical care, the staff of the Queensbridge Medical Unit coordinates the needs of its clients for referrals to social agencies, hospitals, and clinics.

Briefly, the Queensbridge development represents a *compact geographic area* (a housing project) and selects from among all of the residents a *special catgeory of persons,* the aged, to each of whom *comprehensive medical and social care* are offered. To date, the Queensbridge Center has been able to recruit more than half of the available aged population without any intensive advertising of this group. The majority percentage continues to remain under care.

In contrast to the obvious health needs of the aged, a special project has been started to follow through on the young men who are rejected for service in the Armed Forces as a result of their selective service examination. The Health Department is concerned to see that whatever unmet medical needs exist for this group are offered a referral for further care. A secondary emphasis in this program is to inspect previous school health records to learn whether or not the health problems had been noted and what steps were taken to help correct them.

The last project to be discussed took place a great distance, both geographically and culturally, from New York City, yet it is hoped that it will have important consequences for medical care in an urban environment. *The Cornell Navaho Project* offered medical care to a group of widely dispersed members of the Navaho tribe, an ethnic group with its own traditions of medicine. In order to communicate effectively with the members of the group, the project staff developed the concept of the *health visitors*. Health visitors were recruited from among native Navahos and trained briefly in Western concepts of medicine. They served as translators, as advance contacts, and, more significantly, as a cultural bridge between the traditional Navaho patterns and the innovations of Western medicine. Through sensitive and imaginative use of the role of the health visitor, the project was able to reach a large number of Navahos and to offer a wider range of health services than had ever been possible.

Since the New York City Health Department is often faced with similar problems of underutilization of health services by members of some of its ethnic groups, it has been eager to see if any of the lessons learned by the Navaho project are applicable to the New York area, and current plans aim at a demonstration project with an adaptation of this new health visitor to an urban setting.

It seems clear that, for the future, official health agencies must provide the lead in closing the gap that has developed between the modern, highly technical, bureaucratically organized practice of medicine and the traditional social organization of the blue-collar workers. In its search for new techniques of care and treatment, modern medicine has until recently been largely free to develop along lines that were for the most part dictated by the rationality and logic of science or protected from the examination of its own nonrational processes by the immunity of medical practitioners from outside influences. However, it has been obvious for some time now that for modern medicine to continue its advance, it must adapt itself to new forms of social organization that will ensure a return to its original purposes. Some adjustment will have to be made so that the relative alienation of large segments of society will be corrected. The blue-collar group would seem to offer an excellent arena for renewed efforts toward and experience in bringing into line the practice of modern medicine with the needs of society.

The
Underutilization
of
Medical-Care
Services
by
Blue-Collarites

349

Illness Behavior of the Working Class: Implications and Recommendations*

IRVING KENNETH ZOLA

ILLNESS AND POVERTY

TRADITIONALLY, illness has been thought to be the direct and inevitable result of poverty. Although the relationship is no longer considered direct, the two remain somewhat intertwined. Both are generally felt to be evils which ought to be eliminated wherever possible. Although it may be difficult to quarrel with this idea as a value, as a frame of reference for research it has colored our approach to these problems, particularly in what has been studied and how results have been presented.

Running through the social-class literature in the United States is the implicit notion that the middle-class way of life is good and should be striven for. Members of other social strata are, thus, described in terms of how close they approach this model (for example, upwardly mobile, high or low achievers). Likewise, because illness is bad (and perhaps, as Talcott Parsons states, interferes with the capacity to achieve and thus be middle-class), it is good to consult a doctor. Patients are, thus, described in terms of how promptly and appropriately they consult a physician (for example, how much they delay, to what degree they participate in immunization or mass testing campaigns).

Using such implicit models, research in both areas has been concerned with why deviations exist. For example, what is it about the lower class that prevents them from being more middle-class, from achieving, from being upwardly mobile? Is it poor parental supervision, poor planning, poor training? Or are they constitutionally inferior, or naturally lazy and immoral?

* The data on which this paper is based were collected while the author was Assistant Sociologist, Department of Psychiatry, Massachusetts General Hospital, and located in the Medical Out-Patient Department of that institution. I would like to gratefully acknowledge the continuing support, financial and otherwise, given this research by Dr. Erich Lindemann, Department of Psychiatry, and Dr. Walter Bauer, Department of Medicine. I would also like to thank Dr. John Stoeckle, Dr. Philip E. Slater, and Mrs. Leonora K. Zola for their criticisms and comments on the design of the original study as well as the resulting papers.

Similarly, research on illness or, more specifically, when people consult a doctor, has focused on why they delay so long and do not participate. Studies of patient delay have in turn indicated poor parental health supervision and health training, inadequate and inaccurate health information, as well as personal characteristics, such as being obsessed with guilt and fear, having personality problems, or being too "busy" or "lazy" to care. That both the studies of lower-class life, in general, and delay in seeking medical aid, specifically, seem to emphasize a great many similar negative attributes is not accidental. Most "delayers" and "nonparticipators" have usually also been described as being of lower- or working-class background.

A SHIFT IN RESEARCH FOCUS

In recent years, there has been a growing emphasis on the observation of peculiarly lower-class value orientations and the contention that these standards emanate from the nature of their own life situation and not as a reaction or offshoot of middle-class life. Although part of this has been a reaction to the traditional emphasis on negative qualities or lack of middle-class qualities, which lower- or blue-collar class have been observed, or more accurately, interpreted to possess, much of the shift was due to the fact that variation or deviation from the middle-class model simply did not explain a great deal of lower-class behavior. To take a rather simple example, the crime, delinquency, gambling, mental illness, and so forth, observed in the lower class was thought to be indicative of, as well as the result of, social disorganization, a breakdown of traditional (that is, middle-class) norms and of family and neighborhood ties. Closer observation, however, demonstrated that these deviant activities, as well as much of lower-class life, were indeed highly social, highly organized, and infused with traditional ties and loyalties.

The study of delay has similarly led up many blind alleys. For while long lists of cogent reasons have been found as to why people delay, it is a curious fact that these reasons were all culled from people who *had* eventually sought treatment. Although their fears, guilt, dissatisfaction, or ignorance might have been barriers to seeking early treatment, their eventual coming to the doctor did not turn on the resolution of these problems. The answer may lie in what anthropologists call *value orientations*—standards and criteria which help shape what is considered symptomatic, what is and is not worthy of attention and concern. By asking the patient why he comes rather than why he delayed, light might be shed on the specific circumstances surrounding his decision, and thus also on the possible existence of criteria or value orientations which determined when his "limits of tolerance of his symptoms" are reached.

Although interested in the study of the decision-making process, it also seemed to us worthwhile to determine, if possible, some of the sources of these value orientations. Since most "delayers" and "nonparticipators" have usually been described as being of lower-class background, we decided to sample from individuals at that end of the socioeconomic continuum. The lower classes, however, are not a homogeneous group. As has been pointed out by many observers, there are still heavy concentrations of ethnic groups in

Illness
Behavior
of the
Working Class:
Implications
and
Recommendations

this segment of our population. Although our country has traditionally the reputation of being the melting-pot of nationality, there is considerable evidence that one's cultural heritage dies slowly. Because this study was carried out in Boston, and since the importance of ethnic groups in this area had been repeatedly documented, ethnicity was chosen as a further specification of our lower-class sample.

DIFFERENCES IN PRESENTING SYMPTOMATOLOGY

The data from our study were derived from interviews with 196 new patients to the Eye, the Ear, Nose and Throat, and the Medical Clinics of the Massachusetts General Hospital and the Massachusetts Eye and Ear Infirmary. There were almost equal numbers of men and women. All the patients were of lower socioeconomic background (that is, primarily blue-collar workers, their spouses, or their children), white, between the ages of 18 and 50, able to converse in English, and of either Italian Catholic, Irish Catholic, or Anglo-Saxon Protestant ancestry. Each respondent was interviewed before being seen by his examining physician.

What was initially striking about our lower-class patients was the range of responses and reactions to illness and disease—a range unattributable to the disorders for which they sought aid.[2] When a subsample of patients were matched for diagnoses, there were still significant cultural differences in where and how they expressed their chief complaint, whether or not they would admit the presence of pain or irritability, and even in the number of symptoms presented to the doctor.

The most striking (that is, statistically significant) differences were between the working-class Italian and Irish patients. In many of the major symptom comparisons, the Anglo-Saxons occupied a middle position, although in virtually all instances they were "closer" to the Irish. Thus, we found that our lower-class Irish patients tended to deny many aspects of being ill: they denied the presence of pain or any effect of their illness in other than physical behavior, and they tended to be concerned with and express their

---

[2] This paper will report only some of the research highlights, since the detailed findings, methodology, and more general review and discussion are available elsewhere: John D. Stoeckle, Irving K. Zola, and Gerald E. Davidson, "On Going to See the Doctor, The Contributions of the Patient to the Decision to Seek Medical Aid: A Selective Review," *Journal of Chronic Disease,* Vol. 16 (September 1963), pp. 975-89; John D. Stoeckle, Irving K. Zola, and Gerald E. Davidson, "The Quantity and Significance of Psychological Distress in Medical Patients—Some Preliminary Observations About the Decision to Seek Medical Aid," forthcoming in the *Journal of Chronic Diseases;* John D. Stoeckle and Irving K. Zola, "After Everyone Can Pay for Medical Care—Some Perspectives on Future Treatment and Practice," *Medical Care,* Vol. 2 (January-March 1964), pp. 36-41, Irving K. Zola, "Sociocultural Factors in the Seeking of Medical Aid," doctoral dissertation, Harvard University, Department of Social Relations, 1962; Irving K. Zola, "Socio-Cultural Factors in the Seeking of Medical Aid—A Progress Report," *Transcultural Psychiatric Research,* Vol. 14 (April, 1963), pp. 62-65; Irving K. Zola, "Problems of Communication, Diagnosis and Patient Care: The Interplay of Patient, Physician, and Clinic Organization," *Journal of Medical Education,* Vol. 38 (October, 1963), pp. 829-38; Irving K. Zola, "Paths to the Doctor—An Analysis of Patient Decisions," presented at 1963 annual meetings of the Society for Applied Anthropology; Irving K. Zola, "Culture and Symptomatology—An Analysis of Presenting Complaints," submitted for publication.

symptoms in terms of a specific location and to emphasize as their chief complaint a rather specific malfunction or impairment. The lower-class Italians, on the other hand, did not localize their symptoms. They felt that pain was an important part of their disorder. They emphasized complaints of a more diffuse and general malfunctioning and presented more symptoms to the doctor. Finally, they were quite vocal in telling how their symptoms interfered with their daily functioning, often making them irritable and difficult to get along with.

These findings on the variability and range of responses to symptoms set the stage for the crux of the study—the specific timing of the decision to see a doctor.

THE TIMING OF DECISIONS TO SEE A DOCTOR

Most impressive in the study of the decision to seek medical aid was the relative lack of importance of the symptoms themselves in this process. It was not the symptoms themselves that changed or worsened, or that new physical complications arose. Moreover, the timing of the decision did not revolve around the reversal or the resolving of their stated reasons for delay. "Something happened," which could be delineated into five triggers, circumstances, or conditions which spurred the individual to seek medical aid when he did.

The first pattern was called "interpersonal crisis," particularly interesting in the light of all the current work on stress and crisis in the causation of disease. Here, however, it was not the symptoms which led to a crisis, or even vice versa, but rather that an interpersonal crisis called attention to the symptoms —caused the patient to dwell on them and finally to do something about them.

A second circumstance involved "social interference." Although the symptoms did not change, a new or additional perception of them arose. Thus, what was previously a bothersome and endurable difficulty now became a threat to valued social activities. (For example, a high school senior with early-evening headaches sought aid when he discovered he might not be able to attend his prom.)

The third circumstance, "the presence of sanctioning," involved the patient's unwillingness to decide or acknowledge that he wanted or needed a doctor. Instead, he relinquished this responsibility to someone else by placing himself in a position where he was "told" to go.

The fourth trigger, like the second, "social interference," concerns a "perceived threat," but here the nature of the activity was vocational or avocational.

The fifth circumstance, "nature and quality of the symptoms," most commonly involved an inferred attribute of the symptoms: its resemblance to previous ones, or ones like a friend's; some time limit (day, week, month) in his endurance, or attributing to his symptoms a periodic element (for example, once was O.K. but twice. . . . .) It was this imposition of a seemingly arbitrary criterion or standard (that is, according to medical evidence) which these cases had in common.

Other investigators have cited one or more of these circumstances as

Illness
Behavior
of the
Working Class:
Implications
and
Recommendations

reasons why an individual decided or was pushed to seek help.[3] What is striking in our study, in addition to the findings being less retrospective than most, is that these triggers were used differentially within this group of lower-class patients. In short, their use varied significantly (that is, in statistical significance) with ethnic group membership: "Interpersonal crisis" and "social interference" were used more often by the Italians. The third condition, "the presence of sanctions" was overwhelmingly the Irish pattern. The fourth circumstance, "interference with a vocational or avocational activity" was a minor secondary pattern of the Irish but was the most common pattern of the Anglo-Saxons. The fifth trigger, "the nature and quality of symptoms," although used to some extent by all the ethnic groups, was utilized by proportionately more Anglo-Saxons than anyone else.

In addition to these ethnic differences, there is evidence that social-class factors are also operating. Apple has postulated that ". . . to middle-class Americans, to be ill means to have an ailment of recent origin which interferes with one's usual activity."[4] *Usual activities* in her study referred to such things as vocational and avocational activities—the trigger used most often by the Anglo-Saxons in our study. Moreover, "interference in vocational or avocational activity" and "the nature and quality of the symptoms" have an additional characteristic in common. They seem to involve a more impersonal and emotionally neutral decision-making process than do the others, and emotional neutrality is a characteristic commonly attributed to the Protestant middle class.[5]

This similarity between attitudes of our Anglo-Saxon group and what is commonly called "middle-class" attitudes may not be surprising, since on several criteria, such as education, occupation, and parents' social class, they are more "middle-class" than the other two ethnic groups. In this regard, it is worth mentioning the one situation where education (the ladder to success in middle-class society) was directly related to the timing of decisions: Amongst college-educated males (there were an insufficient number of college-educated females to make a similar comparison), there was a blurring of ethnic distinctions. In that educational category, all the men tended to resem-

---

[3] See, for example, Dorrian Apple, "How Laymen Define Illness," *Journal of Health and Human Behavior*, Vol. 1 (Spring, 1960), pp. 219-25; Eliot Freidson, *Patient's Views of Medical Practice* (New York: Russell Sage Foundation, 1961); Charles Kadushin, "Individual Decisions to Undertake Psychotherapy," *Administrative Science Quarterly*, Vol. 3 (December, 1958), pp. 379-411; Erwin L. Linn, "Agents, Timing, and Events Leading to Mental Hospitalization," *Human Organization*, Vol. 20 (Summer, 1961), pp. 92-98; David Mechanic and Edmund Volkart, "Stress, Illness Behavior and the Sick Role," *American Sociological Review*, Vol. 26 (February, 1961), pp. 51-59; Peter Sifneos, "A Concept of Emotional Crisis," *Mental Hygiene*, Vol. 44 (April, 1960), pp. 160-79; Carroll A. Whitmer and C. Glenn Conover, "A Study of Critical Incidents in the Hospitalization of the Mentally Ill," *Social Work*, (January, 1959), pp. 89-94; Edwin C. Wood, John M. Rakusen, and Emanuel Morse, "Interpersonal Aspects of Psychiatric Hospitalization," *Archives of General Psychiatry*, Vol. 3 (December, 1960), pp. 632-41.

[4] Apple, *op. cit.*

[5] As for symptomatology, the Anglo-Saxons presented neither a great many nor an exceptionally few symptoms. They also neither tended to admit nor to deny irritability. They did, however, tend to focus for the chief complaint on a specific malfunction or impairment. Considering their middle position on most items, a case might well be made that this, too, connotes some degree of emotional neutrality.

ble one another and the Irish and Italian patients tended to utilize more frequently the triggers "interference with vocational or avocational activity" and "nature and quality of symptoms"—the two triggers used most frequently by the Anglo-Saxons or more middle-class patients.

Thus, the first three circumstances, "interpersonal crisis," "social interference," and "the presence of sanctioning," may be more working-class mechanisms and the last two, "interference with vocation or avocational activity" and "the nature and quality of the symptoms" more middle-class.

IMPLICATIONS AND DISCUSSION

The analytic emphasis in this study has been on the association between sociocultural background and both differing responses and different reactions to essentially the same experience (that is, similar diseases and disorders). The mechanism whereby this relationship between cultural factors (for example, class and cultural background) and perception is produced has, however, not been investigated. The assumption has been that it was achieved through the transmission of certain cultural values or culturally conditioned ways of responding to a vast array of crises, including illness. With our present data, we cannot prove that this is so, but we can at least note the compatibility of our findings with much of the existing literature on these class and ethnic groups.[6]

This study hopefully, then, has implications beyond the documentation of sociocultural differences. For it seems apparent that, when we talk of making medical care available for all Americans, it must be realized how different in many respects we still are. As has been found in the mental health research, there is an enormous gulf between lay and professional opinion as to when mental illness is present and when as well as what kind of help is needed. Differences such as these are neither simply quantitative nor the result of inaccurate knowledge. These differences are qualitative and, if our theorizing is correct, they reflect not merely something inadequately learned (that is, wrong medical knowledge), but rather something quite solidly imbedded. They are, more likely, part of the value orientations and experiences that one has been subject to from early childhood and that influence what kinds of things and behaviors one considers important and, thus, when one should be upset enough to do something.

[6] See, for example, Dorian Apple, *op. cit.;* Conrad M. Arensberg and Solon T. Kimball, *Family and Community in Ireland* (Cambridge: Harvard University Press, 1948); Sydney H. Croog, "Ethnic Origins and Responses to a Health Questionnaire," *Human Organization,* Vol. 20 (Summer, 1961), pp. 65-69; Marshall McLuhan, *The Mechanical Bride* (New York: Vanguard Press, 1950); Marvin K. Opler and Jerome L. Singer, "Ethnic Differences in Behavior and Psychopathology: Italian and Irish," *International Journal of Social Psychiatry,* Vol. 2 (Summer, 1956), pp. 11-22; Anne Parsons, "Family Dynamics in Southern Italian Schizophrenics," *Archives of General Psychiatry,* Vol. 3 (November, 1960), pp. 507-18; Talcott Parsons, "Definitions of Health and Illness in the Light of American Values and Social Structure," in E. Gartly Jaco, ed., *Patients, Physicians and Illness* (New York: The Free Press of Glencoe, Inc., 1958), pp. 165-87; Mark Zborowski, "Cultural Components in Response to Pain," in E. Gartly Jaco, ed., *Patients, Physicians and Illness* (New York: The Free Press of Glencoe, Inc., 1958), pp. 256-68.

Because there may be a large number of these frames of reference in any given population, this would help explain why medical men have had such difficulty in attempting to set any absolute standards, definitions, and measures of sickness and disability.

The remaining pages of this paper will delineate a number of other implications based on the approach and findings outlined in this study.

RESEARCH AND CAUSATION

There is an implication in our work for the type of research which is generally done to determine the causation of many diseases and disorders. If, as many "evaluation" health surveys are demonstrating, treated illness is only a portion, and not necessarily the largest portion, of the existing symptoms and pathology in a given population, and if, as the present study claims, both the perception of and the reaction to physiological disturbances and aberrations are not necessarily related to the objective nature of the disorder, and if the decision to seek medical aid is based more on social-psychological circumstances than purely biological-physiological ones, then studies of the causation of disorders based only on treated populations may be on shakier grounds than is commonly realized.

Thus, it was formerly believed that Buerger's disease was prevalent in Eastern European Jews. Later it was discovered that this evidence was due not so much to the nature of the disease as to the fact that Dr. Buerger made his observations at Mount Sinai Hospital.[7] Mechanic and Volkart recently reported that persons with a high tendency to seek medical aid were significantly more likely than low-tendency persons to report to the health service for diagnosis of "routine illness" (respiratory, viral, bacterial). Those illnesses classified as "nonroutine" (allergies and skin conditions, poisonings) did not show statistically significant relations to the inclination to seek medical care.[8] Accordingly, clinic and hospital cases used for the study of these "routine" illnesses may represent a biased sample unsuitable for generalization to the larger general population having that illness. A recent study by Cobb has shed doubt on the traditional emphasis on arthritis as being a predominantly female disease. When all the employed males in a factory were surveyed for prodromal arthritic symptoms, regardless of whether or not they were under treatment, their rates were as high as any of those traditionally reported for women.[9] It thus seems that the oft-reported sexual difference in arthritis was due more to a greater tendency for women to seek aid for arthritic-type symptoms and, thus, to appear in morbidity statistics. Finally, Mishler and Waxler, in studying the decision processes in hospitalization for mental illness, came to a similar conclusion about the problems of studying causation in treated populations (italics mine):

---

[7] Melitta Schmideberg, "Social Factors Affecting Diagnostic Concepts," *International Journal of Social Psychiatry*, Vol. 7 (Fall, 1961), pp. 222-30.

[8] David Mechanic and Edmund Volkart, "Illness Behavior and Medical Diagnosis," *Journal of Health and Human Behavior*, Vol. 1 (Summer, 1960), pp. 86-94.

[9] Sidney Cobb, "Epidemiology of Rheumatoid Arthritis," *Academy of Medicine of New Jersey*, Vol. 9 (1963), pp. 52-60.

There is an important implication of these findings for studies that are restricted to populations of patients who are "in treatment" whether the locus of treatment be the office of the private practitioner or the ward of the mental hospital. Our data not only permit but force the conclusion that the patients in treatment, in this instance "admitted" to the hospital, are not a representative sample of patients seeking such care, *nor by implications, of all mentally ill persons.*[10]

PROBLEMS OF DIAGNOSIS AND TREATMENT

Another implication touches on the problems of diagnosis and treatment. Although there has long been recognition of the subjectivity and variability in a patient's reporting of his symptoms and his reasons for seeking aid, little attention has been paid to the fact that this reporting may be influenced by sociocultural factors. In our study, the lack of awareness of such socio-cultural differences in the concern, expression of illness, and reporting on the part of physicians led to an apparent bias in the type of diagnosis given certain patients of our lower class. For example, the Italian responses in our study could be characterized as "overemotional," and in certain instances this could have an effect on the diagnosis they received. When the diagnoses of all patients who had "nothing organically wrong" were analyzed, the Italians were found to have received significantly more diagnoses which implied an emotional origin to their symptoms than did the Irish and Anglo-Saxon patients, who received diagnoses which merely stated that no known organic disease or pathology was present.[11] This situation was no doubt aggravated by the considerable cultural and class differences between the patients and the staff. The latter were predominantly of middle-class Anglo-Saxon Protestant background.

Another situation in which a difference in reactions and perceptions of symptoms is particularly acute is that where the diagnosis is dependent to a large extent on what the patient is able, willing, or thinks important enough to tell the doctor. Two diseases immediately come to mind—appendicitis and certain types of heart disease. In both it is particularly important for the patient to be able to specify the exact amount, type, and location of pain. On what the patient communicates may well depend the decision to operate or, at very least, to hospitalize. If the patient does not define certain types of discomfort or pain, or if, as in Navaho culture, there is simply no terminology (and thus no way of conceiving of) different types (sharp, dull, searing, and so forth) of pain, then diagnosis becomes an exceedingly delicate matter. The physician who is unaware of how the patient's background may unconsciously lead him to respond in certain ways, by not probing sufficiently, may miss important diagnostic cues.

Lack of awareness of what the patient thinks is wrong, as well as of what

[10] Elliot G. Mishler and Nancy E. Waxler, "Decision Processes in Psychiatric Hospitalization," *American Sociological Review,* Vol. 28 (August, 1963), pp. 276-87.
[11] On three general ratings of emotional problems there were no statistically significant differences between the ethnic groups, and thus no objective reason to expect the greater frequency of "psychiatric diagnosis" in one group over another. For more detail, see Irving K. Zola, "Problems of Communication, Diagnosis, and Patient Care: The Interplay of Patient, Physician, and Clinic Organization," *Journal of Medical Education,* Vol. 38 (October, 1963), pp. 829-38.

Illness
Behavior
of the
Working Class:
Implications
and
Recommendations

357

are his chief concerns—a perceived threat rather than a concrete threat to some valued activity—can also have grave effects in the course of treatment. Many of our patients came in for something which they perceived as threatening but which in the eyes of the physician was medically unimportant. In a separate paper it was shown that, where these concerns were ignored, the result was often the premature termination of treatment.[12]

Still another problem in treatment is the patient's ability to follow a medical regimen. Too often the medical instructions were vague and incomprehensible to the patient. Among many lower-class patients, however, there is the habit of acquiescence in the presence of authority. Thus, if matter-of-factly asked whether he understands or if he has any questions, his immediate reply may be, "No." Many of our working-class patients professed a general reluctance to inquire about anything, since they felt that the physician did not want to be asked "foolish" questions and that he was really "too busy" to be bothered. Later follow-ups in this and similar studies have shown that among those who did not fully understand their medical regimen were the highest number of those who failed to follow their prescriptions and instructions.

THE IMPORTANCE OF CRITICAL INCIDENTS IN ILLNESS BEHAVIOR

A rather broader and even more slippery issue to which I would like to devote some space is the potential importance of studying "critical incidents" or triggers as such for the purpose of understanding "illness behavior" and for the more practical aims in the planning of medical-care programs. This discussion starts from an assumption with which many readers may disagree. Based on the existence of a large body of empirical research on patient-delay, as well as on the descriptions and admonitions found in the clinical literature on doctor-patient contacts, I would speculate that, for a large variety of symptoms and problems, there is a general reticence or reluctance to seeking medical aid. Based on the following observations, it is my guess that, if anything, this reluctance is likely to increase:

1. The growing "medical sophistication" (particularly through popoular magazines) of lay population leads them to make more and more self-diagnoses, and, even when they do go, they now bypass the general practitioner and refer themselves to the "appropriate" specialist.

2. With increasing pharmaceutical advertisement, as well as the increased tendency to self-diagnosis, there is the corresponding and concomitant tendency toward self-treatment.

3. The complexity of medical technical knowledge increases, probably even faster than the lay population's sophistication, and this highly specialized knowledge and technique makes for even greater distance between the lay population and the medical profession. This "distance" probably also increases with the disappearance of the "old family doctor" and the tendency to use different doctors for different symptoms and for different people in the family (internists, gynecologist, cardiologist, pediatrician, maybe even a psychiatrist).

---

[12] Zola, *ibid.*

4. The increased attention to the chronic diseases, whether due to an actual increase in the conditions leading to these disorders or to the fact that the longer life span allows for the existence of a greater population at risk, also creates the conditions for delay. With current knowledge, most of these disorders are not amenable to dramatic cures and interventions, but rather to a long, arduous course of treatment, and this has been observed to lead to frustration both on the part of the medical practitioner and on that of the patient.

Each of these elements might act to produce a problem in the following way. The individual's idea of when it is necessary to go to a doctor differs considerably (for both physical and mental disorders) from the professional's view. With his present medical knowledge and the larger variety of drugs readily available, he is, or thinks he is, able to treat himself for a large variety of ills. At the same time, however, it is increasingly likely that he may at some time be afflicted with one or more chronic diseases. Moreover, the onset of many of these is insidious and their course relatively undramatic, thus leading to an almost automatic lull or delay period. With all the emphasis on self-medication, as well as his "knowledge" about chronic disease, the individual might rightly feel that what he himself can't cure requires drastic and somewhat alien measures—psychoanalysis, family therapy, permanent diet control, lifetime reliance on specific drugs, or, finally, highly risky and new surgical procedures, requiring removal of specific parts of the body or organs. In short, if he can't take care of it himself, what he has may really be serious. Some of these people will undoubtedly run rather quickly to a doctor, but the study of those who have many of these chronic conditions leads one to speculate that further delay would be the most common response. It is in this situation that the study of critical incidents or triggers assumes increasing importance, for much of medical care would turn on the issue of getting people to come when they really don't want to or do not see the necessity for it.

If such a situation as described above exists, then it has enormous implications for the future organization of medical and public health programs. We could, of course, attempt to increase the medical knowledge of the general population at least to a level where they could more accurately judge symptoms and signs of early disease. This approach, however, has not proven to be particularly successful.

On the other hand, we could acknowledge the motivational elements that lead an individual to see a doctor, and organize medical-care and health-education programs accordingly. In terms of care, there could be even greater use of "required" periodic examinations (as is done now in many industries). Although this is the subject of some controversy, there is evidence that a great number of otherwise ignored and untreated disorders are picked up in this manner.

As has been suggested for mental-health programs, health education might focus on disturbances in a great array of life-body relationships rather than just the presence of certain physical signs. This might mean encouraging the individual to consult a physician when his work is not up to par or when he notices some interference in his usual activities.

Illness Behavior of the Working Class: Implications and Recommendations

359

If the trigger labeled "sanction" is a pattern for large segments of the population, this fact could be utilized in a number of ways. There could be an increase in "involuntary" participation in certain health campaigns—such as immunizations or mass testing. The "force" aspect to this suggestion is really nothing more than an extension of what goes on today in many hospitals, colleges, and industries, for example, required chest X-rays. This might also take the form of encouraging people to take the responsibility in getting others to consult a physician, as in the recent campaign for eye examinations, where TV "personality" Bill Cullen encouraged wives to have their husband's eyes checked.

To the criticism that no one of the above measures would appeal or work for everyone, perhaps we should take a page out of American advertising. There, a diversity of appeals for the same product are often utilized—whether it be to a certain age or sex group, certain needs, or to different parts of the country. Finally, it should be remembered that the suggestions here are not based on the idea that the specific triggers or incidents delineated in this paper are the major ones, but rather that the idea of specific triggers itself has implications.

SOME FUTURE RESEARCH DIRECTIONS

The very tone of this paper indicates the need for more research. There is a particular lack of knowledge about the mechanisms whereby values and attitudes, particularly those pertaining to health and illness, are transmitted. Our rapidly growing and "developing" society has led us to be increasingly concerned with the influence of rapid change in "underdeveloped" countries as well as our own. In order to understand such phenomena, it is necessary to learn the sources and roots of what is undergoing change. This is particularly important if we are interested in implementing and directing change. For example, as long as the policy of early detection is a cornerstone of the treatment and prevention of many chronic diseases, the issue of overcoming early resistance or delay will be an important and ever-increasing problem.

As the reader can tell from the analysis and suggestions in this paper, it seems unlikely that such information can be garnered by investigating health and illness attitudes in isolation. Attitudes and behavior about sickness simply do not exist, nor are they transmitted in isolation from more general concerns and orientations. Take, for example, our observation that working-class Irish patients in Boston tended to abdicate the responsibility for going to a doctor. It is more likely (as studies of their native homeland have depicted) that this is due to their being taught a general deference of judgment to elders in important (and particularly anxiety-provoking) decisions, and *not* to their having been taught specifically to ask others for medical advice before seeing a physician.

It is thus necessary to recognize that there are important qualitative differences between large segments of our population. Because such differences may be rooted to a large extent in their personal (and, in some cases, unique) cultural background and heritage (for example, class, ethnic, and racial), it would seem necessary to make comparative studies of different sociocultural groupings (including, also, educational, age, sex, and religious ones), not simply to see which is "more important," but to see where and when changes in one's background, attitudes, and behavior occur. Studies which investigate people over time, as in a panel study, are necessary. It should be possible to study individuals for about a year, starting at a point in time when they are not under medical treatment and observations, and then observe under what conditions they do and do not seek medical aid. It should also be possible in a prospective study to investigate some of the mechanisms of their action or inaction. In what situations, for example, is action related to specific medical knowledge and experience, to the acuteness and time span of the "trouble," to attitudes of prevention or self-treatment? Under what circumstances does their behavior reflect more underlying beliefs and orientation, such as concern with certain bodily functions, theories of causation, or even broader issues of time, responsibility, and control of human behavior, and valued spheres of activity in which interference will not be brooked?

While there will, of course, be difficulties in fully answering these questions or in designing and executing such a prospective study, the potential gains seem to present it as well worth the effort.

Illness
Behavior
of the
Working Class:
Implications
and
Recommendations

361

Part VII

MENTAL HEALTH

As frightened as the worker is of a physical diagnosis, so also is he terrified of the various mental ailments. Indeed, the situation here is very much like that in the case of physical health, with the exception that resources for aid are much scarcer, specialists are few in number, the suspicions of the worker are great, and the need for reform is even greater. Freedman opens this section on mental health with an essay that examines the stress of poverty on members of the "new" working class, the significance of the fact that "the poor have rarely rested on the analyst's couch," and the implications of findings for the treatment of economically deprived patients. Bowman reviews the complex interdependencies between social class and mental well-being, and concludes provocatively that "the prospect for improved mental health in the world of manual workers is quite favorable." Looking more sharply at the rehabilitation record of one type of blue-collar mental patient, Bean, Myers, and Pepper find grounds to suggest that the prospects must be better, as the situation can hardly get worse. Social class was found significantly related in 1960 to the treatment status and community adjustment of patients who were schizophrenic in 1950 (note also the insistence of these authors on important differences between "new" and "old" working-class types). Geisel follows with a discussion of the cultural and psychological meanings attached to work by emotionally disturbed (schizophrenic) blue-collar patients in mental hospitals. Finally, and in contrast to much of the popular literature, Price and Levinson focus on rarely mentioned health-producing aspects of work.

Psychopathology and Poverty*

LAWRENCE ZELIC FREEDMAN

THE gifted but socially envious Scott Fitzgerald wrote, "Let me tell you about the very rich. They are different from you and me." He was answered, in the midst of the Great Depression, with a bitter, laconic, "Yes, the rich *are* different. They have more money." Fitzgerald meant that having a lot of money affects personality. I intend here to explore the contrary proposition.

Few of us avoid entirely the threat of economic insecurity or escape the challenge of economic competition. The working-class poor have failed in that race. The thesis upon which this discussion is based is that this adversity affects their personalities, their families, and their other personal relationships and probably influences how and why they fall into psychic illness. We know almost nothing about how these vectors operate.

The economists are not interested, and, until recently, neither have been most psychiatrists. Yet, in the world perspective, the economists recognize that the upheaval of what is euphemistically called the "underprivileged" is neither simply nationalism nor a reaction against poverty in an absolute sense, but a psychic response to an emergent hope, to what we have grown used to calling a revolution of expectation and what may yet be labelled a revolution of neurosis. But this, although it is my concern, is not my business. "After all," as an historian friend once said to me, "you psychoanalysts can't solve the problems of the world, one by one, on a couch."

My present concern is more clinical and more modest, but equally urgent. I propose to examine, rather unsystematically, the impact of this externally imposed disaster, the stress of poverty on people in a Western urban culture. I say "unsystematically" because my peculiar view of man within his community is refracted through the spectacles of my preoccupation with the treatment of emotionally ill persons who have serious failures in their lives.

This concentration on disturbed individuals could seriously distort our perspective, rather as though we expected to find within a slight specimen

* Adapted from a longer, more detailed paper presented at the Thirteenth Annual Human Development Symposium, "The Urban Lower Class," at the University of Chicago, April 14, 1962.

This essay is based on psychiatric investigations concerning social deviancy carried out in the past ten years in collaboration with many colleagues at the University of Chicago and at Yale University and on a study of economic factors affecting mental illness undertaken with Dr. Stanley Leavy.

I am grateful to the Foundations Fund for Research in Psychiatry, and to the Otho S. A. Sprague Fund, for their support.

of human protoplasm the homunculus of mankind, as biologists once thought they could see the tiny figure of the man to be, and within him the seeds of men to come to all infinity, within a drop of sperm. A necessary corrective, however, is provided by the perspectives of social scientists whose methods are designed to study the structure and function of community life. Also, my data are derived not only from the psychoanalysis and psychotherapy of my patients but, in addition, from collaboration with sociologists and social psychologists in studying the *reciprocal* impact of defined community stresses and rewards and individual maturation.

I do not assume that all the effects of poverty are pathological. Poverty is, in our democratic ethos, the royal road or, more appropriately, the wagon trail to rugged character, economic success, and high political office. All significant aspects of human behavior are, in any case, multidetermined; no single parameter, be it biologic, psychic, or social, inevitably produces a predictable result. Thus, a necessary unspoken assumption in our consideration of the effects of economic deprivation must be "other things being equal," even though they never are. They are constant enough for our purposes.

Psychopathology is a term used by the psychiatrist to refer to his impression of a person's unsatisfactory state of being in a given social environment, an impression which the psychiatrist has rather imprecise techniques to measure. The term refers to psychic distortions manifested either by the maladaptiveness of a person within his culture complex, his serious sense of psychic pain, his dissatisfaction with himself, his significant alienation from other human beings, or some combination of these responses. Because the sufferer must somehow concur, or at least react to this view, the diagnosis of psychopathology requires a three-way transaction between the disturbed person, the diagnostician, and the community in which both are living.

Poverty is not easily diagnosible, or quantifiable, either. There are many ways of being poor. The poverty of bohemia or the beatnik, which has been called the *hysterization* of poverty, results from self-selection, in which the psychopathology, if it exists, is an antecedent rather than a consequence of the material deprivation. Similarly, the self-abnegation and asceticism of the religious, creative, or scholarly recluse is not the poverty which we were observing. The poor with whom I am here concerned are those who view themselves as part of the system of over-all social structure of their urban community, but as a materially deprived and politically dominated segment of that community. I shall not discuss, although one cannot ignore, the profound significance of race and ethnicity as preconditions both for existing in a state of poverty, with all that implies, and for affecting the self-image and social identification. My present observations are not intended to be alternative, but rather complementary, to ethnic ones. Poverty also depends not only on the impression of an independent viewer, but on the self-image of the individual concerning his own degree of economic deprivation and on the social and economic milieu in which this judgment is taking place. Poverty and low socioeconomic class are not identical but few would dispute that everyone at the most socially depressed level is poor.

FREEDMAN   The poor have rarely rested on the analyst's couch. The explanation for this does not end with the economics of private medical practice. It is far more complex; what was true of medicine in Plato's day tends to be true in contemporary psychiatry. He wrote: "When a carpenter is ill, he asks the physician for a rough-and-ready remedy—an emetic or a purge, or a cautery, or the knife. And if anyone tells him that he must go through a course of dietetics, and swathe and swaddle his head, and all that sort of thing, he replies at once that he has not time to be ill, and that he sees no good in a life that is spent in nursing his disease to the neglect of his ordinary calling; and therefore, saying goodbye to this sort of physician, he resumes his customary diet, and either gets well and lives and does his business, or, if his constitution fails, he dies and has done with it." (Plato, *The Republic*)

Aside from this impatience with any interruption in the act of living, there are problems of communication, of the quantity of emotional investment in language as contrast to bodily activity, and perhaps, with a substantive difference, in the nature of the psychopathology itself. In recent years, however, the strenuous coordination of the skills and techniques of social scientists and psychiatrists toward a creative investigative synthesis has provided us with some important leads toward understanding these phenomena.

Nonetheless, the diagnoses, theories, and therapies which are applied by psychiatrists and psychoanalysts to those who live in what Oscar Lewis calls the "culture of poverty" are still artificially grafted from the body of observations made upon middle-class persons in what is now called "an affluent society." If there is a "culture of poverty," psychiatric illness within it would have special characteristics—a "psychopathology of poverty." The psychosocial characteristics of being poor are, through the medium of the family or surviving fragments of the family, transmuted into characteristics of personality development.

My hypothesis, which is venerable as a social ethic, is still essentially untested as a social psychiatric variable: *poverty significantly affects the incidence and structure of psychopathology*—specifically, psychoneurosis. I select neuroses rather than the more severe psychoses because of their wider prevalence and because there is reason to believe that the causal impact of biogenetic and biochemical factors is much greater in schizophrenia and manic-depressive psychoses. For the present, then, it is somewhat more efficient, in psychosocial investigations, to emphasize treated neuroses. I shall now summarize, in a necessarily sketchy fashion the results of several studies in which my colleagues and I attempted to test this theory.

Our research has suggested that there are distinct and significant symptomatic and social qualities to each social class. Whether the class profile was drawn according to the percentage occurrence of single, dominant, or complexes of symptoms of patients, we got distinct configurations:

1. Those forms of neuroses which are expressed behaviorally or somatically had the highest treated prevalence in the lower socioeconomic groups.
2. The behavioral manifestation of these neuroses is more likely to occur in a wider community orbit, or family, with greater violence.
3. Contact with psychiatric treatment is likely to be (a) under the duress of

Psychopathology and Poverty

sociolegal intervention for the most deprived groups as the result of violent collision with the laws or mores of the community, or (b) impelled by some sort of somatic pain or disability which is psychic in origin. An interesting corollary of this is that the lowest socioeconomic group came into contact with psychiatry as the result of neurotic manifestations, mainly during childhood and teen age, as an outcome of antisocial behavior, with greater frequency than did the upper-income group. (5)

Poverty is less importantly defined at any absolute level of material deprivation, at least in a Western urban culture. It is more significantly seen in terms of the confluence of larger community values concerning minimum subsistance levels and the self-image of the individual as he relates himself both to his immediate environment and to the larger economically hierarchical social structure. It seems clear, then, that it is not poverty as such, but discontent, viewed from many standpoints, which is most closely related to psychopathology.

But what is the source of this discontent? It probably springs from neither despair nor hope, but from the crisis of conflict of both. Speaking graphically, the threshold for the psychopathology of poverty may be where the rising curve of hope meets the descending curve of despair. It is where the fear of further blows from disinterested or malignant fate and man meets the craving to become incorporated into the community of seemingly sated and satisfied men. Thus, in a sense, an individual decides whether he is neurotic. The degree to which he tolerates or rebels against the role he is assigned in his social milieu may determine whether or not he considers himself neurotic. We might speculate that a more adequate understanding of self-definition as compared with the community definition of *neurosis* would guide us not only to better understanding of prevailing attitudes within the social group concerning psychological sickness and health, but also to seemingly moral questions concerning sin and virtue, and to apparently political questions, such as the degree of democratic self-realization permitted and the nonconformity tolerated, as compared with how much conformity and group immersion is demanded.

Neuroses are not the prerogative of any class. Anxiety, depression, and various unsuccessful psychic maneuvers characterize all the human race, now and always. However, their meaning for the poverty-stricken and disenfranchised—and for those around them—probably differs a great deal from its meaning for those better situated. Where these states are experienced as reactions against an overwhelming impersonal force which deprives, degrades, and punishes—where, in short, the perception of outer reality reinforces the inner perception of psychic pain—the self-image is not likely to be that of an illness to be cured, but of another adventitious blow which, if it cannot be warded off, must at least be shrugged off.

Whatever the general prevalence of neurosis may be, diagnosed and treated neuroses have, in a sense, passed an operational threshold.[1] Social-level dif-

---

[1] The diagnosis of physical illness, also, is not simply a matter of the detection of anatomical or physiological changes. It involves also self-determination on the part of the patient of his degree of disability and pain and assessment by his community of his contagiousness, as well as the diagnostic impression of the physician.

ferences in symptom complexes undoubtedly result from the degree of attention, of emphasis, and of importance given to the particular symptom both by the patient and by the doctor. The obtained differences in the distributions and diagnoses are, to an important degree, a function of class differences in awareness of specific kinds of symptoms, initiative in seeking treatment, and success in obtaining it. (8, 9) Elsewhere I have offered evidence that psychoneurotics of lower socioeconomic groups, when they do come into psychiatric treatment, are more likely to do so in response to some major behavioral anomaly, psychophysical difficulty, or community dislocation, such as conflict with the law, while higher-income persons are more frequently personally propelled in response to subjective malaise, such as a sense of depression. (5)

An important determining factor is the response of his own community to acting out, as well as the opportunities which it provides. The significance ascribed to comparable behavior varies enormously in differing socioeconomic contexts, from hostility, to tolerance, to admiration. For example, vigorous, bold, assertive behavior, which is prized among upper-income groups in the developing boy as wholesome self-expression, is often the reciprocal of similar activity condemned by them as delinquent in the lower-class youth.[2]

Conversely, let us examine the remarkable fact that, although realistic, threatening economic problems were of course endemic in the lower-income group, these people were less likely than those from higher-income levels to suffer from clinical depressions. Depressive patients, to be sure, often verbalized their sense of guilt or fears in economic terms, and among the many dangers to survival which threatened them was economic insecurity. But it was the psychic threat of impoverishment among the well-to-do rather than the reality of such a danger among the poor which precipitated the depression and provided its self-deprecating and self-castigating content. (7, 10, 11) Of course, the lower-income depressives often expressed fear of actual economic deprivation, but it was the middle-class patient who was preoccupied with his *relative* vocational and monetary disadvantage and the handicaps of his lesser training.

Psychic depressions were, to be sure, often brought on by loss—loss which, in turn, threatened absolute destruction. Yet, it was not economic but personal loss which seemed to doom. It was the equivalence of economic insecurity with emotional insecurity which appeared significant, and it was the equivalence of emotional security with love which was at the core of the problem. (10, 11) These relationships, irrational as they may seem to you, are, for the infant, literal *biological* equivalents and not psychic inferences. Every human infant who survives physically and emotionally must have had some adult who cared for him, in both senses of the word. In urban United States, with its welfare policies, poverty itself rarely interferes with the mechanics of the feeding and fostering; physical survival is assured. But the social context of slum living significantly varies the conditions of mothering and fathering for the child. For example, the impact of poverty, deprivation, and over-

---

[2] See Glueck's findings that athletic mesomorphs from lower-class surroundings are most prone to delinquency. (7)

Psychopathology and Poverty

367

crowded living conditions operates in those periods of life when the crucial choice of ego ideals affects future adult character formation. Men or women who can be used as models, frequently through idealizing them as we do in adult forms of love, are essential for the adaptive crystallization of the adult personality. Particularly for young males, the social inadequacy of adult models in slum settings is compounded by their shifting variability and by the disillusioning intimate confrontation in violent and sexual activities with adults. If persons with such a history in early childhood develop psychopathology, they are more likely to be involved in difficulties of adjustment to social values manifested through acting out in the larger community.

Paradoxically, this disillusionment requires defenses against total despair and the denial of brutalizing reality. The reactions of this developmental period may so limit the level of aspiration of such a person and so constrict his community of human relationship that they may *protect* him from the frustrations of disappointment of hopes—by hopelessness. There may be no sense of failure because there is no sense of competition.

The absence or relative inadequacy of an adult identifying figure also impedes or distorts the development of a powerful self-censoring and self-criticizing personality factor which is technically called *superego,* and which is more generally labeled *conscience*. This, again, protects against the self-punishing depressions of the more rigid personalities and the other introversive, self-doubting symptoms of psychic malaise. This, too, predisposes to the behavioral, and community-conflictful, neurotic acting out.

In the treated population, lower-class neuroses are relatively few, but psychoses are comparatively many. Particularly, lower-class patients in state hospitals and other public facilities who are diagnosed as neurotic were likely to be extremely disturbed to the point where their capacity to function was severely impaired, and to exhibit a multiplicity of symptoms indicative of serious personality deterioration. Their symptoms were likely to incapacitate them or to interfere seriously with their ability to work or even to maintain themselves in their society without delinquent acts. Certain forms of social delinquency may, in fact, be the neuroses of the lower class, just as self-punishing doubts may be the neurosis of the middle class.[3]

The jobs of patients in the lower-income group were of a low order of skill, without prestige, and poorly paid. Work was an inconstant means of subsistence; it seemed to rescue the patient neither from dependence on the

---

[3] These observations, in my view, in no way either contradict or reinforce the sociological theories of the genesis of delinquency on the basis of "class conflict," "culture conflict," or "differential association." These speculations on treated neurotics from lower-income groups are not necessarily applicable to a generalized theory of lower-class delinquency. In subsequent studies already completed, we have, in fact, found that socially delinquent behavior may serve as a psychopathological vehicle for a considerable but as yet unknown fraction of psychically deviant individuals; but it is also my impression, reinforced by a variety of observations (5, 3, 6), that greater specificity of study of individuals and precise concern with the psychic significance of the form—whether sexual, aggressive, or acquisitive—which these delinquent acts take are essential complements and correctives to general hypotheses of socially destructive acts.

community nor from inferior status within it. Yet lower-income patients expressed little interest or concern with greater attainments either vocationally or economically, nor, so far as we could see, were their symptoms directly related to the unattainability of such goals.

The occupation of a middle- or upper-class person often provided him not only with an income but with a vehicle for attaining a variety of social values, such as a sense of masculine independence and social status. It may also become a vehicle for carrying aggressive and hostile, in addition to erotic, drives, as well as provide a structuring framework in which to live. We might predict, then, that when work is absent, intermittent, or unpredictable, uncontrolled aggressive and libidinal needs, as well as disorganized and recurrent efforts to achieve masculine reassurance, are likely to result. And this is exactly what happens in the lower-income patient.

The criteria for assumption of the neurotic role differs significantly from class to class. It is quite likely that these group attitudes vary in turn, and that they are undoubtedly affected by cross-class acculturation. From our data there is an apparent difference in concept of self as patient in the social classes if one is (1) uncomfortable or unhappy, (2) if his body hurts or functions poorly, (3) if he is unable to be effective at his work, (4) if he is in trouble with his social community, or (5) if he is in difficulty with the law. Or, as we stated once before, we may indulge ourselves in the following (over)generalizations: the Class V neurotic behaves badly, the Class IV neurotic aches physically, the Class III patient defends fearfully, and the patients in Classes I and II are dissatisfied with themselves. Thus, we have a motor pattern of community dislocation, a "body language" of pain and malfunction, social anxiety, and verbal symbolic dislocation, all called *neurotic* (5, 9).

What implications do these findings have for the treatment of economically deprived patients? We know that not only does the prevalence and type of psychopathology differ for the very poor, but the therapy varies. He is far less likely to be treated at all, unless he becomes psychotic or dangerous, and he is likely to be treated by one or another of the somatic techniques. A relatively short while ago this would have been electro-shock treatment; now it is more likely to be one or another of the available pharmaceutical agents. Psychiatric treatment as a psychological technique involves verbal communication requiring not simply physical presence but a state of receptivity, of motivation. Many lower-class patients tend to come into a psychiatric milieu through official or semiofficial channels—channels in which the element of force is at least implicit. Ultimately, the individual must accept or at least acquiesce in the medical and social value systems which define his condition as neurotic and, hence, himself a proper subject for psychiatric attention. Not only must he acquiesce but he must actually incorporate these values, if the method utilized is to be psychotherapy, because this method employs relationships based on verbal communication. An essential prerequisite is that there exist a shared intention to change something, whether it be the patient's ideas, emotions, or behavior. Many Class IV and Class V patients have nonverbal symptoms—their neurosis speaks a kind of body or motor

Psychopathology
and
Poverty

369

language. Their bodies hurt, or their behavior offends. The judgment that this is a psychiatric illness is often not theirs but that of official or semi-official agencies.

It is at least a possibility that contemporary psychiatrists who have learned to treat upper-class feelings through the manipulation of verbal cues attempt through false analogy to cure the Class IV and Class V bodily and behavioral symptoms in the same way. Perhaps it makes a pragmatic sort of sense that the behavioral and social maladaptions *are·* treated by nonverbal behavioral manipulation of the complex, private verbal symbol. It might make better sense to recognize the often radically differing personal and social significance of the neurosis in different individuals and to develop relevant techniques—perhaps involving behavioral, social, and bodily symbols—more specifically than is now the case.

A wise old doctor once said to me, "The secret of surviving is learning to wear your crown of thorns over one eye." This knack is probably unevenly distributed, and we have no reason to believe that this lesson is better taught among the poor than among the privileged. But until we can cure social illness with appropriate techniques, educational and communal, and until we have learned far more than we now know about how to prevent and heal the psychic ills which I have discussed, it is all too often the only lesson which we have to teach.

BIBLIOGRAPHY

1. Freedman, L. Z., "Impulsive Behavior and Social Conflict." Read at the Symposium on Impulses, Midwestern Divisional Meeting of the American Psychiatric Association, November 16, 1961.

2. _____, "Research and the Mentally Ill Offender." Read at the Symposium on the Mentally Ill Offender, Atascadero State Hospital, California, June, 1960. Published by the Department of Mental Hygiene, Sacramento, California, 1961.

3. _____, "Sexual, Aggressive and Acquisitive Deviates: A Preliminary Note," *The Journal of Nervous and Mental Disease,* Vol. 132, No. 1 (January, 1961), pp. 44-49.

4. _____, *The Varieties of Delinquent Behavior* (to be published).

5. _____ and A. B. Hollingshead, "Neurosis and Social Class. I. Social Interaction," *The American Journal of Psychiatry,* Vol. 113, No. 9 (March, 1957), pp. 769-75.

6. _____ and S. A. Leavy, "Psychiatric Diagnoses and Socioeconomic Levels." Read at the Annual Meeting of the American Orthopsychiatric Association, New York, 1953.

7. Glueck, S., and E. Glueck, *Physique and Delinquency* (New York: Harper & Row, Publishers, 1956).

8. Hollingshead, A. B., and L. Z. Freedman, "Social Class and the Treatment of Neurotics," *The Social Welfare Forum* (New York: Columbia University Press, 1958), pp. 194-205.

9. _____ and F. C. Redlich, *Social Class and Mental Illness* (New York: John Wiley & Sons, 1959).

10. Leavy, S. A. and L. Z. Freedman, "Psychoneurosis and Economic Life," *Social Problems*, Vol. IV, No. 1 (July, 1956), pp. 55-66.

11. —————— and ——————, "Psychopathology and Occupation. Part I, Economic Insecurity, and Part II, Work and Competition," *Occupational Psychology*, January and April, 1961, and July, 1961.

12. Leighton, A. H., *Explorations in Social Psychiatry* (New York: Basic Books, 1957).

13. Redlich, F. C., A. B. Hollingshead, B. H. Roberts, H. A. Robinson, L. Z. Freedman, and J. K. Meyers, "Social Structure and Psychiatric Disorders," *American Journal of Psychiatry*, Vol. 109, No. 10 (April, 1953).

Mental Health
in the Worker's World

I

ONLY recently have we begun to understand the complex interdependencies existing between social class and mental well-being. The psychiatrist views the patient as an individual; his traditional perspective has seldom extended beyond relationships in families of orientation and of procreation. (Indeed, he has usually considered only selected aspects of the total interaction among family members.) In the 1940's, research on stratification by W. Lloyd Warner began to appear, but as late as 1950 very few articles had been published on the class factor in mental illness, and most of those were written by social scientists.[1]

Moreover, psychiatrists, lacking sociological objectivity, tended to exhibit ideological resistances to the very concept of "class," in regard to both their patients and themselves. They seemed to believe that the kind of middle-class people that sought their professional services represented the general run of humanity; and that their criteria of mental health (actually class-related) were universally valid. Many had clinical experience in public mental hospitals or in the outpatient clinics of general hospitals; but, even so, the lower socioeconomic strata remained of peripheral interest.

Even when the realities of social status began to permeate culturally induced defenses, the understanding of stratification was far from adequate. Differences in tangible circumstances—income, housing, education, clothing,

---

[1] Cf. Kingsley Davis, "Mental Hygiene and the Class Structure," *Psychiatry*, Vol. 1, pp. 35-56.
Talcott Parsons, "Psychoanalysis and the Social Structure," *Psychoanalytical Quarterly*, Vol. 19, pp. 371-84.
W. L. Warner, "Society, the Individual, and his Mental Disorders," *American Journal of Psychiatry*, Vol. 94, pp. 275-85.

and manners—where recognized without difficulty, but the more subtle features required study in depth. Until motives, attitudes, and general outlook on life were known—in short, the dynamics of class subcultures—it was still possible to perceive all persons as identical in psychic structure, some having more money or schooling or better clothing than others. Such illusions are probably useful in maintaining an equalitarian ideology, but they vitiate the serious work of behavioral scientists.

II

It remained for August B. Hollingshead, a sociologist, and Fredrick C. Redlich, a psychiatrist, to bridge the gap between these disciplines by raising two fundamental questions: (1) Is mental illness related to class in our society? (2) Does a patient's position in the status system affect the kind of treatment he receives? Their detailed answers have introduced a new sociological dimension into psychiatric conceptualizations.

In the five-class structure of New Haven, manual workers are found in all except the two highest strata. In class III, "16 per cent are plant supervisors or skilled manual workers." [2] Although the exact percentage in the latter category is not given, the inclusion of even a small number of workers in class III points to a fact of greatest importance, namely, that *the category of "manual workers" is far from homogeneous.* In New Haven there appear to be a number of skilled workers whose education, place of residence, mode of family life, and leisure-time activities form a pattern integral with that of small businessmen, semiprofessionals, and clerical workers. Thus, we see that the dichotomy, white-collar and blue-collar, so commonly utilized in social research, fails to take into account the significant variations in psychocultural characteristics existing among different types of manual workers.

Because manual workers comprise 87 per cent of class IV and 98 per cent of class V, we shall limit our discussion to these two strata. Seventy-eight per cent of the psychiatric patients are in these two classes.[3] In regard to type of mental illness, the lower classes show much higher percentages of psychosis. Whereas in classes I and II, 35 per cent of the patients are psychotic, in class IV the figure rises to 80 per cent and in class V, to 90 per cent. Class correlations appear to be reversed for neurotics.

Yet appearances are often deceiving. It cannot be said that classes IV and V have little neurosis, for there are class differences in the use of psychiatric facilities. Hollingshead and Redlich believe that many lower-class neurotics try to handle their problems without going to a psychiatrist.

> Therefore the larger percentage of patients with neurotic difficulties in the higher classes may be the result of the fact that individuals in classes I and II, for example, perceive the psychiatrist in a different way from persons in class IV. Class I and II persons may go to psychiatrists when they have less severe disorders than class IV persons.[4]

---

[2] August B. Hollingshead and Fredrick C. Redlich, *Social Class and Mental Illness* (New York: John Wiley & Sons, Inc., 1958) , p. 95.
[3] Hollingshead and Redlich, *op. cit.,* p. 199.
[4] *Ibid.,* p. 222.

This noteworthy study discovered additional facts bearing upon the heterogeneity of the blue-collar category. Both class IV and class V consist of manual workers, but the difference between them in the proportion of patients to class population is striking. Class IV is *underrepresented,* having 50 per cent of the community's population but only 40 per cent of the patient population. On the other hand, class V is *overrepresented,* having only 18 per cent of the population of the community but 38 per cent of the psychiatric patients. Indeed, this is the only class that is overrepresented in the New Haven community.[5]

III

The Yale study included those who were in a mental hospital or under psychiatric treatment; in other words, it deals with the diagnosed prevalence of mental illness. The Midtown Manhattan Study, while also including a treatment census, featured a Home Interview Study in order to obtain *direct* evidence on the over-all occurrence of illness. This required research "that cuts away from dependence on institutional records and systematically moves out into the open community for face-to-face assessments of its residents and their individual differences in mental health." [6]

This project gives considerable attention to the variable of socioeconomic status (SES). Six strata of nearly equal numerical size were defined, three of these being white-collar and three blue-collar.

When the 1660 respondents are classified according to SES, definite correlations appear. Blue-collar strata include lower percentages of people who are "well" and higher percentages that are "impaired." Some of the results are startling. For example, the sick-well ratio in the lowest of the six strata is *more than ten times* that in the highest. As a matter of fact, the lowest category of manual workers has a sick-well ratio that is more than three times that of the highest stratum of such workers.[7] Leo Srole and his associates suggest that this lowest stratum can claim the highest priority in regard to ameliorative policy. Here is a "downward spiral of compounded tragedy, wherein those handicapped in personality or social assets from childhood on are trapped as adults at or near the poverty level, there to find themselves enmeshed in a web of burdens that tend to precipitate (or intensify) mental and somatic morbidity . . . Here, we would suggest, is America's own displaced-persons problem." [8] This reference, let it be emphasized again, is only to the lowest level of manual workers and not to the entire category.

IV

In *Americans View Their Mental Health,* a nationwide survey of 2,460 adults (one of the monographs published by the Joint Commission on Mental

---

[5] Cf. S. M. Miller and Elliott G. Mishler, "Social Class, Mental Illness, and American Psychiatry," *Milbank Memorial Fund Quarterly,* Vol. 37, esp. pp. 189-91.

[6] Leo Srole, Thomas Langner, Stanley Michael, Marvin Opler, and Thomas Rennie, *Mental Health in the Metropolis: the Midtown Manhattan Study* (New York: McGraw-Hill, Inc., 1962), p. 31.

[7] Srole, *et al., op. cit.,* p. 229.

[8] *Ibid.,* p. 236.

Illness and Health), Gerald Gurin, Joseph Veroff, and Sheila Feld studied the mental health of an interview sample as this is indicated by the self-diagnoses of informants. Their aim was to investigate feelings of adjustment and the methods used in handling emotional problems.

Occupation is, of course, a potent force in determining a man's general life adjustment, and his adjustment, in turn, affects that of his family. What are the mental-health characteristics of various occupations and the life-adjustment patterns peculiar to each?

Skilled workers have few distinguishing characteristics except that they are the least likely to admit to having any worries; nor do their wives stand out as distinctive. Semiskilled workers, along with other blue-collarites, are not especially happy either in general or in their marriages; but their wives frequently report feelings that a nervous breakdown is imminent. Unskilled workers report more general unhappiness and have a more negative self-image than any other group. Their wives are unhappy in their marriages and blame their husbands for this. They, too, feel that they are constantly on the verge of a nervous breakdown. It seems clear that financial deprivation is a major source of worry. "The wives of unskilled workers are perhaps the most deprived of all women. . . . An additional difficulty for them is that their channels of expression are, for the most part, limited to the home. At least their husbands have their jobs to provide another focus for their lives . . . " [9]

It may be concluded, from this investigation, that *the world of semi-skilled and especially of unskilled workers is an unhealthful environment for them and their families.* This conclusion is also supported by the Yale research and by the Midtown Manhattan Study.

Why is this so? What patterns of circumstances in the lowest socioeconomic levels of our society account for these adverse effects? Let us examine this question in detail.

v

A study by Albert K. Cohen and Harold M. Hodges entitled "Characteristics of the Lower-Blue-Collar Class" highlights the adversities experienced at the bottom of the social scale. These investigators analyze the life situation of lower-lowers as follows:[10]

(1) *Simplification of the Experience World*

The LL person experiences a narrow range of situations. "His meager education, the relative inutility to his workaday roles of information about diverse, remote events, and the limitation of his circle of intimates, on and

[9] Gerald Gurin, Joseph Veroff, and Sheila Feld, *Americans View Their Mental Health* (New York: Basic Books, Inc., 1960), p. 227.

[10] Albert K. Cohen and Harold M. Hodges, "Characteristics of the Lower-Blue-Collar Class," *Social Problems*, Vol. 10, pp. 305-7.

off the job, to people very like himself neither facilitate nor encourage vicarious encounters with other, contrasting worlds."

(2) *Powerlessness*

They are powerless because their bargaining power is weak. They are easily replaced and their skills are the least esteemed. There is hardly any autonomy in the work role—"the alternatives are limited to simple compliance, withdrawal or rebellion."

(3) *Deprivation*

A felt sense of deprivation is underlined by the observation that others are getting ahead, even some people like themselves. If a LL youth does not move ahead, he feels all the more frustrated.

(4) *Insecurity*

The meager resources of this class are rapidly expended to meet current needs. Our society, with social-service agencies, insurances, and free clinics, does make provision for these people, but they must have the "ability to move knowledgeably and skillfully through impersonal and bureaucratic channels." This knowledge and skill the lower-blue-collarites typically lack.

A life situation that produces deprivation, insecurity, and powerlessness can hardly mold a psychic structure that is sturdily resistant to the slings and arrows of outrageous fortune. Fear, frustration, a sense of helplessness, and low self-esteem are the nagging concomitants of one's daily life. The wonder is that the mental health of this segment of our population is as good as it is.

VI

When we turn from the general life situation to more specific relationships, the same kind of influences prevail. Lower-class marriages are more frequently broken by death, desertion, divorce, and separation. Class differences in death rates are well-known. Desertion is another case in point. Working with data procured from the Philadelphia Municipal Court, William M. Kephart found that the lower occupational classes are somewhat overrepresented in desertion.[11] Divorce is also more common. William J. Goode calculated the following indices of proneness to divorce:

Professional and proprietary	67.7
Clerical, sales, service	83.2
Skilled, foremen	74.1
Semiskilled, operatives	126.1
Unskilled	179.7 [12]

---

[11] William M. Kephart, *The Family, Society and the Individual* (Boston: Houghton Mifflin Company, 1961), p. 553.

[12] William J. Goode, *After Divorce* (New York: The Free Press of Glencoe, Inc., 1956), p. 47.

375

The class factor is again evident when the subjective evaluations of spouses are studied. Julius Roth and Robert Peck concluded that marital maladjustments increase in prevalence toward the lower end of the social-class scale.[13] This is confirmed by the Gurin-Veroff-Feld survey, where marital happiness was found to be related rather strongly to educational level, those at the higher levels reporting greater happiness.[14]

These results certainly do not give firm and unequivocal support to a simple cause-effect sequence. It is not our intention to suggest that poor mental health is nothing more than a product of marital difficulties. Lower-class men and women undoubtedly take their pre-existing distortions and disturbances into marriage, and out of this dynamic interaction arise a variety of marital problems. Also, a broken marriage is likely to aggravate whatever emotional disturbances already exist in the personality.

The job also seems to be a major influence. In general, it has been found that occupational positions of higher status yield greater satisfactions—although it is easy to exaggerate the extent of the correlations. The nationwide survey by Gurin and associates revealed that 42 per cent of the professionals were "very satisfied" with their jobs, but only 22 per cent of skilled, 27 per cent of semiskilled, and 13 per cent of unskilled workers were happy in theirs. (However, when percentages in the category "satisfied" are added to these figures, occupational differences are less prominent.) These results can be understood better when we juxtapose differentials in ego satisfaction. Whereas 80 per cent of the professional group mention ego satisfactions in connection with the job, with manual workers the percentages range from 54 (skilled) to 29 (unskilled). Also, manual workers feel more inadequate on the job.[15] These findings suggest that

> . . . Self-judgment of one's skill and competence in a given line of work is not only based on skill and competence but on general status considerations as well. . . . Even a highly competent unskilled laborer, in judging his ability to do his work, would be affected by an underlying feeling of inadequacy springing from the generally low status of the job.[16]

In her research on working mothers, Lois W. Hoffman discovered similar differences in attitudes toward work. Those in professional or semiprofessional positions expressed positive attitudes toward their work almost without exception; but in semiskilled or unskilled work, one-third of them expressed negative attitudes.[17]

Occupation is a key factor, to be sure, but self-esteem is linked to social status in a more comprehensive sense. There is also the kind of house and neighborhood in which one lives, the extent of formal education, the personal appearance and manners of oneself and one's associates, and, perhaps most

---

[13] Julius Roth and Robert Peck, "Social Class and Social Mobility Factors Related to Marital Adjustment," *American Sociological Review*, Vol. 16, pp. 478-87.

[14] Gurin, *et al., op. cit.*, p. 105.

[15] *Ibid.*, p. 163.

[16] *Ibid.*, p. 165.

[17] F. Ivan Nye and Lois W. Hoffman, *The Employed Mother in America* (Chicago: Rand McNally & Co., 1963), p. 103.

important of all, the way one is treated by those of higher status. Society provides a multitude of cues that tell men of low status how they have failed to fulfill the hope and the promise of the American dream. Their wives may be even more painfully aware that they are near the bottom, for every object, every situation, every decision in the home is a daily reminder of frustrating impoverishment. Is it, then, surprising that the mental state of these men and women is comparatively unhealthy?

VII

Up to this point the socioeconomic environment has been featured as a help or a hindrance to mental health. Yet environment is not the whole story.

In a competitive, open-class society, processes of selection augment class differentials. Specifically, the fluidity of such a society enables those of motivation and ability to move upward out of their class of origin. At the same time, the system does not guarantee anyone permanent possession of the status of his father's family—those lacking the requisite qualities may move downward.

Now it seems reasonable to believe that good mental health is a factor significantly increasing the chances of upward mobility, with a downward movement occurring where there is impairment. Here, again, the Midtown Manhattan Study supplies relevant data. These researchers compared sick-well ratios by socioeconomic status in two ways: (1) by informants' SES and (2) by SES of the parents of informants. While class differentials were conspicuously present in both instances, the contrasts between the higher and the lower levels were *greater* for informants' SES. Their explanation is in agreement with that suggested above:

> Reflecting the greater tendency of the Well to move upward and the Impaired downward, Figure 4 for the first time reveals that one's own SES stands to adult mental health in a relationship even more sharply accentuated than does parental SES.[18]

VIII

Does the mental health of children suffer as they grow up in the blue-collar world? From the facts and interpretations presented thus far, one would be inclined to think so, and a number of investigations confirm this belief. We have just noted that there are gradations in mental health when adults are classified by the socioeconomic status of their parents. Parental status seems to be an independent variable that is *inversely* related to the prevalence of mental illness among children now grown to adulthood.

Let us examine correlations in more specific areas of socialization. That broken homes occur more frequently in the lower classes has been mentioned. In a review of the evidence on the psychiatric effects of broken homes, Ian Gregory states: "Data recorded to date indicate increased frequencies of parental death in young psychotics and in . . . psychiatric patients (predomi-

---

[18] Srole, *et al., op. cit.,* p. 230.

nantly neurotic). Increased rates of parental separation and divorce are noted in schizophrenic groups . . . and in psychoneurotic groups." [19] To be sure, association does not indicate direct causation. Possibly a third factor accounts for both marital maladjustments of parents and mental disorders in children, the genetic factor coming to mind in this connection. Nevertheless, we cannot dismiss the likelihood that marital disruptions exert an unhealthful influence upon children, especially when the deprivation occurs in early childhood.

Another objective condition that may bear upon the emotional well-being of children is the employment of mothers. Here, too, there are class differences. F. Ivan Nye and Lois Hoffman state that, "although more and more employed mothers are coming from middle and upper socioeconomic levels, they are still overrepresented in the lower and lower-middle classes." [20] Hoffman, as we mentioned earlier, found that mothers in jobs of lower status tend to dislike their work more than those in jobs of higher status. Attitudes toward work, in turn, seem to influence the child's perception of the mother. Mothers who had positive attitudes toward work had children who associated more positive affect with the mother than was the case with those having negative attitudes toward work. Thus, by a process of deduction, we are able to say that the employment of mothers in lower SES seems to have ill effects upon children.[21]

This tentative conclusion is corroborated by the research of Elizabeth Douvan on employment and the adolescent. "The lower-class girl whose mother works full-time is not like other daughters of working women. The girls in this pattern come closest to our original conception of the girl who is neglected and suffers a serious loss of family life because her mother is overextended in her commitments, harassed, perhaps resentful." [22]

In a series of projective tests, J. L. Singer discovered that lower-SES children "portray themselves as relatively isolated from parental figures whom they see as cold and rejecting." Middle-class children, on the other hand, show more positive paternal relationships, the father being more successful and more available for identification. In general, family structure seems more closely knit in the middle class.[23]

F. Ivan Nye's questionnaire research on 1472 adolescents confirms this. He found that adolescents are better adjusted to parents in high than in low socioeconomic levels. (In this particular study, parent-adolescent adjustment consisted of feelings of being loved, feelings that parents trust and have confidence in them, positive feelings about parents as disciplinarians, and favorable attitudes toward parental personalities.) Furthermore, the higher scores of the higher levels are not explained by differentials in such characteristics as broken homes, size of family, or employment of mother. "Significant

---

[19] Ian Gregory, "Studies of Parental Deprivation in Psychiatric Patients," *American Journal of Psychiatry*, Vol. 115, pp. 432-42.

[20] Nye and Hoffman, *op. cit.*, p. 14.

[21] Lois W. Hoffman, "Mother's Enjoyment of Work and Effects on the Child," in Nye and Hoffman, *op. cit.*, pp. 95-105.

[22] Nye and Hoffman, *op. cit.*, p. 159.

[23] J. L. Singer, "Projected Familial Attitudes as a Function of Socio-economic Status and Psychopathology," *Journal of Consulting Psychology*, Vol. 18, pp. 99-104.

socioeconomic differences remain when each of the associated factors is held constant." [24]

Thus, there is a considerable amount of empirical evidence that children in homes of lower SES (which usually means semiskilled and unskilled workers) are growing up in environments where mental morbidity flourishes. Yet, in spite of these psychiatric hazards, many young people from the lower strata do succeed in moving upward. These are the pride and joy of a citizenry that wants to believe that there is equality of opportunity for everyone in this country. Magazines feature the careers of such men and women. Commencement orators exhort youthful graduates to emulate their success. But to what extent do those who commend their ascent appreciate the full dimensions of their struggle? And what about all those who get bogged down hopelessly where they are?

IX

The research passed in review here shows consistently that *mental health is significantly related to socioeconomic status.* However, a word of cautious skepticism must be interjected. Is it possible that a class bias may be present in some of the investigations included in this chapter? Social-science researchers are, after all, middle-class professionals, and they may utilize in their work —subconsciously, if not consciously—the standards and expectations that are integral to their particular style of life and thought. This could be even more true of psychiatrists making mental-health ratings.

The possibility of class bias in psychiatric diagnosis is very real. Let us consider, for example, some of the criteria of positive mental health emphasized by Thomas A. C. Rennie, the first director of the Midtown Manhattan Study. Among others, the following are listed: "ease of social interaction," "capacity for pursuit of realistic goals," "satisfying sense of social belonging: sensitivity to the needs of others," "capacity for utilization of essential creativity," and "conservative handling of hostilities and aggressions." [25] These characteristics are not described in detail, so that we are compelled to guess at their more comprehensive and exact meanings. On the whole, the criteria listed here seem to carry a distinct middle-class flavor. Lower-class people typically lack social skills; their pursuit of realistic goals may be blunted by the time they reach adulthood; they are not satisfied to belong to groups of low status; and opportunities for creativity are much more likely to occur for those of better education. Finally, hostilities and aggressions are expressed more openly in this class—a "conservative handling" of these feelings being the middle-class way. In short, when judged by middle-class criteria, people of low SES will consistently receive unfavorable mental-health ratings.

In this connection, Hollingshead and Redlich interviewed 17 psychiatrists and found that they "disliked" class IV and class V patients. The therapists

---

[24] F. Ivan Nye, "Adolescent-Parent Adjustment: Socio-economic Level as a Variable," *American Sociological Review*, Vol. 16, pp. 341-49.

[25] Srole, *et al., op. cit.,* p. 62.

were "repelled by their crude, vulgar language, their outbursts of violence, at times by their passivity and apathy. . . . The therapists were puzzled and upset over the sexual mores of their class V patients. . . . They complained about the dullness and stupidity of these patients."[26] Similarly, S. M. Miller and Elliott G. Mishler cite a study by William Haase demonstrating "that the same set of presenting symptoms is diagnosed as more severe when the patient is perceived by subtle cues to be a working-class person than when he is seen as in the middle class."[27]

For these reasons we are strongly inclined to believe that current research overstates class differences in mental health. Yet, even when allowance is made for unintentional bias, the significance of the status factor undoubtedly remains.

X

What can be done about the general situation portrayed in the foregoing pages? We can touch only briefly on two approaches to social amelioration.

A. *Treatment*

Because treatment for psychiatric disorders is expensive, many in the lower classes are able to obtain no professional help whatsoever. Those seriously disturbed are often dumped into state hospitals, where they may receive nothing more than custodial care. If this situation is to change, public funds must be spent in unprecedented amounts.

In their recommendations for a national mental health program, the Joint Commission on Mental Illness and Health has said: "Expenditures for public mental patient services should be doubled in the next five years—and tripled in the next ten . . . we recommend that the States and the Federal government work toward a time when a share of the cost of State and local mental patient services will be borne by the Federal government."[28] Among numerous recommendations for such a public program, the Commission underlines the need to develop mental-health centers as part of an integrated community service, with emphasis on outpatient and after-care facilities as well as inpatient services.

Those interested in the mental-health movement were heartened by President Kennedy's special message to Congress on February 5, 1963, urging a comprehensive, long-range program in which Federal funds would stimulate state, local, and private action. He recommended the construction of community mental-health centers which would emphasize prevention, treatment, and rehabilitation at the local level instead of the present "reliance on the cold mercy of custodial isolation" in state institutions.

On October 31 the "Mental Retardation Facilities and Community Mental Health Centers Construction Act of 1963" was signed by the President. This

---

[26] Hollingshead and Redlich, *op. cit.*, p. 344.

[27] Miller and Mishler, *op. cit.*, p. 188.

[28] *Action for Mental Health* (Final Report of the Joint Commission on Mental Illness and Health) (New York: Basic Books, Inc., 1961), p. xx.

act appropriated $150,000,000 of Federal funds on a matching basis to the states over a three-year period for the purpose of constructing mental health centers throughout the country.

B. *Prevention*

Here we shall limit ourselves to a few speculative projections of immediate relevance.

It is generally agreed that the trend in the distribution of income during recent decades has reduced class differentials in living standards. The provision of social services at public expense for those in financial need has augmented this trend. Now it is altogether likely that the rapid acceleration of technological change taking place in the 1960's will give further impetus to this historical development. Industrial changes, stimulated by vast programs of research, are occurring at a dizzy speed in this country. Incredibly complicated machines are taking over the work of unskilled, semiskilled, and even highly skilled men. Under these conditions there will continue to be major changes in the occupational structure of our society, with fewer workers in the lowest categories. The consequences could be salutary. It will be recalled that the research reviewed in this chapter showed consistently that mental morbidity is greatest at the bottom of the social scale. With the shift away from the unskilled occupations and toward those requiring various new skills, it seems plausible to predict that, *other things being equal,* the prospect for improved mental health in the world of manual workers is quite favorable. Yet it is obvious that other things cannot be equal so long as a considerable number of workers remain unemployed.

*Social Class and Schizophrenia: A Ten-Year Follow-Up**

LEE L. BEAN

JEROME K. MYERS

MAX P. PEPPER

THIS article reports on part of an extensive follow-up study of persons enumerated in the 1950 New Haven Psychiatric Census.[1] In the original study,

---

* The research reported in this paper is supported by USPHS, NIMH Grant MH-03569. The authors are from the Departments of Sociology and Psychiatry of Yale University.

[1] For a detailed description of the over-all study, see Jerome K. Myers, Lee L. Bean, and Max P. Pepper, "Social Class and Mental Illness: A Ten-Year Follow-up of Psychiatric Patients," forthcoming in *Connecticut Medicine.*

significant relationships were found between social class and the prevalence, treatment, and development of diagnosed mental illness.[2] Focusing upon what has happened to schizophrenic patients in the ten years following the original study, this paper examines two questions dealing with treatment outcome: Is social class related to (1) 1960 treatment status, and (2) community adjustment for patients who were schizophrenic in 1950?[3]

Schizophrenia is the most prevalent type of serious psychiatric illness. It is a debilitating and chronic disorder, about which relatively little is known. There is increasing evidence, however, that social factors are involved in its etiology and treatment. Our previous research indicates the importance of social class in the development and management of the disorder, but little is known about its long-term consequences.

Previous follow-up research on schizophrenia has tended to be fragmentary. It has focused primarily upon either etiological factors, discharge and relapse rates, or the effect of various therapeutic techniques.[4] A few studies of a limited time span have followed patients in to the community, but scant attention has been given to the effects of social factors upon adjustment.[5] Moreover, measures of adjustment are usually crude and are difficult to replicate or compare with the results of other studies. Finally, by focusing upon a narrowly defined population, follow-up studies generally have limited their scope. For example, most include only a small number of cases, patients from one treatment agency, persons of one sex or age grouping, or some other relatively homogeneous group of patients. All such studies have been limited to a patient population. Without a control population, however, it is impossible to determine whether adjustment variations are unique or whether they are simply reflections of differences to be found among any population.

The present research differs from previous studies at a number of points. All New Haven schizophrenic patients in hospital or outpatient treatment in

---

[2] See August B. Hollingshead and Fredrick C. Redlich, *Social Class and Mental Illness* (New York: John Wiley & Sons, Inc., 1958), and Jerome K. Myers and Bertram H. Roberts, *Family and Class Dynamics in Mental Illness* (New York: John Wiley & Sons, Inc., 1959).

[3] The schizophrenic category includes six schizophrenic reactions: latent, simple, hebephrenic, catatonic, paranoid, and unclassified types plus two paranoid disorders, paranoia and paranoid state. This general category is used in this paper to maintain continuity with the original study. See Hollingshead and Redlich, *op. cit.*, p. 227.

[4] See, for example, Bernhart S. Gottlieb, "Prognostic Criteria in Hebephrenia; The Importance of Age, Sex, Constitution and Marital Status," *American Journal of Psychiatry*, Vol. 97 (1940), pp. 332-41; Benjamin Malzberg, "Cohort Studies of Mental Illness in New York State: 1943-1949," Part VIII, *Mental Hygiene*, Vol. 41 (1957), pp. 420-44; Alexander Gralnick, "A Seven-Year Survey of Insulin Treatment in Schizophrenia," *American Journal of Psychiatry*, Vol. 101 (1945), pp. 449-52; and L. B. Kalinowsky and H. J. Worthing, "Results of Electric Convulsive Treatment in 200 Cases of Schizophrenia," *Psychiatric Quarterly*, Vol. 17 (1943), pp. 144-53.

[5] The major exceptions are the following recent studies, which have dealt with the effect of social factors. However, the follow-up period and patient population have been limited in each case. See George W. Brown, "Experiences of Discharged Chronic Schizophrenic Patients in Various Types of Living Groups," *The Milbank Fund Quarterly*, Vol. XXXVII (1959), pp. 105-31; Arthur Harris, Inge Linker, Vera Norris, and Michael Shepard, "Schizophrenia, a Prognostic and Social Study," *British Journal of Social and Preventive Medicine*, Vol. 10 (1956), pp. 107-14; and Howard E. Freeman and Ozzie G. Simmons. *The Mental Patient Comes Home* (New York: John Wiley & Sons, Inc., 1963).

1950 are followed for ten years.[6] A number of indexes of treatment outcome are investigated, and a control group of nonpatients is employed in measuring community adjustment. Finally, it is one of the first follow-up studies to focus on social class.[7]

METHODOLOGY

Two hypotheses dealing with treatment outcome in 1960 are examined in this paper. First, social class is related to 1960 treatment status; and second, social class is related to the adjustment of patients living in the community relative to a matched control group.

The independent variable, social class, is measured by Hollingshead's Two Factor Index of Social Position,[8] which utilizes occupation and education to rank the study population into five classes, where I is the highest and V the lowest.[9]

The test of our first hypothesis employs the 1950 social-class position of the patients to determine the effect of class position on treatment outcome. Examination of the second hypothesis, however, must take into account the class level at which the individual is living in 1960. Hence, the proportion of individuals in each of the classes examined in the first hypothesis will vary from the proportions in each class examined in the second hypothesis as a result of the mobility of some patients following discharge from the hospital.[10]

To test the first hypothesis, we determined the June 1, 1960 treatment status of all schizophrenics from Greater New Haven, 810 in number, who were in psychiatric treatment between May 31 and December 1, 1950 in psychiatric hospitals or psychiatric outpatient clinics.[11]

The dependent variable in the second hypothesis, community adjustment, is complex and cannot be described adequately by a single index. In this paper we examine two dimensions of adjustment—the biopsychological and the social. *Biopsychological adjustment* is measured in this study by a single index of mental status. Although a comprehensive evaluation of mental status requires an intensive clinical examination in which a composite assessment is made of the individual's behavior, thought, and emotional processes, recent studies have demonstrated that short screening devices may be employed as an alternative to this clinical evaluation. We have adopted the instrument

---

[6] Most medical and psychiatric follow-up studies are limited to a period of five years or less.

[7] Generally, previous studies have been limited to an analysis of hospital discharge rates. See, for example, Robert H. Hardt and Sherwin J. Feinhandler, "Social Class and Mental Hospitalization Prognosis," *American Sociological Review*, Vol. 24 (1959), pp. 815-21.

[8] August B. Hollingshead, *Two Factor Index of Social Position*, mimeographed publication, copyright, 1957.

[9] For a description of the five social classes, see Hollingshead and Redlich, *op. cit.*, pp. 69-135.

[10] A total of 33 of the patients in the community were socially mobile over the ten-year follow-up period. Four class IV patients moved up to class III; one class I moved to class IV; five class III patients moved to class IV; and 23 class IV patients moved to class V.

[11] Of the 810 cases under examination, only 10 were in treatment at outpatient clinics at the time of the original study, and all were in the community, not under psychiatric care, in 1960.

developed by MacMillan and modified by Gurin and associates. It utilizes a list of 20 psychiatric symptoms, which are scored and developed into an index of mental status.[12]

Social adjustment is measured by an index of occupational performance, since its importance in reflecting an individual's community functioning is well documented in sociological literature. As an index of this performance, we have used a modified form of the occupational adjustment scale developed by Adler and associates.[13]

Data for the analyses presented in this paper come from three sources. First, the original records collected in the 1950 New Haven census of the 810 schizophrenic patients were re-examined. Next, patient records were abstracted at the original 1950 treatment agency and at subsequent agencies at which the patient had been in treatment between December 1, 1950 and May 31, 1960. Finally, intensive personal interviews were completed with (1) patients who were in the community in 1960, (2) a "significant other" in the patient's household, and (3) a control group of individuals who have never been treated for mental illness, individually matched with a patient on the basis of the following six variables: sex, race, social class, religion, age, and marital status. This group was selected from a list of names drawn systematically from the city directories of the greater New Haven area.

Eight hundred three, or 99 per cent, of the 810 schizophrenics studied in 1950 were located in 1960. Of the original 810 patients, 127 were no longer hospitalized on June 1, 1960. Of this group, seven could not be located, five refused to be interviewed, and three were in correctional institutions and could not be contacted personally. Thus, 112 of the 127 discharged patients— 88 per cent—were interviewed.

FINDINGS

Hypothesis 1. Social Class Related to
1960 Treatment Status

The data in Table 1 confirm our first hypothesis, that there is a relationship between social class and 1960 treatment status. The proportion of patients hospitalized ten years after our original study increases regularly from 52 per cent in classes I and II to 66 per cent in class V.[14] Even more striking is the distribution of patients who are not hospitalized. Although only 15 per cent of the schizophrenics were not hospitalized in 1960, proportionately, about three and a half times as many class I and II as class V

---

[12] See Allister H. MacMillan, "The Health Opinion Survey: Technique for Estimating Prevalence of Psychoneurotic and Related Types of Disorder in Communities," *Psychological Reports*, Vol. 3 (1957), pp. 325-39; and Gerald Gurin, Joseph Veroff, and Sheila Feld, *Americans View Their Mental Health: A Nationwide Interview Survey* (New York: Basic Books, Inc., 1960), pp. 175-205. We followed the same scoring system which was employed by Gurin, *et al.* Scores range from 22 to 80, with high scores indicating the absence of psychiatric symptoms.

[13] Leta M. Adler, James W. Coddington, and Donald D. Stewart, *Mental Illness in Washington County, Arkansas: Incidence, Recovery, and Posthospital Adjustment*. Arkansas State Hospital and Arkansas State Board of Health, and the University of Arkansas, Institute of Science and Technology, July, 1952.

[14] Classes I and II are combined in the analysis because of the small number of cases.

Table 1

1960 TREATMENT STATUS OF SCHIZOPHRENIC AND PARANOID PATIENTS
BY 1950 SOCIAL CLASS

	Social Class				
1960 Treatment Status	I-II (Per Cent)	III (Per Cent)	IV (Per Cent)	V (Per Cent)	Total (Per Cent)
Hospitalized	52.2	57.4	64.9	66.2	64.5
Dead	13.0	16.1	15.5	24.3	19.8
Not Hospitalized	30.4	25.0	19.2	8.5	14.8
Outpatient* Treatment . . .	(8.7)	(4.4)	(1.8)	(.8)	(1.7)
No Treatment*	(21.7)	(20.6)	(17.4)	(7.7)	(13.1)
Unknown†	4.3	1.5	.3	1.0	.9
Total	99.9	100.0	99.9	100.0	100.0
$N =$	23	68	328	391	810

*This detailed breakdown is not used in the computation of the X^2.
†Excluded from the Chi square test.
$X^2 = 32.91$, $df = 6$; $p < .001$: for the entire table.
$X^2 = 22.83$, $df = 3$; $p < .001$: with the dead excluded from the analysis.

patients were out in the community. The percentage of patients not hospitalized decreases consistently from 30 in classes I and II to 25 in class III, 19 in class IV, and only 9 in class V.

The nonhospitalized group in Table 1 includes both those patients in the community receiving outpatient treatment and those receiving no treatment. Although more class I and II individuals in the community are receiving some outpatient treatment, the proportion of former patients under no psychiatric care is three times as great in the two highest classes (22 per cent) as in the lowest class (8 per cent).

The percentages in Table 1 are based upon the total cohort of 1950 schizophrenic patients, and thus include persons who had died by 1960 as well as those who were still alive. If only those still living in 1960 are considered, the same class differential is found: the percentage of schizophrenics no longer in a hospital declines from 35 per cent in classes I and II to 11 per cent in class V.

*Hypothesis 2. Social Class Related to
Community Adjustment*

Having demonstrated a linkage between social class and one index of treatment outcome, 1960 treatment status, we now focus on ex-patient adjustment to community living. In this phase of the research, a baseline for performance evaluation is required, and hence patient performance is compared with the performance of our matched control group.

*Hypothesis 2a. Social Class Related to
Mental Status*

According to our measure of biopsychological adjustment—an index of mental status—the higher the index score, the better the mental status of the respondent; that is, fewer and less extensive symptoms are expressed by the respondent. To illustrate and summarize the results of our detailed analysis of this index of mental status, we have combined symptoms scores of patients

Social Class
and
Schizophrenia:
A Ten-Year
Follow-Up

385

and controls, rank-ordered the scores, and computed the average rank scores by class. The results of this descriptive analysis are presented in Table 2.

As indicated in Table 2, we found that the patients' average rank scores increase from 73 in classes I-III to 94 in class IV and 102 in class V.[15] Thus, mental status is inversely related to social class for the patient population: the lower the social class, the better the patients' mental status. Little variation is found among the average rank scores of our matched "never-patient" population. However, our primary interest is in the patients' performance relative to the controls' performance. The data presented in Table 2 indicate that, at each class level, the mental status of the matched controls is better than that of the corresponding patients. However, the lower the class, the smaller the difference between patients and controls. Thus, differences decline from 48 in classes I-III to 33 in class IV and to only 18 in class V. It is clear that the lower the class position, the more closely the patients resemble their matched controls on the mental-status index.

Table 2

AVERAGE RANK AND DIFFERENCES OF MENTAL-STATUS SCORES BY 1960 SOCIAL CLASS FOR PATIENTS AND CONTROL[a]

Social Class	Average Rank Scores[b]		Difference[c]
	Patients	Controls	
I, II, III	73	121	48
IV	94	127	33
V	102	120	18

[a] The average scores were computed by combining 108 patients and 108 controls, ordering the mental status scores, and assigning the rank of 1 to the lowest and N (216) to the highest score. Tied scores were handled in the usual manner. Four cases were dropped from the analysis because of insufficient information. Note that the higher the rank, the fewer or less extensive the symptoms expressed by the respondent.

[b] Using the Kruskal-Wallis Analysis of Variance Test for rank-ordered data, the differences among patients are significant at the .10 level, but the differences among the controls are not significant.

[c] Test made by the Wilcoxon Matched Pairs Signed Ranks Test show that differences between patient and control mental-status scores are significant at the following levels:
Classes I, II, and III, $p = <.026$; class IV, $p = <.026$; and class V, $p = <.06$.

In other studies employing this type of index, results have demonstrated that the relatively low scores identify individuals with major psychological problems.[16] Examination of only the extreme cases, presented in Table 3, reaffirms the above findings. The proportion of severely maladjusted former

---

[15] In the analysis of mental status and occupational adjustment, classes I, II, and III are combined because of the small number of cases. The distribution of patients by 1960 class position is as follows: classes I-III—17; class IV—41; and class V—54.

[16] For example, see Leo Srole, Thomas S. Langer, Stanley T. Michael, Marvin K. Opler, and Thomas A. C. Rennie, *Mental Health in the Metropolis: The Midtown Manhattan Study* (New York: McGraw-Hill, Inc., 1962); and Jerome G. Manis, Milton J. Brawer, Chester L. Hunt, and Leonard C. Kercher, "Validating a Mental Health Scale," *American Sociological Review,* Vol. 28 (1963), pp. 108-16. Scores of 66 or lower indicate a significant number of psychiatric symptoms and are considered to represent "impaired" mental status in our research. This grouping of scores follows the procedure of Elton F. Jackson, "Status Consistency and Symptoms of Stress," *American Sociological Review,* Vol. 27 (1962), pp. 469-80.

BEAN
MYERS
PEPPER

386

Table 3

PATIENTS AND CONTROLS WITH IMPAIRED MENTAL STATUS
BY 1960 SOCIAL CLASS[a]

Social Class	Patients (Per Cent)	Controls (Per Cent)	Difference (Per Cent)
I, II, III	41	12	29
IV	37	17	20
V	28	22	6

[a]Mental-status scores range from 22 to 80. This table presents the proportion of respondents with scores of 66 or lower which indicate a significant number of symptoms.

patients is directly related to social class: the higher the social class, the greater the proportion of patients with severely impaired mental status. The percentage of such persons increases regularly from 28 in class V to 37 in class IV and 41 in classes I-III. In contrast to the former patients, we find a pattern among the controls which has been found in similar studies: the percentage of severely maladjusted increases regularly from the highest class level to the lowest.[17] When we examine the difference between patients and controls at each class level, we find that the patients always have a greater proportion of individuals with a high symptom level. However, the differences decline consistently from 29 percentage points in classes I-III to 20 in class IV and to 6 in class V.

Hypothesis 2b. Social Class Related to
Occupational Adjustment

The proportion of persons by class who have not been employed steadily over a maximum five-year period of time is presented in Table 4.[18] At each class level, a higher percentage of patients than controls are poorly adjusted occupationally. The greatest proportion of poorly adjusted individuals in both the patient and the control populations is found in class V. When we compare patients and controls at each class level, the greatest difference is found in class IV and the least in class V. Thus, as in the case of mental status, class V patients most closely approach the occupational performance of their matched controls, but, whereas the higher-class patients were least like their controls for the mental-status index, the class IV patients are least like their controls in terms of occupational performance. The same pattern is found for two other indexes of occupational adjustment which we have examined—the proportion of individuals without earned income during the 12 months preceding the interview and the percentage of persons who have been occupationally downwardly mobile since 1950.

DISCUSSION OF FINDINGS

In our ten-year follow-up study of schizophrenics, we have discovered significant relationships between social class and treatment outcome. Social

[17] For example, see Srole, *et al., op. cit.,* pp. 230-34.
[18] Only those persons in the labor force are included; housewives and retired individuals are excluded from the analysis.

Social Class
and
Schizophrenia:
A Ten-Year
Follow-Up

Table 4

PATIENTS AND MATCHED CONTROLS WITH LOW OCCUPATIONAL
ADJUSTMENT SCORES BY 1960 SOCIAL CLASS[a]

Social Class	Patients (Per Cent)	Controls (Per Cent)	Difference (Per Cent)
I, II, III	40	7	33
IV	50	0	50
V	51	24	27

[a]Patients with low occupational scores have not been steadily employed in the five years prior to the interview.

class is related to 1960 treatment status: the proportion of patients living in the community decreases significantly from classes I and II to class V. Possible reasons for these class differences are suggested by the examination of the mental-status scores of the discharged-patient population.[19] In that examination we found that the highest classes have the poorest mental status. In addition, when patients and controls are compared at each class level, the differences are greatest for the highest classes and decline regularly to the lowest class level.

It appears that class differences in discharge rates cannot be explained solely on the basis of the absence or presence of emotional difficulties. Social-class differences in the ability and willingness of the family to accept a patient back into the community are important. In particular, class V families may hesitate to reaccept a patient who is psychiatrically incapacitated to any degree. Although a hospitalized class V patient is functioning adequately under supervision and care, his family may be unable to undertake the required supervision of the patient at home, no matter how minimal, because of limited resources or restricted living quarters. Furthermore, because of differential values, lower-class families are not so willing to accept back into their midst a member who was hospitalized for mental illness.[20] On the other hand, upper- and middle-class families are not only more willing to have the patient come home, but they have available a greater range of resources to provide for his supervision and care.

Important among the resources available to higher-class families are outpatient treatment facilities. Although public outpatient agencies are ostensibly available to all, previous research has shown the generally greater use of these facilities by higher-class persons as well as the preferential treatment accorded them.[21] Because most outpatient agencies are day clinics, the differential use

---

[19] Findings on mental status and occupational adjustment must be dealt with cautiously in the attempt to explain differences in discharge rates, since, as noted above, we have shifted from the 1950 social class to the 1960 social-class position of the patient in the examination of our two hypotheses. Detailed examination of the mobile and stable patients, however, indicates no reason to assume that the discussion which follows is invalidated by this necessary shift.

[20] Myers and Roberts, op. cit., p. 217, and Appendix Table 22, p. 285.

[21] Jerome K. Myers and Leslie Schaeffer, "Social Stratification and Psychiatric Practice: A Study of an Outpatient Clinic," American Sociological Review, Vol. 19 (1954), pp. 307-10; David Rosenthal and Jerome D. Frank, "The Fate of the Psychiatric Clinic Outpatients Assigned to Psychotherapy," The Journal of Nervous and Mental Disease, Vol. 127 (1958), pp. 330-43.

BEAN
MYERS
PEPPER

of clinics by upper- and middle-class individuals is partially a function of the time an individual has available during the day to attend such clinics. Class differences in occupational demands in this respect provide the upper classes with an advantage. In addition, because of the superior financial resources of the upper-class patient and his family, treatment by private psychiatrists is more readily available. The data presented in Table 1 clearly illustrate the differential use of outpatient agencies. Proportionately, more than eight times as many class I and II as class V patients were receiving outpatient care in 1960. In addition, preliminary analysis of our data on relapse reveals that class I, II, and III patients now in the community have, on the average, a greater number of readmissions to psychiatric treatment agencies over the ten-year follow-up period.

In short, middle- and upper-class schizophrenics who are relatively poorly adjusted psychologically may be more likely to be discharged from hospital treatment because they can and do utilize other therapy facilities. In contrast, once a class V patient is released from hospital care, he is unlikely to receive any further psychiatric therapy. In fact, class V patients in the community have been out of treatment continuously for much longer periods than patients in any other class. Thus, one of the reasons why we find so few class V patients in the community may be that they must be functioning, psychologically at any rate, in a manner superior to higher-status patients before they are discharged.

The relationship we find between social class and occupational adjustment among patients is similar to that reported in many other studies: the lower the social class, the greater the proportion of individuals who are poorly adjusted occupationally.[22] However, these findings alone are misleading, since they do not take into account the occupational performance of nonpatients in the community.

Variations in adjustment by class among our patients relative to our controls clearly indicates the necessity of having baseline data, which can come only from a control population. With such a basis for comparison, we see, in our examination of the occupationally poorly adjusted, the least difference between patients and controls in class V and the greatest difference in class IV.

The reasons for these social-class differences in patterns of occupational adjustment probably are to be found in the economic and occupational structure of society. We have already suggested that one of the reasons why so few class V patients were living in the community in 1960 is that only those are accepted back into the community whose mental status is good and little different from nonpatients. The finding that the class V patients are the poorest adjusted occupationally, relative to the other patient groups, does not contradict this finding, since, relative to the control population, the class V patients are better adjusted than patients at any other class level. Apparently, poor occupational adjustment is not in itself a sufficient condition

---

[22] For example, see Leta McMinney Adler, "Patients of a State Mental Hospital: The Outcome of Their Hospitalization," in Arnold M. Rose, ed., *Mental Health and Mental Disorder* (New York: W. W. Norton & Co., Inc., 1955), pp. 501-23; and Freeman and Simmons, *op. cit.*

for a class V family to rehospitalize the patient, since, relative to nonpatients, this pattern is not unusual. Irregularity and instability are often characteristic of the jobs which are available to lower-class workers. On the other hand, class IV occupations tend to be highly rationalized, requiring stable workers with regular work habits. Employers tolerate little deviant behavior in the skilled and semiskilled factory jobs available to working-class people. Consequently, such jobs are difficult to maintain for the class IV ex-patient who is psychiatrically incapacitated to some degree.

In contrast to the employment opportunities available to class IV persons, the occupations open to class I, II, and III individuals are such that personal variations in mood and affect can be accepted more readily. Even absence from such jobs, if sufficiently irregular, does not affect the person's position, because paid sick leave is generally available. Thus, in the middle and upper classes, where perception of the legitimate sick role more likely includes emotional disturbance, a worker can withdraw from the job for a few days, when under stress, without fear of losing his position. Additionally, because of the differential access to the power structure of the economic world, class I, II, and III families are better able to guarantee regular employment for members of their families who are patients. They are more likely to own or control a business, or have a friend who does, where the former patient can work. Thus, variations in the demands of occupational roles at each class level are probably related to the adjustment patterns, which are found at different class levels.

THEORETICAL IMPLICATIONS

Although the findings reported in this article are most directly relevant to the understanding of the relationship between social class and mental illness, additional theoretical considerations in two areas are implicit in the results of the analysis presented here.

First, the findings have theoretical relevance for the study of social control and deviant behavior. Position in the social structure has been shown to be clearly related to the release of schizophrenics from hospitals which are socially approved control agencies. Indeed, it appears that, for the class V individual, almost complete remission of the deviant psychological manifestations is a requisite for discharge from institutions which have been specifically established for the care and treatment of mental patients. In contrast, it is evident that upper- and middle-class individuals are allowed to operate outside the institutionalized treatment complex in spite of continued manifestations of deviance. Related conclusions concerning the relationship between social class and control of deviance have been reached in studies of delinquency and crime.[23]

Second, our findings cast doubt on the validity of the concept of "blue-collarite" as it has been used traditionally. Our findings support recent attempts to refine the concept. According to customary usage, class IV and class V are considered together as the "blue-collar" class. As Miller and Riess-

---

[23] James S. Wallerstein and Clement J. Wyle, "Our Law-Abiding Law Breakers," *Probation*, Vol. 25 (1947), pp. 107-12; Austin L. Porterfield, "Delinquency and Its Outcome in Court and College," *American Journal of Sociology*, Vol. 49 (1943), pp. 199-208.

man, Cohen, and Hollingshead point out, however, there are important differences between "working" class and "lower" class subculture.[24] Our results show clearly that differences between patients and between patients and controls are greater generally between classes IV and V than between any other two adjacent classes. In fact, patients in class V are so distinctively different from those in class IV that further examination of the concept "blue-collarite" is warranted. The grouping of all manual workers together into one "blue-collar" class masks many crucial differences between the "working" and "lower" classes and hinders the development of a consistent and valid theory of social stratification.

The Meaning of Work and Mental Illness*

PAUL N. GEISEL

WORK in our society is a key value, geared in many ways to another value—achievement. The "normal" state of behavior is largely defined by the degree to which the individual's values and practices regarding work are consonant with those of his community. To the extent that the individual is performing the requisites of an occupational role appropriate to his age, education, training, and talents, he is in large part judged by his community—and judges himself—to be normal.

This project is concerned with the cultural and psychological underpinnings of the meaning of work to the schizophrenic individual, as well as to the individual who has been able to achieve a "normal" life adjustment. This study aims toward (1) increased understanding of the meanings attached to work by emotionally disturbed individuals—in this instance, schizophrenic patients in mental hospitals; (2) increased awareness of normative values attached to work as a comparative base with which to judge the "normality" or "abnormality" of work values and attitudes held by schizophrenic patients; and (3) increased understanding of how such values and attitudes are acquired in the life career of the individual from family, peers, and others who influence the process of growing to maturity.

---

[24] S. M. Miller and Frank Riessman, "The Working Class Subculture: a New View," *Social Problems*, Vol. IX (1961), pp. 86-97; Albert K. Cohen and Harold M. Hodges, "Lower-Blue-Collar-Class Characteristics," *Social Problems*, Vol. X (1963), pp. 303-34; August B. Hollingshead, *Elmtown's Youth* (New York: John Wiley & Sons, Inc., 1949); and Hollingshead and Redlich, *op. cit.*

* This research project on "The Meaning of Work and Mental Illness" is one of several studies in the Social Science Program at the Graduate School of Public Health, University of Pittsburgh. It is partly financed by the Vocational Rehabilitation Administration, Grant No. RD-792-63-C2. The three-year study is now in its second year.

Although schizophrenic mental patients are perhaps the largest single category of handicapped persons in American society, they are not the most easily rehabilitated. (There may even be a causal connection of some kind between these two facts.) Even in a protected workshop where, under ideal conditions, the schizophrenic patient is placed with patients whose disability is also "invisible" (cardiacs and tuberculars), vocational rehabilitation is more difficult for them than for the latter. In state divisions of rehabilitation, over-all rehabilitating of the former patient is considered to be the most difficult for counseling and placement personnel to accomplish. Often experience in counseling these patients leads to reinforced feelings of frustration and hopelessness on the part of counselors and others involved with the former patient.

Much of this despair and lack of rehabilitation "success" may be based upon a general lack of understanding about the meaning of work—particularly as it is related to the onset, treatment, and rehabilitation of the psychoses—to the individual. Learning more of the nature of the relationship between the meaning of work and the development of mental illness should enhance the understanding of counselors and other vocational rehabilitation personnel, in treatment centers, government agencies, and the community generally, and should enable them more effectively to counsel and place in employment the former psychiatric patient.

In addition to the rehabilitation implications of such a study, one must also realize the preventative and habilitative factors. Considerable evidence points to the probability that schizophrenics come primarily from the lower-class strata; they appear to occupy the lowest occupations to a large extent. (4, 3, 5)*

To this date neither the meaning of work nor schizophrenia is well understood. A plethora of hypotheses have been investigated in order to assess the individual's motivation to work, his feelings about particular types of work situations, and stress factors in work. Work has been described as a collection of tasks, activities, statuses, roles; from a cultural perspective, as part of the Judeo-Christian inheritance—the Protestant ethic of life fulfillment through work; from a functional viewpoint, as providing man with economic sustenance; from a sociological view, as providing the individual with participating membership in the society. Only within recent years has there been any systematic attempt to assess the total "meaning of work."

In like manner there is no precise definition of schizophrenia. In Bleuler's classic monograph, we find the concept of schizophrenia used to describe:

> . . . A group of psychoses . . . characterized by a specific type of alteration of thinking, feeling, and relation to the external world which appears nowhere else in this particular fashion. . . . The fundamental symptoms consist of disturbances of association and affectivity, the predilection for fantasy as against reality and the inclination to divorce oneself from reality (autism). Furthermore, we can add the absence of those very symptoms which play such a great role in certain other diseases such as primary disturbances of perception, orientation, memory, etc. (1)

---

* Numbers in parentheses refer to numbered items in the bibliography at the end of the chapter.

GEISEL

Child-rearing practices and styles of family life are often looked upon as being particularly important in creating high vulnerability. Role transitions, severe economic deprivation, and the disruption of primary-group relationships have been regarded as among the stresses that might act directly to induce illness. (7)

Although most classical theories of schizophrenia seem to assume that it is a disturbance of youth, schizophrenic reactions often seem to follow a drastic change in one's pattern of living which is likely to present many new percepts or experiences for assimilation. The changes may be such things as making the transition from dependent adolescence to independent adulthood, entering or leaving the armed service, changing jobs, and losing someone close. The more radical or comprehensive the change, that is, the more new percepts it generates for the individual to assimilate, the more likely a schizophrenic development would be. (11)

In this paper we should like to stress the developmental aspects of the meaning of work for the schizophrenic patient. For, in our empirical findings to date, certain clear patterns are emerging which suggest a strong relationship between the etiology of illness and the meanings associated with work.

According to theories of the socialization process, the child learns to take on many roles. During his childhood, he is in a dependent position in his family and at the same time he is being trained for adulthood. In our society the fulfillment of this training in the home, school, and other social environments is when the individual takes on an adult work role. Taking an adult work role is akin to a "rite of passage" involving change from childhood dependence to adult independence and responsibility. To take an autonomous and responsible work role is not simply an act of working at specific tasks which provide remuneration. When the individual begins working, there is the implication that his training is completed, and the society assumes that the individual is now ready for other adult roles. The "normal" individual is expected to demonstrate qualities of independence from the parental family; he is assumed to be capable and now ready for the roles of husband, father, and breadwinner. The individual is culturally judged to be "mature" or adult by his ability to work but, more than this, by his ability to take on the other meanings associated with work, for example, father-type role independence.

In our analyses of extensive interviews from 110 male schizophrenic patients, 18 to 45 years of age, who have worked, an awareness of this socialization system is beginning to emerge. The schizophrenic, like other deviants in the social system, appears to be quite knowledgeable about the expectations of society with regard to work. Thus, in a comparison with nonschizophrenic workers, matched by age, race, marital status, and occupation, he shows few differences. The schizophrenic defines work in a manner very similar to that of the nonschizophrenic. Work is viewed by both groups as a father-type role in which the individual takes on the responsibilities of adulthood through the acquisition of other adult roles. However, for the nonschizophrenic, it is these other roles which are the fulfillment and motivation sources for work.

It is our basic premise that these other roles, which constitute the attraction for work for the nonschizophrenic, are the source of ultimate anxiety for the

The Meaning of Work and Mental Illness

393

schizophrenic. Rather than assume a process of simple role transition or disruption to induce a schizophrenic reaction, as is generally postulated, we would postulate that the process of preparing for various life roles that constitute maturity operates as a system which either mediates or induces the schizophrenic reaction. The degree to which the schizophrenic-prone individual is compelled to perform these other roles defines his level of vulnerability to hospitalization. Objectively, the schizophrenic, according to his intelligence and physical capabilities, is able to work, but he does not work consistently because he is psychologically incapable of taking on the culturally prescribed meanings of the work role.

Nevertheless, studies (2) of schizophrenic patients, for those who at least begin to assume an occupational role, suggest that the vocational sphere may be the last in which he finds his life situation so distressful that he "completely breaks down." The usual sequence of interpersonal deterioration probably occurs first in the family, where the roots of illness may lie in part within deviant values held toward work and passed on in the socialization process to the growing child. Then he severs relations with the larger circle of friends and acquaintances in the community, from which he also receives work attitudes and values. This circle is able to tolerate him longer because the intensity of emotional ties may not be as strong as in the family; it also is not as deeply affected by impairments in the person's vocational functioning (for example, loss of income, change of psychological image brought about by unfulfillment of cultural expectations regarding the work role, and so on). Finally he is alienated in the occupational sphere, in which the greatest pressures are for performance of the work role, where emotional interpersonal ties are not as intense as in either family or community at large, and where vocational competence may continue for some time beyond the point at which emotional turmoil makes profound interpersonal relationships intolerable. Emotional problems ultimately overwhelm the patient, so that he cannot "pull himself together" enough even to carry out the mechanics of the work role. The family reaches the limits of "tolerance of deviance," and he is hospitalized.

According to these studies, the sequence of rehabilitation is then reversed, with the occupational sphere being the first in which the patient is likely to be rehabilitated to a former or a new level of competence, the larger community sphere of interpersonal relationships usually following this, and finally the affective associations with the family being repaired last of all, if even then. Often, of course, the ex-patient is able to function vocationally even though still suffering in some measure from his neurotic or psychotic symptoms. Where these are too deeply rooted in psychopathology, they may never heal, although the patient receives his sole gratifications from performing his occupational requirements and is once again contributing to the common welfare by carrying out a socially useful vocational task assignment.

Work, then, may be seen as an indicator and central focus of the illness phenomenon. Support for this position from our study findings of the schizophrenic sample is still only suggestive in nature. For example, in our analyses of the lives of these men, we see that, although they are able to define work activities in detail in earlier sections of the interview, in describing a typical day they are unable to differentiate their work activities from family and play activities. They show considerable fuzziness in their time orientations. In their descriptions of an "ideal" day, they structure each setting: family, work, and peer relationships, similarly, along childhood-dependency lines. Work on the ideal day becomes a situation in which we find something akin to a surrogate family. The individual, depending upon his identification with a domineering or passive mother or father, sees himself either in a position with no particular responsibility or at the opposite pole in a position of complete authority. In neither the "typical" or "ideal" day, however, is he able to show any perceived differences in the expectations of his work friends or associates, for example, and those of his family.[1]

Using a measure known as the Semantic Differential (9) to determine the "meaning space" (or evaluation of concepts) for the individual, we find: (1) a universally high evaluation of family, childhood, and mother, in comparison with a rather low evaluation of work, job, and self; (2) life is viewed identically with work, father, and job.

It should be noted, however, that this pattern does not hold for Negroes, who see early life as harsh and life as a whole as identical in meaning with the view of the self as a child. Owing to subcultural differences and discrimination against nonwhites, this is not a surprising difference. The schizophrenic Negro has, in effect, two strikes against him. Not only is he in the lower class, but the jobs open to him are typically menial in nature. No Negro in our sample had attained a white-collar position (possibly owing to the nature of our sample universe).

More generally speaking, the less disturbed schizophrenics—those who were evaluated to be in the best state of remission—relate life as a whole to the meanings of work, the self now, and the job. For those who are most disturbed, life becomes equated with father, self now, childhood self, and work. The pattern here is quite exciting. It shows clearly the relationship of disturbance to the developmental stage of the individual. It also gives some confirmation to the notion of work as a critical indicator of the level of maturity.

Additional evidence for this position is shown by the few schizophrenics who are married. (8) Of course, in a study of hospitalized patients, one must consider the limitations imposed by the illness. Also, there is the qualification that schizophrenia is a disease of the early ages. Nevertheless, in a society where (according to the census) more than 70 per cent of all unskilled workers (blue-collar) are married, we find the vast majority of the schizophrenic patients to be single. The level of occupational achievement is another factor. In our study, 83 per cent of the 110 patients had "blue-collar" work careers, although the median educational level, eleventh grade, was not significantly different from the total population median for this city and county.

Finally, the adult friendship patterns of the schizophrenic are of interest. First we see that the schizophrenic has few adult friends. Second, he equates "best friend" in meaning with father, which may be an indication that he tends to restructure his adult environment along former childhood patternings.

---

[1] Complete tables of empirical findings are not included, owing to space limitations. These are available upon request.

The Meaning of Work and Mental Illness

SUMMARY

In this paper we have attempted to develop a few notions about work and its relationship to the schizophrenic syndrome. We have tried to show how work values and practices play a key role in the psychosocial development of the individual, which is highlighted in a discussion of the etiology of schizophrenia. Work is seen as a primary indicator of "normality." The schizophrenic patient is unable to work effectively. The hypothesis to explain this is as yet only speculative. *We hypothesize that taking on the work role assumes the acquisition of other adult roles and expectations; that these other extra-job expectations pose a significant threat to the schizophrenic.*

The greatest advance to the investigation of the relationship of the meaning of work and mental illness will be in an elaboration of the feelings, attitudes, and practices in these "other social environments." It would seem that a comprehensive theory of social factors in the etiology of schizophrenia and the development of work meanings would have to include the family's influence on the patient in both his formative and his later years, and the family's function as a transmitter of forces from the larger social environment. This is part of our goal and is a primary research need. The meaning of work cannot be evaluated in isolation from developmental factors.

BIBLIOGRAPHY

1. Bleuler, E., *Dementia Praecox or the Group of Schizophrenias.* New York: International U. Press, 1950. Monograph Series on Schizophrenia, No. 1, Translated from the German edition, 1911.

2. Bockoven, J. S., A. R. Pandiscio, and H. C. Solomon, "Social Adjustment of Patients in the Community Three Years after Commitment to the Boston Psychopathic Hospital," *Mental Hygiene,* Vol. 40 (July, 1956), pp. 353-74.

3. Clausen, J. A., and M. Kohn, "The Ecological Approach in Social Psychiatry," *American Journal of Sociology,* Vol. 60 (1954), pp. 140-49.

4. Hollingshead, A. B., and F. Redlich, *Social Class and Mental Illness.* New York: John Wiley & Sons, Inc., 1958.

5. Jaco, E. G., *The Social Epidemiology of Mental Disorders.* New York: Russell Sage Foundation, 1960.

6. Landy, D., and M. P. Linder, "Post-Discharge Experience and Vocational Rehabilitation Needs of Psychiatric Patients," *Mental Hygiene,* Vol. 42, No. 1 (January, 1958), pp. 29-44.

7. Mishler, E. G., and N. A. Scotch, *Socio-Cultural Factors in the Epidemiology of Schizophrenia.* Working paper, from the Cross Cultural Disease Survey, NIMH, Harvard School of Public Health, 1962.

8. Mishler and Scotch, *op. cit.*

9. Osgood, C. E., G. J. Suci, and P. H. Tannenbaum, *The Measurement of Meaning.* Urbana: University of Illinois, 1957.

10. Sanua, V. D., "Sociocultural Factors in Families of Schizophrenics," *Psychiatry,* Vol. 24, No. 3 (August, 1961).

11. Winder, C. L., "Some Psychological Studies of Schizophrenics," Ch. 8, *The Etiology of Schizophrenia,* ed. D. D. Jackson, New York: Basic Books, pp. 191-292.

GEISEL

Work and Mental Health

CHARLTON R. PRICE

HARRY LEVINSON

RECENT years have brought a growing research interest in how work experience can affect mental health, and in the psychological background of effective and ineffective work performance.[1] But while a good deal has been said about the tensions in executive suites and about middle-management anxieties, less attention has been given to relationships between work and mental health in the blue-collar world. In addition, industrial mental-health studies at all occupational levels have tended to concentrate on sources of mental *ill* health, or the incidence and prevalence of mental illness in working populations. Too little is known about the potentially strengthening or health-producing aspects of work experience.

This article summarizes some results of our own research bearing on these issues and draws attention to unanswered questions which have been raised by these and other recent studies.

One of the difficulties in mental-health research is the ambiguity of the term "mental health" itself. What is judged to be good mental health is always somewhat influenced by what the evaluator considers to be "the good life"—the accepted standards of behavior in his own social class and culture. Kingsley Davis demonstrated the middle-class biases which are contained in the popular literature on mental hygiene,[2] and more recently Marie Jahoda's review of definitions of mental health[3] emphasized the same point. Nevertheless a working definition of mental health can be developed with the understanding that the observer's values will inevitably affect the definition to some degree.

Our research purposes required a definition of mental health broad enough to take into account how a person feels about himself, about other people, about the world around him and his place in it, and about his experiences while earning a living for himself and those dependent on him. We also sought a definition which could be derived from observed behavior in ordinary life situations, not clinical descriptions based upon observation of people presumed

---

[1] Harry Levinson, "Industrial Mental Health: Progress and Prospects," *Personnel,* Vol. 38, No. 3 (May-June, 1961), pp. 35-42.

[2] Kingsley Davis, "Mental Hygiene and the Class Structure," *Psychiatry,* Vol. 1 (February, 1938), pp. 55-65.

[3] Marie Jahoda, *Current Concepts of Positive Mental Health* (New York: Basic Books, Inc., 1958).

Work
and
Mental Health

397

to be ill or seeking professional help. Therefore, we undertook to find out how people judged to be in good mental health tended to behave.[4]

Opinions from two kinds of observers were sought. First, we asked a number of psychiatrists and psychoanalysts on the staff of the Menninger Foundation to describe the behavior of people they had known whom they considered to be mentally healthy. We then asked the same question of a group of undergraduates at Wayne State University. Similar kinds of behavior were repeatedly mentioned by both groups of observers. Both the experienced clinicians and the college students described people whom they had known, whom they judged to be healthy, as behaving in these ways:

1. They had a wide variety of sources of gratification, satisfaction, or psychological reward

They tended to have many interests—in other people, in work, in leisure-time activities, in their community. They obtained satisfaction from a wide variety of sources.

2. They were flexible under stress

Stress was conceived of as including both internal pressures and influences from the environment which would tend to disrupt the characteristic way in which a person behaves. The people described were able to "roll with the punch" and to cope successfully with stressful experiences.

3. They treated others as individuals

By this, the observers meant that the presumably healthy people were sensitive to individual differences. They avoided stereotyping: perceiving other individuals as impersonal sources of reward or punishment, or treating others as if they were parents, relatives, or other emotionally significant figures from the past.

4. They recognized, understood, and accepted their own capacities and limitations

These people had a realistic view of themselves; they neither inflated nor ignored their own capacities.

5. They were active and productive

This behavioral characteristic was, in a way, an outcome of those previously listed. Given an ability to obtain gratification from a wide variety of sources, to deal flexibly with stressful experiences, to understand and accept other people as having individual differences both from oneself and from others, and to understand one's own assets and limitations, it was possible for the people described to use their capacities in the interest of their own self-

---

[4] C. M. Solley and K. J. Munden, "Toward a Description of Mental Health," *Bulletin of The Menninger Clinic,* Vol. 26 (July, 1962), pp. 178-88. See this for a more complete discussion of Mental Health definitions.

fulfillment and in the service of others. They did not, for example, characteristically have a neurotically driven need to achieve, nor were they apt to experience difficulty in completing tasks which they had undertaken.

These ways of describing healthy functioning are so general that they could be illustrated in any life situation. Our interest, of course, was in the work situation. Each of the aspects of behavior identified as indicative of good mental health could be affected in various ways by working conditions.

For example, jobs in some parts of an organization might involve people in a wider variety of ties to the environment than others. Some work situations would offer people many chances to learn about themselves and their capacities, whereas in other jobs—perhaps highly routine work or work involving limited responsibilities—such opportunities would be less likely. Perception of other people might depend upon how regularly the job requires contact with others, and work situations clearly varied in this respect. Work-related stresses and the resources available for coping with stress also vary according to the type of job involved. Similarly, some jobs are more likely than others to permit a sense of accomplishment through initiating and completing tasks.

The next step was to test these assumptions by direct observation. We sought, in short, to identify and describe aspects of people's work experience in an organization which tended to enhance or inhibit behavior indicative of good mental health.

Clearly, our conception of the definition of the work environment also had to be a broad one, because there was no way of establishing in advance which aspects of the work situation would be the most closely related to mental health as we had defined it. Therefore, in an extended study of a public utility[5] and subsequent briefer studies in four additional organizations,[6] we undertook to describe each organizational "culture": the firm's public reputation, its history of management-union relationships, habitual work practices, formal policies and informal working rules, the kinds of people who tended to seek work in each organization and how they differed from those entering employment in other kinds of organizations, common work-related stresses and satisfactions, and other characteristics of the work environment which were referred to or could be inferred from the interviews and observations.

One major conclusion from these studies has been that *people's perception of the organization and their relationship to it are of greater significance for mental health than prior research has indicated.* This became evident from what was learned about work expectations, a prominent theme in the data.

Some of these expectations were quite apparent, such as those about wages, hours, and working conditions. Others, however, were implicit, even outside conscious awareness. For many, there seemed to be an implicit expectation that, by providing work opportunity, the organization would help the person clarify questions he had about himself, that he would be able to find out

---

[5] Harry Levinson, Charlton R. Price, Kenneth J. Munden, Harold J. Mandl, and Charles M. Solley, *Men, Management and Mental Health* (Cambridge: Harvard University Press, 1962).

[6] Division of Industrial Mental Health, The Menninger Foundation, *Interdisciplinary Research on Work and Mental Health: A Point of View and a Method* (Topeka: The Menninger Foundation, 1961).

more about who he was and what he could do. The company and the union, through attitudes and actions of their leadership, also convey expectations to organization members. The employee is not told, "We want you to be loyal," or "We want you to be identified with the free enterprise system," but both managements and unions certainly have these or similar expectations of their membership.

The obligatory quality of these expectations was striking. The fact of being hired was assumed to mean that each party—the employee and the organization—had incurred certain obligations to the other. And, should either party not meet these obligations, especially those which remained implicit, people behaved as if a contract had been violated.

But employees' expectations which seemed most central were not the sort to be found in a collective-bargaining agreement. They stemmed from three basic concerns about the work situation. The first of these was a concern with dependence upon the organization. The second was a concern with psychological distance, and the third was a concern with change.

Interdependence

In a society such as ours, in which there is an extended period of dependence on parents, growing up involves a struggle to become relatively independent. Yet an adult is also expected to be able to establish and maintain various kinds of interdependent relationships: in marriage, with family and friends, on a job. Within broadly defined limits, which vary from organization to organization, it is considered legitimate for an employee to expect a certain degree of job security in exchange for adequate work performance. He has to depend upon the organization to keep its part of the bargain. But there is often a parallel, though usually latent, fear of the organization: that its power will envelop the employee and make him excessively dependent, or that the organization is too unstable and inconsistent to be depended upon.

The importance of the concern with dependency was illustrated by what happened when a serious auto accident partially crippled a utility company lineman. The company had no formal obligations to the man, because the accident did not happen on the job. But there had been a tradition in the company of altering work assignments if an accident or illness prevented a person from carrying out his regular job. The rest of the injured man's work group felt that not to keep him in some kind of job was a violation of the psychological contract. They did not put it in these terms, of course. Their expressed view was that the company should find and maintain a place for this man even though he was low on the seniority list and the accident had not occurred while he was on the job.

Distance

Achieving and maintaining the right amount of psychological distance was another important theme in our data. The concern with distance had essentially to do with people's attempts to cope with the drives of love and hate. Linemen working in crews to repair or install electric lines are forced to be extremely close to each other both physically and psychologically. They must be able to tolerate and control each others' aggression. Therefore, each man has to be hypersensitive to how each other member of the crew feels. If one of them comes to work in the morning with his "toast burnt," as they put it, his working partner, sensing his tension, may not go up the pole with him, because a man who is upset, preoccupied with his distress, might hand another a "hot wire" accidentally. The foreman tries to be close enough to the men to anticipate such possibilities and to keep an "edgy" crew member from going up the pole on that day. For such problems to be handled with skill, the members of the crew must be able to tolerate extreme closeness in work relationships.

On the other hand, many men who work in electric generating stations, where the environment is one of widely separated work locations, a high noise level, and relatively few people, seem to prefer a situation requiring greater distance than prevails on the line crews. The power-plant men can talk with each other only infrequently, and then only by shouting. They work on rotating shifts, which means that their social life is disrupted. Though all of the power-plant people complained about these working conditions, most apparently are not made so uncomfortable that they seek to change jobs. For them the greater psychological distance enforced by the plant environment seems comparatively comfortable.

However, even in the power plant, the psychological distance can become too great and therefore disturbing. Every member of the plant crew is aware that at any moment one of them could accidentally turn a wrong valve and blow the place up. Each man, then, has to be concerned to some degree about what each other man is doing. But because he can watch or talk with others on the work crew only at rare intervals, there is a good deal of opportunity for imagining all the things which might go wrong and wondering whether or not the others are doing what they are supposed to do. Furthermore, people who choose and stay with jobs precluding close contact with others probably are somewhat more suspicious of other people than the average. A supervisor who intuitively understood this problem dealt with it by constantly making the rounds among the men. Thus he brought them closer together psychologically, using himself as a medium for reducing the psychological distance.

In isolated work locations like the power plants, much suspicion and latent hostility is also directed toward the larger organization. The company is seen as a distant, powerful "they," who create and maintain the work environment in which the power-plant men live. Hostile fantasy about the distant "they" can turn into open anger in situations of labor-management conflict, particularly when the actions of management or union leadership trigger the hostility or increase it.

In short, optimal psychological distance involved appropriate degrees of affection, privacy, and control. People needed to be close enough to superiors, peers, and subordinates so that they could feel that what happened to them was of concern to others, but not so close that it was "too personal." There needed to be enough freedom so that each man could feel he was doing his job as he would like to do it, but not so much that nobody knew or cared about what a man was doing. People needed to feel close enough to each other

Work and Mental Health

401

to be confident that the work situation could be brought and kept under control, but not so close that they felt that they were being overcontrolled and made overdependent.

Change

The third set of expectations centered around the problem of coping with change. Any change in the work situation is apt to involve a certain psychological loss. A man who has come to see himself as a man because his work requires a good deal of physical stamina may lose part of his favored self-image when automation makes his skill and strength unnecessary. He may have difficulty learning a new skill if he has had limited formal education and has learned mostly from experience. Change in the work environment thus inevitably takes away from a person a certain sense of who he is and what he is, and requires a new adaptation. The new adaptation is seen as a demand from outside himself which occurs simultaneously with the psychological loss. The combination of psychological loss and demand creates a stress situation.

Older employees, with limited education or long experience in a single job assignment, were particularly likely to retreat from situations of change which involved simultaneous experiences of loss and demand. Many said, in effect, "Why don't they leave me alone doing some small job until I can retire?" If, however, both man and organization work on the change process together, then the change seems to be much more easily dealt with and not to produce psychological and physiological symptoms. The psychological tie between the man and the organization seems to be a critically important one. Other research indicates that adaptation to change will be most successful if it can be made by the work group as a unit, in the context of their own community and retaining the ties to the organization.[7]

Incidentally, the implications of these findings seem relevant to the design of retraining programs for people in economically distressed areas. Once the tie between a man and his work organization has been lost, in many cases it is extremely difficult for the employee to cope with the added demand of retraining.

In summary, the expectations of organization members, sought as opportunities, include these:

1. To plan some part of one's work life, an area of freedom to function;
2. To identify with people in authority positions in both management and union leadership, to have an authentic relationship in which one is recognized as an individual;
3. To act upon both company and union organization, shaping them to some extent to conform to one's life goals;
4. To have the experience of dealing successfully with stress and responsibility in the work situation;
5. To be controlled by the reality demands of the task, including the feeling that the organization depends on the individual to get his task accomplished;
6. To be stimulated and strengthened (not stripped of psychological resources) by the experience of growth and change.

---

[7] Charles R. Walker, *Toward the Automatic Factory* (New Haven: Yale University Press, 1957).

Reciprocation

The process of moving toward fulfillment of these expectations, involving a give-and-take between man and organization, we have called *reciprocation*. We found that, when reciprocation is operating in such a way that it fulfills the psychological contract for both parties, then people are more likely to act in ways which our criterion study had established were indicative of positive mental health.

These conclusions do not imply that work situations in which the reciprocation process does not occur *cause* mental illness. Mental illness is too complex a phenomenon to be attributed to any single cause. Nor do we imply that a company could make people well if they are sick. We postulate, however, that there are ways in which an organization can be managed which can enhance the psychological strength of the people within it, or which, conversely, can to a certain extent diminish that strength.

We found that when the psychological contract was being fulfilled, when reciprocation was operating well, the five kinds of behaviors indicative of good mental health tended to appear. When reciprocation was not operating well, other kinds of behavior occurred more frequently. Among these were outright hostility, sabotage of the organization, accidents, rejection of relationships with other people in the organization, running away from the job as quickly as one could, the destruction of social groups on the job, and physical symptoms.

IMPLICATIONS FOR RESEARCH AND ACTION

Future research could well concentrate on more detailed description of the kinds of behavior which the criterion study indicated are characteristic of healthy functioning. For example, it is not yet known what kinds of experiences and what amount of variety of experience provide the kinds of gratifications which meet the psychological needs of people in various life circumstances.

Our pilot research indicates that the wider the range of gratifications, the more adequate are the resources available to the individual in maintaining his mental health. But one man's variety may be another's confusion or distraction. Mental-health research in industry summarized here and a recent review of organization theory[8] both underline the value of understanding the "fit" between the individual's psychological processes and structure of the organizational system: its psychologically rewarding and stressful features, the kinds of interpersonal relationships involved, and the kinds of task activities required by the work flow. Similar importance is attached to the problem of "fit" in recent research on personnel selection.[9] Although such considerations are increasingly taken into account in the selection and development of people

[8] Alex Inkeles and Daniel J. Levinson, "The Personal System and the Sociocultural System in Large-scale Organizations," *Sociometry*, Vol. 26, No. 2 (June, 1963), pp. 217-29.
[9] George Stern, Morris I. Stein, and Benjamin S. Bloom, *Methods in Personality Assessment: Human Behavior in Complex Social Situations* (New York: The Free Press of Glencoe, Inc., 1956).

for managerial jobs, little attention has been given to psychological aspects of selection at the line level. Our view is that these studies point dramatically to the value of more attention to the psychological dimension of *all* work assignments, not just of the positions at the top of the organizational pyramid.

A second direction for further research should be comparative studies of "the psychological contract" which this exploratory research indicates is a crucial part of everyone's work experience. Our hypothesis is that the reciprocation process is a universal. It can be seen as an effort to deal with three problems inherent in all work situations: the problem of dependency, the problem of achieving optimal distance between the individual and his work associates, and the problem of coping with both sudden and long-term change, both in personal life circumstances and in the organization. But little is known as yet about the ways in which different kinds of company and union structures may serve to carry forward or impede the process of reciprocation.

That the kind of organization structure involved does make a difference is suggested by a comparison of our findings with the results of research in large-scale manufacturing industries. In the mass-production situation which Kornhauser[10] studied, it seems clear that blue-collar jobs are less likely than white-collar and executive positions to provide the kinds of work experience conducive to optimal mental health. Robert Dubin[11] and Daniel Bell[12] have claimed that the work experience of more and more Americans provides fewer opportunities for individual accomplishment, particularly for those on the lower rungs of the organizational ladder. For people at the blue-collar level, says Dubin, work is less and less a "central life interest." Robert Weiss and David Riesman[13] point out that so many blue-collar jobs are psychologically unrewarding that it would be odd if the man on the line were to say that he "enjoys" his work. Weiss and Riesman also observe that opportunities for advancement from blue-collar to white-collar ranks are becoming more limited. Thus, in a predominantly white-collar culture, "the unskilled laborer or service worker, despite the pieties that may be uttered periodically about the dignity of labor, knows that he has not gotten very far." Seemingly, these conclusions dovetail with the findings of Gerald Gurin and his fellow researchers at the University of Michigan.[14] They found that the lower the status of a person's job, the less likely he was to report "ego gratifications" stemming from work experience. But if there is less opportunity for a sense of personal accomplishment in nonsupervisory jobs, this is not experienced as "a lack of frustration, at least at the conscious level," according to the Michigan researchers.

In the utility company we studied, however, blue-collar work assignments were carried out within a less impersonal work environment, and work

---

[10] Arthur Kornhauser, "Toward An Assessment of the Mental Health of Factory Workers: A Detroit Study," *Human Organization*, Vol. 21, No. 1 (Spring, 1962), pp. 43-46.

[11] Robert Dubin, "Industrial Workers' Worlds: A Study of the Central Life Interests of Industrial Workers," *Social Problems*, Vol. 3 (January, 1955), pp. 131-42.

[12] Daniel Bell, *Work and Its Discontents* (Boston: Beacon Press, 1956).

[13] Robert S. Weiss and David Riesman, "Social Problems and Disorganization in the World of Work," in *Contemporary Social Problems*, eds. Robert K. Merton and Robert A. Nisbet (New York: Harcourt, Brace & World, Inc., 1961), pp. 459-514.

[14] Gerald Gurin, Joseph Veroff, and Sheila Feld, *Americans View Their Mental Health* (New York: Basic Books, Inc., 1960), Ch. 6.

routines involved for the most part *service* rather than small segments of a very large and complex *production* process.[15] In this type of work organization, more of the kinds of behavior indicative of positive mental health did occur even in blue-collar work experience when an effective process of reciprocation between man and organization was operating.

Clearly, further study of the latent meanings of work is badly needed. If work were not psychologically important, there would not be either the pressure Dubin describes toward seeking satisfactions exclusively in family life and leisure activities, nor would symptoms of stress appear in those job situations in which the reciprocation process is not evident.[16] But, as we have emphasized repeatedly in this discussion, many of the significant aspects of the man-organization relationship, work expectations, and psychological needs motivating work performance are not within the conscious awareness of either the individual organization member or those who shape personnel policy. These meanings of work remain hidden both when the reciprocation process functions well and when, for personal or structural reasons, the work situation is experienced as chronically stressful.

We think that the psychological distance between both management and union leadership and the rank-and-file industrial worker (both as employee and as union member) is increased by the fact that so many work expectations remain implicit. Robert McMurry[17] blames the inability to "tune in on" the kinds of unspoken expectations which people bring to the work situation on differences in *values* characteristic of various social strata or occupational groups. The research reviewed in this discussion indicates, in addition, that behind expressed values and beliefs are basic psychological needs which are pressing for fulfillment through work experience. These psychological forces are at the root of work expectations.

The implications for action by both management and union leadership seem clear. A leadership policy which ignores the psychological meaning of the organization to its members, or fails to take account of the compelling quality of people's expectations of the organization, can have destructive consequences, both for the individual worker and for the viability of the organization itself. Sheer self-interest in survival would seem to require management and union executives to take a closer look at the reciprocation process.

---

[15] The psychological significance of organizational purpose for organization members, and a preliminary catalog of types of purposes, have been suggested by Warren G. Bennis, but the effects of an organization's purposes on the mental health of its members has yet to be systematically studied. Warren G. Bennis, "Leadership Theory and Administrative Behavior," *Administrative Science Quarterly*, Vol. 4 (December, 1959), pp. 259-301.

[16] Stanislav V. Kasl and John R. P. French, Jr., "The Effects of Occupational Status on Physical and Mental Health," *Journal of Social Issues*, Vol. 18, No. 3 (July, 1962), pp. 67-89.

[17] Robert N. McMurry, "Conflicts in Human Values," *Harvard Business Review*, Vol. 41, No. 3 (June, 1963), pp. 130-45.

Part VIII

LEISURE

HOW does the worker seek fun, excitement, pleasure, novelty, knowledge, and other leisure experiences? How successful a pursuer is he?
What is the impact of the mass media on the adult blue-collarite,
and the impact of television on the working-class child? Why do
"new" working-class Negroes react to television in the ways that
they do, and why do blue-collarites gamble in their particular
fashion? How might the blue-collarite be helped to make more
constructive use of his leisure? These are the key questions of the
six essays in this section, five of which appear here for the first time
anywhere. Gordon and Anderson explore what, in fact, the worker
is doing with his increased leisure time and why. They also consider
contrasts and similarities in blue- and white-collar uses of leisure
(note their stress, as earlier in Hamilton's essay, on the significance
of working-class socialization). Bogart challenges cliché images of the
blue-collarite's experience of the mass media, and characterizes the
mass media as "perhaps the most powerful current by which blue-
collar workers are swept into the mainstream of conformity to
middle-class values and aspirations." Gomberg (the wife of a co-
editor) finds, similarly, that the working-class child today is led by
his considerable exposure to television to admire the middle-class
setting of the situation comedy and to aspire after such arrangements.
Blum explores the reaction of "new" working-class Negroes in the
television-viewing situation and challenges the notion of blue-collar
passivity and defenselessness against the medium. He observes, instead, that hostility toward the dominant white society is expressed
in the joking relationship the Negro television-viewer establishes
with the performer. Zola similarly analyzes the significance of blue-
collarite gambling in local bars, and finds, quite like Blum, that the
activity is a way of harnessing or channeling or venting otherwise
destructive frustrations. Finally, London and Wenkert explore some
of the obstacles that inhibit greater participation by blue-collar
workers in adult education. "The task for the future," they conclude, "is not to cast blame, but to rethink the objectives of adult
education and to bring together the educators and the blue-collar
workers into a dynamic harmony."

The Blue-Collar Worker at Leisure

MILTON M. GORDON

CHARLES H. ANDERSON

CLASSICAL conceptions of the laboring man in the reformist and radical literature, both Marxist and non-Marxist, have included either implicitly or explicitly the idea that the blue-collar worker, if freed from his brutal bondage and long hours of work on the machine, would use his time in advantageous and profitable ways to improve himself educationally, to develop his esthetic sensitivity, and to fulfill his need for creative activity and work. In the critical comment of Marx, the capitalistic system left the worker no "time for education, for intellectual development, for the fulfilling of social functions and for social intercourse, for the free play of his bodily and mental activity . . ." [1]

Thus the question arises in twentieth-century America and in other countries where a social-welfare system has emerged from the early exploitative stage of capitalism, bringing with it a considerably reduced work day: What, in fact, is the worker doing with his increased leisure time? Is he using it to improve himself educationally and intellectually, to engage in constructive civic activity, to develop esthetic interests—that is, in ways which classical reformers and critics of society predicted? Or is he not? And, if not, why not? It should be understood, of course, that the general desirability on humane and moral grounds of the substantial decline in hours of labor (and improvement in conditions) for blue-collar workers is not at issue here.

A second theoretical proposition of considerable interest is the question raised in stratification analysis, after one distinguishes among the various dimensions of stratification, as to whether a change in one dimension, such as economic power, leads to a change in another dimension, such as social status. [2] Both Max Weber and W. Lloyd Warner have stressed the importance of life style and group life as intervening variables in the process of the transition from low to higher social status following an increase in income. [3] Changes in cultural behavior systems, such as clique activities, associational relation-

---

[1] Karl Marx, *Capital* (Chicago: Kerr & Company, 1912), Vol. I, p. 291.

[2] For a germinal discussion of the multidimensional approach to stratification analysis, see Max Weber's essay, "Class, Status, and Part," in H. H. Gerth and C. Wright Mills, *From Max Weber: Essays in Sociology* (New York: Oxford University Press, 1958); a more detailed theoretical formulation can be found in Milton M. Gordon, *Social Class in American Sociology* (Durham, N. C.: Duke University Press, 1958).

[3] Especially, W. Lloyd Warner and Paul S. Lunt, *The Social Life of a Modern Community* (New Haven, Conn.: Yale University Press, 1941).

ships, family interaction, and life style, are said to be produced by the dynamic operation of the economic variable, and these changes then act as intervening variables contributing to mobility in the social-status dimension. In this context, accordingly, the question can be asked: Has the modern worker translated his well-attested-to gains in the economic dimension by adopting group ties and cultural attributes that are classically associated with the middle classes, and that would therefore connote real social mobility? Here, again, in view of the rising income levels of workingmen during and following World War II and the earlier and continuing favorable governmental climate for union activity and workers' welfare, we have the opportunity to derive at least some tentative answers to this question.

Thus, two basic questions about blue-collar workers have been raised in these introductory comments. A literature of theoretical and empirical studies on blue-collar culture has grown up, particularly in the postwar period, which gives us a picture of the blue-collar way of life over a time span of some magnitude. Most of the studies have been carried out in large metropolitan settings. Our proposal is to describe the results of a small exploratory study in which intensive interviews were completed on 15 relatively high-income workers in a small city with a rural environment, and to relate these findings to the other studies in terms of the theoretical questions we have raised. Our interview schedule included questions dealing not only with the workers' current leisure-time activities, but also, through recall, with their leisure pursuits ten years ago when their incomes were significantly lower. Obviously, the number of interviews is far too small to enable us to claim proven validity for our findings. Rather, our statements based on these data should be thought of as hypotheses suggested by these exploratory interviews. (Nevertheless, there is a highly suggestive uniformity in much of the data.) After exploring the model of blue-collar leisure depicted in the existing literature, we shall be able to compare our findings on the current leisure-time activities of these small-city workers with their recall data for the early 1950's and with the model derived from existing studies.

Clark,[4] White,[5] and Reissman[6] have carried out studies comparing blue-collar with white-collar workers and reported similar findings: namely, that the blue-collar worker differed from his white-collar counterpart in reading fewer books and periodicals, attending fewer movies, lectures, concerts, and theaters, and displaying less interest in artistic and musical pursuits, while spending more time watching television, working on automobiles and going for automobile rides, playing cards, fishing, and tavern-visiting.

Geiger and Sokol argue that television watching has become symbolic of the working class, and that, because of this fact, television has been stigmatized in other classes, hence influencing their findings of a disproportionate

[4] Alfred C. Clark, "The Use of Leisure and Its Relations to Levels of Occupational Prestige," *American Sociological Review*, Vol. 21 (June, 1956), pp. 301-7.

[5] Clyde R. White, "Social Class Differences in the Uses of Leisure," *American Journal of Sociology*, Vol. 61 (September, 1955), pp. 145-50.

[6] Leonard Reissman, "Class, Leisure, and Social Participation," *American Sociological Review*, Vol. 19 (February, 1954), pp. 76-84.

GORDON
ANDERSON

amount of time devoted to television watching in working-class homes.[7] Graham, in interpreting his findings of greater working-class acceptance of television, proposes that the cultural equipment of those lower in socioeconomic level is more compatible with television viewing than is the case for those higher in socioeconomic status.[8] Be that as it may, television watching was found to consume a considerable portion of the leisure hours for those residing in the working-class suburb studied by Berger.[9] Approximately 50 per cent of the respondents said that they spent more than 16 hours a week before their sets, Westerns and sports events being the favorite kind of programs. Previous findings regarding low movie attendance were substantiated, for only 15 per cent go often, and more than half rarely or never see a movie at a theater.

Havighurst and Feigenbaum found the leisure style, that is, the pattern formed when one observes the kind and number of activities of what would be the stable working class in terms of our study, to be home-centered.[10] Family activities, keeping the house in good repair, craft hobbies, and watching television exemplify the home-centered style of leisure. And this picture is in essence little different from the one provided in 1924 by steelworkers who had recently acquired more leisure time in a switchover to the eight-hour day —"I like putterin' around the house. I'm growin' a garden." In the words of another worker, "I putter around the house and make myself a nuisance to the missus. I take her out for a ride when it's hot." [11]

Free time devoted to associational life—that is, to formal organizations— by the blue-collar worker has been found to be minimal in scope. The working classes of Middletown[12] and Yankee City[13] belonged to few organizations; and when they did, it tended to be a lodge, veterans' group, or labor union. Organizations emphasizing social and artistic functions tended to be white-collar in composition. Empirical studies by Mather,[14] Dotson,[15] Axelrod,[16] Scott,[17] and Berger,[18] covering nearly a 20-year period, portray the working-man's associational life in much the same fashion. Both Dotson and Berger, focusing directly on the working class, found that a definite minority had no organizational contacts whatsoever, and that those who did belonged to

---

[7] Kent Geiger and Robert Sokol, "Social Norms in Television Watching," *American Journal of Sociology*, Vol. 65 (September, 1959), pp. 174-81.

[8] Saxon Graham, "Cultural Compatibility in Television Watching," *Social Forces*, Vol. 33 (December, 1954), pp. 166-70.

[9] Bennett Berger, *Working Class Suburb* (Berkeley: University of California Press, 1960).

[10] Robert Havighurst and Kenneth Feigenbaum, "Leisure and Life Style," *American Journal of Sociology*, Vol. 64 (January, 1959), pp. 396-404.

[11] Rose C. Feld, "Now That They Have It," *Century*, Vol. 108 (1924), pp. 747-56.

[12] Robert S. Lynd and Helen Lynd, *Middletown* (New York: Harcourt, Brace & World, Inc., 1929).

[13] Warner, *op. cit.*

[14] William Mather, "Income and Social Participation," *American Sociological Review*, Vol. 6 (June, 1941), pp. 380-83.

[15] Floyd Dotson, "Patterns of Voluntary Associations Among Urban Working-Class Families," *American Sociological Review*, Vol. 12 (October, 1951), pp. 687-93.

[16] Morris Axelrod, "Urban Structure and Social Participation," *American Sociological Review*, Vol. 21 (February, 1956), pp. 13-18.

[17] John Scott, "Membership and Participation in Voluntary Associations," *American Sociological Review*, Vol. 22 (June, 1957), pp. 315-56.

[18] Berger, *op. cit.*

athletic, church, union, or veterans' groups. For all studies cited, the average number of memberships for working-class people is less than one.

At the level of informal associations and social cliques, the issue of social participation becomes more critical than it does at the level of organizational relationships, for it is this more personalized aspect of group life that is particularly decisive with respect to the initial theoretical statements. In Middletown, nonassociational patterns of leisure are implied to be divided along class lines so as to exclude primary social relationships between business and working-class people, be it in their homes or in their play activities. The same picture appears in Yankee City, where the various status levels define to a considerable extent the social systems within which the respective members carry on most of their intimate social contacts. Blue-collar people form informal groups largely from their own numbers, and, in many instances, the extended family has particular saliency for social contacts. The fact of working-class reliance upon the kin group for intimates is stressed by Dotson, who found that two-fifths of the respondents had no close friends outside of relatives.[19] This dependence on kin is also borne out in a recent study by Cohen and Hodges, where it was found that interaction with relatives varied inversely with social class, the upper-middle showing 16 per cent who claimed "most frequent" informal contacts with relatives; the lower-middle, 21 per cent; the upper-lower, 41 per cent; and the lower-lower, 59 per cent.[20]

Berger found that the kinship system provided most of the social relationships for the workers in his sample, and that mutual visiting between friends and neighbors was infrequent. Unlike upper- and middle-class visiting patterns, most of the visiting was not planned or invited, but rather was spontaneous and casual, typically involving informal chats or advice on do-it-yourself projects or discussion about the merits of the respondents' automobiles. In view of what has previously been said pertaining to Berger's study, it is apparent why he concluded that, despite a substantial improvement in physical comfort and standard of living gained by his respondents' move to a suburb, there had been no changes in group ties or cultural behavior, and therefore there had been no individual social mobility.

Gans gives us an excellent description of Italian working-class subculture in Boston, emphasizing the overriding importance of what he terms a "peer group society." [21] These ethnically second-generation, blue-collar workers have a body of close relatives and a few friends who come over to the house regularly to engage in conversation. Because of an insatiable appetite for this sort of group experience, their leisure hours are frequently consumed by interaction within this assemblage of familiars. This primary group is also a peer group, because most of the relationships are with peers, that is, with people of the same sex and age; siblings, cousins, and in-laws are the group's most important component. Within the context of this kind of group and within the confines of the home, these workers strive to fulfill their own individuality, rejecting achievement goals and other forms of middle-class

---

[19] Dotson, *op. cit.*

[20] Albert Cohen and Harold Hodges, "Characteristics of the Lower-Blue-Collar Class," *Social Problems*, Vol. 10 (Spring, 1963), pp. 303-34.

[21] Herbert J. Gans, *The Urban Villagers* (New York: The Free Press of Glencoe, Inc., 1962).

status and culture. The remainder of their social life largely takes place on the street, and watching this social life from an apartment window is a popular spare-time activity.

Thus, the picture of blue-collar leisure, as it is portrayed in the literature, appears to flow quite naturally from what are held to be the basic themes of the stable working-class subculture: a desire for stability and security and an unwillingness to take social and economic risks which could disrupt the old security found in a group of solidary familiars, an anti-intellectualism which aspires for the understood result and the concrete, and a person-centeredness which is illustrated by the comment, "one learns more from people than from books." [22]

Our small exploratory study is based on intensive interviews with 15 factory workers[23] who are employed at a factory in "Smithville" (a fictitious name), a small city of 30,000 population with rural environs located in Western Massachusetts. The respondents are skilled and semiskilled in their jobs, and their incomes range from $5,000 to $7,000 annually, a substantially higher figure than their incomes of ten years ago. All are natives, and an analysis of the names indicates that they include individuals of Irish, Polish, French-Canadian, and English ethnic background. Nearly all appear to be Roman Catholic. The interview schedule contained questions which were designed to discover what respondents do in the evenings, on weekends, and on vacation, the extent and nature of their reading, television-viewing, and movie-going, what organizations they belong to and why they belong or why not, what visiting patterns prevail and with whom, and so forth. Recall questions were used in an attempt to get a picture of what their leisure habits were ten years ago.

We propose to compare our tentative findings for the current leisure-time activities of our 15 respondents with the model set by the literature and with our own respondents' recall data. The effect of the small-city, rural environment will also be discussed, since this feature appears to be salient in the interpretation of the results.

Responses to questions directed at ascertaining favorite pastimes had a marked similarity. Working out of doors around the house, on gardens, lawns, and do-it-yourself projects, occupies a large amount of the respondents' leisure time. Typifying this activity is a remark made by a shirtless respondent who was working among his flowers in the backyard when the interviewer arrived —"I'm inside working at the shop all day, and I want to get outside in the evenings and on weekends. I could name a dozen guys who work with me at the shop that do the same thing [gesturing toward his garden]." In addition to this outside activity, woodworking and mechanics in the basement or garage are esteemed spare-time activities. Building or repairing furniture and fixing automobiles were mentioned frequently, and a pride in ownership of tools was openly expressed in several instances. One eager respondent invited the interviewer to observe his finished wood products, and claimed that

---

[22] S. M. Miller and Frank Riessman, "The Working Class Subculture: A New View," *Social Problems*, Vol. 9 (Summer, 1961), pp. 86-97.
[23] Names were derived from the employment roster of the factory concerned without pretense of randomness.

his tools and production apparatus were worth $10,000; from the appearance of such electrical equipment as lathes, drills, and saws and other expensive woodworking instruments, his estimate could not have been too far wrong. The direction of leisure is further indicated by answers to a question regarding expenditures of over $10 for objects related to spare-time activities. Such things as garden and ship tools, a tune-up kit, auto parts, and fishing equipment were mentioned.

Automobile rides through the surrounding countryside are popular among these workers, and many declared that their wives in particular enjoyed "getting away from the house." When asked specifically what they did the night before, two nights ago, and what they usually do in the evening, another spare-time pursuit became apparent: merely sitting on the front porch or lawn enjoying the cool of the evening. Relatives or a neighbor might pay a casual visit, and this may mean a game of cards on the porch or badminton in the yard, but usually it means light conversation, a cold drink of some kind, and a slight repast before the evening is out. In the words of one worker,

> "I'm a homebody. We don't go out much. I chew the rag with my wife, or someone stops in. Like last night. The friend that lives across the street, the tinsmith, was here . . . we had a beer. Not that the beer was important. Just something to talk on."

In only a few instances did the questions regarding the previous evening's activities bring answers other than those involving work around the house or casual visiting; and these described pursuits such as auto rides with the family, swimming with the children, fishing in a nearby stream, and having a beer at a tavern. Large back yards and proximity to scenic countryside and hills, lakes, and streams are obviously crucial in shaping the kinds and location of leisure activities of the workers in this sample.

Weekends differ very little from evenings in leisure-time consumption. It appears that the longer period of free time on weekends simply permits additional amounts of time to be devoted to approximately the same things that are done on weekday evenings. All-day trips to homes of relatives, watching baseball games on television, fishing excursions, and jobs around the house requiring more time than is available on weekday evenings are representative activities. The desire for part-time work and its additional income committed a few respondents to regular or occasional Saturday work.

As for vacations, activities similar to the above again predominate. Nearly all of the respondents split their two-week vacations into a short trip to the beach or mountains, which often combines fishing, visiting relatives, or family reunions, and loafing; and a second week usually spent at home relaxing, completing a project such as building a patio, or preparing the residence for winter by putting on storm windows and bringing in flower bulbs.

Several respondents mentioned reading as a favorite pastime, but only three could say they had read a book in the last three months; these turned out to be Western and detective paperbacks, *Reader's Digest* condensed books, and an automobile tuning manual. All read at least one newspaper, among which the Springfield *Union* (Springfield, the largest city in western Massachusetts, 175,000, is about 20 miles distant from "Smithville") is the favorite.

GORDON
ANDERSON

412

A few read the Boston *Advertiser* on Sunday. Magazines were also present in every home, with the *Saturday Evening Post* and *Reader's Digest* being the most prevalent. Other magazines which are purchased regularly or subscribed to are in the sporting, mechanical, adventure, or home and housekeeping vein. No periodical with a literary orientation is read, and only two homes had magazines in them which specialize in current events.

Four out of five respondents expressed a positive attitude toward television, but viewing time is low during the summer months. It is quite apparent that outdoor activities replace television-viewing to a large extent in the summer. Otherwise, the average amount of time the television set is on is three hours a day. There was only one emphatic rejection of television, and this, too, was qualified—"There is too much crap on TV. I like good whodunits if they're difficult to figure out and make you think." When asked if he cared for movies on television, this respondent's reply was, "Only the type where I can learn something." In general, Westerns, detectives, musical programs featuring such performers as Lawrence Welk and Mitch Miller, and sports events are, in that order, seen most frequently. Panels, drama, and the family-comedy type do not attract much attention from these workers. Over half rarely or never go out to movies, and only one in five had seen a movie in the last month. What movies were seen were those which appeared on television. The model taste for these is Western and adventure.

As is true in the Berger and Gans studies, nights out with the boys are infrequent, if they occur at all. One younger respondent, who answered questions while cooling off his two small children with a garden hose, asserted that "Before I was married I used to spend time with a bunch of friends, making all the bars. Was out raising hell a lot. Now I bring my beer home." Of the ten who said they drink, seven do most of their drinking at home, and the popular drink is beer.

Visiting is frequent, and, fitting the model set by the literature, it is done more with relatives than with friends. In fact, contacts with relatives occur at least twice a week for almost half of the respondents, while a few visit with relatives almost every day. Eleven of the 15 said that three or more of the people they feel closest to are relatives. Contacts are usually casual after-dinner affairs, with virtually none of them involving formal entertainment of a planned nature. On several occasions the interviewees were engaged in informal conversation with a neighbor when the interviewer arrived, or some close relatives "dropped in" for a chat while the interview was in progress.

Ninety per cent of close friends and relatives are blue-collar workers. This indicates that the cultural milieu of the workers in this sample is homogeneous in occupation, just as it was in Middletown and Yankee City. Participation in social networks dominated by middle-class or white-collar individuals is a rare phenomenon.

The number and types of organizational affiliations coincided fully with the model derived from previous studies. In our sample, six had no memberships in organizations, and another six had only one. In all, the frequency of membership is 13, for an average of less than one per person. Church accounted for eight of the memberships and is the only kind of formal group where attendance achieves regularity for a significant portion of the sample.

Veterans' and fraternal organizations account for the remainder, but none of those who belonged were active; they held only token memberships.

A positive disposition toward organizations could be detected in only two of the respondents. Typifying the prevalent attitude are remarks such as "They are good and mean well, but are made up too much of cliques. The top clique runs it for their own enjoyment to the detriment of others"; and, "Organizations are all right if you get the right crowd. You can get a bunch of bums in there and that ruins it for the rest." Others stated that they had no interest or didn't have time for such activities. The wives showed even less interest, for only two had memberships, and these were both in women's church groups.

Recall information for ten years ago revealed no significant differences in the salience of most of the above current leisure practices. Faulty memories may partially be responsible for the apparently remarkable continuity of these leisure styles, but in most cases the responses were made with a seeming confidence, indicated by such a comment as "Things have been pretty much the same since World War II." One exception is that more of the respondents spend time working around the house now than they did at the earlier date. What did change for many was their material surroundings. The entire group is, on the average, driving newer automobiles than they did in 1953, and one in three moved to improved houses during the course of the past ten-year period. And, in general, the living situation of all those in the sample appears quite comfortable, with ample space inside and outside of the home.

Although the sample itself was small, there was a peculiar uniformity of response throughout the interviewing. It was almost with mechanical regularity that each respondent duplicated the preceding one in terms of the answers given. *Leisure for these blue-collarites has a stamp of constancy and fixedness.* It means puttering in the garden, trimming the hedge and bushes, tinkering with the automobile, working on a do-it-yourself project, watching a favorite television program, playing a game of cards with friends on the front porch, taking an evening drive through the country, or simply sitting in a lawn chair having a beer with some relatives. The outdoor setting for these activities is a note of considerable importance, because, in most instances, these several activities are pursued out of doors. And, appropriately enough, a majority of the respondents were outdoors engaged in one of the above activities when approached for an interview. Not only were many of the respondents either busy with outside activities or relaxing on the porch or lawn with some friends, but the same pattern was visible throughout what were each predominantly working-class neighborhoods. And, to be sure, the interviewer did not go unnoticed, but was the object of considerable staring and whispered remarks by those in the vicinity of the respondent's house— actions which are not characteristic of upper- and middle-class neighborhoods, where a stranger can come and go without attracting special notice.

The regularity and similarity of leisure activities, the chatting with relatives and friends, the home-centeredness, and the close watch on neighborhood activities are certainly familiar characteristics of leisure in the working-class subculture, especially as set forth by Gans. The differences for our sample are manifestly in the greater use of the hands and the utilization of an outdoor and more spacious physical setting. Thus, the leisure-time pursuits of the workers in our study are very comparable with those depicted in other empirical studies and with our workers' recall data.

Does the work on the lawn and garden indicate a shift to a middle-class suburban style? It is our view that the changes are mechanical changes which do not basically modify the classic model of the workingman's way of life, but are adaptations of this model which provide opportunities for outdoor activity. They are differences due to the functioning of environmental setting, but they do not upset the basic orientations of blue-collar workers' lives.

Thus, to the extent that our findings substantiate this hypothesis and Berger's, we conclude that a rise in income is not likely to produce a change in the way of life and subculture of the workingman, and that working-class individuals are not, on the whole, rising in social status, even though their collective economic mobility is unquestioned.[24] In other words, *although their lives are more comfortable than they once were, workingmen have not converted this economic rise into changes in subcultural life style and group affiliations which would effect status mobility.* Moreover, with regard to the classical model of worker self-improvement and creative activity presumably attendant upon a reduction of hours of labor, it appears that creative work involving the use of manual skills around the house does develop in the "new leisure" of the blue-collar worker, but that, insofar as the model includes self-education, development of a higher esthetic sense, greater civic participation, and more sophisticated political and ideological orientation, little of this is borne out by the findings of studies reviewed here or by our tentative exploratory study.

In interpreting these findings, two explanations are possible and they are not mutually exclusive: First, the working class may represent a biologically less able portion of the population which is less likely to develop these intellectual, esthetic, and civic interests. This hypothesis is unlikely to be true for a society with little mobility; but, regardless of one's ideological beliefs, it is conceivable that, in a society which has had considerable social-class mobility over a long period of time, some approximation of this model may be valid. Of course, neither our data nor any other data reviewed here cast any light on this question.

Second, a hypothesis may be advanced which embraces a larger range of phenomena than the topic of blue-collar workers and stratification; this is, that the socialization process is such that, once adults have completed their substantive socialization, their subcultures are relatively fixed, particularly if they are supported by a group of peers. A corollary of this hypothesis is that, in quantitative statistical terms, changes in subculture are likely to take place only for the children of a given social stratum before socialization is completed, and, even then, only providing that stimuli from the outside world are

---

[24] For discussions of "collective mobility," see Seymour Lipset and Reinhard Bendix, "Social Status and Social Structure: A Re-examination of Data and Interpretations. ii," *British Journal of Sociology*, Vol. II (September, 1951), pp 230-54; Gordon, *op. cit.*, pp. 116-17; and Berger, *op. cit.*, pp. 93-94.

sufficiently present and sufficiently powerful to affect those who have initial biological and personality qualities which would predispose them to be receptive to such stimuli.

Another way of stating this theoretical proposition is that the power of the socialization process is such that, barring unusual circumstances, the socialization that has been consistent into adulthood and has socialized a person into a particular subculture and provided the person with a social structure which sustains that subculture, makes subcultural changes within the life of the person unlikely, regardless of changes in material circumstances. Social mobility, therefore, which requires subcultural changes (and it does, by classical models), is likely to be found largely among the children of workers, rather than among the workers themselves; these are the children who will take advantage of the educational pathway to a white-collar way of life and who will never work as blue-collar people themselves.

In short, just as the urban working class in Gans's study had no interest in changing life orientations after they had grown up in a peer-group society, so has the working class in a rural environment no desire to alter the behavioral systems inculcated in them during their period of socialization. It seems very probable, therefore, that there are intangible, psychological variables mediating the relationship between low-status position and lack of upward mobility despite economic gains, and that such more subtle correlates of the objective class structure are systems of beliefs and values which de-emphasize traditional achievement goals instrumental for social mobility and which have been inculcated during youth.[25]

If hypotheses such as the above are tenable, then the fact of arrested development of leisure pursuits among blue-collar workers, despite vastly improved economic position and increased free time, is no paradox, but a logical consequence.

The Mass Media and the Blue-Collar Worker

LEO BOGART

THE blue-collar worker's experience of the mass media is something which readily summons up a series of cliché images. We see him now, after his day

---

[25] Further elaboration of similar propositions can be found in Herbert H. Hyman's essay, "The Values Systems of Different Classes: A Social Psychological Contribution to the Analysis of Stratification." in Reinhard Bendix and Seymour Martin Lipset, eds., *Class, Status and Power* (New York: The Free Press of Glencoe, Inc., 1961).

of toil, perspiring in his undershirt, staring fixedly at the wrestling matches on TV, grunting empathically and swilling his beer. We see him flipping the dial, rejecting an educational documentary and relaxing with satisfaction as he encounters the familiar hoofbeats and gunfire of a Western. How he indulges his displaced aggressive feelings, inflamed by the tense tedium of his unrewarding job! His hostile fantasies run riot again as he turns to the latest murder reports and divorce scandals in his tabloid, skipping the serious news to find a chuckle in the comic strips. In the background the radio wails rock 'n' roll, or perhaps a hymn. His other reading is confined to the captions in girlie magazines, to racing forms, or to abandoned copies of *Confidential*. If his wife drags him to the movies, his taste runs to scenes of lust and carnage. As for her own media habits, the parallel stereotypes are equally familiar—and equally misleading.

A review of the evidence suggests that there is no simple, clear-cut distinction to be drawn between the place of the mass media in working-class family life and their place in other sectors of American society. To the contrary, *the mass media represent perhaps the most powerful current by which blue-collar workers are swept into the main stream of conformity to middle-class values and aspirations.*

The opportunity for exposure to the media has become well-nigh universal. Television sets are today in 92 per cent of United States households; radio is in 94 per cent; one or more newspapers are read every day in 86 per cent of the homes. Magazines, being more costly commodities, have a more restricted readership, but even so, 69 per cent of the population describe themselves as readers of at least one magazine. Motion pictures, despite growing admission prices, report an increase in attendance after a long period of attrition wrought by TV.

With such broad coverage, mass media in the United States do not have the same self-conscious social-class orientation which characterizes their counterparts in many other countries. We do have snob magazines, with a definitely aristocratic outlook and audience, and, at the other end of the scale, the weekly or monthly newspapers published by trade unions for their membership. Many publications and some broadcast programs maintain editorial formulas that aim at particular specialized segments of the public. The specialization is usually that of a sex, ethnic, age, avocational, or occupational interest-group role which may only indirectly be related to social class.

We must infer that a good many periodicals (including successors to the old "pulps") attract a predominantly working-class audience, although there is no solid evidence to support this assumption. Union newspapers are a special case, and so is the Macfadden Group of women's publications (whose time-tested content formula of true confessions, romances, and the heart throbs of Hollywood idols has been translated into marketing terms to make an advertising sales package). With these exceptions, it is almost impossible to speak of publications or programs which are perceived as particularly blue-collar media by readers, publishers, or advertisers.

Two broad explanations may be offered for this phenomenon, one related

The Mass Media and the Blue-Collar Worker

417

to the American social structure and one to the economic structure of the mass media themselves:

1. In the United States, occupation does not have the same determinant relationship to social-class position as it does in more traditional societies.[1] Great social mobility (both geographically and up and down the social ladder) has meant that cultural or leisure-time interests may reflect class orientations which in turn reflect an individual's antecedents or his aspirations and not necessarily his present environment. The classic American pattern of conflict between immigrant parents and their native-born children has been replaced by more subtle distinctions in outlook, as between a city-bred generation and its suburban offspring. At a given occupational level, and even within the same family, one often encounters diverse cultural patterns which reflect differences in age, education, and income.

Family income and life style no longer relate as closely to occupation as they did in the past, because of the enormous changes of recent years in the American occupational pyramid, the rise in the average level of education, and the substantial growth in the number of working housewives (with its implication for the total income of the working-class household). Residential neighborhoods whose housing appears homogeneous increasingly harbor families whose breadwinners have widely differing occupations.

All this has meant that the analysis of life style along social-class lines, as in the studies of W. Lloyd Warner, has placed little stress on occupation by itself as a determinant of cultural taste. Burleigh Gardner and other followers of Warner prefer to think in terms of a "middle-majority" element of society which combines the solid, respectable working (upper-lower) class along with the lower-middle class. The rationale for this classification came out of analyses of many thousands of interview records of opinion and preference with respect to consumer goods as well as to the mass media.[2]

2. The second reason why mass media in the United States rarely express an occupational or social-class orientation arises from the economic structure of the media themselves. The technology of all the mass media is such that the lowest unit cost of production is, as in many manufacturing industries, obtained at the point where the maximum-size audience is achieved. Because United States broadcasting is almost entirely supported by advertisers, and magazines and the press primarily so, there is a constant financial motivation to get the largest possible return on investment (or the lowest cost per thousand people reached) by winning the largest possible number of readers, listeners, or viewers.

In an open society with virtually universal literacy and relatively easy access to the distribution channels for broadcasting, print, and the cinema,

---

[1] Richard Hoggart's *The Uses of Literacy* (London: Chatto & Windus, Ltd., 1957) has portrayed brilliantly the place of the mass media in the everyday life of the English working class. However, Hoggart tells us more about how the media are experienced (in a working-class setting, to be sure) than about working-class media as such.

[2] The "middle-majority" concept, employed in most of the marketing reports of Gardner's Social Research, Inc., was abandoned in a recent book by his associates: *Workingman's Wife*, by Lee Rainwater, Richard P. Coleman, and Gerald Handel (New York: Oceana Publications, 1959).

there has been every incentive for media operators to look toward a very broad target. Because the content of the media is prepared by middle-class professionals, any working-class orientation necessarily reflects artifice ("talking down") rather than the genuine, spontaneous expression of the blue-collar group itself. In rare cases, it has been possible for a medium to define its character and carve out an advertising market along strictly social-class lines. But, for the most part, a restricted social-class orientation would appear to be at variance with a medium's economic self-interest. Where media managers have gone after a limited audience, they have generally judged that this could be more easily designed by appealing to people who share common preoccupations rather than a common occupation.

The social-class differentiation of the mass media in England is perhaps most clearly seen in the three services of BBC radio and in the Sunday national newspaper. The characteristics of the readers of these papers show a wide range which can be explained better in terms of their individual content and editorial style than in political terms.

Because American mass media are produced with little conscious reference to the occupational characteristics of their audiences, the sociologist must resort to a good deal of conjecture in any attempt to describe how the blue-collar worker responds to them. Most studies of media audiences analyze reader or viewer characteristics in terms of broad socioeconomic groupings like education or family income, which relate only in a general way to blue-collar occupational status.

Some media are far better researched than others. There is more information about aggregate exposure to a medium than there is on variations of exposure within it to specific editorial elements or programs. Yet it is precisely in these finer areas of analysis that one would expect to find significant differences in outlook and in taste. Moreover, the available data are not always comparable, because they have been collected at varying intervals over a period of years. The same period has seen the rise of television and of paperback books, so that the media themselves have undergone considerable shifts in position and function.

The relationship between occupational status and mass-media exposure or preference is highly indirect. Occupation tends to place an individual in a social setting which carries its own particular cultural environment. Thus, occupation affects taste primarily insofar as it places the individual within a given income range, with consequent limitations on his access to various kinds of cultural experiences. Every occupation calls for skills which fall within a given range of schooling, and these educational limits are also reflected in the individual's media tastes. In a far less significant way, occupation might be said to affect media behavior, insofar as different kinds of jobs set up different types of work stress or tension which call for different kinds of symbolic release in leisure-time activity.

The blue-collar sector does not occupy the very lowest rung of the occupational scale. Below it is a low-income rural element and a substantial population of marginal individuals, including institutional inmates, migratory workers, chronically unemployed, elderly indigents, and others who, either because they are incapacitated or have no fixed residence, are virtually outside the sphere of all the mass media. Conventional classifications of media audiences, in terms of a few major categories of income, education, and socio-economic status, present a distorted picture insofar as they lump together individuals in stable working-class families with substantial media exposure and those marginal individuals with very little exposure.

In a 1957 study made by Batten, Barton, Durstine & Osborn, Inc.,[3] the advertising agency, exposure to magazines, newspapers, books, radio, and television was measured for "yesterday." The proportion of individuals who were exposed yesterday to four or five media ranges from 11 per cent in the case of those who had not progressed beyond grade school to 32 per cent on the part of the college graduates. Thus, the blue-collar public experiences fewer media in a given period of time than is true of their white-collar counterparts (largely because fewer read magazines and books).

PRINT VERSUS TV ORIENTATION

In the days of radio's peak popularity, it was observed that people of lower income and education were oriented to the "easier to absorb" broadcast medium, while those of higher income and education gravitated toward print.[4] This has been borne out by a variety of studies conducted over recent years. For example, a study by Foote, Cone & Belding reported by Cornelius DuBois[5] compares the characteristics of "print-oriented" and "broadcast-oriented" people. Of the women classified as "readers," 54 per cent had husbands in white-collar occupations, compared with 21 per cent of those classified as "viewers." Similarly, a study made for the Magazine Advertising Bureau[6] by the Market Research Corporation of America examines exposure to television by households divided into five groups. The distribution of viewing by blue-collar households runs very close to the national average:

TELEVISION VIEWING BY BLUE-COLLAR HOUSEHOLDS

	TV Viewing Per Week	
	All U. S. Households	All Households Headed by Operatives and Laborers
Heavy exposure (40 or more telecasts)	21%	23%
Medium heavy (27-39 telecasts)	21	23
Medium light (16-26 telecasts)	21	21
Light (1-15 telecasts)	23	20
No exposure (0 telecasts)	14	13

---

[3] "The Communicators: An All-Media Study," a talk presented by Ben Gedalecia of BBDO at the ARF Conference, November 14, 1957.

[4] Cf. Paul F. Lazarsfeld and Patricia Kendall, *Radio Listening in America* (Englewood Cliffs, N. J.: Prentice-Hall, Inc., 1948); and Paul F. Lazarsfeld, *Radio and the Printed Page* (New York: Duell, Sloan & Pearce, Inc., 1940).

[5] "What Is the Difference Between a Reader and a Viewer?" Part 2 of a two-part series by Cornelius DuBois, *Media/scope*, October 1959, pp. 46-51.

[6] *The Profitable Difference—A Study of the Magazine Market . . . its size, quality and buying*, Magazine Advertising Bureau of the Magazine Publishers Association, 1960.

On the other hand, magazine reading in blue-collar households runs to considerably less than the national average:

MAGAZINE READING BY BLUE-COLLAR HOUSEHOLDS

	Magazine Issues Looked at in Calendar Year	
	All U. S. Households	All Households Headed by Operatives and Laborers
Heavy exposure (10 or more issues)	23%	15%
Medium heavy (6-9 issues)	21	17
Medium light (3-5 issues)	19	19
Light (1-2 issues)	18	21
No exposure (0 issues)	19	29

Persons of lower education feel relatively closer to electronic media and not so close to the printed word, according to a 1961 study prepared by Audits and Surveys for the Newsprint Information Committee.[7]

Question: "Generally speaking, which do you feel closest to—the television channel you watch most often, the radio station you listen to most often, or the newspaper you read most often?"

DEPENDENCE UPON MEDIA ACCORDING TO EDUCATION

	Grade School	High School	College
Television channel	34%	39%	18%
Radio station	17	12	14
Newspaper	34	39	53
All the same, don't know ..	16	10	15

Gary Steiner, in his book, *The People Look At Television*,[8] analyzes viewing habits and attitudes in terms of education and income rather than by occupation. He finds that the lower-educated have the most favorable attitude toward television, compared with radio, magazines, and newspapers. At the very lowest educational bracket (less than grade-school education), television actually receives higher marks than newspapers as "the most important and the most educational medium" which "presents things most intelligently." Among the high school-educated, newspapers and magazines assume far greater importance.

TELEVISION

Steiner used psychological projective techniques to compare feelings about television versus reading. His lower-educated respondents tended to characterize viewing as "a perfect way to relax" and were relatively unlikely to express feelings of guilt ("I really should be doing something else"). They were far less likely than the better-educated to agree that "I watch because there is

---

[7] "A National Study of Newspaper Reading," Newsprint Information Committee, March-April, 1961.

[8] Gary Steiner, *The People Look At Television* (New York: Alfred A. Knopf, Inc., 1963).

The Mass Media and the Blue-Collar Worker

nothing else to do at the time." These attitudes are reflected in actual reports of viewing behavior, as shown in the estimated average number of hours viewed per day.[9]

HOURS OF TELEVISION VIEWING PER DAY, BY AMOUNT OF EDUCATION

```
0-8 years' grade school . . . . . . . . . . . . . . . . 4.3 hours
1-3 years' high school . . . . . . . . . . . . . . . . . 4.4 hours
4 years' high school  . . . . . . . . . . . . . . . . . 4.2 hours
1-3 years' college . . . . . . . . . . . . . . . . . . . 3.6 hours
3-4 years' college . . . . . . . . . . . . . . . . . . . 3.5 hours
Beyond college . . . . . . . . . . . . . . . . . . . . . 2.9 hours
```

The proportion here who report that the programs they watch are "extremely enjoyable" ranges from 49 per cent among grade school-educated respondents to 38 per cent of those who had gone to college.

People with less education look to television for entertainment rather than for information, and this is reflected in their favorite programs. They show a greater preference for action shows (Western, crime, adventure, and so forth), for light drama, and for sportscasts. They show a relatively low interest in heavy drama, news, and public affairs programs. But there are smaller differences of program choice than one might suspect among different educational groups (apart from the small maverick professional group with postgraduate training).

TELEVISION PROGRAM CHOICE, BY AMOUNT OF EDUCATION

	Favorite Programs	
	Action (Western, crime, adventure)	Comedy, Variety
0-6 years' grade school . . .	27%	18%
7-8 years' grade school . . .	30	24
1-3 years' high school	33	24
4 years' high school	29	29
1-2 years' college	26	24
3-4 years' college	23	21
Beyond college	18	14

Within the category of comedy-variety shows, however, there are interesting differences by type of program. For example, among those with less than six years of grade-school education, the proportion preferring situation comedies is 29 per cent while for "stand-up" or star comedians the proportion is 9 per cent. In the best-educated category (professionals with postgraduate education), only 14 per cent prefer situation comedies and 22 per cent, star comedians.

An early (1950) study by the National Broadcasting Company[10] shows that less-educated persons express markedly greater preference for feature films and quiz shows and markedly less for public affairs shows. But there were only small differences for such staple types as news, musical, dramatic, sports, and mystery shows.

---

[9] According to the American Research Bureau, persons with less than 8 years' grade-school education report viewing an average of 40 programs per week, compared with 25 for those with some college.

[10] National Broadcasting Company, "The Hofstra Study: A Measure of TV Sales Effectiveness" (New York: National Broadcasting Company, 1950).

In general, the statistics of the rating services do not show very marked educational or income differences in the audience composition of various shows. The evidence suggests that people at every social level watch a great many programs of types they do *not* necessarily "prefer."

Steiner reports that the less-educated are more likely to describe TV commercials as "helpful," "entertaining," and "welcome." This finding is borne out by a study by Social Research, Inc., for Campbell-Ewald.[11] Compared with the lower-middle class, the blue-collar man is reported to be relatively more concerned with the entertainment than the educational value of TV; he spends more time with the medium and "does the most indiscriminate viewing" with the "least explicit evaluating standards." He is also said to be least critical of television advertising, most readily involved in commercials, most willing to admit that commercials influence him, and most passive and undiscriminating in his viewing of commercials.

The A. C. Nielsen Company conventionally divides its sample panel of households into five groups of equal size, ranked in terms of the total amount of their evening television viewing (as measured by an "audimeter" electrical measuring device attached to the set). A recent unpublished analysis shows that, among the heaviest-viewing fifth of the homes, 29 per cent of the family heads had not progressed beyond grade school. Among the lightest-viewing fifth, the proportion is 25 per cent—not a great difference. However, the heaviest-viewing fifth had 54 per cent of its membership drawn from homes where the family head was not a high school graduate. In the lightest-viewing quintile, only 42 per cent were drawn from this group. Thus, Nielsen corroborates the other evidence that blue-collar families view more TV than white-collar families do.

RADIO

Despite their predilection for TV, members of blue-collar families contribute a disproportionately low amount of the total amount of radio listening, according to another recent study of the radio audience conducted by The Pulse, Inc.[12] In this analysis, radio-listening homes were divided into four equal groups based on the total hours of radio listening by individual members of the household. Blue-collar households contributed 31 per cent less than the average to the heaviest-listening fourth and 26 per cent more than the average to the lightest-listening fourth. However, blue-collar homes do more listening in the daytime (63 per cent between 9 and 3 P. M., compared with 56 per cent in the sales and clerical group).

A national study done by R. H. Bruskin Associates in 1962 for the Radio Advertising Bureau[13] reports that 89 per cent of blue-collar workers listen to the radio at least once during the week. Seventy-eight per cent hear the

---

[11] Campbell-Ewald Company, "The Television Viewer—His Tastes, Interests and Attitudes," 1961. This report, incidentally, characterizes the "lower class" as primarily made up of "semi-skilled blue-collar workers, (who) while striving for a 'respectable' life, give emphasis to attaining the more limited pleasures available to them."

[12] The Pulse, Inc., *Dimensions '62*, 1963.

[13] Radio Advertising Bureau, *The listening habits of . . . Blue-Collar Men*, October, 1962.

radio at least once on an average weekday for an average of 2 hours and 44 minutes, and 54 per cent report hearing the radio every day of the week. (No comparable statistics are given for other social levels.)

NEWSPAPERS

Daily newspaper reading is as nearly universal in working-class homes as it is among the population as a whole, according to the study (already cited)

PER CENT OF HOUSEHOLDS IN WHICH A PAPER IS READ ON THE AVERAGE WEEKDAY

	All U. S. Households	Skilled Manual Employees	Machine Operators and Semiskilled Employees	Unskilled Labor
Households in which a paper is purchased	80%	86%	80%	73%
Households in which a paper is read though not purchased	6	3	10	11
Total reading households	86%	89%	90%	84%

of the Newsprint Information Committee. Households headed by a worker, of course, include persons other than the worker himself. Readership may also be looked at in terms of the occupation of the individual adult. The number

AVERAGE WEEKDAY NEWSPAPER READING, BY OCCUPATION

Readers		All U. S. Population	Skilled Manual Workers	Machine Operators Semiskilled Workers Farmers	Unskilled Workers
Total	No.	89,567			
	%	80	83	82	69
Subscribers and purchasers	No.	80,940			
	%	72	76	72	61
Other readers	No.	8,627			
	%	8	6	10	8

of papers read per day on the average shows no significant difference between working-class readers and the national average (1.4).

However, regularity of newspaper reading increases with education. Among persons who have never been beyond grade school, only 53 per cent read the paper every day, compared with 77 per cent of the college-educated. Among the former group, only 27 per cent read more than one paper a day, compared

WEEKDAY NEWSPAPER READING HABITS, BY EDUCATION

	Grade School	High School	College
Reading Regularity:			
Read every day	53%	65%	77%
Read less often	47	35	23
Average Number of Weekday Newspapers Read Per Day:			
One paper	73	67	54
Two or more papers	27	33	46
Average Reading Time Per Paper:			
Up to 30 minutes	25	37	34
30-39 minutes	22	22	29
40 minutes or more	53	41	37

BOGART

with 46 per cent of the college-educated. However, the less well-educated reader spends more time, on the average, with each paper he reads, probably because his reading skill is less efficient. Interestingly enough, there is no difference among educational groups in the proportion (68 per cent) who say that they look forward more to reading the news items as opposed to those who look forward more to reading the regular features which are largely of an entertainment nature.

However, the lower the education, the more parochial the reading interests are, as the following table shows:

INTEREST IN LOCAL VERSUS NATIONAL AND INTERNATIONAL EVENTS, BY EDUCATION

	Grade School	High School	College
I am personally <u>much more</u> interested in what is happening in my own city or town. . .	38%	26%	19%
I am personally <u>slightly more</u> interested in what is happening in my own city or town. . .	24	27	17
Total Own City or Town	62%	53%	37%
I am personally <u>slightly more</u> interested in what is happening on the <u>national or international scene</u>	15%	20%	24%
I am personally <u>much more</u> interested in what is happening on the <u>national or international scene</u>	16	25	37
Total National or International Scene . .	31%	46%	61%
No preference	7%	2%	2%

The lower the education, the less active the use of the newspaper also. This may be so because the workingman regards the newspaper (and media generally) as among the remote and impersonal institutions of the established power structure, or simply because he feels altogether less confident in his ability to manipulate the forces of the world around him. He does not think of the people who run the mass media as people like himself, people whom he can influence and whose services he can command. The following table illustrates this point:

USE OF THE NEWSPAPER, BY EDUCATION

	Grade School	High School	College
Per cent showing or reading an item aloud to someone else	62%	80%	89%
Clipped a newspaper item within the past year	50	64	82
Ever wrote a letter to the editor	2	7	17
Ever wrote or phoned for information	12	23	36
Ever placed a classified ad	30	45	64
Ever visited a newspaper office	28	41	63

In a study of newspaper-comics reading by working-class men in a New York slum,[14] the writer found, contrary to his expectations, that significantly more of the high school-educated respondents (71 per cent) report discussing the comics than those with less education (53 per cent). Many studies of public opinion have shown that persons of superior education are most likely to

---

[14] Leo Bogart, "Comic Strips and Their Adult Readers" (Ph.D. dissertation, University of Chicago, 1950).

discuss politics and current events. But the comics are popular symbols. One might well have expected to find the poorly educated *more* likely to talk about the comics because they presumably have fewer things to talk of. But the data show that to engage in discussion has less to do with a particular subject than with a generalized confidence or articulateness, which education helps to provide. The better-educated are better oriented to the mass media; they absorb more of their content, even the trivia.[15]

Some indication of how newspapers in a highly competitive newspaper market differ in their capacity to attract working-class members of the public may be shown by the following breakdown of data from a study of W. R. Simmons for the New York *Daily News*.[16] It is interesting to note that the gradation reflects the editorial tone and content of the papers rather than their political alignments with working-class causes or opinions. Such a sharp

BLUE-COLLAR* READERS AS A PER CENT OF TOTAL

All adults 47%

Mirror 58
News 56
Journal-American 40
Post 33
Times 24
World-Telegram & Sun 20
Herald Tribune 17

*Craftsmen, foremen, operatives, service workers and manual laborers.

segmentation of the newspaper-reading public is, of course, not apparent in cities with a more limited choice of papers.

MAGAZINES

Magazines are normally thought of as the most specialized and selective of the mass media. Although the blue-collar person's exposure to magazines in any given week is less than the average, over a period of time—either by purchase or by "pass-along"—he is brought into contact with the principal mass publications. The *Life* "Study of Consumer Expenditures," [17] conducted by Alfred Politz Research, reports that 19 per cent of "operatives and service workers" see the average single issue of *Life* (compared with 22 per cent of the general public). Over a 13-week period, it is estimated that 56 per cent of these blue-collar people (compared with 58 per cent of the general population) see at least one issue of *Life*.

To get an idea of the extent to which the major publications are able to reach a massive audience, we may look at the following abstract from another survey made by Politz for *Look* magazine in 1958:[18]

[15] On this point see also O. N. Larsen and R. J. Hill, "Mass Media and Interpersonal Communication," *American Sociological Review*, Vol. XIX (1954), pp. 426-33, and Leo Bogart, "The Spread of News on a Local Event," *Public Opinion Quarterly*, Vol. XIV (1950), pp. 769-72.

[16] New York Daily News, *Profile of the Millions*, 3rd ed., 1962.

[17] "Magazine Coverage of Consumer Expenditures," Volume Two, *LIFE Study of Consumer Expenditures* (New York: Time, Inc., 1958).

[18] Look Magazine, *The Audiences of Nine Magazines*, 1958.

READING OF MAGAZINES BY INDIVIDUALS, BY OCCUPATION
(15 years of age and over)

	All Individuals Employed Full Time	Craftsmen, Foremen, Service Workers	Operatives Nonfarm Laborers
Life	29%	26%	23%
Look	25	21	20
Saturday Evening Post	19	19	11
Time	11	8	5
Better Homes and Gardens . . .	12	11	9
Good Housekeeping	7	5	8
Ladies' Home Journal	8	5	7
McCall's	6	7	2
Reader's Digest	30	29	17

It is interesting to note that (except in the case of the picture magazines, *Life* and *Look*) differences between skilled and unskilled workers are greater than those between skilled workers and the general public.

A similar finding is echoed in a study (by Sindlinger & Company[19]) of the readers of the three leading news magazines. These publications have negligible readership among unskilled workers (operatives and laborers), but their readership among skilled craftsmen, supervisory workers, and semiskilled blue-collar workers is actually higher than the national average.

PER CENT OF READERS IN EACH OCCUPATIONAL GROUP
(12 years of age and over)

	Newsweek	Time	U. S. News & World Report
Total United States	6%	6%	4%
Craftsmen, foremen, kindred . .	8	8	5
Operatives and laborers	1	2	1

To be sure, some specialized magazines, because of their character and orientation, cannot be expected to find a substantial working-class audience. For example, a study done among readers of *Harper's* and the *Atlantic* (by Erdos & Morgan[20]) shows that only six per cent of the subscribers fall into the skilled, semiskilled, and laborer category.

A survey made by W. R. Simmons and Associates, for the Macfadden publications,[21] demonstrates that magazines which are deliberately edited to reach a blue-collar audience manage to achieve their purpose. A total of 13,325,000 women 15 and over had read one or more average issues of magazines in the Macfadden Women's Group (*True Story, Photoplay, TV Radio Mirror, True Romance, True Experience,* and *True Love*). Of these, a total of 8,903,000, or 67 per cent, were in households headed by a skilled, semiskilled, or unskilled worker. The editorial content of these magazines is directed to the portrayal of situations and problems which the working-class reader can realistically identify with her own.

---

[19] *The Characteristics of the Reading Audiences of Newsweek, Time and U. S. News & World Report*, Newsweek, 1959.

[20] *The People Next Door—A Comparison Between Subscribers to Harper's Magazine and The Atlantic and Non-Subscribing Neighbors*, Harper-Atlantic Sales, Inc., September, 1962.

[21] *The Women Behind the Market*, Macfadden-Bartell Corporation, 1962.

The
Mass Media
and the
Blue-Collar
Worker

The available evidence suggests that, *contrary to stereotyped expectations, the mass-media experience of blue-collar workers and their families hews remarkably close to the American main line.*[22] Thus, the mass media provide a common source of widely shared information, values, symbols, heroes, and fantasy figures for workers as for other elements in American life.

In general, the working-man's use of the media is less active than that of his middle-class counterpart; his media experience, like his social experience, takes place within a more narrow and constricted range. He tends to be distrustful of fantasy and to prefer media content which runs closest to his own day-to-day personal experience.

Working-class and middle-class media orientations are often contrasted in terms of broadcast versus print. This may actually disguise a paradox. It appears that the life of the working-class family is not so much more positively centered on the broadcast media than that of middle-class people. It is, rather, that broadcasting assumes greater importance within the total array of media experience because of the blue-collar family's lower interest in print, which is associated with fewer years of schooling and less ease and skill in reading.

Differences in taste and preference within both broadcast programs and print media are clearly apparent between working-class and middle-class families. The differences always run in the direction one might expect, with blue-collar folk placing greater emphasis on easy entertainment and correspondingly less on information. However, the small size of the differences is of even greater interest than the fact that they exist. The explanation may well lie in the fact that most mass-media experiences represent pastime rather than purposeful activity with a strong emotional charge. The choice of one magazine or program over another, or even a choice of one medium over another, as a way of filling time very often reflects chance circumstance within the range of availabilities rather than the expression of psychological motivation or need. This very fact would tend to obscure those class differences in audience composition which might reflect personality differences.

The mass media, through their widespread distribution, open up windows to areas of life that lie beyond the range of the blue-collar worker's daily personal orbit. Their psychological importance in orienting him to the Great Society may be even more critical than it is to the middle-class man, who feels more confident of his place in the world.

Thus, the mass media represent a powerful force for conformity, a source of nourishment for the American Dream of apple pie, convertibles, ranch houses, and the eventual move to middle-class status.

---

[22] The motion pictures have been neglected in this analysis simply because there is no publicly available evidence on audience composition.

BOGART

The Working-Class Child of Four and Television

ADELINE GOMBERG

DURING every period of our civilization, young children, whatever their social or economic background, have been influenced by those who reared them. From this primary source came the foundations for their future attitudes, prejudices, biases, values, moral and ethical codes of behavior, as well as for their future levels of aspiration, academic and economic.[1] Today's young child has acquired a new and most successful teacher who greets him daily and gives him information that may have some far-reaching ramifications not contemplated by his parents. The teacher, influencing all children—of every age, class, color, or creed—is television.

The four-year-old learns best the things he both sees and hears. This knowledge is then reflected in his play. It is through research into children's play that television's impact upon children of different socioeconomic groups becomes apparent.[2] Because children now have fewer unique experiences, their play has become less variegated. In fact, the banal or flattening effect of television proves most significant. Television is an integral part of their natural environment[3] and completely captivates, fascinates, entertains, and informs them. Although they watch primarily for entertainment, what they see also presents covert instruction in social attitudes, morals, and behavior. Television is a new source of authority: "My mommy said . . ." or "My daddy said . . ." has almost given way to "The man on television said. . . ."

Any observer who takes the time to listen, to watch, and to talk to a child of four discovers that the child is a bundle of energy searching for the why's and how's of everything he encounters in his environment.[4] He spends his waking moments in manipulating objects, ideas, concepts, and behavior patterns. He reveals in play what he understands or what confuses him. And while psychologists and sociologists and educators seek the reasons for his playing,[5] the four-

---

[1] Gordon Allport, *The Nature of Prejudice* (New York: Doubleday Anchor Book, 1958), Chapter 3.

[2] Adeline W. Gomberg, *The Four-Year-Old Child and Television,* unpublished dissertation, Teachers College, Columbia University, 1960.

[3] According to the 1960 Census, over 46 million homes had TV sets—*The New York Times,* May 17, 1962.

[4] A. Gesell et al. *Infant and Child in the Culture of Today* (New York: Harper & Row, Publishers, 1943), pp. 224-45; F. Ilg and L. Ames, *Child Behavior* (New York: Harper & Row, Publishers, 1955), pp. 30-33; W. Olson, *Child Development* (New York: D. C. Heath & Company, 1949), Ch. 1.

[5] H. S. Sullivan, *The Interpersonal Theory of Psychiatry* (New York: W. W. Norton & Company, 1953), pp. 209-226; C. W. Valentine, *The Normal Child* (London: The Whitefriars Press, Limited, 1957), Ch. 10; E. H. Erikson, *Childhood and Society* (New York: W. W. Norton & Company, 1950), pp. 207-218; S. Isaacs, *Social Development in Young Children* (London: Routledge & Kegan Paul Limited, 1952 Ed.), p. 425.

year-old is unconcerned—he just plays. Today, much of what he plays comes straight out of television.

WORKING-CLASS CHILDREN AT PLAY PRIOR TO TELEVISION

Pieter Breughel, in his famous mural of 1560, "Children's Games," depicted some of the activities and games of the peasant child: spinning tops, blindman's buff, stunting and climbing, hoop-rolling, stilt-walking, swimming, playing house, and the like. Based upon her own research, the author has concluded that the child of this century plays in much the same fashion as did the child of the sixteenth century.[6] There are some differences, however.

During the depression thirties, most children from working-class families were subjected to a situation rarely experienced by children born into more privileged homes. Husbands, in all too many cases, were compelled to take over the household chores of their wives. The typical male—hale, hearty, but harassed—was unable to find work. If he were lucky, his wife was employed. Thus, the child at home, too young to go to school, was cared for by the father. When mother left for work each morning, father remained to cook, clean, and care for the offspring.

In addition, the child heard in the conversation of his parents and others troubled words relating to the adult concern for having and holding a job. He sensed, and reflected in his own behavior, the insecurity of his parents. But through it all, whether indoors or outdoors, he played. For the most part, he played traditional games. The words he used in his play were sprinkled with the phrases of his parents; but the games were of the past. In this latter respect, his play was not unlike the play of the upper-class child. However, the upper-class child had begun to leap the "here and now," and his experiences included the vaster world of the theatre and of travel.

A closer look at the play of the working-class child is provided by the author's observations at the BD Nursery from December, 1938 through March, 1939.

The BD Nursery was in operation from 7:30 A.M. until 5:30 P.M., five days a week. Twenty-three children attended the nursery for a minimum fee of twenty-five cents a day. Twelve of the children came from families which had two or more additional children. The remaining eleven were in the "only child" category. Three children in the group were the product of broken homes.

What did our observations tell us about these children. What games did they play? What did they talk about? What influenced their behavior? In general, they played traditional games and spent the greatest part of their school day imitating their parents. The girls assumed the role of mother. They cooked, cleaned, sewed, shopped, ironed, and cared for "their family." The boys played at "earning a living"—or engaged in active and aggressive games such as "cops and robbers." Both sexes played "fear" games: the "bogey man" was much in evidence and games in which the children played "sick" were also common. The words used by the children in their play provided a clue to what they saw and heard at home, in comics, or on the radio. Here are some typical examples:

---

[6] Data was assembled from 1937-40 while the author was with the International Ladies' Garment Workers Union. Over 500 working-class homes were visited. Children's play was investigated while working for the Master's and Doctorate degrees at Teachers College, Columbia University, from 1938-40, and from 1958-60.

G (*Speaking to her doll*): You gonna eat or do I gotta hold your nose? Come on, open your mouth. I can't be bothered with you all day. I got work to do.

M (*Wearing necktie and playing father*): Aw shut up, won't you? Let the kid alone.

G: Aw right. Easy does it. Here—nice baby. It's good for you. Eat it.

———

B (*To child lying in a crib*): If I told you once, I told you a hundred times. Go to sleep!

———

H (*Dressed as mother, rocking*): I'm so sick, and he never cares nothing about it. I could die and he won't care.

M: If you get sick, teach him a lesson. Drop dead!

H: O.K. I'm dead. (*Sinks to floor, lies quietly for less than a minute—sits up.*)

M: (*Pushing her down*): No, H. . . . , you be dead. You gotta lay down. You be dead.

———

D (*Shouting into telephone*): Hello. Give me Dick Tracy. Tracy? Crooks went into the store. Come quick. I'll hold them until you get here. Come quick, you hear me? O.K. Tracy. (*Runs off wielding an imaginary gun.*)

———

Like children of all generations, they concocted imaginary games and episodes. A favorite of the boys was the daily encounter of the "good guys" and the "bad guys." The hero was either a policeman—any policeman—or Dick Tracy, the comic-strip hero of the day. In fantasy, they mounted horses, drove cars, shot guns, and climbed ladders.

It is interesting to note that these pre-television children were interested in things they saw or heard in their daily lives. They did, on occasion, slip into sheer fantasy. Yet, they knew the difference between the real and the make-believe. Their aspirations were the normal aspirations of four-year-olds. All but two of the children wanted to be "like daddy" or "like mommy." The exceptions chose to be like Dick Tracy.

WORKING-CLASS CHILDREN AT PLAY SINCE TELEVISION

Will a child who has seen and known television since infancy play in the same way as a child who has not? An examination of the behavior of some post-television children of the fifties, as observed by the author at the BW school of New York City from November, 1958 through March, 1959, may shed some light on this question.

Fourteen children attended the school five days a week, from 7:30 A.M. until 5 to 6 P.M. The children lived in walk-up apartments within a radius of ten blocks of the school. Six of the children lived with both parents, four lived with mother only, and the remaining four lived with relatives. The family incomes, according to the school's director, were all under $5,000 per year. The average income was at about $3,000 a year. Some of the families received city welfare. Nevertheless, television, which was considered a necessity, was in all but three of the homes. Of the three children in these homes, two managed to see television at their neighbors. Thus, only one child did not see television on a regular basis.

Listed in order of preference are the television shows the children watched daily or weekly.

Cartoons: Popeye, Mickey Mouse, Woody Woodpecker, Terry Tunes
 The Little Rascals, The Three Stooges

431

Cowboy Shows: The Lone Ranger, Zorro, Annie Oakley	American Bandstand
Superman	Twentieth Century Films
Shirley Temple/Walt Disney	Huckleberry Hound
Situation Comedies (family-type):	The Price is Right
I Love Lucy/Danny Thomas/	Wonderama
Leave It to Beaver/This is Alice	Captain Kangaroo
	Romper Room

The spontaneous play encouraged at some other schools (for middle- and upper-class children) was pointedly discouraged at the BW school. The children were closely supervised. The school's policy is evidenced in the following:

1. Children were encouraged to work independently so that they could plan and carry out their own "constructions" without interruption. This was in contrast to their play situations at home where little privacy was afforded and the presence of brothers and sisters usually resulted in the disruption of their play.

2. Noise within the classroom was kept to a minimum. "Correct" behavior was stressed. A quiet tone of voice was encouraged.

Middle-class mores were imposed. Excitement, whether in voice or play, was to be gently, but firmly, quelled. The policies were designed to forestall the kind of raucous behavior that television-prompted play situations might provoke.

INFLUENCE OF TELEVISION ON THE PLAY OF THE WORKING-CLASS CHILD

Television's influence on the play activities in which the children engaged, the vocabulary they used, and the movements and gestures they employed was found to be great indeed. It was as though the children were following a prescribed television script. Their play had a definite sequence. They knew when and how to start and terminate their activity.

Here are some examples which help to illustrate the influence of television on these children:

1. Bryan played alone. He piled rubber figures onto a radiator shelf. He crouched and whispered aloud as he moved each figure. He peopled his stage with many different characters and used his voice to represent each one. He was, in addition, a most expert sound-effects man. Although his play area adjoined that of others, he played alone.

   "Yaikes, look where the airplane is! (*Moves plane.*) "Here?" (*New voice.*) "Who got the gun? (*New voice.*) "I have, Who you? Who you? Quiet! Who gotta gun? Yaikes! (*New voice.*) Hey men, look out—look out. (*Screams.*) Look out—airplanes. (*Drops two planes to the floor.*) Gee—eee—eee (*whining and zooming sound.*) Hey men, look—we got him (*Drops another plane.*) Gee—eee—eee!"

   Teacher: Bryan, keep your voice down, please.

   Bryan: O.K. (*Continues his monologue, voice almost inaudible. After a few minutes, his voice rises in imitation of the whine and zoom of a plane.*)

   Teacher: Bryan ... ! Bryan!

   (*Bryan stops, stares at teacher, throws his figures on the floor and runs from the room.*)

2. Frank's vocabulary reflected what he heard at home and on the street. When constructing, he always peopled his buildings with a boss, a foreman, and workers. Whenever he introduced a TV character, his play situation would

GOMBERG

432

switch to one of conflict. On the particular day in question, he had constructed a "United States Building."

"Now, that's right. All these men—all gotta go to the doctor. O.K. Foreman, you hear? All these men gotta go to the doctor. Nobody gonna get sick at my plant. O.K. foreman, get them going. To the doctor—to the doctor. United States Building—. This worker goes there. This worker goes here. Hi boss. Hi, boss. Good morning, boss. Say good morning to the boss."

Danny: (*Looking at Frank.*) What's 'that?

Frank: (*Grimaces and whispers.*) That's Hawkeye.

Danny: (*Shivers.*) Ooooh. He scares me.

Frank: Good. Hawkeye. Get the guys moving. Fast. Hurry up. Get moving. (*Twists upper blocks to one side and then to another.*) United States is falling! United States is falling! (*Topples figures.*) Good. They're dead. Now, let's have a war. (*Sound effects of planes whizzing and falling as he knocks over every block.*)

3. Robson reacted peculiarly to his televiewing. Whether he called his figures or players "crooks," or "pirates," or "Indians," or "bad guys," he always concluded his play in this way:

"Now I got yeh! Bleed! Bleed! Bleed! Bang! Bang! Bang! Bleed until you die. You're no good. A bad lot—no good. Bleed! Bleed! Now, die!"

One morning Robson tripped in the corridor and cut his lip, which bled. He became hysterical. His teacher tried to soothe him, but to no avail. Robson screamed, "I'm bleeding. I don't want to die. Only bad guys bleed. I don't want to die." Obviously, Robson's televiewing had gotten beyond him. He had developed misconceptions about the relation of television happenings to real events and was in dire need of help.

Common to all schools was the same aggressive form of play. Whether it was called "cops and robbers" or went by some other name, was just incidental. The tone, tempo, and pattern of action were virtually the same. For example, an extended finger represented a gun. The boys extended their fingers as they galloped about. They would crouch behind furniture and shout, "Bang! Bang!" or "take that, and that, and that!" Facial expressions, posturings, and movements were also routinized. The boys swaggered, talked out of the sides of their mouths, spat on the ground, and practiced endlessly the western-style "fast draw." Boys who posed as "Superman" practiced simulating flight. Commandoes practiced crawling and wriggling through rough terrain.

As for the girls, they prattled about what they had seen on television. They talked about the products they had seen advertised. They compared shows and discussed products that they thought they would like to own and use. They were prone to tease those who did not conform. A girl whose views differed, suffered the taunts of the majority. The following brief episode illustrates the point.

Dawn: Caryn, know what? I saw Sleeping Beauty and the Princess Aurora.

Caryn: I saw it on the Disney show. And you know what? My mother took me to see it at the movies, too.

Jackie: Yeah, me too. I saw it on Disney.

Mary: Aw, you and the Sleeping Beauty. Every day—Sleeping Beauty! She's a witch.

Dawn: Oh, no! Mal-e-ficient. She's the witch. You didn't see it, so how do you know.

All: Yeah! How do you know?

Dawn: (In sing-song fashion) Mary don't kno—ow! Mary don't kn—ow!

All: (Taking up the chant.): Mary don't kn—ow! Mary don't kn—ow!

The
Working-Class
Child of Four
and Television

At the work tables, girls and boys often talked with one another as they manipulated their blocks, puzzles, tiles, or pegs. They talked about the "funny things," their favorite cartoon characters or puppets said or did. For example:

Joey: I'm going to get a little car and take off your neck.
Danny: No. I'll get a big car and take off your neck. Hey, I'm not your friend. (*Pinches Joey's arm.*)
Joey: Ow. I not hit you. Only fun-pretend. Here. (*Gives Danny two magnets.*) I'm your friend.
Danny: I'm big. Like the Rangers.
Joey: I'm bigger—like the "Lone Ranger."
(*Frank comes galloping into the room*), Hi, ho, Silver.
Teacher (*Putting her finger to her mouth*) Shh! Frankie.
Joey: Hi, cuckoo head!
Frank: Who you calling cuckoo head?
Joey: (*Grinning broadly*) Nobody.
Vickie: Hi, cuckoo head!
Caryn: Who you calling cuckoo head!
Mary: Nobody (*Grins at others who return her grin*).
Teacher: Who is cuckoo head? What are you talking about?
Joey: Nobody. I'm just foolin' around.
Mary: I know! Cuckoo head is Clowney!
Frank: What she telling for? Nobody!

The foregoing illustrates a typical pattern. The children in this case are the "in" group. They can share their information, but not with adults in authority. Mary was chastized for violating the code. Once the teacher moved beyond hearing distance, the children began reciting Clowney's entire repetoire: "skinny bones," "noodle puss," and ending with "Aw shut up, you cuckoo head. Who's saying cuckoo head? Nobody!"

An offshoot of televiewing was the introduction of a novel play. The children called it, "watching television." This was unlike any other play either in structure or content. It closely resembled mutual day-dreaming. Here they lined up chairs and stared fixedly ahead at some imaginery screen. Occasionally one child would twist a "dial" and the viewers would sigh. Infrequently some viewer would express annoyance: "Why did you change that? I wanted 'Lassie',"; or "No, 'Little Rascals'! Boy—leave that channel alone."

"Watching television" was also done in the housekeeping area. Then the girls would open the "oven door," insert a puzzle, announce, "TV is on." Those cooking, washing, or ironing, would relax momentarily and watch. Their only comment was, "Ain't that cute." All children played this new game. What they saw was their own mental creation. They stood or sat transfixed, seldom talking or moving. Their annoyance at being interrupted was clearly demonstrated by this illustration:

Teacher: Whatever are you doing?

Dawn: Gee whiz, don't you know nothing, watching television.

Television's influence on the children in their choice of attire and toys was also apparent. Some of the girls wore cowgirl skirts and jackets. The boys wore boots, jackets, and holsters. Hand puppets ("Lamb Chops," "Mickey Mouse," "Cuckoo Head") were also popular. In general, the clothes and toys favored by this working-class group of children matched closely the clothes and toys favored by children in upper- and middle-class groups. Thus television not only provided the "scripts" for their play, but determined to some extent their attire and their equipment.

Needless to say, commercial messages had their own special impact. The children were drawn to the products they saw advertised on television. The desire to conform—to own or use those products the commercial suggested that others owned and used—was very strong in the children.

INTERVIEW WITH CHILD AND PARENT/GUARDIAN

Further probing into the meaning of each child's role-taking was afforded by means of interviews. Each child, in a separate interview, was asked to explain terms he had used, roles he had taken, equipment he had used, and concepts he had derived from television. The following data was compiled:

1. *Exposure to Television*

As estimated by parents			*As estimated by the children*		
Watched 5 hours —	1 child		Watched 0 hours —	1 child	
" 8 "	" "		" 8 "	" "	
" 9 "	" "		" 15 "	" "	
" 22 "	11 children		" 22 "	4 children	
			" 25 "	" "	
			" 30 "	3 "	

2. *Reason for watching television*

   (a) Entertainment
   (b) Security (sense of)
   ı(c) Aesthetics
   (d) Boredom

3. *Concepts or new information derived from television*

   (a) The world is a glamorous stereotype in which the major cartoon figure (or hero or heroine) acts in a predictable fashion. It is a world of action, violence, and destruction—a world of kill or be killed.
   (b) Good people—the hero or heroine—must kill.
   (c) Bad people are bad because they start the fight. They must be taught a lesson. They deserve to be killed.
   (d) A hero is easily identified. He has his own particular trademark, i.e., he wears a white hat, rides a white horse, wears a special cape or costume, etc.
   (e) Bad people bleed and then die.
   (f) Superman is real and will help you if you really need him. But he knows when you are fooling and that's why he doesn't come.
   (g) All Indians are bad, with the exception of Tonto.
   (h) All "Japs" are bad and must be killed.
   (i) The good lady, the "girl" always marries the good guy.
   (j) All the products advertised are good and everyone should buy them.

4. *Ethical Standard*

   What is seen on television becomes a basis for behavior. It is the way people act, and the authority should not be questioned.

   The interviews with the parents provided insights into conditions at home. Television, it developed, was used "to keep the kids out of trouble"—serve as

The Working-Class Child of Four and Television

435

a baby-sitter. But parents saw an educational value, too. They felt that their children had become more knowledgeable because of television. They believed that learning to read—at any rate, the ability to distinguish some words and letters—was a by-product of the child's televiewing. They illustrated this by reference to shopping trips during which the children would run from counter to counter picking out products they recognized from television. In one case, the parents reported: "He knew the name right off . . . found the Bosco and brought it to me . . . 'see this spells Bosco—B-O-S-C-O:'"

CONCLUSIONS

Basically, the children found television to be wonderful entertainment. It brought them excitement, glamour, fun, and an escape from boredom. But influence of television appeared to overshadow the influence of parents. The child of the 1950's did not make what his parents said or did the basis for his behavior as did the child of the 1930's. The *"seeing and hearing"* experiences of television had a greater learning impact than did the comic strips and radio programs of the thirties. The actions, behavior patterns, expressions, and attitudes of television personalities were more readily assimilated than were those of the comic-strip and radio heroes. And there was, in addition, pressure to conform. The one child in our study who rarely watched television was nevertheless driven to adopt the behavior of her companions in order to stay in their good graces and to share in the fun. Thus television—the ideas derived from it—dominated their play. This was true of children regardless of their socioeconomic background. For some children, fantasy and reality became indistinguishable. They readily assimilated the attitudes and prejudices of the unreal and stereotyped world they saw on television, and in their immaturity, could not accept or tolerate a challenge to the authority of television.

As the survey of shows discussed earlier suggests, some of the children were accustomed to seeing adult programs. How did these children respond to "I Love Lucy," "Danny Thomas," and the rest? This question is difficult to answer. However, we do know that the homes of "Lucy" and "Danny Thomas" were a far cry from the walk-up apartments to which these children were accustomed. Television invited them regularly into these new and glamorous homes. Might there be in this comparison the beginning of dissatisfaction? Time, and possible future research, may give us the answer.

Today, children are avid televiewers. Their exposure to television has greatly influenced their play and general behavior. The working-class child of the thirties shared a common experience but only with children of his own class. His play activities reflected what he understood best—his home and his parents. The working class child of the fifties, because of television, shares an experience with children of all classes. The context of his play activities, and his behavior at play, are similar to the activities and behavior of children of all classes. And although his childlike aspirations of the 30's was to be like his parent, today *all* working class children want to be like or marry television performers. Finally his fascination with the world of television is overwhelming. Listen to Joey: "I'm gonna make a lot of money and buy three . . . four . . . no . . . a hundred TV sets . . . and watch anything I want . . . even late at night"

Lower-Class Negro Television Spectators: The Concept of Pseudo-Jovial Scepticism*

ALAN F. BLUM

IN this paper we analyze the peculiar type of social relationship which is established between lower-class Negro spectators and white performers in the television-viewing situation. The essential nature of this encounter—the fact that it appears as a joking relationship between two interactants with divergent interests—suggests that the lower-class Negro television spectator uses jocularity to reduce the hostility he feels toward the society which the white *persona* represents. In what follows we shall argue that traditional sociological conceptions of the working-class personality and of the interrelations between social class and cognition have tended to obscure the recognition of such facts.

I.   THE CONCEPT OF WORKING-CLASS PRIMITIVITY

For some time sociologists have accepted an image of the working-class personality which has emphasized the concreteness of their cognitive processes and their emotion-laden, particularistic orientations to objects. The sociological formulation easily lent itself to the development of a concept of working-class cognitive primitivism which differed radically from the way in which sociologists conceptualized middle-class thought, which its assumed richness and capacity for abstraction. Lipset has stated this position well.

> Working-class life as a whole emphasizes the concrete and immediate . . .
> This concern with the present leads to a concentration on daily activities, without
> much inner reflection, imaginative planning of one's future unrelated to one's
> daily activities. . . . They do not have a rich inner life, indeed their imaginative
> activity is meagre and limited.[1]

---

* Parts of this essay first appeared in "The Concept of Working Class Primitivity," a paper read at the 33rd Annual Meetings of the Society for Social Research, May 1961, at the University of Chicago; "The Dynamics of Pseudo-Jovial Scepticism," a paper read at the Social Psychology Seminar at the University of Chicago, October, 1962; and, "The Mass Media Relationship as an Interaction Episode," unpublished paper, 1963.

[1] S. M. Lipset, *Political Man* (New York: Doubleday & Company, Inc., 1959), p. 116.

Lower-Class
Negro
Television
Spectators:
The Concept
of Pseudo-Jovial
Scepticism

It is not our purpose in this paper to challenge the validity of this representation of the working-class mentality, but rather, to suggest that the propositions which have been derived from it are not altogether appropriate for explaining certain forms of lower-class behavior.[2]

The sociologist's model of working-class cognitive primitivity has generated an order of consequences which are somewhat questionable: it has usually been assumed that the working-class person is incapable of defending himself against the organized assault of the mass media because he is not sufficiently competent to make the complex cognitive discriminations necessary for a reflective assessment of media fare. In contrast with this, we shall maintain that it is the worker's very concreteness of perception, his pragmatic and "primitive" cognitive orientation to people and ideas, which produces in the lower-class television consumer a critical distrust of various forms of reality which are created and sustained by the medium.

II.   THE IMAGE OF THE LOWER-CLASS AUDIENCE IN
THE WRITINGS OF THE POPULAR CULTURALISTS

Most of the broad-gauge commentary and speculation on the effects of the mass media upon American audiences have been produced by a group of social scientists, essayists, and journalists whom we identify as the *popular culturalists*.[3] They have traditionally portrayed the media consumer as a passive and narcotized spectator whose responses are controlled by an omnipotent medium. From this perspective, the viewer is not seen as energetic or discriminating in his use of the media, but, rather, as a lethargic receptor whose behavior is guided by media against which he is helpless. These media have the power to condition him to new modes of adaptation and commitment, to transform his beliefs and rechannel his passions in the service of goals which are not in his interests, to create new needs, to gratify base and frivolous needs, and to distract him from a serious involvement in the polity. The major theme of the popular culturalists is that the media consumer lacks the energy, initiative, and cognitive competence to evaluate the media fare to which he is exposed and to defend himself effectively against such fare.

If this is a general picture of the American audience, the lot of the lower-class person is even more hopeless: with his senses dulled from continuous participation in repetitive industrial routines, and his attention absorbed by the concrete, the tangible, and the immediate, he is presumably too tired and indifferent to become critically involved in the media context.

---

[2] We do not mean to imply that this model of working-class cognition should not be challenged. However, the available evidence suggests that it is appropriate. See B. Bernstein, "Some Sociological Determinants of Perception," *British Journal of Sociology*, Vol. 9 (1958); Schatzman and Strauss, "Social Class and Modes of Communication," *American Journal of Sociology*, Vol. 60 (January, 1955).

[3] See B. Rosenberg and D. White, *Mass Culture* (New York: The Free Press of Glencoe, Inc., 1956), for a representative sample of these writings.

III.   THE TV-VIEWING CONTEXT AS AN
INTERPERSONAL ENCOUNTER

A reckless transformation is involved when this model of working-class cognitive simplicity is adapted for use as an intervening variable in the analysis of the television-viewing situation. The television-viewing relationship is, to a great extent, an interpersonal encounter which is characterized by the spectator's high level of involvement. Horton and Wohl have underscored this point in a classic paper in which they called this type of interaction routine between spectator and *persona* "para social interaction." [4] They conceptualized the performer-spectator relationship within the context of the television-viewing situation as a simulated, vicarious interpersonal encounter in which the spectator personalizes the *persona* and particularizes the communication which is transmitted. The notion of "para social interaction" suggests that, although the performer does not literally "talk back" to the spectator, the viewer often reacts as if he does by defining their relationship as concrete, personal, and reciprocal.

The argument which we develop in this paper follows from our acceptance of the description of the "para social nature" of the television-viewing situation. The traditional image of working-class impotence in the face of a powerful medium does *not* correspond with the facts we observed in studying the television-viewing behavior of 40 lower-class Negro families in Chicago. These facts can be more reasonably interpreted from a perspective which acknowledges the fundamental hostility of the lower-class Negro toward the image of reality which the medium attempts to sustain. *The cognitive "primitivism" of lower-class Negroes does not make them especially vulnerable to the message of the medium, but, rather, serves to mobilize their scepticism and defenses.* The lower-class viewers in our sample succeeded in controlling their hostilities by channelizing them into the highly stylized personal relationships which they developed between themselves and the television performers.

IV.   THE FUNCTIONS OF PSEUDO-JOVIAL SCEPTICISM FOR
LOWER-CLASS NEGRO TELEVISION-VIEWERS

A most important and unanticipated finding which we repeatedly observed while studying the television-viewing behavior of 40 lower-class Negro families in Chicago[5] was the jocular quality of their interaction with the medium performer, with the accompanying fact that they seemed to carry on a continuous joking dialogue with the television persona. The lower-class Negro television spectator in these cases tended to personalize the media relationship

---

[4] D. Horton and R. Wohl, "Para Social Interaction and Mass Communication," *Psychiatry*, Vol. 17 (1954).

[5] The research operation is not described, because it was designed for other purposes. Our subsequent comments must be understood as largely impressionistic.

Lower-Class
Negro
Television
Spectators:
The Concept
of Pseudo-Jovial
Scepticism

to a great extent and to inject himself actively into the ongoing interaction between media performers, either as a third party or as an actual interacting participant. The kinds of repartee developed in these relationships—the spectator would chide the performer, cajole him, answer his questions directly, warn him of impending dangers, compliment him, and so on—were executed lightly, humorously, and freely, in a highly personal manner. Because most media spectators maintain identifications of a serious nature with media performers, it was the very frivolity and joviality characterizing the responses of those lower-class Negro viewers which sensitized us to other factors. It was precisely because these relationships were couched in such jocular terms that they were suspect: the understanding that humor often conceals basic hostilities directed our inquiry.

The notion of pseudo-jovial scepticism is merely an extension of the familiar anthropological concept of joking relationships which suggests that interacting participants with disjunctive interests will minimize the probability of occasioning occurrences of conflict by developing a ritualized exchange of insults and jocular banter in their interpersonal encounters.[6] Pseudo-jovial scepticism is suggested from our observations of the television-viewing styles of these lower-class Negro audiences: the pseudo-jovial quality of the relationship is reflected in the lower-class Negro's defensive humor toward the television performer; the jocularity which appears seems to reflect the viewer's suspiciousness and distrust of the medium more than any genuine delight in consumption; the scepticism which we identify refers more directly to the tenor of the relationship and to the fact that the lower-class Negro viewer does not appear to internalize the goals of the interaction. This scepticism is probably the natural derivative of the lower-class Negro's disenchantment with a normative order that has been, and promises to continue to be, quite unrewarding.

The mechanism of pseudo-jovial scepticism appears to serve a protective function for the viewer against the attractive, technologically organized appeals and promises of the medium. In this sense, the lower-class Negro television-viewer tries to resist the attempts of the media to mobilize his aspirations, commitments, and loyalties in the service of normative goals which he regards as hypocritical and illusory.

This concept of pseudo-jovial scepticism necessarily assumes that the spectators participating in the media relationship tend to translate the relation into a concrete, reciprocal, personal encounter. By considering the relationship between performer and spectator in this way, while holding the notion of joking relationships in mind, the concept of pseudo-jovial scepticism can be better understood. Although the lower-class Negro responds to the medium and its presentation, he does not seem to take it seriously—he is "putting the medium on" and he seems to believe that the medium is reciprocally "putting him on." Compared to other television viewers who seriously

---

[6] See A. R. Radcliffe-Brown, *Structure and Function in Primitive Society* (New York: The Free Press of Glencoe, Inc., 1952), Ch. 4.

commit themselves to the medium presentation, the lower-class Negro viewer achieves considerable distance; he is typically involved with the medium in a joking relationship in which conflict is imminent; the possibilities of conflict are occasioned when the lower-class Negro is confronted by media which serve as spokesmen for a normative order which he regards as highly deficient. When the media relationship is simulated in personal and concrete terms, the possibilities of conflict can be reduced only through the establishment of ritualized jocularity.

The type of argument advanced here could be developed only from the assumption that the spectator and performer are involved in a personal relationship. The notion of a joking relation in such a context requires the assumption of a basic hostility between participants. We shall now enumerate some of the sources of this interpersonal hostility.

The media relationship tends to engender its own world—its own reality, events, roles, and identities—but one which is predominantly a white cosmos, and not easily accessible to Negroes. When the Negro viewer is invited to project himself into a role, an identity, an event, or a setting which he knows from experience to be restricted to whites, he must mobilize a remarkable single-mindedness in order to blot out the view of external reality which contradicts the norms of the relationship in which he is involved. As an interaction, the media relationship generates its own schema of interpretation, and this interpretation is derived from the perspectives of spokesmen for a white society. At every point in the encounter, the media performer's interaction, his simulation of sociability and intimacy, his attractiveness and appeal, must be reassessed. The Negro spectator cannot internalize the goals of the interaction because he is incapable, even if he desires, of mobilizing a complete identification with the reality of the media context.

In the media relationship, the Negro lower-class television-viewer must adapt to at least three types of strain. First, he must somehow resolve the dissonance which he senses between the image of the world which is produced by the media and his own image of the world which is derived from his life in it. Second, the Negro viewer must in some way develop an empathic relationship with the white *persona;* he must be able to internalize the mutual goals which they establish concertedly for the duration of the interaction. All of this requires that he simulate a close, personal relationship with a white *persona* whom he would not find as approachable under other circumstances. Finally, the Negro spectator must adjust to the fact that none of the performers to whom he is responding are Negroes—a blatant reminder of his peculiar status as a participant in the interaction.

Thus, we would argue that the Negro lower-class television spectator is, to a greater extent than other viewers, involved in a strained interaction episode when he relates to the performer. The joking relationship which he establishes with the television performer serves to keep him in character and to control his affect while simultaneously providing him with a margin of expressiveness which he requires more urgently than other television spectators.

Lower-Class
Negro
Television
Spectators:
The Concept
of Pseudo-Jovial
Scepticism

V. SUMMARY AND IMPLICATIONS

We have argued that the hostility of the lower-class Negro toward his white society is expressed in the joking relationship he establishes with the performer in the television-viewing situation. Furthermore, we have suggested that the cognitive orientations of these viewers do not render them more affectionate to the media presentation, but rather serve to articulate their awareness of the discrepancy between media reality and their own experiences as underprivileged members of the society.

The conventional sociological conception of working-class thought—with its emphasis upon the concreteness and simplicity of their cognitions—has usually been incorporated in explanations of working-class television-viewing behavior which have stressed their greater defenselessness against the medium. However, by accepting this image of working-class cognition in conjunction with the description of the television-viewing situation as a "para social encounter," we have succeeded in casting some doubt upon this traditional sociological conception of the lower-class television spectator.

Rather than appearing as the docile and submissive viewers so frequently described by the students of popular culture and the mass media, the lower-class television viewers whose behavior we have discussed in this paper reacted with decided hostility to the performers and programs to which they were continually exposed. We discovered this hostility by searching for the latent implications of the joking relationships which they sustained with the performer in the television-viewing encounter.

Thus, our interpretation directly challenges the sociological tradition which has assumed that working-class submissiveness follows from their greater cognitive primitivism. We have implied that this concreteness of cognition has certain positive consequences for lower-class spectatorship, which middle-class observers might not ordinarily recognize: it is possibly this very lack of cognitive sophistication which enables the lower classes to "see through" the façade of media reality more readily than do sophisticated middle-class viewers. Through the exercise of their cognitive capacities, lower-class viewers manage to defend themselves from commitment to the image of reality that is manufactured by the medium. Paradoxically, then, we suspect that *lower-class television spectators succeed in resisting identification with media reality precisely because they are socialized into deficient modes of cognitive adjustment.*

It is true that the ideas presented in this paper were derived from observations of a particular segment of the working-class subculture—lower-class Negro television-viewers—and not from a representative working-class sample. Thus, there is the problem of whether the behavior reported here is a function of a generalized lower-class orientation, or whether it is a culturally patterned response specific to lower-class Negroes. It is our feeling that both factors of cognitive primitivism and underprivilege interact to produce such television-viewing styles. The lower-class Negroes in our sample might serve to illustrate the interaction of these factors more dramatically, because they do represent an extreme case.[7]

The effects of underprivilege and low status upon the viewer's perception of media reality are quite direct: he is exposed to a picture of reality with which he has no experience, and of a performer who is a type of person that he has never confronted in his everyday existence. The dissonance which he experiences when he attempts to match his own image of life with the perspective created by the medium generates a resentment in him which must be discharged in some way; the lower-class Negroes whom we observed invested this hostility into personal, joking relationships with the television performers.

In conclusion, the tentative and highly conjectural nature of this essay must be re-emphasized, since these findings were neither initiated by theory nor anticipated in a research design. Furthermore, the ambiguities in the theoretic explanations which have been adduced to account for these findings have not been systematically explored in subsequent research. We do feel, however, that the implications of the concept of pseudo-jovial scepticism are sufficiently challenging to warrant discussion and further consideration at this time.

Observations on Gambling in a Lower-Class Setting*

IRVING KENNETH ZOLA[†]

INTRODUCTION

STUDIES in gambling have often focused on matters of individual pathology[1] and yet, on a number of psychological dimensions, no significant differences

---

[7] There is one paper which suggests that the personalization of relationships is more characteristic of Negroes. See E. Barth, "The Language Behavior of Negroes and Whites," *Pacific Sociological Review*, Fall, 1961. Dollard and Goffman, among others, have discussed the use of joviality by Negroes in their relationships with whites as one strategy of control which they attempt to exert.

* Reprinted from *Social Problems*, Vol. 10, No. 4 (Spring, 1963).

† Now, Department of Sociology, Brandeis University.

This report is part of a study entitled "Relocation and Mental Health: Adaptation Under Stress," conducted by the Center For Community Studies in the Department of Psychiatry of the Massachusetts General Hospital and the Harvard Medical School. The research is supported by the NIMH, Grant #3M 9137-C3. The author wishes to acknowledge Edward Ryan and Leonora K. Zola for their repeated readings and criticisms, and Frances Morrill, Stanton Wheeler, and George H. Wolkon for their valuable suggestions.

[1] Edmund Bergler, *The Psychology of Gambling*, (New York: Hill and Wang, 1957); and "The Gambler—A Misunderstood Neurotic," *Journal of Criminal Psychopathology*, Vol. 4 (1943), pp. 379-93.

have been found between gamblers and nongamblers.[2] Part of the explanation for this lack of difference is the fact that so widespread an activity as gambling can be "many things to many people." [3] Another reason is that while recognized as one of our major social problems, gambling also constitutes a major American paradox, fluctuating as it does between tolerance and condemnation, with a very thin line drawn between legal and illegal forms.[4] It seems obvious that to exist in this state of limbo, gambling must serve important social and psychological functions. This report is an attempt to delineate some functions of one form of gambling as it occurs in a small lower-class residential community.

THE SETTING

East Side was a small working-class area within a large New England city. Successive waves of immigrants once flooded the streets, but in recent years the population had become more stable, predominantly Italian with smaller segments of Eastern European Jews and Poles. As part of an anthropological field team, the observer spent several months in East Side, becoming a habitué of meeting places, bars, and taverns and participating actively with several subgroups. His identity and role were, however, unknown to the community. Most of the observations on gambling were made at Hoff's Place, one of many taverns along the main street of East Side. It was a bar and grill frequented mostly by Italians and Poles who were either present or former residents of the immediate neighborhood. At Hoff's one type of gambling predominated: off-track betting where wagers are made with a "bookie" or "bookmaker." Though the men spent much of the day here, virtually all over thirty were married and relatively few were unemployed. Some were on vacation or on their day off. Some worked nearby, drove delivery trucks or taxis and dropped in and out while ostensibly working. Others worked on split shifts and visited between them. Still others had jobs which ended early in the day or started very late.

One of the first observations made of Hoff's was the dissociation of the bar from other spheres of the men's social life. Violent reactions often greeted any invasion or intrusion.

> One wife became concerned when her husband did not return for supper and so she called and asked the bartender about his whereabouts. Although he knew, he gruffly denied any knowledge. Whereupon she burst into tears, pleading with him, "Please don't tell him I called, 'cause he would beat the shit out of me if he knew."

---

[2] James Hunter and Arthur Bruner, "Emotional Outlets of Gamblers," *Journal of Abnormal and Social Psychology*, Vol. 23 (1928), pp. 38-39; and Robert P. Morris, "An Exploratory Study of Some Personality Characteristics of Gamblers," *Journal of Clinical Psychology*, Vol. 13 (1957), pp. 191-93.

[3] Edward C. Devereux, Jr., "Gambling and the Social Structure—A Sociological Study of Lotteries and Horse Racing in Contemporary America," Unpublished doctoral dissertation, Harvard University, 1949.

[4] Herbert A. Bloch, "The Sociology of Gambling," *American Journal of Sociology*, Vol. 57 (1951), pp. 215-22; and "The Gambling Business; An American Paradox," *Crime and Delinquency*, Vol. 8 (1962), pp. 355-64.

"One day my mother sent me after my father. It was gettin' late. When he came home was he mad! He kicked her all the way down Lawrence Street and back and said to her, 'Don't you never send anyone after me here. No buts, anything can wait till I get here.' And she never did it again."

A further distinction was made between gambling and other spheres of economic activity. A man was not expected to share his profits with his family and was thought a "damn fool" if he even told them of his winnings. The fact that most gambling activities take place in a context institutionally defined as "recreation" helps to emphasize this dissociation from ordinary utilitarian activities.[5]

A GROUP IN PROCESS

The men at Hoff's, however, did not constitute a group in the formal sense. Regardless of when in the day one entered, the men in the bar seemed only to be whiling away their time drinking, barely taking notice of one another. On any day the pattern would be quite similar.

In the first booth, Hal reads the Morning Telegraph while Sammy naps in a corner. Behind them Smiley studies the Star Racing Section and Silvio looks at Phil's Armstrong. Phil, the bookie, sits at the bar going over his slips. Beside him Nick stares blankly at the wall and not two stools away Johnnie and Joe sip beer without speaking. Further down the bar sits an unidentified man and next to him stands Al, the bartender, gazing aimlessly out the window as he washes glasses.

Ten minutes before the start of each race, however, this changed. Men who were outside came in and those previously silent began to talk.

"Do you think he's got a chance?"
"I don't like the jockey."
"He likes muddy tracks."
"He's long overdue."
"They've been keeping him for this one."

Some of the remarks were addressed to one's neighbor, some to no one in particular. The bookie began to take bets. Gradually, the conversation became more agitated.

"Get your bets in while you can," kids Phil. Silvio turns and hands him five dollars while Smiley shakes his head, "He'll never win." Sal laughs, "Here Phil, a bean on the nose, number seven, a 'sure thing.' " "I'm the one who's got that," roars Al, reaching into his pocket and taking out a twenty-dollar bill. "Twenty thousand on number one. C'mon Irv, stick with me." "Uh, uh," I answer, "You're bad news, I like Principio." Meanwhile Phil proceeds gingerly down the bar as others turn and bet, rise from their booths or motion him toward them.

Some last minute bets or changes were made and then the race began. If the race was broadcast, a group formed near the radio. The cheering was restrained and muffled.

---

[5] Devereux, *op. cit.*

Observations
on Gambling
in a
Lower-Class
Setting

445

"See, look what's happening."
"Why is the jockey holding him back?"
"Just watch him finish with a spurt."

Regardless of whether the race was broadcast, the announcement of the winner always led to the same discussion. All attention focused on the winners.

"How did you figure it?"
"How come you picked her?"
"How did you know?"

And their answers. . . .

"I've noticed that jockey. . . ."
"Did you see the weight shift? Well. . . ."
"I figure they've been saving him. . . ."
"His last time out, he. . . ."

If no one picked the winning horse, the discussion was still the same, but more philosophical and not as prolonged. Within five minutes, however, it was quiet again.

Al is back washing glasses. Silvio and Smiley return each to a separate booth. Hal goes outside and Sammy goes back to sleep. Joe and Johnnie leave but Paul and Charlie replace them at the bar sipping beer without speaking. Nick studies the chart for the next race. Sal stands at the door looking at the sky and Phil, slips of paper in his hand, walks slowly toward the phone.

Once more they appeared to be strangers . . . until the next race.

Yet gambling is more than a mode of communication. It creates a bond between the men—a bond which defines insiders and outsiders. This function of gambling first became apparent when a newcomer arrived at Hoff's.

Joe did not live in East Side, though he was distantly related to one of the bookies. He worked on a nearby construction gang and gradually began to patronize Hoff's. At every opportunity, he would come in, order a drink, and sit at the bar or in one of the empty booths. Although he was through work at 4:00 P.M., he often remained until 5:00 or 6:00. When he offered to buy someone a drink, he was gently, but firmly, refused. All he gained was an occasional nod; until, in an off-hand manner, he asked questions about the races, horses, odds, and ways to bet. At first he bet the choices of others and then finally his own. Only when he started betting did others begin to interact with him, respond more than monosyllabically, and "allow" him to join them as they sat at the bar or in the booths.

For the younger residents of East Side, gambling seemed a way of preparing them for later adulthood. A number of teen-agers always hung around Hoff's; and, although they were not allowed in the bar to drink, they were welcome to place bets. It was during such times that they first initiated conversation with the younger men (19-21)—a preliminary step in "anticipatory socialization."

Thus, even though someone might appear at the same time every day, or the same day every week, this was insufficient to designate one a "member," a "regular," or an "insider." At Hoff's, this was accomplished only by off-track betting—an activity which served as the entrance fee, defining membership and initiating newcomers.

THE PRESERVATION OF GROUP ATTACHMENT

Three observations made by Devereux in his analysis of gambling and the social structure are relevant here: (1) Although the making of a wager polarizes the field and artificially creates the gambler's bond of interest in the event, it does not follow that winning money is the dominant motivational force; (2) many gamblers go to great lengths to deny their emotional involvement in specific events; (3) the importance and relevance of competition to gambling varies with the social context in which it occurs.[6] Each of these observations were found to hold true for Hoff's, but here in East Side, they have yet a secondary function. In de-emphasizing emotionality, monetary gain, and competition, not only were several basic sources of hostility often emanating from gambling eliminated but, at the same time, attachment to the "group at Hoff's" was thereby reaffirmed.

While the excitement accompanying any sporting event was present, it was restrained. The extremes of overexcitement and depression were both negatively sanctioned. On more than one occasion, a person who went "over the line" when he won was called "nuts" or told to stop "acting like a jerk"; or if one persisted in bemoaning his "hard luck," he too was reprimanded. Even overconcern during a race or contest was regarded with scepticism.

> Donnie was disturbed about the ball game—he had bet $10 on the outcome. He would get up, pace back and forth, sit down again. Each time he asked questions about the ability of the players or the manager. "Do you think he knows what he's doing?" As he returned to his seat once more, Mario shook his head indicating Donnie. He commented on his nervousness, adding, "After all, it's only money."

While these men cared when they lost, such depression was remarkably short-lived, perhaps until post-time of the next race. Little systematic effort was made to retain one's winnings. These men never stopped while ahead, nor reduced or even maintained the size of their bets after having won. If a person was ahead at the end of the day, it was more likely because there were no more races than through any conscious effort to accumulate profits. At Hoff's, there was no prototype of the conservative gambler who quit while ahead. People who did were disliked, and not only by the bookies. Instead of admiring them, the regulars shook their heads and called them "cheap bastards." One would have to increase the bet continually in order to gain any substantial amount of money, and yet there is still the problem of a stopping or cutting-off point. The following legend is illustrative of this:

> Bob was relating the experiences of an old East Sider. "I know a guy who won a $100,000. First here and then he wanted to gamble so badly he flew to New

[6] Devereux, op. cit.

York and then back here and kept losing till he had nothing." "Yeah," added Spike, "It could happen. You lost twenty G's and figure you've still got eighty, so you take another shot, and finally you've got nothing."

Thus, if no limit, no matter how theoretical, exists then monetary gain *per se* becomes an indefinite goal and one impossible of attainment. Finally, individual competition was almost nonexistent. Within the group itself, members were not explicitly compared with one another as being better or worse players. In part to salve the wounds of defeat, and to share the fruits of victory, there was the common practice of mutual treats where the winner paid for the drinks of his closer acquaintances.

Particularly striking was the shift of competition from within the group to "the system." There was continual talk of "beating the system," "cracking the system," "not letting the system beat you." While this ostensibly referred to the scheme or principle governing the results of races, the actual hostility was more often expressed against the agent of that system—the bookie. The group complained that "he can't be hit" or dubbed him "the undertaker," and alluded to how they would "like to bury him . . . in an avalanche of losses."

> Joe told of one bookie. "Why, you know why that son-of-a-bitch makes more money than anyone else? It's because all the bettors hate his guts, so they make all bets with him, even 'hot tips' just in the hope they'll break him."
>
> "Remember the time that 'Happy' bet 20-20-0 on a long shot and won. Do you remember Sam's face. I thought he would bust a gut."
>
> "Well, I took care of that bookie. I bet $5 on the fifth and kept betting it all on each race. By the eighth, he had to close up shop."

In this situation, the bookie served a dual function. As the personification of the system they were trying to beat, he facilitated the shifting of competition from within the group to outside the group; and by serving as the target for their hostility, he also became an integrating force of the group—their scapegoat.

Thus the de-emphasis on thrill, money, and competition not only prevented the individual member from becoming too involved with his own personal success and failure; it also made him more dependent on the group and reinforced his attachment to it and the rewards which it alone can bestow—prestige and group recognition. To understand these rewards, it is necessary to examine their dispensation.

SYSTEMS OF BETTING AND THE PRESTIGE HIERARCHY

As depicted in the opening illustration, at Hoff's all available attention and admiration was focused on those men who had chosen winners. Everyone clustered about them, prodded them to reveal the basis of their choice, praised them on their good judgment, and regarded their subsequent opinions highly. Rewarding someone in this manner assumes that he has *done* something to merit such an action. Not all types of gambling warrant such behavior. In the "numbers" or "policy game" where full rein is given to hunches, omens, dreams, and where a person may have his own special number and play it

ZOLA

448

day after day, year after year, no one is congratulated on his ability if he wins, nor asked to explain the rational basis for his choice; he is rather congratulated on his good fortune or luck. In short, methods of selection and the social rewards for winning reflect a conception of the numbers as a game of chance, whose outcome is beyond human control and comprehension, explainable only in terms of luck, fortune or fate.[7]

The methods and social rewards of off-track betting reflect a different assumption, i.e., the existence of an underlying order, a principle which can be figured out and mastered by a skilled observer.[8] While segments of the larger society deny this in their educational and legal attempts to eliminate gambling, there is hardly a single major newspaper which does not publish the opinions of at least one professional racing expert. As a rule, the latter not only names his choices but gives his reasoning. This was similar to the behavior of the bettors at Hoff's, who consulted with the winners or joined in a general discussion to explain the results, to figure out why it happened or what factors had not been sufficiently considered.

Not all criteria for making decisions were equally regarded. Basically, there were two positively valued modes, one subtype of these, and one devalued mode. Generally, an individual was characterized by his reliance on a particular mode, though it was possible that he might use more than one method on any given day. The four systems were differentiated not only by their basis of selection but also by the degree, amount, and quality of attention and recognition the group bestowed on the successful user of such methods.

Handicapping, the method which elicited the highest respect, was based on some pragmatic system of integration of available information such as past performances of horses and jockeys, weight shifts, post position, track conditions, etc. Using any available factual data, there was an attempt to *figure out* one's choice. Calling an individual a "handicapper" was the highest compliment that could be paid. When someone wanted information about a particular horse or race, the "handicappers" were the ones to whom questions were directed. Moreover, their opinions were solicited even though their total losses might actually outweigh their gains.

> At one time, I hit upon a system of betting a number of horses in combination. For three straight days, I won the daily double and in the next five days, at least one of my choices won while the other finished second or third. Each of these bets, however, was only for fifty cents and thus the net profit on each day was between five and ten dollars and after the first three days I lost. For this eight-day period I was operating at a loss, and yet for the next few weeks I was consulted by other bettors and kidded by the bookies as being "too good." One even joked about barring me.

Thus, it seems apparent that the "handicapper" gains and retains prestige not because of monetary profits or a preponderance of winners, but because he has demonstrated some technique or skill enabling him to select winners or at least come close.

---

[7] Gustav G. Carlson, "Number Gambling—A Study of a Culture Complex," Unpublished doctoral dissertation, University of Michigan, 1939; and Devereux, *op. cit.*

[8] Devereux, *op. cit.*

Observations
on Gambling
in a
Lower-Class
Setting

The "hot tip" was the second positively valued mode. It was based on the use of "inside information," facts about the horses not published or known to the general public. Though the knowledge was supposedly secret, "hot tipsters" usually revealed its possession. For only in so doing could they be acknowledged by the group. While the method of selection is a rational one, the distinguishing feature is *access* to information and not the exercise of any particular skill. This fact was recognized by the men at Hoff's and though they would ask tipsters, "Got anything hot?," "Any inside dope?," their seeking of advice would not usually go beyond this. Nor were the personal choices of such men given undue weight or consideration unless they had also achieved some recognition as handicappers.

The "hedge" is more complex and seems to be a subtype of the above two methods. One or more of the following statements usually introduced the "hedge."

"You saw me give that to Spike and Angelo and the others and I told them it it would win and then I go and bet on another. Whatta dope!"

"I couldn't decide which one of these would win so I didn't bet any."

"I had him [the winning horse] but I had to do an errand before I got here so I arrived too late to bet."

"Remember how I figured it out at home and picked number three to win but then I came here and saw the Armstrong so I bet the six. If only I hadn't seen 'the Arm.' "

The groundwork was usually laid before the race and the sequence was often as follows:

Before: "I like Ocean Rock but Principio is long overdue and that blasted Pilot's Express is always a threat with Hobbes aboard."

After: The fact that he bet Ocean Rock is ignored. "See, what did I tell you, that son-of-a-bitch Hobbes brought him in. I told you that would happen."

These remarks not only covered the bettor if his choice did not win, but also communicated to the group, "See, I also picked the winner, even though I didn't play it." For the most part, it succeeded. The group listened to the "hedgers," included them in the discussion of the results, and so allowed them to share to some extent the rewards of picking a winner. Considering their verbalization, it also seems likely that acceptance hinged on the presumption that the basis of their "unbet" choice was really handicapping or a "hot tip."

At the bottom of this prestige ladder was the hunch or random choice bet—lowest because it embodied a denial of the rationality which underlies the concept of "system" and hence "figuring out" of race results. Although "hunch betting" was chided as a "woman's bet," it was difficult to ignore if it produced a winner. Congratulations might be offered, but the reasoning behind the choice was never seriously solicited nor was future advice sought. The underlying attitude toward this technique was best shown when it produced a loser.

Jack bet on a dog called Cerullo because it was the name of a local hockey player. When it finished second, he was furious. "Damn it, that's what happens when you only have a bean [a dollar]—if I'd had more, I'd have bet him for second too." He barely uttered this when his friends began to tease him. "Say Mickey Mantle is running in the third and Williams in the ninth." They harped on the "why" of his bet. Jack fought back, shouting, "You wouldn't act that way if the shoe was on the other foot." But this only encouraged them. They continued berating him till he began to sulk and finally walked out.

Only in "hunch" betting and only when it lost did such hostility occur in the group.

THE FUNCTIONAL ASPECTS AND SATISFACTIONS OF BETTING

A rational-cognitive dimension seems to pervade these methods of selection. Since the races were considered capable of human understanding, this emphasis on rationality reflected and manifested the idea of understanding. By using these methods, the players were "beating the system." The "system," which they frequently mentioned, referred to more than a principle underlying the races but rather to life or fate. Miller claims that many lower-class individuals feel that their lives are subject to a set of forces over which they have relatively little control and that furthermore this world view is associated with a conception of the ultimate futility of direct effort towards a goal.[9] Gambling can help deny this futility, as illustrated by the response of one "regular."

> Joe continually talked about "hitting it big." Today was no exception as he spoke of just missing a $1000 double. I looked at him quizzically, "You know you always talk about your ship coming in. Do you ever think it will?" Startled, he raised his head and without looking at me, muttered, "No . . . but what else have I got besides this?" [betting on the races].

By "beating the system," outsmarting it by rational means, these men demonstrated they *can* exercise control and that for a brief moment they *can* control their fate. Off-track betting is thus a kind of escape. It denies the vagaries of life and gives these men a chance to regulate it. At Hoff's, there was an emphasis on rewards rather than punishments, on how much can be gained rather than lost. One was rewarded by increased attention and recognition when he won but never punished or ignored when he lost except when the very structure of the group was threatened. "Hunch" betting was just such a threat because it not only denied the concept of an underlying order but also was a way of admitting defeat, of granting that everything *was* beyond one's control.

Recognition was the supreme reward of the winner. By competing against the system rather than against themselves, however, recognition was no longer a scarce commodity, for theoretically there was no limit to the number of winners. Thus, wherever possible success and recognition were shared, whether by extending the definition of winners in the acceptance of "hedgers" or sharing the fruits of victory by "mutual treats." One regular revealed the

[9] Walter B. Miller, "Lower Class Cultures as a Generating Milieu of Gang Delinquency," *Journal of Social Issues*, Vol. 14 (1958), pp. 5-19.

Observations on Gambling in a Lower-Class Setting

meaning of being a winner when amid the talk and praise of his selection, he yelled, "What do you think I am, a nobody?" It was a statement so appealing that it was taken up as a byword and used over and over again by the group. In some ways, it was an insightful joke, for in picking the winner and becoming the center of attention, the winner leaves the realm of the nobody for the realm of the somebody.

CONCLUSION

Although betting doubtless serves many idiosyncratic needs, much of its structure, function, and persistence can only be understood by an examination of the social context in which it occurs. Gambling offers these men more than a means of recreation, just as Hoff's offers them more than a place to drink. Though such betting may produce neither recreation nor monetary gain, this does not necessarily mean that it is a sterile, nonproductive, or even dysfunctional activity. As many observers have pointed out, these men are aware of the major goals and values of middle-class society but are either unwilling[10] or incapable of achieving them by the use of the ordinary methods.[11] However, as recent empirical[12] and theoretical[13] literature has demonstrated, deviance may be more than a symptom of dysfunctional structures. For these men, gambling may be a way of harnessing or channeling their otherwise destructive frustrations. Instead of lashing out at society, they lash out at "the system." In this sense, gambling may be an activity which helps reinforce and preserve some of the major values of the larger social system. At Hoff's, they *can* "achieve" and *can* gain recognition for their accomplishments—by exercising skill or knowledge in the selection of horses.

Moreover, these goals of achievement and recognition can be aspired to with few of the conventional risks. In the society at large, one's success or failure alters and affects one's whole way of life while here it is completely incidental to it—a reflection of the isolation of gambling from other spheres of life. Here there is an emphasis on rewards rather than punishments, on gains rather than losses, on being a "somebody" and not a "nobody." For these men, gambling, or at least off-track betting, is not simply the flight, the withdrawal, or the escape as so often claimed. By making success and recognition possible, it allows the players to function in the larger society without suffering the consequences of the realization that they indeed have little else.

This paper is necessarily limited by the way the observations were made and thus depicts only one small but significant slice of the social context of gambling—the relation of bettors to one another. Unfortunately little was

---

[10] *Ibid.*

[11] Albert K. Cohen, *Delinquent Boys* (New York: Free Press of Glencoe, Inc., 1955); and Robert K. Merton, *Social Theory and Social Structure*, rev. and enl. ed. (New York: Free Press of Glencoe, Inc., 1957), Ch. IV and V.

[12] Robert A. Dentler and Kai T. Erikson, "The Functions of Deviance in Groups," *Social Problems*, Vol. 7 (1959), pp. 98-107.

[13] Lewis A. Coser, "Some Functions of Deviant Behavior and Normative Flexibility," *American Journal of Sociology*, Vol. 68 (1962), pp. 172-81; and Kai T. Erikson, "Notes on the Sociology of Deviance," *Social Problems*, Vol. 9 (1962), pp. 307-14.

known of the lives of these men outside this particular setting, so no explanation is possible of how or why the groups at such places as Hoff's originated nor of the origins of gambling in general. As with so many other phenomena, the sources or causes have long faded into the background and may even be unimportant. This report is but a single case study—an attempt to delineate some of the possible reasons for the persistence of gambling and some of the functions it may presently serve. Whether similar observations hold for different settings[14] and for different types of gambling will have to be settled by further empirical and more systematic investigations.

Obstacles to
Blue-Collar Participation
in Adult Education*

JACK LONDON

ROBERT WENKERT

THE facts are plain and thoroughly established—the blue-collar worker is less likely than his white-collar peers to participate in adult education. There are differences within the blue-collar world, in the sense that skilled workers have a higher rate of participation than the unskilled laborer, just as there are differences in the white-collar world, where the professional groups have a much higher rate than small businessmen. Indeed, the two worlds overlap somewhat, so that the participation rate of the top blue-collar category is somewhat higher than the rate of the lower rungs of the white-collar groups. Nevertheless, it is generally true that the blue-collars participate less than the white-collar strata.

So what? Why should these facts be of concern to anyone? The answer lies in certain trends of the American economy, particularly the trend toward the continuing reduction in the number of hours spent at work. The amount of time available for leisure pursuits is growing, and it is growing proportionately faster for the blue-collar than for the white-collar segment of society.[1] The

---

[14] Robert D. Herman, "Gambling Institutions: The Race Track," Unpublished manuscript presented at the 1963 Meeting of The Pacific Sociological Association.

* This is publication A-30 of the Survey Research Center, University of California, Berkeley.

[1] Harold L. Wilensky, "The Uneven Distribution of Leisure: The Impact of Economic Growth on 'Free Time,'" *Social Problems*, Vol. 9, No. 1 (Summer, 1961), pp. 32-56.

increasing automation in industry will accelerate this trend, and the blue-collar worker is likely to be the major recipient of these reductions in work time.[2] The constructive use of leisure time is, then, one of the major dilemmas to be faced by blue-collar workers, and it is one for which they are, of all the groups in society, least prepared.[3]

Ironically, support for the occupational training or retraining of individuals is much more readily available than is support for aid in the fruitful utilization of one's time away from work. As Harry L. Miller has noted:

> It is a truly astonishing feature of present educational policy that public funds may be used to subsidize vocational training enabling individuals to benefit personally by increasing their incomes, but not for education devoted to raising either the cultural level of the society or the available and dangerously low supply of thoughtful citizens trained to make independent judgments on important public matters.[4]

Certainly, an emphasis on vocational preparation is a necessary feature of adult education and of formal education as well. However, the initiative shown by society's members is not based on narrow job qualifications alone, but also depends on the free use of broader perspectives. The most important resource of any society lies in its people, and societal progress requires the free thought and action of all segments of the population. If opportunities for education are readily available, if becoming educated has a high value in society, if there are adequate rewards and incentives for pursuing a program of learning for adults, and if there is a receptive climate for the need and importance of life-long learning, then we may expect an increase in the collective ability of the population, in contrast to other countries where such conditions do not exist.[5]

Adult education consists of the most diverse educational experiences, including in its province cultural, vocational, recreational, religious, and (minimally) political subjects. Regardless of the motivation which brings the blue-collar worker to adult-education courses (and such motivation is most likely to be vocational), the artificial distinction commonly made between vocational and liberal education tends to retard efforts to develop meaningful and vital educational experiences for adults that will benefit them as individuals, and not only in their social and work roles. Although vocational courses may attract blue-collar workers, and may thus be used as part of a broader strategy to obtain their minimal participation in adult education, such courses should be used not only for transmitting vocational information,

---

[2] Robert E. Cubbedge, *Who Needs People?* (Washington: Robert B. Luce, 1963), and Gerard Piel, *Consumers of Abundance* (An Occasional Paper on the Role of the Economic Order in the Free Society) (Santa Barbara: Center for the Study of Democratic Institutions, 1961).

[3] Dan Wakefield, "Labor Shudders at Leisure," *The Nation*, Vol. 196 (April 20, 1963), pp. 325-27.

[4] Harry L. Miller, "Liberal Adult Education," in *Handbook of Adult Education in the United States*, ed. Malcolm S. Knowles, (Chicago: Adult Education Association, 1960), p. 510.

[5] Robert E. L. Faris, "Reflections on the Ability Dimension in Human Society," *American Sociological Review*, Vol. 26, No. 6 (December, 1961), pp. 835-43.

LONDON
WENKERT

but also for broadening social horizons so that their appetite is whetted for educational experiences which will enhance personal growth as well as develop vocational skills. It is our conviction that blue-collar workers, without possessing academic credentials in the form of diplomas and degrees, can learn and come to grips with great ideas if such material is presented in a manner that is both familiar and meaningful to them. This is, then, the basic task which confronts the adult educator vis-à-vis the blue-collar worker.

Our emphasis in this paper will be to identify some of the obstacles that inhibit greater participation by blue-collar workers in adult education. These obstacles are of two kinds: (1) myths about the nature of blue-collar life, about the learning process, about the blue-collar worker's interest in education, and so on; and (2) obstacles which inhere in the social conditions of the blue-collar world. Some of these myths and obstacles have been identified through the senior author's long experience with adult education in general and with workers' education in particular; the others were revealed in an empirical study concerned with the relations between social class and adult education, carried out in Oakland, California, of a sample of men between the ages of 20 and 60.[6]

MYTHS RETARDING PARTICIPATION

Myth 1: Workers are naturally apathetic and uninterested in the larger society

The myth of worker "apathy" is one of long standing, and has been used at least since the establishment of the early Mechanics Institutes in Great Britain, organizations which were originally intended to serve workers but which turned quickly into middle-class institutions.[7] The view associated with this myth assumes that no amount of effort will succeed in bringing working-class adults into adult education proportional to their numbers in the population, and it further assumes that the reason for this lack of success is the "natural" disinterest of the blue-collar worker in the important educational experiences of life.

The first thing to be noted about this view is the kind of assumption which underlies use of the word *apathetic,* because this word is symbolic for the attitudes which adult educators and others bring to the issue. *Apathy* is not a descriptive term, but a moral one. That is, its use implies a moral stance, from which judgments are made about what people *should* be doing, how they *should* be spending their time, and how what they are *not* doing is morally reprehensible. A good example of this kind of moral stance is to be found when *apathetic* is used to designate people with reference to other issues. For example, to say that the "masses" are "apathetic" about civil rights (or birth

---

[6] Jack London, Robert Wenkert, and Warren Hagstrom, *Adult Education and Social Class,* Survey Research Center Monograph (Berkeley: University of California, 1963).

[7] C. Hartley Grattan, *In Quest of Knowledge: A Historical Perspective on Adult Education* (New York: Association Press, 1955), pp. 86-90, 152.

control or fluoridation or peace or federal and local elections) implies not only that they are inactive, but also that they should be active and concerned and spirited about the issues involved. In short, they should agree with the person who is characterizing them, with regard to both the importance of the issue and the suggested solution. Use of the word *apathetic* takes for granted the moral validity of the position taken by the persons engaged in characterizing other people.

In the context of educational institutions, the characterization of blue-collar workers as "apathetic" usually implies the moral position that workers should be middle-class, should fit themselves into the institutional structure which exists, and should take courses which educators deem to be important for workers to be informed about. The word thus hides what should be called into question, namely, whether it is the worker who should fit himself to the existing institutions or whether the institutions should fit themselves to the life styles of the blue-collar worker.

As Frank Reissman has argued with regard to children's education, the emphasis on the "cultural deprivation" of the working-class child has inhibited attention to the positive aspects of working-class life which are worth support-ing and which can be used as steppingstones to the broadening of educational perspectives.[8] The same is true for adults: the methods, techniques, and con-tent of adult education must be surveyed from the perspective of the blue-collar worker, to determine which are most congruent with his values and interests. Unfortunately, adult administrators and teachers are predominantly middle-class, and their "trained incapacity" to understand the worker's per-spective restricts their ability to organize adult-education activities in a manner which will appeal to his interests and outlooks.

The myth of the "apathetic" lower socioeconomic strata is thus detrimental to efforts which might be undertaken for increasing the participation of these strata in adult education, because it finds fault with the potential clientele rather than with the serving institutions. The myth thus inhibits the use of imaginative programming, even though the literature hints at the types of programs which could increase participation. For example, Abraham Kaplan has pointed out that Negro participation was increased enormously in one New England town when a program relevant to Negro life was presented.[9] Similarly, we suspect that worker participation would increase substantially if labor unions could be persuaded to bargain for the inclusion of worker educa-tion during working hours. The British experience with day release classes for workers is an interesting model to follow in experimenting with ways of negotiating "educational time off" to attend classes. In Britain, programs vary from liberal studies to apprenticeship training, as well as job training and trade-union education.[10]

---

[8] Frank Reissman, *The Culturally Deprived Child* (New York: Harper & Row, Publishers, 1962).

[9] Abraham Abbott Kaplan, *Socio-Economic Circumstances and Adult Participation* (Teach-ers College, Columbia University, Contributions to Education, No. 889), 1943.

[10] H. A. Clegg and Rex Adams, *Trade Union Education* (London: Workers' Educational Association, 1959), pp. 48-50; A. H. Thornton, "Liberal Studies for Factory Workers," *Adult Education*, Vol. XXXIII, No. 1 (May, 1960); and F. J. Bayliss and J. T. Rhodes, "Courses in Factories," *Adult Education*, Vol. XXXV, No. 3 (September, 1962).

Myth 2: Workers are not capable of sustained intellectual effort,
and therefore are not able to benefit from continuing education

This view stems from the common assumption that all members of society want to belong to the middle-class or the white-collar strata, and that those who do not get the requisite education as children simply do not have the ability or capacity to do passing work in school.

Like the other myths outlined here, this assumption is not supported by the facts. As a number of studies in the last decade have shown, a relatively high proportion of school children do not continue their education after graduation from high school even though their I. Q. scores indicate that they have the necessary ability to do so. Heavily represented in this group of "underdeveloped manpower" are the children from the lower socioeconomic strata.[11] It is also sometimes conveniently overlooked that, although the mean I. Q. for white-collar occupations tends to be higher than that for the blue-collar occupations, the range within each occupation is so large that there is considerable overlap between the various occupations. There are intelligent men in all occupations.[12]

Aside from the recent studies which undermine the myth that workers are not intellectually capable, history itself attests to the fact that, when sufficiently challenged, all men are capable of thought and deed beyond what are commonly imagined to be their limits. Over 100 years ago, when public argument raged over the question of providing free public education to the general population, one of the arguments against such a provision was that the mass of people were incapable of profiting from such education. A letter to the editor of a North Carolina newspaper in 1829 complained that:

> Gentlemen, it appears to me that schools are sufficiently plenty, and that people have no desire they should be increased. Those now in operation are not all filled, and it is very doubtful if they are productive of much real benefit. Would it not redound as much to the advantage of young persons, and to the honour of the State, if they should pass their days in the cotton patch, or at the plow, or in the cornfield, instead of being mewed up in a school house, where they are earning nothing? . . . Gentlemen, I hope you do not conceive it at all necessary that everybody should be able to read, write and cipher. If one is to keep a store or a school, or to be a lawyer or physician, such branches may, perhaps, be taught him; though I do not look upon them as by any means indispensable; but if he be a plain farmer, or a mechanic, they are of no manner of use, but rather a detriment. . . . Should schools be established by law . . . our taxes must be considerably increased . . . and I will ask any prudent, sane, saving man if he desires his taxes to be higher?[13]

---

[11] Torsten Husén, "Educational Structure and the Development of Ability," in *Ability and Educational Opportunity*, ed. A. H. Halsey (Paris: Organization for Economic Co-operation and Development, 1961), p. 127; Patricia Cayo Sexton, *Education and Income* (New York: The Viking Press, Inc., 1961); Brian Jackson and Dennis Marsden, *Education and the Working Class* (London: Routledge and Kegan Paul, Ltd., 1962).

[12] Naomi Stewart, "AGCT Scores of Army Personnel Grouped by Occupation," *Occupations*, Vol. 26, (1947), pp. 5-41; Donald E. Super, *The Psychology of Careers* (New York: Harper & Row, Publishers, 1957); pp. 38-39; Lawrence G. Thomas, *The Occupational Structure and Education* (Englewood Cliffs, N.J.: Prentice-Hall, Inc., 1956), pp. 288, 310.

[13] From *The Raleigh* (North Carolina) *Register*, November 9, 1829, in Edgar W. Knight and Clifton L. Hall, *Readings in American Educational History* (New York: Appleton-Century-Crofts, Inc., 1951), p. 341.

Obstacles
to Blue-Collar
Participation
in Adult
Education

It seems highly unlikely that anyone of sound mind would make such an argument today, at least in its more blatant forms. Nevertheless, such assumptions seem to be prominent among self-righteous and self-satisfied educators who see no sense in making special efforts to attract and educate the lower strata of society.

The view that these strata are "naturally" incapable is also to be doubted on other grounds, when one reflects on the fact that a number of societies which were formerly colonies of European powers, and which have emerged as powerful and self-sufficient nations in their own right, were originally settled by malcontents, indentured servants, heretics, and (in the case of Australia) convicted criminals. Yet, these pioneers built total societies largely by their own efforts, a fact which should make one uneasy about facile generalizations regarding the "incapability" of the lower strata.

Myth 3: The blue-collar strata do not have an interest in or appreciation of the value of education

The apparent "apathy" and relative lack of participation in adult education by blue-collar workers is sometimes interpreted as stemming from lack of interest rather than lack of capacity. This is, again, one of those myths which support inaction and lack of effort on the part of adult teachers and administrators.

Actually, a substantial majority of the lower socioeconomic strata place a high value on education, as is indicated by national polls which have investigated this topic.[14] If the working class is negative, it is most likely to be so with regard to the schools, rather than toward education itself. This is no surprise, because the schools generally fail to deal effectively with the style of thinking, background, and values of blue-collar workers and their children.

Indeed, it is no wonder that many working-class children are disaffected by their schooling, because much of this schooling is simply irrelevant to their interests and their knowledge of social reality. This disaffection is supported by the reluctance of educators to revise their curricula so as to incorporate in it a realistic appraisal of American life as it actually exists rather than as the textbooks and the traditional methods of teaching pretend it to be. How can a history course be convincing or effective in attracting the interest of lower-class students when it neglects important facts about American life, such as the growth of the labor movement or the impact of racial and ethnic groups on the fabric of our society? The "melting pot" image, which is so popular when we wish to present ourselves to foreigners as a hospitable and democratic country, seems to have melted away by the time it gets to high school textbooks.

The schools, oriented to and administered by the middle class, and increasingly emphasizing their role as mere steppingstones to the colleges and universities, tend to assume that they know best what is needed to enable someone to "succeed" on their terms and with their values. School children who do not share such values, who are not neatly dressed and docile to the

---

[14] Herbert H. Hyman, "The Value Systems of Different Classes," in *Class, Status, and Power*, eds. Reinhard Bendix and Seymour Martin Lipset (New York: The Free Press of Glencoe, Inc., 1953), pp. 426-42.

LONDON
WENKERT

school's authority, are rejected as stupid, unmanageable, or tramps who just do not have the ability to profit from what the school has to offer. As a result of such experiences in school, workers and their children tend to suffer a loss of self-respect and self-esteem, and subsequently they shun existing opportunities for education.

Experiences in school affect, at least indirectly, participation in education during adult life. The published data on adult-education participation clearly indicate that the level of formal education achieved is more important than the occupational level in bringing people into adult education. Thus, at each occupational level, those with more formal education are more likely to participate than those with less formal education. In contrast, the participation rates of people in different occupational strata, but with the same level of formal education, are quite similar. Those who drop out of school early, because of disaffection with the school system or for other reasons, are therefore less likely than their more persistent and patient peers to engage in adult-education activities later in life.[15]

Myth 4: Intellectual ability is demonstrated early in life—
if it does not appear then, it will never appear

A myth that works to the detriment of the blue-collar worker is the belief that all individuals mature in the same fashion. The system of age grading, whereby children are expected to progress at the same speed through elementary, secondary, and higher educational institutions, as if chronological age were a sure sign of intellectual maturity, serves to penalize the "late bloomer." And, we suspect, it is especially the children of working-class homes who are most likely to be "late bloomers," because they enter the school system without having had the benefits which many middle-class children have had. Some of these benefits are homes in which books are plentiful and widely read, in which children become acquainted with a relatively large vocabulary through listening to their parents and relatives, and in which children have broadening experiences by being taken on trips, to restaurants or other public places, and perhaps being taught to read prior to their entrance into the school. It is in this sense that the currently popular term "culturally deprived" has a clear meaning.

The problem is that early intellectual immaturity may be considered a sign of stupidity rather than an indication of a different pattern of growth. As Talcott Parsons has argued, children are "typed" in elementary school, and the attitudes of their later teachers depend to a great extent on the children's very early performance.[16] The school records precede children to the next grade; and even before a child enters the grade, his new teacher will be "prepared" for him according to his prior performance. Such typing affects not

[15] Bert I. Greene, "Continuing Education and the High School Drop-Out," *Adult Education,* Vol. XII, No. 2 (Winter, 1962), pp. 76-83; Louis J. Cantoni, "Stay-Ins Get Better Jobs," *Personnel and Guidance Journal,* Vol. XXXIII (1955); Ephraim Mizruchi and Louis M. Vanaria, "Who Participates in Adult Education?", *Adult Education,* Vol. X, No. 3 (Spring, 1960), pp. 141-43.

[16] Talcott Parsons, "The School Class as a Social System: Some of the Functions in American Society," *Harvard Educational Review,* Vol. 29, No. 4 (Fall, 1959), pp. 297-318.

only the efforts which the teacher may expend on the student, but also the image which the student has of himself. Thus, in the manner of a self-fulfilling prophecy, a student who is treated as dull, stupid, or ignorant may react by fully meeting the expectations of those who treat him in this manner.[17]

The consequence of this early typing is that efforts are not made to raise the aspiration or achievement levels of the children involved. Thus, a vicious cycle is set into motion whereby improvements in performance are disregarded or unrewarded because they do not meet the low expectations of the teacher. Because the educational experiences of such children are a series of "failures," their motivation is adversely affected even if their abilities are equal to the tasks at hand. They continue to do inferior work, their work is properly acknowledged as inferior, and their next task will continue to be inferior, because they ordinarily do not perceive their own improvement or even what an "improvement" entails. As likely as not, they will subsequently engage in truant activities, delicately called "behavior disorders," because the school situation is patently unfair, and will thereby merely reinforce the teacher's previous conception of them.[18]

When something is considered impossible, this is in itself a barrier which a person will feel himself incapable of exceeding. A good example of such an achievement barrier is the four-minute mile run, which most experts conceived as the absolute limit beyond which an athlete could not penetrate. Since Roger Bannister accomplished the feat in 1954, the four-minute mile has been exceeded over 100 times. The moral of this story is that the individual who establishes his goal (or has it established for him) at a low level will be restrained by what he perceives to be his limits, and not by his innate capabilities.

Early school failure tends to follow a person throughout his lifetime because of the increasing tendency to characterize individuals as bright or dull according to the level of formal schooling which they acquired. Thus, if an individual drops out of school before obtaining a high school diploma, he is likely to be labeled unintelligent, ignorant, stupid, boorish, ill-mannered, and so on, without any efforts being made to know the individual more intimately. This is especially true if he applies for a job, because most jobs now automatically require a high school diploma. Thus, lacking the official *credentials* of "brightness," the person is treated with a lack of respect, on the easy assumption that his lack of an official degree indicates a lack of talent or ability. It is a saddening experience, and unfortunately a frequent one, to meet intelligent people who feel inferior (or have been made to feel inferior) because they do not have a college education or have not in some other way met some formal educational requirement. The blue-collar worker is, of course, most likely to be in this predicament, since he is also most likely

---

[17] Orrin Klapp, *Heroes, Villains, and Fools* (Englewood Cliffs, N.J.: Prentice-Hall, Inc., 1962) is an interesting examination of how social types operate to categorize people in various ways. Klapp depicts how social typing operates to mediate relationships between people. Lewis A. Dexter, "On the Politics and Sociology of Stupidity," *Social Problems*, Vol. 9 (Winter, 1962), also points out how the characterization of an individual as being stupid serves as a self-fulfilling prophecy to determine an attitude of stupidity.

[18] Cf. Carl Werthman, "Delinquents in Schools: A Test for the Legitimacy of Authority," *Berkeley Journal of Sociology*, Vol. VIII (1963), pp. 39-60.

LONDON
WENKERT

to have less formal education (this situation being partly due to the fact that he tends to be older, and therefore reflects the average educational achievements of an earlier generation).

Myth 5: People lose the ability to learn with increasing age.

This view, contrary to the existing research evidence, declares that adults deteriorate mentally as they age, and that therefore the resources expended on them can be better utilized for the education of the young. The provision of opportunities for the education of adults commensurate with the need for such education is, thus, not forthcoming.

Although aging is accompanied by a deterioration in certain capacities, such as hearing, seeing, and the speed of reaction time, these physical changes do not extend to a slowing down of the ability to learn. On the contrary, the evidence shows that the loss of an ability to learn new materials results from disuse of one's intellectual faculties rather than from the physical fact of aging.[19] Nevertheless, the view that aging is accompanied by loss of learning ability continues to persist despite the evidence to the contrary, derived from longitudinal studies of the influence of aging and from evidence of the remarkable intellectual works which have been produced by older adults.

The internalization of an attitude that one's ability to learn deteriorates with age operates as a self-fulfilling prophecy which may actually retard the ability to learn or the motivation to engage in educational activities. Of course, an adult may fear learning for a number of reasons—because of prior unfortunate experiences with schooling, lack of success in intellectual activities, failure to acquire the requisite skills of learning, or not remaining mentally alert through a systematic program of lifelong learning. Each of these may serve as obstacles to perceiving adult education as a viable element in one's leisure activities.

OBSTACLES IDENTIFIED BY EMPIRICAL STUDY

Individuals will not participate in adult education unless they know that educational opportunities exist and that there are organizations which sponsor activities to meet their interests and needs. Although the community we studied had a wide variety of organizations sponsoring adult-education activities, many men in our sample were not aware of them. This was particularly true of unskilled and semiskilled blue-collar workers—even those who expressed an interest in taking courses now or during the next few years. How can one account for this puzzling fact? One way to do so is by examining how those already participating learned about the courses in which they were enrolled.

By comparing the different occupational groups with regard to their sources of information, it became clear that personal sources—friends, neighbors, and acquaintances—are much more frequently used by the unskilled and semiskilled blue-collar workers than by the skilled blue-collar or lower

---

[19] Irving Lorge, "The Adult Learner," Ch. I in Wilbur C. Hallenbeck, ed., *Psychology of Adults* (Chicago: Adult Education Association, 1963), p. 109.

white-collar, professional, and managerial groups. The latter, in turn, relied much more frequently on the mass media, employers, supervisors, or being on a mailing list and receiving an announcement by mail, although a minority also relied on personal contacts.

Not only are personal sources relied on, although they are more important for the lesser skilled, but men also tend to participate in adult-education activities with their friends. That is, adult education takes place in a network of interpersonal relations. Yet, there are differences between the occupational strata with regard to the likelihood of having friends who are also participating in adult-education activities. Although the blue-collar worker is more likely to find out about adult-education courses through friends, acquaintances, or neighbors, he is less likely to know people who are participating in such activities. The upper white-collar participants are twice as likely to have participant friends as are the less skilled blue-collar participants. Similarly, because blue-collar participation is relatively lower than white-collar participation, the blue-collar nonparticipant is less likely to know a participant and is therefore also less likely to have friends who are good informants about adult-education opportunities.

The relative lack of information about adult education by blue-collar nonparticipants was also revealed on another question. Thus, a larger proportion of blue-collar nonparticipants than their white-collar peers felt that they could not afford to pay for the cost of further education, even though in most instances they were unaware of the exact cost of such programs. Mass-media reports about the congressional controversies regarding federal aid to education, or arguments when bond issues for schools are voted on, may create a popular image of the high cost of education. Vague and diffuse though these may be in the mind of the general public, such reports may contribute to the view that education is beyond the means of blue-collar workers, whose economic resources tend to be below those of the more economically advantaged groups in society.

Many individuals report that they do not participate in adult education because they feel too tired after a full day of work. Being tired is correlated with age, since those over 40 are twice as likely to say that they are "too tired" than those under 40. In addition, however, blue-collar workers are more apt to mention this reason for nonparticipation than are white-collar workers. This is so despite the fact that the white-collar groups tend, on the whole, to work longer hours, although the blue-collar workers may be engaged in more physically tiring work. It is also relevant to note, in this connection, that white-collar workers are more likely to be members of voluntary associations and to attend weekly meetings, so that the time they have available for adult-education participation tends to be more restricted than the time available to the lower occupational strata. In contrast, the latter are more apt to watch television and to engage in more home-oriented and neighborhood-oriented leisure activities, many of which are "relaxing."[20]

With regard to being "too old to go back to school," the blue-collar worker

[20] Jack London and Robert Wenkert, "Leisure Styles and Adult Education," Paper delivered to the session on The Sociology of Leisure at the national meeting of the American Sociological Association, August, 1963.

is much more likely than the white-collar to feel that this is an important reason for not participating. Similarly, blue-collar workers are more likely than white-collar workers to report that they would "feel kind of childish" going to evening classes, and the younger blue-collar workers are most likely to say that this applies to them. In addition, a larger proportion of blue-collar workers stated that their friends "discouraged or kidded them" about participating in adult-education activities. Thus, we may draw the general conclusion that blue-collar workers tend more than others to define education as something for children and adolescents. The widespread image of education as designed for preparing the young for adulthood—an image which the current labor and economic trends have largely destroyed in reality—is more nearly held by those who will be most affected by these powerful changes in the economy.

Blue-collar workers are also more likely than white-collar workers to agree that they are not "bookish" types. Similarly, older blue-collar workers are more apt than older white-collar workers to assert that they can learn what they need to know without attending classes. These two patterns of responses may stem from (1) a lack of skill with "bookish" activities because of inferior educational experiences in the past, or (2) a lack of prior success in school, leading to a rejection of school-like activities. Those with more success and greater experience in school are more apt to look upon schooling as an important source of information and knowledge. The responses to our questions in the manner reported above may be more a protection of self-esteem than an indication of a negative attitude toward education.

Among the adult-education participants, there is a tendency for the more educated to be more articulate about their reaction to adult-education courses than those with less formal education. That is, blue-collar workers find it more difficult to verbally appraise the value of their adult-education experiences. This suggests that the organizations which serve the educationally disadvantaged have less "feedback" in searching for program deficiencies than do the institutions which cater to the more educated adults. The importance of this deficiency is highlighted by the fact, mentioned earlier, that adult educators tend to have a middle-class orientation and are therefore less knowledgeable about working-class values and interests. Thus, the bias against the blue-collar worker tends to be compounded, because the adult educator serving a blue-collar clientele is not likely to get criticisms or suggestions about the kinds of educational experiences which his adult students find most rewarding.

This lack of visible reaction thus allows the educator to allocate blame for failures to the students, rather than assessing the extent to which such failures are caused by a lack of skillful teaching or competency in subject matter.[21] As W. W. Sawyer has noted, an inappropriate approach to a subject may be more influential in causing a failure to learn than any lack of ability by the students involved.[22]

It is evident that a student's satisfaction with adult education depends

---

[21] George Williams, *Some of My Best Friends Are Professors* (New York: Abelard Schuman Limited, 1958).

[22] W. W. Sawyer, *Mathematician's Delight* (London: Penguin, 1943).

largely on how well he perceives himself to be doing. Participants were asked to compare their ability as students in adult education with their prior ability when they were in school as adolescents. By and large, participants who felt that they were now better students were more likely to report satisfaction with adult education than those who thought that they had been better when engaged in full-time schooling. Thus, a favorable attitude toward education may result both from prior educational experiences and from subsequent favorable experiences in adult education. Some success in learning serves to transform a prior feeling of inferiority to one of confidence and heightened interest. The person with poor experience in schooling may thus be helped to realize the value of education, if the educational experience engaged in as an adult is meaningful and effective.

In addition to acquiring information regarding gross participation rates, we also asked a number of questions about the reasons why participants enrolled in adult-education courses. These questions enable us to distinguish between those who enrolled for nonvocational reasons and those who enrolled for vocational reasons. Among the latter, we are also able to distinguish between the men who wished to get help on their present job and those who desired aid in getting a new job. About half of the men interviewed participated for nonvocational reasons, the proportion being somewhat higher among the lower strata, who were relatively overrepresented in religious instruction and in citizenship courses.

When examining the pattern of participation for vocational reasons, one is struck by the differences between the occupational groups. The blue-collar groups are much more likely than the white-collar groups to participate in order to get a new job, while the latter are much more interested in obtaining aid for their present job. Thus, while the low-skilled workers who want to change jobs constitute only 17 per cent of the matched sample, they constitute 47 per cent of those who have taken a course during the past year to help get a different job. On the other hand, the low-skilled workers who do not indicate a desire to change jobs are least likely to have participated in education of any sort during the past five years. Thus, the greater the degree of dissatisfaction with one's present job, the greater the likelihood of taking adult-education courses. Apparently the vocational motivation is very strong, especially among the lower occupational groups.

It is also true, however, that a considerable number of workers who desire to secure another job are not participating in adult education. An important factor for such a lack of participation may be the condition of the labor market and the availability of opportunities for employment. If unemployment is high and new jobs are difficult to secure, nonparticipants may not wish to devote the requisite time and effort to obtaining further education. This may also be partly caused by the fact that adult-education courses are not clearly meshed with the openings in the labor market, so that participation in adult education is no sure guarantee that a new and better job can be obtained. Current efforts to upgrade the skills of unemployed workers through retraining programs may fail unless the available and emerging employment opportunities are known and this information is used to improve the retraining curricula. In addition, a clearer image of existing opportunities must be portrayed to the potential clientele for such retraining.

Our study also revealed that men take courses to help them on their jobs if they hold positions which require continuing education. The prototype of such positions is found in the professions—almost all professionals had taken at least one adult-education course during their careers, a vast majority reported that they studied at home for their jobs, and a substantial proportion were engaged in current adult-education courses. In addition, those who held supervisory positions and who think their chances for promotion are good are also more likely to participate in vocational education in order to help themselves in their present job. Because most blue-collar jobs, particularly at the lower levels of skill, do not require continuing education and do not involve the supervision of others, one can readily see why blue-collar workers have a lower rate of participation than other segments of the labor force. Because job requirements for continuing education is one of the factors in participation, we may expect a continuing growth of adult education as the changes in the economy put a premium on jobs with high levels of skill and knowledge.

In conclusion, we have sketched a picture portraying some of the obstacles which inhibit the participation of the lower socioeconomic strata in adult education. Involved in this portrait are myths about the learning process and about the character of blue-collar groups, myths which detract from imaginative programming by adult teachers and administrators. The other dimension involves some of the aspects of the life situation faced by blue-collar groups —aspects which tend to detract from educational objectives. The task for the future is not to cast blame, but to rethink the objectives of adult education and to bring together the educators and the blue-collar workers in a dynamic harmony.

Obstacles
to Blue-Collar
Participation
in Adult
Education

465

Part IX

UNEMPLOYMENT
AND RETIREMENT

EVEN as leisure itself is surrounded by misgivings on the part of
workers who fear too much of a good thing, unemployment and
retirement directly raise the specter of unwanted leisure—of leisure
without meaning or purpose. In this section, a few of the many
ramifications of both unemployment and retirement are considered,
special attention being paid to the extra-work aspects of the subjects.
Schwartz and Henderson, for example, lead off with a discussion of
the impact a father's prolonged unemployment has on the adolescent
son of a "new" working-class Negro. The children of the unemployed,
they warn, "do not perceive the payoff." Miller and Harrison, in a
provocative contrast, discuss a predominantly white group of adolescent dropouts who have quit school and are thought unemployable.
Even this type, they assert in conclusion, "has attitudes which offer
possibilities for more effective school and job adjustment." Ferman
and Aiken go to the other end of the life scale and explore the
emotional adjustment to unemployment made by older white
workers. Similarly, Smith and Fowler relate how adult blue-collarites
react to the situation of a plant shutdown and relocation (they note
the greater flexibility of "new" as contrasted with "old" working-class
types). Leggett and Street focus on unemployed urban Negroes and
seek to demonstrate the connection between economic crisis, extremist
views, the probability of violence, and the desirability of federal
intervention. Ferman pulls much of this together in his essay on
problems of sociological relevance in unemployment research, and
Miller contributes a blueprint for reform. In the separate but related
matter of retirement, Loether considers the extent to which the
older worker is successful in making the transition from work to
retirement. He contrasts blue- and white-collar records, and concludes
concerning blue-collarites that "without their occupational roles as
anchors, their lives fade into insignificance."

The Culture of Unemployment: Some Notes on Negro Children

MICHAEL SCHWARTZ

GEORGE HENDERSON

PERSONNEL managers and others concerned with personnel functions will, of course, agree that among their prime problems is that of keeping the level of personal motivation at an optimum level for organizational efficiency. The assumption is that the motivation to work exists within the individual, and the primary problem is to maintain, increase, or direct that motivation. Only upon rare occasions does one find himself thinking that John Jones does not really want to work. And even with such thoughts, one might only mean that he does not want to work on this job or in this organization. Rarely does one believe that the individual does not want to work at all. In at least one way, the beliefs that men do not want to work does not fit one of the most salient elements in our system of beliefs: the belief in hard work and striving as the key to success.

It is argued, and with no minor degree of emotionality buttressing the argument, that men—all men—want to work, in fact, must work; not only must they work simply to acquire money, but they must work, moreover, to maintain some kind of personal integration. Work is the prime source of self-respect; it meets the needs for affiliation and for self-actualization. Work, in a society that provides men with so much free time (but so little leisure), is mandatory for all men—all men seek it, all men *need* it, all men desire it. Or so the argument runs on. It is a very uncomfortable situation in which one finds himself when he discovers that there may be at least a grain of truth in the argument of those who insist that *some men do not want to work*. We would like to briefly explore such a "grain," noting also that the concept of work and working in American society is not static or fixed, but seems to vary according to life situations.

When Max Weber wrote *The Protestant Ethic and The Spirit of Capitalism*, describing the necessity for developing and maintaining a moral compulsion to work, strive, and achieve as the key to the development of mature capitalism, he provided later scholars with a broad theoretical base for describing one major portion of the American belief system. The ethic of hard work, individual initiative, laissez-faire democracy, and free enterprise still survives in America today. The ethic survives even though culture change has taken place at a rapid rate, providing objective situations and social structures which, to some degree, at least, preclude the individual's operating in terms of the value structure. For example, the possibilities for a single individual, within his lifetime and largely through his own efforts, to develop a huge corporation or to amass a large fortune have been curtailed in very large measure. The opportunities for social mobility still exist, of course, but the bases for mobility seem to have changed and are still changing.

Indeed, if David Riesman[1] is correct, we, as Americans, are considerably more concerned with consumption and consumer activities than we are with work and working as highly valued activities. That is not to say that Americans devalue work; that is not the case, generally. But work today has come to have a fairly clear-cut "means orientation." Work is a means to consumer activities; in and of itself, work, as so many scholars have been quick to point out, has come to lose its "ends orientation," although this is probably not the case for the professions and skilled trades. In essence, then, work and working are still highly prized aspects of the American belief system. Individuals engage in work activity today just as they did 100 years ago. But the motivation for the same activity has apparently changed. Success in work—that is, high achievement—generally no longer represents a sign that one has been chosen and will be saved from eternal damnation. Work today provides the individual with resources that enable him to engage in consumer activities which, in turn, permit him to present himself to others in terms of, say, an appropriate life style. Work permits him to give signs to others that, when decoded, mean: "These are things that I have been able to acquire; this is what I believe is in good taste; judge me in these terms."

Money becomes a key to mobility and to the acquisition and maintenance of preferred and valued styles of life. Generally speaking, acquisition of money is an intermediate goal, intervening between some motivation or need and the final goal, such as preferred life style. Obviously, work is a means to the intermediate and ultimate goals, while acquiring work can be viewed as an intermediate goal as well. We do not mean to ignore the fact that work permits individuals to meet needs other than simply acquiring money. The needs for affiliation, for self-actualization, and so on, are also met through work. But it must be pointed out that these needs are also met through other quite acceptable manners as well. A poker game can fill the need for affiliation just as readily as can the work environment; the same is true for a meeting of avid stamp collectors. But the work situation is the one that is culturally defined as *the* appropriate one for meeting the need for the acquisition of money.

The value of working, then, is still an integral part of the belief system. Young children are socialized to a need to work; they play at work roles—fireman, policeman, store clerk, and so on. They are neverendingly asked the question: "What would you like to be when you grow up?" Daddy leaves in the morning for some mysterious place variously called "work" or "the office." The school systems reinforce the pattern with "career conferences" and other work-oriented activity; students compete with one another for grades and

---

SCHWARTZ
HENDERSON

[1] David Riesman, *The Lonely Crowd* (Garden City, N. Y.: Doubleday & Company, Inc., 1955).

honors—or they learn that they are expected to compete for these juvenile and adolescent pay-offs. They are imbued with the American Dream and tales of Horatio Alger. They become work-oriented. In effect, children seem to develop two expectations: first, that work is good and, second, that it is available.

The question that must arise is, What happens when the process of socialization to the ethics of work either fails or is subverted? When a value system, such as the one of achieving and hard work, comes to be preceived as not in accord with reality, some sort of intra-individual imbalance or "cognitive dissonance" must exist.[2] The dissonant situation creates tension within the individual that causes him to seek some solution to the conflict that will reduce the motivating tension or anxiety. (A very vivid example of the dissonant state can be had if one will take the role of the Negro child living in Mississippi as he learns on the one hand, that all men are created equal and on the other that he cannot use the white man's rest room. Such a dissonant state must bring with it a good deal of anxiety and tension for the youth whose "idealism" has yet to be corrupted by local folkways.)

Specifically, it is felt that children from lower socioeconomic class environments are confronted with work-value dissonant situations. On the one hand they do receive a work orientation, and on the other hand they are daily confronted with chronic long-term unemployment in the family and in the community. Moreover, among the lower-class Negro population, the situation must be somewhat more severe—even in good times, the structure of opportunities for the Negro is considerably more closed than it is for the lower-class white.

The question is: *How does the adolescent lower-class male Negro respond to the dissonance between the stated societal work values and his perception of a closed opportunity structure and chronic unemployment?*

Some restructuring of values must occur if the dissonance is to be resolved; we propose that what occurs is a general devaluation of work as a means of obtaining money and the substitution of other means. Moreover, it is reasonable to propose that a new community, in both the ecological and the social-psychological sense, comes into existence in which new values are communicated and shared and to which adolescent males are resocialized. Just as the delinquent gang develops a code for members, so do the unemployed develop a code. Their code reveals how to fake illnesses to avoid taking some jobs; who to see successively for different types of aid; how to take employment tests and whether to fail them or pass them. All of this, and more, is controlled by the cultural system.

James Baldwin, in "Letter From a Region of My Mind,"[3] pointed to a situation much like the one being proposed here. In describing his youth, he noted that "The boys, it was clear, would rise no higher than their fathers.

---

[2] Leon Festinger, *A Theory of Cognitive Dissonance* (Stanford, California, Stanford University Press, 1962).

[3] James Baldwin, "Letter From a Region of My Mind," *The New Yorker Magazine*, Vol. 38 (November 17, 1962), p. 59.

School began to reveal itself, therefore, as a child's game that one could not win, and boys dropped out of school and went to work." [4] The Jeffersonian conception of men as perfectable through education became absolute nonsense for Baldwin: "I no longer had any illusions about what an education could do for me; I had already encountered too many college-graduate handy men." [5]

If one were to follow Professor Merton's model of social structure and anomie,[6] it is apparent that several alternative roads are open to the individual whose perceptions of his own life-chances in the market, that is, dissonant ones, are like those held by Baldwin. Such an individual may accept the culture goals, such as money, as valid or legitimate but reject the institutionalized means for achieving those goals. Merton calls this type of adaptation "Innovation." Baldwin points to this alternative when he writes, "Crime became real, for example—for the first time—not as *a* possibility but as *the* possibility. One would never defeat one's circumstances by working and saving one's pennies . . ." Merton describes "Ritualism" as another possible adaptation. The pattern is reflected by giving up or drastically reducing the cultural goals to the extent that the scaled-down goals can be met. But even though one gives up the institutionalized goals, "one continues to abide almost compulsively by institutionalized norms." Thus, the college-graduate handymen. "Retreatism"—the giving up of both the institutional goals and the institutionalized means to their achievement—proves a form of adaptation not uncommon among the so-called "doomed" or "defeated" classes. Merton notes that they are largely autists, pariahs, outcasts, vagrants, vagabonds, tramps, chronic drunkards, and drug addicts. And Baldwin describes the people of "the Avenue" in much the same manner. The final technique or adaptation to perceptions of lack of access to the opportunity structure is termed "Rebellion." In this mode, the existing goals and means are rejected, but the rejectors subscribe to plans that require replacement of the old means and goals with new ones. Baldwin's discussion of the Black Muslim movement does not paint the picture of rebellion in this sense, but rather in terms of what must be known as *ressentiment*. As Merton points out, "In ressentiment, one condemns what one secretly craves; in rebellion, one condemns the craving itself." Yet others remain, in terms of the model, conformists—they accept and operate in terms of the institutional goals and the institutionalized means. Baldwin does not discuss such people. Either they are of the middle class, which does not concern him, or he fails to recognize the potential of the human psyche for compartmentalization, repression—perceptual defenses in general. There are, to be sure, lower-class Negroes who do fit the conformist pattern.

Baldwin's discussion of his own entry into the church is fascinating. In it he found a lever for power. For at least a time, he had control of this particular institution. For him it was a kind of "Innovation"; his own cynicism

---

[4] *Ibid.*, p. 59.
[5] *Ibid.*, p. 59.
[6] Robert K. Merton, *Social Theory and Social Structure* (New York: The Free Press of Glencoe, Inc., 1957), pp. 131-60.

toward his role reflects that clearly. His orientation had never become what one could realistically call "other-worldly." However, he omits the function that the church serves for others. Clearly, a different function was performed for the members of the congregation. As Professor Herrick has pointed out to me,

> Some of the sect/cult groups are serving society by turning potential rebellion into retreatism or ritualism (these show less immediate danger to the social structure than does rebellion). Further, they are able to do this by serving as structural alternatives, i.e., structures within which behavior is allowed which would otherwise be termed and treated as deviant. They are "lymph nodes" which collect and enclose elements which could potentially destroy the organism.

The community of the unemployed, in terms of restructured values including a devaluation of work and working and of the acquisition of large amounts of money, apparently represents a hybrid type of adaptation to the closed opportunity structure. It would seem to show elements of Retreatism as well as elements of Innovation. The dynamics of choice patterns with respect to each of the adaptations of Merton's model is still a mystery. Why should some clearly react in terms of Innovation while others react clearly in terms of Retreatism? That Negro youth of the lower class confront situations through patterns of Ritualism, Innovation, Retreatism, and Rebellion as often as through the pattern of Conformity is relatively clear. But why they choose one pattern rather than another is not at all clear.

Dai[7] has shown the development of personalities among lower-class Negro children to be largely determined by broken homes and the influence of maternal authority. The pattern of the matriarchy is found in homes that are not broken but where fathers are no longer important. Karon[8] has noted that an average Negro cannot fulfill the role of "provider" because to find or keep a job is harder for him. In frustration, he may find the situation intolerable and leave, or live in a weak position. Negroes are, of course, the worst sufferers in wage differentials. Rose has noted that "Poverty is almost a tradition among Negroes." [9] And Myrdal writes, "The American Creed permeates instruction, and the Negro as well as the white youths are inculcated with the traditional American virtues of efficiency, thrift, and ambition. The American dream of individual success is held out to the Negroes as to other students. But employment opportunities—and, to a lesser extent, some other good things of life—are so closed to them that severe conflicts in their minds are bound to appear." [10] In this connection, the school systems, traditionally in the control of the middle-class whites, particularly contribute to the Negro child's aspirations.

At the same time, the mother, who is dominant in the Negro home, con-

---

[7] Bingham Dai, "Problems of Personality Development Among Negro Children," in *Personality in Nature, Society and Culture,* eds. Kluckhohn and Murray (New York: Alfred A. Knopf, 1959), p. 552.

[8] B. P. Karon, *The Negro Personality* (New York: Springer Publishing Co., 1958), p. 32.

[9] Arnold M. Rose, *The Negro's Morale* (Minneapolis: The University of Minnesota Press, 1949), p. 71.

[10] Gunnar Myrdal, *An American Dilemma* (New York: Harper & Row, Publishers, 1944), p. 1010.

tributes to the same ethos. Work opportunities are more available for her than for her husband. She is, more often than not, at least a partial provider of the family income. She values work and working, and she values the notion of a man's supporting his family. And she communicates these values to her children. She is a strong, powerful figure within the family. The matriarchy itself may have implications for the Negroes' acceptance of an achieving ethic. Fromm discusses Bachofen's thoughts in this direction when he points out that the positive aspect of attachment to the mother figure "is a sense of affirmation of life, freedom, and equality which pervades the matriarchal structure." The negative aspect is seen "as being bound to nature, to blood and soil; man is blocked from developing his individuality and his reason. He remains a child and incapable of reason." [11]

What, then, has occurred? If one combines the effects of caste and class, matriarchal family patterns, the myth of opportunity, and an other-worldly orientation, it is not difficult to begin to perceive as emerging from a total constellation of factors a unique subculture that by virtue of its own structure, not to mention the manner in which it is related to the dominant culture, cannot be expected to participate wholly and freely in the dominant culture in terms of that culture's value and means orientations. We may in very large measure be breeding *a subculture of unemployables,* that is, individuals who, by virtue of the total pattern of institutions with which they come into contact, reject the ethics of work and striving for culturally defined goals— individuals who come to have the work ethics socialized "out."

The white culture demands that the lower-class Negro conform to middle-class white values while the structure of opportunities for participation remains largely closed to him. Certainly, many of the conditions that must inevitably bring to the Negro youth the despair that Baldwin communicates so brilliantly are beginning to decay—by executive order. The process is slow; the Negro middle class and its leadership are impatient. One hundred years is too long to wait to be given what is rightfully the Negroes' in the first place. Whether the lower class is equally impatient is not known. No condition in which the Negro finds himself today is his by choice—not his family pattern, not his religious sects or cults, not his skill levels. In every case, one can point only to adaptations to situations created for him by the white culture.

And the truly fearful aspect lies in the high probability that if tomorrow the lower-class Negro were to be completely free and integrated into the dominant culture, having free access to opportunities of all forms, the situation might be no better for him. The adaptations over generations have in many cases become "functionally autonomous." They are, for many, now a preferred way of life; an appropriate life style that includes "bunking in," welfare chiseling, borrowing from working women or women on relief, and so forth. The concept of "culture lag" has never meant more than it means in this instance. The road to mobility depends more and more upon education. But the very route to entrance into the opportunity structure also depends upon education. The technology advances, requiring greater and greater skill levels; the semiskilled and unskilled bases shrink each year. Requiring more

[11] Erich Fromm, *The Sane Society* (New York: Holt, Rinehart & Winston, Inc., 1955), p. 45.

and more education of youth requires that they accept more and more the so-called "middle-class deferred-gratification pattern." The lower-class Negro today is not prepared to do this; he does not value education. Equality of opportunity is mandatory. But the self-fulfilling prophecy looms large. "The Negro is lazy, indolent; they are indifferent." The structure opens to the Negro; the influx is immediately "underwhelming." The racists can be expected to have a field day, and once again the desperate appeal on the part of Negro and white liberal leadership for time and more time.

Culture patterns decline slowly, and the community of the unemployed will not dissolve overnight—especially when it is not so visible to the layman. Furthermore, we do not find it surprising that some personnel managers have complained that, even though their organizations have opened all positions to qualified Negroes, none have applied. There is an enormous time lag. Access to the structure of opportunities is a very new phenomenon for the Negro. Motivation to work depends upon the perception of the ability to find work and to do it well.

GENERAL PROCEDURE

It is our intention now to describe empirically even as we have already described more generally some social-psychological characteristics of Negro children of the unemployed. Accordingly, in the fall of 1962 we conducted 130 interviews with boys ranging in age from 13 to 19 years, the mean age being 15 years 8 months. The sample was drawn from welfare records for the City of Detroit, and the following restrictions were employed: First, the boy's family must have been on the welfare rolls for at least six consecutive months, in order to insure their exposure to long-term unemployment. Second, both mother and father must have been residing in the dwelling unit with the boy during that time. All respondents were Negro, as were the interviewers, and all were guaranteed anonymity. All of the cases were drawn from the central city.

The interview schedule provided the following information. First, level of Alienation as measured by Dean's Alienation scale[12] (modified). Second, level of Mastery and Independence as measured by Strodtbeck's V-scale[13]; third, a series of items designed to elicit responses which would permit us to categorize each respondent as Conformist, Innovator, Ritualist, or Retreatist.[14] Fourth, we wished to know the types of churches attended by our respondents and the frequency of participation. Fifth, we asked each respondent to tell us whom he perceived as being "the boss" in his family—mother or father. Sixth, we developed a single, independent item, "Does it pay to be honest but poor?" "Why?" Except for this last item and the item concerned with church attendance and participation, all the items above were of the simple agree-disagree

---

[12] Dwight G. Dean, "Meaning and Measurement of Alienation," *American Sociological Review*, Vol. 26, No. 5 (October, 1961), pp. 753-57.
[13] Fred L. Strodtbeck, "Family Interaction, Values, and Achievement," in David C. McClelland, Alfred L. Baldwin, Urie Bronfenbrenner, and Fred L. Strodtbeck, *Talent and Society* (New York: D. Van Nostrand Co., Inc., 1958), pp. 168-69.
[14] Merton, *op. cit.*

The Culture
of Unemployment:
Some Notes
on Negro
Children

variety. In addition, there were several open-ended items, dealing with feelings about being on welfare, difficulty in finding work, making money without having a steady job, and so forth.

GENERAL RESULTS

Although, in general, the sociological literature has pointed to the Negro matriarchal family pattern, particularly among the lower class, this is *not* what our respondents perceived. Of the 130 boys, exactly one-half (65) perceived their fathers as being "the boss" in their families. Reasons for selecting father varied from "When we eat, he gets his (food) first, then we get ours," to "He tells us what to do, and if we don't do it, he kicks hell out of us." In any case, unemployed, lower-class fathers may not give up their role of authority because of feelings of insecurity, shame, and worthlessness as a result of being unemployed. On the contrary, many may be well adjusted and resigned to a life of unemployment. When asked how their fathers felt about being unemployed, most boys replied that they (their fathers) "don't like it but can't do nothing about it." A few boys noted that their fathers "don't mind being on welfare" or simply "don't want to work."

Further, it is generally believed that women participate in church activities to a greater extent than do men. If this is the case, then we would expect to find more boys attending church regularly when they perceive that their mothers run their families than would be the case when fathers are perceived as dominant. But in homes where the boys perceived strong fathers, they showed a relatively high level of church attendance; whereas in homes where the boys perceived weak fathers and strong mothers, they showed a lower level of church attendance. A boy explained: "When my mother tells me to do something and I don't, nothing usually happens. But when my dad tells me to do something and I don't, I can't sit down for a week 'cause my behind is sore. He don't take no stuff off us." Even with the less physically dominant fathers, the degree of obedience was admitted to be higher than with dominant mothers.

The relatively high level of reported obedience to fathers, plus the higher frequency of church attendance reported by boys who perceived their fathers as the dominant parent, leads us to believe that the father-dominated home is the more stable home—even when the father is not working and has been unemployed over a long period of time.

These data lead us to form some after-the-fact hypotheses (which, although not scientifically legitimate, are most reasonable in view of existing theory). In homes where boys perceive weak fathers and strong mothers, and where the boys show a relatively low level of institutional attachment (measured by frequency of church attendance), it is not unreasonable to expect a level of alienation, or rootlessness, somewhat higher than would be the case for boys who had strong male images and/or relatively high levels of institutional attachments.

On an over-all measure of alienation, the boys from perceived mother-dominant homes with low levels of institutional attachment are in fact more alienated than any of the other groups. This would indicate the interaction effect of high maternal dominance and low institutional attachment. But, as Dean has pointed out, alienation may have at least three dimensions. Usually, it has meant normlessness and anomie, but it may also mean feelings of powerlessness or feelings of isolation in the environment.

The boys who see their mothers as dominant and who are infrequent church attenders have feelings of alienation which are based primarily upon the feeling of powerlessness, whereas they show no more feeling of isolation or normlessness than do the other boys. These findings lead us to some possible hypotheses.

Although the boys who perceive their mothers as dominant and who attend church infrequently are more alienated than the others, they feel powerless but not normless. We would expect that more of these boys would, therefore, be found in Merton's categories of Ritualism and Retreatism than in the categories of Conformity and Innovation. That is, they should appear to be more passive than active in their responses to alienation. Our interviews indicate that this is precisely the case, although no more so than for the other boys. In the main, the boys are consistently more passive than aggressive. Perhaps the most impressive aspect of our interviews is the fact that we seemed to find far fewer Conformists than we would have expected and many more Ritualists and Retreatists. Nor did we find a disproportionate number of Innovators.

As a further check on the passivity of the boys, we may examine the data from the "poor but honest" question. These data were categorized in the following manner: All those boys who responded by saying "Yes," it pays to be poor but honest, *and* who did so for reasons which the researchers felt were based on internalized norms, for example, "keep your self-respect," "good people are like that," were placed in one category while those who responded "No" *or* "Yes" but for reasons judged to be fear of external sanction, for example, "I don't want to go to jail," were placed in a second category.

The major differences are in the group of boys who perceive their mothers to be the dominant parent. Those boys who are frequent church-attenders in this group show significantly more responses which seem to indicate the internalization of cultural norms, whereas the boys who are infrequent church attenders show significantly more responses which indicate their accepting the statement on the basis of the fear of external sanctions or of rejecting the statement outright. Typically, one of the boys in the latter group told the interviewer, "Being poor but honest ain't never got my folks anywhere," another noted that, "It won't feed you," and still another said, "I'd rather be rich and dishonest." Although it is true that there were fewer innovating responses than we would have anticipated, there were more of them among these boys than among any of the others. Furthermore, significantly more of the boys who perceived their mothers as dominant and who were infrequent church-attenders said that they believed it to be very difficult to find and hold a steady job than was the case for any of the other boys. Although we found this to be the case, we did not find them to be substantively more sophisticated with respect to making money without the antecedent of a steady job than any of the other boys. But it should be pointed out that, in general, the boys were quite sophisticated.

An example which is not too extreme comes from one boy who, when asked, "How could you get enough money to live on if you can't get a job?" responded, "I guess I could get me a good hustle—hit a number—something." Although most respondents did not openly admit aspiring to a life on welfare, they did state that "if you can't do no better, it's better than starving." One boy came to one of the authors at the Urban League to ask, "How old do you have to be to get your own (Welfare Case) number?" Welfare, unlike Aid to Dependent Children (ADC) and Old Age Assistance (OAA), distributes very little cash to the recipients. Whereas the welfare department pays most of the client's bills directly, ADC and OAA clients are given cash to meet budget needs. Thus one seldom hears of welfare "parties," but ADC "mothers' day parties" in which funds are misused are frequently reported by the boys.

Luck—"hit a number" or "find some money"—was perceived by most of the boys as their only means to escape poverty. Interestingly, most respondents did not view playing numbers as being equivalent to gambling. Although gambling is perceived to be illegal, playing the numbers is seen as an acceptable subcultural pattern of behavior. Consequently, within the subculture, people working in numbers are socially acceptable and, in many cases, admired.

Following an interview, a fifteen-year-old boy asked the interviewer, "How much do you make a week?" Upon hearing the answer, the boy frowned and replied, "My brother ain't got no college education—he ain't even got a high school education, but he makes more than you do." His brother "picked up" numbers.

DISCUSSION

This brief and descriptive study, of course, needs replication. That is not a mere academic disclaimer; we must know the extent to which these attitudes and beliefs and structural patterns are prevalent in other communities. But the initial evidence is clear enough; the boys do not perceive an open opportunity structure; they feel powerless in the environment, but not necessarily normless. Consequently, we see passive and, in some ways, passive-aggressive response patterns. They know the norms and they know "the situation." The consequence seems to be at best a ritualism about the belief system and at worst a propensity to youth crime and, for some, individualistic retreat into addiction. In the main there seems little willingness to accept the hard-work-and-striving ethos. The children of the unemployed do not perceive the pay-off. The implications for a "culture of unemployment" are clear.

Types of Dropouts: "The Unemployables"*

S. M. MILLER

IRA E. HARRISON

A good indication of our lack of understanding of dropouts[1] and the dropout process is the absence of a typology of dropouts. The literature on dropouts abounds in discussion of "the dropout," ignoring the great variations which exist among dropouts. The limited efficacy of dropout-prediction instruments suggests that dropouts differ considerably in their characteristics, and that the *process* of dropping out takes many different routes. Most dropouts are from relatively low-income families, but a considerable percentage are not; for many dropouts, it is possible to see an early pattern of school difficulty and adjustment, but many others have not been retarded in school. The prospects of dropouts also are varied; an investigation of Syracuse dropouts two years after leaving school shows that one of five males is able to attain a white-collar or skilled job.[2] These and other studies show that dropouts have varying experiences and characteristics both before and after leaving school.

There is urgent need for a typology of dropouts and of the processes of dropping out; we have had many studies of the properties of dropouts and

* The collection of the interview data reported in this paper has been largely supported by a contract with the New York State Division for Youth. A grant from the Social Security Administration has facilitated analysis of the data. Neither agency is responsible for the formulations presented here. This paper has been presented at the annual meetings of the American Orthopsychiatric Association, Washington, March, 1963.

[1] The term "dropout" may be a misnomer. "School leavers" is a more descriptive and inclusive term than "dropout." As pointed out later, the majority of our subjects did not feel that they dropped out. The word *dropout* however, is customarily used to refer to all those who did not graduate from high school, for whatever reason, and we shall continue to employ it in this paper despite its connotation of a voluntary move.

[2] Kenneth Baldwin, *et al.*, *The Syracuse Dropout—Two Years Later.* Unpublished group master's thesis, School of Social Work, Syracuse University, 1962. This study was supervised by Maurice Connery. We have reanalyzed these data in Betty L. Saleem and S. M. Miller, *Two Years in The Syracuse Labor Market—Work Experiences of Dropouts* (Syracuse, N. Y.: Syracuse University Youth Development Center, 1964).

few of the process of dropping out. In this paper, we deal with one type of male dropout—those who have left school and are thought to be "unemployable." Our analysis of the attitudes of these boys largely ignores the outside world which determines their fate; in other work we have concentrated on economic and political aspects of school dropout problems.[3] In this paper, we are moving to a discussion of the attitudes of these boys rather than to the conditioning events and to the economic structure which facilitates or retards their economic advance.

We have interviewed 50 boys (37 white, 13 Negro) under the age of 18 who have left school, have had difficulty in obtaining or keeping jobs, have gone to the New York State Employment Service in Syracuse for placement help, and have been classified by the office as "presently unemployable" in the Syracuse labor market.[4] They have been referred to a work and training program sponsored by the Onondaga County Youth Board and the New York State Division for Youth. These are boys who have had decidedly more economic and social difficulties than is true of the Syracuse dropout group as a whole.[5] Although one-quarter of those in our census of 1959-1960 dropouts were known to have been apprehended by police, at least two-thirds of our "presently unemployable" dropouts have had police records, and many have been in penal institutions. The fathers of about a fifth of the boys are dead. This, of course, is a remarkably high figure. Of the surviving fathers, less than half live with their families. Several boys have been brought up in foster homes. Mothers support one-quarter of all the families. At least 60 per cent, and possibly 90 per cent, of the families have been on welfare at one time or another. Public assistance is much more frequent among Negroes than among whites.

We are dealing with a difficult group of dropouts who probably pose the gravest kinds of problems; we have called them "unemployable" dropouts to distinguish them from other types of dropouts. In turn, it is important to recognize, as we have only partially done in this paper, that there are important variations among them.

---

[3] S. M. Miller, "Dropouts—A Political Problem," *Integrated Education*, Summer, 1963; it is reprinted in Meyer Weinberg, ed., *Living Together*, Chicago: Integrated Education Associates (1964). A fuller version appears in Daniel Schreiber, ed., *The School Dropout*, Washington: National Education Association (1964). See also S. M. Miller, "Youth and the Changing Society," *Journal of Social Issues*, forthcoming.

[4] The concept of "presently unemployable" is a difficult one to specify and apply. It means that, under the present conditions of the labor market, a job is not available for this boy. It implies that the boy is difficult to place generally, but it need not indicate that the boy has no capacity for work and could never obtain a job. The use of the adverb *presently* correctly points out that "unemployability" is not an individual characteristic alone, but is related very deeply to the economic and social characteristics of the labor market. Because conventional thinking has taken the labor market as a given, the emphasis has been on individual inadequacies for employment. The fluctuations, from periods of high to low employment demand, in the number of those thought to be "unemployable" underlines the inadequacy of the stress on personal characteristics to explain "unemployability."

[5] S. M. Miller, Carolyn Comings, and Betty Saleem, *The School Dropout Problem: Syracuse* (Albany: New York State Division for Youth and the Syracuse University Youth Development Center, 1963).

In response to a series of questions about their attitudes toward school, about half of our dropouts declared that they did not drop out of school but were asked or forced to leave. An example from an interview:[6]

I   Why did you drop out of school?
NDO I didn't drop out of school. They dropped me.
I   Why did they drop you?
NDO Well, when they dropped me there were a few other boys. . . .
I   How was it possible for you to remain in school?
NDO Oh, it was impossible for me to stay in school. I had to go down to Board of Education and see Dr. _____, and he said that all my actions indicated that I didn't want to stay in school. So by going to night school and passing in my grades in March, maybe by next September I'd be allowed to get back into day school . . .

They would have stayed, most contend, if this pressure had not been exerted on them. They define themselves as "pushouts" rather than "dropouts." Obiously, such reporting cannot be taken at face value, and undoubtedly many acted so as to incite action to expel them from school, whether they intended that result or not. Most have been suspended from at least two schools.

The pattern is generally a great deal of residential mobility, so that many have attended eight different schools before leaving school in the tenth grade. In school they meet their friends and acquaintances; frequently, as they report it, these friends and others "wise around" and sometimes it is admitted that they themselves have done this as well. As one boy expressed it:

I   What did you like about school?
WDO The only thing I liked about school was recess and lunch.
I   Recess and lunch, huh?
WDO Yeah.
I   Okay. What didn't you like about school?
WDO Really to come right down to it, you know, I really didn't dislike school. I just didn't have time to do my work. I was always monkeying around. I think that was my biggest downfall. I think that if I hadda kept my mouth shut in class, you know, and never mind about my buddy next door, I wouldda got along okay. I don't know.

"Wise around" can include talking out loud, laughing, throwing paper, hitting students, drinking whisky. This action frequently ends in trouble—reprimands by the teacher, being grabbed or shoved by the teacher, having to stay after school, stand in a corner, or sent to the principal's or counselor's office. A boy explained his school departure in the following way:

I   Why did you come back up here?
WDO You see I was getting kind of old. You see they don't take anybody up to

[6] "I" refers to the interviewer; "WDO" to a white dropout and "NDO" to a Negro dropout. Interviews averaged two hours. A limited number of the boys have so far been interviewed twice; the second time, some six months after they entered the program. Some parents have been interviewed. Italics and parenthetical materials in the interview excerpts are the authors'. The interview schedule and coding were primarily constructed by Dr. Arthur Pearl and the staff of the New York State Division for Youth.

Types of Dropouts: "The Unemployables"

sixteen. That's all. When I went back to this (rural school) everything was going great. You see they got this new principal and this new principal wouldn't take it from the old principal about me, so he figured he'd try me out. So I was good. No trouble or nothing. Then all of a sudden one day this kid comes up and slugs me as hard as he could on the back. They'd been doing this because I'm from the city and they don't like city kids.

I   City? What city?

WDO Oh, this city (Syracuse) and New York. I told them I'd been down to New York and they don't like it. And so they kept on hitting me as hard as they could. Then this one guy come up and hit me as hard as he could and then moved back. I turned around and swung and he moved and I hit the teacher and that was it.

I   What do you mean he moved? Where was the teacher?

WDO The teacher was standing in back of him. You see we were lined up and going down to the gymnasium and this kid was in back of me and he let me have it. You go by height and in the line I was near the end and the teacher was after you. So when this kid let me have it. . . .

I   Your back was turned?

WDO Yes. I was facing front. And he let me have it in the middle of the back. And so. . . .

I   The teacher didn't see him hit you?

WDO Yes. But the teacher didn't say nothing. Or he didn't have time. Once he hit me I let him have it.

I   What happened then?

WDO He dragged me down to the office and that was it.

I   Did you tell your side?

WDO I told my side.

I   What did the principal say?

WDO He says he didn't believe me but it would be better for me to get out.[7]

Sometimes, the principal suspends them from school. And sometimes, it is two or three days before dropouts' parents discover that their child has been suspended. The dropout, however, usually returns to school or is able to re-enroll unless his sixteenth birthday is near. If this is the case, he is usually not returned to school, or, if he has past offenses, is not permitted to re-enroll.

This picture has been reported frequently in other communities. We want to make two comments which seem not to have been reported elsewhere:

(1) The boys are aggrieved by school: they frequently contend that they were not immediately involved in the event for which they have been kicked out and the teacher's misinterpretation of what was occurring led to their involvement in the event leading to their school dismissal.

They see the school personnel as "bugging" them, constantly keeping after them, until they finally have turn to defend themselves. The following excerpt relates this feeling:

I   I see. Now, do you feel any teachers were unfair to you?

WDO No. They were all fair to me.

I   Did you have any teacher that you didn't like?

---

[7] A number of our respondents claim to have been pressured by fellow students because they were new to a school and community. In contrast to the stereotype of the friendliness of the rural life, a number of urban boys reported, as in this interview, getting a rough reception when they moved to a rural school.

WDO	No. Up to a certain point.
I	Well, tell me about it.
WDO	I had an English teacher. He was a man too. Ah . . . I was doing my best to work, you know, and he always kept telling me I hadda do better and he *kept after me.* So one day I told him off and walked out of class and never went back.

We shall return to the "bugging" question later.

(2) The boys, to our initial surprise, were not negative about school. School is a convenient place for meeting one's friends, and they miss it for this reason frequently. In reply to a question about the "fairness" of teachers, most indicated that they felt that teachers were fair. These excerpts from one interview indicate the general feeling of fairness:

I	What do you like about school?
NDO	I like going to school. I enjoyed going to school, yeah. I don't know whether or not it was so much what I was learning, but I enjoyed going to school. One year I went to school every day and I still failed. . .
I	Was there anything about school that you didn't like?
NDO	No. Not really. Only a few teachers. From time to time. . . . .
	. . .
I	Could you tell me something about the teachers that you mentioned before? What kind of people become teachers?
NDO	More or less people who enjoy working with children or get some sort of a good feeling about helping young people and regardless of who they are.
	. . .
I	Do you feel that any of your teachers you had in school were unfair to you?
NDO	Oh, all my teachers were fair to me.
I	Weren't any unfair?
NDO	No. Not really.

Further, many volunteered that some particular teacher had been particularly fair or interested in them. Yet, as one boy expressed it, "School and I just aren't friends."

What has struck us is that in a dropout population that has been particularly afflicted with school problems, there was not a pronounced rejection of school. Perhaps in retrospect after a difficult experience in the work-world, they romanticized school, but the important thing in terms of educational policy is to see the possibilities in their views. The youth are perplexed by school because it places great constraints on their behavior, is not intrinsically interesting, and does not have visible connection with the actual content of jobs on the outside. They recognize, however, that a high school diploma is a necessary *credential* for many jobs, although not an aid in these jobs.

The formal organization of schools may be an obstacle. One dropout was absorbed by drawing. When he could not continue his art classes because he was doing poorly in all his other classes, he left school. School personnel are perplexed by what they see as school-antagonism on the part of these youth, but the latter do not reject school out-of-hand. Teachers and administrators

481

and difficult students have not learned how to become "friends," but there is more of a potential for this on the dropouts' side than has been realized. As one of the boys replied when asked, "How important is school?" "Well, I can't rightly say. I've never had a chance to know what school really is."

Now that they are out of school and have experienced the difficulties of the labor market, the majority of boys wished they had not left school, although many do not see on what basis they could have remained in that environment. It may be that, once boys in eighth grade or later have begun to move onto the school-leaving track, little will keep them in school. Perhaps it is after they have entered the labor market and tasted its possibilities and pitfalls that they then offer the greatest potential for satisfactory school performance. But in very few cities is there the flexibility which permits readmission any time during the year and provides special programs for the returnees.[8]

Ninety per cent of our dropouts liked the following school subjects: math, science, physical education, art, and shop. English and social studies were courses our dropouts had the most difficulties with; they were dull and uninteresting. The potential of these generally disliked courses is revealed by a Negro dropout whose social studies teacher had the class "act out" historical events. He relates:

> You might think it was crazy, but you actually felt that you were there, at the Boston massacre. Now, why can't other teachers do that?

The great interest in science fields among our male dropouts and the "culturally deprived" generally has not been developed. Martin Mayer has pointed out that it is regrettable that the innovational programs in science teaching are mostly beamed at the elite schools, public and private, rather than at the slum schools, where they might capture the imagination of youth who find many school subjects uninteresting but not those in science. The constant reporting that many dropouts are too poor in mathematics to be able to benefit from advanced vocational and technical training underlines the inadequacy of science teaching.

All but 10 per cent of the boys feel that a high school education is all that is necessary for them. They seem to tailor their occupational (and consequently their educational) expectations to what they can reasonably get.

THE "NOW" AND THE "IF" WORLDS

The question of occupational and educational aspirations and expectations has become very cloudy in contemporary analysis. How realistic are the outlooks of our boys? On questions which ask what they would like to be, implying that they should not consider immediate limitations, they often indicate quite high aspirations and hopes. If they had their choice, white dropouts would become factory owners, majors in the army or air force, mechanics,

---

[8] We estimate that from 10 per cent to 25 per cent of Syracuse dropouts continue their education or training in some form *after* leaving school. See Betty L. Saleem and S. M. Miller, *The Neglected Dropout: The Returnee,* Syracuse University Youth Development Center (July, 1963).

truck drivers, and factory workers. Negro dropouts, if they had their choice, would become doctors, lawyers, scientists, majors in the army, and garbage collectors. On questions that deal with what they are expecting to do in some immediate time span, they are very rooted in reality. Forty-eight per cent of the dropouts have a specific job aspiration (mechanic, and so forth); eight per cent of our dropouts have a very specific job, place, and time in mind (for example, a forester, in New York State); six per cent of our dropouts state a broad area of work (skilled, semiskilled, for example, construction work, and so forth); eight per cent of our dropouts were inconsistent (one time mentioning one job and later another, for example, lawyer, then construction worker); 10 per cent were diffuse with respect to type of job (no specific ideas at all); and for the remaining 20 per cent, future job expectations were either not obtained or impossible to classify. Dropouts frequently indicated the routes by which they expect to get to these occupations. Job expectations are realistic and related to their experiences.

A number of boys responded negatively to questions about whether they would like to enter certain occupations because "I can't get that kind of job." "Don't have the brains for it." When asked whether they would *like* to have it, many repeated that they could not obtain such a position. In this excerpt, the interviewer is eliciting responses to a series of pictures involving work situations:

I	Okay. What about this type of job? What is going on here?
WDO	Mailman.
I	Do you like that type of work?
WDO	Nah.
I	Why not? What's the matter with that?
WDO	I don't know the city that good.

They find it difficult to think in terms of an abstract job that they might like or dislike apart from the possibilities of their attaining it.

Many of the boys do profess a concern with high-level occupations which they have little chance of achieving. One boy spoke about the possibilities of becoming a doctor, if he applied himself. Another would like to be an artist. Yet this boy, who prided himself on his vivid dream-world, was sharply aware of what was fantasy and what was the life of the possible. Another boy related his hopes and fears:

I	Well, just how important is school to you? School in general, how important is it to you?
NDO	It's very important to me.
I	Why?
NDO	Because I figure I'm going to need a job and everything, so that's why . . . because I might be getting married pretty soon, so that's why I gotta go to college. See, I want to be a doctor, but I doubt if I'll ever be, though.
I	Why is this?
NDO	'Cause I might not finish school. See, I want to finish high school and go on to college.
I	Why might you not finish?
NDO	Might get in some more trouble or something. I'm trying not to, though.
I	Why might you get in some more trouble?

Types
of Dropouts:
"The
Unemployables"

483

NDO	Might get in with the wrong boys.
I	How is this going to come about?
NDO	No . . . when you . . . see, you see, I live on Grace Street, and I always stay up there, but then sometimes I come down on Henry Street. Then the kids down there, they be rowdy and I be with them and then they get in trouble and the next I know, the cops got us.

The world of today, the "now" world is a world of concretes, of boundaries, of limited possibilities among which one can roam. But the "if" world is—the world of what might happen, the world of the possible rather than the world of the probable, and that is seen quite differently. For in the world of the possible, one might get the lucky breaks, or settle down for the training which is necessary. But for almost all the boys, the important world is the "now" world; when they think of the "if" world, they are aware that it is not "now" and that they have to live immediately in the "now" world.

I	You can't complain about what?
WDO	About what kind of job I get right now. If I get a job, that's it. Later on in life, cleaning and sweeping, I'm not going to have that kind of job later on. It's a job. What can I do. I can't complain. Later on, I'm not saying that I'm going to be a real businessman, but I'll make a go of it. When I finish school, I'll be in better hands, let's say of getting a job. Maybe not getting it, but it will be a help.
I	Are you going to school now?
WDO	Yes.
I	Where?
WDO	I'm attending night school.
I	When do you expect to finish high school?
WDO	About another year and a half.
I	Then what are you going to do?
WDO	Most likely go into the service.
I	What branch?
WDO	Air Force.
I	What are you going to take up?
WDO	Administration.
I	What kind of administration?
WDO	Clerical work.
I	Good. What do you think you'll be doing 10 years from now?
WDO	Well, what I'd like to be doing is, I don't know. After I get in the service and if they train me in the field that I like, I don't know. I may go on and take up some kind of business course, after I'm finished with the service and go in the business field, which I want to do, but I'm undecided right now.
I	Good. Now, is there any job that you wouldn't take right now?
WDO	No. I'd take any job right now.

While most of the boys think more education would be desirable for them (and generally), the amount of education which they see as helpful is not very great. A high school diploma is enough in their eyes because they have gauged their occupational expectations on a scale of the "now."

I	What is your idea of a good job? For a boy your age?
NDO	Wash dishin' machine. (dishwasher)
I	Say what?

NDO	Wash dishin' machine.
I	Anything else?
NDO	No.
I	Why is this a good job?
NDO	Because it's what I figure I could get.

JOB EXPECTATIONS

The kind of jobs they want has real likelihood for them, and their present-day educational aims are not out of line with these modest but realistic goals. These are not boys looking to conquer the world and expecting the "easy buck." They see themselves as working and are willing, in the main, to accept what would generally be deemed low wages. Perhaps after marriage when they become more fully cognizant of the problems in attempting to support a family at this low income, their views might change. Our guess is that most will not; rather, they will scale what they expect close to what can be achieved.

It is not that they are satisfied with too little. What they would be satisfied with is always greater than what they now have. What they actively want is in the realm of their possible world. We detect what appears to be a self-protecting element of not investing emotionally in the "now" world things that can be obtained only in an "if" world. It is not that many things are not wanted, but that there does seem to be some hesitation in soaring freely in thinking about the "now" world. The following are excerpts from one interview:

I	Well, you've sort of confused me now. . . . First you tell me that you like office jobs, and then you start talking about construction, and now you started telling me about G.E. Now, first I'd like to know what job you'd like to have?
NDO	I'd like to have the one out to G.E. 'cause some of them people out there work in offices, some of them don't.
I	G.E. Doing what? What would you like to do at G.E.?
NDO	I mean fix tubes, meters and all, fix you know, bulbs and all that other stuff. I'd like to be in one of them kind of jobs.
I	In other words, you really want to be a factory worker. You really don't want to be in office work. You want to be in factory work.
NDO	Yes.
I	All right. When you think about work or working, what first comes to your mind?
NDO	The first thing that comes to my mind would be a dishwashing job.
I	Why a dishwashing job?
NDO	I just want to work in a restaurant, that's all, instead of being out in the cold.
I	Why don't you want to be a chef or cook? Why do you want to be a dishwasher?
NDO	I'd like to be a cook, too, but I don't know how to cook.

· · ·

I	Do you think the fact that you have a record will keep you from getting a job?
NDO	I couldn't work in no office, nobody might not trust me. I couldn't work in no school 'cause that's where they teach the kids. 'Cause they might think I teach them how to steal or something. I couldn't work in no

Types of Dropouts: "The Unemployables"

485

construction work or work in a restaurant or work in a bakery or something like that.

I   I noticed earlier that one of the first jobs you said that you wanted was an office worker and I noticed when I started asking you about it, you forgot about it. Why did you do this?

NDO   'Cause I know I can't get no job in an office. Nobody would let me work in no office. 'Cause I have a record.

. . .

I   All right. Which job would you like to have of any jobs on the list? Shall I read them again? Okay. Teacher, janitor in a building, sales clerk in a small store, carpenter, garbage collector, lawyer, factory worker, a bus boy in a restaurant. Which would you rather have?

NDO   I'd rather be a lawyer.

I   Why a lawyer?

NDO   Well, a lawyer see, a lawyer, he have a steady job unless somebody try to take his contracts or something and he has a steady job and he helps people what get in trouble. People what try to do something to him, he get to try to get out, try, if they get, if they have 10 years, well, he'll try to get it broken down to five or three. . . .

I   Do you think you'll become a lawyer?

NDO   Unless I go to school and take up lawyer.

I   Can you do that?

NDO   No.

I   Why can't you?

NDO   Well, I ain't, don't have no money to go, see, after you go to high school, you have to go to college, some kind of law college, you gotta take up law in college and I don't have enough money to pay to get through.

Our impression is that there is no effort to bring the "now" and "if" worlds together. It is not a process of alleviating a cognitive dissonance, but an effort at perseverating the two worlds, keeping them apart with little interplay among them. Obviously, mistakes may be made. A "now" job possibility may really be only an "if" chance.

I   Why is it the best job?

WDO   The florist would have been the best. After a while I would have gotten a raise, man, it would have been pretty good. I would have got good money after a while. I had to work myself up. I would have been doing pretty well *if* I was working there. This is the next best, the one I'm working now.

I   Well, what's the future in this job you have now? (sales clerk in produce market)

WDO   Ah . . . ah . . . I don't know.

I   Does this job have any future—that you're working on now?

WDO   I might become a manager some day—something like that.

I   What do you think your chances are?

WDO   Of becoming a manager? I don't know. What do you think?

One implication of this analysis is that the enlarging or raising of aspirations and expectations has only limited value. If coping with the world frequently consists of riding with it rather than directing it, of accepting its concrete possibilities as goals rather than harboring higher goals which are constantly frustrated, then the attacks must be of a different order. It would be necessary to raise possibilities somewhat in order to encourage more thinking about the "if" world by transmuting part of it into the "now" world. Experiences with acquaintances or neighbors who have obtained high school or college diplomas but have not been able to do well occupationally reduce the willingness to believe that the "if" world can be incorporated into the "now" world. What we are saying may apply only to our specific group of dropouts, who have had more job difficulties than others, but undoubtedly some elements of this thinking is found among many other types of dropouts.

PARENTS

Parents have the same orientations to jobs as the boys. They want their sons to get a job: "Anything that he can do." They seldom state a specific job, just any job that the boy can get. One parent indicated an important school problem: "It is embarrassing for a kid his age remaining in the eighth grade. I let him quit. . . . I want him to get a job working eight hours a day, so he can be home at night."

Several parents express a feeling of not being able to direct the boys. Once the boys are "grown up," they cannot be treated like kids and told what to do. Words are not effective with them and physical force—frequently important in regulating child behavior in working-class families—is no longer easily usable with fully grown boys. A substitute force has not developed nor is it always thought to be desirable to pressure the youth into a given direction.

Hylan Lewis[9] has described a somewhat similar orientation among some Negro mothers in Washington:

> As children grow older there seems to be a cut-off point at which parents express impotence and bafflement. Although there are anxieties, the fate of these growing children is often written off as out of parents' hands. There recurs in the records a mixture of hope and resignation: "I do hope they don't get in trouble. I tried to raise them right." "The Lord will have to look out for them." "I'm glad mine are little. I kinda hate to see them grow up. At least I can do something for them now."

ORIENTATIONS TO PROBLEMS

We were concerned to see to what extent this group of "unemployable" dropouts identified their problems as products of their behavior or as essentially arising from external causes over which they had little control. We classified as "impunitive" responses those that indicated self-deprecatoriness, tendency to blame self for outcomes and the like, and as "extra-punitive" responses in which others are blamed, causes are seen as external, or problems are not perceived. (The distribution had to be dichotomized into two such omnibus categories because of the small number of cases.) We estimate that 55 per cent of the boys were impunitive and 45 per cent extra-punitive. Since many, if not most, of these boys would be classified as "acting out," these results raise further questions about that overworked and overstretched cate-

---

[9] Hylan Lewis, "Child Rearing Among Low Income Families," Washington Center for Metropolitan Studies (July, 1961), pp. 4-5.

Types
of Dropouts:
"The
Unemployables"

487

gory. Similarly, it raises questions about the category of "sociopathic personality," and the like, which presumes a lack of concern for social values that does not seem to be exhibited by these boys.

Our Negro dropouts showed a higher incidence of extra-punitiveness than did the white dropouts. Although 40 per cent of whites are extra-punitive, 55 per cent of the Negroes were so classified. The Negro dropouts may have a point here in identifying outside pressures as causing difficulties. Negroes who have been in the work-training program have had greater difficulties getting jobs than the white participants. The training program does not primarily provide any skills; it has been mainly aimed at developing a more positive orientation toward work. Improving the outlook of whites seems to enhance their chances of getting low-level interstitial jobs, but not those of Negroes. The latter seem to know this and are less willing to take low-level jobs, in the hope of being able to move up. White boys have this hope; Negro boys see the first job as the terminus, not as the gateway station to further occupational advance. Similarly, many white dropouts are willing to become policemen, but almost no Negro is—it is a dirty job in their experience, as they have seen what they consider to be prejudiced behavior against them.

"BUGGING"

A frequent explanation of difficulties, especially with police, employers, or school, is that someone was "bugging me." Two examples of "bugging":

I	What did they (teachers) do when they picked on you?
NDO	Like sometimes, you know, I ain't doing nothing, they just start bugging me. They just started talking and all this trash.
I	What did they say?
NDO	Oh, like, what you doing, do your work and all that. Sometimes I can't quit talking 'cause I ain't been talking and it be somebody else that been talking.
I	Anything else you dislike about school?
NDO	No.
I	Why did you drop school?
NDO	I got expelled.
I	Can you tell me about that?
NDO	Well, you see, I was getting in a little bit of trouble, so one day, in the cafeteria; you know they have teachers that be in there, so this one teacher, he thought I snuck ahead in line but I didn't, so when I got up to get my milk, he told the boy not to give it to me, and then, so I said something, so then he grab me and then, you know, we sort of tussled a little bit and then I had to go down to the principal's office and he . . . ah . . . he . . . ah, Mr. ___, the principal, he expelled me. He kicked me out. . . .
I	Why did you leave school?
WDO	Got sick and tired of school.
I	Got sick and tired of school? How did you get sick and tired of school? What happened?
WDO	Oh, the teachers keep on bugging me.
I	"Bugging" you?
WDO	Yes.
I	How do teachers "bug" students? I have heard this expression time and again. But I don't understand what it is. How do teachers "bug" a student?

WDO	They push me around, or something like that.
I	Push you around how?
WDO	Shove me or something.
I	Where do they shove you? Who shoves you?
WDO	The teachers.
I	Why do they shove you?
WDO	I talked in class or something like that. Fooled around a couple of times.
I	Why do you think they did that?
WDO	Oh, they got mad at me, and pushed me around, so I started pushing them around.

These boys frequently report that the precipitating incident for their getting kicked out of school or being fired from a job was a situation in which they were not deliberately trying to do something wrong. (The earlier excerpt from the interview with the New York City boy in a rural school is a good example.) They contend that a teacher was constantly nagging them, misinterpreting what they were doing; the adults' misperception led to the action which the adults feared.

WDO	Well, the teachers were okay up until the 7th grade. Then they started getting down my neck.
I	How they'd get down your neck?
WDO	Well, it started out when I moved into the 7th grade and there was a bunch of guys I knew that had failed. They were in my class. We started monkeying around and the teachers started to get mad.
I	Monkey around with you?
WDO	Yes.
	. . .
WDO	Ug . . . oh boy . . . I can't right remember her name but it will come back to me. She was my homeroom teacher in _____ School and . . . well, she always jumped on all the boys' necks. It's like when we had study hall and when we had to go back to our room for a study hall 7th period and we did all our work during the class and she tell us to do anything we want. We go over and start talking to the girls: we start asking them questions and things like that, she started jumping on the boys' necks about that. Then she goes down to the principal and say we were molesting her. And I didn't like that a bit.
I	Is that the worst teacher you've had?
WDO	Oh boy, that's the worst teacher I've had yet—ever had.
I	Has she ever hit you, or anything like that?
WDO	She's hit me. One time she wish she hadn't.
I	With what? Why did she hit you?
WDO	I was . . . well, she told us to do anything we wanted to cause I did my . . . we only had English homework one night and I did that all during English class. We have . . . I think it's 15 minutes at the end of the class there to do our homework or anything like that or any homework we've got, so I did all my homework in that 15 minutes so she told us that if we were tired, to lay our heads down on our desk or something like that, so I laid my head down on the desk and she come over with a ruler and hit me in the back of the neck just as hard as she could and that hurt too. She cut me with the edge of the ruler there. So I got up and hit her.

The boys, in using this mode of explanation, do not claim that they had always been good-little-conformists; no, they had been in trouble before, but the incident which led to their exile was not initiated by them.

Types of Dropouts: "The Unemployables"

489

They see the adults' behavior in the situation as "unfair," for they are falsely accused. This injustice seems to provide a basis for neutralizing the norms which restrain behavior in school or in the job world. Perhaps more importantly, they see many supervisory adults as "buggin'" them, always "buzzing around," "riding" them, going "after them," looking for trouble even when it is not there. The boys frequently recognize that they are doing things which are difficult for teachers or bosses to accept, but they do not do them to antagonize. These outcomes are the result of trying to have a good time, "kidding around," and the like. The constant nagging and riding, which is their interpretation of what is taking place, is thought of as "picking on" them and excessively irritating. Yet, they accept the idea of structure and discipline; it is the particular form of it which "bugs" them. They see the adult mode of control as entrapment: "They're after me all the time" until I finally get real angry and do something that is too much.

Yablonsky[10] reports the poignant feeling of being "bugged":

> The essential meaning of the "permanent" clubroom to the gang was revealed by Jay. He would come regularly, pay his ten-cent dues, then go and lie down in a corner on the floor and stare quietly at the ceiling. One day I questioned him about what seemed to be a waste of money:
>
> L.Y.: Jay, how come you pay your dime and just lie around? Why don't you play checkers or talk to the guys or something?
> Jay: Look, man, this is the only place in the world they leave me be. *Don't bug me.* I hang on the corner or the park—the cops boot me. I go home—they throw me out. They don't let me in the (community) center no more. I hang in my hallway—the janitor yells. I go on the stoop—the neighbors bitch. I get a little peace here—so leave me be.

THE JOB

In the job world, the boys frequently mention that they have been fired because one boss wanted them to do one thing; another, a different thing and they got fed up and told off the boss.

> Makes me sick. I got so many bosses, I don't know who to mind. Even the bus boys had bus boys. "You bus that table!" "No. I want you to bus that table! Come over here and bus this table." So I said, "Don't none of you say nothing to me. If you do, we're going to fight. I'm not taking any orders from anybody but the big boss. If I see something that needs to be done, I'll do it."

The precipitating incident is again that of a false accusation of aberrant behavior. Yet, here again, as in the school situation, they accept the idea of authority and supervision. It is its concrete manifestation with which they have difficulty.

> I Is it ever really necessary for someone to give orders?
> NDO Yes, if nobody don't give no orders and everybody do what they want to do, somebody might not do the right thing.

[10] Louis Yablonsky, *The Violent Gang* (New York: The Macmillan Company, 1962), p. 78.

Another boy:

I	Well, is having someone give orders ever really necessary?
WDO	Well, in ways it is and in ways it isn't. Because, let's say, one guy gives you orders and you go to do it and another guy gives you orders when you're just doing this one. When you're doing the other one, the other one come by and ask you why you aren't doing this one and then you get all mixed up and then you. . .
I	That happen to you?
WDO	It happened to me six times.
I	Where was this?
WDO	This company. Till the 7th time, I got sick and I slammed him. I gave him a black eye and a bloody nose. He said I was fired and I said, sorry, I quit two minutes ago and I want my check and he said he wasn't going to give it to me. So I took it to the labor board and I got $20 extra.

The frequency with which contradictory orders may be involved may be due to these boys' working in situations (such as restaurants) where work rationality is limited and the organizational structure leaky. Their jobs are frequently in establishments where there is not a well-formalized work situation. (One action suggestion would involve setting up regularized grievance systems in places which employ many youths. Training programs might experiment with providing a neutralized mode of handling grievances.)

A central tension is that the boys seem to take criticism in a very personal way (not that all of us do not have difficulty in separating criticisms of our products from criticisms of ourselves). It is all right for a boss to exert authority—that's what being a boss is—but that is not the same thing as criticizing me, telling me what is wrong with what I do, especially if such comments are made in heat.

What does it mean to these boys to accept criticism? Is it considered a sign of weakness to let someone get away with it? Or is it taken as a sign of total rejection by the adult? Or as an effrontery and an invasion of privacy? We do not know; we suspect that the boys are asking for respect, a "rep," a status which we adults tell them has to be earned. But the boys frequently are not sure it is worthwhile to try to earn it, if it is not first accorded them.

THE STRUCTURE OF OPPORTUNITY

John Miner concludes that all but 15 per cent in unskilled occupations are capable of working in higher-level occupations.[11] Lockwood reports that in Baltimore only 5 per cent of high school students overstate their occupational potential while 37 per cent understate it.[12] With the growing emphasis on formal credentials, a sizable number of people will never be able to move close to what they can do and will lose the chance to obtain a decent income.

A touching story of his travails is told by a boy whose father is in a mental hospital:

---

[11] John B. Miner, *Intelligence in the United States* (New York: Springer Publishing Company, 1957).

[12] William V. Lockwood, *Realism in Vocational Preference* (Ph. D. dissertation, Johns Hopkins University, 1957). A summary is published as "Realism of Vocational Preference," *Personnel and Guidance Journal*, Vol. XXXVII (1958), pp. 98-105.

Types of Dropouts: "The Unemployables"

WDO   No, I quit. I went to school in September, 1962, this year. I started in September. I guess it was just about the end of the month, I quit. And then . . . the reason why I quit was that my mother wanted me to help her out. So I went to work and I lost a job. I was laid off. So then I couldn't find another job. My mother asked me to go back to school so she could get welfare assistance for me. So I went back to school. And then when I went back to school, I just completely lost interest in it, you know, didn't care too much about it. After that I didn't feel like doing my work or anything. I wanted to go to work.

Getting youth to stay in school is difficult if courses do not have any clear connection with their occupational future or do not otherwise enrich their lives but are merely ways of accumulating credit for a credential. Going to school is not seen as a way of learning something which is of value later for a job or for enjoyment of living, but a mode of getting a high school diploma that opens up the possibilities of a greater range of jobs and higher pay. And in truth, it is the diploma as such, not the courses, which provide the opening wedge into the educationally cleavaged upper levels of the occupational pyramid. We suspect that this situation makes it more difficult to put up with school than would be the case if courses were providing something useful for later activities. If high school graduation does not advantage or does not seem to advantage youth they know (a likely occurrence where racial discrimination is involved and in our kind of economy where layoffs are likely with recurring recessions and an extending wave of declining industries), they are not likely to think of investing further time in school.

This report on a group of "unemployable" dropouts is far from definitive. But we have been surprised enough by our results to assert that even this type of dropout has attitudes which offer possibilities for more effective school and job adjustment. We adults at present have not done much to capitalize on them. As in love and song-making, it is in the accentuation of the positive that we have a chance of eliminating the negative.

MILLER
HARRISON

492

The Adjustment of Older Workers to Job Displacement

LOUIS A. FERMAN

MICHAEL T. AIKEN

STUDIES of the labor market have traditionally emphasized economic considerations in a discussion of worker adjustment to job displacement.[1] The analysis of adjustment has centered around such variables as the number of months unemployed, the loss in savings, the increase in debt, and the reduction in expenditures. Adjustment to job displacement has been thought of as problem-solving behavior made necessary by a change or a depletion in economic resources. Some of the questions posed in such research include these:

> How does the displaced worker find a new job? Does the displaced worker move from one labor market to another seeking work? How does he allocate scarce economic resources following job displacement?

Completely neglected in this conceptualization has been the study of *emotional adjustment to job displacement* and, even more important, *the relationships between economic factors and emotional adjustment.*

In this article we shall sketch a few partial results from a study dealing with workers' adjustment to job displacement, a study relating economic dimensions of adjustment to workers' emotional states. Besides citing study

* The authors of this paper would like to express their appreciation to the Institute of Labor and Industrial Relations, University of Michigan–Wayne State University, and particularly its co-directors, Ronald W. Haughton and Charles Rehmus, for their support and encouragement in the analysis of the data on the adjustment of older workers to job displacement. The Packard study has been primarily supported by funds from the Institute since the project began in 1957.

The senior author would also like to thank the American Philosophical Society for financial aid on the project during the summer of 1959 and the National Institute of Mental Health for a small grant in 1960—project number M-3839 (A); MH (A).

[1] Leonard P. Adams and Robert L. Aronson, *Workers and Industrial Change* (Ithaca, N.Y.: Cornell University, 1957); Ewan Clague, Walter J. Couper, and E. Wight Bakke, *After the Shutdown* (New Haven, Conn.: Yale University, 1934); Charles A. Myers and George P. Shultz, *The Dynamics of a Labor Market* (Englewood Cliffs, N.J.: Prentice-Hall, Inc., 1951); Harold L. Sheppard and James Stern, "Impact of Automation on Workers in Supplier Plants," *Labor Law Journal*, Vol. 8 (October, 1957); Richard C. Wilcock, "Impact on Workers and Community of a Plant Shutdown in a Depressed Area," *Monthly Labor Review*, Vol. 80 (September, 1957).

findings, we shall discuss their implications, and suggest certain problems for further research.

The present paper utilizes data from interviews conducted in 1958 with 314 ex-automobile workers who were left jobless when the Packard Motor Car Company closed its Detroit plant about 18 months earlier.[2] Two hundred and sixty interviews were used for the analysis presented in this paper; interviews with Negro workers were eliminated, because there were not sufficient cases for significant comparisons between whites and Negroes. The sample, then, includes only white, older workers who had many years of seniority at the Parkard Motor Car Company. Seven out of every ten workers were over 40 years of age; seven out of every 20 workers were 60 years of age or over. Nearly one-half of the respondents had at least 25 years of service with the company; five per cent had started with the company between 1900 and 1915. The workers represented various levels of blue-collar occupations in the automotive field.

THE MEASURES OF ECONOMIC AND EMOTIONAL ADJUSTMENT

Two sets of measures were constructed from the responses in the interviews. The first, attempting to gauge the amount of workers' loss of economic security, was an *Index of Economic Deprivation*. A scoring procedure was utilized which gave a high score to a respondent who reported that his savings had declined since leaving the company, that his debts had increased, and that it was necessary for him to cut down on at least two types of expenditures for such things as food, clothing, house repairs, medical care, recreation, and transportation. Conversely, a respondent who reported more savings, less debts, and no cutback on expenditures was give a low score. The relationship of each item to the over-all index is as follows:

INDEX OF ECONOMIC DEPRIVATION

	Pearsonian Correlation Coefficient
Cutback on two expenditures since being laid off . . .	.75
Savings are less since being laid off	.69
Debts are more since being laid off	.54

The second set of indicators was designed to measure emotional adjustment. By "emotional adjustment" we do not mean the absence or presence of classical forms of mental illness (for example, schizophrenia). Instead, we refer to an attitudinal set of responses frequently used by researchers to designate mental health or morale. This attitudinal set, of course, has many facets, but we limited our measures to two dimensions which seemed to be quite basic to adjustment: the degree of satisfaction with life and the absence or presence

---

[2] The study of ex-Packard workers was initiated in 1957 by Dr. Harold L. Sheppard, currently with the Area Redevelopment Administration. An earlier report on the study has been published: Harold L. Sheppard, Louis A. Ferman, and Seymour Faber, *Too Old to Work—Too Young to Retire: A Case Study of a Permanent Plant Shutdown*, U.S. Senate, Special Committee on Unemployment Problems, 86th Cong., 1st Sess. (Washington: Government Printing Office, 1960).

of feelings of anomie. The actual construction of the measures was based on the results of a factor analysis of a series of items in the interview designed to measure these two dimensions.

The Anomie Index was obtained by assigning one point for each of the items below to which respondents gave a positive response. The relationship of each item to the over-all Index of Anomie is shown in the table.[3]

INDEX OF ANOMIE

	Pearsonian Correlation Coefficient
1. "No one is going to care much about what happens to you when you get right down to it." . .	.75
2. "You sometimes can't help wondering whether life is worthwhile any more."	.68
3. "In spite of what some people say, the lot of the average man is getting worse, not better."	.67
4. "These days I get a feeling that I'm just not a part of things."	.67
5. "Most people don't really care what happens to the next fellow." . . . . : . . .	.66
6. "It is hardly fair to bring a child into the world today, the way things look now."	.65
7. "These days a person doesn't really know whom he can depend on."	.64

The *Index of Satisfaction with Life* was designed to measure a mental posture of general happiness and satisfaction with everyday life. The index gave a high score to respondents who provided a positive response to the four items below and a low score to respondents who gave a negative response to these four items. The relationship of each item to the over-all index is as follows:

INDEX OF SATISFACTION WITH LIFE

	Pearsonian Correlation Coefficient
1. Find a good deal of happiness in life.	.76
2. Very satisfied with life.	.76
3. Hardly ever or never get the feeling that life is not useful.	.75
4. Generally feel in good spirits most of the time . .	.61

As one would expect, the two measures of emotional adjustment—the Index of Anomie and the Index of Satisfaction with Life—are highly related to each other. The correlation coefficient between these two measures is —.49, indicating that a worker who is highly satisfied with life is less prone to have feelings of anomie, and vice versa.

THE ANTECEDENTS OF ECONOMIC ADJUSTMENT

Are there differences in economic adjustment based on predisplacement statuses (age, education, and skill level) and unemployment experiences (length

---

[3] These items were provided by Leo Srole. For some discussion of the measure of this concept, see Leo Srole, "Social Integration and Certain Corollaries: An Exploratory Study," *American Sociological Review*, Vol. 21, No. 6 (December, 1956), pp. 709-16.

of unemployment and finding and holding a job)? Let us look at predisplacement statuses first. Age and education are highly related to each other; the younger the worker, the more likely he is to be better educated. Both age and education are related to the length of unemployment and to the frequency of finding a job and holding it. The younger worker and the more educated worker experienced less unemployment and had less difficulty in finding and holding a job than did the older and less educated workers. Similarly, the more skilled workers in the sample were unemployed for shorter periods of time and had less difficulty in finding a new job and holding it. Although age, education, and skill level were significantly related to the length of unemployment and to finding and holding jobs, these variables were not related to the degree of economic deprivation as measured by our index. The younger workers, the more educated workers, and the skilled workers were as likely as other workers to experience a loss of savings, an increase of debt, and a reduction in expenditures. In other words, we could *not* predict the extent of economic deprivation in the sample using only the predisplacement variables of age, education, and skill level.

When we turned to unemployment experiences, such as the length of unemployment and the frequency of finding and holding a job, we found a significant relationship between these experiences and the degree of economic deprivation. A prolonged period of unemployment and difficulty in finding and holding a job were manifested in a high degree of economic deprivation. Thus, such unemployment experiences were significant variables in predicting the extent of economic deprivation in this sample. The following "causal link" is suggested from these findings: certain predisplacement statuses (age, education, and skill level) are associated with certain kinds of unemployment experiences (prolonged unemployment and the ease or difficulty in finding and holding a job). The latter experiences significantly influence the degree of economic deprivation (loss of savings, increase of debt, and reduction in expenditures).

THE ANTECEDENTS OF EMOTIONAL ADJUSTMENT

We now turn to the factors which are related to emotional adjustment as measured by the *Index of Satisfaction with Life* and the *Index of Anomie*. Let us consider the predisplacement statuses and unemployment experiences discussed in the previous section. Age, education, and skill level are not significantly related to scores on the Index of Satisfaction with Life. Age and skill level are not significantly related to the Index of Anomie, but education is strongly related to it. The more educated workers were less likely than other workers to have high anomie scores. It would seem, then, that with the exception of education, we could *not* make any predictions about the emotional adjustment of the workers in the sample using only the predisplacement statuses.

The relationships between unemployment experiences and emotional adjustment are similarly not significant; although there is a weak relationship between the length of unemployment and scores on the Index of Anomie, prolonged unemployment results in only a slightly higher tendency to give

FERMAN
AIKEN

496

anomic responses. Therefore, the knowledge of the unemployment experiences of the workers does *not,* in and of itself, permit one to predict emotional adjustment to job displacement.

ECONOMIC DEPRIVATION AND EMOTIONAL ADJUSTMENT

Is there a relationship between the two kinds of adjustment? In terms of our measures, is the *Index of Economic Deprivation* related to the *Indices of Satisfaction with Life* and *of Anomie?* The answer is affirmative. There is a strong relationship between economic deprivation and both measures of emotional adjustment. The most economically deprived workers are the least satisfied with life and are most likely to give anomic responses.

It now becomes possible to chart a network of relationships between predisplacement statuses, unemployment experiences, economic deprivation, and the measures of emotional adjustment. Predisplacement statuses give rise to certain types of unemployment experiences, such as length of unemployment and finding and holding a job. These experiences, in turn, determine the extent of economic deprivation. Finally, the degree of economic deprivation will influence the emotional adjustment of the worker, as evidence by responses indicating his satisfaction with life and lack of anomie. Knowing the level of economic deprivation among the respondents permits us to predict certain aspects of their emotional adjustment to job displacement. The network of relationships, illustrated by two "pure types," is as follows:

RELATIONSHIP BETWEEN ECONOMIC DEPRIATION AND EMOTIONAL ADJUSTMENT

Predisplacement Statuses	→	Unemployment Experience	→	Economic Adjustment	→	Emotional Adjustment
a. Young age High education High skill level		Finds and holds a job Short duration of unemployment		Low economic deprivation		Low anomie score High satisfaction with life
b. Old age Low education Low skill level		Difficulty in find- ing and holding a job Long duration of unemployment		High economic deprivation		High anomie score Low satisfaction with life

The importance of economic deprivation as an influence on emotional adjustment seems quite clear. The relationship between economic deprivation and emotional adjustment remains even if we introduce predisplacement statuses and unemployment experiences as controls. It is also interesting to note that economic deprivation is highly related to stability in rates of social contact with relatives and friends, and somewhat related to stability- in rates of contact with former co-workers and neighbors. The most deprived workers were less stable in these social contacts than other workers. The significance of the latter finding is that it reinforces our general inference about the impact of economic deprivation on emotional adjustment, because stability in rates of social participation may be a behavioral reflection of emotional adjustment.

The findings reported here suggest the following: The adjustment to job displacement must be conceptualized as a social process involving a close interplay between economic and noneconomic variables. Economic adjustment is an important dimension in this process, but it is only one consideration. *There is no denying that emotional adjustment is closely linked to economic deprivation and that the solution to a range of emotional problems may depend on some amelioration of the worker's economic position.*

Two comments would seem appropriate. First, Roethlisberger and Dickson[4] suggested in the Hawthorne study that a worker's morale is more closely related to how a worker feels about a situation than the structure of the situation itself. The unfortunate consequence of this finding has been the development of a strong tendency in industrial relations to probe the worker's feelings about a situation rather than to examine the situation itself. The findings in the present study suggest that the situation, if it is characterized by a high degree of economic deprivation can have an important influence on a worker's attitudes. A worker cannot "think away" or "feel away" a loss of savings, an increase in debt, or a necessary reduction in expenditures for essential items.

Second, one could pose the argument that economic deprivation results from emotional factors, rather than the reverse. That is, the worker who is emotionally upset or agitated may not function rationally and, thus, may engage in behavior which leads to economic deprivation. It could also be suggested that people who become economically deprived are "poor planners" or have been socialized in a manner which predisposes them to become economically deprived. These are arguments for which there are no conclusive answers in this study. It is our view that social structural factors, such as a worker's relationship to the economic order, have consequences not only for social behavior—for example, changes in the amount of participation with relatives, co-workers, or friends—but are also reflected in psychic states.

Such issues as these cannot be conclusively resolved with a cross-sectional approach such as this, but would necessitate a longitudinal study with adequate before-job-displacement measures of economic and emotional states of workers as well as periodic post-job-displacement evaluations. Further, there may be some aspects of this process of economic and emotional adjustment to job displacement which are unique not only to the automotive industry, but also to the Detroit labor market. Economic deprivation—its meaning and its consequences—may vary from one labor market to another. Therefore, further study of these issues should reflect adequate sampling of labor markets along such dimensions as region, predominant industry, and general standard of living.

---

[4] F. J. Roethlisberger and William J. Dickson, *Management and the Worker* (Cambridge: Harvard University Press, 1939).

FERMAN
AIKEN

Plant Relocation and Worker Migration

LUKE M. SMITH

IRVING A. FOWLER

A. THE PLANT-RELOCATION STORY

IN January, 1958, in the middle of the 1957-1958 recession of the auto industry, the Ford Motor Company announced that within a month its assembly plant in Buffalo, New York, was to be closed. The local plant had become obsolescent and too costly to operate amid intensely competitive conditions. Its operations and equipment were to be transferred to Lorain, Ohio, approximately 40 miles west of Cleveland and 200 miles southwest of Buffalo. Under the terms of a national contract and a newly negotiated supplementary agreement with the local union, the 1,100 UAW-CIO workers were promised jobs with seniority and job-classification rights in the Lorain plant. Faced with job loss in one community and the promise of similar job rights so far away that residential changes would be necessary, amid recession conditions in the local and the national economy, the workers were in a difficult decision-making situation. How many workers decided to move, how many to stay, and how many endured a long period of indecision? Were there any distinct social characteristics of the workers which seemed to produce one or another of these decisions, or indecision?

B. PRACTICAL AND THEORETICAL PROBLEMS IN WORKER MIGRATION

The problem of obtaining an adequate labor supply at those places where production can occur most efficiently is an old one in human history. It has been solved by such devices as slavery, penal transportation, conscription, politically coerced movement of whole populations, and the more subtle coercions of the labor market. In American society of the latter twentieth century, with plant obsolescence occurring through automation, and national markets moving in a southwesterly direction, labor problems in plant relocation have been arising again and again and are likely to arise repeatedly in the future, especially in the older, industrialized sections of the country. The

Plant Relocation and Worker Migration

practical problem is more than that of an efficient deployment of the labor force or the reduction by the welfare state of economic and social costs. For a free society, the basic problem is that of the optimal mobility for personality development and for the progressiveness of the local community and the larger society.

In its theoretical aspects, worker migration for jobs has long troubled social scientists. Workers sometimes refuse to move from areas of unemployment to areas of job opportunities, and then again will move about with little or no regard for the conditions of the labor market. It is difficult to explain many of the random facts of worker migration by systematic economic theory, and assumptions are often made about the *psychological* characteristics of the individual decision makers which explain why they act in ways which are now rational, now irrational from the standpoint of the total economy. It is also possible, however, that the worker choosing to be mobile or immobile has certain *social* characteristics—a set of positions occupied in the structure of the community or of the society—which make his decision rational for him in the world as he is *socially* able to perceive it.[1]

Solutions to these practical and theoretical problems were sought in interviews with 145 blue-collar employees of the Buffalo Ford assembly plant. Because all of these workers had lost their jobs in the same organization at the same time, and all had been offered the same jobs with the same company at a place beyond commuting distance, this research was conducted under conditions affording unusual quasi-experimental control of the "push" and "pull" factors in migration, at the same time giving access to people who were in the midst of decision making and, therefore, were often very willing to talk freely about themselves.[2]

---

[1] See Donald J. Bogue, *A Methodological Study of Migration and Labor Mobility in Michigan and Ohio in 1947* (Athens, Ohio: Scripps Foundation Studies in Population Distribution, No. 4, June 1952); Theodore Caplow, *The Sociology of Work* (Minneapolis, Minn.: University of Minnesota Press, 1954), pp. 88-98; Evan Clague, *et al., After the Shutdown* (New Haven, Conn.: Yale University Institute of Human Relations, 1934); Irving A. Fowler and Luke M. Smith, *Do Workers Move When Their Plant Is Relocated? The Case of the Ford Motor Company Plant Relocation* (Buffalo, N.Y.: The University of Buffalo, 1960, mimeographed); Herbert S. Parnes, *Research on Labor Mobility* (New York: Social Science Research Council), Bul. 65 (1954); William Petersen, "A General Typology of Migration," *American Sociological Review*, Vol. 23 (1958), pp. 256-66; Lloyd G. Reynolds, *The Structure of Labor Markets* (New York: Harper & Row, Publishers, 1951); C. R. Walker, *Steeltown* (New York: Harper & Row, Publishers, 1950); Richard C. Wilcock and Irvin Sobel, *Small City Job Markets* (Urbana, Ill.: University of Illinois Institute of Labor and Industrial Relations, 1958).

[2] *Method*. There were 145 interviews from among 256 Ford plant workers or their wives, a sample taken from the seniority list of 1,100 furnished by the union with company approval. These interviews, each of about 45 minutes, were obtained by undergraduate students in several Introductory Sociology sections at the University of Buffalo during May, 1958, four months after the announced plant closing. It became difficult to obtain an *effective* sample because of the growing obsolescence of the seniority list, worker movement out of or within Buffalo, an unusually wide geographical scatter of worker residences (where the interviews were made), the pressure of the end of the school semester on student performance, and, as always when using field interviewing as a teaching device, a wide range of student compliance with class assignments. Some technical accuracy had to be sacrificed in order to execute the study within a few months of the plant shutdown.

C. SOCIAL CHARACTERISTICS OF THE WORKERS

The social characteristics of the all-male, blue-collar employees of the assembly plant seemed to be those of a typical work force in the older industrialized areas of the United States.

The values of the workers, manifested in life patterns of stability rather than mobility, seemed to indicate a tendency to solve life problems by remaining in the locality rather than by moving. Only one-tenth had lived in Buffalo for less than five years, and nearly three-fourths had lived there for 20 years or more. A little over half had been born in Buffalo or had wives who were native to the locality, and one-tenth were living in the same house where they had been born. Nine-tenths were married, and the work force was distributed over all the stages of the family life cycle. Three-fifths owned or were buying their homes.

Their social ties were concentrated in the locality rather than being regional or national. Most of the workers and their wives who were interviewed had about an equal number of relatives elsewhere and in Buffalo, only 26 per cent had all their kinship ties out of Buffalo, and 18 per cent had all their relatives in Buffalo.

Workers met *less frequently* with their fellow workers than with friends who were not in the plant, with relatives, and with neighbors. Thus, it was not the mobile plant which was the chief source of primary group relationships, but nonmobile groups in the locality. Correspondingly, there was a weak tie to the union, judging from the fact that nearly two-thirds of the workers reported attending union meetings "sometimes or hardly ever." There was also marked civic participation, 74 per cent of the workers or their wives reporting membership in one or two local clubs (in addition to union and church), 83 per cent and 87 per cent, respectively, voting in the last local and presidential elections, 31 per cent having collected charity funds, and only seven per cent reporting no formal community participation.

In addition there were, as in the Buffalo community generally, large and solidary ethnic minorities which were identified with their local ethnic groups rather than with the nationwide cultural majority. For only eight per cent of the workers and their wives was the original nationality on the father's side British or Irish, whereas for 22 per cent it was German or Italian and for 21 per cent Polish. Only 15 per cent of the workers had no friends who were identified with the paternal nationality, 44 per cent had some, and 41 per cent all.

All workers were in a similar economic position: all had lost their jobs with the same company in Buffalo, and all had been offered jobs by this company in its relocated plant several hundred miles away. However, there were differences also: 42 per cent were in the lower skill brackets, 61 per cent had not completed high school, 72 per cent had not yet found another job in Buffalo, and 55 per cent were pessimistic about getting another job in Buffalo as good as the one they had held in the plant.

In learning about jobs in Buffalo, workers reported that they would seek information from newspapers (mass communication) and from friends outside

Plant Relocation and Worker Migration

the plant, rather than from employment offices, relatives, fellow workers, or, least of all, personal canvassing (self-reliance). On the other hand, when it came to seeking aid in financial trouble, workers said that they would rely more on relatives than on neighbors, church, lodge, banks, or other loan agencies, and least on friends outside the plant. Some said that they did not know from whom they would seek aid. Thus, workers relied on the more extensive and the more flexible channels of communication only for learning about jobs in Buffalo.

D. HOW THESE SOCIAL CHARACTERISTICS AFFECT WORKERS' DECISION MAKING

Only 20 per cent of the 145 workers interviewed decided to take advantage of the job offer in Lorain, 51 per cent decided to stay in Buffalo in spite of the widespread unemployment there, while 29 per cent were undecided. The workers took a negative attitude toward the move. They felt that they were being "pushed" by economic crisis rather than "pulled" by economic advantages; and they desired to stay in Buffalo mainly because of social ties, but also because of fear of no job security in Lorain, reports of a lower standard of living there, and the cost and trouble of moving, although one-sixth reported having jobs or other economic resources in Buffalo. Workers expressing fear of unemployment in Buffalo and those attracted by the job in Lorain tended to be *Movers,* whereas those mentioning social ties to Buffalo and various economic resources there tended to be *Stayers.*

Not only were these different attitudes toward the move associated with different decisions, but also certain social characteristics or social positions of the workers—differences in life patterns of mobility or stability, in local and extra-local social ties, in economic position, and in channels of communication for obtaining economic information—were associated with different decisions.

Workers who had life patterns of mobility were likely to be mobile in this kind of crisis. Those who had never been married or who were at the time of the decision divorced or widowed, who had made two or more moves between communities in the last ten years (exclusive of Armed Service moves), who were not native to Buffalo, who had lived there less than 20 years, who had spent most of their lives in less urbanized communities than Buffalo, and who were renting their homes tended to be *Movers.* On the other hand, it was the older workers (50 years and over), the married ones, those who had moved only once or not at all in the last ten years, those who had lived in Buffalo 20 years or more, and those who had been born in Buffalo or had lived there most of their lives, who tended to be the *Stayers.*

Workers whose kinship ties were concentrated in Buffalo rather than elsewhere, who had intense and varied social involvements in the locality (kinship, neighborhood, plant and nonplant friendships, union and civic activities, and ethnic minority identifications) were more likely to be immobile in a crisis; whereas those whose kinship ties were more extra-local, who were less involved in the affairs of the local community, and who identified them-

SMITH
FOWLER

502

selves with the nationwide culture group tended to meet the crisis by migrating for a job opportunity.

Workers who were marginal economically as well as socially were more likely to move than were workers in better economic and social positions. For instance, those with the lower job skills, with an education less than high school graduation, those who believed that they had poor chances of getting another job in Buffalo as good as the one they had held in the plant—all tended to be *Movers*. But high plant seniority (ten years or more employment) was not associated with moving. This economic position meant for the worker a community status rather than a tie to the mobile work organization; it was part of the whole constellation of social characteristics which produced a life pattern of stability.

There was also a tendency for workers who obtained their information about income opportunities through the more extensive and the more flexible channels of communication to be more mobile, and *vice versa*. Workers who reported that they would personally canvass for jobs or sell their property to finance the move (both evidences of self-reliance), and those who would rely on social welfare agencies in financial trouble, were more likely to move. However, employment offices and banks were, from the workers' viewpoint, part of a local rather than a regional or national community.

Not every worker was clear in his own mind as to whether he would move or not move. Twenty-nine per cent of those interviewed were, four months after the comany's announcement, still in the Undecided group. This was greater than the per cent who had decided to move (20 per cent). Indecisiveness was associated with several social characteristics which point to a *social structure* of indecision—cross-pressures in the decision-making situation—rather than to confusion or slowness in thinking. Thus, having a *lone* parent or parent-in-law produced higher per cents of Undecided than having no parents in the locality or having the parental couple *intact*. Also, having *all* of one's relatives in Buffalo and, paradoxically, meeting infrequently (less than once a month) with relatives produced comparatively high per cents of Undecided. Identification with a highly solidary ethnic minority in the locality (Polish ancestry on the father's side, and having most or all of one's friends of the paternal nationality), instead of tying the worker unquestionably to the locality, was associated with high per cents of Undecided.

It is also remarkable that an exceptionally stable life pattern was associated with high per cents of Undecided, as evidenced by 15 or more years of residence in Buffalo and by even having lived all of one's life there. On the other hand, none of the various economic factors—seniority, job skill, education, and perceived chances of getting another job in Buffalo as good as the one held in the plant—produced any marked numbers of undecided workers, although most of these economic factors had been associated with either *Movers* or *Stayers*.

The cross-pressures in the social structure of indecision did not lie, then, in contradictory economic opportunities or demands. Cross-pressures occurred as a result of a weakening or breakup of exceptionally strong social ties to the locality. In the Buffalo situation, this probably meant the gradual assimilation of the highly solidary Polish-American group. Likewise, broken parental

Plant Relocation and Worker Migration

503

couples rather than intact ones produced indecision. The category of the undecided worker shows that the conflict between economic and social factors is actually a conflict *within* a social structure which is becoming sufficiently expanded and flexible to take advantage of greater economic opportunities.

E. THE SOCIAL DYNAMICS OF THE DECISION MAKING

By December of 1958, after an unemployment crisis of more than half a year in a severe local recession, 106 workers' families were reinterviewed.[3] Thirty-three per cent had changed their minds. The Undecided had changed mostly in the direction of staying (25 out of 35). Of the 61 *Old Stayers*, only one had changed his mind—and had become a *Mover*. Thus, the social structure of the *Old Stayers* had been a stable one, and their decision had remained stable also; whereas the social structure of the *Undecided* had been a dynamic of cross-pressures which eventually produced a decision in one direction or another rather than permitting them to remain in permanent tension.

In some respects, the economic positions of the *Old* and the *New Stayers* had become similar. Three-quarters of each had been able to find jobs, although often at lower wages (two-thirds of each so reported). In about three-quarters of each group, no other family member had had to go to work, but three-fifths of the families had had to use some of their savings. The decision to remain had been economically possible, but at some economic cost.

In other respects, however, the *New Stayers* were now better off than the *Old Stayers*. Two-thirds reported a job security *better* than the one at the plant, whereas over half of the *Old Stayers* reported it to be *worse*. Correspondingly, nearly half of the *New Stayers* reported a *better* total life situation, whereas almost this same fraction of the *Old Stayers* reported a *worse* one. Thus, the resolution of indecision in the direction of staying had not come about through hopelessness in a deteriorating socioeconomic situation, nor because the *Undecided* had simply been slow to make up their minds, but rather because these people saw their local situation improving. On the other hand, many of the *Old Stayers* reported at least a relative deterioration of their formerly superior socioeconomic situation.

It would seem, then, that an early decision to stay in the community, in the face of local economic crisis, was actually the producer of two different patterns in the work force. On the one hand, there was a superior socioeconomic position which made the decision an economically rational one. On the other hand, there was the well-known poverty pattern: restricted and inflexible social relationships which made rational adaptation difficult or impossible, and the resulting economic deprivation in turn reinforcing the original social relationships.

---

[3] The reinterviewing was done by graduate students at the University of Buffalo School of Social Work (now the State University of New York at Buffalo School of Social Welfare). Taking only the married among the current *Stayers*, there were 84 cases available for analysis, 68 per cent of which were *Old Stayers* and 32 per cent *New Stayers*. *New Stayers* included four cases of former *Movers* who had changed their minds, thereby producing a little statistical contamination in this category.

SMITH
FOWLER

504

F. CONCLUSION

The relocation of the Ford assembly plant from Buffalo, New York, to Lorain, Ohio, furnished a quasi-experimental case for studying worker migration. Not only was the economic "push" standardized for all workers— the loss of their jobs with the same employer at the same time in one locality —but also, the economic "pull" was standardized—a simultaneous offer to all of similar jobs by the same employer in a new locality at such a distance as to require a change of residence. Because individual workers and their families could be interviewed before they moved, it was possible to see worker mobility as a product of decision making rather than as a yielding to inexorable economic forces or an irrational resistance to them.

Worker immobility in the Buffalo case was the result of (1) a value system, as expressed in a life pattern of stability, which made stability an end in itself and predetermined the nonmigration answer when the worker was faced with a problem, (2) social ties and identifications which were locally strong and concentrated rather than diffused over a larger area, and which were not attached to mobile occupational or ethnic primary groups, (3) economic positions which were meaningfully part of a local community pattern rather than part of a regional or national one, (4) channels of communication which were limited and inflexible, so that participation in these social relationships predisposed the workers to a decision to stay when they received economic information through them. An early decision to stay reflected either a good socioeconomic position in the community or else the vicious circle of a poverty pattern. A late decision to stay seemed to reflect an expanding and more flexible set of social relationships which allowed the worker to take advantage of expanding economic opportunities.

However, the workers had a negative attitude toward *this* particular move. Satisfactory income opportunities were being taken from them in the locality, whereas the move offered no better opportunities than the ones they had lost; and, furthermore, the move was from a higher- to a lower-status community. It is possible, therefore, that absolute rather than relative economic improvement, and a style of life in the new community which would raise rather than lower one's status, would have attracted the socially and economically more substantial workers rather than the peripheral ones who in this case seemed to be pushed into the move by virtue of their weak position.

Plant
Relocation
and Worker
Migration

505

Economic Crisis and Expectations of Violence: A Study of Unemployed Negroes*

JOHN C. LEGGETT
DAVID STREET

THE FOCUS

THE rapid mechanization of Southern agriculture and the marked instability of Northern industry have jointly contributed to the formation of extremist beliefs among uprooted Negroes.[1] The presence of a new agricultural technology and the rapid pace of its introduction have revolutionized the cultivation of crops such as cotton and rapidly eliminated jobs hitherto filled by these rural workers. The latter have in many cases attempted to solve the problem of unemployment by moving to industrial towns located in the North, where, until recently, occupational positions demanding few skills and offering union protection have provided many of these immigrants with a standard of living markedly superior to what they had left behind. The 1958 recession threatened these improvements, as a sizable proportion of the Negro labor force became unemployed.

The development of this crisis within the Negro community led to our concern with the initial impact of the 1958 recession as it affected the attitudes of these workers toward (1) the probable consequences of economic depression for the country as a whole and (2) the preferred role of the federal government in the areas of control and ownership of crucial industries. In examining these two subjects, we seek to demonstrate that *severe and widespread economic insecurity within the Negro community engenders the formation of extremist*

* This paper is based upon information reported elsewhere. See John C. Leggett and David Street, "Conflict Response, Detroit Negroes Face Unemployment," an unpublished paper delivered before the 1959 American Sociological Association meetings, and David Street and John C. Leggett, "Economic Deprivation and Extremism: A Study of Unemployed Negroes," *The American Journal of Sociology*, Vol. LXVII (July, 1961), pp. 53-57. The 1960 data were taken from a study of class consciousness conducted by John Leggett and supported largely by the Social Science Research Council.

We wish to thank Gerhard Lenski, Morris Janowitz, Werner Landecker, and R. O. Richards for helpful suggestions.

[1] For a discussion of uprooted workers and several sources of their militancy, see John C. Leggett, "Uprootedness and Working-Class Consciousness," *American Journal of Sociology*, Vol. LXVIII (May, 1963), pp. 682-92.

beliefs, the content of which includes both the probability of violence and the desirability of federal intervention.

The findings of many social scientists indicate that economic insecurity leads to hostility toward the economic order, antagonisms between political groupings, and commitment to political radicalism.[2] At the same time, it should be noted that Marie Lazarsfeld Jahoda and Hans Zeisl's classical study of mass unemployment during the Great Depression found that *long*-term and very widespread unemployment contributed to collective lethargy, political disengagement, and, presumably, a diminution of extremist views.[3] This setting, however, was anything but identical with conditions in Detroit in 1958, since unemployment, however widespread, was as yet *short*-term.

Both theoretical expectations and previous research led to a small, exploratory study of the relationship between economic insecurity and extremist beliefs. The principal settings were depressed segments of a depressed community—two predominantly Negro neighborhoods in Detroit. Both were studied during the summer of 1958. In addition, comparative data are reported from a sample of Detroit blue-collar workmen interviewed during the spring and summer of 1960. At that time, unemployment was considerably less severe.

Within these settings we investigated the conditions under which violence becomes an expected outcome of severe economic crisis. Of course, such views, when they do occur, cannot be equated with readiness to engage in violent behavior. However, the development within a group of a definition of the situation in which sanguinary activities become plausible may well constitute an important precondition for the actual initiation of violence.

PROCEDURE AND EXPECTATIONS

The information on the two neighborhoods was based upon interviews of heads of households selected on a nonrandom, door-to-door basis in May and July, 1958. Our initial aim was to explore the problem within a single neighborhood where there was considerable indigenous political activity and some radical leadership (West Side Neighborhood, $N=40$). Soon after, we decided to repeat the study in a neighborhood matched, as far as possible, on all variables except political activity (East Side Neighborhood, $N=52$).

---

[2] There is considerable material on the relationship between economic insecurity and orientations toward the economic order. For a sampling, see F. A. Rundquist and R. F. Sletto, *Personality in a Depression: A Study in the Measurement of Attitudes* (Minneapolis, Minn.: University of Minnesota Press, 1936); and O. M. Hall, "Attitudes and Unemployment," *Archives of Psychology*, Vol. XXV, No. 165 (1934). Interesting information of political radicalism and economic dislocation can be found in E. W. Bakke, *The Unemployed Man* (New York: E. P. Dutton & Co., Inc., 1934); R. Heberle, *Social Movements* (New York: Appleton-Century-Crofts, Inc., 1951); B. Zawdski and P. F. Lazarsfeld, "The Psychological Consequences of Unemployment," *Journal of Social Psychology*, Vol. VI (1935), pp. 224-51; H. O. Lasswell and D. Blumenstock, *World Revolutionary Propaganda* (New York: Alfred A. Knopf, Inc., 1939); and L. Pope, *Millhands and Preachers* (New Haven, Conn.: Yale University Press, 1942). On attitudes toward violence during periods of economic stress, see Pope, *ibid.*, and A. E. Jones, *Life, Liberty, and Property* (Philadelphia: J. B. Lippincott Co., 1941).

[3] Marie Lazarsfeld Jahoda and Hans Zeisl, *Die Arbeitslosen Von Marienthal* (Leipzig: Verlag Von S. Hirzel, 1933).

Although this new research site did not furnish us with an area wholly free from political organization, we were able to contrast the political activity of the two neighborhoods.

The West Side area was considerably more active than its counterpart on the East Side. The former contained a social club which, in the months just before our interviewing, had added the function of political pressure group to its principal concerns of cleaning up the area and sponsoring recreational and other social activities. This group had joined a score of such clubs in Detroit in order to persuade the governor to declare a moratorium on home-mortgage payments for the unemployed. Three "ex-radicals" residing in the neighborhood were active in the movement, both in the local and the city-wide groups.

The East Side neighborhood had no such club. The interviewers, although sensitized to uncover any evidence of political activity, learned only of discussions initiated by a Jehovah's Witness. These meetings were decidedly political but poorly attended. Although the East Side meetings were said to have had, at the most, an attendance of 25 people, the West Side group organized one political-action meeting which attracted an audience of 300 to 400.

In many ways the two neighborhoods were similar. Internally, both were highly homogeneous. Almost all residents were homeowners or home buyers. In addition, it should be noted that from 75 to 85 per cent of the respondents in both samples were Negroes, the vast majority of whom were born in the South and located in blue-collar, unionized occupations, mainly in auto. From 50 to 60 per cent of the Negroes interviewed in both settings were unemployed or were working part-time. Many of the remainder feared unemployment.

In order to gauge the importance of *lessened* unemployment, 375 male blue-collar residents of the city of Detroit were interviewed in the spring and early summer of 1960. A random-sample procedure was used to select respondents from seven residential districts. Of the 375 interviewed, 120 were Negroes resident in neighborhoods very similar to those studied in 1958. The more recent study, however, was conducted during a period of relative economic prosperity for the community as a whole, although its economic structure was obviously not up to par. The 1957-1958 recession had ended and the percentage of unemployed had dropped from 20 per cent of the total labor force to six per cent in April and May of 1960. However, even though unemployment had declined considerably, many men laid off during the recession had failed to find work after the automobile industry had recovered. The percentage of fully unemployed in the total sample was still 7.7 per cent, whereas among the Negroes it was 13.3 per cent. Unemployment in the Detroit Metropolitan Area at the time ranged between 7.1 and 8.1 per cent of the labor force. In 1958, the comparable figures were between 18 and 19 per cent.[4]

Expectations of violence were gauged by asking the following question:

[4] Information presented on unemployment for the Detroit Metropolitan Area is based upon data gathered by the Michigan Employment Security Commission.

"If a bad depression were to happen, what do you think would happen in this country?" When violence was anticipated, the reply was classified according to the form it was expected to take—either collective (for example, revolution, rioting, civil war) or individuated (for example, killing, robbing, stealing, crime waves).[5]

Previous research suggested the incidence and location of violence expectations within the two neighborhoods. Specifically, predictions to violence should be frequent in both of them, since the two areas had suffered extensive unemployment.[6] We also hoped to demonstrate that the expectation of collective violence would be more prevalent in the neighborhood classified as socially and politically active, for, after all, collective coloration of opinions should correspond with collective activities, particularly when the latter are often guided by left-wingers. In addition, we presumed that unemployed Negroes would take more extreme views than their employed counterparts. Furthermore, we thought that there would be a higher incidence of extremist views among Negroes than whites, since the frequency and consequences of unemployment were more striking in the Negro ghetto than in the white community. Finally, it was hypothesized that these extremist views would be more widely shared among Negroes interviewed in 1958 than in 1960, because unemployment was more severe during the earlier period.

THE SALIENCE OF VIOLENCE

In general, the information gathered supports our predictions. The findings can be summarized as follows: First, a very large percentage of those interviewed in both neighborhoods during 1958 felt that some form of violence

---

[5] In the few cases in which respondents spoke of both kinds of violence, the one mentioned first was treated as the response. Expected outcomes other than violence included "government aid," "much loss of property," "change in parties," "impossible to have," "people will accept it," "industrialists will help the people," and "bad (undifferentiated) consequences."

In the East Side neighborhood, when respondents were asked about the likelihood of a bad depression, 46 per cent of the Negroes felt that it was either imminent or already in progress.

[6] Unemployment, considered by itself, is not the only source of extremist views. Rather, it would seem that several interrelated conditions common to many industrial towns facilitate the formation of militant opinions: (1) denial of full-employment opportunity to many workmen, (2) spatial concentration of large numbers of these and other workers, and (3) their informal and formal channels of communication. The modern industrial community operates to create medium and high levels of working-class unemployment, as firms continue to use the age-old practices of discharging and laying off many workmen when markets contract, plants mechanize, factories relocate, and businesses fail. At the same time, the community functions so as to concentrate large numbers of both employed and unemployed workmen in relatively small, culturally homogeneous residential districts. A population density and homogeneity of this sort facilitate discussion between workers who share common problems, particularly in the area of employment opportunity and retention. Interaction along these lines is certainly prevalent within many Negro residential districts. There, neighborhood organizations often deal with class and race questions, such as unemployment, educational facilities, and similar matters. In many instances, however, discussions among workers who later become unemployed may occur within the confines of work groups and unions which are racially mixed. Under these circumstances, racial heterogeneity and associated interracial hostility no doubt curtail, but certainly fail to eliminate, activities which generate a militant point of view.

Economic
Crisis
and
Expectations
of Violence:
A Study
of Unemployed
Negroes

would occur if and when a bad depression took place. Sixty-three per cent of the West Side Negroes and 57 per cent of the East Side Negroes expected violence. Second, on the West Side, 35 per cent of them predicted *collective* instances while 28 per cent mentioned *individuated* forms. The less organized neighborhood provided an interesting but not unexpected reversal among Negro respondents: 22 per cent foresaw collective and 36 per cent referred to individuated patterns of violence. Third, the Negro unemployed studied in 1958 proved to be singularly concerned with its occurrence. On the West Side, 71 per cent of the unemployed, as opposed to 53 per cent of the employed, expected violence. The same pattern occurred among the East Side Negroes, although the percentage differences were not so great. Fourth, the Negroes were more likely than the whites to expect violence, except among the unemployed interviewed in 1960. Finally, it should be noted that the Negro and white workmen studied during the latter period were less inclined to expect violent acts than were those observed in 1958.[7]

EXTREMIST RESPONSES

Many replies to our question were notable for their strident quality:

"There would be a tremendous crime wave."

"Widespread riots, people would be out after hunger and clothes (*sic*). Those with money won't be very comfortable."

"Don't know, but I think they'd rob, steal, and kill for food."

"I don't want to think about it. If we had a depression, people starving and ragged, don't know what might happen, maybe a revolution."

"I think people might turn Communist. They'd look for a different way of living."

"There'll be a lot of hungry people—there's no telling what a hungry person would do. They could do *anything*—if he doesn't *get* something he'll *take* something. Right now there's a lot more robbery."

"We won't have no country. There'll be fighting, stealing, starving. No one will have no chance. Not even the rich man."

"Everyone would lose everything they've got, and might revolt. Not the head people, of course, but people like around here—they've got something to lose now. There've been good times over twenty years. They have cars, houses, homes now, and so they'll miss them if they lose them. When many are hungry, they're liable to do anything."

"There'd be destruction by the people, breaking into homes, they'd rob banks. Some guys with jobs would be scared to walk home. There would be a civil war between the rich and poor. They'd kick the shit out of some of these people."

"It may be called a revolution. If he gets hungry, he won't stand for it. The young people won't take it. They will steal. A lot of them steal now because they aren't working."

"I'm almost scared to say. So many things could happen. . . . The younger generation won't take it; a lot of bad things would happen. Couldn't hardly go out

[7] For a more detailed statement of the findings, see David Street and John C. Leggett, *op. cit.*, pp. 55-56.

of their doors. In fact, they might have a war here in the U.S. People are used to a good way of living. Every time you pick up a paper, you hear about robbery and killing. Take me. I got kids, think I'm going to let them go hungry? Even the welfare won't give you anything. This is the first time I've ever been out of a job. I've always worked. I don't know what I'll do when my compensation runs out. People got homes and cars now, and they aren't going to stand around and lose them. Take this place. I just bought it. I haven't got enough paint to paint it. Have to use my money to feed my kids."

"Could not be nothing but a war. The people would start fighting because people have to have something to feed their family on. I know I would. If things don't pick up, God knows what will happen. If they don't stop this discrimination there is going to be a civil war. A man is a man; that's all I think about it."

"The poor would be trying to get food and things and the rich would try to keep theirs."

"Oh hot! Everybody would get a ball bat and start swinging!"

AN ADDITIONAL CONSIDERATION

Views such as these may be correlated with militant attitudes regarding governmental intervention in the economy. In other words, we expected a consistency in outlook. In order to test this notion, all of those interviewed in the East Side neighborhood were asked a series of questions dealing with the desirability of governmental intervention. On the basis of their replies, the *attitudes* of those interviewed were ordered so as to distinguish degree of approval of all governmental action, ranging from those which indicated disapproval of such activity to those which favored extensive governmental participation in economic affairs, including its ownership of all industries.[8] Among Negroes, it was found that a disproportionately large number of unemployed or part-time employed respondents who favored considerable intervention also expected violent consequences in the event of a bad depression. These findings strongly suggest that *during periods of marked economic distress, lack of full-employment opportunity helps to create a crystallization of radical beliefs among workmen located within a ghettoized group which has experienced a modicum of prosperity.*

CONCLUDING REMARKS

Our study of economic crisis and extremist views has noted certain predictable relationships. However, because of the nonrandomness and rather small size of the 1958 neighborhood samples, any conclusions drawn must be tentative. Nevertheless, it would be foolish to ignore the implications of our findings for the current behavior of American Negroes. During the present period, tens of thousands of them are engaging in forms of direct action designed to improve their economic lot. Oddly enough, violence has seldom been initiated by Negroes involved in their liberation movement, although this predilection

---

[8] A series of questions used to measure attitudes toward government intervention in the economy formed a Guttman scale. The latter's coefficient of reproduceability was .95, and the Menzel coefficient was .81.

may stem largely from tactical considerations rather than felt predispositions. Indeed, our findings strongly suggest that not a few Negroes are prepared to engage in collective violence if and when the occasion merits such participation.

Sociological Perspectives in Unemployment Research*

LOUIS A. FERMAN

THIS is an attempt to sketch in very rough form some problems of sociological relevance in unemployment research. Two basic assumptions underlie this paper: (1) *unemployment is not simply an economic problem but involves a number of noneconomic considerations;* and (2) *future research in unemployment will increasingly utilize the concepts and tools of a variety of social sciences.* Studies of unemployment in the 1958 and 1960 recessions largely emphasized unemployment as an economic problem, and few attempts were made to relate unemployment to kinship structure, work values, mental health, community structure, and mass social movements. The sociological and psychological studies of unemployment made by Bakke,[1] Komarovsky,[2] Lazarsfeld,[3] and Angell[4] during the 1930's were largely ignored in the research concerns of the 1950's and early 1960's. Two exceptions were the studies of displaced automobile workers in Detroit and Buffalo.[5,6] In the latter studies, some attempt was made to go beyond traditional economic problems and to deal with sociological factors in unemployment.

Although the field of unemployment research is still young, an impressive body of data has been accumulated on the mobility patterns of unemployed workers, the dynamics of finding a job after becoming unemployed, and the

---

*I should like to extend my appreciation to Professors Guy L. Swanson and Charles Rehmus who read an early version of this paper and made a number of valuable suggestions. My gratitude is also expressed to the Institute of Labor and Industrial Relations, University of Michigan—Wayne State University—and especially to its co-directors, Ronald W. Haughton and Charles Rehmus, for the support and encouragement given to me in this work.
[1] E. Wight Bakke, *Citizens Without Work* (New Haven, Conn.: Yale University Press, 1940).
[2] Mirra Komarovsky, *The Unemployed Man and His Family* (New York: Holt, Rinehart & Winston, Inc., 1940).
[3] Philip Eisenberg and Paul Lazarsfeld, "The Psychological Effects of Unemployment," *Psychological Bulletin,* Vol. XXXV (1938).
[4] Robert Cooley Angell, *The Family Encounters the Depression* (New York: Charles Scribner's Sons, 1936).
[5] Harold L. Sheppard, Louis A. Ferman, and Seymour Faber, *Too Old to Work—Too Young to Retire: A Case Study of a Permanent Plant Shutdown* (Washington, D.C.: United States Printing Office, 1960).
[6] Irving Fowler and Luke M. Smith, *Ford Relocation Follow-up Study* (Unpublished data on file in the School of Social Work, University of Buffalo, Buffalo, N.Y.) 1957.

correlates of unemployment. This "piling up" of data has been one of the most striking trends in unemployment research since 1940. For the most part, these data have been descriptive statements or statistical summaries with few attempts at intensive analysis. We know that large numbers of the blue-collar unemployed are geographically immoble, but we have yet to discover the dynamics and social processes that account for this. We know that, frequently, unemployed workers refuse jobs, but their motives for doing so remain a mystery. Unemployment seems psychologically to incapacitate some workers while other workers are able to deal with unemployment problems. There is no doubt that when an analysis of these questions is made, sociological and psychological schema will play a prominent role.

It is beyond the scope of this paper to suggest or to develop a comprehensive sociological framework that may be useful in such analysis. My presentation will be limited to a discussion of a number of unemployment problems which can be studied through the use of sociological concepts.

FAMILY STRUCTURE AND UNEMPLOYMENT

Unemployment is a family rather than an individual experience. The loss of employment may affect the family in a number of different ways. A reduction in purchasing power may be felt by all members of a family and frustrate certain needs and wants. It may mean a realignment of family responsibilities as the worker's spouse or children enter the labor market. There may be changes in the frequency and kind of contact with kin outside of the immediate household. Unemployment may also affect the prestige of family members in the eyes of the community and reduce the opportunities for certain kinds of social participation.

These relationships between unemployment and family structure have been generally recognized but rarely studied in any systematic research. Komarovsky,[7] Bakke,[8] and Angell[9] did study the relationship between unemployment and family structure in the 1930's, but these studies had a limited research emphasis. These investigators emphasized the isolated patriarchal family with centralized authority as the prototype of the unemployed American family. Attention was focused on the male head of the family and the problem of maintaining his authority in the face of a diminished economic role. Almost completely neglected was the impact of unemployment on the matriarchal, extended family, where the locus of decision making and authority may not coincide with the status of the chief male breadwinner. It is hard to imagine that the authority structure of a Negro family, such as that described by Lorraine Hansberry in *Raisin in the Sun,* would be in jeopardy if the chief male breadwinner lost his job. The pattern of authority in such a family flows around and past the male breadwinners and is only incidentally influenced by them.

There are two aspects of the unemployment problem which may be

---

[7] Komarovsky, *op. cit.*
[8] Bakke, *op. cit.*
[9] Angell, *op. cit.*

markedly affected by the family structure. The most important of these is the degree to which an individual's ties to his extended family enable him to weather the problems of unemployment. The second aspect takes in the differences in adjustment to unemployment required by families at different points in the family life cycle. Let us discuss each of these in turn:

In the United States, most individuals have family relationships which extend beyond the members of the immediate household. There has been some disagreement as to the existence of an extended family and the importance of these relationships for the individual. It has been argued that an industrial society demands high geographical and occupational mobility and must discourage intense, extended family bonds. This results in a series of isolated nuclear families. Recent research findings in contempory family structure, however, have contradicted this picture of isolated nuclear families.[10] For some individuals, relatives were indicated to be the most important informal group in cities and were important to the individual as a source of companionship and support. Litwak has proposed the emergence of a modified extended family type which differed from the classical extended family in that the new type consisted of a series of nuclear families joined together on an equalitarian basis for mutual aid but lacking a single authority head, geographical propinquity, or occupational dependence.[11]

The influence of extended family relationships on the unemployed worker may be considerable. Relatives may be a source of affective support and functional aid in meeting the problems of unemployment. In cases where the unemployed worker's elders or in-laws have key roles in maintaining contact within the extended family and provide ritualized opportunities for security and recognition, the emotional impact of unemployment may not be so severe. Such contacts may be particularly influential in offsetting the effects of disappointments and frustrations in the search for a new job.

Besides providing a stable social environment and affective support, relatives may aid the unemployed worker by functional aid—financial loans; job leads; care of the children when both spouses are absent from the household; or the loan of an automobile for the job search. These services may act as evidence of affective support and at the same time can shorten the period of unemployment. The important consideration is that the unemployed worker has open to him a reservoir of informal services to supplement the aids from official community agencies. His range of alternatives in obtaining aid is never completely limited by the impersonal standards and requirements of community aid programs.

Extended family relationships may influence the re-employment opportunities and geographical mobility of the unemployed worker. It is clear from a number of research efforts that the worker relies more on his friends and relatives than on formal agencies for job leads, and that such job leads are

---

[10] Eugene Litwak, "The Use of Extended Family Groups in the Achievement of Social Goals: Some Political Implications," *Social Problems*, Vol. VII, No. 3 (Winter, 1959–1960), pp. 177–87.

[11] Angell, *op. cit.*

frequently successful.[12] The efficacy of these informal job leads may be explained by the fact that friends and relatives have a higher awareness of existing and impending job openings through their own work experiences. This awareness can often be supplemented by intimate knowledge of working conditions and supervisory-worker relations in a particular business organization. There can be no doubt that these informal relationships are linked to opportunities for re-employment.

Whether an unemployed worker decides to move from his immediate labor market and seek a job elsewhere may also be influenced by extended family relationships. In his present location, the unemployed worker may feel that he has a fund of affective and functional resources that will not be available to him if he moves. The decision to move is not simply a function of differential job opportunities. The presence and promise of support from relatives may permit the worker to remain in a labor market where there are few opportunities for employment. Certainly other factors may contribute to immobility (for example, home ownership), but one cannot deny the influence of extended family relationships.

This discussion suggests the need for an intensive study of unemployment against the background of extended family relationships. Some suggestive questions are the following: Does frequent contact with the extended family affect the adjustment to unemployment? If so, in what ways? Are there any particular status roles within the extended family that exert an influence in adjusting to the loss of work? What specific affective satisfactions and functional services result from contact between the unemployed worker and his relatives? It is clear that an answer to these questions requires both a greater understanding of extended family structure and specific knowledge of relationships between the unemployed and their relatives.

Family structure may affect unemployment behavior in another way. The family at different points in the family life cycle will be required to make different adjustments. Geographical mobility, for example, may be less of a problem for the family of a young unemployed worker than for the family of a middle-aged unemployed worker. The latter may be more hesitant about moving because he has established strong psychological and social ties in the community; owns a home; or has children quite advanced in school. For his family, a move would pose considerably more difficulties than for younger families.

There are at least four ways in which the family life cycle may affect unemployment behavior: (a) the availability of family members to enter the labor market to relieve financial pressures, (b) receptivity to retraining programs, (c) availability of affective support and functional aid from relatives, and (d) extent of economic resources to blunt the impact of unemployment.

The number of family members who can enter the job market will vary at different points in the family life cycle. The newly married couple may both

---

[12] William Haber, Louis A. Ferman, and James Hudson, *The Impact of Technological Change* (Kalamazoo, Michigan: W. E. Upjohn Institute For Employment Research) March, 1963, pp. 29–30.

work without the necessity of diverting time and energies for the care of children. The coming of children may take the wife out of the labor market periodically or permanently. In the middle years, the wife may re-enter the labor market and be joined by one or more children. In the later years, the family may lose the income from the children as they marry and leave the family. In this last case, financial responsibilities may be shifted back completely to one or both of the spouses. The availability of family members for employment to relieve the pressures of unemployment will vary.

It should also be noted that the compromise and shifting of family responsibilities to enter the labor market will vary with points in the family life cycle. Where there are young children in the household, there must be some calculation of cost relative to income in providing substitute care. The female spouse may find that this will limit her job possibilities to part-time work, especially when her presence may be required in the household at specific times. Compromises may be worked out where the husband assumes some of her duties in the household or where some of the responsibilities are shifted to the older children. It is possible that each set of compromises generates particular tensions, and the latter will vary with the points in the family life cycle when unemployment occurs.

Receptivity to state, federal, and community retraining programs will vary with points in the family life cycle. The unemployed worker with a wife and a number of dependent children may feel that family obligations demand that he spend his time actively seeking work rather than in a retraining program, especially if the retraining period is going to mean a considerable reduction in income for him. A younger worker or an older worker with few family obligations may not see retraining as posing such hardships. In some cases, there may be some hesitancy in moving from some financial aid program (for example, unemployment compensation or public welfare) to retraining, because the latter offers less financial support and the family may experience hardship as a result.

There is some evidence to indicate that contact with the extended family (relatives) decreases as the family ages.[13] The newly married couple has more frequent contacts with kin than does the family with grown children or the family with spouses in their later years. The significance of these findings is that opportunities for affective support and functional aid would seem to be optimal in the "new family" and minimal in the "older family." The chances, then, for the unemployed to gain affective support and functional aid from the extended family would vary with points in the family life cycle.

Finally, it seems likely that "older families" may be in a better position than "young families" to weather the financial threats of unemployment. A family at a late point in the family life cycle is more likely than other families in the same economic stratum to have economic resources to blunt the impact of unemployment. The economic demands for subsistence may be considerably

---

[13] I am indebted to Michael T. Aiken, Department of Sociology, University of Wisconsin, for this information. Kin contact was highest for newlyweds, decreased in the middle years of the family, and was lowest in the older years of the family. A full discussion of family life cycle and kin contact in Detroit will be found in his forthcoming doctoral thesis, "Kinship in an Urban Community" (The University of Michigan, 1964).

less than in the families with young children. The "older family" is also more likely than other families to have savings, other sources of income (for example, investments or rental property), and a learned capacity to budget and manage economic resources in a period of economic crisis. These resources may give these families an advantage in dealing with problems of unemployment.

WORK VALUES AND UNEMPLOYMENT

Whether unemployment experiences influence attitudes toward work and the "will to work" is not known. There is no doubt that prolonged unemployment may have negative consequences for the worker: loss of income, loss of feelings of personal worth, and loss of authority in the family. The relationship between these effects and attitudes toward work or belief in the worthwhileness of work has not, as yet, been systematically studied.[14]

One point that would have to be considered in such a study is that workers may achieve some gain from an unemployment status and thus prefer unemployment to re-employment. The worker may be under less pressure from creditors when he is unemployed than when he is working. While working, the worker who has not met his financial obligations may be under the constant threat of garnishment of wages. While he is unemployed, the worker is insulated from this threat: first, by the loan company's reluctance to press for payment when money is scarce, and second, by the legal sanctions which forbid garnishment of relief payments. Going back to work may not be viewed with enthusiasm if it brings about a recurrence of these financial pressures.

The worker may also find other advantages in being unemployed. Receiving a regular payment from a state agency (unemployment compensation or public welfare payments) makes economic expenditures and payments more predictable. While working, income may fluctuate owing to periodic unemployment or underemployment. Landlords very often express satisfaction with the unemployment status of their tenants, since it means regular payments of rent direct from the government agency. Shopkeepers may also extend credit readily to the unemployed because (a) the dole is considered more *predictable* and *regular* income than income from work; and (b) relief checks are administered through the woman in the household, who is regarded as being more dependable in paying bills.

What is suggested here is that, far from placing new pressures on the worker, unemployment may actually provide a relief from certain pressures and permit a more predictable existence through state aid. The relevance of this thesis to a discussion of work values among the unemployed is obvious. Sociological investigation must recognize the unintended consequences of an unemployment status and the significance of these consequences in problems of re-employment as well as of unemployment.

There have been some recent statements about a "culture of unemployment," where the unemployed stress nonwork values and the negation of the

---

[14] A study of the work values of unemployed workers has been undertaken by Dr. Jesse Pitts and myself.

worthwhileness of work as a meaningful social activity. The logical consequences of this thesis is to suggest that today there exists a social grouping resistant to job opportunities, willing to accept an unemployment status as a way of life, and largely committed to values which deny the utility of employment. This is an interesting thesis and deserves comment.

As Hylan Lewis has noted, present-day social science abounds with the uncritical and loose usage of the culture concept.[15] There is reference to a "culture of the uninvolved," to a "culture of violence," and to a "culture of poverty." The term *culture* is widely applied to numerous dimensions and components of aggregates, groups, and persons. One common fallacy is to confuse *culture* with *class*. In a *culture* context, we speak of norms and values which regulate behavior in some form of *organized social grouping*. In a *class* context, we refer to certain attitudes and motives that are common to a *category of individuals* sharing the same life chance or economic resources.

Granted that many people have a particular experience and reach certain conclusions about it, these conclusions may not be normative in any customary sense. *Normative behavior* is behavior that is prescribed and made obligatory in a given group. It is learned through specific socialization mechanisms in the group. *Class behavior*, on the other hand, is a function of sharing like experiences, but it is not prescriptive or obligatory in the sense that cultural behavior is. It is one thing to say that workers in a particular work group engage in organized restriction of output, and quite another to say that workers who see overproduction as a threat to their continued employment restrict their production. In the first case, we refer to individuals who are in an organized social grouping and who share prescriptive, obligatory behavior. In the second case, we refer to individuals who are in a given category and who have given a common reaction to the same experience. In the same way, we may confuse different behavior patterns of the unemployed. When Allison Davis spoke of "underprivileged worker" attitudes and behavior, he was referring to class behavior, not cultural behavior.[16]

It seems to me that this is one of the problems of an "unemployment culture" thesis. It would have to be demonstrated that such values and attitudes arise out of a definite, organized social grouping rather than being derivatives of a life-chance situation; that there were definite mechanisms for the socialization of these values; and that a system of rewards and punishments existed to reinforce such values.

The other problem associated with the thesis concerns a specification of unemployment. The unemployed of today are not a homogeneous population, but contain a number of types. The "technologically displaced" is one category of unemployed, the "hard-core unemployed" is another, and the young people entering the labor market for the first time and unable to find jobs constitute still another category. It would seem that the "culture of unemployment" thesis would be most applicable to the "hard-core" category, if it, indeed, fits

[15] Hylan Lewis, "Culture, Class and the Behavior of Low Income Families," unpublished paper presented for the Conference on Lower Class Culture, Barbizon Plaza Hotel, New York City; June, 1963, pp. 3-4.

[16] Allison Davis, "The Motivation of the Underprivileged Worker," in *Industry and Society*, ed. W. F. Whyte (New York: McGraw-Hill Book Company, 1946), pp. 84-106.

FERMAN

518

any of the categories. If this is the case, then the thesis must be limited to certain unemployment problems and cannot be applied indiscriminately to unemployment in general.

The importance of an inquiry into work values among the unemployed is undeniable. But such an inquiry would need to consider some of the points raised above.

MENTAL HEALTH AND UNEMPLOYMENT

The concern with the mental health of unemployed workers dates back to the work of Bakke,[17] Komarovsky,[18] Lazarsfeld and Zawdski,[19] and Angell[20] in the 1930's. Their concern was not with the incidence of classical forms of mental illness, but rather with questions of maintaining self-esteem, ability to make plans for the future, and competence to deal with interpersonal tensions in the family. There has not been any attempt to test or extend their findings on the unemployed of the 1950's and 1960's. One consequence of this has been a tendency of the part of researchers and popular writers to make inferences about the emotional problems of the unemployed today using the research findings of 30 years ago.

There are several reasons to believe that the mental-health problems of unemployed workers today are different from those of the unemployed workers of the 1930's. The first point to consider here is the nature of unemployment today as against unemployment in the 1930's. Whereas the depression of the 1930's was characterized by widespread national unemployment, the recessions of the 1950's and 1960's have been characterized by "islands of unemployment." The majority of the unemployed are concentrated in specific geographical areas: Michigan, West Virginia, and Pennsylvania. At the same time, the national economy has continued to grow, with employment and gross national product at an all-time high.

The unemployed of the 1930's were part of a national economic crisis, and it was assumed that new economic growth would remedy unemployment. Although his life-work pattern had been disrupted, the unemployed worker could hopefully look ahead to a resumption of work once the economy began to move again. It is far different in the unemployment of today. The technologically displaced worker cannot resume his work career without a period of retraining, and even this may not guarantee him a job. The youngster who enters the labor market finds himself cut off from a number of job opportunities because his educational and training background have not prepared him for a job in the new technology. For these workers, economic growth will have little effect on job opportunities. The emotional problems of these workers who see no clear-cut solution to their unemployment will undoubtedly be different from the emotional problems experienced by unemployed workers in the 1930's.

---

[17] Bakke, *op. cit.*

[18] Komarovsky, *op. cit.*

[19] Bohan Zawadski and Paul Lazarsfeld, "Psychological Consequences of Unemployment," *Journal of Social Psychology*, Vol. VI (1935), pp. 224-51.

[20] Angell, *op. cit.*

We must also consider that changes in the norms and structure of the American family over the past 30 years which will make a difference in the type of emotional problems among the unemployed today in contrast to the unemployed of the 1930's. The increase in the number of working wives suggests that family responsibility and authority may not be so highly centralized today as in the 1930's. The democratic ethic which pervades the modern American family may mean a greater emotional stability of the family unit than in the family of the 1930's. The loss of functions of the family over the years may mean fewer interpersonal tensions, because affective and functional needs can be fulfilled through other institutional activities.

The social and political climate of the times must also be considered as a relevant factor in the mental health of unemployed workers. In the 1930's, a number of mass social movements developed which permitted the unemployed to express their frustrations and resentments by blaming the political and economic system for their troubles. The 1950's and 1960's have not been characterized by such opportunities to externalize resentment. This has been an age of the discouragement of political and economic dissent. The advent of McCarthyism and the Cold War has stifled the development of radical ideologies or social movements through which the unemployed could express their resentment. It might well be that, in the absence of such movements, the unemployed of the 1960's have resorted to mechanisms of self-blame to deal with frustration. This would certainly be a problem worthy of investigation.

These remarks suggest the need for a re-evaluation of the emotional problems of the unemployed today. Our perspectives must not be limited by the research findings of the 1930's, but must develop from intensive empirical investigation of the present situation.

COMMUNITY POWER STRUCTURE AND UNEMPLOYMENT

Unemployment does not occur in a vacuum, but always within a specific geographical setting. The economist recognizes this fact in the use of the labor-market concept. He refers to a specific land area dominated by a given industrial complex and labor force. The sociologist has been slow to recognize the utility of the community concept, and particularly the community power structure, in the study of unemployment.

A number of problems of unemployment are directly related to the power structure of a community. We can recognize that decisions to close plants or to relocate them elsewhere may be a result of power relationships in a community. The absentee owner has relatively little compunction about closing a plant if business logic dictates it. The local owner, especially if he is involved in the community, does not find it as easy to make such a decision. He must balance business logic against his loss of social standing and influence in the community. The relocation of new plants in the community may also be related to problems of community power relationships. Businessmen speak of a community providing a favorable "climate for business." It is clear that economic factors are only part of the total considerations which enter into the "climate for business." The businessman may be concerned with the relative participation of labor unions in community decisions; the willingness of community influentials to press for tax concessions; the extent to which his company will fit in with the existing industrial pattern; the receptivity of other business leaders in the community to the new firm. These social facts will influence not only the level of unemployment in the community but also the facility with which the community is able to provide new employment opportunities.

Community structure can influence the rate of recovery from unemployment in other ways. The community influentials may be only segmentally involved in the industrial problems of the community. This may be particularly true of service communities, where the emphasis is on the retail and wholesale trade with a hinterland and not on the industrial units in the community. The community leaders may divert few resources to deal with problems of job displacement or retraining in the industrial sector. In such cases, the burden for solutions and programs falls on state agencies. The latter may be relatively ineffective because of their remoteness from the scene. Research findings indicate that community effectiveness in dealing with problems of unemployment varies from community to community. Some communities mobilize a number of resources quickly and efficiently, although others do relatively little.

Communities also differ in their receptivity to state and federal aid in dealing with the problems of unemployment. Hawley has indicated that the occupational structure of a community relates to the acceptance or rejection of urban renewal funds from the federal government.[21] Area Redevelopment Administration loans are predicated on a minimum mobilization of local resources, and apparently there is considerable variation in communities in meeting these minimum requirements.[22] There is some evidence that communities dominated by large, absentee-owned industrial units, such as Detroit and Pittsburgh, are less able to generate support on the local level for these federal aid programs.[23]

It would be desirable to specify the factors in community structure which account for these differences between communities in unemployment problems. We can do this by: (1) studying community reaction to unemployment in a number of different community structures and (2) analyzing the census data for communities that have differed in mobilizing community support for federal aid programs. There is no doubt that this could prove to be a very productive area of sociological investigation into unemployment.

MASS SOCIAL MOVEMENTS AND UNEMPLOYMENT

It is important to note that *the* social movement of the 1960's—the Negro movement toward equality—may be closely related to present-day unemployment problems. In an age when genuine dissent and protest movements are

[21] Amos H. Hawley, "Community Power and Urban Renewal Success," *American Journal of Sociology*, Vol. LXVIII, No. 4, pp. 422-31.
[22] I am indebted for this information to several staff members of the Area Redevelopment Administration in the Department of Commerce.
[23] This finding was reported by Dr. Benjamin Chinitz of the University of Pittsburgh in a paper prepared for the Special Seminar on Problems of the Large Industrial City held at Inglis House, The University of Michigan, February 12, 1962.

Sociological
Perspectives
in
Unemployment
Research

rare, it is significant that the only social movement of note is dominated by members of a social category with the highest rate of unemployment. The links between unemployment and the Negro mass-protest movement of the 1960's are surely worthy of study.

Two points on this subject deserve comment. The first is the question of the relative importance of economic deprivation to the Negro social movements. Becker has indicated that among unemployed German youth in the thirties the degree of economic deprivation was related to the level of class consciousness—the greater the degree of economic deprivation, the higher the level of class consciousness.[24] This may be an important insight into the enthusiasm for sit-ins, boycotts, and street demonstrations shown by Negro workers. It would be important, however, to show how *various* Negro movements may stem from economic deprivation and how others may result from other factors (for example, religious motives).

The second point has to do with the consequences of these movements. Given that strong Negro movements have developed in the sixties, what does this mean for the unemployed Negro? How much will be gained, and at the possible expense of what other groups in society? Negro youth will have achieved a greater opportunity for jobs at a time when the competition for jobs is increasing largely as a result of the impact of technological change and high birth rates in the forties. Will Negro success spark a series of social movements among other groups who will feed deprived or threatened by this development? Unemployed Negro youth of today have an opportunity for the release of frustrations and tensions stemming from unemployment experiences that is not open to unemployed white youth. What consequences will these differential opportunities for affective release have among Negroes and whites? We cannot answer these questions at this time.

CONCLUDING REMARKS

We are only now becoming aware that the unemployment of the last decade may not be a temporary phenomenon and that it differs in many important respects from the unemployment of the thirties. This awareness should make us question and possibly reconsider some of the long-accepted findings in the field. Implicit in this paper is the thesis that a proper understanding of unemployment problems involves a persistent refusal to indulge in oversimplified and stereotyped notions about unemployment. There are no ways to answer the questions raised in this paper other than through rigorous field investigations of the unemployed of today. Only through updating our knowledge will we be able to formulate meaningful social policies to deal with the economic and human distresses of unemployment.

---

[24] Howard Becker, *German Youth: Bond or Free* (London: Kegan Paul, Trench, Trubner and Co., Ltd., 1946).

Further Thoughts on Reform*

S. M. MILLER

WE are increasingly moving into a dual economy in which the main economy of the United States is characterized by the provision of high standards of living, somewhat stable employment, and other rewards for those who are able to stay in it. On the other hand, the marginal economy is centered around low-level service trades and occupations, peopled by individuals of low skill who are from minority groups or left-over immigrant populations, receiving relatively little of what the economy is producing, especially in regard to housing amenities. Those in the marginal economy frequently are unable to get jobs; when they do work, wages are low. (Twelve per cent of all those receiving welfare assistance in New York City, including the aged, are in families whose head is employed. The pay of these heads of households is inadequate to support their families.) Moreover, job insecurity is great, and individuals are frequently unemployed for considerable periods of time. In this kind of colonial situation of a successful "white economy" and a meager "bush economy," there are wide disparities; furthermore, gains in the main economy do not rapidly trickle down to those in what Harrington has called the "other America."

The high profits, high productivity, and high wages of the affluent economy have limited effects on those in the marginal economy. Indeed, increasing productivity has meant that many are being squeezed out of the affluent economy (for example, auto workers in Detroit who are permanently laid off despite the high production of cars). Those who can make the affluent economy —and making it depends largely upon education—do relatively well. Those who live in the marginal economy do not automatically progress with the gains of the affluent economy. This segmentation within the economy accentuates inequality.[1]

---

* This essay is part of a larger chapter entitled "Poverty, Race and Politics" in Irving L. Horowitz, ed., *The New Sociology: Essays on Social Values and Social Theory in Honor of C. Wright Mills* (New York: Oxford University Press, 1964).

[1] Increases in employment in the various governmental levels are becoming the important source of new jobs in the economy. This has been especially true for Negroes who in recent years have had to rely on governmental jobs as a source of employment. The important work of Oscar Ornati and his associates at the New School for Social Research will report these developments in detail.

In economically undeveloped societies, the rise of a middle class is expected to mitigate the extreme variation in standards of living in the society. In present-day United States, the expansion of what Mills emphasized was a new middle class is no longer reducing the size of the poor class. In some ways, the growing affluence of the upper and middle classes is increasing the *relative deprivation* of the poor.

The great decline in poverty took place during World War II. Since then, the rate of decline in the percentage who are poor has sharply slackened. There has actually been an increase since 1949 in the concentration of wealth assets owned by the upper one per cent.[2] This important finding has been ignored in the stress on Kuznets' debated conclusion that the concentration of income in the hands of the upper one per cent has decreased. The end of the war and the postwar boom have meant that economic forces which reduced income inequality are no longer effective. The income advantage of the "diploma elite" over those who have only "some college," have secured high school diplomas, or are school dropouts is increasing. The income spread between skilled workers and the unskilled, which was narrowed during this century, is beginning to widen. Upper-level blue-collar workers, who were improving relative to lower-level white-collar workers, are now losing ground to these white-collar groupings. And the lower-level white-collar occupations are falling behind the upper white-collar occupations.[3]

The inability of our economic system in recent years to sustain a high level of economic activity and to provide jobs for the growing labor force indicates that the optimistic hopes following the war are no longer well-based. The sputtering of our economic system has been reflected in rising unemployment and the maintenance of a large group in poverty.

UNEMPLOYMENT

In World War II the percentage of the labor force who were unemployed was reduced drastically. The concept of "unemployables" was disregarded. Many who had not been able to work for a long period, and perhaps regarded themselves as unable to perform on a job, discovered that their abilities and effort were needed.

A period of high employment demand is a situation where poverty is rapidly reduced because of the functioning of the economic market. When the economy is not geared to this level of production and activity, many people

---

[2] Robert J. Lampman, *The Share of Top Wealth-Holders in National Wealth, 1922-56*, National Bureau of Economic Research (Princeton, N.J.: Princeton University Press, 1962), p. 24.

[3] I have discussed various aspects of these issues in "Youth and the Changing Society," *Journal of Social Issues,* forthcoming, and in "Poverty and Inequality in America: Implications for the Social Services," *Child Welfare,* November, 1963. See also S. M. Miller, Carolyn Comings, and Betty Saleem, *The School Dropout Problem: Syracuse* (Albany: New York State Division for Youth and the Syracuse University Youth Development Center, 1963), p. 8; S. M. Miller and Martin Rein, "Poverty, Inequality, and Social Change;" *American Child,* Vol. 46, March, 1964, pp. 10-15.

are thrown on the unemployment scrap heap. They face long periods of unemployment and frequently find themselves described after a while as and may believe themselves to be "unemployable." A conclusion to draw from this is that we need sustained economic growth, high production, and high employment in order to solve many of the problems of the unemployed and the poor today in America.

The Meaning of Work and Adjustment to Retirement*

HERMAN J. LOETHER

THE older worker in contemporary American society finds himself on the horns of a cultural dilemma. At an early age he learns that the worth of a man is measured in terms of his ability to find a job, work steadily at it, and make a success of it. Again and again he is reminded of this fact. However, when he reaches the age of retirement, he is expected to refrain from working—to take it easy and enjoy his "twilight" years. He is expected to change his whole orientation from one of work to one of nonwork.

American society is a work-oriented society. The most important role which the average man plays in his lifetime is his occupational role. It is his occupational role which anchors him to his society. Morse and Weiss[1] asked a national sample of employed men whether they would continue to work even though they inherited enough money to live comfortably without working. Eighty per cent said that they would continue to work. Nearly two-thirds of them gave positive reasons for wanting to continue. They gave such reasons as the following: to keep occupied, to keep interested, work is good for a person, to keep healthy, to justify one's existence, work gives one a feeling of self-respect. The authors conclude,

> The typical employed man does not *at present* have alternative ways of directing his energy and internal resources and does not *at present* have alternative ways of gaining a sense of relationship to his society which are sufficiently important to take the place of working.[2]

* This study was supported by a grant from the National Science Foundation administered by the Faculty Grant and Research Committee of Los Angeles State College. The author wishes to acknowledge the cooperation of the Alumni Employees Association of Los Angeles County, the Los Angeles County Employees Association, and Mr. Ernie O. Adler, Membership Services Coordinator.
[1] Nancy C. Morse and Robert S. Weiss, "The Function and Meaning of Work and the Job," *American Sociological Review,* Vol. XX (April, 1955), pp. 191-98.
[2] *Ibid.,* pp. 192-93.

In earlier days, work had a definite religious significance. Max Weber hypothesized that the rise of Protestantism gave religious meaning to work and stimulated the development of capitalism.[3] Wright contends that the Protestant Ethic took on greater importance in the United States than in Europe because "labor was scarce, the returns from an individual's work were unusually high, and the opportunities to rise from a lower to a higher economic and social status were relatively constant." [4]

There has undoubtedly been some carryover of the Protestant Ethic to the present day. It is likely, however, that the meaning of work has evolved so that, although it is still positive, it no longer has religious significance for most men.[5] Friedmann and Havighurst suggest that work now serves five functions for the worker: (1) it provides him with an income, (2) it regulates the pattern of his life activity, (3) it gives him identification in his group, (4) it fixes his patterns of association, and (5) it provides him with a set of meaningful life experiences.[6]

Of course, work has different meanings for different individuals. Whatever meaning work has for a man, his success will be judged largely in terms of his occupational career. Even those who see no particular value in work can seldom avoid it. The average man comes to accept work as a natural part of his life.

Retirement is a relatively new stage of the life cycle. As Orbach says,

> Retirement is a phenomenon of modern industrial society. This emerging pattern of social life has no precedents in the past, and represents the development of a new and distinct social role available universally for ever increasing numbers of persons. While prior socioeconomic systems have had varying numbers of older people, none has ever had the number or proportion of aged that obtains in the industrialized societies of the present, and, more important, the older persons of previous societies were not retired persons. There was no such thing as a retirement role in the past.[7]

Retirement has become a social institution primarily because people are now living longer than ever before. In 1900 the life expectancy for men was a little over 48 years. Only one person in 20 was 65 years or older—and most of these were women. There was no retirement problem because few men lived long enough to retire. By 1961 the average life expectancy had increased by 21 years. About one person in 11 today is 65 years or older. In the 10 years between 1950 and 1960, the aged population increased nearly 35 per cent while the general population increased only 19 per cent.[8]

---

[3] Max Weber, *Protestant Ethic and the Spirit of Capitalism*, trans. by Talcott Parsons (London: George Allen and Unwin, 1930).

[4] Louis B. Wright, *The Cultural Life of the American Colonies* (New York: Harper & Row, Publishers, 1957), p. 23.

[5] Cf. William H. Whyte, Jr., *The Organization Man* (New York: Simon and Schuster, Inc., 1956).

[6] Eugene A. Friedmann and Robert J. Havighurst, *The Meaning of Work and Retirement* (Chicago: University of Chicago Press, 1954), p. 4.

[7] Harold L. Orbach, "Normative Aspects of Retirement," in *Social and Psychological Aspects of Aging*, eds. Clark Tibbitts and Wilma Donahue (New York: Columbia University Press, 1962), p. 54.

[8] Staff Report to the Special Committee on Aging, United States Senate, *New Population Facts on Older Americans*, 1960 (Washington: U. S. Government Printing Office, 1961).

Employment opportunities are not expanding fast enough to accommodate these older men and still absorb all of the young men entering the labor force. Thus, there is pressure on the older worker to withdraw from the labor force to make room for the youngster. The virtues of retirement are being widely extolled.

This, then, is the nature of the dilemma which faces the older worker. For the greatest part of his life, he has pounded into him the importance of an active work life. Then, suddenly, upon reaching retirement age, he is expected to abandon his daily routine, forget what he has heard about the dignity of work, and retire gracefully.

To what extent is the older worker successful in making the transition from work to retirement? What relationship is there between the meaning that work has for him and his success in adjusting to retirement? Do white-collar workers make the transition more successfully than blue-collar workers? Are differences in the adjustments of retired white-collar and blue-collar workers attributable to the different meanings which work has for them? These are some of the questions which it is the purpose of this paper to examine.

THE STUDY

In the summer of 1963 the writer conducted a pilot study of retired men in the Los Angeles metropolitan area.[9] A random sample was drawn from among the 2,177 active members of an association for retired county employees. Interviews were successfully completed for 101 (69 per cent) of the cases in the sample.[10]

The Subjects

The 101 men who were interviewed may be described as follows: Ninety-two per cent were Caucasian and eight per cent were Negro. Their mean age was 69 years. Eighty-three per cent of them were married, five per cent, never married; four per cent, divorced; and eight per cent, widowed. An overwhelming majority, 84 per cent, lived with their spouses; while 11 per cent lived alone. The mean number of years of school completed was 11.39, with a range of one to 20 years.

Former white-collar workers constituted 55 per cent of the sample and blue-collar workers, 45 per cent. Eighty-one per cent said that they were in very good or good health. Eighty-five per cent said that they had enough money to live on comfortably.

Half of the men retired voluntarily; 26 per cent were compelled to retire upon reaching retirement age; the rest retired for reasons of health. The length of time retired ranged from less than one year to 23 years, with a mean of 6.62 years. Since retirement, 20 per cent of them had worked or were working full-time. Thirty-three per cent had worked or were working part-time. The remaining 47 per cent had not worked at all.

---

[9] The writer was assisted by Joan Harris, Homer Metcalf, Bill D. Miller, Robert Vilmur, and Ronald White.

[10] Ten men refused to be interviewed and 36 were unavailable for various reasons.

Blue-Collar—White-Collar Comparisons

The blue-collar workers in the sample did not differ strikingly from the white-collar workers. The fact that all were former county employees probably had a leveling effect. Nevertheless, there were some noteworthy differences between them.

As might be expected, there was a significant difference in the level of educational attainment. The mean years of school completed by blue-collar workers was 9.25, as compared with 13.11 for white-collar workers. Sixty per cent of the blue-collar workers had not completed more than eight years of school, as compared with 12 per cent of the white-collar workers, whereas 54 per cent of the white-collar workers had attended college, as compared with nine per cent of the blue-collar workers.

Blue-collar workers tended to be less optimistic about their health than were their white-collar counterparts. Twenty-four per cent of the blue-collar workers said that they were in only fair health, as compared with 11 per cent of the white-collar workers.

Although both classes of workers were relatively satisfied with their finances, the white-collar workers were slightly more so. The respective percentages for white-collar and blue-collar workers who said that they had enough money to live on comfortably were 89 per cent and 80 per cent.

When asked how well they liked their former jobs, most of the subjects expressed satisfaction. However, white-collar workers tended to be more enthusiastic than blue-collar workers. Eighty-seven per cent of the white-collar workers said that they liked their former jobs very well and nine per cent, fairly well. By comparison, 62 per cent of the blue-collar workers liked their former jobs very well and 31 per cent, fairly well. Seventy-one per cent of the white-collar workers said that, if they could start over again, they would go into the same kind of work, as compared with 60 per cent of the blue-collar workers.

Those men who had not worked since retirement were asked what they missed most about not working. The most frequent response for white-collar workers was that they missed nothing at all (38 per cent), and second, that they missed their associates at work (27 per cent). The most frequent response by blue-collar workers was that they missed their associates at work (37 per cent); 34 per cent of them missed nothing.

Blue-collar workers were more likely than white-collar workers to have retired voluntarily (53 per cent versus 46 per cent) or for health reasons (27 per cent versus 20 per cent). White-collar workers were more likely than blue-collar workers to have been compelled to retire (32 per cent versus 18 per cent). Furthermore, there was more of a tendency for white-collar workers to have worked full-time since their retirement. Twenty-seven per cent of the white-collar workers had worked or were working full-time, as compared with 11 per cent of the blue-collar workers. The primary reason given by white-collar workers for going back to work was for enjoyment or to relieve the boredom of not working (62 per cent). Blue-collar workers who went back to work were most likely to explain their action as a means of earning more money or qualifying for Social Security benefits (44 per cent) or to relieve the boredom of not working (38 per cent).

LOETHER

528

The Meaning of Work

The subjects were asked whether or not they thought it was important for a man to work. They were then asked to explain why it was or was not important. These questions were used as indicators of the meaning of work. On the basis of their responses, the subjects could be placed into four categories.

First, there were those who saw a religious significance in work. Representative of the remarks made by men in this category were the following: "It's (work) a fundamental need in this world. You have to keep occupied. It is a rule of life—ordained by God." "Man was put here by God to work!"

Second were those men who valued work in a positive sense but did not attach religious significance to it. Representative of the remarks made by these men were the following: "Work gives a person purpose—something to live for. I'd hate to think I'd just work for money alone. The feeling of creativity is a big reward." "Man works for creativeness. You want to feel you have done something good in the world to justify your existence."

Third were the men who valued work in a negative sense. To them, work was not a vehicle for achieving good but, rather, for avoiding the bad. Witness the following remarks: "Work keeps you out of mischief." "You have to keep occupied. You'll get into trouble if you don't."

Finally, there was a group of men who did not feel that it was necessary or important for a man to work, if he could possibly avoid it. These men said such things as the following: "I worked for income. I didn't dislike it, but if I didn't have to work, I don't think I would have. Work was a necessary evil." "I don't know whether it is important for a man to work. It all depends on the individual's mentality—if he can get along without working, good!"

The data of the present study support the proposition that the importance of the Protestant Ethic has declined among American workers. Only three of the 101 men interviewed (three per cent) attached religious significance to work. Two were white-collar workers and one a blue-collar worker. Most respondents saw work either as a means of self-expression (a positive value) or as a means of keeping out of trouble (a negative value). Twenty-five per cent of the sample saw work as a positive value and 61 per cent saw it as a negative value. Eleven per cent placed no value on work.

White-collar workers more often than blue-collar workers placed a positive value on work (29 per cent versus 20 per cent). Blue-collar workers were a little more likely than their white-collar counterparts to place a negative value (64 per cent versus 59 per cent) or no value (13 per cent versus nine per cent) on work.

Adjustment to Retirement

Three measures of adjustment to retirement were utilized. First, the direct question, "In general, what kind of adjustment would you say that you have made to retirement?" was used. The subjects rated their general adjustment along a five-point scale. Second, the subjects responded to a four-item Guttman-type scale designed to measure personal self-conception. The items dealt with the individual's conception of his success, satisfaction, happiness, and usefulness. Finally, the subjects responded to a six-item Guttman-type scale designed to measure social self-conception. These items were concerned with the individual's conception of his dependableness, popularity, likableness, respectability, friendliness, and acceptability.

On all three measures of adjustment there was a decided tendency for the subjects to respond positively. Not one person said that he had made a very poor adjustment to retirement. Forty-nine per cent said that they had made very good adjustments and 36 per cent, good adjustments. Only two per cent of the subjects had unfavorable social self-conceptions, although 56 per cent had favorable self-conceptions. The highest percentage of unfavorable responses occurred on the personal self-conception scale. Twelve per cent of the subjects had unfavorable personal self-conceptions. But on this scale, as on the others, the majority of the subjects (61 per cent) gave favorable responses.

There are several possible explanations for the tendency for so few men to see themselves as being poorly adjusted. First, the sample was drawn from the membership list of an association for retired county employees. Those who have made an adequate adjustment to retirement are probably more likely to join such an association than are those who have made a poor adjustment. Second, the men who refused to be interviewed may have been those who had made poor adjustments. Third, there may well be more men who make an adequate adjustment to retirement than who do not.

White-collar workers and blue-collar workers differed in their responses to the adjustment question. A higher percentage of white-collar than of blue-collar workers described their adjustment to retirement as very good (54 per cent versus 42 per cent). Although no white-collar worker described his adjustment as poor, 11 per cent of the blue-collar workers did.

On the personal self-conception scale, 70 per cent of the white-collar workers had favorable self-conceptions, as compared with 48 per cent of the blue-collar workers whose self-conceptions were favorable. Conversely, 20 per cent of the blue-collar workers had unfavorable self-conceptions as compared with five per cent of the white-collar workers.

Differences between white-collar and blue-collar workers were slight on the social self-conception scale. Fifty-eight per cent of the blue-collar workers and 53 per cent of the white-collar workers had favorable self-conceptions. Four per cent of the blue-collar workers and none of the white-collar workers had unfavorable self-conceptions.

The Meaning of Work and Adjustment

The scores of the three measures of adjustment were cross-tabulated against responses to the meaning-of-work questions. However, because of the relatively small number of cases involved, the findings should be considered suggestive rather than definitive.

Comparisons of the meaning-of-work responses with responses to the general adjustment question produced the following results: A larger percentage of white-collar workers for whom work had positive value had favorable adjustment scores than did their blue-collar counterparts (95 per cent versus

70 per cent). None of the white-collar workers for whom work had positive value had unfavorable adjustment scores, but 20 per cent of the blue-collar workers did. Slightly more of the white-collar workers than of the blue-collar workers for whom work had negative value had favorable adjustment scores (85 per cent versus 80 per cent). None of the white-collar workers for whom work had negative value had unfavorable adjustment scores; but 10 per cent of the blue-collar workers with negative work value did.

There were only five white-collar workers who did not value work. All five had favorable adjustment scores. It is interesting to note that, of these five, four had not worked since retirement and one had worked full-time. There were six blue-collar workers who did not value work. Five of these had favorable adjustment scores and one had a moderately favorable adjustment score. The five who had favorable adjustment scores had not worked since retirement, whereas the one who had a moderately favorable adjustment score had worked part-time.

Sixty-seven per cent of the white-collar workers for whom work had positive value had favorable personal self-conceptions and five per cent had unfavorable personal self-conceptions. Fifty-six per cent of the blue-collar workers for whom work had positive value had favorable personal self-conceptions and 22 per cent had unfavorable personal self-conceptions.

Seventy-three per cent of the white-collar workers for whom work had negative value had favorable personal self-conceptions and three per cent unfavorable. Among the blue-collar workers, 52 per cent of those for whom work had negative value had favorable personal self-conceptions and 24 per cent unfavorable.

Of the five white-collar workers who did not value work, three had favorable personal self-conceptions; one, moderately favorable; and one, unfavorable. Two of the three with favorable personal self-conceptions had not worked since retirement and the other had worked full-time. Neither the white-collar worker with the moderately favorable self-conception nor the one with the unfavorable self-conception had worked since retirement.

Of the six blue-collar workers who did not value work, two had favorable personal self-conceptions and four had moderately favorable self-conceptions. One of the two with the favorable self-conceptions had worked part-time and the other had not worked since retirement. None of the four with moderately favorable personal self-conceptions had worked.

Blue-collar workers for whom work had positive value had a higher percentage of favorable social self-conceptions than did their white-collar counterparts (80 per cent versus 67 per cent). Fifty-five percent of the blue-collar workers for whom work had negative value and 52 per cent of such white-collar workers had favorable social self-conceptions.

Of the six blue-collar workers who did not value work, two had favorable social self-conceptions and four had moderately favorable social self-conceptions. Of the five white-collar workers who did not value work, one had a favorable social self-conception and four had moderately favorable self-conceptions.

CONCLUSIONS

The percentages of favorable responses to the general adjustment question were higher than the percentages of favorable personal self-conceptions. Why was it easier for a man to say that he had made a favorable adjustment to retirement than it was for him to have a favorable personal self-conception? The most logical explanation is that these two measures tap two diverse aspects of adjustment. Possibly responses to the general adjustment question reflect the person's recognition of his retired status and his resolve to make the best of it. Thus, the man who says that he has made a very good adjustment to retirement may, in effect, be saying, "Given the situation in which I find myself, I am making out very well." However, it may be that, given a choice, he would prefer not to be in the situation in which he finds himself.

On the other hand, the personal self-conception scale calls for the man to take stock of himself, of what he has accomplished, and of what he is now. The man who scores high on the personal self-conception scale may be saying, "My life has been worthwhile. I am satisfied with what I have been and what I am."

If this explanation does, in fact, account for the difference in the two measures, then the personal self-conception scale would seem to be preferable to the general adjustment question as a measure of adjustment.

White-collar and blue-collar workers did not differ significantly in the meanings that they attached to work. The meanings attached to work were related to adjustment, but they did not account for the adjustment differentials between white-collar and blue-collar workers. Such adjustment differentials did exist and were generally in favor of the white-collar workers. How can these differentials be accounted for?

It should be noted that, although white-collar workers expressed greater job satisfaction than that of blue-collar workers and seemed more reluctant to retire voluntarily, they were more likely to have favorable adjustment scores and favorable personal self-conceptions. Furthermore, they were more likely to say that they missed nothing about work.

The following is a possible interpretation of these findings. The average white-collar worker has positive feelings about his job. Therefore, he may look with some dread at the prospect of retirement and the loss of his occupational role. But when he does retire, the transition to the retired state is smoother for him than it is for the blue-collar worker. He is able to make the transition more smoothly because he has greater role flexibility.[11] He is able to compensate for the loss of his occupational role because he has other roles to play and because he has not put disproportionate emphasis on his occupational role as a means of relating himself to the social system. In addition, his personal self-conception tends to be more favorable and more stable because he can look back at his life as a whole with a sense of accomplishment. His occupation is an important source of his feeling of accomplishment, but not

---

[11] Cf. Robert J. Havighurst, "Flexibility and the Social Roles of the Retired," *American Journal of Sociology*, Vol. LIX (January, 1954), pp. 309-11; and Elaine Cumming and William E. Henry, *Growing Old* (New York: Basic Books, Inc., 1961).

the sole source. Accomplishment is an integral part of his whole life experience. Furthermore, he may retain such tangible evidences of accomplishment as a college degree or avocational interests.

Although the blue-collar workers had lower job satisfaction than the white-collar workers and were more likely to retire voluntarily, they were less likely to have favorable adjustment scores and favorable personal self-conceptions. Apparently, the average blue-collar worker enjoys his work less and looks forward to retirement with more anticipation. But, alas, it is less probable that he will make the transition to retirement smoothly. This may be so because blue-collar workers put proportionately more emphasis on their occupational roles as a means of relating themselves to the social system and, thus, suffer more from the loss of such roles. They do not particularly like their jobs, so they do not realize how central their occupational role is to their existence. When they retire, they miss, not the job itself, but the association which the job made possible for them, because they depend more on the job as a source of social relationships than do the white-collar workers. They lack the role flexibility of white-collar workers, so that when they lose their occupational roles, they are less likely to have other roles to fall back on successfully. Furthermore, any sense of accomplishment that they have in life is more directly related to their occupational roles and to the status derived therefrom. Therefore, when blue-collar workers are separated from their occupational roles, they suffer a proportionately greater reduction in personal self-conception. They are not left with any tangible evidence that they have accomplished anything. Probably, all that they really had to make them feel important was their occupational roles and the associations that these afforded. Without their occupational roles as anchors, their lives fade into insignificance.

The Meaning
of Work
and Adjustment
to Retirement

Part X

TRENDS AND PROSPECTS

OUR concern in this concluding section of the book is with the near future of the country's blue-collarites. What explains the gradual disappearance of many blue-collar positions and the abrupt disappearance of some others? (Chaplin examines the position of the domestic worker, a type seldom before discussed in the sociological literature.) How reasonable is it to expect blue-collarites to succeed in alternative work careers? (Mayer and Goldstein evaluate the performance of blue-collarites as small businessmen, as do also Berg and Rodgers.) What are some implications of the white-collarites' "flight to the suburbs"? (Hoult and Mayer, using Detroit as an illustration, point out that the city is, "by and large, being abandoned by all except those who suffer from relatively great housing, educational, and general economic deprivations.") Gross turns our attention next to the sweeping matter of the future of toil and the impact of automation. He injects a rare note of optimism into the proceedings with his suggestion that a new and positive view of the role of work and the rights of workers is gradually developing—a view that may yet transform the workers' situation into a more satisfying and enlarging one than it is at present. In the final essay, Rodman asks readers of the volume to critically reappraise the curative efforts of practitioners and to address new attention to preventive measures. He declares, in a closing, provocative challenge: "If the 1960's are to be the decade for an ideology of Negro rights, perhaps the 1970's will be the decade for an ideology of lower-class rights. The members of the lower class, however, do not have their own spokesmen and fighters as do the Negroes. A special obligation therefore rests upon the intellectuals—to come out of their end-of-ideology corner fighting for lower-class, as well as Negro, rights."

Domestic Service and the Negro

DAVID CHAPLIN

I.   INTRODUCTION

THE passing of domestic service, imposing as it does on the daily comfort of the well-to-do, has been one of our most recognized and lamented occupational trends.[1] A less-noticed feature of its decline has been the change in its structure. Always a predominantly female and minority group refuge it has become more so, not because more women and Negroes are entering, but because white men are leaving it faster.

by those interested in either the assimilation of minority groups or the process of industrialization. Besides acculturating immigrants, domestic service has also served as an escape from industrial labor-market norms for minorities unable, or individually unwilling, to take their place in the mainstream of our economic system. The crutch or escape function of domestic service has been especially important to the declining proportions of spiritually unemancipated Negroes. It seems that this occupation may be disappearing faster than the desire or necessity for it on the part of Southern Negroes in Northern cities faced with the decline in unskilled jobs due to automation.

Therefore, to understand what happens when such an occupational role is assigned to a socially visible minority group, it would be worthwhile to look at some of its general features.

[1] Currently, the census figures for domestic servants show an increase of 22 per cent between 1950 and 1960 after a sharp drop of 32 per cent between 1940 and 1950. The latter decline followed a steady pattern from 1900. In terms of our definition, however, this recent change is misleading, since it arises largely from the inclusion of the greatly increased number of part-time baby sitters. Max Rutzick and Sol Swerdloff, "The Occupational Structure of U.S. Employment 1940-60," *Monthly Labor Review*, Vol. 85 (November, 1962), p. 1213.

We would prefer to exclude them on the grounds that (1) they are not domestic servants if we consider domestic service as a self-identifying full-time occupation; (2) they are frequently the social equals of their employers, a fact made necessary by the class-homogenized suburbs in which the employers of such short-time workers live; and (3) they do not normally live-in. They are, thus, not viewed by others nor do they view themselves as domestics.

As a working definition of domestic service, the conventional, "direct employees of private families, engaged to assist in household operation" seems less useful than the following: workers with a socially inferior status, paid for goods and services produced in the home of the employer and consumed only by his household and his personal guests. The latter definition unfortunately still leaves undetermined the matter of the residence of the servant, but the frequent lumping together in governmental statistics of those living-in with those living-out makes this necessary. Sociologically, the "ideal type" domestic would be an unmarried resident servant whose world would be bounded by the employer's family.[2]

Our definition, therefore, excludes slaves, artisan apprentices, and unpaid relatives, however similar their duties. Some questionable types would be private governesses, secretaries and "companions," nurses, tutors, family chaplains, and foster children, for whose care parents are paid but who nevertheless work as domestics.

A final problematic element in our definition is the location of domestic service in the blue–white-collar continuum. The pay, social status, and origin of these workers certainly put them in the blue-collar class. However, not only does the frequent "over"-identification with management prevent their unionizing and give them much in common with white-collar "organization men," but the type of labor they offer is a service which has much in common with that expected from salesmen, public relations specialists, and clerks in expensive and luxury goods shops and all the "public service" occupations from shoe-shining to medicine. The stock in trade of the top domestic servant is the style as much as the technical skill (as a cook, for instance) with which he serves his employer; his ability to adjust to his employer's moods, his sensitivity to the degree of subservience expected, and so forth.

It would appear that services involving aspects of this type of personal deference are on the increase. As the relative amount of discretionary income rises in the United States, more emphasis will be put on the nonfinancial aspects of services. As for the supply of such labor, it can be suggested that, whereas domestic service, street vending, and similar occupations "stretched" to absorb the surplus labor arising in the early phases of the first Industrial

---

[2] Additional elements in an ideal-type definition of domestic servants would be: (1) the wearing of livery; (2) strict hierarchies *between* servants *within* one household and *among all* servants in a society in terms of both the type of families they serve and their own backgrounds and characteristics; (3) the use of first names for "lower" servants and last names without marital-status titles for "higher" servants (This characteristic is accompanied by snobbish attitudes on the part of "professional" domestics, concerning the class of employers they are willing to serve, which in turn constitutes the main source of occupational pride available to them.); (4) extensive sumptuary control over all aspects of the servants' lives, such as forbidding the growing of beards as presumptuous, controlling marital choices, and other behavior during their time off; (5) conversing as though servants were not present during meals and in front of guests, except for orders.

Revolution,[3] other services must "give" in a comparable fashion to take care of labor displaced by automation[4] in the "second" Industrial Revolution.[5]

The Employer-Employee Relationship

Domestic service is almost universally defined as a problem, but generally from the employer's perspective. Not even in England have domestics successfully organized on their own behalf. Such organizations as do exist are employer- or government-created, as befits the paternalistic tradition which complements this servile subculture. Therefore, to get beyond a superficial and biased view, it would be helpful to work out the domestic servant-master relationship in order to clarify the internal contradictions involved, since it seems that their expectations are neither internally nor mutually consistent.

The Employer's Expectations

Employers who express the greatest concern over the "servant problem" have been largely of the urban middle class, dating well back in European history.[6] Those suffering the fewest problems have been the rural aristocracy whose homes represented the best local employment available and whose authority was bolstered by far more than legal contracts.

The primary inconsistencies in the employer's expectations would seem to be the following:

1. Expressing a desire for an extensive range of services based on an aristocratic model, while at the same time being unwilling or unable to hire the number of servants that such a style of service implies.[7] Employers persistently blocked the rationalization of domestic service by not allowing specialization, yet their qualifications for servants followed the model of homes in which a proliferation of workers was allowed.

2. Employers limiting their own obligations to servants to the terms of

---

[3] P. T. Bauer and B. S. Yamey, "Problems of Classifying Economic Activity," in *Underdeveloped Areas,* ed. by Lyle W. Shannon (New York: Harper & Row, Publishers, 1957), p. 148.

[4] It was during the early stages of industrialization, 1750-1914 in England, and currently in underdeveloped areas, that domestic service involves the largest labor force and perhaps most deserves the damning economic term of "disguised unemployment." Here the rising urban middle class meets a swarming proletariat as a product of population growth and, especially in current nonwestern countries, migration to cities far in excess of demand. The desperate need for employment, the pretensions of a growing bourgeoisie, and the cultural gap between the bulk of the migrants and industrial labor-force requirements, make domestic service the easiest "entrant" occupation. Domestic service, street vending, and begging are the classic occupational opportunities which can stretch when all others seem full:

"Overpopulation can be measured not only by the extent of underemployment in agriculture but also by the amount of disguised unemployment. Sixteen to twenty percent of the labor force is in domestic service. Servants at the top of the wage scale themselves hire servants at the bottom of the wage scale." [Walter Galenson, *Labor and Economic Development* (New York: John Wiley & Sons, Inc., 1959), p. 265.]

[5] Colin Clark, *The Conditions of Economic Progress* (New York: The Macmillan Company, 1957), p. 492.

[6] Dorothy M. Stuart, *The English Abigail* (London: Macmillan & Co., Ltd., 1946), p. 2.

[7] "The one servant plan adopted in the large proportion of American homes (1900) seems to impose conditions that would be entirely inadmissible in any other branch of industry, particularly in view of the fact that most employers insist on maintaining a degree of style compatible with the employment of several servants." Gilson Willets, *Workers of the Nation,* Vol. II (New York: The Crowell-Collier Publishing Co., 1903), p. 1035.

their contracts while expecting from them a diffuse personal loyalty and a wide and undefined range of duties limited only by the employer's imagination. This, of course, constitutes the classic "exploitation" situation, found so often in manufacturing during the early stages of industrialization, in which management initiates a withdrawal from paternalistic obligations while continuing to expect feudal servility from its workers.[8] (Within domestic service, it is hard to decide which of the following situations would be more abusive: that of the socially pretentious petty clerk employing the cheapest, least experienced country girl or city orphan, or that of a *déclassé* family taking out their frustrations on the single old retainer too faithful to leave them, convinced as he is that they are too helpless to survive without him.)

Workers' Reaction

Unlike factory workers, domestics have not reacted collectively, nor in most cases aggressively, to the denial of their expectations of paternalistic care.[9] The techniques that domestic servants have employed have been characteristically different, owing to the type of workers self-selected for such work, as well as to the nature of their employers and their labor market. In conformity to the solitary nature of their employment situation and their lack of encumbering property, domestics have shown, especially since 1900, *a high rate of mobility*. Rather than negotiate for better conditions, they often leave without notice to try out a new home in hopes of improvement.[10] Those who choose to stay can have recourse to *personality manipulation* as a means of increasing their security and bettering their working conditions and perhaps, even, their job satisfaction: for example, the highly intimate and personal nature of living-in domestic service makes possible the personal intimidation of employers. Such a turning of tables would, of course, be a delicate psychological trick easily spoiled by the arrival of another adult and dependent on a rare combination of submissive-employer and dominant-servant personalities. It need not depend on a bizarre setting, however, as in "The Admirable Crichton." The frequency with which such situations have cropped up in literature and in popular culture since 1800, for example, Uriah Heep or Hazel (of the cartoon, not the watered-down TV version), suggest that such personalistic variations of formal relationships are not highly extraordinary.

---

[8] Reinhard Bendix, *Work and Authority in Industry* (New York: John Wiley & Sons, Inc., 1956), p. 88.

[9] Among the obstacles to the unionization of domestic servants are: (1) the high proportion of casual labor; (2) the isolation of individual workers; (3) personalistic ties to employers —a factor inhibiting the few dedicated careerists; (4) racial and ethnic cleavages, and the high proportion of women (95 per cent), which by itself would tend to prevent collective aggressive action; (5) the impracticality of the strike against so many scattered employers, on the basis of a service which is increasingly being replaced by machine and "packaged services." An additional factor relevant to Negroes would be the tendency of this occupation to select out of the total Negro labor force the "Uncle Tom's."

[10] Charles Booth, *Life and Labor of the People of London, Vol. VIII* (London: Macmillan & Co., Ltd., 1897), p. 214.

Even if we assume a cultural situation in which there is some respectable "place" for domestic servants, in which they, along with all manual workers, need not feel, by the very nature of their jobs, like failures, what frustrated expectations have they which *still* make job satisfaction unlikely?

1. *The absence of fellowship.* The majority of domestic servants, since before 1900 in England and the United States, have been in "single-handed" homes in which they were the drudge-of-all-work. Consequently, aside from the opportunities for intrinsic job satisfaction, they were denied the recently much-discussed chance, at least, to have pleasant primary relations with fellow workers.

2. *The absence of any objective criteria for an adequate performance of their duties.* Their primary duty is to please someone rather than to perform in any impersonally measurable fashion.[11] Servants have no recourse to outside judges to determine whether they have cleaned enough or been sufficiently obedient.[12] There are no public fairs where they can receive an outside and impersonal evaluation of their worth. They, therefore, can judge themselves only through acquiring a thorough knowledge of all the peculiarities of their employers. Moreover, the multiplicity of their duties prevents any serious over-all professionalization. The few cases of the deliberate training of domestics concentrated largely on their "character" and personality rather than on skills.[13]

3. *Invasion of privacy.* Whether or not domestic servants consciously desire privacy, it can be safely asserted, on the basis of general knowledge of the human personality, that a minimal degree of autonomy is necessary if an adult is to survive psychologically outside of a completely fixed social situation. It is true that lower-class people, in this respect like many so-called primitives, are more gregarious in that they have not received the full amount of formal education which leads many of the middle and upper class to want to be alone occasionally, even from their closest peers. This is revealed most strikingly in hospitals, in which lower-class patients frequently suffer if given

---

[11] Another way of approaching this problem would be to clarify *what* is being purchased. A worker can hire out his physical strength, appearance, character, personality, and skills. Each type of occupation calls for a different mix of these traits or services. Most occupations tend to require much more of one of the five than of the others, thus simplifying the problem of self-esteem and objective evaluation of the worker and his work.

Domestic service, though essentially manual labor, is as demanding of personality involvement as is selling, and as demanding of character as is clerking in a bank. "These different (domestic service) occupations for the most part call for different types of workers. A butler or chambermaid-waitress who is tall and comely may have access to a larger number and to better places than one who is short. . . ." Elizabeth Ross Haynes, "Negroes in Domestic Service in the United States," *Journal of Negro History*, Vol. 8, No. 4 (October, 1923), p. 428. Such a typology of salable workers' traits and services allows us to go beyond the statement that too many duties are expected of too few people.

[12] Vilheim Aubert, "The Housemaid—An Occupational Role in Crisis," *Acta Sociologica*, Vol. I (1955-1956), p. 421.

[13] Booth, *op. cit.*, p. 216.

the luxury of a single room. Long accustomed to "overcrowded" living conditions, a virtue has been made of a necessity.

The invasion of the servant's privacy is not limited to those who live-in, although this group naturally finds it hardest to resist such impositions. A comparable situation was found among a Negro population of 150 in a small New England town in which the majority were domestic servants.[14] None lived in the homes of their employers, but many found themselves drawn into a peculiar relationship involving self-abasing exposés of the most intimate details of their private lives as part of a quite unconscious bargain with paternalistic employers. Female domestics were subject to a sort of verbal voyeurism on the part of their mistresses.[15] This situation suggested to the servants, consciously or otherwise, the possibility of playing on the sympathy or lurid imagination of their employers by elaborating, and often inventing, debasing anecdotes about their private lives. They were, in effect, catering to the least complimentary elements of the Negro stereotype in return for receiving the type of paternalistic protection and extra rewards in kind and in cash, which has long been the Southern Negroes' technique for dealing with a generally hostile and unjust world.[16]

American Negroes, until recently, have rarely found collective resistance or overt aggression useful for individual needs. Also, the demoralized state of the lower-class Negro family made Negro domestics especially prone to emotional involvement in their employers' families—if the employers chose to "play it that way," that is, according to the expectations Negroes had developed as household servants during slavery. Negroes have been pressured into seeking physical and financial security through personal ties to a white protector in much the same manner as the lower class, especially Indians, in Latin America elaborated on the Spanish *compadrazgo* (godparenthood) institution in cultures pervaded by a spirit of *desconfianza* (lack of trust). Compadrazgo, once found largely among peers, has developed increasingly between the rich and the poor as the only meaningful protection which the latter feel they can obtain in a world of corruption and injustice.[17]

4. *The absence of a "paternalistic-servile" tradition.* This "absence" applies, of course, to non-Negroes, not only whites but Orientals and Indians as well. At this point we must question the tentative assumption on page 531

---

[14] David Chaplin, "The Amherst Negro." Unpublished Honors Thesis, Amherst College, 1953.

[15] ". . . conversation is regimented both in form and content . . . with few exceptions, there can be no serious discussions between Negroes and whites concerning politics . . . nor about problems of their daily lives. The one exception is that some white women use Negro servants as a source of gossip. . . ." Bertram P. Karon, *The Negro Personality* (New York: Springer Publishing Co., 1958), p. 20.

[16] A more public version of this Negro approach to white society, until World War II, was the side-show human-baseball target whose stock in trade consisted of a self-deprecating repartee and quick reflexes. "Come on, white man. See if you are smart enough to hit this nigger."

[17] "One very great advantage of the peon-hacendado relationship . . . is the protection which the mestizo patron may give to his Indian peons. Any mestizo is better able to obtain justice than an Indian . . . the Indian is disparaged because he is Indian. Moreover there is a certain broad solidarity of "mestizoness" as opposed to the Indian social category. . . ." William W. Stein, *Hualcan: Life in the Highlands of Peru* (Ithaca, N.Y.: Cornell University Press, 1961), pp. 40-41.

that there was a respectable "place" for servants in our society. It applied, if ever, to Negroes only as long as they accepted the myth of their racial inferiority. It is very difficult for the rest of the American poor, whose persistent condition has only recently regained some scholarly attention, to avoid condemnation as "failures." Doing a menial job well is not doing well enough, as middle-class values pervade our entire society. Moreover, as state-welfare paternalism replaces traditional *noblesse oblige,* domestic service loses one of its primary "advantages."

III. THE CURRENT SITUATION OF DOMESTIC SERVICE

As the number and proportion of workers in domestic service decline, the structure of employment changes. An occupation which once normally meant living-in now rarely requires or allows servants, especially Negroes, to be resident.[18] The replacement of physical distance, as far as Negro homes are concerned, for the narrowing caste distinction, added to the general absence of servants' quarters in modern urban homes, has meant that most employers prefer help by the day. For Negroes this is a special burden, because they are usually imprisoned in downtown ghettos, while their middle- and upper-class employers live as far from them as possible. The next stage in the dissolution of the full-time resident-servant tradition is that servants come only part-time, sometimes for only a few hours a week, and increasingly for more specialized duties.

The implications of these changes for the paternalistic master-servant relationships are drastic. First of all, new categories of employers, many with no experience in handling servants or employees of any type, are now able to afford some domestic service. This is especially the case because the effective employer is normally the woman of the house, who at any class level is unlikely to have had outside administrative experience. Second, besides having employers who have not learned their "part" in the traditional relationship, part-time domestics have to have many employers, thus seeing too little of any one to establish the personal ties on which the old relationship was based. In addition, except for the newest arrivals from the deep South, who are not likely to be competent servants if this is their first job, Negro domestics are increasingly "overeducated" for their work. Consequently, the growing proportion of female entrants must include a larger number for whom such work represents a bitter defeat at some better job.

IV. TRENDS IN DOMESTIC SERVICE

Although the continued decline of the living-in domestic seems assured, like most social changes, this trend is the result of forces working in both directions. Among the factors, however overwhelmed, which would favor an *increase* in this occupation are the following:

1. *Urbanization and the growth of the middle class.* Domestic service in

---

[18] St. Clair Drake and Horace R. Cayton, *Black Metropolis,* rev. ed. (New York: Harper & Row, Publishers, 1962), p. 244.

the post-feudal period has been associated with the rise of the urban middle class. The patterns to be emulated were aristocratic, but the latter group was not large enough to employ more than a small fraction of the labor force, even in the most lavish households. Consequently, other things being equal, as these trends continue they would, by themselves, favor an increase in demand for domestic service.

2. *The migration of Negroes and Puerto Ricans to Northern cities.* The role of domestic service in "processing subordinate or traditional ethnic and racial minority groups suggests that if the supply were to increase, demand might rise to the occasion." On this score one can only conjecture as to how much more the percentage of domestic servants might have dropped if these two groups were not available.

3. *The appearance in the labor force of a rising proportion of women,* long the majority sex in domestic service. This factor should increase demand in the cases of middle-class working mothers as well as increase supply.

4. *The rising qualifications for skilled labor.* The increasing hard core of unemployables turned out by automation at both ends of the working-age span suggests that those at the younger ages, at least, might become a future supply of domestic servants. Michael Young proposes that, by the year 2033 (1984 is too close to be used any longer as the apocalyptic year), the lower end of the I. Q. span will, or should be, used as servants in the homes of the brilliant.[19] Young is not suggesting, in the style of Huxley, that people can be or should be bred for menial tasks; he merely asks, What else are we to do with those who end up that way naturally?[20] The only escape from this biological support for social inequality would, indeed, be to manipulate the development of intelligence in order to keep the minimum in line with the rising demands of industrial society.

Among the factors which would favor a continued decline in this occupation are:

(1) *The mechanization of housework* through home appliances.

(2) *The rationalization of consumer services* through specialization and commercialization, laundresses being one of the first types of domestics to cease "living-in."

(3) *The increasing desire of the middle class for privacy* (or the increasing proportion of our society with middle-class values), impossible with living-in servants.

---

[19] Michael Young, *The Rise of Meritocracy, 1870–2033* (New York: Penguin Books, Inc., 1961), p. 120.

[20] In fact, it has been the custom for some time in the United States for institutions for the feeble-minded to hire out their more capable charges to presumably sympathetic employers at nominal wages. It would appear, however, that inmates intelligent enough to be of any practical help as domestic servants and yet not sensitive to their menial status or loss of conventional social opportunities, constitute a very narrow segment of the intelligence spectrum, if, indeed, such tests can measure the ideal traits for this work. As medical science enables more and more biologically unfit children to survive, the proportion of social incompetents incapable of even domestic service is bound to rise. Such a suggestion, then, however serious or humane in intent, would not solve either the "servant problem" or the problem of economic incompetents. The suggestion that we may be developing a scientific rationale for a class system, however, seems highly probable.

(4) *The increasing cost of housing space.*

(5) *The decline in boarders and in the number of children and dependent relatives to be cared for at home.*

(6) *The increase in public manual-service jobs,* such as hotel work, a type of occupation long open to Negroes. These opportunities are draining off that segment of the Negro labor force which might otherwise have offered itself for private domestic service.

(7) *The shrinking supply of spinsters,* the declining age at marriage and the increasing amount of formal education, together with the rising proportion of people getting married. These factors leave fewer spinsters available for housework as a prelude to marriage.

(8) *The decreasing willingness of workers to suffer the stigma of being a domestic or to endure the hours and invasion of privacy usual in this field.* This change in mood was partly due to the rise in the percentage married in the population as well as to the closing off of immigration. The basic problem in the United States has always been the absence of an ethnically stable "servile subculture," with the obvious exception, until recently, of Negroes.

In short, we are obliged to agree in part with Levenstein when he asserts that:

> The moralists who lament the refusal of people to take menial jobs forget that we have cut off the traditional American sources of supply of such labor. . . . The virtual disappearance of domestics in this country, which makes conversation under the beauty parlor dryers, is somehow believed to be evidence of a change in the American character. It is evidence principally of a change in our immigration laws. . . . Certain types of labor could be obtained only through immigration. The servant class was never native American; even in Colonial days domestics came as indentured servants who ultimately moved up to higher-status jobs once their service was over.[21]

The most effective forces operating against domestic service have been (1) the closing of supplies of foreigners, many of whom were obliged to enter American culture through Victorian cellars, and (2) the equalization of income which has reputedly taken place in the United States.

CONSEQUENCES

Some implications of changes in the organization of domestic service are the following:

1. The kitchen again is the center of the United States middle-class family. Also, large mansions have been abandoned, even by the very rich.

2. The status of housework has been raised, owing to the vast improvement in home appliances and packaged services, as well as to the resulting performance of such work by middle-class wives, however unwillingly.[22]

3. On the other hand, in areas of the United States and in countries

---

[21] Aaron Levenstein, *Why People Work* (New York: Crowell-Collier Publishing Co., 1962), p. 38.

[22] See Betty Frieden, *The Feminine Mystique,* for the latest feminist attack on the status of housework.

such as England, where the improvement of domestic facilities lagged behind the disappearance of domestic servants, middle-class wives, indeed, became the "slaveys" of their families. So concerned was even the postwar Labor government with the plight of servantless housewives that special permits were issued for the importation of foreign girls.[23]

4. Other consequences of the disappearance of the servant have been the increasing participation of American husbands (and children?) in housework as well as a lessening of the formality of family life. These changes have several aspects. In the first place, with no servants present, adults need not feel obliged to strike a dignified posture, especially before their children and guests. Also, parties have to be less formal if the hosts are to have the time to mingle with their guests. There may well have been a time when, owing to a lag in standards of hospitality behind the loss of servants, pretentious or proud families simply ceased entertaining.[24]

CONCLUSION AND SPECULATION

In the case of domestic service, we have seen the demise of this traditional occupation both hastened and retarded by the declining status of its "final" entrants. The low prestige of this work—the most frequently offered objection to it—is certainly made even lower as the status of its (final) recruits declines. On the other hand, the tapping of new reservoirs of low-status or marginal workers could have postponed the reduction in available labor.

It must be emphasized, however, that both demand and supply factors have worked against the persistence of domestic service. Along with the desire for privacy on both sides, we find an increasing proportion of possible employers unprepared to "handle" servants. Traditionally, the middle-class family expected to have to train "green" country girls or immigrants, whereas in well-staffed wealthier homes the older servants took over this task.

This combination of worker and employer distaste for domestic service has created a demand for, and then been reinforced by, home appliances and "packaged" services. It is possible, persistent complaints about the servant shortage notwithstanding, that the decline in demand for servants preceded that of the decline in supply, at least for Negroes, whose rate of unemployment is twice that of whites. It may well be that, as in the case of the English, owing to employer initiative in backing away from paternalism, the remaining unemancipated Negroes will find this traditional escape from the industrial labor market taken from them before they are fully ready for this challenge.

It is for this group, especially males, that the Black Muslim movement seems to be especially suited. This cult is outstandingly masculine in leadership, lower-class in origin, and middle-class in values. At last an ideology of self-respect has been provided the sons of the traditionally matriarchal Negro lower class. For these men domestic service in white homes should offer no lure. It remains to be seen if jobs adequately satisfying their newly acquired manhood will be provided by the American social and industrial system.

---

[23] Lewis and Maude, *op. cit.*, p. 311.
[24] Russell Lynes, "How America 'Solved' the Servant Problem," *Harper's Magazine,* Vol. 227 (July, 1963), p. 51.

CHAPLIN

Manual Workers as Small Businessmen

KURT B. MAYER

SIDNEY GOLDSTEIN

INTRODUCTION

THE traditional American emphasis on "independence" and "being one's own boss" finds expression in the desire for business ownership. Indeed, the magic formula that "any ambitious American youth with industry, average intelligence, and thrift can save enough money to start a small business and, if he has real initiative and ability, can develop it into a profitable business of considerable size"[1] has long fired the imagination of millions of Americans in many walks of life. For example, in two nationwide polls conducted by *Fortune* magazine, the respondents were asked whether they would like to go into business for themselves. Both times approximately one-half of the employed respondents answered, "Yes."[2] Those answering in the affirmative were then asked: "Do you think you will ever actually try to go into business for yourself?" This much more specific question was also answered affirmatively by half of those asked.

Further evidence which fully corroborates the findings of the *Fortune* polls was provided by a labor-market study conducted by the University of California Institute of Industrial Relations in Oakland in 1949-1950.[3] Two of the questions dealt specifically with business aspirations, and the answers reveal that the majority of the respondents in every occupational category admitted to having had the goal of going into business. More important than mere aspirations, a considerable proportion of men in all occupational groups had actually attempted to implement their hopes at some time during their career.

The Oakland data also show that both the desire for business ownership and the actual attempts to realize this aspiration were greater among blue-collar workers than among those in white-collar occupations.[4] The authors

---

[1] P. D. Converse, *Should I Start My Own Business?* (Urbana, Ill.: University of Illinois, 1945), Special Bulletin No. 5, p. 4.

[2] *Fortune*, Vol. 45 (February, 1940), p. 28; also Vol. 52 (January, 1947), pp. 5-16.

[3] Seymour M. Lipset and Reinhard Bendix, "Social Mobility and Occupational Career Patterns," in *American Journal of Sociology*, Vol. 67 (January and March, 1952), pp. 366-74 and 494-504.

[4] *Ibid.*, pp. 501-3.

Manual Workers as Small Businessmen

545

of the study interpret this differential between manual and nonmanual workers as an indication that today, the creed of individual business ownership has become largely a working-class goal. It is one of the few positions of higher status attainable today by manual workers whose educational limitations preclude an executive or professional career. That the desire to run a business is high among manual workers is borne out by Chinoy's case study of automobile workers who see an opportunity to gain in business ownership what they rarely achieve in the factory—a rich and full sense of self.[5] As one of the machine operators put it:

> The main thing is to be independent and give your own orders and not to have to take them from anybody else. That's the reason the fellows in the shop all want to start their own business. Then the profits are all for yourself. When you're in the shop, there's nothing in it for yourself. When you put in a screw or a head on a motor, there's nothing for yourself in it. So you just do what you have to in order to get along. A fellow would rather do it for himself. If you expend the energy, it's for your own benefit then.[6]

The strong attraction of business ownership for manual workers also was one of the major findings of a 1958-1960 longitudinal field investigation of a group of 81 newly formed small business establishments in the Providence Metropolitan Area.[7] This study was an attempt to identify those factors which distinguish small businesses that survive the first two years of their existence from those that close during this founding period. Although not designed specifically as a study of manual workers, the results provide new insights about the precise circumstances under which blue-collar workers go into business and the fate which they encounter.

THE RESEARCH DESIGN

The research design employed in this study involved the selection of 81 newly established retail and service enterprises in three sectors of the Providence Metropolitan Area. The monthly lists of businesses which had newly registered with the Rhode Island Division of Taxation or with the Department of Employment Security provided the basic roster from which the business concerns included in this study were serially selected. For purposes of this study, a "new" business was defined as one which had either been newly established or just changed ownership.

In order to know who opens a business and why, as well as the specific circumstances which accompany its inception, development, and demise, information was obtained through direct contacts with the business owners themselves over an extended period of time. Reasons for success or failure cannot be identified completely through questioning a business owner. They may be identifiable only through direct observation of the business behavior of the owner and of the physical environment in which he operates. The need

---

[5] Ely Chinoy, *Automobile Workers and the American Dream* (Garden City, N.Y.: Doubleday & Company, Inc., 1955).

[6] *Ibid.*, p. 86.

MAYER
GOLDSTEIN

[7] Kurt B. Mayer and Sidney Goldstein, *The First Two Years: Problems of Small Firm Growth and Survival* (Washington, D.C.: Small Business Administration, 1961).

for these diverse types of information requires a combination of interviewing and observation techniques.

Following selection of the sample, the owner of each concern was contacted, and his cooperation for the study was solicited. In the initial interview, data were obtained on: (a) social background of the owner; (b) circumstances underlying the establishment of the recently opened business; (c) the type of business and its financial structure; and (d) the enterpriser's own expectations concerning the future success of the firm. The interview was supplemented by observations recorded by the interviewer concerning: (a) the physical features and the population composition of the neighborhood; (b) the appearance of the business proper; and (c) the personal characteristics of the owner.

Following the initial interview, personal contact was maintained with each firm through follow-up interviews for a two-year period. The two-year period was selected because all previous studies have shown that a high percentage of business discontinuances occur within a year or two after the opening of new firms. In the beginning, the follow-up interviews were conducted at monthly intervals; thereafter, the interval between interviews was allowed to vary from four to 10 weeks, depending upon the circumstances revealed by the previous contracts. These interviews were designed to ascertain the progress of the business. At the end of both the first and second years of the business' existence, the interviews were specifically designed to review the developments of the preceding year. Apart from the responses to the interview schedule, the interviewers were required to report after each contact all changes which they observed in the business area, in the business establishment, and in the behavior and attitude of the owner.

For all firms which closed before the end of the two-year observation period, all the materials were obtained to the point of discontinuance. In addition, a special interview was designed to collect information regarding the factors which led to the discontinuance of the concern. In order to evaluate more fully the circumstances underlying discontinuances and success, interviews were also conducted with leading suppliers and creditors of both the closed and the surviving firms.

THE OCCUPATIONAL BACKGROUND

Of the 93 owners involved in the 81 firms, no less than two-thirds (64) had at some time been employed in manual work (see Table 1). Thirty-six of these owners—almost 40 per cent of the total—had done nothing but manual work prior to opening their present enterprise. Mr. Beck, for example, who had been a mechanic employed by an automobile dealer for four years, decided to go into business for himself as a gas station operator because he saw this as "a good chance to make a buck"—an opportunity to make more money as a businessman than as a wage earner. Another example: Mr. Green's only work experience had been 14 years as a farm worker, but he had always wanted to start a business—"something the children could take over later"; he saw an ad in the newpaper, offering a diner for sale, and finally embarked on his venture.

Manual Workers as Small Businessmen

547

Twenty-one of the 64 enterprisers with manual work experience had also owned other businesses previously. Some of these had started their occupational careers as manual workers, but they had then consecutively operated a series of business enterprises; others had changed back and forth

Table 1

PREVIOUS OCCUPATIONAL EXPERIENCE OF BUSINESS OWNERS

Occupational Category	Previous Business Ownership	No Previous Business Ownership	Total
Manual	13	36	49
Manual and white-collar	8	7	15
White-collar	12	10	22
Business experience only	4	–	4
No previous occupational experience..	–	2	2
Total	37	55	92*

*No information on previous occupational experience was obtainable in one case.

between manual work and self-employment. Mr. Commo, for example, a barber-shop owner, began his career as a professional dancer. Next he owned a small candy store for three years. He then migrated to the West Coast, where he held a variety of manual jobs for three years. Then followed service in the Army. Upon discharge, he opened a small doughnut shop in Los Angeles, which he closed after a few months. He next went to work as a journeyman barber, first in California, then in Rhode Island, for a total of 12 years. Finally, he decided to open his own barber shop.

In eight cases, the occupational career pattern had been even more complex, alternating between manual work, white-collar employment, and business ownership. Thus, Mr. Friendly, a café owner, started out as a truck driver, becoming successively a beer salesman, ice cream salesman, job printer, sign painter, clerk of the probate court, and bartender during a 12-year period. Thereafter, he took over the operation of a clubhouse, while simultaneously being employed as a bus driver. He gave up the club operation after three years but continued to drive the bus for another four years, before acquiring the café.

Although perhaps an extreme case, Mr. Friendly's career vividly illustrates the fact that an important aspect of social mobility in American society consists of repeated crossings between white-collar, blue-collar, and self-employment, with relatively little permanence at any level. This is further borne out by the fact that many of the newly established businesses in the sample eventually closed, with the owners returning to manual employment. Small-business ownership, thus, appears as one of the main avenues of social mobility open to manual workers, but it is a precarious route and seldom assures the permanent achievement of the higher social status associated with business ownership.

MOTIVATION FOR BUSINESS OWNERSHIP

The actual reasons for going into business depend on many factors, such as age, sex, education, previous occupational experience, employment conditions, and, in some instances, the whole family history of a given individual.

MAYER
GOLDSTEIN

Although any or all of these factors may influence or determine the actual decisions of an individual, he does not always clearly apprehend these considerations consciously and weigh them rationally, as economic theory would have us assume. As a result, direct questions on reasons for going into business tend to be answered in terms of cultural stereotypes—"to be independent" and/or "to make money." When it is feasible to probe more deeply, it often becomes apparent that such clichés are rationalizations rather than basic motives. Indeed, the data of this study indicate that the blue-collar owners in many cases did not consciously know why they went into business; often they had no clear goals in mind, having little if any appreciation of the business world in general.[8]

The most striking fact is the small number of business owners who conform to the classical stereotype of the capitalistic entrepreneur as an individual who sets out deliberately to make a maximum profit from his business endeavor. In order to qualify for the traditional designation of an entrepreneur seeking maximum money rewards, a prospective business owner would have to make an attempt to isolate the most profitable opportunities by careful calculation of costs, sales volume, location, competition, and, above all, comparison of financial gains to be expected from self-employment with potential income from paid employment. The data show, however, that the overwhelming number of manual workers in the sample did not bother to make any such rational calculations and comparisons.

In the large majority of the cases, monetary motives were, of course, present; but they take on a very different meaning. Thus, 21 openings were prompted by a desperate need for providing some income because the prospective owner had either already lost his job or was in imminent danger of becoming unemployed. Mr. Satti, for example, who at the age of 50 was laid off from his job as a handyman through a reduction in the labor force of the factory in which he was employed, said: "If you want to know the truth why I really went into business, I would have taken anything. I was out of a job and couldn't find work. I was desperate for anything, so when the opportunity to go into business came along I jumped at it." Illustrative of those who went into business because they were afraid that they were going to lose their jobs is Mr. Friendly, who had been driving a bus for 11 years. As he put it: "You're bound to get laid off after that many years, especially if you're getting old." Because he was married and had four children to support, he thought he had better get himself "something steady." According to him, "This boils down to going into business for yourself in order to get security—not to get rich, just to make a living."

Many others who were not under the immediate pressure of unemployment viewed business ownership in much the same way as Mr. Friendly. To them, this was simply a way of making a living as an alternative to working for others. The 32 cases in this category were largely former manual workers who felt perfectly satisfied if their income as business owners were comparable to the amount of money they had earned as wage workers. To be sure, in

---

[8] For a review of the literature dealing with the motivation of economic behavior, see C. Addison Hickman and Manford H. Kuhn, *Individuals, Groups, and Economic Behavior* (New York: Holt, Rinehart & Winston, Inc., 1956).

answering the direct question: "Why did you go into business?" most of these respondents included some mention of money, as illustrated by the comments, "I like the green stuff" and "To make money, naturally."

Despite this frequent reference to money, however, the analysis of these cases indicates quite clearly that they were not thinking in terms of sizable business profits, but were primarily interested in just making enough money for an adequate living. These respondents viewed self-employment as a preferable alternative to paid employment because they believed that it offers greater security, higher prestige, and more independence. It is quite significant that independence was listed as a secondary motive in 28 of these 32 cases. The following comment by a mechanic who opened his own gas station is typical: "I went into business for myself to make money and so I don't have to take no guff from anyone." As has been pointed out, both of these reasons reflect general cultural goals in our society and therefore provide acceptable and easy answers to the direct question, "Why did you go into business?"

Further probing by the interviewers suggested, however, that although the respondents' expressed desires for money were probably sincere, this motive was usually intricately combined with others. For example, a respondent may have said: "I went into business to make a living." When asked, "Why did you not stay on your job or look for a better job?" he would then reply, "I want to be my own boss," or "I don't want to spend the rest of my life working for someone else." A typical example of this type is represented by Mr. Mangia, a taxi driver who opened a pizza place: "I thought I could make money for a living by working for myself. I didn't expect to get rich, but I always wanted to be my own boss." Clearly, many of these workers who became self-employed knew perfectly well that they would not be better off economically than if they continued as manual workers, but the ideal of independence was strong enough to prompt them to escape the dependent status of an employee by setting themselves up in business despite dubious prospects.

Nevertheless, in some cases, the owners eventually came to feel that the price of independence was much higher than they had anticipated, and that the expected advantages of making a living as their own bosses were outweighed by long hours and the anxieties which ownership entails. To be sure, one man, a meatcutter who opened a meat delivery service, said: "Being in business for yourself means more work, but the freedom is worth it." Yet he, too, turned out to have been unrealistic in his appraisal of his chances of success, since he had to close down after only three months of "freedom."

However, there are eight cases in the sample where the desire for independence stands out as unquestionably the major motive. For example, Mr. Gam—who had been a cook for 28 years, the last 14 years in a leading restaurant in Providence—established his own restaurant simply because he was "sick and tired of working for someone else" and wanted to be his own boss. Quite similarly, another 30-year-old man, who had been a cook since he was 18 years old, answered the question by asking back: "Doesn't every man want to be in business for himself?" He had been looking for a restaurant of his own for a long time, because he likes "to be on my own, make my own decisions, and run the restaurant the way it should be run." Unfortunately, he found that he was a much better cook than a businessman.

Lacking a pleasant disposition, he did not manage to attract sufficient patrons, and thus decided to give the business up after only four months and to return to work as a cook in another man's restaurant.

The picture uncovered by the motivational analysis in most cases has, thus, little resemblance to the image of the traditional enterpriser as he appears in the popular mind as well as in economic theory. It explains, however, why so many business owners came from a manual background, and it accounts for the frequent movements back and forth between paid employment and self-employment pointed out earlier. To the extent that these owners view self-employment simply as another means of making a customary living, business ownership appears to them as not fundamentally different in nature from a paid job. Some of them make the transition to business ownership with no more effort or forethought than they would employ in applying for a paid job. This appears most pronounced in the 21 cases where business ownership represented an alternative to, or escape from, unemployment. It is not irrational for such persons to open a business in the hope of providing themselves with at least a minimum income and thereby avoiding the social stigma of joblessness, even though the chances for success may be small. On the other hand, it also appears that, even in those cases where self-employment was viewed as an alternative to working for others, some businesses were opened in a kind of reckless, gambling spirit, "just to see what would happen." Some respondents, for example, stated that they had a few dollars saved, had often thought about starting a business sometime, and had simply decided "to give it a try." Although this is understandable in terms of another American cultural stereotype, "nothing ventured, nothing gained," it is hardly conducive to solid business success. It helps to explain why many enterprises are started with insufficient preparation and lack of foresight, and why so many former owners of enterprises rejoin the ranks of the paid labor force.

CHOICE OF LINE

Closely allied to the decision about going into business is the question of what kind of business to choose. The great majority of both white-collar and manual workers cite previous experience as the most important single factor influencing them to establish a particular type of business. For the manual worker, previous experience in a given line is an even more decisive factor, because he generally does not have the perspective and knowledge which would permit him to investigate different kinds of businesses. A blue-collar worker who has experience as an employee in a particular line of business, therefore, is likely to open an enterprise in the same line when he decides to go into business for himself.

Mr. Bono, for example, had been a mechanic in a large machine-tool plant and was laid off in July, 1957. Having worked as a tune-up man in various gas stations for five years previously, he felt that he knew something about cars and therefore thought that opening a filling station might be a good idea. He turned out to be mistaken, however, because he knew nothing about repair work, nor had he any capital. Consequently, the two filling stations he took over successively lasted only a short time. Again, Mr. Singer, who had started a meat delivery service, chose this line of business because he was familiar with it as a result of his 12 years' experience as a union butcher. However, as he came to realize too late, knowing how to cut meat expertly still does not teach one how to buy meat wholesale and how to sell it profitably. He overbought, the meat spoiled, and he went back to cutting meat again for a major packing firm within three months.

These cases illustrate the close connection between the general motivation for going into business and the selection of the particular line of business. Because the desire to make a living as one's own boss represents the major motivation for business ownership, it is only logical to expect that such persons will choose a line of business which presumably enables them to draw upon their past experience. However, as illustrated by Mr. Singer, experience as an employee in a business is not *business* experience. Therefore, what appears rational reasoning in the eyes of the prospective owner may be an erroneous assumption in many instances.

In a limited number of instances, manual workers made their choice because the opportunity came at a time when they were unemployed or anticipating imminent layoffs and were desperately looking for any kind of business. For example, Mr. Werner, anticipating loss of his factory job, began to watch the newspapers for advertisements of the availability of a package store. No opportunities of this nature came along, so, as his layoff was coming closer, he began looking for some other business. At this time, he saw an advertisement of a grocery store for sale. After discussing it with his wife, he bought the store; he felt that experience in his uncle's grocery store during high school vacations justified the decision—a rationalization which proved to be erroneous.

THE EXPERIENCE OF THE BLUE-COLLAR BUSINESS OWNERS

During the two-year observation period, the 81 firms in the sample followed quite different courses of development. Although the experience of each firm was unique, the basic distinction was between the 40 firms that closed and the 41 firms that survived the full two-year period. It is significant that the survival experience of the 49 owners who had had only manual work experience prior to their present business venture *was less favorable than that of the other owners.* As Table 2 shows, only 20 of them remained in business for the entire two-year period, compared with 27 out of 43 of the other owners.

Table 2

SURVIVAL EXPERIENCE BY PREVIOUS OCCUPATION

Occupation Before Business Ownership	Total	Survivors	Closures
Manual Work	49	20	29
Mixed White-Collar and Manual Work	15	12	3
White-Collar Work	26	14	12
No Previous Occupational Experience	2	1	1
	92	47	45

An effort was made to ascertain the fate of those who went out of business during the two-year period. Of the 26 former manual workers for whom information could be obtained, 17 returned to blue-collar jobs when their business venture ended and two each entered white-collar employment and new business careers. Of the remaining five, four were unemployed when last contacted and one had become a housewife.

Comparison of the case histories of the surviving and closed firms suggests the following reasons for the higher mortality rate of the businesses operated by former blue-collar workers:

1. The rate of survival varied inversely with owner's age. The blue-collar workers were more concentrated in the younger age groups and tended to view business as an alternative to paid employment, to which they returned when the opportunity presented itself.

2. Owners with less education had a higher rate of discontinuance because they were more haphazard in establishing a business than those with better education.

3. Contrary to a widespread notion, experience as an employee in a given line of business did not result in a higher survival rate as an owner in that type of business. Thus, of the 26 owners who had previously worked as an employee in the same line, 17 were out of business by the end of the study.

4. Within the sample, the smaller firms, as judged by capital investment and number of employees, were less stable than the larger ones. Those going into business from manual work generally had only very limited capital resources. Those with initial investments of $7,500 and over had the best survival record—13 out of 17 survived, but there were only a couple of manual workers in this category.

5. As would be expected from these previous points, owners' motivation and expectations were related to their survival experience. Those who were more rationally motivated and had planned more extensively had a better survival rate. Firms that were opened by blue-collar workers either because of the owner's immediate need for a job or as an alternative way for the owner to make a living showed poorer survival records. Over half of the openings that were prompted by these motives failed. On the other hand, of those that established businesses in the hope of making "real money," less than one-fifth closed.

Those who escaped from either unemployment or the discipline of a supervised job in quest of the independence of entrepreneurship were haphazard about the decisions involved in the opening, as well as in the operation of their firms. Illustrative of such a situation is the case of John Satti, the owner of Satti's Spa, who, after closing his business said: "I should never have gone into business in the first place because I did not have the experience and any business know-how." Disgusted with the outcome of his venture, he swore that he would commit suicide before he ever went into business again. An unskilled laborer all of his life, the 50-year-old, Italian-born Satti went into business after he had lost his job and felt that he was too old to find employment. When he heard about a grocery store for sale, he decided "to grab it" out of sheer desperation. His spur-of-the-moment decision to purchase the store and to expand it into a combination grocery store and lunchroom was the first time he had even considered going into business for himself. Having invested $2,600 worth of savings in the venture, he admitted to the interviewer that he knew nothing at all about operating a business:

"I haven't got the faintest idea about running a business, and I feel I would probably be doing much better if I knew more. This lack of knowledge is my most important business problem."

From the beginning, business was poor. Satti reported that he had not realized much of any profit during the first two months. Business was doing well enough to enable him to pay his bills and to permit his family to eat out of the store, but it left no cash profits. No change in the situation was reported during the following two months. Feeling perplexed and unable to cope with the complexities of business operation, he sold the enterprise the same way he had bought it—on the spur of the moment. A man hearing of Satti's dissatisfaction came in one day and offered him $500; Satti accepted the offer on the spot, even though it meant a $1,500 net loss. Subsequently, he found work in a jewelry factory. He told the interviewer, "This is more up my alley. I'm through with business forever. I learned the hard way."

The 41 firms in the sample which survived were classified, according to the degree of success, into four categories: (a) the "marginal survivors"; (b) the "limited successes"; (c) the "potentially profitable enterprises"; and (d) the "profitable enterprises." Eighteen out of the 20 former manual workers ranked in the first two, that is, the less successful, categories, compared with 21 out of 27 other owners. In most instances the income of the 18 former manual workers in the first two categories was not higher than what these individuals could have earned in paid employment.

In the case of the "marginal survivors," continuation in business was possible only because of other sources of income, usually from outside employment by the owner or his spouse. Because the aspirations and expectations of these owners were very low, they could continue their enterprises, even though they yielded less than a normal living.

An example of a "marginal survivor" is Larry Pemberton, who operated a small grocery store. He had been employed as an electrical maintenance man for 35 years when a heart attack put an end to his days of heavy work. His reason for going into business three years later was to supplement the meager income provided by his wife's Social Security. His choice of the grocery line was dictated largely by the availability of a grocery store and the fact that it did not require physically strenuous work. As he put it: "I heard about the vacancy from a friend, slept on it for a night, and then bought it for $1200." Throughout the entire period of observation, the business fluctuated between actually losing money and just barely meeting expenses "plus a few dollars left over." The total net income for the second year of operation was only $700. In his effort to keep the business going, Pemberton had also taken a part-time job driving a school bus. Without this job and his wife's Social Security, he would never have been able to continue the grocery business. As long as these additional sources of income were available, he was determined to continue the business indefinitely despite its marginal character.

The survival of the "limited successes" depended on the degree to which the businesses provided their owners with a return equivalent to what the owner could have expected to receive through paid employment. Although some of these owners indicated that they hoped to do better, most were satisfied if minimum returns were obtained. The idea of being one's own boss appealed to these ex-blue-collar workers and led them to prefer business ownership to paid employment even when the returns were not greater.

An illustration of this is Mr. Pasquale, who was an unemployed mechanic when he located a vacant Texaco station and decided to become a filling-station owner. He reached a level of $500 to $600 weekly gross sales after the first three months of operation, and thereafter volume fluctuated at this level for a year and a half. This permitted him to make a modest living for his family. He was satisfied with the business and expected to continue indefinitely.

Pasquale suffered an on-the-job accident, which required him to stay home for two weeks and prevented him from actively participating in the work for several more weeks. During his absence, his help "ran the business into the ground." They were rude to customers and stole equipment. As a result, his gross sales fell off considerably, but his costs increased sharply because he needed additional employees and had to replace equipment. The continued survival of the business depended on his ability to obtain a loan, which he was able to do. Pasquale's experience indicates how precarious even a stable business may be. His business had been sufficient to meet his everyday needs, but he had been unable to accumulate any reserves to meet an emergency situation. Although no similar emergencies occurred in any of the other cases in the "limited success" category, they all would have been in serious difficulties if a comparable situation had arisen, since all had their resources tied up completely in the business and none had any liquid reserves.

Only two of the total of 20 former manual workers who were still in business two years later could be classified as "potentially profitable enterprises," whereas none qualified for the most successful category of enterprises that had already become really profitable. In contrast to the firms in the "limited success" category, these firms show a pattern of growth which, by the end of the first two years, provided the owners with a living and, in addition, gave indication that the growth may continue to the point where these firms will yield a profit. Although both qualify for inclusion in this category, it should be pointed out that the growth pattern of these firms was not always smooth.

One illustration is provided by the experience of Mr. Gam. With 29 years of experience as a restaurant cook behind him, Gam decided to become his own boss by opening a seafood restaurant. He began seeking a location as far away as possible from the two major seafood restaurants in Providence, which he considered his main competitors. He rented a vacant store on a major traffic artery in the best residential area of Providence. He invested $17,000—$2,000 from his savings and $15,000 obtained through a three-year commercial bank loan—to remodel and furnish the restaurant and kitchen. The result was a small but modern and attractive-looking restaurant.

Upon opening, he placed some advertisements in the local newspapers. He hired a chef and two waitresses, but fired them all after the first week of operations, because he found that he was losing money. He appointed his wife waitress and himself chef. This saving of salaries enabled him to pull through a very tight spot.

The difficulties continued for quite a while. The location was far from ideal and the heavy indebtedness to the bank was burdensome. Gam also had to contend with teen-agers from a nearby high school, who were using his place as a hangout and were damaging his furniture, until he categorically refused them service. He discontinued advertising as he began to realize that his true competitors were the numerous small neighborhood restaurants, not the leading seafood places that he had originally envisaged as his major competitors.

After six months, Gam was disgruntled enough to talk about closing, but he realized that new restaurants tend to undergo a slump after their novelty wears off. He tried to overcome this by experimenting with different menus and specials, by rearranging the booths to provide more privacy, and by repeatedly varying his hours of business.

Eventually his stamina and resourcefulness won out. At the end of the first year, business had definitely improved, and Gam was more optimistic. During the second year, he was able to close on Sundays and holidays. As the interviewer pointed out: "There has been a slow transformation in this business which becomes more obvious with each visit." When the Gams opened, they had hoped to do a really large business—one which would allow them to run things but have other people do most of the labor. It was not long before they realized that this was not going to happen. As they put it: "We had to make a decision right then: either to get out or to pitch in ourselves and work hard." They decided to continue even though they knew that long hours and hard work would be required to build up their business.

The carry-out business which they had instituted was booming and accounted for about half of the weekly gross volume of $800. At the two-year mark, the Gams had succeeded in completely paying off their indebtedness to the bank. During this period, they had kept their cash withdrawals at a minimum and had eaten all their meals in the restaurant. With the heavy burden of debt removed, tension relaxed considerably. The Gams saw a rosy future ahead for themselves, since all the profits, which had previously been applied to paying off the loan, could now go into their pockets. Gam was highly pleased about his prospects. He reported that he was making considerably more money now than he had ever earned as an employed cook. In addition, he was his own boss. His credit rating with the bank was excellent and the bank was urging him to borrow again for expansion purposes.

CONCLUSIONS

The limited sample on which this study was based requires that caution be used in generalizing the conclusions reached. However, the longitudinal character of the study and the opportunity it provided for observation of and contact with the small business owners resulted in an unusual body of information on the conditions under which blue-collar workers decided to go into business and the experiences they had as owners. In this respect, the analysis provides insights which cannot be obtained either by a cross-sectional interviewing study or by a statistical analysis of business records.

The fact that a majority of the individuals under observation who established a new business enterprise were blue-collar workers bears out the conclusions of other studies cited earlier, undertaken in various parts of the

MAYER
GOLDSTEIN

556

country. The desire to become a businessman has largely become a working-class dream. The typical avenues of upward social mobility for white-collar workers today are more likely to be in an office bureaucracy or corporate hierarchy. However, blue-collar workers who wish to move out of the working class find their opportunities to do so sharply limited by their lack of education. With few exceptions, their channels of mobility are restricted to sales work or business ownership. The attractiveness of the latter is greatly enhanced by the element of independence from supervision and the chance of "being one's own boss," which represents one of the most traditional values of the American ethos. Although other studies indicate that many more manual workers talk about going into business than actually do, the data of this study suggest that substantial numbers of them in fact realize their plans.

Unfortunately, it is considerably easier to open a business than to keep it in operation. Although many of the owners in this sample had long entertained hopes of becoming businessmen, they had done little if any substantial planning. Rather, the idea was latent in their minds and was brought to fruition very suddenly in either of two ways: (1) A worker heard about a going concern that was available or noticed a location, or (2) he was actually unemployed or threatened with unemployment and turned to business ownership as an alternative. In both instances, the worker tended to throw caution to the winds and plunge with minimum capital, relying on the idea that his previous experience as a worker in a particular line would be sufficient to operate an enterprise successfully.

It is hardly surprising, therefore, that the business careers of 60 per cent of the former manual workers did not last even two years. Moreover, almost all of those who were still in business at the end of the two-year observation period had only very limited success. They were either operating at a subsistence level, in which the profits from the business did not exceed the income they had earned as blue-collar workers, or they were relying on the business only as a means of supplementing cash from other sources. Of the 49 owners with a blue-collar background, only two had established firms which promised better profits than a manual worker's wages. The experience of these two firms suggests that, if there is any formula of business success for manual workers, the ingredients consist largely of the ability to evaluate objectively, to plan carefully, and to be prepared emotionally to persist long enough to overcome temporary setbacks until the business reaches its full potential. The record shows, however, that these characteristics were conspicuously absent in the overwhelming majority of the blue-collar entrepreneurs.

If the experience of the blue-collar business owners interviewed and observed in this study is in any way typical, it would appear that *the dream of business ownership is badly tarnished.* It continues to lure substantial numbers of workers into an adventure in which most of them fail. Because their investments tend to be small, the financial losses are not exorbitant; but they nevertheless tend to deplete the individual's savings. Because most of the blue-collar owners who fail return again to manual work, one may conclude that ventures into business contribute substantially to the two-way mobility between the blue-collar and white-collar worlds which is characteristic of contemporary American society. The high proportion of those who return to manual work, coupled with the fact that even those who stay in business are operating at economic levels which differ little from paid employment, raises grave doubts as to whether business ownership constitutes a channel of permanent upward mobility for more than a very small proportion of manual workers. It is essentially a waste of motion and resources, and it provides no more than an alternative way of earning a living. Significantly, while most of the blue-collar owners were not very rational in establishing their enterprises, they were quite realistic in their expectations. They viewed business ownership as merely another way of making a living and did not expect to "strike it rich."

Former Blue-Collarites
in Small Business

IVAR BERG

DAVID ROGERS

SMALL businessmen occupy an important niche in traditional democratic theory, in orthodox economic thought, in popular ideology, and in the American market place. In the face of such cultural emphasis, it is not surprising that thoughts of becoming a small businessman occupy a correspondingly important place in the minds and lives of many Americans. Thus, it is well known to students of the American scene that many people in all occupational and class groups have given thought to entering the world of small business; that, despite the growth of large corporate behemoths, there are still over six million self-employed; and that blue-collar workers, in particular, often accommodate to the bureaucratic and technical complex of their industrial environment by dreaming of an escape into small-business ventures.

Surprisingly little, however, is known about the social characteristics, aspirations, and satisfactions of those comparatively few from blue-collar backgrounds who have moved into small-business ranks (from factory to small shop, and from payroll to self-employed status)—people who have, in short, honored the social and cultural commitments to the values of upward mobility and small business.

I

As part of a larger study of the contemporary position and ideology of small retailers, we have collected information on the social backgrounds, aspirations, present business circumstances, and satisfactions of 200 randomly selected service-station dealers in the Greater New York City area. Among the 200 were 117 with blue-collar family backgrounds or job histories, or both, whose interview protocols provide highly interesting evidence on both the varieties of work situations confronting former blue-collarites and their reactions to them.

Because our study is not based on a representative sample of small businessmen from all trades or industries, and because of differences in ethnic, religious, and class composition of different regions, we are obliged to point out that our results may not be easily generalized. Furthermore, the modest size of our sample compels us to underscore the limitations of any analysis, however suggestive, resting on small numbers. It should be noted, however, that some evidence does exist suggesting that small retailers, regardless of trade, come from different social backgrounds in roughly similar proportions, and that they share a number of work-related attitudes and even motives for entering small business.[1] Our dealers, moreover, were not unlike a representative national sample of service-station dealers studied by the Du Pont Corporation in the mid-1950's with respect to education, class background, job history, and a number of dealership characteristics.

Having at least briefly acknowledged academic conventions, we may pass to our findings, aware of the qualifications that our sampling procedures imply.

MOTIVES FOR ENTRY OF FORMER BLUE-COLLARITES

First, we can confirm the results reported in one other study with respect to the modest motives of former blue-collarites for entering small business. Thus, as Table I shows, a scant *two per cent* expressed the kinds of reasons for becoming small businessmen that conformed to what Mayer and Goldstein have described as the "classical stereotype of the capitalistic entrepreneur," [2]

Table 1

MOTIVES AND ASPIRATIONS OF DEALERS WITH BLUE-COLLAR
OCCUPATIONAL BACKGROUNDS
(Percentages)

	N (%)	"Drifted in" (%)	"To make a living"; "enjoy nature of tasks" (%)	"Drifter" plus "tasks" interest (%)	To gain high income and to achieve upward mobility (%)	Independence and no answer (%)
Why did you enter small business?	83	29	52	10	2	7
What aspirations did you have when you entered small business?	82	22	9	10	2	26*

*This question was not asked of dealers during early interviews; the overwhelming majority of dealers in this category represent this early segment of the research sample.

---

[1] Seymour Martin Lipset and Reinhard Bendix, *Social Mobility in Industrial Society* (Berkeley: University of California Press, 1959); G. F. Lewis and C. A. Anderson, "Social Origins and Social Mobility of Businessmen in an American City," *Transactions of the Third World Congress of Sociology*, Vol. III (London: International Sociological Association, 1956); Alfred Oxenfeldt and Gertrude Oxenfeldt, "Determinants of Success in a Small Western City," *Social Forces*, Vol. 30 (December, 1951); P. E. Davidson and H. Dewey Anderson, *Occupational Mobility in an American Community* (Stanford: Stanford University Press, 1937).

[2] Kurt Mayer and Sidney Goldstein, *The First Two Years: Problems of Small Firm Growth and Survival* (Washington, D.C.: Small Business Administration, 1961).

Former
Blue-Collarites
in Small
Business

that is, an interest in business expansion—more generally, in substantial income and status mobility. Nearly 30 per cent stated that they had "drifted" into their businesses ("It was all I knew. . . ." and ". . . to avoid unemployment. . . ."). Slightly more than half indicated very modest reasons for going into small business (". . . to make an honest living. . . ," ". . . so I could work in the open air. . . ," ". . . because I like cars and like to work with 'em"). A smaller number gave us both "drifter" responses and more positive expressions of interest in specific job components and concrete tasks. Like Mayer and Goldstein's small businessmen, and contrary to popular mythology, our dealers mentioned the quest for "independence" only rarely as a reason for entering their businesses.

When we asked a different question, we obtained, as the saying predicts, different answers. Asked about their *aspirations* at the time they entered small business—in contrast to their *reasons* for entry—our dealers expressed traditional entrepreneurial themes somewhat more often. The fact that this was the case may reflect a reaction to the interview situation in a society that puts a considerable premium on success-striving.

When we then asked our dealers to discuss whether their reasons for becoming small businessmen had been justified by their subsequent experiences, we found that only a small minority had been completely disappointed (see Table II). Well over three-quarters felt that their experiences had justified some or all of their earlier reasons. The drifters apparently felt that whatever

Table 2

OUTCOME OF REASONS FOR ENTRY INTO SMALL BUSINESS
(Percentages)

	"Yes" without qualification (%)	Qualified or equivocal "Yes" (%)	Unqualified "No" (%)
Were your reasons for entry into small business justified by your subsequent experience? (N = 83)	41	42	17

residual motives they might have had for entering small business (given their allegedly constrained occupational choice) had been largely vindicated.

The results reported so far would not be predicted from a reading of anecdotal and speculative writings on small business and the American "radical right," and from recent studies of the values of small-business spokesmen.[3] In many of these sources, small retailers are characterized as an ambitious but frustrated group. They are seen to be caught in a system in which their marginality renders them helplessly vulnerable to the effects of self-serving policies of larger and more powerful groups—for example, competition from mass retailers and wage demands from unions. As a result of their distressing circumstances, it is argued, small businessmen are predisposed toward such politics of disenchantment as are espoused by Texas oil kings, Bible-belt

---

[3] See Daniel Bell, ed., *The Radical Right* (Garden City, N.Y.: Doubleday & Company, Inc., 1963), pp. 281 ff.; Martin Trow, "Small Businessmen, Political Tolerance, and Support for McCarthy," *American Journal of Sociology*, Vol. 64 (1958), pp. 270-81; S. M. Lipset, *Political Man* (Garden City, N.Y.: Doubleday & Company, Inc., 1960), pp. 134-40; and John Bunzel, *The American Small Businessman* (New York: Alfred A. Knopf, Inc., 1962).

patriots, deviant martinets, modern Midwest populist types, and other so-called "dispossessed" groups. Our data suggests that such estimates of alienation may be somewhat wide of the mark.

An exploration of the responses of our former blue-collarites to questions about specific features of their situations serves to inform somewhat more fully the skeptical judgment we have advanced.

Dealers who expressed either unqualifiedly negative or mixed feelings about their experiences as small businessmen specified three features of their situation that caused them to equivocate when asked to balance these experiences against their reasons for entry: (i) long hours (on the average, 72 hours per week); (ii) low income (often expressed in relation to hours worked); (iii) supplier insincerity in public relations statements regarding their interest in dealers' welfare. The first two complaints might well be particularly galling to such former blue-collar workers, many of whom had worked in organized industries where there have been substantial improvements on both counts in recent years.

The third complaint might be thought to denote a generalized dissatisfaction with the company, a point that our data did not bear out, as Table III indicates. Indeed, dealers expressed favorable evaluations of relationships with

Table 3

ATTITUDES TOWARD SUPPLIER CORPORATIONS

Occupational Background	Per Cent Satisfied with Supplier-Dealer Relations	Per Cent Skeptical About Sincerity of Suppliers' Public Statements Concerning Dealers
Blue-Collar N = 83	74	36
White-Collar N = 37	68	35
Small-Business N = 42	64	40

suppliers despite a tendency to regard the company as insincere. In a word, the perceived lack of company sincerity is apparently accepted as a fact of life, growing out of the often conflicting interests of companies and dealers and does not affect seriously the dealer's general evaluation of the relationship.

The prevalence of such contradictory attitudes toward corporations among our former blue-collarites is not surprising. These views are not essentially different from the seemingly compartmentalized attitudes of their former industrial peers who joined unions even in countless shops where labor-management relations had been amicable, and where puzzled managers greeted workers' desires to organize in a voice of injured innocence, with the irrelevant and uncomprehending protest: "But my door is always open." Because oil companies confront no strong dealer organizations, they are probably not even aware of what superficially appears to be a paradox in dealer attitudes.

It is our impression, unlike that of commentators who see small businessmen as candidates for radical rightist movements, that these former blue-collarites (like those who remained in the factory)[4] are for the most part

---

[4] Robert Blauner, "Work Satisfaction and Industrial Trends in Modern Society," in W. Galenson and S. M. Lipset, eds., *Labor and Trade Unions* (New York: John Wiley & Sons, Inc., 1960).

accommodated to their situations. The misgivings they have about corporate sincerity, like those of industrial workers, are of the sort that cause them to be alert to problems not resolved by company assertions of good will. In the next section we shall see who former blue-collarites may be able to act, in modest ways, upon this alertness.

BACKGROUNDS, PRESENT CIRCUMSTANCES, AND
SATISFACTIONS OF DEALERS

The foregoing materials on company-dealer relations suggest that former blue-collarites by and large are not an alienated lot. When we asked a number of additional questions concerning dealers' feeling about their small-business experiences, we found that, although former blue-collarites are generally contented, the patterns of response preclude a simple and sovereign interpretation of attitudes based entirely on dealers' previous occupational experience.

Table 4

PER CENT OF DEALERS FROM DIFFERENT WORK BACKGROUNDS EXPRESSING SATISFIED/ACCOMMODATED FEELINGS ON WORK-RELATED ISSUES

	Blue-Collar (N = 83)	White-Collar (N = 87)	Small-Business (N = 42)
1. Would you like to see a son enter a small business?	40	27	43
2. Do you feel that supplier companies are sincere in their stated concern for dealers' welfare?	36	35	40
3. How do you feel about the number of hours you work?	55	54	59
4. How do you feel about the amount of income you earn as a small businessman?	45	52	57
5. How do you think others see your occupation?	64	60	69
6. Do you feel there is a harmony of interests between dealers and corporate suppliers?	57	46	57
7. Would you like a different occupation if you could change?	56	40	78
8. How would you evaluate the behavior of company sales representatives?	64	70	55
9. How do you feel about the degree of prestige you enjoy as a small businessman?	69	64	65
10. How do you feel about the security you enjoy as a small businessman?	66	67	62
11. How do you feel about your occupation, compared with other occupations?	72	73	57
12. Does your occupation provide your family the prestige you would like them to have?	78	76	79
13. How do you feel about your relations with your supplier?	74	68	64
14. How do you feel about demands customers make?	72	71	74

Another more likely possibility, according to many writers, is that dealers have different proprietary arrangements, and that these account in large part for job-satisfaction differences. It has been argued, for example, that although some dealers own their establishments, many others are but "employees" of large suppliers, tied to one-sided lease-and-franchise agreements over which

BERG
ROGERS

562

suppliers exercise more than a little control.[5] It would then follow that any effort to estimate the impact of small-business experiences on former blue-collarites should take account of such proprietary differences.

Tables V and VI, respectively, show the distribution of dealers from different backgrounds in the various proprietary arrangements and their satisfactions on the issues noted above. In Table V we see that former blue-collarites, along with dealers from small-business backgrounds, are more likely than the total population (and, obviously, than dealers from white-collar backgrounds) to be company lessees. At the same time, former blue-collarites are underrepresented in the "owner" category, in sharp contrast to men from small-business backgrounds who become owners in disproportionate numbers.

Table 5

PERCENTAGE OF DEALERS FROM DIFFERENT OCCUPATIONAL BACKGROUNDS, ACCORDING TO PROPRIETARY ARRANGEMENTS

Previous Occupation	Per Cent of Research Population	Company Lease (%)	Third-Party Lease* (%)	Owner (%)	Total (%)
Blue-Collar (N = 83)	43	53	34	13	100%
White-Collar (N = 37)	19	40	38	22	100
Small-Business (N = 42)	21	57	15	28	100
Other (Student, Military, etc.) (N = 32)	17	34	44	22	100
Total Study Population (N = 194)	100	48	32	20	100

*This dealer type is not easily described; some of these dealers lease from large gasoline jobbers, while others lease from investors, real estate syndicates, and the like. Some of our dealers reported that both refiners and oil companies were actually seeking to buy the stations they were leasing from third parties.

If critics of the modern corporation are right in their portrayal of lease-and-franchise arrangements as constraining, if not exploitative, in their effect on small businessmen and contributive to their disenchantment, we would expect either (1) that lessees would be less contented over-all than owners, regardless of occupational background; (2) that lessees would be less contented than owners but that their *degree* of contentment might conceivably vary, depending on occupational background; or (3) that it depends largely on the

[5] See C. Wright Mills, *White Collar* (New York: Oxford University Press, 1953), Part I; Paul A. Baran, *The Political Economy of Growth* (New York: Monthly Press, 1957); Walter Adams, ed., *The Structure of American Industry; Some Case Studies*, rev. ed. (New York: The Macmillan Company, 1955), Ch. 14; Joseph Palamountain, *The Politics of Distribution* (Cambridge: Harvard University Press, 1955), Ch. 1. See also *TNEC Monographs* Nos. 3, 17, 21, 29, and 41.

Table 6

PERCENTAGE OF DEALERS EXPRESSING SATISFACTION/ACCOMMODATION WITH
OCCUPATIONAL EXPERIENCES ACCORDING TO JOB HISTORY AND PROPRIETARY
ARRANGEMENTS*

Previous Occupation and Station Type	Blue-Collar:			White-Collar:			Small-Business:		
	Lease	Third Party	Owner	Lease	Third Party	Owner	Lease	Third Party	Owner
N	44	28	11	15	14	8	24	6	12
Son in small business	41	22	40	23	17	13	52	16	36
Corporate sincerity	48	33	18	46	33	43	47	50	42
Hours	40	35	43	45	43	37	45	50	62
Pay	48	43	55	50	57	50	73	50	55
How others see me	70	46	64	23	84	63	67	67	60
Harmony of big- and small-business interests	65	58	60	36	50	75	75	33	70
Would like a different occupation	77	54	36	46	33	0	65	66	82
Salesman relations	65	61	50	58	56	75	50	50	58
Prestige	79	60	55	86	57	50	75	66	45
Security	75	61	60	80	57	63	71	50	55
View of own occupation compared with others	80	64	64	67	75	75	62	50	50
Family prestige	84	74	50	84	54	88	74	100	75
Evaluation of relations with suppliers	73	79	82	73	67	75	74	83	42
Evaluation of customer relations	82	80	74	80	77	75	91	84	100
Returns in light of aspirations at entry	66	57	73	67	57	38	71	83	75
Average percentages across work-related issues ($\bar{p}$)	63	53	53	56	52	55	64	58	54

*These work-related issues are abbreviated versions of questions itemized in Table 4.

issue, with job history influencing degree of contentment on some issues and
property arrangements doing so on other issues; where property arrangements
are determinant, company lessees would be the least contented dealers.

As Table VI shows, these hypotheses are not confirmed by our data. It
is true that on some issues job history seems to make a difference in degree
of satisfaction although on others it is the dealer's proprietary arrangements.
But it turns out that, within each occupational-background group, the highest
over-all levels of satisfaction are expressed by company lessees. This suggests
that we either drop the assumption made by the critics of corporate marketing
practices) that lease arrangements are repressive or write off the findings as
meaningless. The findings might be disclaimed by the contention that satisfied

lease dealers, much like accommodated blue-collar workers, "don't know how bad off they are"—Marx's false consciousness. Aside from involving the questionable procedure of imputing to the dealer "interests" and "needs" which he may not have, this would unfortunately divert attention from the intriguingly mixed responses of lease dealers to their working conditions.

We note, for example, that, although lease dealers are the most contented of the property-types within each of the three occupational groups, some lease dealers are more contented than others. There is a considerable difference, for example, between the "average contentment" of lease dealers from blue-collar and small-business backgrounds on the one hand and former white-collar workers on the other.

Moving from the over-all "average of accommodation" to a consideration of the sheer number of issues on which different property-types within each occupational group are most contented, we find once again that the lessees, regardless of background, are the most contented. Moreover, the rather striking differences in contentment between company lessees and owners seem to be greatest among former blue-collarites. Within this occupational group, company lessees are most content on 11 of 16 issues and least content on only one, compared with lessees from small-business or white-collar backgrounds who were most satisfied on fewer issues and most dissatisfied on more relative to others from the same past jobs. Yet, although lessees are more content than other property-types within each occupational group, there does not appear to be any pattern to the contentment. As one compares dealers from the three past-job groups, one finds that lessees are not consistently more satisfied than owners on particular clusters of issues.

We then compared company-lease dealers with one another, and found that those from small-business backgrounds are most contented on eight of 16 issues, followed by former blue- and white-collarites, with six and three, respectively, a pattern much like that discerned from average satisfaction/accommodation scores.[6] Although a more detailed, issue-by-issue analysis is necessary for a fuller understanding of the sources and patterns of discontent, our present aim has simply been to review evidence showing that company-lease dealers are the most contented, especially if they have not moved into small business from white-collar occupations.

The significance of the data that have already been reported on the lessees' satisfactions resides in their implications for understanding the sentiments of former blue-collarites. The latter are becoming more numerous among small retailers generally and among lease-type dealers in particular. This is a trend that is likely to continue in the petroleum and other industries where lease-and-franchise arrangements, requiring minimal entry capital, are adopted by suppliers. It is relevant in this context to note that the proportion of dealers from blue-collar backgrounds has nearly doubled from the pre- to post-World War II eras, although the proportion of dealers from other occupational backgrounds has declined over the same period (see Table VII).

---

[6] The nonprofessional reader is reminded that averages can be deceptive; hence the tediousness of this second measure of accommodation/satisfaction.

Table 7

PERCENTAGE OF DEALERS ENTERING SMALL BUSINESS IN DIFFERENT ERAS,
ACCORDING TO OCCUPATIONAL BACKGROUND

Occupational Background	Time of Entry		
	Before World War II	During World War II	After World War II
Blue-Collar	28%	23%	54%
White-Collar	21	11	19
Small-Business	40	22	12
Other (student, military, etc.)	11	44	15
Total	100%	100%	100%

Because the lease plays such an increasingly important role in the small-business experience of former blue-collarites, a fuller examination of the lease dealership is in order.

THE COMPANY LESSEE

First it should be noted that, in contrast with other property types, lease dealers benefit from the favorable locations owned by large suppliers able to afford expensive real estate investments, and from the favored treatment—for example, discounts—they often receive from oil companies during recurring gasoline price wars. They also benefit from the supplier's interest in maintaining his property as well as from his contributions to promotional programs.

We do not by this logic seek to discount the significance of the grievances that lease dealers have voiced in Congressional hearings and elsewhere about the pressure tactics of refiners and oil companies. That there are conflicting interests between companies and their lease dealers seems evident. Consider the following sources of strain: chronic oversupply; tie-in agreements between the supplier and other manufacturers which limit the dealer's product line; the sale by companies of gasoline to price-cutting, unbranded dealers; supplier real estate and building investments requiring high rent returns; cancellable and short-term rental agreements. Such are some of the sources of pressures and constraints circumscribing the dealer's margins of choice, or profit, or both.

Yet all this should be seen in some comparative perspective. Although lease dealers are vulnerable to supplier pressures, paradoxically they are less disadvantaged than dealers, who, because they own their stations, are supposedly independent. Owners have not only the expenses of station maintenance and improvement but the immobilizing constraints of a considerable property investment limiting their freedom as well. It is indeed ironical that the lease dealers—many of them former blue-collarites—like their propertyless peers in the plant—are freer in many respects than property-owning dealers, the supposed entrepreneurial heroes of traditional democratic theory. The owners' property investment alone limits their mobility. Further, compared with lease dealers, they have little bargaining power, faced as they are with competition from suppliers' own retail outlets.

One of the issues is especially revealing in this regard. The greater sense of security expressed by lease dealers, regardless of occupational background, reflects the protection which their suppliers give them from the chaos of competition, a favor not bestowed on owners. Service-station dealers are, in this respect, little different from other businessmen, large and small, who have traditionally sought to blunt the effects of competition through legislation, conspiracy, and artful dodging in the market place.

LESSEES FROM DIFFERENT BACKGROUNDS

Although we offer these comments in explanation of the over-all differences in satisfaction/accommodation as between lease and nonlease dealers, we must also note that lessees differ in degree of contentment. The least satisfied are those from white-collar backgrounds, who, to take one compelling example, are much less likely to see a harmony of interests in relations with the supplier than are lessees from blue-collar and small-business backgrounds. This fact is probably due to the former white-collarites' higher levels of education, giving them both higher aspirations[7] and levels of sophistication on economic matters that make for skepticism about supplier-dealer harmony. This general interpretation is further corroborated by the considerably lower levels of satisfaction of white-collar lessees as reflected in their views on how others rank their occupation and with respect to whether they would choose different occupations if given an opportunity to do so.

Conversely, one explanation for the high levels of satisfaction of the former blue-collarites is that this group is able to engage in implicit bargaining of the type that takes place in both organized and unorganized shops between first-line supervisors and workers. Such dealers had already developed bargaining skills in the factory. More importantly, the situation of the lease dealer has many features conducive to limited horse trading. Dealer complaints before the F.T.C. and Congressional committees are embarrassing, adding fuel to ever-smoldering fires eagerly fanned by Congressional champions of small business who seek to divorce refining from retailing; vacant stations or ones with a new operator (replacing a canceled dealer or one who has decided to move to a more advantageously located station owned by another major oil company) are not so profitable for the supplier as are those operated by experienced and competent dealers; and company salesmen have some considerable influence over the allocations made from sales-promotion and station-remodeling budgets. It is, therefore, not surprising that, as some informants reported, quids and quos are more easily exchanged by lease dealers and company salesmen than in the nonlease situation. For former blue-collarites there is much continuity between their present relations with salesmen and those they once had with the foreman, whether in organized shops or otherwise.

At the same time, higher levels of contentment for lease dealers generally, and for former blue-collarite lessees in particular, are so generalized as to suggest other explanations, in addition to locational and competitive advantages, favorable supplier relations, and bargaining opportunities. The fact

[7] It is likely that former white-collarites had higher standards of living in mind than did former blue-collarites when responding to questions tabulated in Table I.

that lessees from small-business as well as from blue-collar backgrounds were very contented and to roughly the same degree suggests that factors other than previous occupational experience should be considered. The role of educational differences, already mentioned, is suggestive in this regard. (See Table VIII.)

Table 8

EDUCATIONAL ACHIEVEMENTS OF DEALERS, ACCORDING TO
OCCUPATIONAL BACKGROUND

Previous Occupation	8 years and less (%)	9-11 years (%)	High School Graduates (%)	College or Technical Training (%)	No Answer (%)	Total
Blue-Collar (N = 83)	25	25	31	16	3	100
White-Collar (N = 37)	0	24	32	38	6	100
Small-Business (N = 42)	26	33	31	0	·10	100

Table 9

SATISFACTION/ACCOMMODATION OF DEALERS, ACCORDING TO PREVIOUS
OCCUPATION AND DEGREE OF AUTHORITARIANISM (F)

Previous Occupation and Degree of Authoritarianism (F)*	N	Mean Satisfaction/Accommodation Score on Work-Related Questions†
Blue-Collar, High F	33	62
Blue-Collar, Low F	11	43
White-Collar, High F	16	58
White-Collar, Low F	6	35
Small-Business, High F	13	71
Small-Business, Low F	4	65

*The familiar 10-item "short form" of the F Scale was utilized to measure authoritarianism, providing a possible range of scores from 10 to 70. We used the following cutting points, having omitted the "medium" group in this report: 10 to 36 and 51 to 70, for High F and Low F, respectively.

†These scores, and those reported in Table 10, were derived by computing an over-all average from the percentage of satisfied dealers (p̄) on each of the above six categories, using the questions listed in Table 4.

In Tables IX and X we see that when personality differences, as measured by the well-known California F (Authoritarianism) Scale, are considered we can inflate the differences already reported as associated with proprietary arrangements. Unfortunately, our small sample prevents a consideration of previous occupation, proprietary arrangements, and authoritarianism simultaneously as a composite set of characteristics associated with work satisfactions. But if we consider (1) that high F dealers, regardless of occupational background, were more content than low F's; (2) that lease dealerships are more likely to be chosen by men from blue-collar and small-business backgrounds; (3) that high F's are more likely to become lessees than are low F's; and (4) that contented dealers are more likely to be lessees than owners, then it is reasonable to suggest that we cannot fully appreciate the impact of small-business experience on former blue-collarites without knowing, first, something about their personality (since F, or authoritarianism score, is the single best predictor of contentment) and, second, their proprietary arrangements. The finding that former blue-collarites who are both high in "authoritarianism" and prevalent in lease-type stations are more contented than authoritarian blue-collarites under different proprietary arrangements is consistent with theoretical thinking about the authoritarian personality and with empirical work on authoritarianism reported in many places. The lease station provides these dealers with a situation congruent with their personality needs. Such personalities thrive on their highly structured subordination to the supplier and the opportunity to exercise authority over their station help. For low-F men (especially well-educated former white-collarites, some of whom are lease dealers), such hierarchical organizational arrangement may well seem insufferable.

Table 10

PERCENTAGE OF DEALERS IN DIFFERENT PROPRIETARY
ARRANGEMENTS, ACCORDING TO DEGREE OF AUTHORITARIANISM (F)

	Company Lease	Third-Party Lease	Owner	Total
High F ($N = 76$)	55	25	20	100%
Low F ($N = 27$)	26	59	15	100
Population of Dealers ($N = 194$)	48	32	20	100

We thus conclude that former blue-collarites are not all of a piece but respond to their situations as do dealers from other occupational backgrounds —in accordance with their personalities and with their proprietary circumstances. Much of this analysis parallels the suggestive interpretations of "working-class authoritarianism"[8] advanced by others.

II

Before we move to an alternative conceptualization of "former blue-collarites," we would point out that the lesser contentment of white-collar dealers relative to other lease dealers may also be associated with differences in aspiration levels that are obscured by the similar language used in response to that question (see Table I). It is likely that former white-collar workers had higher living standards in mind when they told us that they had aspired, at entry, to "make a living."

The notion "former blue-collarites" may obviously refer to class background as well as to former occupation. A long tradition of social inquiry, at least since Marx, suggests the importance of class background in the shaping of social attitudes. A review of findings on the association of class background with work satisfactions shows the same general pattern as for job histories, although in a much less dramatic fashion. Dealers from blue-collar origins are somewhat more accommodated than are those from small-business or

---

[8] Seymour Martin Lipset, *Political Man: Essays on the Sociology of Democracy* (Garden City, N. Y.: Doubleday & Company, Inc., 1960), Ch. IV.

white-collar families. Because we found these differences, we decided to analyze the combined effects of father's occupation and previous job on dealer satisfactions. We chose the five combinations that included some blue-collar past experience. They included the following:

		N
(1)	Blue-Collar Fathers + Blue-Collar Job History	=54
(2)	Blue-Collar Fathers + Small Business Job History	=21
(3)	Blue-Collar Fathers + White-Collar Job History	=18
(4)	Small Business Fathers + Blue-Collar Job History	=18
(5)	White-Collar Fathers + Blue-Collar Job History	= 6

An examination of Table XI will suggest that these five subgroups may not be distinguished by any combination of common background characteristics on which we have data, by their present station circumstances, by their personalities (as measured by the F scale), or by their age at entry into small business. Yet some intriguing differences in scores on work satisfaction appeared which, we concluded, could be linked to dealers' *total* mobility experiences. More specifically, dealers with a mixture of white- and blue-collar pasts (that is, those with white-collar fathers and blue-collar job histories, and vice versa) are only a fraction as accommodated across all the satisfaction/accommodation items as are dealers from other backgrounds, suggesting that the mobility experience itself deserved further examination. In a word, the accommodated dealers experienced less radically discontinuous changes in their class positions during their lives than had the others.

Radical discontinuities in their social relationships—which movement in and out of substantially different class groups surely implies—have apparently left the dissatisfied dealers with a disquieting sense of what-might-have-been in the white-collar worlds of their fathers or former peers, as the case may be. They have, in short, "skidded"; their social and psychological disappointments are reflected in their situation as small businessmen. Although their attitudes are not directly comparable with those encountered among skidders in a blue-collar shop, neither are they inconsistent with them.[9] Responses by skidders to a question dealing, for example, with big-business practices were much like those we reported earlier concerning dealers' attitudes toward corporations.

Confidence in our conclusion concerning the importance of continuities and discontinuities in social experience would be greater if we could validate it, because it rests in part on an analysis of small numbers. A crude test of its validity is fortunately possible if we consider the extent of work satisfaction of all our dealers, including those from neither blue-collar families nor blue-collar occupational backgrounds.

Our sample then grows from 117 to nearly 150, and we would predict that those who have experienced no change in social-class status prior to becoming dealers would have the highest levels of satisfaction, those with the greatest discontinuities in mobility experience would have the lowest levels of satis-

9 Harold Wilensky and Hugh Edwards, "The Skidder: Ideological Adjustments of Downward Mobile Workers," *American Sociological Review*, Vol. 24, No. 2 (April, 1959), pp. 215-31.

Table 11

EDUCATION, RELIGION, TIME OF ENTRY, AND STATION CHARACTERISTICS OF DEALERS, ACCORDING TO FATHERS' AND PREVIOUS OCCUPATION
(Percentaged by Rows)

	Education (Per Cent)				Religion (Per Cent)			Time of Entry (Per Cent)			Proprietary Arrangement (Per Cent)		
	8 years or less	9-11 years	High School Graduate	Some College Technical School	Protestant	Catholic	Jew	Pre-WW II	During WW II	After WW II	Company Lease	Third Party	Owner
Blue-Collar Father, Blue-Collar Job History (N = 54)	31	30	26	13	21	63	15	80		20	11	52	37
Blue-Collar Father, Small Business Job History (N = 21)	29	48	24	0	10	53	38	62	5	33	33	52	14
Small-Business Father, Blue-Collar Job History (N = 18)	22	17	39	22	12	47	41	17	11	72	10	61	28
Blue-Collar Father, White-Collar Job History (N = 18)	0	35	41	23	0	53	47	22	11	67	33	39	28
White-Collar Father, Blue-Collar Job History (N = 6)	0	33	33	33	0	50	50	66	0	33	33	67	0

Former Blue-Collarites in Small Business

571

Table 12

SATISFACTION/ACCOMMODATION OF DEALERS ON WORK-RELATED ISSUES*
ACCORDING TO FAMILY AND PREVIOUS OCCUPATIONAL BACKGROUND†

	Blue-Collar Fathers, Blue-Collar Job Histories ($N = 54$)	Blue-Collar Fathers, Small-Business Job Histories ($N = 21$)	Small-Business Fathers, Blue-Collar Job Histories ($N = 18$)	Blue-Collar Fathers, White-Collar Job Histories ($N = 18$)	White-Collar Fathers, Blue-Collar Job Histories ($N = 6$)
Son in small business	−28	−30	−30	−66	−66
Corporate sincerity	−28	−20	22	6	−66
Hours	−16	−18	0	−54	−34
Pay	−10	36	12	− 6	−34
How others see me	38	48	6	− 6	0
Harmony of big- and small-business interests	34	34	34	−22	−100
Would like a different occupation	38	36	22	−76	−34
Salesman relations	32	10	6	38	−20
Prestige	40	40	56	22	32
Security	44	40	22	34	0
View of own occupation compared with other occupations	44	30	66	54	0
Family prestige	66	34	66	56	32
Evaluation of relations with suppliers	52	36	44	10	32
Evaluation of customer relations	68	68	52	64	0
Over-all average computed from percentages accommodated on individual items ($\bar{p}$)	27	23	27	4	−18

*Issues are described in detail in Table 4.

†Figures in cells are scores derived by subtracting the percentage of dealers who gave
alienated or dissatisfied responses from the percentage expressing satisfaction/accommoda-
tion. Negative scores resulted when the number of dissatisfied on a given issue exceeded the
number expressing satisfaction. Where a group divided evenly on an issue, the resulting
score was zero.

Table 13

MOBILITY EXPERIENCE AND SATISFACTION/ACCOMMODATION ON WORK-RELATED ISSUES*

Mobility Experience	Little Discontinuity (Blue-Collar Father, Blue-Collar Job History; White-Collar Father, White Collar Job History; Small-Business Father, Small Business Job History) (N = 69)	Moderate Discontinuity (Blue-Collar Father, Small-Business Job History; White-Collar Father, Small Business Job History,† Blue-Collar Job History) (N = 42)	Considerable Discontinuity (Small-Business Father, White-Collar Job History;† White-Collar Father, Blue-Collar Job History; Blue-Collar Father, White-Collar Job History) (N = 35)
Son in small Business	−30	−26	−64
Corporate sincerity	−22	2	−30
Hours	−8	−12	−26
Pay	−4	26	0
How others see me	38	28	4
Harmony of big- and small-business interests	34	28	−20
Would like a different occupation	36	38	−52
Salesman relations	30	16	4
Prestige	42	46	32
Security	36	26	32
View of own occupation, compared with other occupations	42	36	36
Family prestige	62	52	54
Evaluation of relations with suppliers	54	40	32
Evaluation of customer relations	64	64	58
Over-all average computed for scores on individual items	27	27**	4

*Scores in cells were computed as in Table 12 and added (or subtracted) for the mobility groups.

†Dealers with white-collar job histories in many instances had higher-status white-collar jobs than did dealers' fathers with white-collar occupations. Our data unfortunately do not permit us to determine whether this holds in every case.

**Note: While the first two groups have nearly identical scores, the second group is, generally speaking, less alienated (negative scores) on issues on which both groups are alienated and less accommodated on issues on which both groups are accommodated. The over-all scores conceal these qualitative differences.

Former Blue-Collarites in Small Business

573

faction, whereas those with some but not radical changes in class would be midway between the two extremes. The data in Table XIII would seem to confirm our prediction and thereby increase our confidence in our interpretation of the effect of discontinuities in the lives of blue-collarites-turned-small-businessmen.

CONCLUSION

By and large, former blue-collar workers who moved into the type of lower-middle-class position we examined, like their former peers who remained in the factory, are an accommodated lot; they are favorably situated in a structure of work relations which provides them a range of opportunities in some respects continuous with those they experienced as blue-collar workers. If, however, they came from white-collar family backgrounds, their earlier experiences in industry did little to temper their reactions to the world of small business, which they found considerably less than rewarding. This was less true of small-business sons who entered dealerships after blue-collar work experiences. The lifetime blue-collarite, meanwhile, joins other dealers who have had a similar continuity in class experience in viewing his situation with not a little equanimity.

Although space does not permit our developing materials that we have on the political-economic ideologies of the dealers, a short statement will help round out the findings we have reported. Dealers who were most resentful about their lot as small businessmen had typically the most liberal attitudes on a series of 30 questions dealing with the issues that political sociologists claim divide the left from the right.[10] Such dealers were also the most educated and least authoritarian in our sample. Meanwhile, those with the most totalitarian and radical rightist attitudes viewed their occupational situation with the greatest equanimity; the latter dealers were largely our former blue-collarites. Liberal intellectuals, restive about the impact of work dissatisfactions, conservative extremism, and authoritarian personality characteristics on the politics of these twentieth-century heirs of traditional capitalism's legacy, should feel somewhat reassured, because the three together might be more likely to foster a militant political posture than would the force of these variables acting separately and, to a degree, in opposite directions.

Readers may join us in our concern for the well-being of democratic institutions were there ever a direct rather than an inverse relationship between the degree of work alienation and the degree of general ideological disenchantment within the small-business community. The fact that our data do not indicate this suggests that blue-collarites in small business who realize the American Dream may not end up contributing to an American nightmare.

[10] These questions treated a number of contemporary political, economic, and social issues.

The Blue-Collarite Abandoned in the Big City

THOMAS F. HOULT

ALBERT J. MAYER*

THE much-discussed "flight to the suburbs" has meant, among other things, that blue-collar workers are being abandoned in the big cities to fend for themselves. The specific consequences of the entire process have been noted in detail for Detroit, Michigan.[1] Because Detroit, as shown in "Midwestern Minority Housing Market" and in the works of Sharp and Schnore[2] is largely representative of the wave of the future so far as large-city population and housing trends are concerned, it is appropriate to concentrate attention on this one city.

I

By 1970, present trends continuing, the population of the City of Detroit[3] will:

Include only one-quarter of the most productive age group (25-44 years) of all persons living in the metropolitan area;[4]

Include only one-third of all producing-age persons (15-65 years) living in the metropolitan area;

Have an age distribution such that between one-third and one-half (41 per cent) of its total will consist of persons in the age groups considered generally nonproductive (under 15 and over 64 years of age).

The revolutionary effects of such population changes will be accentuated

* With the assistance of Susan Sheffield.

[1] Thomas F. Hoult and Albert J. Mayer, with the assistance of Susan Sheffield, "The Population Revolution in Detroit" (Detroit: Wayne State University Institute for Regional and Urban Studies, 1963).

[2] "Midwestern Minority Housing Market, A Special Report by the Advance Mortgage Corporation," issued December 1, 1963; Harry Sharp and Leo F. Schnore, "The Changing Color Composition of Metropolitan Areas," *Land Economics*, Vol. 38 (May, 1962), pp. 169-85.

[3] Unless otherwise noted, the term "City of Detroit" as used in this report includes the enclave cities of Highland Park and Hamtramck.

[4] "Metropolitan area" as used here refers to the Standard Metropolitan Statistical Area—Wayne, Oakland, and Macomb Counties.

by the accompanying alterations in the relative size of the two major racial groups living in the city. By 1970, present trends continuing, Detroit will:

Be approximately 44 per cent Negro in its total population;

Have a school population that is almost two-thirds Negro (63 per cent);

Have only 18 per cent of all white metropolitan-area residents in the child-bearing ages (15-44 years);

Include only one-seventh (15 per cent) of the most productive age group (25-44 years) of all white persons living in the metropolitan area;

Have 91 per cent of the metropolitan area's aged Negroes (those 65 years of age and over).

If the projected 1970 racial and age-group distribution for the City of Detroit actually occurs—and it will occur unless there is a significant change in present trends—the political, economic, and general social effects will be literally massive. White residents of the city will be well on the way to a numerical minority status; politicians, to be successful, will increasingly have to consider the needs of the Negro voter; long-established economic handicaps of Negro workers will have a profound impact on business and on the tax resources needed to provide even minimal city services; the increasing proportion of dependent residents will result in an increasing demand on decreasing revenue sources; school programs, to be effective, will have to concentrate on the needs of pupils whose attitudes and aspirations have been adversely affected by economic deprivation and by various forms of segregation and discrimination.

II

The foregoing predictions about the changing nature of Detroit's population are based on an analysis of census data, the relevant portions of which were included in the publication entitled "The Population Revolution in Detroit."[5] Those interested can refer to the original. Here we need only point out that the magnitude of population changes in Detroit constitute nothing less than a revolution. This ongoing revolution has a qualitative nature which seems far more important than the quantitative decline of total population being experienced by Detroit and other large cities.

The data show that from 1940 to 1960 (and, by projection, to 1970),[6] there is a constantly increasing proportion of Negroes,[7] particularly younger and older Negroes, living in the City of Detroit. The decade-by-decade percentage increase of Negro Detroiters, by age, was (or will be from 1960 to 1970) as follows:

---

[5] Hoult and Mayer, *op. cit.*

[6] Note that the projections are conservative, based as they are on 1950-1960 findings; racial and age changes from 1940 to 1950 were affected by the war effort and were therefore more extreme than were those in the later decade.

[7] In this report, the terms "Negro" and "nonwhite" are used interchangeably, since in the Detroit area 98 per cent of those included in the frequently used "nonwhite" census classification are Negro.

HOULT
MAYER

DECADE-BY-DECADE INCREASE OF NEGROES
IN DETROIT, BY AGE

Under 15 years of age

1940-1950	113%
1950-1960	131%
1960-1970	51%

15 to 24 years of age

1940-1950	87%
1950-1960	25%
1960-1970	74%

25 to 44 years of age

1940-1950	228%
1950-1960	23%
1960-1970	− 16%

45 to 64 years of age

1940-1950	119%
1950-1960	62%
1960-1970	59%

65 years of age and over

1940-1950	143%
1950-1960	130%
1960-1970	70%

Note that the only age group of Negro Detroiters experiencing any decrease at all is that from 25 to 44 years of age; this age group will decline 16 per cent between 1960 and 1970.

In addition to the decade-by-decade percentage increases and decreases shown above, 20-year and 30-year percentage changes in the relative size of the Negro group, by age, in the City of Detroit have been noted. Thus, by 1970 —using 1940 as the base—there will be a 640 per cent increase in the proportionate number of Negro Detroiters under the age of 15; during the same period, there will be a 305 per cent increase in the proportionate number of Negro Detroiters aged 15 to 24, a 465 per cent increase in the proportionate number of those aged 45 to 64, and an 850 per cent increase in the proportionate number of those aged 65 and over. Negro Detroiters aged 25 to 44 constitute the only age group with a relatively "moderate" 1940 to 1970 proportionate increase (94 per cent). These percentage increases are spectacularly large—but not because they describe the doubling and tripling of very small numbers of people; this is not a case of 10 people growing to 40 and being described as "increasing by 300 per cent." In 1940, there were 155,495 Negro Detroiters; by 1960 there were 500,275, constituting 29 per cent of the total population of the city. It is the changes and trends in major subdivisions of this very large group that are described by the percentage increases indicated.

In view of the trends just described, it is not surprising to learn that, from 1940 to 1960 (and, by projection, to 1970), there has been a constantly decreasing proportion of whites living in the City of Detroit. The decrease has been at all age levels except among the oldest residents, with the decrease being greatest (75 per cent decline by 1970) in the most productive age group (25 to 44 years of age). Some of the decrease in the latter age group may be attributed to factors other than the city-to-suburbs movement—it is probably due to low birth rates during the depression era—since a general decline

The
Blue-Collarite
Abandoned
in the
Big City

in the age group is apparent in the suburbs as well as among city whites. But the age-group decline among city whites will be three times that of suburban whites (75 per cent versus 25 per cent) by 1970.

When projected percentage changes from 1960 to 1970 are noted, it becomes clear that some of the most significant aspects of the 1940 to 1970 changes are occurring during the current decade. For example, the data shows a 50 per cent decline from 1940 to 1970 in the number of white Detroiters under 15 years of age; but they also indicate a projected 45 per cent decline of the same age-group from 1960 to 1970. In other words, approximately nine-tenths (that is, 45 per cent is nine-tenths of 50 per cent) of the 1940-to-1970 decline of white Detroiters under age 15 is occurring (or will occur) during the last ten years of the 30-year span. Similarly, about four-fifths of the 1940-to-1970 decline of white Detroiters from 25 to 44 years of age is occurring (or will occur) during the last 10 years of the 30-year span between 1940 and 1970. But the larger part of the 1940-to-1970 city increase in the number of older whites has already occurred (that is, the increase for this group will be only 13 per cent from 1960 to 1970; whereas the 1940-to-1970 increase for the group is a very impressive 165 per cent). Similarly, most of the 1940-to-1970 decrease in city whites aged 15 to 24 has already been experienced; the same is true for the 1940-to-1970 increase in suburban whites under age 15.

The following two sets of figures show the final 1970 population distribution which will result from the trends described above:

PROJECTED 1970 POPULATION DISTRIBUTION

	Per Cent of Total City Population in 1970	
Age Group	Nonwhite	White
Under 15	17.96%	10.75%
15-24	6.57	9.21
25-44	8.18	8.01
45-64	9.22	17.48
65 and Over	2.42	10.20
Total	44.35	55.65

PROJECTED 1970 POPULATION DISTRIBUTION
(Cont.)

	Per Cent of Total Detroit Suburban Population in 1970	
Age Group	Nonwhite	White
Under 15	0.87%	35.03%
15-24	0.44	16.27
25-44	0.47	23.53
45-64	0.52	18.15
65 and Over	0.13	4.59
Total	2.42	97.58

The first set of figures shows that young (under 15) Negro Detroiters will greatly outnumber young white Detroiters, and that there will be approximately equal proportions of Negro and white Detroiters from 15 to 44 years of age.

The only instance where white Detroiters will constitute a larger proportion than Negro Detroiters will be in the age groups over 44 years—there will be twice as many whites as Negroes from age 45 to 64, and four times as many whites as Negroes over 64 years of age.

Thus, the total picture conveyed is that of a city population that will have very large proportionate numbers of young Negroes and older whites.

The second set of figures constitutes a "suburban version" of the first set and indicates that in 1970 Detroit's suburbs will continue to be almost totally white in their population make-up. The white suburbanites will consist mainly of young people and of people in the most productive age group (25 to 44 years of age). Relatively dependent oldsters will constitute only about five per cent of the total suburban population; in contrast, 12½ per cent of the City of Detroit's total population will be age 65 and over by 1970. Thus, speaking proportionately, in 1970 Detroit, as contrasted with its suburbs, will have two and one-half times as many older citizens.

When the population trends described are analyzed in terms of the technique known as the "method of expected cases," details of the city's loss of total population—both relative to the metropolitan area and absolutely in recent years—become manifest. Only the nonwhite group shows a gain that is more than expected during the last two decades of the 30-year span. The discrepancy between actual size and expected size of the white group in the City of Detroit grows larger with the passing of each decade. Between 1960 and 1970, the number of white Detroiters will be more than 35 per cent (36.65 per cent) less than could be expected if white Detroiters increased in numbers at the same rate as white residents of the total metropolitan area. The opposite is true for the suburbs, where the size of the white group is always larger than one would expect if the suburbs grew at the same rate as the total metropolitan area.

When the method of expected cases is used with an age-group breakdown, it becomes clear that the number of Detroit City whites of all ages in all three of the decades between 1940 and 1970 is (or will be) less than expected, *not excepting* whites over age 65. That is, as described above, Detroit will have what amounts to a "surplus" of aged whites; but, even so, the increase in the number of aged whites in the city is less than should be expected if the age group were growing at the same rate as it is in the total metropolitan area.

The latter fact epitomizes the enormity of what is happening to Detroit from the standpoint of population change—even its fastest-growing group of whites (those over 65) is increasing at a slower rate than in the metropolitan area as a whole. In contrast, the numbers of suburban whites in all age-groups have increased (1940 to 1960) or are increasing (1960 to 1970) between nine per cent and 70 per cent (the former figure refers to those over age 65 during the 1940-1950 decade) faster than the growth rate for the same racial age groups in the total metropolitan community.

III

Population trends in the Detroit area have been described in detail because, to a large extent, Detroit illustrates America's big-city "demographic wave of the future." Hence, it is particularly significant to note, the data clearly demonstrate that *Detroit is, by and large, being abandoned by all except those who suffer from relatively great housing, educational, and general economic deprivations.* As a consequence, the central city will be increasingly unable to support itself, and even less able to continue its much-needed support of the suburbs. Although many suburbanites are loath to admit it, each suburb has been able to grow and function primarily because there has been a nearby central city with a complete set of urban facilities —large-scale industry, highly specialized services such as adequate libraries, centers of communication and transportation, the means and techniques needed to provide proper water and sewage systems for a concentrated population, and the like. These are the types of services that the typical dormitory suburb almost never provides yet must have to exist.

It should be noted in conclusion that there are some who will assert that the writers are equating a large increase in nonwhite population with a decline of the central city. We feel that it is very important to disabuse those who would make this inference—an inference that can only divert attention from the major point of this report. That point is, present trends continuing: *Fact*—By 1970, Detroit's population will consist of very large proportionate numbers of younger Negroes and older whites; *Fact*—Younger Negroes and older whites are relatively more dependent and are relatively poor sources for tax revenue; *Fact*—Negroes as a total group, in comparison with whites, are economically and educationally handicapped because of job discrimination and because of housing and school segregation; *Conclusion*—By 1970, officials of the City of Detroit will be called upon to give greatly increased social and economic services to a population having greatly decreased opportunities for providing even minimal tax revenues.

These facts, and the almost inevitable conclusion to which they lead, do not suggest anything at all negative about race and color. On the contrary, the facts and the related conclusion suggest that America's great cities, Detroit among them, now must pay for the long-standing American tendency to segregate and to discriminate against minority groups, particularly Negroes.

For those interested in possible solutions to problems such as those being faced by Detroit, the improving status of Negroes may be regarded as one hopeful sign—*but* it is doubtful that this improvement is occurring at a rate fast enough to fill the gap left by departing whites. Furthermore, it can be assumed that Negroes with increased status will themselves move to the suburbs just as fast as open-occupancy housing becomes available. A city income tax, applied (as in Detroit) to nonresidents as well as to residents, may be seen as a saving feature—*if* the completion of more and more suburban shopping centers and office and industrial facilities does not make a hollow mockery of the attempt to tax nonresident workers. Urban renewal is mentioned by some as the ultimate solution—*but*, Detroit is typical in the sense that urban renewal is, to date, mostly talk, mostly "cleared acres," with precious few residents. Indeed, despite all of the millions of dollars and effort expended so far, only about 1,000 housing units have been built in Detroit's renewal projects, and at this date only several thousand more are contemplated for subsequent projects.

There are, finally, those who regard the development of metropolitan-area government as the best solution to the problems being faced by large cities —but, with few exceptions, is it realistic to believe that suburbanites, who already outvote their big-city brethren by far, can be convinced that they must integrate their areas with the area whose problems and difficulties they assumed they had left behind?

The Future of Toil*

RONALD GROSS

DOES toil have a future? If so, what are its lineaments? These questions are central to the prospects of blue-collar workers, for it is precisely the kind of work they do which defines them as blue-collar, working-class people.

In our society, Everett Hughes has pointed out, a man's occupation is "a combination of price tag and calling card."[1] This is increasingly true as widespread affluence erodes the connection between income and class status. When Bennett Berger studied a California working-class suburb[2] populated by semiskilled automobile production workers who had acquired all the accoutrements of lower-middle-class life, he found little of the standard suburban syndrome. Far from exhibiting conformity, anxieties about getting ahead, social hyperactivity, lack of privacy, concern about status, and transcience, these families remained in most respects indomitably working-class. One reason was that they defined their class on purely occupational criteria: they worked with their hands, for an hourly wage, in a factory. This gave them their blue-collar status; one respondent, acknowledging that he and his neighbors did enjoy all the domestic comforts of white-collar suburbanites, explained that "around here, the working class *is* the middle class." To discern the future of the blue-collar world, then, we must consider the future of blue-collar work, for it is their toil which gives its defining character to these people's lives.

As C. Wright Mills noted, American unions have the simple ideology of alienated workers: more and more money for less and less labor.[3] Actually, there are three significant attitudes toward toil in America today. To the

* The writer would like to acknowledge the valuable research assistance of Mr. Philip Springer, at the time of writing associated with the Bureau of Applied Social Research, Columbia University, in reviewing data concerning the effects of automation at the workplace.

[1] Everett C. Hughes, *Men and Their Work* (New York: The Free Press of Glencoe, Inc., 1958), p. 42.

[2] Bennett M. Berger, *Working-Class Suburb: A Study of Auto Workers in Suburbia* (Berkeley: University of California Press, 1960).

[3] C. Wright Mills, *White Collar: The American Middle Classes* (New York: Oxford University Press, 1956), p. 230.

extent that the working life of the blue-collarite is thought about at all, by himself or by others, these are the guiding viewpoints:

1. *We are on the brink of a workless world; leisure will henceforth move to the center of men's lives.* Thus John Kenneth Galbraith argues that "the greatest prospect we face" as a nation is to "eliminate toil as a required economic institution."[4] Gerard Piel assures us that this will occur inevitably, making blue-collar workers as scarce as farmers by the year 2000.[5] Sooner, says Donald Michael in his pamphlet on *Cybernation.*[6]

2. *Work must be stepped up, not reduced,* for reasons summarized succinctly by W. W. Rostow:

> It is too soon for a four-day week and for tolerance of substantial levels of unemployment. . . . A society like the United States, structurally committed to a high-consumption way of life; committed also to maintaining the decencies that go with adequate social overhead capital; committed by its own interests and the interests of those dependent upon it or allied to it to deal with a treacherous and extremely expensive world environment; committed additionally, out of its own internal dynamics, to a rapidly enlarging population and to a working force which must support more old and more young . . . such a society must use its resources fully, productively, and wisely.[7]

Michael Young's *Rise of the Meritocracy*[8] is a satiric projection of this line of thought—a society in which individual worth is measured solely by the person's contribution to the nation's efficiency.

3. *Work is still the center of men's lives, but its quality, not its quantity or efficiency, is the important consideration.* The vacuousness and corruption of work in a profit-driven society saps the morale of the people. We need neither more work nor less work, but *better* work. "It's hard to grow up," writes Paul Goodman, "when there isn't enough man's work."[9] Other social critics, like Harvey Swados[10] and Erich Fromm,[11] agree. Some of them, like David Riesman, see automation as providing the opportunity to humanize work for the first time in history:

> . . . we are not necessarily the prisoners of our technological fate, of our given forms of mass production and of the organization of work . . . a rich, heavily automatized society is precisely one that can afford to reorganize work so that attention is focused no longer exclusively on the product, but on the worker himself as a product of his work.[12]

---

[4] John Kenneth Galbraith, *The Affluent Society* (Boston: Houghton Mifflin Company, 1958), p. 340.

[5] Gerard Piel, *Consumers of Abundance* (Santa Barbara, Calif.: Center for the Study of Democratic Institutions, 1961), p. 7.

[6] Donald Michael, *Cybernation: The Silent Conquest* (Santa Barbara, Calif.: Center for the Study of Democratic Institutions, 1962).

[7] W. W. Rostow, *The Stages of Economic Growth: A Non-Communist Manifesto* (Cambridge: Cambridge University Press, 1960), p. 81.

[8] Michael Young, *The Rise of the Meritocracy* (London: Thames and Hudson, 1958).

[9] Paul Goodman, *Growing Up Absurd* (New York: Random House, 1960), p. 17.

[10] Harvey Swados, "The Myth of the Happy Worker," *The Nation,* Vol. 185 (August 17, 1957).

[11] Erich Fromm, *The Sane Society* (New York: Holt, Rinehart & Winston, Inc., 1955).

[12] David Riesman and Michael Maccoby, "The American Crisis: Political Idealism and the Cold War," *Commentary,* Vol. 29 (June, 1960), p. 470.

Is it realistic to give weight to these value-laden *attitudes* when considering the future of toil? Or should one rely more on projecting *technological* potentialities and their implications? It would seem evident from the work of sociologists like W. Lloyd Warner and political scientists like A. A. Berle[13] that moral sentiments and value judgments will play an increasing role in determining national policy in the United States. Increasingly, the imperatives of technological efficiency are subordinated to political purposes broadly expressing a moral consensus. As Warner writes:

> . . . although the society increasingly is using a nonmoral technology and the cold rationality of science, American capitalistic enterprise is less and less dominated by the rational values of the technology (and those of classical economics); increasingly, it feels and yields to the influence of the nonrational value system of the moral order.[14]

Ivar Berg put it more bluntly, observing that "the values in American society are changing and inexorably will focus far more on the man than on the product and the dollar."[15] It therefore seems justifiable to consider emerging value judgments and moral aspirations as potent though hardly decisive determinants of the future of toil.

On the other hand, the burgeoning technology of automation will certainly dictate the character and contours of the industrial environment of tomorrow's blue-collar worker. The currently available data suggest that the advent of automation will have the following short-range effects on the blue-collarite's world of work:

1. Improved physical working conditions, especially in regard to bodily exertion, health, safety, and nervous strain due to excessive sound levels reduced.

2. Increased emotional problems, such as gastric ulcers, resulting from isolation from other workers and prevention of daydreaming by the need for increased, constant attention. These effects may be temporary or characteristic only of transitional phases of automation; they have sometimes been mitigated by training programs.

3. Little upgrading of workers, contrary to popular opinion and hope. Skill levels seem to decline more than they rise. In the case studies undertaken by the Bureau of Labor Statistics in a variety of representative industries, the general effect of automation was to substitute one low-skilled job for another.[16]

4. Decreased control of work pace and less handling of materials.[17] A representative automobile worker told one interviewer:

---

[13] Adolf A. Berle, *The American Economic Republic* (New York: Harcourt, Brace & World, Inc., 1963).

[14] W. Lloyd Warner, *The Corporation in the Emergent American Society* (New York: Harper & Row, Publishers, 1962), p. 38.

[15] Quoted from Robert B. Cooney, "Democracy in the Workplace," *AFL-CIO American Federationist* (March, 1962), p. 11.

[16] Walter Buckingham, *Automation: Its Impact on Business and People* (New York: Harper & Row, Publishers, 1961), p. 98.

[17] This analysis of four major effects of automation in the work place follows Buckingham, *ibid.*, pp. 93-108, but with some changes and shifts in emphasis.

(I don't like) the lack of feeling responsible for your work. The feeling that you're turning out more work but know it's *not yours really* and not as good as you could make it if you had control of the machine like before.[18]

What generalization might we make about these working conditions under automation?[19] The worker's function seems to shift from the physical to the mental level; he operates as a cognitive rather than a mechanical component of the production process. No one who has worked on an assembly line, or glimpsed its horrors in the works of Harvey Swados,[20] Patricia Sexton,[21] or Daniel Bell,[22] will regret the passing of the tension and danger of a steel mill or automobile plant. But despite this change, the worker is still, under automation, being used as an instrument of production, and one wonders if he is not gaining many of the disadvantages of white-collar work without its psychological advantages. For it seems that the worker who up to now has been thought of as a low-level handling machine is now to be thought of as a low-level computer. His eyes and brain, rather than his hands, are linked to the other machines. Gone is whatever distinctive self-image was provided by the "sexual frenzy of the factory,"[23] or by the feeling expressed by a British worker in comparing himself with white-collar clerks: "He works in a collar and a tie and has clean hands, and I have to dirty my hands. What he does can be rubbed out while what I do stays."[24]

There is, however, a promising pair of developments which could alter the basic concept of the role of the blue-collar worker; at one significant point the emerging *ideas* about work and the emerging *technology* of the work place intersect. It is here that we find the most exciting possibilities regarding the future of toil. Georges Friedmann, in *Anatomy of Work*, reviews experiments in Europe and the United States since the war—experiments which endeavor to overcome the "orthodoxy of scientific management" which decrees that maximum efficiency demands specialization and routinization of the work process. Such firms as IBM, Detroit Edison, and Equitable Insurance have reversed the division of labor through "job enlargement," giving each worker a whole sequence of tasks constituting a complete job and providing some sense of achievement, or letting workers handle their jobs in small groups, rotating among different tasks and setting their own working conditions. The results have been good for the workers, and also good for business. Although the workers do not perform their more complex

---

[18] W. A. Faunce, "Automation and the Automobile Worker," *American Sociological Review*, Vol. 28 (August, 1958), p. 401.

[19] Additional research is sorely needed in this area. The best studies, such as those by Mann and Hoffman, Walker, and Faunce, are not really comparable, since their categories and approaches differ. For example, Walker's work is not quantitative. Again, Walker cites the ill effects of night shifts, but we do not know how typical these are in automated factories. What is needed is a body of multi-case research with controls for the major variables: types of industry, organizational factors, and so forth.

[20] Swados, *op. cit.*

[21] Patricia Cayo Sexton, "The Auto Assembly Line: An Inside View," *Harper's Magazine*, Vol. 224 (June 1962), pp. 54-57.

[22] Daniel Bell, *Work and Its Discontents* (Boston: Beacon Press, 1956).

[23] Cited by Leo Steinberg in *Harper's Magazine*, November, 1961, p. 88, from Marcel Jean, *History of Surrealist Painting* (New York: Grove Press, 1960).

[24] George Cyriax and Robert Oakeshott, *The Bargainers* (London: Faber & Faber, Ltd., 1960), p. 142.

and varied tasks with the same robotlike efficiency with which they executed only one minute task, the reduction in absenteeism, botched work, and employee turnover has usually more than made up for the relaxed pace of work.

Friedmann argues that these experiments have brought us to a turning point in the managerial belief that efficiency demands increasing specialization and simplification of work:

> The subdivision of jobs, constantly on the increase during the development of the machine age from the end of the Eighteenth Century onwards, will in future appear, not as a one-way process of unlimited duration, but as a transitory form of labor, and often a pathological one, if we consider it in relation to some of our deeper human needs.[25]

What is most interesting and little noted is that strikingly similar conclusions emerge from studies of the impact of automation. In his comprehensive study, *Automation,* for example, Walter Buckingham writes:

> With mass production, and now with automation, trivialization of work and its resulting specialization of labor ·may have reached its economic limits. At first mechanization reduced the physical exertion of labor by transferring the heavy, back-breaking jobs to machines but it left workers with an endless number of routine, repetitive, monotonous trifles. Automation permits many of the most petty tasks to be assumed by machines. Electronic control equipment can perform the more undistinguished jobs of counting, sorting, filing, deciding between two clearly defined alternatives, moving something from one fixed location to another at precisely the right time and so on.[26]

But the fact that upgrading is anything but endemic in automated plants at present indicates that this happy result will come about only as the result of conscious and strenuous action by management, prodded, if need be, by organized labor. A concrete example of the possibilities is revealed in the study of an automated power plant by Mann and Hoffman:

> In building the new power plant, technological changes and management decisions resulted in the redesigning of the operating jobs. This redesign consisted of enlarging the jobs of each operator by job rotation among different types of jobs and by increasing the scope of responsibility on each of these jobs. The results of transferring men from more specialized jobs in the older plants to the enlarged jobs in the new plant were for the most part positive. Expressions of increased job interest and job satisfaction were found in a large proportion of these transferred operators. The combination of job enlargement and of job rotation increased for many of these men—at least temporarily—the intrinsic satisfactions which could be derived from the work itself.[27]

Walker and Guest, in *The Man on the Assembly Line,*[28] also recommended

---

[25] Georges Friedmann, *The Anatomy of Work,* translated by Wyatt Rawson (New York: The Free Press of Glencoe, Inc., 1961), p. 120.

[26] Buckingham, *op. cit.,* p. 106.

[27] Floyd C. Mann and L. Richard Hoffman, *Automation and the Worker* (New York: Holt, Rinehart & Winston, Inc., 1960), p. 103.

[28] Charles R. Walker and Robert H. Guest, *The Man on the Assembly Line* (Cambridge: Harvard University Press, 1952).

job enlargement and rotation to alleviate auto workers' lack of control over their work process.

Will automation be used to rectify the excesses of the industrial division of labor, or will the blue-collar worker merely become a cognitive rather than a manipulative instrument? The answer lies in the interplay between the imperatives of technology and those of moral valuation, both of them mediated by the social institutions of corporation, government, union, and public opinion. The likeliest outcome is that American industry will neither overturn the "cult of efficiency," as Daniel Bell has been urging for years, nor merely succumb to the compulsions of technology. A middle course seems to be taking shape in a broadening of the concept of efficiency itself to include the workers' morale as an intangible but important outcome of his work. Cold War sophistication is encouraging the widespread realization that the idea of efficiency, if it is to serve as an effective national goal, must be given a broad and enlightened interpretation. It can no longer stand for the simple exploitation of human beings in the service of mechanical output. "Human resources," it turns out, are the most valuable raw material and source of productivity in a highly industrialized society.[29] The idea of efficiency has thus been inverted, turned back upon the worker himself, enabling the Indian H. C. Ganguli to write that:

> . . . for the development of an organization, of a society and a country it is not only efficient work that is needed, but also effective work. The criterion for evaluating a worker's performance should include all aspects of the individual and how he functions not only as a worker, but also as a citizen, as a family man, etc. An effective worker, not simply an efficient one, is a person who not only does his immediate job well but also carries out the other roles he plays in society appropriately. This, it will be noted, is an extension of the concept of efficiency to the larger social environment.[30]

The blue-collar worker, produced by industrialism and its correlates, faces a radically changed world of work in what Daniel Bell has called the "post-industrial" society. Ultimately, of course, this worker is slated for extinction by the developing technology of automation. But the question is whether, during his remaining decades, he will continue to be used as a mere instrument in the interstices of the machine-man system of modern industry, or whether a new view of the role of work and the rights of workers may transform his situation. Granted that the central life interests of blue-collar workers do not focus on their jobs; still, as a French worker told Georges Friedmann, "It's what you spend the most time doing that counts."[31] As automation proceeds, it will encounter the growing moral awareness that work should provide the worker with some intrinsic fulfillment. Out of this interplay of technical and moral demands will come the future world of work for the blue-collarite. He will have little say as an individual about how this interplay is resolved. That is up to the organizations which exercise their countervailing

[29] See, for example, Eli Ginzberg, *Human Resources: The Wealth of a Nation* (New York: Simon and Schuster, Inc., 1958).

[30] H. C. Ganguli, *Industrial Productivity and Motivation* (New York: Asia Publishing House, 1961), p. 80.

[31] Friedmann, *op. cit.*, p. 138.

GROSS

powers in this arena: corporations, unions, government. But there is some indication that technical compulsions and moral awareness intersect at an important point: the broadened concept of efficiency. Increasingly it is felt that the wider community outside the particular productive enterprise in which the worker works has a legitimate concern with the impact of his job on his social character. If true efficiency entails effective operation in a wider context than that of the individual factory, then society cannot condone, even if it must tolerate, the subordination of men to machines. If the nation's greatest wealth and productive power lie in its human resources rather than in the material output of its factories, then we must begin to be alarmed by the paradox noted by Pius XI, that "from the factory dead matter goes out improved, whereas men there are corrupted and degraded."

The Lower Classes and the Negroes: Implications for Intellectuals

HYMAN RODMAN

THERE is a great deal of prejudice and discrimination in our society against the lower classes and against Negroes. Stereotypes that are used about the lower classes, such as *obscene, dirty, loud, lazy, promiscuous, happy,* and *irresponsible,* are also used about Negroes.[1] These stereotypes reflect prejudicial attitudes, and ultimately such attitudes must be changed. A more immediate step, however, is to change the social, economic, educational, political, and legal discrimination that gives rise to these attitudes.

NEGRO RIGHTS

What role can whites play in the present battle for Negro civil rights? Whites must, on the whole, content themselves with a relatively minor role, since the battle has effectively been taken over by Negroes. The temporizing, compromising, gradualist position taken by many whites in past years has clearly been superseded. There are, nevertheless, a number of areas within which whites can still be active. As financial contributors, as members in the ranks, or even as occasional leaders, whites have participated in the 1963 "Negro revolution." The white intellectual, however, in a different way, can still play an important role. He can do this by raising and exploring and pur-

---

[1] See my paper in this volume: "Middle-Class Misconceptions About Lower-Class Families," pp. 56-69.

The
Lower Classes
and the
Negroes:
Implications
for
Intellectuals

suing questions that are important in the area of Negro-white relations in the United States and that are nevertheless usually ignored by whites.

Should serious consideration be given to favored, rather than merely equal, treatment for Negroes? Should this be aligned with compensation for past slavery and discrimination? Is the use of quotas (in occupations or housing) necessarily a retrograde step, or are such quotas, judiciously used, a temporary step in the march toward equality?

Should *all* public schools be integrated *immediately,* despite the existence of residential segregation? Is such a step, under present circumstances, constitutionally required in order to provide equal educational opportunities? Will such a step have an important influence in maintaining stable, integrated neighborhoods?

Is it not time to remove all state laws that bar interracial marriages and adoptions? Should white intellectuals now be encouraging interracial marriages and adoptions? Is it still necessary to hesitate when the bigot asks, "Would you want your sister to marry a Negro?" Or to reply, "Perhaps not, but I shouldn't want her to marry you either"?[2] Is it not time for a straightforward "Yes," or for a sensible "It depends upon the man"?

In following through questions such as these—in a serious and scholarly manner, or in an active and passionate manner—the intellectual can open up a variety of alternatives that will be beneficial to the Negro civil rights movement. In quite a different fashion, the Black Muslims have opened up a variety of alternatives that have been beneficial to the Negro civil rights movement. In my own estimation, the Black Muslims, by virtue of their uncompromising stand in the area of race relations, have done more than any other single group to bring about the series of events that make up the "Negro revolution" of 1963. It is true that only a very small percentage of American Negroes belongs to the Black Muslims, and that very few of them go along with the Muslims' desire for a separatist, black state. Most American Negroes are, nevertheless, in sympathy with the forthright statements that Black Muslim leaders have been making about the racial situation in the United States. The Black Muslims have voiced angry Negro sentiments about racial exploitation that few before them uttered. Their assessment of the racial situation is basically similar to that of the Negro rights groups, such as CORE and the NAACP. Their goals, however, differ. With the passing of time and the increasing militancy and success of the Negro civil rights movement, I predict that the goals of the Black Muslims will become much more like those of the Negro rights groups.[3]

LOWER-CLASS RIGHTS

I referred earlier to the way in which lower-class stereotypes are extended to Negroes. They are also extended to stable, working-class groups. Miller and

[2] See Gordon W. Allport, *The Nature of Prejudice,* abr. ed. (Garden City, N. Y.: Doubleday & Company, Inc., 1958), pp. 354-55, 358-59. This book still remains the best general social science treatment of prejudice.

[3] This is a highly truncated account of a longer statement which I am currently preparing about the Black Muslims.

Riessman, who are concerned about this confusion, make the following very apt statement:

> One of the greatest sources of difficulties in understanding non-upper and non-middle class behavior is that social scientists have frequently used the omnibus category of "lower class" to encompass the stable, and frequently mobile, fairly high income skilled workers, the semi-skilled factory worker, the worker in varied service trades, the unskilled worker and the irregular worker.[4]

Many differences may be concealed by the use of such an omnibus category —and the category is variously referred to as "lower class," "working class," "low status," and the like. Many differences between some of these workers and the middle classes have by now become blurred:

> A major contribution to this blurring has been the high income of the elite labor groups, largely though not wholly enforced by strong union pressure, so that there is a considerable overlap in income. But along with this has gone the assimilation of styles of life so that it is difficult to draw clear differentiations.[5]

A more important differentiation, within the United States, is the one between the stable and skilled workers and the irregularly employed and unskilled workers. An important implication, as I see it, is that intellectuals, social scientists, and professional practitioners must not expend all their energies in trying to save the stable worker from the stereotypes of the unstable, or in trying to ameliorate the conditions of the unstable on a case-by-case basis. A good deal more energy must go into altering some of the social and economic and political deprivations of the unstable workers, the truly "lower-class" individuals.

A recent report by Walter B. Miller deals with an intensive effort in the Boston area to cut down juvenile delinquency within a selected number of gangs. In a coordinated effort, work was done with local citizens' groups, professional agencies, problem families, and the gangs themselves. After three years of effort, what was the result?

> It is now possible to provide a definite answer to the principal evaluative research question—"Was there a significant measurable inhibition of law-violating or morally-disapproved behavior. . . ?" The answer, with little necessary qualification, is "No."[6]

One failure does not signify that we should abandon such efforts. But it does perhaps signify that we should not put too much faith in the practitioners' curative efforts. More attention must be directed to preventive measures. Part of the answer—perhaps the major part—lies in establishing greater occupational and economic security for members of the lower class. Further

[4] S. M. Miller and Frank Riessman, "The Working Class Subculture: A New View," *Social Problems,* Vol. 9 (Summer, 1961), p. 88.

[5] Talcott Parsons, "A Revised Analytical Approach to the Theory of Social Stratification," in *Class, Status and Power,* eds. Reinhard Bendix and S. M. Lipset (New York: The Free Press of Glencoe, Inc., 1953), p. 124.

[6] Walter B. Miller, "The Impact of a 'Total-Community' Delinquency Control Project," *Social Problems,* Vol. 10 (Fall, 1962), p. 187.

The
Lower Classes
and the
Negroes:
Implications
for
Intellectuals

extensions in unemployment insurance and minimum-wage coverage would provide some of this security. More appropriate and basic, however, are the proposals to establish a "guaranteed annual wage" on a society-wide rather than merely on a corporation-wide level. Such a step would not eliminate crime and delinquency and other problems overnight, because these are not merely economic problems. But it may take us a longer way in the direction of eliminating many social problems than any other recent step that has been taken, especially if such a step is coordinated with other simultaneous efforts.

Have we truly reached the end of ideology? Daniel Bell has suggested that "the ideological age has ended" and that "in the West, among the intellectuals, the old passions are spent." He is merely noting a trend that has also been observed by others, and he is undoubtedly right in the broad, historical view. It is nevertheless curious to read, in the context of the 1963 civil rights movement among American Negroes, that "the driving force of the old ideologies were social equality and, in the largest sense, freedom"—and that these ideologies are dead.[7]

Have we truly reached the end of ideology? If most whites have, this is clearly not true for Negroes. As a matter of fact, within the civil rights field, ideology is now in full flower, as it has never been before. In addition, Galbraith, Lipset, Bullitt, Harrington, and many others have pointed out that there are still plenty of voiceless lower-class men around, white as well as Negro.[8] If the 1960's are to be the decade for an ideology of Negro rights, perhaps the 1970's will be the decade for an ideology of lower-class rights. The members of the lower class, however, do not have their own spokesmen and fighters as do the Negroes. A special obligation therefore rests upon the intellectuals—to come out of their end-of-ideology corner fighting for lower-class, as well as Negro, rights.

---

[7] Daniel Bell, *The End of Ideology*, rev. ed. (New York: Collier Books, 1962), pp. 403-4 *et passim*.

[8] J. K. Galbraith, *The Affluent Society* (Boston: Houghton Mifflin Company, 1958), pp. 328-29; S. M. Lipset, *Political Man* (Garden City, N. Y.: Doubleday & Company, Inc., 1963), pp. 48-49, 51, *et passim*; Stimson Bullitt, *To Be a Politician*, rev. ed. (Garden City, N. Y.: Doubleday & Company, Inc., 1961), pp. 172-84; Michael Harrington, *The Other America: Poverty in the United States* (New York: The Macmillan Company, 1962). See also Dwight MacDonald, "Our Invisible Poor," *The New Yorker*, Vol. 39 (January 19, 1963).

RODMAN

APPENDIX

FREEMAN and Lambert, Jr., point up the fact that the notion of distinct social classes and the use of objective characteristics to identify their boundaries are still in vogue, despite serious questions about the adequacy of such characteristics. The two writers subject a number of objective characteristics to a test of consistency between measures, a test that casts further doubt on the ability of such tools to demarcate distinctive social classes. In a provocative concluding warning to colleagues, the authors note that "even if the current lack of specificity in defining classes is tolerable within the frame of sociological analysis, it poses a neat problem of responsibility for the sociologist . . . [who] may be affecting the thinking and activities of practitioners without an adequate empirical basis." As the contributing authors in this volume join the editors and Freeman and Lambert, Jr., in a special concern with this entire matter, it was thought appropriate to conclude the volume with an unsettling, rigorous test of basic assumptions and methodology: indeed, our intent throughout has been to raise questions, stir new concern, and provoke new study of *any* and *all* aspects of "the blue-collar world."

591

The Identification of "Lower-Class" Families in an Urban Community*

HOWARD E. FREEMAN

CAMILLE LAMBERT, JR.

THE measurement of social-class status has been the subject of many methodological analyses, and rightfully so because this variable is a key one in social research.[1] Critics of research on social stratification have commented most sharply on the conceptual confusion and methodological weakness of class research, and particularly on the "status-continuum—class structure issue." [2] Serious questions have been raised about the possibility of identifying discrete classes, especially by means of objective characteristics; nevertheless, the notion of distinct social classes and the use of objective characteristics to identify their boundaries are still in vogue.[3] Sometimes the identification of the members of a particular class provides the starting point for an investigation, and class membership determines the inclusion of persons as objects for study—for example, the study by Rainwater and his associates of workingmen's wives.[4] At

* This paper draws on data collected in an investigation supported by United States Public Health Service research grant No. D-1301, National Institute of Dental Research. The research is sponsored jointly by The Florence Heller Graduate School for Advanced Studies in Social Welfare, Brandeis University, Waltham, Massachusetts, and the Brookline Health Department, Brookline, Massachusetts. Investigators participating in the study, in addition to the authors, are Robert Morris, Brandeis University, Leon J. Taubenhaus, Brookline Health Department, and Louis J. P. Calisti, Tufts University School of Dental Medicine. Walter Miller and Stanton Wheeler have commented on this paper, and their criticisms were most useful, although not always taken into account. This paper was read at the 1963 Eastern Sociological Meeting.

[1] Ozzie G. Simmons, *Social Status and Public Health* (New York: Social Science Research Council, 1958).

[2] See, as examples, Milton M. Gordon, "Social Class in American Sociology," *American Journal of Sociology,* Vol. 55 (November, 1949), pp. 262-68; Llewellyn Gross, "The Use of Class Concepts in Sociological Research," Vol. 54 (March, 1949), pp. 409-41; Gerhard E. Lenski, "American Social Classes: Statistical Strata or Social Groups," *American Journal of Sociology,* Vol. 58 (September, 1952), pp. 139-44; Paul K. Hatt and Virginia Ktsanes, "Patterns of American Stratification," *American Sociological Review,* Vol. 17 (December, 1952), pp. 670-78; Joseph A. Kahl and James A. Davis, "A Comparison of Indexes of Socio-Economic Status," *American Sociological Review,* Vol. 20 (June, 1955), pp. 317-25; and Weiner C. Landecker, "Class Boundaries," *American Sociological Review,* Vol. 25 (December, 1960), pp. 868-77.

[3] Lenski, *op. cit.;* Landecker, *op. cit.;* and Robert A. Ellis, "Social Stratification and Social Relations: An Empirical Test of the Disjunctiveness of Social Classes," *American Sociological Review,* Vol. 22 (October, 1957), pp. 570-78.

[4] Lee Rainwater, Richard P. Coleman, and Gerald Handel, *Workingman's Wife: Her Personality, World and Life Style* (New York: Oceana Publications, Inc., 1959).

other times, the activities and values of a particular social class are used in explanations of social or cultural phenomena, such as Miller's thesis that gang delinquency is primarily "lower-class" behavior.[5]

Many of the investigators who make use of the notion of distinctive classes, such as Rainwater and Miller, are most sophisticated about the risks involved in regarding certain persons in the community as members of a discrete aggregate. In the two studies cited, for example, the fuzziness of class lines is pointed out, and problems involved in identifying members of given aggregates by objective measures are described. Nevertheless, the selection or description of aggregates of persons within the community on the basis of selected status characteristics implicitly assumes congruence between class measures, that is, that most persons identified as belonging to a particular aggregate on one measure would be so identified if another were used instead.

In this paper, we wish to consider whether or not different class measures currently in vogue provide a way of selecting, with consistency, the members of disjunctive social classes. We are concerned specifically with the consistency with which different measures serve to identify members of a community as "lower-class." Assessment of the utility of social-class measures in identifying the lower class is most pertinent at this time. Stimulated by the provocative work of investigators such as Miller, there is a flurry of activity and concern with the "lower class" by health and welfare practitioners as well as by social scientists. The building of a body of knowledge and the synthesis of findings of studies that use diverse criteria for delineating social-class aggregates can move forward only if one has confidence that there is a sufficient degree of consistency between measures.

It should be pointed out that this analysis is concerned with the use of objective measures in identifying disjunctive social classes. This is not, of course, a relevant issue in many substantive investigations. Often investigators who make use of objective class measures look upon social class as a continuous dimension; thus, the major methodological concern is with the adequacy of a particular index as a measure of the *relative* position of persons in "socio-economic prestige" or in "style of life." The use of multiple indicators in serveral studies and correlational analyses of different class measures suggest that findings remain fairly consistent despite the particular variables chosen to reflect relative status position. Indeed, when social class is looked upon as a continuum and used as an independent variable, there may be virtue in the employment of various indicators by different investigators.[6]

Our analysis is relevant to the use of social class in "community studies." In many community studies there is an awareness of the problem of using objective criteria in identifying distinct social classes and a recognition that class labels derived from compressing a continuum of scores into score groups

---

[5] Walter B. Miller, "Lower Class Culture as a Generating Milieu of Gang Delinquency," *Social Issues,* Vol. 14 (1958), pp. 5-19; and "The Impact of a 'Total-Community' Delinquency Control Project," *Social Problems,* Vol. 10 (Fall, 1962), pp. 168-91. Concern with the lower class as the locus of deviant behavior is undoubtedly one of the stimuli for descriptive studies of this group. For example, see Albert K. Cohen and Harold M. Hodges, Jr., "Characteristics of the Lower Blue-Collar Class," *Social Problems,* Vol. 10 (Spring, 1963), pp. 304-34.

[6] Paul F. Lazarsfeld, "Problems in Methodology," in *Sociology Today,* eds. Robert K. Merton, Leonard Broom, and Leonard S. Cottrell, Jr., (New York: Basic Books, 1959), pp. 60-67.

The
Identification
of "Lower-Class"
Families
in an
Urban
Community

are primarily of heuristic value. Nevertheless, there is usually the assumption that ". . . the differences *between* the score groups are greater than the differences *within* each score group in terms of class status characteristics." [7] Our primary concern, however, is with the utility of objective measures for identifying classes in the types of investigations referred to in the introductory paragraph, when the identification of the members of a particular class determines the inclusion of persons as objects for study and when the activities and values of a particular social class are used in explanations of social phenomena. *In such instances the particular criteria used to identify members of a particular class are a major determinant of the findings of the study.* The point is well illustrated by Cohen and Hodges' analysis of the characteristics of the lower blue-collar class, in which they report a number of important differences between the lower-lower class and the remainder of their study group.[8] Their class categorization is based on a modified version of the Hollingshead Two-Factor Index.[9] Would the findings be the same if another measure of class were employed, such as rent or total family income? It is obvious that, if a different measure resulted in the inclusion of a large proportion of persons from the adjacent class (which they label *upper-lower*) or in the identification of a significant number of persons in their lower-lower class as belonging to the upper-lower, many of their findings might not hold. It is to this particular problem that we are addressing ourselves in this paper and not to the utility of different measures of class when social status is looked upon as a continuum.

1. THE STUDY GROUP

The data for this analysis were obtained as part of a study of the utilization of a public health dental clinic by lower-income families. The study group consists of 298 families in Brookline, Massachusetts, who had at least one child between five and eight years of age. These families were obtained by examining the school records of all children in the grades one through four in one-half of the census tracts in Brookline. All families were included who lived in the same census tract for three years and had a breadwinner, if anyone in the household was employed, in a "low-status"—typically a blue-collar—occupation. Interviews were completed with 265 mothers in these families by trained social workers using a precoded schedule.[10] Adequate data were not available in six of these cases, and this small number are not included in the

---

[7] August B. Hollingshead and Frederick C. Redlich, *Social Class and Mental Illness* (New York: John Wiley & Sons, Inc., 1958), p. 395. Some sociologists maintain, of course, that objective measures cannot ever capture the social-class differences in a community, although, with the exception of Centers' work, noted later, there have been limited attempts at measurement of subjective dimensions. See R. M. MacIver, *Society* (New York: Holt, Rinehart & Winston, Inc., 1937), Ch. 9.

[8] Cohen and Hodges, *op. cit.*

[9] August B. Hollingshead, *Two Factor Index of Social Position* (Dittoed publication) (New Haven, Conn.: Yale University Press, 1956).

[10] The questionnaire and other data-collection instruments have been deposited as Document number 7100 with the ADC Auxiliary Publications Project, Photoduplication Service, Library of Congress, Washington 25, D. C.

analysis. We began the analysis, then, with a group of families who, at least in terms of occupation of chief breadwinner, are at the lower end of the class continuum.

2. RESULTS

As part of the study, ratings were obtained for each family on 13 different class measures, namely, the following ones:

1. Warner's I.S.C.[11]
2. Hollingshead's Two Factor Index[12]
3. Hollingshead's Room/Person Index[13]
4. House Type
5. Dwelling Area
6. Rent
7. Occupation of Breadwinner
8. Source of Income
9. Total Family Income
10. Education of Husband
11. Education of Informant
12. Clinic Eligibility
13. Class Identification[14]

The first three measures are composite indices that take into account several different class variables and which currently are in many studies; the next eight are "objective" measures which often are employed either as single indicators of class or as dimensions of standard, composite indices. The next-to-last variable, clinic eligibility, is a measure of per-capita family income and is used routinely by many local medical clinics and welfare departments.[15] The last variable—class self-identification—although not an "objective" measure of class, is quite commonly used, and it was thought that, for completeness, it should be included.

We attempted, on each measure, to dichotomize the study group so that one part of it could be designated reasonably as "lower class." In doing so, two criteria were employed. For some of the measures, such as Warner's I.S.C., the classification system designates certain scores as cutting points for distinguishing particular classes. For other measures, we had to decide on the cutting points. In these cases we divided the study group so that the dichotomization of families would provide maximum agreement when cross-classified with the other class measures. In an appendix, we describe in detail the data-analysis procedures as well as give a summary of the statistical findings. Both a careful inspection of the tables and the application of several different measures of correlation indicate that families identified as "lower-class" on

---

[11] W. Lloyd Warner, Marchia Meeker, and Kenneth Eels, *Social Class in America* (Gloucester, Mass.: Peter Smith, 1957).

[12] Hollingshead, *op. cit.*

[13] *Ibid.*

[14] Richard Centers, *The Psychology of Social Classes* (Princeton: Princeton University Press, 1949).

[15] These standards are similar to those used in the Premature Program, Division of Maternal and Child Health, Department of Public Health, Commonwealth of Massachusetts.

The
Identification
of "Lower-Class"
Families
in an
Urban
Community

one measure are likely to be so identified on another only to a most limited degree. The cross-classification between Warner's I.S.C. and rent shown in Table 1 illustrates the limited overlap between persons classified as lower-class on two different measures. Of the total 253 families that comprise the study group, 199 would be classified as "lower-class" in terms of Warner's scoring scheme. When the families are dichotomized into those paying less than $60 a month rent and those paying over this amount, we do find that most of the "middle-class" families on Warner's measures fall into the higher-rent category, but so do more than one-half of the lower-class families on Warner's scale as well. As shown in the summary data reported in the appendix [to this article], dividing the families at a different point on the rent measure (that is, at $80 per month) results in somewhat more congruence between the two measures but still leaves over 25 per cent of the families classified in different categories on the two measures. The results illustrated in Table 1 are typical of the relationships between the various class measures. On the average, the classification of families by different measures is consistent in only about 60 per cent of the cases. Moreover, as shown by the summary values shown in the appendix [to this article], the proportion identified as belonging to the lower class on any two measures fluctuates considerably with the use of different cutting points. For example, when Warner's I.S.C. (variable 1) and Hollingshead's Two-Factor Index (variable 2) are compared, quite high agreement results if "lower-lower" and "lower" on the former are classified as one group and compared with "class V" on the latter. Likewise, when "lower-lower," "lower," and "upper-lower" are defined as one group on the former and compared with "classes IV and V" on the latter, a high degree of agreement is obtained. But other combinations of these two measures result in agreement in less than half the cases. The analysis clearly indicates that there is limited congruence between most measures, and lack of agreement between *all* measures except when certain specific classification points are employed.

Table 1

RELATIONSHIP BETWEEN RENT AND WARNER'S I. S. C.

Rent	Warner's I. S. C.		
	Lower-Lower, Lower, and Upper-Lower	Middle	Total
Under $60	92	7	99
$60 and Over . . .	107	47	154
Total	199	54	253

$r\phi = .28;\ Q = .70;\ A = .55*$

*See the appendix to this essay for a discussion of these three coefficients.

3. CONCLUSIONS

It is quite clear from the data that different measures of class status fail to identify the same population as "lower class." If there is so limited congruence on which persons are lower-class, it seems at least as likely that other disjunctive aggregates—for example, "working-class" families—are at least as difficult

FREEMAN
LAMBERT

to identify with consistency. The findings of this study may be related, of course, to characteristics of the community from which the study group was drawn, or to the procedures used in selecting the sample. It is a predominantly "white-collar" and "bedroom" community, and the study group constitutes only a small proportion of families living in Brookline. There may be greater congruence between class measures in communities with more depressed economic profiles and in which more families cluster at the lower end of the various continua. Likewise, we were concerned only with families with young children, and our sampling procedures eliminated households that are not organized on a conjugal family basis, such as persons who live alone or couples who are childless. Moreover, our study group does not include the residentially unstable family. Households less "organized" and less residentially stable may cluster more consistently on different class measures.

Arguments also can be raised about the appropriateness of the procedures undertaken to test the degree of agreement between the measures. The approach involves assessing the degree of agreement among families preselected on occupation. It could be that the restriction of the families to those in lower-status occupational categories provides so homogeneous a study group that little correlation can be expected between the various measures. Indeed, if homogeneity of the study group explains the findings, this would suggest that "blue-collar" families, who constitute a rather extensive group, are the narrowest definable stratum—a position rather inconsistent with the distinctions about lower-class culture raised, for example, in the work of Miller.

There is little doubt that, if the analysis had been undertaken with a sample of the general community, the extent of agreement would have been higher; the identification of adjacent classes is a most stringent test of the utility of objective measures for distinguishing discrete social classes. But it seems most reasonable to assert that the meaningfulness of the notion of disjunctive classes depends upon distinguishing between members of adjacent classes. If the findings cannot be dismissed because of limitations in method or study group selection, *the results of this analysis raise serious question about the use of a variety of measures in the identification of distinct or disjunctive classes.*[16] Unless the findings of this study are idiosyncratic, the measures of social status that we currently work with in large sample studies, and which appear useful in identifying the *relative* status position of community members, do not permit the development of a body of knowledge that pivots about the notion of distinctive social classes.

One obvious solution would be for persons in the field with an investment in class-linked frames of reference and in lower-class families to agree upon a single criterion—either some measure, such as occupation, or one of the composite indexes now in vogue—and to use it with consistency. Another solution would be to construct an entirely new index, more reflective of the ideas held regarding the boundaries of different classes, including perhaps measures of

---

[16] In this regard, the studies of status inconsistency should be noted. The utility of the notion of disjunctive classes may indeed be limited because of the multidimensionality of the status system. For a discussion of status consistency, see Leonard Broom, "Social Differentiation and Stratification," in *Sociology Today*, eds. Robert K. Merton, Leonard Broom, and Leonard S. Cottrell, Jr., (New York: Basic Books, Inc., 1959), pp. 430-33.

subjective class-identification, and to use it with consistency.[17] As was pointed out in the previous section, relationships between several measures, when certain cutting points are used, do result in high coefficients of agreement. The identification of measures that yield consistently high degrees of agreement with one another is a possible approach to the development of a common definition. Secondary analysis of completed research could be the starting point for the construction of such a measure.

Considering the range of training and the differences in orientation of individual researchers currently interested in class variables, one cannot be too optimistic that either of these alternatives will be adopted. But without some sort of action which will provide a way that studies can be compared directly and their findings synthesized, it is unlikely that the notion of disjunctive classes will have enduring utility for sociological analyses.

Finally, it should be pointed out that the notion of distinctive social classes is being utilized extensively in the development, planning, and execution of practice programs in the fields of health, education, and welfare. Practitioners in these fields cannot be expected to grasp the apparent lack of congruence between various definitions of class boundaries. Even if the current lack of specificity in defining classes is tolerable within the frame of sociological analysis, it poses a neat problem of responsibility for the sociologist; social class is used perhaps more frequently than any other concept by the social scientist who wishes to display the efficacy of his discipline to the practicing professions. The sociologist may be affecting the thinking and activities of practitioners without an adequate empirical basis. The notion of distinctive social classes, and certainly the means for identifying their members, need to be re-examined.

METHODOLOGICAL APPENDIX

In analyzing the data, three summary measures—"$r\phi$," "Q," and "A"—were used, since no single measure is entirely satisfactory. For the relationship between rent and Warner's I.S.C. reported in Table 1, the "$r\phi$," "Q," and "A" values are shown at the bottom of the table. The differences between the values of the three coefficients illustrate the problem of relying on any single measure. The phi-coefficient is most sensitive to differences in the skewness of the two variables.[18] In this table and in the matrix reported as Table 2, the variations in "one-sidedness" of the distribution serve to reduce the $r\phi$ values.

The second value indicated—Q—usually is higher than $r\phi$, particularly in cases where one cell is close to zero. Indeed, Q equals 1.00 in a two-by-two table in which there is a cell with a zero frequency, regardless of the distribution of cases in the other three cells.[19] The relationship between rent and I.S.C. shown in Table 1 is much higher if one looks at the problem as one of predicting a "necessary but not sufficient condition" rather than as one of "linear" correlation. The third coefficient—A—assesses the extent of agreement between classifications. Robinson and others have commented

---

[17] For example, see Robert A. Ellis, W. Clayton Lane, and Virginia Olesen, "The Index of Class Position: An Improved Intercommunity Measure of Stratification," *American Sociological Review*, Vol. 28 (April, 1963), pp. 271-77.

[18] Allen L. Edwards, *Statistical Methods for the Behavioral Sciences* (New York: Holt, Rinehart & Winston, Inc., 1954), pp. 185-88.

[19] Wayne McMillen, *Statistical Methods for Social Workers* (Chicago: University of Chicago Press, 1952).

on the appropriateness of using a measure of agreement rather than of correlation in problems such as the one being considered here.[20] In the case of two-by-two tables, a satisfactory measure of agreement can be obtained by subtracting from unity the value obtained from dividing the number of disagreements by N. This measure is most sensitive to the marginal distributions, however; high A values are much more likely when both measures are extremely skewed than if they are split evenly. There is, of course, no substitute for the careful inspection of the tables, but the results on the three measures are useful in reaching an over-all assessment.

In Table 2, $r\phi$ and A values are presented for 23 variables (signs are not shown). As noted previously, for some of the measures, we had to decide on the cutting points, and selected those which maximized the magnitude of agreement or correlation between variables (that is, which resulted in the highest mean correlation between one variable and the other 12). In several cases, we felt that other cutting points best reflected the degree of agreement or correlation between measures, either because the initial point selected resulted in unusually one-sided marginals, or because the average correlation of a variable with the others was influenced too strongly by a few of the interrelationships. We wished to provide as fair a test as possible of the degree of congruence between the measures, and consequently used several different cutting points for some of the measures; the matrix therefore contains 23 "variables."

The correlational values above the diagonal in Table 2 are phi-coefficients. An examination of this part of the table indicates that there is only limited relationship between any two measures. The highest correlations are between composite measures and single variables which are included as subdimensions in these measures. The average correlation is less than .3, and it would be foolhardy to regard the persons identified as "lower-class" on different measures as the same aggregate. Although the Q coefficients are not shown, they were calculated for all the interrelationships and they usually are much higher than the phi values; the measures are related, but only in the sense of "necessary but not sufficient" prediction.

The coefficients of agreement shown below the diagonal indicate the limited congruence between measures as well. These A values sharply point up the fluctuations that result from the use of different cutting points. Many of the high coefficients are derived from the cross-classification of measures with most skewed distributions, and the high A values for the relationships between certain measures, such as I.S.C. (variable 1a) and class self-identification (variable 13b), should not be regarded too optimistically, for they may not obtain in another study group.

[20] W. S. Robinson, "The Statistical Measurement of Agreement," *American Sociological Review,* Vol. 22 (February, 1957), pp. 17-25.

The
Identification
of "Lower-Class"
Families
in an
Urban
Community

Table 2*

CORRELATIONAL VALUES OF OBJECTIVE MEASURES USED TO IDENTIFY SOCIAL CLASSES

		Cutting Point	1(a)	1(b)	2(a)	2(b)	3	4
1(a) I. S. C.	Lower-Lower and Lower (34)†	Upper-Lower and Middle (225)	−	−	.54	.14	.18	.61
(b) I. S. C.	Lower-Lower, Lower, and Upper-Lower (203)	Middle (56)	−	−	.24	.64	.21	.29
2(a) Two-Factor Index	Class V (53)	Class IV and Higher (206)	.86	.41	−	−	.16	.25
(b) Two-Factor Index	Classes V and IV (231)	Class III and Higher (28)	.24	.86	−	−	.17	.14
3 Room/Person Ratio	Ratio of 1.00 or Less (162)	Ratio of 1.01 and Higher (97)	.47	.66	.29	.65	−	.16
4 House Type	Very Poor and Poor (75)	Fair and Higher (184)	.84	.49	.71	.37	.52	−
5(a) Dwelling Area	Very Low and Low (38)	Below Average and Higher (221)	.87	.36	.75	.25	.48	.83
(b) Dwelling Area	Very Low, Low, and Below Average (89)	Average and Higher (170)	.76	.53	.67	.41	.55	.84
6(a) Rent	Under $60 (99)	$60 and Over (154)	.70	.55	.66	.48	.59	.74
(b) Rent	Under $80 (165)	$80 and Over (88)	.47	.72	.51	.67	.70	.58
7(a) Occupation of Breadwinner.	Unskilled and Skilled Manual (185)	Clerical and Higher (53)	.35	.86	.45	.89	.63	.44
(b) Occupation of Breadwinner.	Unskilled and Semiskilled (84)	Skilled Manual and Higher (154)	.76	.56	.87	.47	.50	.63
8(a) Source of Income	Welfare (13)	Wages, Salary, and Profit (246)	.86	.27	.76	.16	.39	.70
(b) Source of Income	Welfare and Wages (226)	Salary and Profit (33)	.26	.79	.31	.85	.61	.34
9(a) Total Family Income	Under $4,000 (34)	$4,000 and Over (221)	.82	.34	.87	.24	.43	.69
(b) Total Family Income	Under $5,000 (98)	$5,000 and Over (157)	.66	.51	.62	.44	.55	.65
10(a) Education of Husband	Completed Grammar or Less (26)	Some High School and Higher (220)	.87	.31	.83	.22	.43	.74
(b) Education of Husband	Some High School or Less (80)	Completed High School and Higher (166)	.74	.48	.78	.43	.57	.67
11(a) Education of Informant	Completed Grammar or Less (19)	Some High School and Higher (240)	.82	.22	.75	.18	.40	.69
(b) Education of Informant	Some High School or Less (70)	Completed High School and Higher (189)	.72	.42	.72	.37	.53	.66
12 Eligibility	Eligible (155)	Ineligible (104)	.48	.68	.52	.64	.69	.54
13(a) Class Identification	Lower and Working (135)	Middle (119)	.48	.61	.48	.56	.56	.49
(b) Class Identification	Lower (6)	Working and Middle (248)	.87	.23	.78	.13	.39	.72

	5(a)	5(b)	6(a)	6(b)	7(a)	7(b)	8(a)	8(b)	9(a)	9(b)	10(a)	10(b)	11(a)	11(b)	12	13(a)	13(b)
1(a)	.45	.46	.35	.24	.21	.47	.17	.15	.22	.24	.41	.34	.07	.18	.16	.00	.17
(b)	.22	.30	.28	.33	.60	.37	.12	.28	.18	.19	.12	.20	.00	.15	.32	.22	.02
2(a)	.14	.20	.25	.25	.29	.72	.03	.11	.72	.03	.40	.46	.00	.23	.20	.00	.05
(b)	.11	.12	.22	.18	.65	.27	.08	.28	.14	.10	.12	.24	.10	.18	.20	.10	.05
3	.21	.19	.25	.36	.14	.09	.03	.04	.06	.16	.13	.24	.03	.20	.34	.10	.07
4	.55	.63	.43	.32	.13	.15	.05	.01	.13	.22	.25	.23	.05	.17	.19	.01	.07
5(a)	−	−	.38	.26	.05	.09	.05	.04	.13	.22	.16	.23	.09	.21	.21	.02	.01
(b)	−	−	.37	.28	.11	.10	.06	.06	.18	.16	.28	.29	.14	.27	.19	.09	.11
6(a)	.71	.71	−	−	.15	.12	.18	.05	.28	.30	.26	.33	.08	.22	.22	.10	.09
(b)	.48	.58	−	−	.20	.14	.09	.06	.19	.29	.16	.27	.02	.15	.25	.15	.12
7(a)	.32	.45	.50	.66	−	−	.05	.36	.06	.08	.09	.12	.05	.06	.21	.11	.06
(b)	.63	.59	.59	.52	−	−	.12	.17	.27	.35	.25	.22	.03	.16	.26	.04	.07
8(a)	.83	.65	.64	.38	.23	.66	−	−	.54	.26	.12	.12	.07	.02	.19	.04	.20
(b)	.23	.36	.43	.63	.81	.44	−	−	.10	.04	.08	.09	.02	.02	.01	.10	.02
9(a)	.79	.67	.67	.45	.29	.70	.91	.20	−	−	.20	.33	.06	.12	.33	.07	.25
(b)	.66	.61	.67	.60	.44	.71	.66	.40	−	−	.13	.16	.02	.15	.62	.18	.15
10(a)	.81	.71	.67	.42	.30	.69	.89	.22	.85	.65	−	−	.35	.33	.07	.05	.12
(b)	.70	.68	.69	.57	.45	.65	.68	.39	.73	.62	−	−	.29	.34	.14	.13	.12
11(a)	.82	.67	.61	.38	.25	.62	.89	.19	.82	.60	.89	.72	−	−	.05	.17	.15
(b)	.73	.69	.64	.49	.39	.63	.71	.34	.70	.62	.77	.72	−	−	.11	.11	.08
12	.50	.56	.58	.65	.63	.60	.45	.57	.54	.78	.45	.53	.43	.50	−	.24	.08
13(a)	.48	.53	.54	.58	.55	.52	.48	.56	.50	.58	.50	.55	.50	.54	.62	−	−
(b)	.84	.67	.62	.38	.23	.65	.94	.13	.88	.63	.89	.69	.92	.73	.42	−	−

*The correlational values above the diagonal are phi-coefficients; those below the diagonal are coefficients of association.

†Number in parentheses equals *n*; difference between *N* for each variable and 259 equals number of cases with no information.

Index

"Educational and Social Consequences," 190n.

Educational Status, College Plans, and Occupational Status of Farm and Nonfarm Youths: October 1959, 187n.

"Educational Structure and the Development of Ability," 457n.

Edwards, Allen L., 598n.

Edwards, Hugh, and Harold Wilensky, 15n., 212, 570n.

Edwards, Rheable M., *et al.*, 249n.

Eels, K., *et al.*, 140n., 595n.

Effects of Mass Communication, 49n.

"Effects of Occupational Status on Physical and Mental Health," 405n.

Egalitarianism as expression of class consciousness, 239, 240, 241

Ego-functioning of the individual, 18

"Eighteenth Brumaire of Louis Bonaparte," 236n.

Eisenberg, Philip, and Paul Lazarsfeld, 512n.

Elasticity, concept of, in sociological thinking, 18-19

Elementary School:
  and basic skills, 176
  dropouts, 179n.

Ellis, Robert A., 592n.

Ellis, Robert A., *et al.*, 598n.

Elmtown's Youth, 59n., 196n., 391n.

"Emergence of Fun Morality," 27n.

Emile Durkheim, 176n.

"Emotional Outlets of Gamblers," 444n.

Empey, LaMar T., 142n., 158

Employed Mother in America, 158n., 376n.

Encounters, 197n.

End of Ideology, 24n., 590n.

Endleman, Robert, 307, 308-16 *(reading)*, 309n., 315n.

Engels, Friedrich, 1, 236n.

Engels, Friedrich, and Karl Marx, 236n.

Engineering, attraction of working-class youth to, 30n.

English Abigail, The, 537n.

"English Fabian Socialism," 236n.

Ennis, Philip H., 217n.

"Entry" job, 129

"Epidemiology of Rheumatoid Arthritis," 356n.

Epstein, Irwin, and Richard A. Cloward, 301n.

Erdos & Morgan, 427

Erikson, Kai T., 452n.

Erikson, Kai T., and Robert A. Dentler, 452n.

Ernst, Charles F., *et al.*, 250n.

Essays in Sociological Theory, 315n.

Essays on the Welfare State, 19n., 300n.

"Ethnic Differences in Behavior and Psychopathology: Italian and Irish," 355n.

Ethnic group occupational distribution in Detroit (1958), 238n.

Ethnicity, importance of, as source of working-class consciousness, 236, 237, 238, 241

Excitement, workers' appreciation of, 33, 34, 209, 211, 214

"Expectations of Psychotherapy in Patients of Lower Socioeconomic Class," 64n.

Expectations of teen-agers different from aspirations, 184-87

Expenditure patterns, 37, 41

"Experiences of Discharged Chronic Schizophrenic Patients in Various Types of Living Groups," 382n.

Exploitation:
  as factor in working-class consciousness, 243
  racial, 588

"Exploratory Study of Some Personality Characteristics of Gamblers," 444n.

Extended family, decreased importance of, for working class, 40

External restraint of behavior, 198

"Externalized conscience," 312, 313

F

Faber, Seymour, *et al.*, 494n., 512n.

"Factors Related to College Attendance of Farm and Non-Farm High School Graduates: 1960," 123n.

Familial security, 30

Familial stability/instability, 13, 17
  stable poor, 14-15, 19
  the strained, 15, 19-20
  copers, 16, 20
  the unstable, 16-18, 20

Families in Trouble, 63n.

Families Under Stress, 9n.

Family:
  age, relation of, to reactions to father's job, 88, 91
  assistance through homemaker help, 18
  behavior, working-class changes in, 37, 39-40
  contribution to, as reason for curtailing of education, 184, 186
  discord in, 30
  and home as focus of working-class life, 209
  relationships, 13
  status and husband's job, 98
  structure and unemployment, 513-17

Family and Class Dynamics in Mental Illness, 92n., 382n.

Family and Colour in Jamaica, 60n.

Family and Community in Ireland, 355n.

"Family Dynamics in Southern Italian Schizophrenics," 355n.

Family Encounters the Depression, 512n.

"Family Interaction, Values, and Achievement," 473n.

Family and Kinship in East London, 72n., 203n.

"Family Reactions to the Father's Job," William G. Dyer, 86-91 *(reading)*

Family and Social Network, 71n., 197n.

Family, Society and the Individual, 375n.

Family Spending Patterns and Health Care, 325n.

Marz, Roger H., 44*n*.
Masculine-values, emphasis of working-class on, 209
Maslow, A. H., 18*n*.
Mass Culture, 438*n*.
Mass media:
  behavior patterns toward, 45, 49, 53, 75
  effects of, on blue-collar wife, 95, 98, 106
  effects of, on young skilled workers, 56
  role of, in value homogeneity, 44*n*.
"Mass Media and the Blue-Collar Worker," Leo Bogart, 416-28 *(reading)*
  magazines, 426-27
  newspapers, 424-26
  radio, 423-24
  television, 421-23
"Mass Media and Interpersonal Communication," 426*n*.
"Mass Media Relationship as an Interaction Episode," 437*n*.
Mass movements, working class susceptibility to, 213-14
Mass social movements and unemployment, 521-22
Mathematician's Delight, 463*n*.
Mather, William, 409
Matrifocality, 17, 22*n*.
Matthews, Charles V., and Paul H. Bowman, 128*n*.
Matthews, Dom Basil, 61*n*., 66
Matza, David, and Gresham Sykes, 314*n*.
Mayer, Albert J., and Thomas F. Hoult, 534, 575-81 *(reading)*, 575*n*., 576*n*.
Mayer, Kurt, 42, 43, 44, 45, 47, 48, 52, 53, 54, 55
Mayer, Kurt, and Sidney Goldstein, 534, 545-58 *(reading)*, 546*n*., 559*n*.
Mayer, Martin, 482
McCarthyism, 520
McClelland, David C., *et al.*, 473*n*.
McKay, Henry D., and Clifford R. Shaw, 165*n*.
McLuhan, Marshall, 355*n*.
McMillen, Wayne, 598*n*.
McMurry, Robert N. 405*n*.
McPhee, William N., *et al.*, 48*n*.
"Meaning and Measurement of Alienation," 473*n*.
"Meaning of Work," 299*n*.
"Meaning of Work and Adjustment to Retirement," Herman J. Loether, 525-33 *(reading)*
"Meaning of Work and Mental Illness," Paul N. Geisel, 391-96 *(reading)*
  Bibliography, 396
Meaning of Work and Retirement, 526*n*.
"Measurement of Marital Strain," 94*n*.
Mechanic, David, and Edmund Volkart, 354*n*., 356
Mechanical Bride, The, 355*n*.
Media/scope, 420*n*.
Medical Care, 352*n*.

Medical care for indigent groups in New York City:
  Cornell Medical Welfare Demonstration Project, 347
  Health Insurance Plan of Greater New York, 348
  Queensbridge Health Maintenance Service, 348
  St. Vincent's Medical Care Project, 347-48
Medical-care services, factors affecting underutilization of, by blue-collarites, 341-49
  anomie, 346
  demographic shifts, 342-43
  economic and cultural factors, 343
  education and belief in rationality, 345
  impersonality and bureaucratization of medical care, 346
  organization of medical care, 347-49
  prejudice, 345-46
  preventive behavior, 344
  treatment by professionals, 343-44
  lay referral system, 343
Medical care, worker's attitudes toward:
  perception of physician's interest in patient's welfare, 326, 328-29, 331
  skepticism toward medical care, 326, 328-29, 331
Medical practices of blue-collar workers, 291-92
Medicare, 7
Meeker, M., *et al.*, 140*n*., 595*n*.
Meier, D. L., and W. Bell, 205*n*.
Meltzer, Bernard N., and Jerome G. Manis, 240*n*.
"Membership and Participation in Voluntary Associations," 409*n*.
Men, Management and Mental Health, 399*n*.
Men and Their Work, 581*n*.
Menninger Foundation, 398, 399*n*.
Mental health, 362-405
  behavior patterns of, 398-99
  definition of, 397-98
  and unemployment, 519-20
Mental Health and Mental Disorder, 389*n*.
Mental Health in the Metropolis: the Midtown Manhattan Study, 92*n*., 373*n*., 386*n*.
"Mental Health in the Worker's World," Claude C. Bowman, 371-81 *(reading)*
  children's adjustments, 377-79
  class mobility as factor in mental health, 377
  job competence and ego satisfactions, 376
  marital maladjustments, effects of, 375-76
  Midtown Manhattan study, 373, 374, 377, 379
  prevention of mental disorders, 381
  socioeconomic environment and mental health, 373-76, 379
  treatment for psychiatric disorders, 380-81
  Yale study, 372, 373, 374
Mental Hygiene, 354*n*., 382*n*.
"Mental Hygiene and the Class Structure," 371*n*., 397*n*.

Saleem, Betty L., *et al.*, 9n., 126n., 478n., 524n.

Saleem, Betty L., and S. M. Miller, 125n., 129n., 477n., 482n.

Sane Society, The, 472n., 482n.

Saturday Evening Post, 413

Sawyer, W. W., 463n.

Schaeffer, Leslie, and Jerome K. Myers, 388n.

Schizophrenia, *see* "Social Class and Schizophrenia"; *see also* Work values and the schizophrenic

"Schizophrenia, a Prognostic and Social Study," 382n.

Schmideberg, Melitta, 356n.

Schneider, Louis, and Sverre Lysgaard, 24n.

Schnore, Leo F., and Harry Sharp, 575n.

"Scholars," 172

"School Class as a Social System," 459n.

School clubs, study and analysis of, 229-32
  comparison to block clubs, 232-34

School Dropout, The, 478n.

School Dropout Problem—Syracuse, 9n., 126n. 478n., 524n.

School dropouts, *see* Dropouts

School leavers, *see* Dropouts

School-retention efforts, 179, 180-81

School, role of, with working-class youth, 123

School withdrawals, *see* Dropouts

Schreiber, Daniel, 131n., 480n.

Schumpeter, Joseph A., 300

Schwartz, Michael, and George Henderson, 466, 467-77 *(reading)*

Scotch Irish in America, The, 260n.

Scott, John, 409

Scripps Foundation Studies in Population Distribution, 500n.

Sears, Robert R., *et al.*, 24n.

Security, striving for, 1, 29-30

Segregation:
  as source of working-class consciousness, 243
  Supreme Court decision against, 177

Seidman, Joel, *et al.*, 151

Selected Writings in Sociology and Social Philosophy, 236n., 237n.

Self-depreciation of worker, 96, 97, 98, 99, 100, 103, 106

Seligman, Ben, 2n.

Separation in marital relationship, 68, 119

"Serial monogamy" mating patterns, 11n., 122n.

Service-type industries, 189

Services, expenditures for, 41

"Seven-Year Survey of Insulin Treatment in Schizophrenia," 382n.

Sewell, W. H., and A. O. Haller, 141 n.

Sexton, Patricia, 58, 63, 81-85 *(reading)*, 122n., 179n., 307, 457n., 584

Sexton, Patricia, *et al.*, 2n., 9n.

Sexual relations, greater mutuality in conjugal-role relationship, 73-74

Shannon, Lyle W., 537n.

Share of Top Wealth-Holders in National Wealth, 1922-56, 524n.

Sharp, Harry, and Leo F. Schnore, 575n.

Shaw, Clifford R., and Henry D. McKay, 165n.

Sheatsley, Paul B., 325n.

Sheffield, Susan, 575n.

Shepard, Michael, 382n.

Sheppard, Harold L., *et al.*, 494n., 512n.

Sheppard, Harold L., and James Stern, 493n.

Shils, E. A., 196, 197n.

Short History of the British Working Class, 237n.

Short, J., and A. Henry, 198n.

Shorter Work Week, 190n.

Should I Start My Own Business? 545n.

Shryock, Richard H., 324n.

Shultz, George P., and Charles A. Myers, 493n.

"Sids," 172

Sifneos, Peter, 354n.

Sigerist, Henry N., 324n.

Silva, Ruth M., 186

Simey, T. S., 65

Similarity of poor to other groups, 3-4

Simmel, G., 196

Simmons, Ozzie G., 592n.

Simmons, Ozzie G., and Howard E. Freeman, 382n., 389n.

Simmons, W. R., and Associates, 426, 427

Simpson, George E., and Y. Milton Zinger, 60, 61n.

Simpson, Richard L., 186

Sindlinger & Company, 427

Singer, Jerome L., 378

Singer, Jerome L., and Marion K. Opler, 355n.

Sitwell's Fallacy, 182

Size of family, planning and limiting of, 286-87

"Skeptical Note on the Relation of Vertical Mobility to Education," 139n.

Skepticism as expression of class consciousness, 239, 241

Skid rowers, 6

"Skidder, The: Ideological Adjustments of Downward Mobile Workers," 15n., 570n.

"Skidding," 15n., 212, 570
  and white-collar groups, cleavage between,

Skilled workers:
  as autonomous status group, 53, 55, 56
  behavior and values of, 42-57
  and white-collar groups, cleavage between, 54

Sklare, Marshall, 175n.

Slater, Philip E., 350n.

Sletto, R. F., and E. A. Rundquist, 507n.

Slum areas:
  and delinquency, 165
  of large cities, 4

"Slum landlords," 251

Slum settlers as element of urban poor, 5, 16

Sykes, Gresham, and David Matza, 314*n*.
Symposium on School Dropouts, 176*n*.
Symposium on Sociological Theory, 259*n*.
Syracuse Dropouts—Two Years Later, 130*n*.,
    477*n*.
Syracuse Herald-Journal, 21*n*.
Syracuse University Youth Development Center, 9*n*., 10*n*., 22*n*., 123*n*., 125, 128*n*.,
    131*n*., 302*n*., 303*n*., 477*n*., 478*n*., 482*n*.

T

Tagliacozzo, Daisy, *et al.,* 151*n*.
Talent and Society, 473*n*.
Tangent, Pierre, 29*n*.
Taubenhaus, Leon J., 592*n*.
Taves, Marvin J., *et al.,* 187*n*.
Teachers:
    and their lower-class pupils, difficulties
        faced by, 63
    approach toward lower-status youngsters,
        182
"Techniques of Neutralization: A Theory of
    Delinquency," 314*n*.
Technological change, 190
    see also Automation
Teen-ager in the labor force, 183
Television and the blue-collar worker, 56,
    408-9, 413, 421-23
"Television Viewer—His Tastes, Interests and
    Attitudes," 423*n*.
Television-viewing context as an interpersonal
    encounter, 439
Textile industry of the East, death of, 4
Themes in working-class life, 27-28
Theory of Cognitive Dissonance, 469*n*.
Third-generation immigrant population, 4, 14
Thomas, Lawrence G., 457*n*.
Thompson, Edgar T., 60*n*.
Thornton, A. H., 456*n*.
"Threat and Potential of Urban Renewal: A
    Workable Program for Better Race Relations," 257*n*.
Tibbitts, Clark, and Wilma Donahue, 526*n*.
Timing of decisions to see a doctor, 353-55
Titmuss, Richard, 19, 124, 300
TNEC Monographs, 563*n*.
To Be a Politician, 590*n*.
Toby, Jackson, 142*n*., 175*n*.
Toby, Jackson, and Larry Karacki, 121, 165-
    76
Too Old to Work—Too Young to Retire,
    494*n*., 512*n*.
"Tory workers," 55
"Tough guys," 172
"Toward an Assessment of the Mental Health
    of Factory Workers, 404*n*.
Toward the Automatic Factory, 402*n*.
Toward a Democratic Work Process, 151*n*.
"Toward a Description of Mental Health,"
    398*n*.
Townsend, Peter, 22, 23*n*.
Townsend Plan, 7

Toynbee, A., 272*n*.
Trade magazine reading, pattern of, 49
Trade Union Education, 456*n*.
Trade-union membership, *see* Union membership
Traditionalism of working class, 30-31, 33
Training for Jobs in Redevelopment Areas,
    190*n*.
*Transactions of the Third World Congress of
    Sociology,* 42*n*., 559*n*.
Transcultural Psychiatric Research, 352*n*.
Transition from adolescence to adulthood and
    its work roles, 183, 191
Transplanted Southern whites, 34
"Trends in Inter-Generational Occupational
    Mobility in the U.S.," 137*n*.
Trow, Martin, 560*n*.
Tumin, M. M., and A. S. Feldman, 138*n*.
Two-Factor Index of Social Position, 383*n*.,
    594*n*.
*Two Years in the Syracuse Labor Market—
    Work Experiences of Dropouts,* 477*n*.
"Types of Dropouts: The Unemployables,"
    S. M. Miller and Ira E. Harrison, 130*n*.,
    477-92 *(reading)*

U

Ulam, Adam, 237
"Uncommitted Adolescent: Candidate for
    Gang Socialization," Larry Karacki and
    Toby Jackson, 165-76 *(reading)*
Underdeveloped Areas, 537*n*.
Underprivileged, the, 10, 34, 37
"Underutilization of Medical-Care Services
    by Blue-Collarites," Daniel Rosenblatt
    and Edward Suchman, 341-49 *(reading)*
Unemployables, 18, 299, 472, 478, 492, 524-25
Unemployed Man, The, 507*n*.
"Unemployed of Marienthal," 112*n*.
Unemployed Negroes, study of, 506-512
Unemployment, 3, 8, 16, 29, 75, 84, 101, 129,
    183, 187, 188, 191, 554
    and community power structure, 520-21
    culture of, 467-76, 517, 518
    date on adolescents and unskilled labor,
        179
    and family structure, 513-17
    and mass social movements, 521-22
    and mental health, 519-520
    of the 1930's, 23
    social-psychological effects on Negro children, 473-76
    sociological perspectives in research, 512-22
    and work values, 517-19
"Uneven Distribution of Leisure: The Impact of Economic Growth on 'Free
    Time,' " 453*n*.
Unfinished Revolution, The, 237*n*.
Union attitudes toward worker's wife, 83-85
Union membership, 46-47, 291, 418
    among city and suburban residents, study
        of, 218-23